CHRONOLOGY

OF

AMERICAN

MILITARY

HISTORY

VOLUME III

★ ★ ★

Cold War to the War on Terror
1946 to the Present

CHRONOLOGY OF
AMERICAN MILITARY HISTORY

Volume I
Independence to Civil War
1775 to 1865

Volume II
Indian Wars to World War II
1866 to 1945

Volume III
Cold War to the War on Terror
1946 to the Present

CHRONOLOGY

OF

AMERICAN
MILITARY
HISTORY

VOLUME III

★ ★ ★

Cold War to the War on Terror
1946 to the Present

JOHN C. FREDRIKSEN

Facts On File
An imprint of Infobase Publishing

Chronology of American Military History

Copyright © 2010 by John C. Fredriksen

All rights reserved. No part of this book may be reproduced or utilized in any form or by any means, electronic or mechanical, including photocopying, recording, or by any information storage or retrieval systems, without permission in writing from the publisher. For information contact:

Facts On File, Inc.
An imprint of Infobase Publishing
132 West 31st Street
New York NY 10001

Library of Congress Cataloging-in-Publication Data

Fredriksen, John C.
   Chronology of American military history / John C. Fredriksen.
      v. cm.
   Includes bibliographical references and index.
   Contents: v. 1. Independence to Civil War, 1775 to 1865–v. 2. Indian wars to world war, 1866 to 1945–v. 3. Cold War to the War on Terror, 1946 to the present.
    ISBN 978-0-8160-7761-8 (hardcover : alk. paper) 1. United States–History, Military–Chronology. 2. United States–History, Naval–Chronology. 3. United States–Biography. 4. United States. Army–Biography. 5. United States. Navy–Biography. I. Title.
   E181.F85 2010
   973.02'02–dc22   2009022198

Facts On File books are available at special discounts when purchased in bulk quantities for businesses, associations, institutions, or sales promotions. Please call our Special Sales Department in New York at (212) 967-8800 or (800) 322-8755.

You can find Facts On File on the World Wide Web at http://www.factsonfile.com.

Excerpts included herewith have been reprinted by permission of the copyright holders; the author has made every effort to contact copyright holders. The publishers will be glad to rectify, in future editions, any errors or omissions brought to their notice.

Text design by Kerry Casey
Maps by Pat Meschino
Composition by Hermitage Publishing Services
Cover printed by Sheridan Books, Ann Arbor, Mich.
Book printed and bound by Sheridan Books, Ann Arbor, Mich.
Date printed: May 2010

Printed in the United States of America

10 9 8 7 6 5 4 3 2 1

This book is printed on acid-free paper.

CONTENTS

INTRODUCTION

After victory in World War II, the United States rushed to demobilize the mighty military machine it had assembled, a move that coincided with the first rumblings of the cold war with the Soviet Union and its satellites. At this time the American monopoly on nuclear weapons seemed like a safe bet for several years, while the Russians and Chinese were still viewed favorably as former allies. Still, despite dwindling manpower and military expenditures at home, the United States managed to win a startling victory of sorts during the Berlin Airlift of 1948–49. Moreover, political expedients such as the Truman Doctrine, NATO, and the Marshall Plan put the Communist bloc on notice that the West would be neither militarily intimidated from without nor submit passively to political subversion from within. Despite such bold posturing, the American military was roundly unprepared for the Korean War (1950–53), the West's first military challenge from the East. The U.S. Army, U.S. Navy, U.S. Marine Corps, and U.S. Air Force all recovered from their initial surprise, which included modern MiG-15 jets and hordes of fighting Chinese, but, for the first time in its history, the United States was forced to accept a draw instead of complete victory. Such were the geopolitical realities of limited war in the nuclear age, when neither side dare risk an all-out conflagration that might result in total annihilation for all involved. The decade of the 1950s was nonetheless a golden age of American rearmament in which jet bombers of the Strategic Air Command formed the first rank of nuclear deterrence, pending the development of even newer land- and submarine-based nuclear missiles. The Americans were superbly equipped and determined to confront the next challenge when it arose in Cuba, and they forced the Soviets to withdraw offensive weapons from that island without a shot being fired. However, the Kennedy and Johnson administrations were also increasingly drawn into Southeast Asia to halt what, on the surface, appeared to be an overt attempt by Communist North Vietnam to subjugate South Vietnam. To North Vietnamese leaders the struggle centered more on a long-desired goal of vanquishing colonial influences than anything else and, despite the tremendous firepower brought to bear by American forces, and the huge toll in lives and materiel it extracted, they proved unrelenting in their quest for national unity. The United States, having propped up the losing side as long as possible, had to accept its first strategic defeat. The experience also soured public opinion on military matters and, for a while, it appeared as if the American armed forces were in decline. Fortunately, attitudes and preparedness experienced an abrupt turnaround with the election of Ronald Reagan in 1980, who not only rebuilt and modernized the American military, but also evinced clear determination to intervene abroad whenever deemed necessary. Reagan and his successor, George H. W. Bush, successfully accomplished American goals in Grenada and Panama by force of arms, and Nicaragua and Afghanistan by clandestine means. The Vietnam-era anti-intervention mania evaporated completely after the smashing victory of Desert Storm in January 1991, after which American soldiers were again hailed as heroes and honored with ticker-tape parades. Reagan and Bush also conducted a comprehensive rearmament strategy that literally bankrupted the Soviet Union when it attempted to follow suit, bringing the cold war to a victorious conclusion in 1991.

Since the collapse of the Soviet Union, the American military has been principally involved in small, brush fire wars in Somalia and Bosnia with varying results. Its status as a military superpower nonetheless lay unchallenged until the horrendous terror attack on the World Trade Center on September 11, 2001, a date that marked America's struggle with fanatical Muslim extremists worldwide. Operation Enduring Freedom cleared the violent Taliban regime out of Afghanistan in less than 90 days while Operation Iraqi Freedom laid the dictatorship of Saddam Hussein to waste in only three weeks. Militarily victorious, the United States found itself embroiled in seemingly intractable sectarian-based insurgencies in both countries. By 2008 the corner appeared to have turned in Iraq, once Sunni tribesmen agreed to unite in a common cause against al-Qaeda terrorists lurking there, but the Taliban, safely ensconced in neighboring Pakistan, has proved a durable, tenacious foe. It appears that the new administration of Barack Obama will rely more on diplomacy than on military force to resolve these pressing issues, as well as grapple with the acquisition of expensive new weapons systems in an age of declining economic strength. The United States still remains the greatest military power in the world and, having acknowledged the limits of that power, the nation remains all the more secure because of it.

This volume contains extensive chronological coverage of U.S. military history from 1946 to 2009, from the beginning phases of the cold war through Operations Enduring Freedom and Iraqi Freedom. Thematically, entries are listed by service with *Military* denoting army, militia, and National Guard, *Naval* for navy, *Marines* for marines, and *Aviation* dealing with individual events in the Army Air Service, Army Air Corps, and Army Air Force. *Technology* highlights important inventions with significant military applications as they appear in the time line. Finally, a handful of topical entries such as *Diplomacy* and *Politics* are included when necessary for greater clarification. Given the vast geographical expanse covered, this volume also delineates military events by a strictly ordered geographical region (East, South, then West) while naval events are listed by geography (Atlantic, Pacific, then rivers). For World War II, multiple entries are listed in the order of Europe, North Africa, and Asia. Most entries cover single events, but wherever two or more military or naval events fall under a given date, they are listed in this strict geographic order for uniformity. Also, the exact locale is spelled out in each entry for clarity. Moreover, the scope of this series is inclusive and an "event" might entail coverage of a battle, a noted person's activities, a congressional law, or policy concerning some facet of the army and navy, such as the debut of a new military weapon or system. Space constraints limit most entries to a few lines at best, but significant events may command up to a paragraph according to their importance. The text is interspersed with 46 capsule biographies of significant military figures (generals, admirals, officers, Native Americans) who deserve greater attention than these citations allow. Finally, a 5,000-word bibliography is included of all the latest scholarship on U.S. military history, listed by subdivisions to promote ease of use. The text is also replete with numerous illustrations, which serve both as embellishments and as visual points of reference.

By perusing these pages even a casual reader can grasp the great complexity and richness of the American military experience, which has done so much to influence the history and politics of the nation and the world at large. I am indebted to my editor, Owen Lancer, for accepting this project at my suggestion; it was an arduous endeavor but also a learning experience for which I am much obliged.

—John C. Fredriksen, Ph.D.

CHRONOLOGY

1946

January

AVIATION: At Wright-Patterson Airfield, Ohio, engineer J. W. McGee begins investigating the properties of various high-temperature alloys at the Materials Laboratory. Within a year he develops the new "ML" alloy, so-named after the laboratory where it was developed.

MILITARY: The army now numbers 1.8 million officers and men, down from 8 million a year previous, with many of these men slated for demobilization. However, owning to the nation's new overseas commitments in Germany, Italy, Japan, and Korea, along with mounting tensions with the Soviet Union, the standing establishment is not reduced as readily as had been the case in previous conflicts.

January 1

NAVAL: The Coast Guard is returned to the Treasury Department for the first time since November 1941. Throughout World War II it fell under the purview of the U.S. Navy.

MARINES: At Yokosuka, Japan, the 3rd Battalion, 4th Marines assumes security duties once the 2nd Battalion returns to the United States for disbandment.

January 4–15

MILITARY: In Washington, D.C., the War Department announces that complete demobilization would be slowed down to preserve sufficient army personnel to meet current international obligations. This change in policy triggers an outpouring of anger from many soldiers still deployed overseas, and Congress is besieged by letters of protest.

January 6

MARINES: In light of increasing security commitments on the mainland, the headquarters element, 4th Marines, ships from Yokosuka, Japan to Tsingtao, China.

January 8

MARINES: At Camp Pendleton, California, the 12th Marines are disbanded.
• In Japan, the 2nd Marine Division continues with occupation duty on Kyushu once the last corps-level element of the V Amphibious Corps ships out for the United States.

January 10
AVIATION: Over Stratford, Connecticut, a Sikorsky R-5 helicopter flown by C. A. Moeller and D. D. Viner sets an unofficial world altitude record by reaching 21,000 feet.
DIPLOMACY: In China, former general and now U.S. special envoy George C. Marshall arranges a cease-fire between Nationalist (KMT) and Communist (CCP) factions to take effect beginning January 13.
MARINES: In Hawaii, a group of disgruntled NCOs petitions Major General Roy S. Geiger for an early discharge to civilian life, much as army counterparts have done. Geiger responds by demoting all of them to private, ending all further protests in the Marine Corps at present.

January 11
MARINES: In Washington, D.C., a marine honor guard is present at ceremonies attending the return of the original Magna Carta from the Library of Congress to the British ambassador. It had been kept there secretly during the war for safekeeping.

January 13
MARINES: At Camp Pendleton, California, the 3rd Marines are deactivated.

January 15
AVIATION: In China, transport aircraft from Marine Air Group 25 (MAG-25) drop leaflets announcing the cease-fire between Nationalist and Communist factions.

January 16
AVIATION: A panel of scientific experts is cobbled together to found the U.S. Upper Atmosphere Research Panel. They are tasked with testing and evaluating the 60 captured V-2 rockets presently in American hands. Their findings also give rise to similar programs at Johns Hopkins University and the Naval Research Laboratory.

January 19
AVIATION: Over Pinecastle Army Air Force Base, Florida, test pilot Jack Wollams takes the Bell XS-1 rocket research airplane on its first glide test.

January 20
MILITARY: In Washington, D.C., President Harry S. Truman signs an executive order establishing the Central Intelligence Group, forerunner of the Central Intelligence Agency (CIA).
• General Dwight D. Eisenhower, in light of discontent over demobilization practices, addresses Congress to assure legislators that there has been no dramatic change in army policy respecting discharges and, in fact, the military is actually ahead of stated goals.

January 22
MARINES: In Washington, D.C., Commandant Archie Vandegrift orders that an expeditionary brigade be held in readiness for service in any troubled parts of the Caribbean.

January 26
AVIATION: At Eglin Field, Florida, the army activates the 1st Experimental Guided Missile Group to guide the development and research of drones and guided missiles.

1946

• A Lockheed F-80 Shooting Star piloted by Colonel William H. Council sets a new transcontinental record by flying coast to coast in four hours and 13 minutes at 584 miles per hour.

January 28
MARINES: At Quantico, Virginia, and Camp Lejeune, North Carolina, the 1st Special Marine Brigade is created from the three separate battalions numbered 1–3.

January 29
AVIATION: The carrier *Philippine Sea* launches six R4D transports under Rear Admiral Richard E. Byrd as part of Operation Highjump. This is the most ambitious plan yet to chart and map the Antarctic.

February 3
AVIATION: In a nod to the future, the Army Air Force declares that it is developing an aircraft with a completely automated flight profile system, whereby the onboard pilot has little to do but monitor engine controls for safety reasons.

February 4
AVIATION: Lieutenant General James H. Doolittle (retired) becomes the first president of the new Air Force Association (AFA). This is a civilian organization dedicated to promoting public awareness of aeronautics and its centrality to national defense.
MARINES: At Quantico, Virginia, Major General Oliver P. Smith assumes command of the 1st Special Marine Brigade, now strengthened by the addition of Marine Air Group 11 (MAG-11).
• On Kyushu, Japan, the 2nd Marine Division is assisted in its garrison duties by advanced elements of the British Commonwealth Occupation force.

February 5
MARINES: At Camp Pendleton, California, headquarter elements of the 5th Marine Division are disbanded, removing that unit from the duty roster.

February 9
AVIATION: In Washington, D.C., General of the Army Henry H. Arnold relinquishes command of the Army Air Force, which he was so instrumental in developing, to General Carl A. Spaatz. The latter officially takes charge as of March 1.

February 10
MARINES: On Wake Island, the marine detachment in garrison is transferred to Eniwetok Atoll to cooperate with forthcoming atomic bomb testing to be held there.

February 15
AVIATION: The 2nd Marine Air Wing (MAW) ships from Okinawa, Japan, for its usual billet at Cherry Point, North Carolina.
MARINES: At San Diego, California, the final headquarter elements of V Amphibious Corps disband and that hard-fighting formation ceases to exist.
• In Yokosuka, Japan, the 3rd Battalion, 4th Marines is redesignated the 2nd Separate Guard battalion and assigned primary guard duties at that naval base.

1946

February 19
MARINES: In Washington, D.C., the secretary of the navy creates the Marine Air Reserve Training Command (MARTC) to oversee training functions within Marine Corps Reserve aviation units. Shortly after, it is activated at Glenview Naval Air Station, Illinois.

February 26
AVIATION: In England, the Army Air Force closes the last of its 112 former air bases with a special ceremony held at Honington Air Station, Suffolk. The weather refuses to cooperate, however, and the departure of the last remaining B-17 bombers in the British Isles is delayed due to a heavy snow storm.

February 28
AVIATION: The prototype Republic XP-84 is flown by Major William Lien for the first time. It enters service as the F-84 Thunderjet and renders distinguished service in the Korean War.

March
AVIATION: In Los Angeles, Project RAND is founded as a division of the Douglas Aircraft Company by the Army Air Force. It is tasked with studying the possibilities of missiles, earth satellites, and supersonic flight.
• In light of the fact that ballistic missiles are a military reality, the Army Air Forces commences studies to develop a ballistic missile defense system.

March 1
AVIATION: In Washington, D.C., General Carl A. Spaatz formally replaces General Henry H. Arnold as commanding general, Army Air Forces.

March 1–22
NAVAL: In the Davis Strait north of Greenland, the carrier *Midway* steams to the Arctic Circle to conduct Operation Frostbite, an extensive series of cold-weather operational tests to evaluate the navy's performance there.

March 3
MILITARY: In Berlin, Germany, a Soviet sentry kills ordnance officer Lieutenant James Wilson in a sign of increasing hostility between the West and the Communist bloc.

March 5
DIPLOMACY: Former prime minister Winston Churchill, speaking at Westminister College in Fulton, Missouri, declares that an "Iron Curtain" has descended across Soviet-controlled sections of Central and Eastern Europe. This speech is considered by many to signal the start of the cold war between the United States and the Soviet Union.

March 8
AVIATION: The two-seat Bell Model 47 helicopter, distinct with its bubble canopy, is certified by the Civil Aeronautic Agency (CAA) for public use. This is the first rotary-wing aircraft so designated and it is adopted by the military as the ubiquitous UH-13.
MARINES: In northern China, the 6th Marine Division reincorporates the headquarters of the 4th Marines; all subordinate elements will be reconstituted from recently deactivated units elsewhere.

March 11

AVIATION: An afterburner is successfully tested under simulated high-altitude conditions by the NACA Lewis Altitude Wind Tunnel. This device enhances jet propulsion by having fuel poured directly into it.

MARINES: In Washington, D.C., the Basic Post-War Plan No. 2 is issued. This plan sets personnel levels at 8,000 officers and 100,000 enlisted men, divided into a Fleet Marine Force (FMF) for the Atlantic and Pacific Oceans. Ground forces are reduced to two divisions at Camp Lejeune, North Carolina, and Guam, with an additional brigade at Camp Pendleton, California. Marine aviation is also reduced to two wing-sized commands, although those marine units assigned to carrier groups will retain their own headquarters.

March 12

AVIATION: The new Air University is created at Maxwell Field, Alabama, to draft the curricula of the Air Command and Staff School and the Air War College.

March 15

AVIATION: At the White Sands Proving Ground, New Mexico, technicians and scientists conduct the first static firing of a captured German V-2 rocket.

March 21

AVIATION: The Army Air Force is reorganized to include the new Air Defense Command (ADC), the Strategic Air Command (SAC), and the Tactical Air Command (TAC).

March 22

AVIATION: A WAC missile, jointly developed by the Jet Propulsion Laboratory and Army Ordnance, becomes the first American-made projectile to enter Earth's outer atmosphere by reaching an altitude of 50 miles.

April

MARINES: In Washington, D.C., Congress sets personnel levels for the Marine Corps at 7,000 officers and 100,000 enlisted men.

April 1

AVIATION: Bell Aircraft acquires one of the few remaining missile contracts when it signs on to develop a guided missile capable of hitting targets at a distance of 100 miles. This is the origin of the Rascal missile, also known in military circles as Project MX-776.

MARINES: In northern China, the newly activated 3rd Marine Brigade replaces the 6th Marine Division, which is demobilized. This consists of the 4th Marines plus several supporting remnants of the 6th Marine Division.

April 5–14

NAVAL: The battleship *Missouri* arrives in Turkey to retrieve the body of the U.S. ambassador who died there in 1946 and convoy him back home. It also serves as a show of force to deter communist activity in the eastern Mediterranean.

April 15

AVIATION: At the White Sands Proving Ground, New Mexico, military scientists and technicians successfully launch a captured German V-2 rocket for the first time. The effort is being assisted by Project Paperclip, a clandestine program to incorporate German technology, research, and scientists into

American military defense. White Sands conducts over 40 such tests in the next two years.

MARINES: Consistent with peacetime footing, the 1st Marine Division demobilizes one battalion from each of its three infantry regiments, along with one artillery battery in each battalion of the 11th Marines.

April 19

AVIATION: In San Diego, California, Consolidated-Vultee (Convair) contracts with the Army Air Force to design and build an intercontinental ballistic missile (ICBM), Project MX-774.

April 22

AVIATION: In Maryland, the Glenn L. Martin Company signs a contract with the Army Air Force to develop a surface-to-surface guided missile capable of hitting targets 600 miles away. This is the origin of the Matador missile, or MX-771.

• The U.S. Weather Bureau with the Army Air Force, navy, NACA, and several university research institutes join forces to better understand weather-related phenomena. Both piloted and unpiloted glider and aircraft are flown under a variety of conditions to gather the requisite scientific data.

April 27

MILITARY: In Washington, D.C., the Gillem Report is released by the War Department, which purports to be a comprehensive study of African Americans serving in the ranks. Many of the reports are inconclusive and do little to improve the status of blacks in the military, although they do call for an end to racial discrimination.

May

MARINES: Throughout the month, the 1st Special Marine Brigade conducts the first postwar training exercise in the Caribbean.

May 1

MARINES: Leathernecks being released from active duty are advised by Marine Corps Reserve Bulletin No. 1 that they can maintain connections to the corps by joining its reserve component.

• In China, the theater command is eliminated and operational command of all marines reverts back to the U.S. Seventh Fleet.

May 2

MARINES: In San Francisco, California, marines are called upon to assist local police put down a prison riot on Alcatraz Island in the bay.

May 6

MARINES: As the battle of defense service unification heats up, Commandant Major General Archie Vandegrift angrily testifies before Congress, insisting that if the corps is to be abolished after 175 years of unparalleled service to the nation, it should be "with dignity and honor, not by subjugation to the status of uselessness and servility planned . . . by the War Department." Vandegrift's tough words stop Congress in its tracks and no further attempts to abolish the marines are considered. Apparently, army leaders wanted to reduce the marines to a small force restricted to operating landing craft.

☆ ☆ ☆ ☆ ☆ ☆ ☆ ☆ ☆ ☆ ☆ ☆ ☆ ☆

Vandegrift, Archie (1887–1973)
Marine Corps general

Alexander Archer Vandegrift was born in Charlottesville, Virginia, on March 13, 1887, and he joined the Marine Corps in January 1909 as a second lieutenant. Over the next three decades he completed a series of wide-ranging assignments in Nicaragua, Veracruz, Mexico, and Haiti, where he served with distinction under legendary major Smedley D. Butler. A capable officer, Vandegrift rose steadily through the ranks and, shortly after American entry into World War II, he became a major general commanding the 1st Marine Division. In this post, Vandegrift spearheaded Operation Watchtower, the first American offensive action of the Pacific theater, by landing at Guadalcanal on August 7, 1942. A tremendous trial of strength ensued as the air, naval, and air forces of Japan were marshaled against the marines, who were outnumbered and isolated once Admiral Frank J. Fletcher withdrew his carriers from the Solomons. However, Vandegrift was an old hand at jungle warfare at this point, and his marines defeated Japanese veterans in several determined efforts to storm Henderson Field. That November the tide had turned in America's favor and the exhausted 1st Division was relieved by the 2nd Marine Division. Guadalcanal, moreover, was the first major ground victory over the heretofore invincible Japanese, and U.S. forces seized the strategic initiative and kept it for the remainder of the war. Vandegrift, for his part, won a Medal of Honor and promotion to lieutenant general before returning to the Pacific to plan and lead the successful landings at Bougainville. In January 1944

Alexander Vandegrift *(U.S. Marine Corps)*

he succeeded General Thomas Holcomb as commandant of the Marine Corps and orchestrated the expansion of that force to half a million men. In March 1945 Vandegrift became the first marine officer to become a full general while still on active service.

The postwar period proved even more challenging to the survival of the Marine Corps than World War II. The advent of nuclear weapons meant that present amphibious tactics had to be completely overhauled. President Harry S. Truman,

(continues)

(continued)

determined to slash military expenditures, also embarked on a "unification" program to bring all three services under a single command. Vandegrift, realizing that this meant abolishing the corps, took his case before Congress and pleaded that it be maintained as an integral part of America's defense establishment. So forcefully did Vandegrift make his case that Congress forced the president to scuttle the plans altogether. In light of Vandegrift's perfor-

mance, Truman subsequently stated that the Marine Corps possessed a propaganda machine nearly equal to that of Soviet dictator Joseph Stalin. The general spent his final years as commandant exploring new helicopter technology and new amphibious doctrines before resigning in March 1949. Vandegrift died in Bethesda, Maryland, on May 8, 1973, another legendary marine commander who epitomized the motto of "first to fight." His impressive victory at Guadalcanal serves as a major part of Marine Corps tradition.

May 14
MILITARY: The War Department announces its first postwar reorganization scheme for the army, whereby Army Ground Forces and the Army Air Force continue on as separate entities, with the latter slated to become an independent service. Also, the wartime corps areas nationwide are to be replaced by six army areas.

May 16
AVIATION: At Wright Field, Ohio, the Army Air Force Institute of Technology opens; it is tasked with graduating 350 technically minded officers every year.

May 17
AVIATION: At Muroc, California, the Douglas XB-43 jet bomber completes its maiden flight. This is the Army Air Force's first jet bomber and, while it demonstrates impressive performance, the AAF believes that four-engine designs hold more promise and performance.

May 20
MARINES: On Okinawa, the 8th Military Police Battalion (Provincial) is redesignated a Marine Barracks.

May 21
MARINES: Near Tientsin, China, Communists open fire on a marine patrol, killing one serviceman. Truce violations are growing more frequent and violent between the Communists and their Nationalist opponents.

May 28
AVIATION: Project NEPA is initiated by the Army Air Force to investigate the possibility of atomic energy in aircraft propulsion. The endeavor continues over the next decade.

May 29
AVIATION: A report issued by the War Department Equipment Board recognizes the military implications of missile technology in future warfare. It also recommends pursuing no less than seven surface-to-surface systems with ranges from several hundred to several thousand miles.

June 3
AVIATION: A P-80 Shooting Star jet fighter flown by Lieutenant Henry A. Johnson finishes a 1,000-kilometer course in a record one hour and 20 minutes; his speed averages 462 miles per hour.

June 5
AVIATION: The Army Air Force reveals that it has ordered prototypes of two multijet engine bombers: North American's XB-45 and Boeing's XB-47.

June 10
MARINES: In China, force restructuring continues as the III Amphibious Corps headquarters disbands and its responsibilities are assumed by the 1st Marine Division.
•   On Saipan, Central Pacific, the 5th Military Police Battalion (Provisional) is redesignated Marine Barracks Saipan.

June 13
AVIATION: The Navy Flight Demonstration Squadron, or Blue Angels, gives its maiden performance.
MARINES: In Kyushu, Japan, the first elements of the 2nd Marine Division begin embarking for the United States and army forces assume more responsibility for occupation duty.

June 15
MARINES: On Kyushu, Japan, the army 24th Infantry Division assumes occupation duties formerly held by the 2nd Marine Division. However, at Yokosuka, the 2nd Separate Guard Battalion (Provisional) is redesignated a Marine Barracks.

June 17
AVIATION: In Washington, D.C., the first meeting of the Scientific Advisory Board (SAB) meets at the Pentagon under the aegis of Chairman Theodore von Karman. This is an outgrowth of an earlier group of 33 scientists who participated in Operation Lusty, which helped acquire top-secret German technology at the end of World War II. Presently, it functions as a sounding board for new ideas and concepts relative to the Army Air Force.

June 22
AVIATION: Two P-80 Shooting Stars make the first jet-powered mail delivery when they take off from Schenectady, New York; one heads for Chicago, Illinois, while the other descends upon Washington, D.C.

June 25
MILITARY: In Washington, D.C., the Selective Service Act is extended by Congress to March 31, 1947, for all able-bodied men between 19 and 34 years of age. The length of service, however, is reduced to 18 months.

June 26
MILITARY: The Army Air Force and the navy adopt the Knot (one nautical mile per hour) and the Nautical Mile (1.15 statute mile) as standard measures of speed and distance.

June 27
MARINES: In Washington, D.C., the Marine Corps Reserve, Division of the Reserve, is removed from the Personnel Department and reassigned to the Commandant's Office. This is undertaken to boost the status of reserve forces.

June 28
AVIATION: The Boeing Company signs an agreement with the Army Air Force to develop a long-range, intercontinental bomber, which eventually emerges as the B-52 Stratofortress.

June 30
MARINES: At this time, Marine Corps strength is 14,028 officers and 141,471 enlisted men; roughly one-third higher than personnel levels mandated by Congress.

July 1
MILITARY: In Bamberg, Germany, the U.S. Constabulary is made operational to meet the need for a highly mobile security and border force in Germany and Austria. Drawn from elements of the 1st and 4th Armored Divisions, it is organized into a headquarters, three Constabulary brigades, and 10 Constabulary Regiments under Major General Ernest Harmon. In addition to the usual jeeps, armored cars, and motorcycles, horses are also employed, making it the military's last mounted unit.
MARINES: In order to expedite reductions in Marine Corps personnel levels, draftees and reservists possessing 30 months of active service are now eligible for immediate discharge, if desired.
TECHNOLOGY: Operation Crossroads commences as the United States conducts atomic weapons testing at Bikini Atoll in the Marshall Islands. The objective is to assess damage inflicted on an anchored armada of 73 obsolete warships acting as the target. The experiment unfolds as a 23-kiloton Fat Boy–type fission device is dropped by the B-29 *Dave's Dream* from 30,000 feet. The ensuing air burst is several miles off target yet sinks five old warships anchored around the bomb site. Nine more are heavily damaged.

July 7
MARINES: In China, Communist Party authorities release a manifesto accusing the United States of supporting the Nationalist government of Chiang Kai-shek. This stance increases tensions with marines presently deployed throughout the country.
• At Camp Leujene, North Carolina, advanced elements of the 2nd Marine Division begin arriving at this, their new home and headquarters.
• In China a patrol of seven marines disappears after visiting a village near Peitaiho; no trace can be found by subsequent patrols.

1946

July 12

MILITARY: At Ursina on the Italian-Yugoslavian border, Communist partisans ambush a squad from L Company, 351st Infantry Regiment and are driven off with two killed; the Americans sustain no losses.

July 15

MARINES: At Tangku, China, marines oversee the final demobilization of the few remaining Japanese troops still overseas. Over 2 million soldiers and civilians have been repatriated back to their homeland.

July 16

MARINES: In Washington, D.C., in accordance with presidential wishes, the Marine Corps abolishes its Paymaster Department while also redesignating the Quartermaster Department the Supply Department.

July 21

AVIATION: A McDonnell XFD-1 Phantom piloted by Lieutenant Commander James J. Davidson becomes the first true jet fighter to land on the carrier *Franklin D. Roosevelt*.

TECHNOLOGY: President Harry S. Truman signs the McMahon Act, which establishes the Atomic Energy Commission (AEC) and places future nuclear development under the control of civilians, not the military.

July 24

MARINES: In China, negotiations unfold that lead to the release of seven Marines abducted from Peitaiho.

July 25

TECHNOLOGY: At Bikini Atoll, Pacific, Operation Crossroads continues as the first underwater nuclear test sinks or heavily damages 75 vessels anchored around the site, sending a plume of water 6,000 feet into the air. Radioactive contamination in the immediate vicinity is also intense and forces the evacuation of many participants.

July 29

MARINES: On the road to Peiping, China, Communists ambush a supply convoy run by the 1st Battalion, 11th Marines and the 1st Marines, the attackers are rebuffed but the Americans lose four dead and 10 wounded.

August 1

AVIATION: In Washington, D.C., Commandant Major General Archie Vandegrift proposes marine aviation strength at 1,498 aviation and 2,149 ground officers, and 11,848 aviation and 36,493 ground enlisted personnel. Moreover, the bulk of Marine Corps aviation is to be concentrated either on the West Coast of the United States or in the Pacific region.

August 6

AVIATION: A pair of radio-controlled B-17 bombers successfully fly from Hilo, Hawaii, to Muroc Dry Lake, California.

August 7

MARINES: In Washington, D.C., Commandant Major General Archie Vandegrift orders 100 women reservists to be retained on active duty to perform clerical chores at headquarters until June 30, 1947; the number is soon after increased to 300.

August 8
AVIATION: The massive, six-engine XB-36 bomber prototype flies for the first time at Fort Worth. Texas. This huge machine was originally designed for service during World War II, but it performs a useful role during the cold war.
NAVAL: The carrier *Franklin D. Roosevelt* embarks on a Mediterranean cruise lasting several months, and it makes a port of call at Athens, Greece, as a strong signal against communism there.

August 9
AVIATION: A Yugoslavian Yak-3 fighter downs an American C-47 transport over Slovenia, although the crew is unhurt and eventually released.

August 12
AVIATION: In Washington, D.C., President Harry S. Truman signs a congressional appropriations bill, which includes $50,000 to found the National Air Museum at the Smithsonian Institution. It opens its doors in 1976 and remains the most visited museum in the world.
MILITARY: In another sign of rising tension, three American soldiers belonging to the 32nd Infantry Regiment, 7th Infantry Division, are seized by Soviet forces in Yohyon, northern Korea. They are detained for 13 days before being released.

August 13
NAVAL: In Washington, D.C., a plan drawn up by a board chaired by Rear Admiral James L. Holloway for preserving the structure of the U.S. Naval Academy and strengthening the Naval Reserve Officer Training Corps is signed into law by President Harry S. Truman. The plan is intended to provide sufficient ensigns to meet the needs of a global navy cannot be met by Annapolis alone.

August 17
AVIATION: Over Ohio, Sergeant Larry Lambert is the first American pilot to "punch out" of an aircraft when he uses an ejection seat from his P-61 Black Widow at 7,800 feet.

August 19
AVIATION: In Ohio, aviation pioneer Orville Wright receives a plaque from Major General Laurence C. Craigie in recognition of his contributions to the field of aeronautics.

August 21
NAVAL: In Washington, D.C., the Office of Naval Research is founded to facilitate planning and carry out the most modern scientific research.
MARINES: Major General Roy S. Geiger, having observed atomic bomb tests at Bikini in person, concludes that World War II–style amphibious operations, traditionally based on concentrated naval and ground forces, are no longer viable in the atomic age. He therefore urges that new amphibious warfare techniques be developed and quickly.

1946

August 31

AVIATION: Colonel Leon Gray, flying a Lockheed P-80 Shooting Star, wins the first postwar Bendix Race, Jet Division, by racing from Los Angeles, California, to Cleveland, Ohio, in four hours and eight minutes at an average speed of 495 miles per hour.

MARINES: At Camp Lejeune, North Carolina, and Quantico, Virginia, the 1st Special Marine Brigade and allied units are demobilized.

September 6

MARINES: In light of recent attacks upon marine personnel in China, Nationalist troops are delegated sole responsibility for guarding their own supply convoys. Henceforth, marines will guard only trains carrying American supplies or personnel.

September 10

POLITICS: In Washington, D.C., President Harry S. Truman, having failed in his attempt at defense unification, instructs the secretaries of war and the navy to write a compromise bill that Congress can pass.

September 11

MARINES: At Camp Pendleton, California, parts of the 6th Marines are ordered to serve as the headquarters and weapons company of the 3rd Marine Brigade.

September 13

MARINES: In Washington, D.C., Commandant Archie Vandegrift appoints a Special Board tasked with developing new concepts and principles for adapting traditional amphibious war techniques to the atomic age.

September 18

AVIATION: Over Muroc Dry Lake, California, the experimental Convair XF-92, the first true delta-wing design, performs its maiden flight with test pilot Sam Shannon at the controls.

September 29

AVIATION: Commander Thomas Davies and his crew of three men fly a Lockheed P2V-1 Neptune named *Truculent Turtle* a distance of 11,235.6 miles from Perth, Australia, to Columbus, Ohio, in 55 hours and 17 minutes. It is a record-breaking long-distance flight.

September 30

AVIATION: At Muroc, California, 13 engineers of the new Muroc Flight Test Unit begin assisting the X-1 Program; their success leads to the eventual founding of the NASA Flight Research Centers at Edwards, California.

MILITARY: At Fort McKinley, Manila, Philippines, a detachment of American military police are attacked by Communist Huk guerrillas; the Americans lose one dead and one wounded.

October 1

AVIATION: At Point Mugu, California, the Navy Air Missile Test Center is founded to help guide the development of such weapons.

1946

NAVAL: In light of the strategic significance of the Mediterranean region, the government establishes U.S. Naval Force, Mediterranean, a progenitor of the future Sixth Fleet. Shortly afterwards, the carrier *Randolph* is ordered to cruise the region.

MARINES: Today the Marine Corps slips slightly below its assigned personnel levels with 95,000 serving on peacetime contracts.

October 2

MILITARY: In Washington, D.C., the War Department announces plans to replace the Selective Service with a new scheme calling for Universal Military Training (UMT). All participants, while not part of the regular army, are subject to six months of military instruction. In light of resistance from many civic groups and veterans organizations, the plan is not adopted.

October 3

MARINES: At Hsin Ho, China, Chinese Communists raid the 1st Marine Division's main ammunition depot but they are driven off by the guards.

October 4

MARINES: To expedite the process of demobilization, Headquarters Marine Corps orders the discharge of all remaining personnel who entered the corps as either reservists or draftees, or those whose regular enlistments had expired.

October 4–6

AVIATION: The B-29 *Pacusan Dreamboat* piloted by Colonel C. S. Irvine completes the first, nonstop unrefueled flight over the North Pole from Hawaii. The flight takes almost 40 hours to complete the 10,000-mile mission.

October 7

AVIATION: At Niagara Falls, New York, the Bell Company ships out its first XS-1 rocket-powered test plane to Muroc, California. A total of three are built and they are subsequently redesignated the X-1.

October 10

AVIATION: Space science officially begins after a V-2 rocket fitted with spectroscopic reading equipment is launched high into the atmosphere over the White Sands Proving Ground, New Mexico.

October 16

MILITARY: At Nuremberg Germany, an army executioner carries out the death sentence by hanging the last 10 Nazi war criminals who had been condemned by an international court.

October 24

AVIATION: At the White Sands Proving Ground, New Mexico, a V-2 rocket carries a De Vry 35mm movie camera to an altitude of 65 miles while its film records 40,000 square miles of the Earth's surface.

November 21

NAVAL: President Harry S. Truman observes naval maneuvers off Key West, Florida, from aboard a captured German U-boat.

December 1

MARINES: The Marine Corps streamlines its existing rank structure for enlisted men to seven pay grades: private, private first class, corporal, sergeant, staff sergeant, technical sergeant, and master sergeant.

• At Parris Island, South Carolina, the Marine Barracks is redesignated the Marine Corps Recruit Depot.

December 6
AVIATION: Navy Attack Squadron VA-19A takes delivery of the first Douglas AD Skyraiders (or "Spad"), an outstanding propeller-driven carrier aircraft that serves well through the Vietnam War, and in a wide variety of attack and electronic countermeasure roles.

December 8
AVIATION: At Muroc, California, the first powered flight of the Bell XS-1 by Bell pilot Chalmers Goodlin takes place as it is dropped from the belly of a B-29 carrier aircraft. The XS-1 then ignites its RMI XLR-1 rocket engine and zooms to 35,000 feet at a speed of Mach .75.

December 10
AVIATION: In Washington State, a Marine R5C transport disappears without a trace with 32 marines onboard. The wreckage is recovered on the South Tacoma Glacier in July 1947.

MARINES: In the Pacific, the provisional detachments on Wake Island and Eniwetok are disbanded while the unit on Kwajalein is redesignated as a Marine Barracks.

December 16
MARINES: The headquarters of Fleet Marine Force Atlantic (FMFANT) is created and is initially the purview of the commanding general of the 2nd Marine Division. This office is subordinated to the commander of the Atlantic Fleet.

• Major General Lem Shepherd, reporting the result of a board charged with evaluating the impact of atomic weapons on amphibious warfare, concludes that dispersal of assets at sea is essential and that helicopters, seaplanes, or any other means of rapidly deploying ashore is necessary to achieve concentration of forces at the last possible moment to deny an enemy a potential target. Shepherd therefore requests that a helicopter squadron be formed to begin experimenting with this possibility.

December 17
AVIATION: In Washington, D.C., President Harry S. Truman forwards a telegram of congratulations to Orville Wright on the 43rd anniversary of his first manned flight at Kitty Hawk, North Carolina.

• At the White Sands Proving Ground, a German V-2 establishes a velocity and altitude record for single stage rockets: 3,600 miles per hour and 116 miles in altitude. The rocket also carries a collection of fungus spores aloft for an experiment.

MEDICAL: At Holloman Air Force Base, New Mexico, the National Institutes of Health begin a space biological research program. It includes subjecting volunteers to high-G acceleration in rocket sleds.

December 31
DIPLOMACY: In Washington, D.C., President Harry S. Truman declares World War II formally over and terminates all hostilities with the former Axis powers of Germany, Italy, and Japan.

1946

1947

January 1
NAVAL: Admiral John H. Towers is appointed to the new post of commander in chief, Pacific Command, becoming the first naval aviator so honored.
MARINES: Cognizant that every marine is a rifleman, the pre–World War II practice of paying extra money for good marksmanship is reinstituted.

January 6
DIPLOMACY: In Washington, D.C., President Harry S. Truman orders an end to American efforts at truce-making between Communists and Nationalists in China. The 7th Marines, 3rd and 4th Battalions, 11th Marines, and several air elements sail from Chinwangtao for Hawaii.

January 11
AVIATION: The McDonnell XF2H-1 Banshee, the navy's first twin-jet fighter plane, makes its maiden flight.

January 13
AVIATION: At Eglin Field, Florida, a drone launched by the 1st Experimental Guided Missile Group successfully flies nonstop to Washington, D.C.; the flight is intended as a simulated, long-range bombing mission.
• Aeronautics and popular culture merge in the new comic strip *Steve Canyon,* drawn by Milt Caniff, which highlights the contributions of military aviation to America.

January 15
NAVAL: At Annapolis, Maryland, Rear Admiral James L. Holloway gains appointment as the 35th superintendent of the U.S. Naval Academy.

January 16
MILITARY: In Washington, D.C., President Harry S. Truman submits a new unification defense bill, based on input from the secretaries of war and the navy, to Congress for its approval. To placate the Marine Corps and its supporters, Truman also promises to more clearly define its role and mission in the national defense establishment.

January 23
AVIATION: At White Sands Proving Ground, New Mexico, Project Hermes gets underway when a V-2 rocket is fitted with special telemetry equipment that is transmitted in flight. A ground receiving station records and evaluates its flight performance.

January 28
AVIATION: At Mission Inn, Riverside, California, General of the Army Henry H. Arnold holds a special ceremony during which he affixes a pair of wings autographed by Orville Wright to the commemorative "Flier's Wall."

January 29
NAVAL: Rear Admiral Richard E. Byrd directs the first phase of Operation Highjump, during which six R4D Skytrain transports are launched from the carrier *Philippine Sea* for landing at Little America in the Antarctic. From there

they will aerially map 150,000 square miles of the ice cap over the next three months.

January 31
MARINES: After months of official tabulations, the Navy Department declares that of 88,939 dead and missing in the naval services during World War II, 24,479 were members of the Marine Corps.

February 3
MARINES: At Chicago, Illinois, the first Volunteer Training Unit is created to allow reservists not attached to a tactical unit to acquire some basic skills in staff or specialty fields.
•   In China, the 1st Marine Division is ordered to prepare to evacuate all U.S. personnel from Beijing in light of an impending showdown between Communist and Nationalist forces.

February 5
MILITARY: In Washington, D.C., President Harry S. Truman is urged by the Atomic Energy Commission and the secretaries of the army and navy to continue with the production and testing of atomic weapons; the president concurs.

February 10
AVIATION: Over Dayton, Ohio, a Sikorsky R-5 reaches an altitude of 19,167 feet, an unofficial world record for helicopters.

February 12
AVIATION: The submarine *Cusk* becomes the first such American vessel to launch a guided missile when it unleashes a Loon—a copy of the German V-1 rocket.

February 17
AVIATION: At the White Sands Proving Ground, a WAC rocket is launched to an altitude of 240,000 feet.

February 20
AVIATION: At the White Sands Proving Ground, Project Blossom unfolds as a V-2 is fitted with canisters that are ejected once the rocket reaches its maximum altitude.

February 27
AVIATION: The North American F-82B Twin Mustang *Betty Jo,* piloted by Lieutenant Colonel Robert Thacker and John M. Ard, flies nonstop from Hickham Field, Hawaii, to LaGuardia Airport, New York, a distance of over 5,000 miles. The craft makes the record-breaking flight in 14 hours and 33 minutes.

March 5
MARINES: At Camp Pendleton, California, the 7th Marines disband and the bulk of personnel are reassigned to the 3rd Marine Brigade.

March 6
AVIATION: At Muroc Air Force Base, California, the North American XB-45, America's first jet bomber, arrives on a flat-bed truck for flight testing.

March 10
MARINES: In China, the 1st Pioneer Battalion embarks for Guam, where they are to begin constructing a camp for the forthcoming 1st Marine Brigade.

1947

March 12

DIPLOMACY: In Washington, D.C., President Harry S. Truman outlines what becomes known as the Truman Doctrine by requesting millions of dollars in financial aid for the governments of Greece and Turkey to help them defeat Moscow-backed Communist insurgencies. Such assistance defines U.S. cold war foreign policy over the next five decades.

March 15

MILITARY: General Joseph McNarney, current military governor of Germany and commander in chief, Europe, is replaced by General Lucius D. Clay.

NAVAL: Ensign John W. Lee becomes the first African-American officer to receive a regular navy commission. During World War II, blacks could hold commissions only in the Naval Reserve.

March 16

AVIATION: At San Diego, California, the Convair 240 airliner prototype makes its maiden flight. It is adopted into the military and flies for many years as the T-29 trainer and C-131 MedEvac aircraft.

Clay, Lucius D.   (1897–1978)
Army general

Lucius Dubignon Clay was born in Marietta, Georgia, on April 23, 1897, a descendant of Henry Clay, the noted 19th-century politician. He graduated from West Point in 1918 as a second lieutenant of engineers and held down a number of routine assignments. His big break occurred in 1933 when President Franklin D. Roosevelt initiated a large public construction project, the Works Project Administration (WPA) to help fight the Great Depression. Clay, who enjoyed a reputation as a fine organizer, became liaison for the Corps of Engineers to Congress. He excelled at orchestrating public works projects, including the Denison Dam on the Red River in Texas, and, in 1940, Clay was authorized to direct the improvement of 277 airports for possible military use. During World War II he rose to major general in 1942 and oversaw the coordination of industrial production and procurement of supplies for the war effort. Clay sought out a

combat command, but in 1944 he arrived in France to untangle allied logistical arrangements at Cherbourg, France, in the wake of the D-Day invasion. He quickly sorted matters out, achieved a 20-fold increase in supplies delivered to the front, and ended the war as deputy of the War Mobilization and Reconversion Agency in Washington, D.C. However, in May 1945 he was summoned back to Europe to serve as General Dwight D. Eisenhower's civilian affairs deputy in Germany.

Clay arrived in a German nation emaciated by war and divided into Western and Soviet zones of occupation. The civilian populace was suffering from the postwar depression and a devastated industrial base. Clay, who was appointed military governor in 1947, set about instituting remedial reforms. First, he insisted that Germany be treated like a sovereign nation and not a conquered province. Second, Clay sepa-

March 17

AVIATION: At Muroc Dry Lake, California, the North American XB-45 prototype flies for the first time with company test pilots George Krebs and Paul Brewer at the controls. This is also America's first four-engine jet bomber and it enters service as the B-45 Tornado.

MARINES: Technical Sergeant Mary E. Wancheck is the first female marine to earn a four-year service stripe ("hashmark") on her uniform.

• On Peleliu, a force of 62 marines are flown in from Hawaii and Guam to hunt down a Japanese holdout who tossed a grenade at a marine patrol.

March 27

AVIATION: Over northern China, transports of VMR-153 have airlifted 750,000 pounds of food and medicine in support of United Nations relief efforts.

March 31

MILITARY: In light of high rates of voluntary enlistment, the War Department declines to ask the Selective Service for an extension of the military draft and it expires; this is the first time since 1940 that the country does not rely on conscription.

rated military from civilian functions, a concept alien to central European traditions, and he encouraged the first free elections in Germany since the 1920s. Moreover, when the Soviets instituted their blockade of Berlin, in June 1948, Clay proved instrumental in helping to orchestrate Operation Vittles, the so-called Berlin Airlift, which provided 2.3 millions tons of supplies to the city's residents and completely thwarted Soviet intentions. Consequently, Clay advanced to lieutenant general in 1948. His final official act as governor was to help draft a constitution for the new Federal Republic of Germany. On May 12, 1949, he retired from the military a full general. He then served as chief executive for several corporations. In 1961, when the Berlin Wall crisis erupted, he returned to West Germany as President John F. Kennedy's personal ambassador to assure German citizens of America's commitment to that nation. He ordered all Western diplomats to be given armed escort convoys while visiting the Soviet zone, as

Lieutenant General Lucius Clay (*National Archives and Records Administration*)

was allowed by treaty. After the crisis subsided, Clay returned home to resume his business interests. He died in Chatham, Massachusetts, on April 16, 1978, a pivotal figure of the early cold war period.

April 3
MARINES: On Peleliu, a Japanese soldier surrenders to marines looking for him and he relays information as to the whereabouts of other survivors.

April 4
NAVY: The Reserve Officer Training Corps program is reinstituted on college campuses by the Navy Department.

April 5
MARINES: At Hsin Ho, China, Communist guerrillas attack an ammunition supply point while another band waits to ambush a relief company sent by the 5th Marines. Five Americans are killed and 16 are wounded while the Chinese leave six dead on the field.
• On Peleliu, another 25 marines arrive to bolster the effort to round up all remaining Japanese holdouts.

April 15
AVIATION: The A-26 Invader *Reynolds Bombshell* flown by Captain William P. Odom establishes a new, round-the world flight record in 78 hours, 56 minutes. The distance covered is over 20,000 miles.

April 16
MILITARY: In Washington, D.C., President Harry S. Truman signs the Army-Navy Nurses Act of 1947 into law; this makes the Army Nurse Corps a part of the regular army establishment. The Women's Medical Specialist Corps also comes into being, although in 1955 it is renamed the Army Medical Specialist Corps.

April 20
MARINES: On Peleliu, a force of 26 Japanese infantry under a lieutenant turn themselves in to a party of marines looking for them. They are joined by seven additional soldiers on the following day.

April 22–24
MARINES: In Washington, D.C., Commandant Major General Archie Vandegrift again appears before the Senate Armed Services Committee, where he expresses only moderate concern about the new defense unification bill.

April 30
AVIATION: A standard nomenclature for guided missiles is adopted by the army and navy. Henceforth, designations will contain either A (Air), S (Surface), or U (Underwater) to indicate the missile type and its target.

May 1
MARINES: At Tsingtao, China, the Fleet Marine Force Western Pacific (FMF-WESPAC) becomes the sole controlling force for the region following the departure of the 1st Marine Division and the 1st Marine Air Wing.

May 12
MARINES: A chapter closes in Marine Corps history once the final elements of the 5th Marines depart Beijing and head for redeployment on Guam.

May 21
AVIATION: At NACA Langley, Virginia, engineers test what is probably the first stealth airplane, an almost silent machine employing a special, five-bladed propeller, or muffled exhausts.

May 22
AVIATION: At White Sands Proving Ground, New Mexico, the Corporal E missile is successfully launched and tested; this is the army's first ballistic missile to be designed solely in the United States.

May 23
MARINES: At Peitaiho Beach, China, marines rescue and evacuate 66 American and foreign nationals after Communist troops began attacking the area.

May 24
MILITARY: To thwart a potential Communist takeover of Greece, President Harry S. Truman authorizes creation of the U.S. Army Military Group-Greece (USAMGG), which facilitates delivery of modern weapons and training to Greek forces. This is one of the earliest manifestations of the Truman Doctrine to help fight the spread of communism.

May 27
AVIATION: At the White Sands Proving Ground, the new Corporal E surface-to-surface rocket exceeds all technical expectations on its maiden flight.

June 1
MARINES: On Guam, the 1st Marine Division is reactivated; at the time, it consists of the 5th Marines and the 1st Battalion, 11th Field Artillery.

June 5
AVIATION: The Air Materiel Command (AMC) contracts with New York University to construct the army's first research balloon.
DIPLOMACY: Secretary of State George C. Marshall, speaking at Harvard University, delineates his program for providing massive amounts of aid to the struggling democracies of Western Europe to thwart any potential Communist takeovers. His program to rebuild economic infrastructure to insure political stability gains fame as the Marshall Plan. Aid is also offered to the Soviet Union and its satellites, but dictator Joseph Stalin refuses.

June 17
MARINES: In Washington, D.C., retiring brigadier general Merritt Edson testifies before the House Committee on Expenditures in the Executive Department. He opposes the new unification bill because of the perceived threat it represents toward civilian control of the military.

June 18
MILITARY: Colonel Florence Blanchfield, Army Nurse Corps, becomes the first woman tended a regular army commission.

June 19
AVIATION: Over Muroc Dry Lake, California, Colonel Albert Boyd, the Army Air Force's chief test pilot, sets a new world air speed record of 623.8 miles per hour in a P-80R Shooting Star jet fighter.

June 20
MARINES: By this date, the majority of the 1st Marine Division has shipped out to Guam. All that remains at Tsingtao, China, are the headquarters and 2nd Battalion, 1st Marines, some aviation detachments, and the 12th Service Battalion; their purpose is to protect the few remaining American citizens still living in the area.

1947

June 23
NAVAL: In Washington, D.C., Secretary of the Navy James V. Forrestal issues a statement to senior U.S. Navy and Marine Corps personnel that they are free to express their opinion about the unification bill before Congress. Thus assured, several leader go on record opposing the bill as written.

June 25
AVIATION: The Boeing XB-50, an improved version of the classic B-29 bomber, makes its maiden flight. It serves as a bomber until 1955 and as a tanker until 1965.

June 30
AVIATION: In light of rising friction between the Army Air Force and NACA, a meeting of representatives at Wright Field, Ohio, parcels out responsibilities for the ongoing X-1 program. Henceforth, the army will be responsible for breaking the sound barrier while NACA will monitor, collect, and evaluate research information obtained from these activities.
MILITARY: World War II demobilization ends when the last wartime draftee is discharged back to civilian life.
MARINES: In Washington, D.C., President Harry S. Truman signs legislation posthumously promoting Lieutenant General Roy S. Geiger to full general (four-star).
• By this date, Marine Corps manpower levels have dipped to 7,506 officers and 85,547 enlisted men, far below the 108,000 ceiling established by Congress.

July
DIPLOMACY: In an essay signed anonymously by "X," published in *Foreign Affairs* magazine, foreign service officer George Kennan suggests that the United States adopt a policy of "containment"–shifting U.S. political, economic, and military resources to threatened regions–to counter Soviet expansionism. In concert with the Truman Doctrine and the Marshall Plan, containment is the third and final policy guiding American foreign policy throughout the cold war period.

July 1
AVIATION: In light of postwar fiscal retrenchment, the MX-774 program, destined to create the first intercontinental ballistic missile, is cancelled. Revived later on, it creates the Atlas missile.

July 3
AVIATION: A 10-balloon cluster designed by New York University scientists is released by the Army Air Force. Rigged to carry aloft a 50-pound instrument package, it reaches an altitude of 18,550 feet.

July 4
MARINES: On Guam, the 1st Marine Brigade names its cantonment Camp Witek after Private Frank P. Witek, who received a posthumous Medal of Honor there in 1944.

July 6
MARINES: At Camp Pendleton, California, the headquarters unit of the 1st Marine Division arrives; Pendleton has since served as its permanent home station.

July 7
MARINES: In Quantico, Virginia, the first postwar Platoon Leaders Class officer training course begins.

July 16
MARINES: In Washington, the tussle over defense unification continues as Clare Hoffman, chair of the House Committee on Expenditures in the Executive Department, reports a new version of the bill that clearly delineates the roles and mission of the Marine Corps in national defense and also minimizes the merger between the War and Navy Departments. Once passed by the House it goes to a Conference Committee, with the Senate version preferred by President Harry S. Truman.
•   At Camp Pendleton, California, the 3rd Marine Brigade is disbanded and its personnel are absorbed into the 1st Marine Division.

July 18
AVIATION: In Washington, D.C., President Harry S. Truman appoints Thomas K. Finletter to chair a five-man board tasked with sounding out the best ideas for providing the United States with the greatest benefits from aviation.

July 19
MILITARY: In Washington, D.C., Robert P. Patterson is replaced as secretary of war by Kenneth C. Royall; Royall also becomes the first man to hold the title secretary of the army.

July 22
MARINES: The *Freedom Train,* which carries treasured documents and artifacts of American history on a national tour, is guarded by a detachment of 26 marines.

July 26
MILITARY: In Washington, D.C., President Harry S. Truman signs the National Security Act of 1947 into law; this mandates a "National Security Establishment" consisting of the U.S. Army, U.S. Navy/Marines Corps, and a new, independent U.S. Air Force. A National Air Guard also is established as a reserve unit of the air force. Moreover, the new cabinet post of secretary of defense is created as the chief presidential adviser in military affairs while the various department heads serve under him; current secretary of the navy James V. Forrestal is the first appointee. Furthermore, the Joint Chiefs of Staff (JCS) receives statutory recognition, although the commandant, Marine Corps, is not a member. The Central Intelligence Agency (CIA) and National Security Council (NSC) emerge as separate entities.

August 4
MILITARY: To improve administrative efficiency, all ancillary organizations of the Medical Department are now collectively grouped under the new Medical Service Corps. The four sections involved are Pharmacy, Supply, and Administration; Medical and Allied Sciences; Sanitary Engineering; and Optometry.

August 7
MARINES: In Washington, D.C., Congress passes a new law that raises the permanent rank of the commandant, Marine Corps, to four stars.

August 20
AVIATION: Over Muroc, California, a Douglas D-588-1 Skystreak piloted by Marine Lieutenant Colonel Marion Carl establishes a new world speed record of 640.6 miles per hour. Carl beats his own record with the same aircraft five days later.

Carl, Marion   (1915–1998)
Marine Corps general, aviator

Marion Carl was born near Hubbard, Oregon, on November 1, 1915, and, in 1936, after graduating from the University of Oregon, he joined the Marine Corps as a private. After attending the flight school at Pensacola Naval Air Station, he received his wings and a lieutenant's commission. Carl served several years as a flight instructor, then transferred to Midway Island in the Pacific with Marine Air Group 21. On June 3, 1942, the Americans there were roughly handled by highly maneuverable Japanese aircraft, but Carl managed to flame a A6M Zero in his F4F Wildcat. He was one of three surviving pilots in his squadron and he received the Navy Cross. Soon after, Carl transferred to VMF-223 on Guadalcanal, where he shot down four more Japanese aircraft, becoming the first Marine Corps ace of the war. He also entered into friendly competition with his commanding officer, Major John Smith, to see who could down more enemy planes. On September 9, 1942, Carl was himself shot down and spent five days in the jungle making his way back to American lines, rather disturbed that, in his absence, Smith's tally had exceeded his own. By the time he left Guadalcanal, Carl's score stood at 16 kills, which won him a second Navy Cross. He rose to captain stateside and then returned to the Solomon Islands flying the new F4U Corsair fighters, bagging additional Zeroes for a total of 18. At this juncture, Carl drew a staff assignment at Jacksonville Naval Air Station and, despite his protests, spent the final months of the war behind a desk.

After the war, Carl volunteered as a test pilot and spent two years flying experimental jets. In 1946 he made some of the earliest carrier landings in jet aircraft and he also became the Marine Corps first helicopter pilot. On August 25, 1947, he became the fastest man alive by flying the Douglas D-558-1 Skystreak at 650 miles per hour. Carl rose to lieutenant colonel, and, on August 21, 1953, he broke another world speed record by piloting the Douglas D-558-2 Skyrocket to an altitude of 83,000 feet. He resumed military flights in 1955 by piloting reconnaissance aircraft over Red China as a colonel, and, in 1958, he was allowed to attend the Air War College at Maxwell Air Force Base. Carl next served as a brigadier general in Vietnam by commanding the First Marine Expeditionary Brigade at Da Nang. He personally flew over 40 jet and helicopter combat missions. In April 1967 he transferred back to command the Marine Corps Air Station at Cherry Point, North Carolina, and, that fall, he rose to major general commanding the Second Marine Aircraft Wing. In May 1973 Carl concluded 35 years of active service by retiring, having accumulated over 14,000 hours of flight time in 250 different types of aircraft. This singular aviator died in a robbery attempt at his home in Roseburg, Oregon, on June 25, 1998. Close acquaintances once described him as the "ultimate fighter pilot."

August 22
AVIATION: At Langley, Virginia, Dr. Hugh L. Dryden, a former confidant of Theodore von Karman, is appointed the director of NACA Aeronautical Research.

August 27
MARINES: The pullout of the 1st Battalion, 1st Marines from Tientsin, China, leaves the Fleet Marine Force Western Pacific (FMFWESPAC) at Tsingtao as the only marine contingent left on Chinese soil.

August 28
AVIATION: At Carswell Air Force Base, Texas, the first of 22 production model Convair B-36A Peacemakers makes its maiden flight. This initial version is intended as a training raft for future combat crews.

September 6
AVIATION: The first American launching of a German V-2 rocket at sea is completed onboard the carrier *Midway*.

September 15
MILITARY: The army-led occupation of Italy officially ends. Moreover, because Italy is now a member of the new North Atlantic Treaty Organization (NATO), American forces will remain at several leased bases.
MARINES: In light of declining military budgets, the Marine Corps adopts the J-series tables of organization whereby infantry regiment headquarters are abolished and battalion landing teams are redesignated as regiments.

September 18
AVIATION: After a long struggle, the U.S. Air Force finally emerges as an independent arm of the American military. W. Stuart Symington is seated as the first secretary of the air force.

September 18–23
MILITARY: In Washington, D.C., once the National Security Act of 1947 takes effect, Secretary of the Navy James V. Forrestal becomes the new secretary of defense. Meanwhile, Kenneth C. Royall is appointed the first secretary of the army, while John L. Sullivan becomes the 49th secretary of the navy. Also, the former National Military Establishment is renamed the Department of Defense.

September 19
MILITARY: General Albert C. Wedemeyer reports back to President Harry S. Truman concerning recent events in China and proposes a five-year military assistance program to shore up the Nationalist regime of Chiang Kai-shek.

September 22
AVIATION: At Stephenville, Newfoundland, a remote-controlled C-54 transport aircraft lifts off and flies nonstop to Brize Norton, England. This is the first aircraft to cross the Atlantic and safely land under these conditions.

September 25
AVIATION: At White Sands Proving Ground, New Mexico, the new Aerobee sounding rocket is successfully launched for the first time; this liquid-fueled device performs useful scientific research over the next 40 years.

1947

September 26
AVIATION: In Washington, D.C., General Carl A. Spaatz officially becomes the first chief of staff of the U.S. Air Force. Accordingly, Secretary of Defense James V. Forrestal orders all personnel, facilities, and aircraft transferred from the army to the new service.
• Major General William E. Kepner, who commanded the Eighth Air Force during the war, is appointed to head the new Atomic Energy Division within the U.S. Air Force.

October 1
AVIATION: At Muroc Dry Lake, California, the North American XP-86, America's first swept-wing jet fighter, successfully flies for the first time. It enters service as the legendary F-86 Sabre.
• At Bethpage, New York, the Grumman XJR2F-1 amphibian prototype makes its maiden flight. This aircraft enters production as the SA-16 and HU-16 Albatross and saves thousands of downed pilots during the Korean War.

October 6
AVIATION: The Firebird XAAM-A-1, the first U.S. Air Force air-to-air missile, is successfully tested, However, production of such weapons is still a decade away.

October 14
AVIATION: Over Muroc Dry Lake, California, Captain Charles "Chuck" Yeager flies an experimental Bell XS-1 research plane through the sound barrier for the first time. Once dropped from the belly of a B-29 mothership, Yeager rockets upward at a speed of Mach 1.06 in level flight, winning the Mackay Trophy for most memorable flight of the year.

October 21
AVIATION: The futuristic Northrop YB-49 "Flying Wing" makes its maiden flight over Muroc Dry Lake, California. Despite an impressive performance, it is unstable as a bombing platform and does not enter production.

October 24
AVIATION: At Cherry Point, North Carolina, VMF-122 becomes the first marine jet squadron to fly McDonnell FH-1 Phantoms under the command of Major Marion Carl.

November 10–14
MARINES: Off the Southern California coast, the 1st Marine Division holds large-scale amphibious exercises during the next five days.

November 14
DIPLOMACY: In New York, the United Nations establishes a Korean commission to oversee elections in Korea despite objections by the Soviets, who boycott the proceedings.

November 15
AVIATION: The air force reveals the existence of its one-man XH-20 *Little Henry* ramjet helicopter, which first flew the previous May 5. A novelty, it does not enter production and the prototype is on display at the Air Force Museum, Dayton, Ohio.

Yeager, Chuck (1923–)
Air Force officer

Charles Elwood ("Chuck") Yeager was born in Myra, West Virginia, on February 13, 1923, the son of an oil driller. He joined the Army Air Corps in 1940 and trained as an airplane mechanic but developed an affinity for flying and earned his pilot's wings at Luke Field, Arizona, in July 1942. Yeager subsequently flew P-51 Mustangs with the 363rd Fighter Squadron in England, where, in 55 missions, he shot down 13 German aircraft, including five in one day. In the course of intense aerial combat, Yeager was himself downed over France and fled across the Pyrenees to Spain with the help of the French underground. He returned to combat soon after and his most notable kill came on November 6, 1944, when a futuristic Messerschmitt Me-262 jet fighter fell before his guns. After the war, Yeager reported to Perrin Field, Texas, where he trained pilots as an instructor. However, the new jet age had dawned and he yearned to be a part of it. In 1947 he was selected to fly the top-secret Bell XS-1 rocket-powered research aircraft owing to his excellent reputation for piloting and his relative short

(continues)

Captain Charles E. Yeager is shown here standing in front of the U.S. Air Force's Bell-built X-1 supersonic research aircraft. *(U.S. Air Force)*

(continued)

stature, for the cockpit of this streamlined machine was extremely cramped. On October 14, 1947, Yeager was released by a B-29 bomber and broke the sound barrier at Mach 1, faster than 660 miles per hour, for the first time. He accomplished this despite the fact that two days earlier he had fallen from his horse and broken two ribs. His feat won him the prestigious Mackay Trophy for the year's most outstanding flight. Yeager continued flying out of Edwards Air Force Base, California, where, in December 1953, he piloted a new Bell X-1A to 1,650 miles per hour, roughly three times the speed of sound. Tragedy nearly struck when the craft began tumbling and he fell nearly 50,000 feet (10 miles) before regaining control. President Dwight D. Eisenhower awarded him the Harmon trophy for outstanding airmanship.

In 1954 Yeager left flight testing to command an F-100 Super Sabre squadron in Germany. He returned home three years later a lieutenant colonel. In 1961 he assumed command of the Air Force Flight Test Center at Edwards Air Force Base, where, from 1962 to 1966, he trained 19 astronauts. In 1969 he resumed combat operations in commanding the 405th Tactical Fighter Wing, and he flew an additional 127 missions over Vietnam in Martin B-57 Intruders. He retired from active duty in 1975 as a brigadier general and retained his celebrity status. In 1983 actor Sam Shepard played Yeager in the movie *The Right Stuff* and, two years later, President Ronald W. Reagan awarded him the Presidential Medal of Freedom. On October 14, 1997, the 50th anniversary of his record-breaking flight, Yeager once again broke the sound barrier in his supersonic F-15 Eagle jet fighter for the last time at an Edwards Air Force Base air show. He has since retired and resides in Cedar Ridge, California. In an active career spanning 50 years, Yeager flew and tested no less that 330 different types of aircraft.

November 21

NAVAL: The prototype Grumman XF9F-2 jet fighter makes its maiden flight, and it enters service as the F9F Panther.

November 23

AVIATION: In San Diego, California, the gigantic Convair XC-99 prototype makes its maiden flight. This huge cargo plane is capable of lifting 400 fully armed troops and is based on the B-36 Peacekeeper but, unlike the bomber version, it does not enter production.

November 24

AVIATION: At the White Sands Proving Ground, New Mexico, technicians fire a liquid-fueled Aerobee rocket to an altitude of 190,000 feet.

November 26

AVIATION: At Langley, Virginia, NACA scientists successfully operate the first hypersonic flow wind tunnel to study airfoils faster than the speed of sound.

December 1
AVIATION: At Quantico, Virginia, HMX-1, the first experimental marine helicopter squadron, assembles. It is to be equipped with Sikorsky H3S-1 and Piasecki HRP-1 helicopters.
NAVAL: Admiral William H. P. Blandy is appointed the first commander in chief, Atlantic Command, and commander in chief, Atlantic Fleet.

December 10
AVIATION: Lieutenant Colonel John P. Stapp becomes the first human being to study the effects of rapid acceleration along a 2,000-foot track while strapped to a rocket sled. No serious injuries result.

December 15
NAVAL: In Washington, D.C., Admiral Louis E. Denfield is appointed the 11th chief of naval operations.

December 17
AVIATION: Over Seattle, Washington, the swept-wing Boeing XB-47, the most important multijet bomber in aviation history, flies for the first time. It has been designed with a cruising range of 1,500 miles at speeds of up to 500 miles per hour and inspires other significant designs, such as the B-52 bomber, the KC-135 aerial tanker, and the 707 commercial airliner.

December 25
MARINES: In China, five marines stumble into Communist-held territory while on a hunting expedition and are ambushed; one American is killed and the others are taken captive.

December 30
AVIATION: In Washington, D.C., the National Military Establishment assigns the U.S. Air Force sole responsibility for developing the Joint Long-Range Proving Ground at Cape Canaveral, Florida, and other down-range sites.

1948

January
MILITARY: In three years, army personnel levels have dropped from 8 million to a mere 554,000; moreover, many of its major weapons systems are verging on technical obsolescence.

January 1
MARINES: In Washington, D.C., Major General Clifton B. Cates is appointed the 19th commandant of the Marine Corps.
• In California, the Marine Corps Base San Diego is redesignated Marine Corps Recruit Depot San Diego.

January 2
AVIATION: At Patterson Field, Ohio, the Air Force Technical Museum opens its doors for the first time.

January 4
AVIATION: At the University of California, scientists complete a pilot model for the world's first low-pressure supersonic wind tunnel.

January 5
MARINES: In the Mediterranean, the 2nd Marines are designated to join the Sixth Fleet for an extended tour afloat. This initiates a high visibility for marines as a landing force in that region.

January 7
MARINES: Admiral Chester W. Nimitz warns the government of Yugoslavia not to threaten the 5,000 army troops garrisoned in the free city of Trieste, and he orders the Sixth Fleet and the 2nd Marines into the Adriatic to back up his threat.

January 11
MARINES: In Philadelphia, Pennsylvania, the Marine Corps sponsors National Marine Corps Reserve Week to help spur a recruiting drive.

January 31
MARINES: Near Tsangkou Airfield, China, a marine patrol is attacked by Chinese Communists, although no casualties result. This is also the home base of air elements belonging to the Fleet Marine Force West Pacific (FMFWESPAC).

February
AVIATION: Throughout this month, Marine Corps air transports evacuate American and foreign nationals from Changchun, Manchuria, just ahead of victorious Communist Chinese forces.

February 6
AVIATION: At the White Sands Proving Ground, New Mexico, a V-2 fitted with a Hermes A-1 flight control system is launched and controlled for the first time by ground control. The dawn of guided missiles is at hand.

February 7
MILITARY: In Washington, D.C., General Omar N. Bradley gains appointment as the 17th chief of staff, U.S. Army, to replace outgoing General Dwight D. Eisenhower. Eisenhower has resigned from active duty to serve as president of Columbia University, New York.

February 9
AVIATION: At Quantico, Virginia, the Marine Experimental Helicopter Squadron (HMX-1) begins operating its first two Sikorsky HO2S-1s.

February 13
MARINES: In China, the Communists admit they have captured five marines on December 25, 1947, and that one has since died in captivity. They also demand a formal apology from the United States for having sided with the Nationalists during the civil war there.

February 16
AVIATION: B-29 bombers of the Strategic Air Command (SAC) deploy to airfields in Germany as part of a long-distance training exercise; on the return trip, they are "intercepted" by Royal Air Force fighters.

February 19
MILITARY: Command of the new Joint U.S. Military Advisory and Planning Group (JUSMAPG) goes to Lieutenant General James A. Van Fleet. This orga-

nization is tasked with providing arms and training to the Greek army and replaces the earlier USAMGG. There are presently 400 American military personnel in Greece, including 182 army advisers, and they prove instrumental in orchestrating the ultimate Greek victory over Communist insurgents by October 16, 1948.

February 20
AVIATION: The first Boeing B-50 Superfortress is delivered to the Strategic Air Command (SAC). Though superficially similar to the B-29 it replaces, the new machine boasts more powerful engines, a higher tail section to absorb the torque, and inflight refueling capabilities for virtually unlimited range.

February 24
DIPLOMACY: The legitimate government of Czechoslovakia is toppled in a coup orchestrated by the Soviet Union, underscoring for many in the West that the Iron Curtain is a political reality and the cold war is real.

March 5
SCIENCE: A U.S. Navy missile reaches speeds of 3,000 miles per hour and an altitude of 78 miles at White Sands, New Mexico.

March 10
AVIATION: Over Muroc Dry Lake, California, the air force reports that a B-29 has dropped a bomb weighing in excess of 42,000 pounds, larger than any aerial ordnance dropped during World War II.

MILITARY: General Jacob L. Devers gains appointment as commander of the newly created Army Field Forces, which replaces the earlier designation of army Ground Forces. This entity oversees army responsibilities within the continental United States.

March 11–14
MILITARY: In Key West, Florida, Secretary of Defense James V. Forrestal meets with the Joint Chiefs of Staff in an attempt to iron out traditional interservice rivalries. Ultimately, the navy halts its opposition to the air force monopoly on strategic bombing, while the air force will no longer oppose the new carrier under construction. Nor are the marines allowed to form a second land army. They will be restricted to only four divisions in wartime. Significantly, the new field of rocket research will not be allocated to one service. It is hoped that these arrangements will also end mounting friction in the field of nuclear warfare planning.

March 17
POLITICS: In Washington, D.C., President Harry S. Truman advocates before Congress that the military draft be resurrected and universal military training be instituted in light of the current world situation. He also urges speedy passage of the Marshall Plan to thwart the spread of communism in war-ravaged western Europe.

March 22
AVIATION: At Van Nuys, California, the prototype two-seat TP-80C successfully flies. It enters the service as the T-33 jet trainer, which trains thousands of American and allied jet pilots over the next two decades.

March 25
MARINES: Commandant General Clifton B. Cates testifies before Congress, calling for resumption of the military draft and a gradual implementation of universal military training. He is seconded in these opinions by the secretary of defense, the three service secretaries, and members of the Joint Chiefs of Staff.

March 28
AVIATION: To extend the range of strategic bombers, the Strategic Air Command begins testing KB-29M tanker aircraft in aerial refueling exercises. These craft can unload 2,300 gallons of fuel from a tank in the bomb bay from a hose and reel system in the tail.

March 31
DIPLOMACY: Beginning today, Soviet troops in East Germany begin repeatedly interrupting the flow of Western supplies and traffic to West Berlin, which come to a complete halt on June 24.

April 1
AVIATION: At Naval Air Station Lakehurst, New Jersey, HU-1 becomes the navy's first helicopter utility squadron.
MARINES: In China, the Communists release the four marines seized on Christmas Day last.

April 10
AVIATION: A marine air transport makes an emergency landing in Communist-held territory in China and the four crewmen are taken prisoner.
AVIATION: In Washington, D.C., Secretary of Defense James V. Forrestal assigns the U.S. Air Force the mission of protecting the United States from attack.

April 26
AVIATION: The air force, a technically oriented, forward-thinking service, orders that all ranks be racially integrated. Henceforth, African Americans will be employed wherever their talents best suit the service. This order anticipates President Harry S. Truman's antidiscrimination order by three months.

April 30
AVIATION: In Washington, D.C., General Hoyt S. Vandenberg becomes the second chief of staff of the Air Force.

May 6
AVIATION: Fighter Squadron VF-11, operating new McDonnell FH-1 Phantom fighters on the carrier *Saipan*, is established as the navy's first jet squadron.

May 10
MILITARY: Faced with a national railroad strike, President Harry S. Truman orders the army to seize control of all U.S. railroads until labor peace can be restored on July 19.

May 19
AVIATION: The marine experimental helicopter squadron HMX-1 goes to sea for the first time onboard the escort carrier *Palau*.

1948

Vandenberg, Hoyt S. (1899–1954)

Air Force general

Hoyt Sanford Vandenberg was born in Milwaukee, Wisconsin, on January 24, 1899, and raised in Lowell, Massachusetts. He passed through the U.S. Military Academy in 1923 near the bottom of his class and became a second lieutenant assigned to the Air Service. Vandenberg, a natural flier, rose steadily through the ranks after winning his wings at Kelly Field, Texas, and, in 1927, he served as a flight instructor at March Field, California. Vandenberg subsequently attended the Air Corps Tactical School and the Command and General Staff School, where he met and befriended Carl A. Spaatz, another future air leader. Following American entry into World War II, he served on the staff of General James H. Doolittle in North Africa, rising to brigadier general as of December 1942. A year of distinguished service in the Mediterranean ensued. In March 1944 Vandenberg rose to major general and helped plan Operation Overlord in England. The following August he took charge of the Ninth Air Force and provided close support mission for General George S. Patton's Third Army as it raced across France. Shortly before World War II ended, Vandenberg, who rose from lieutenant colonel to lieutenant general in the space of three years, was back home functioning as assistant chief of staff for the Army Air Force.

In April 1947 Vandenberg's friend, General Spaatz, appointed him deputy chief of staff of the newly independent U.S. Air Force. He succeeded Spaatz the following year and became, aged 48 years, the youngest four-star general in service. Sub-

Hoyt S. Vandenberg *(U.S. Air Force)*

sequently, he made several critical decisions that catapulted the air force to the forefront of national defense. Vandenberg realized that, in an age of fiscal restraint, the greatest firepower available would be in the form of nuclear weapons, so he opted to spend most of his budget on expensive, impressive systems like Convair's giant B-36 bomber and a host of new jet aircraft. He also instituted the new Strategic Air Command (SAC) under General George C. Kenny to usher in the age of nuclear deterrence. Throughout 1948 he responded to the challenge of com-

(continues)

1948

(continued)

munism by authorizing Operation Vittles, a massive airlift that broke the Soviet-inspired Berlin blockade. The cold war became much hotter once North Korean Communists invaded South Korea, and Vandenberg orchestrated a massive air campaign that help beat them back. The conflict also led to a resurgence in defense spending, for which the air force was the major beneficiary, and Vandenberg proved instrumental in expanding its nuclear, tactical, and airlift capabilities. During his tenure, the service expanded from 49 to 90 combat wings, becoming the largest aerial force in the world. Unfortunately, poor health forced Vandenberg to resign from office, and he died of cancer in Washington, D.C., on April 2, 1954. He was a far-sighted aviation leader who put the U.S. Air Force on a sound footing for the remainder of the cold war.

May 20

AVIATION: Over Inglewood, California, the first production F-86A Sabre jet fighter flies. This is the first of 6,000 aircraft constructed in several versions.

May 23

AVIATION: During Operation Packard II at Camp Lejeune, North Carolina, experimental helicopter squadron HMX-1 ferries 66 marines from the escort carrier *Palau* to positions on land.

May 24

AVIATION: Noted aviatrix Jacqueline Cochran sets a world speed record for propeller-driven aircraft over a 1,000-kilometer course by reaching 432 miles per hour.

May 26

AVIATION: In Washington, D.C., President Harry S. Truman signs legislation creating the Civil Air Patrol as an auxiliary of the U.S. Air Force.

June 1

AVIATION: The air force and navy transport commands are combined and unified under a single, U.S. Air Force–controlled entity, the Military Air Transport Service (MATS) under Major General Lawrence S. Kuter.

June 10

AVIATION: The air force confirms that the Bell X-1 rocket plane has exceeded the speed of sound on several occasions since Chuck Yeager's landmark flight was publicized.

June 11

AVIATION: The air force updates its aircraft designations: henceforth "F" is used to signify fighters, "R" stands for reconnaissance, and "H" is used for helicopters. These replace the P, F, and R designations in use since before World War II.

June 12
MILITARY: In Washington, D.C., Congress passes the Women's Armed Services Integration Act granting the Women's Army Corps (WAC) both regular and reserve status as part of the standing U.S. Army, U.S. Air Force, U.S. Navy, and Marine Corps. However, although women may now serve in the regulars, they are restricted to 2 percent of each service. The present WAC director, Colonel Mary A. Halloran, is also retained in office.

June 16
AVIATION: Colonel Geraldine P. May, the first female in the air force to achieve that rank, is appointed the first director of Women in the Air Force (WAF).

June 18
AVIATION: At Davis-Monthan Air Force Base, Tucson, Arizona, and Roswell, New Mexico, the air force activates the first two aerial refueling squadrons in its inventory; both are equipped with Boeing KB-29Ms.

June 24
AVIATION: A Soviet land blockade of Berlin commences, which requires the Western powers to supply the city's inhabitants by air. It becomes known as the Berlin airlift, or Operation Vittles.
MILITARY: In light of cold war realities, President Harry S. Truman signs the new Selective Service Act, requiring all males between 18 and 25 to register for possible military service.

June 26
AVIATION: At Fort Worth, Texas, the first B-36 Peacekeeper intercontinental bomber is accepted into service by the Air Force's 7th Bomb Wing. This is also the

Transport airplanes taking part in the Berlin airlift *(National Archives)*

world's largest bombardment aircraft, with a wingspan of 230 feet and a length of 160 feet. By year's end, 35 of the giant craft are operational.

• Responding to the Russian-imposed land blockade of Berlin, the American European Command authorizes Operation Vittles. Transport aircraft begin flying in food and other essential supplies for the city's beleaguered inhabitants. The first aircraft deployed are C-47s while U.S. Air Force Europe (USAFE) commander General Curtis E. LeMay begins gathering aircraft elsewhere.

June 30
MARINES: In Washington, D.C., President Harry S. Truman signs the Reserve Retirement Law into effect, which allows reserve members to receive retirement pay for their time in uniform.

• Present manpower levels have dipped to 6,907 officers and 78,081 enlisted men, largely on account of budgetary constraint and fiscal retrenchment.

July 2
MARINES: In China, the Communists release four captive airmen seized on April 5.

July 13
AVIATION: The Convair MX-774 rocket is successfully tested and features moveable (gimballed) directional nozzles that later show up on the Atlas ICBM in the late 1950s.

July 17
AVIATION: Air Force B-29s belonging to the Strategic Air Command (SAC) arrive in England for training. Because these aircraft are capable of delivering atomic weapons, their presence send a powerful signal to the Soviet Union.

July 18
MARINES: As the first Arab-Israeli War rages, the 21st Marines are tapped to serve as a provisional consular guard to protect the U.S. consul general in Jerusalem.

July 20
AVIATION: At Selfridge Field, Michigan, a squadron of 16 F-80 Shooting Stars commanded by Colonel David Schilling takes off and flies nonstop to Scotland while en route to Furtsenfeldbruck, West Germany. This is the first mass west-to-east transatlantic flight by jet fighters and takes nine hours and 20 minutes.

MILITARY: In Washington, D.C., President Harry S. Truman orders all males between the ages of 18 and 25 to register for the draft by September 18; the actual draft begins on October 1.

July 22
MARINES: The Marine Corps declares that it will not accept draftees this year as its recruiting quotas are being met.

July 23
AVIATION: In light of the Soviet blockade of Berlin, West Germany, the Military Airlift Transport Service (MATS) establishes the Airlift Task Force under Major General William H. Tunner to counter it.

July 26
MILITARY: In a major development, President Harry S. Truman signs Executive Order 9981, mandating an end to segregation in all U.S. armed forces–although the last segregated unit is not disbanded until 1954. The president also calls for an immediate end to racial discrimination in federal employment.

July 30
AVIATION: The air force accepts delivery of its first operational North American B-45A Tornado. This is the first large jet bomber in aviation history and it serves capably over the next decade in a variety of roles.

August 6
AVIATION: Two B-29s from the 43rd Bomb Group, *Gas Gobbler* and *Lucky Lady,* complete a 20,000-mile flight around the world in 15 days

August 8
AVIATION: A Convair B-36 Peacekeeper touches down in Fort Worth, Texas, after flying 9,400 miles round trip and nonstop from Hawaii. Aerial refueling proves unnecessary.

August 9
MARINES: As amphibious CAMID exercises unfold at Camp Lejeune, North Carolina, all branches of the armed forces participate for the first time since World War II.

August 15
AVIATION: The marine experimental helicopter squadron HMX-1 accepts delivery of its first Piasecki HRP-1 twin-rotor helicopters. Due to its distinctive curved shape it is known as the "Flying Banana."
MILITARY: In light of the recent division of the Korean Peninsula into Western and Soviet halves, the Provisional Military Advisory Group (PMAG) is established to funnel logistical support and equipment to the South Korean constabulary force. It presently consists of 100 officers and men.
POLITICS: In South Korea, Syngman Rhee becomes the first democratically elected president through U.S.-sponsored elections. North Korea, a sphere of the Soviet Union, does not allow elections.

August 16
AVIATION: At Muroc Dry Lake, California, the Northrop XF-89 prototype flies for the first time. It enters the service as the F-89 Scorpion and is the air force's first all-weather, radar-guided interceptor.

August 20
NAVAL: At Newport, Rhode Island, Secretary of Defense James Forrestal convenes a second meeting of the Joint Chiefs of Staff at the Naval War College. He attempts to solidify and define the roles and missions of the respective services, whereby the air force temporarily receives control of all atom bombs.

August 23
AVIATION: Over Muroc Dry Lake, California, an XF-85 Goblin parasite fighter flown by test pilot Ed Schoch collides with its hookup trapeze dangling from a

B-36 bomber and is forced to crash-land. The notion of "parasite fighters" dates back to the 1930s when several were stored on dirigibles, but it never becomes operational.

August 25
MARINES: At Quantico, Virginia, Lieutenant John E. Rudder becomes the first African-American marine officer to receive a regular Marine Corps commission and begins his training at the Basic School.

September 3
AVIATION: In England, Operation Dagger unfolds as U.S. Air Force B-29s and Royal Air Force aircraft hold a joint defense exercise.

September 9
AVIATION: The navy founds Composite Squadron VC-5 to develop tactics for delivering atomic weapons from the decks of aircraft carriers. It is initially equipped with specially modified P2V Neptune patrol planes.
POLITICS: In North Korea, former Red Army member Kim Il Sung proclaims establishment of the Communist People's Democratic Republic. Little known in the West, he intends to unify the Korean Peninsula under his rule by force, if necessary.

September 12–16
AVIATION: Over newly renamed Edwards Air Force Base (previously Muroc Dry Lake), California, the Convair XF-92 prototype flown by Sam Shannon is successfully flown. This sleek, delta-configured jet was inspired by Alexander Lippisch, a radical German aircraft designer and the information it gathers leads to several air force delta fighters a decade later.

September 15
AVIATION: Over Muroc Dry Lake, California, an F-86A flown by Major Richard L. Johnson sets a new world airspeed record of 671 miles per hour.

October 1
AVIATION: The seaplane tender *Norton* is converted into a guided missile test ship and is eventually designated AVM-1.
MARINES: By this date, the Marine Corps Reserve has risen to a strength of 116,000; of these, 37,742 presently serve in active duty units.

October 15
AVIATION: In Europe, Major General William H. Tunner, who successfully organized and commanded the cargo flying effort over the Himalayas in World War II, takes charge of the Berlin airlift. A logistical wizard, Tunner completely turns the flagging airlift around, making it highly successful.

October 18
MARINES: At Headquarters Marine Corps, Colonel Katherine A. Towle becomes the director of Women Marines and the first head of the female corps component.

October 19
AVIATION: In a major development, General Curtis E. LeMay gains appointment as the new head of the Strategic Air Command (SAC). Within a decade he trans-

forms it into the world's greatest bomber fleet and a major component of American nuclear deterrence.

October 20
AVIATION: The McDonnell XF-88 prototype flies for the first time, although it is subsequently cancelled and never enters production. However, the lessons learned lead to development of the highly successful F-101 Voodoo.

October 31
AVIATION: Air force authorities announce that an F-80 fighter has been flown at high altitude, powered by two wingtip ramjets. This is the first known instance of ramjet propulsion on a piloted craft.

November
AVIATION: Helicopter use now dawning, the Marine Corps publishes its first doctrine on the subject, *Amphibious Operations-Employment of Helicopters (Tentative)*.

November 4
AVIATION: In Santa Monica, California, the research-oriented RAND Corporation is established as a result of the joint Air Force–Douglas RAND project. It serves as an advisory body to the air force and draws upon noted scientists, industrialists, and military thinkers.

November 9
AVIATION: To contribute to Operation Vittles, the navy sends Transport Squadrons VR-6 and VR-8 to fly as part of the ongoing Berlin airlift. By the following July, they will have flown 45,990 flight hours and hauled 129,989 tons of cargo.

November 10
MEDICAL: At Randolph Air Force Base, Texas, the medical problems associated with space flight are the topic of the first-ever School of Aviation Medicine symposium.

November 14
MARINES: In Beijing and Tientsin, China, small detachments of marines arrive to escort the few remaining Americans to safety as Communist forces begin closing in on those cities.

November 16
NAVAL: At the Boston Navy Yard, Massachusetts, the heavy cruiser *Des Moines* is commissioned into service. This is the first of a three-ship class and, equipped with automatic 8-inch guns, it is the largest heavy cruiser ever launched.

November 17
MARINES: In light of the deteriorating situation in China, Secretary of the Navy James V. Forrestal directs that 1,250 marines on Guam will be immediately transported to Tsingtao to reinforce the 3,000 men comprising the Fleet Marine Force Western Pacific (FMFWESPAC). A platoon of marines is also deployed to Nanking to protect the American embassy before the city falls to Communist forces.

November 18
MARINES: In Haifa, Israel, a detachment of 62 marines is tapped to serve in the U.S. Military Observer Group and help conduct truce supervision.

November 20
AVIATION: A U.S. Army Signal Corps balloon reaches an altitude of 140,000 feet (26.5 miles).

November 28
MARINES: On Guam, BLT-9, consisting of the 9th Marines and reinforcing elements, embarks on the transport *Bayfield* for China. It is tasked with evacuating 2,500 American citizens from Shanghai before it falls to Communist forces.

November 30
AVIATION: A Douglas C-54 Skymaster transport, fitted with Curtis-Wright reversible propellers, manages a controlled descent from 15,000 feet to just 1,000 feet in only one minute and 22 seconds.

December 1
AVIATION: While created over a year ago, the Continental Air Command (CAC) is finally activated.

December 2
AVIATION: The prototype Beech Model 45 demonstrator performs its maiden flight. It enters the service as the T-34A Mentor, the first primary trainer adopted since the end of World War II, and it remains in the inventory until 1961.

December 8
AVIATION: Today a B-36 Peacekeeper flies nonstop from Carswell Air Force Base, Texas, to Hawaii, flying all 9,400 miles without refueling. Concurrently, a B-50 also makes the same trip, assisted by three inflight refuelings. Both feats demonstrate the range potential of Strategic Air Command (SAC) bombers.

December 9–27
AVIATION: In Greenland, a severe storm forces a C-47 to crash land on the icecap, stranding seven airmen there. An attempt to reach them through a glider towed by a B-17 fails, stranding another five would-be rescuers as well. An attempt is launched to rescue them before they freeze to death.

December 10
MILITARY: At Ceska Kubie, Czechoslovakia, two American soldiers from the 6th Armored Cavalry Regiment are detained by Communist forces and kept prisoner until February 1949.

December 15
MILITARY: The head of the U.S. Military Advisory Group in China declares that the Nationalist Army is not fighting effectively against Communist forces and, in all likelihood, will lose control of the entire country.

December 16
AVIATION: At Edwards Air Force Base, California, the tailless Northrop X-4 Bantam jet performs its maiden flight. Two X-4s are built to test the characteristics of tailless, swept-wing designs.
MARINES: BLT-9 arrives at Shanghai, China, although Secretary of State George C. Marshall declares that they will not get involved in the Chinese civil war unless violence threatens American lives.

December 17
AVIATION: In Washington, D.C., the original Wright flier, history's first heavier-than-air aircraft, is donated to the Smithsonian Institution for permanent display. Today is also the 45th anniversary of the first heavier-than-air flight.

December 28
AVIATION: A ski-equipped C-47 cargo plane flown by Lieutenant Colonel Emil Beaudry safely lands on the Greenland icecap and rescues 12 airmen who had crashed there on December 9. This daring rescue earns Beaudry the Mackay Trophy.

December 29
AVIATION: In Washington, D.C., Secretary of Defense Forrestal declares that the country is developing a program to place objects in low Earth orbit.

December 31
AVIATION: At this juncture, Operation Vittles has made its 100,000th flight during the Berlin airlift.
MARINES: By this date, the Marine Corps boasts 24 women officers and 300 enlisted on active duty.

1949

January
MILITARY: With the aid of the draft, army manpower levels have increased to 660,473 officers and men.

January 3
MARINES: In Jerusalem, the formal marine guard is organized for the U.S. consulate there.

January 3–March 15
AVIATION: In the wake of severe snowstorms throughout the Midwest, air force transports commence Operation Hayride, bringing 4,700 tons of livestock feed and other supplies to snow-bound ranchers.

January 5
AVIATION: At Edwards Air Force Base, California, a Bell X-1 piloted by Chuck Yeager makes the first standard takeoff by a rocket-propelled airplane, rising to 13,000 feet while making an unofficial climbing record. This is the only such takeoff in the rocket research program.

January 8
AVIATION: Boeing's new, swept-wing XB-47 jet bomber makes a transcontinental flight in three hours, 46 minutes, at an average speed of 607 miles per hour.

January 19
AVIATION: At Holoman Air Force Base, New Mexico, the Martin XB-61 Matador surface-to-surface missile is successfully fired.

January 21
AVIATION: Marine fighter squadron VMF-211 leaves China and is reassigned to the carrier *Rendova* in the western Pacific.

January 22
AVIATION: An Air Force AT-6 is shot down by Communist guerrillas in Greece and the pilot is killed.

January 25
AVIATION: A new slate blue uniform is adopted by the air force to replace the World War II–vintage olive drab uniforms.

February 8
AVIATION: A B-47 Stratojet lifts off from Moses Lake Airfield, Washington, and shatters all existing transcontinental records by touching down at Andrews Air Force Base, Maryland, in three hours and 45 minutes. The raft maintained an average speed of 600 miles per hour, faster than most fighter jets of the day, and cuts the previous record nearly in half.
MARINES: At Tsingtao, China, the bulk of the Fleet Marine Force Western Pacific (FMFWESPAC) embarks and sails for the United States. They leave behind a detachment of the 3rd Marines to maintain order as the Chinese civil war rages around them.

February 9
MEDICAL: At Randolph Air Force Base, Texas, the School of Aviation Medicine establishes a Department of Space Medicine.

February 23
MARINES: At Parris Island, South Carolina, the 3rd Recruit Battalion is activated for the purpose of training female recruits, the first of whom arrive five days later.

February 24
AVIATION: The army supervises launching of a two-stage WAC-Corporal missile at the White Sands Proving Ground, New Mexico. The device is basically a modified German V-2 rocket with a nose attachment, but it reaches a record altitude of 244 miles at 5,150 miles per hour, becoming the first human object to skirt the fringes of outer space.

February 25
MARINES: In Alaska, 20,000 sailors and marines conduct a month-long amphibious exercise.

February 26
MARINES: At Camp Pendleton, California, the Fleet Marine Force Western Pacific (FMFWESPAC) disbands and its personnel are absorbed into the 1st Marine Division.

February 26–March 2
AVIATION: A Boeing B-50 Superfortress named *Lucky Lady II,* piloted by Captain James Gallagher, completes a round-the-world flight with four inflight refuelings over the Azores, Arabia, the Philippines, and Hawaii. The 23,452-mile trip was completed in 94 hours, one minute. It also puts potential aggressors on notice that the United States possesses viable intercontinental strike capability with atomic weapons. The crew wins the Mackay Trophy for outstanding flight of the year.

1949

February 28
MILITARY: In Washington, D.C., the Hoover Commission on the Organization of the Executive Branch suggests that the secretary of defense be given greater authority over all branches of the armed forces so as to diminish interservice rivalry.

March
AVIATION: A P2V Neptune from Composite Squadron VC-5 launches from the carrier *Coral Sea* off the Atlantic Coast, then flies a 23-hour mission simulating an atomic strike on the West Coast before landing at Naval Air Station Patuxent River, Maryland.

March 2
MARINES: On Vieques Island, Puerto Rico, marines, army troops, and several platoons of Canadian soldiers conduct the largest amphibious exercise since World War II.

March 4
AVIATION: Since June 1948, the Berlin airlift has delivered over 1 million tons of coal, food, and supplies to the city's inhabitants.

March 5
MILITARY: In Washington, D.C., President Harry S. Truman adheres to the recommendation of the recent Hoover Commission in changing the National Security Act of 1947 to strengthen the secretary of defense's office at the expense of the service secretaries.

March 15
AVIATION: The Military Air Transport Service (MATS) establishes the Global Weather Service to assist operations of the Strategic Air Command (SAC).

March 23
AVIATION: The air force begins deploying four-engine North American B-45 Tornado jet bombers, the first such aircraft in the world, with the 47th Bomb Group at Barksdale Air Force Base, Louisiana, under Colonel Willis F. Chapman. A tough, two-year shakedown period ensues, but the Tornado achieves operational status.

March 26
AVIATION: At Fort Worth, Texas, the new Convair B-36D Peacekeeper debuts and features two wingtip pods housing four J-47 jet engines. The 10-engine behemoth is now capable of reaching 440 miles per hour in level flight and can lift an 85,000 lb. payload. Success, however, triggers an internecine struggle with navy officials, who hotly dispute the notion of atomic-armed strategic bombers in an age of fiscal retrenchment.

March 28
MILITARY: In Washington, D.C., Louis Johnson replaces James V. Forrestal as the second secretary of defense.

March 30
AVIATION: In Washington, D.C., President Harry S. Truman signs legislating mandating the nation's first, permanent radar defense network.

1949

Marines: In Shanghai, China, the 3rd Marines assume protection duties for American civilians in the city once BLT-9 embarks for the United States.

April

Marines: In round two of the defense unification battle, Secretary of the Army Kenneth C. Royall testifies before Congress that the Marine Corps ought to be abolished.

April 4

Diplomacy: Lines of the cold war harden when 10 European nations join the United States and Canada in a mutual defense pact called the North Atlantic Treaty, which lays the groundwork for the North Atlantic Treaty Organization (NATO). Its charter members are the United States, Great Britain, France, Italy, Canada, Belgium, Luxembourg, Portugal, the Netherlands, Denmark, Norway, and Iceland. All signatories are committed to the military defense of Western Europe; this is also the first time that the United States has joined a military alliance in peacetime.

April 6

Aviation: Curtiss-Wright declares that the XS-1 rocket research aircraft (built by Bell, powered by a Curtiss-Wright engine) has established an unofficial world speed record of 1,000 miles per hour.
• The Berlin airlift reaches its highest point of efficiency with one cargo plane landing at Templehof Airfield every four minutes for six consecutive hours.

April 16

Aviation: At Van Nuys, California, the Lockheed YF-94 makes its maiden flight. This is a stretched version of the F-80 Shooting Star intended to serve as an all-weather interceptor, and it enters the service as the F-94 Starfire.
• By this date, 1,398 aircraft sorties of the Berlin airlift have delivered 12,940 tons of supplies to the citizens of that beleaguered city.

April 20

Naval: Military violence against foreigners in China reaches a new peak when Chinese forces shell a Royal Navy frigate moving up the Yangtze River to rescue British citizens marooned in Nanking. The British suffer 40 dead and 78 wounded. The Communists are playing for keeps.

April 21

Marines: Because of escalating violence against foreign troops in China, the naval commander there orders the solitary Marine platoon, 3rd Marines, in Nanking to be evacuated by air to Shanghai as soon as possible.

April 23

Naval: In Washington, D.C., Secretary of Defense Louis Johnson cancels the new carrier *United States* only five days after its keel has been laid in Newport News, Virginia. Because this move was arbitrarily performed without consulting either Secretary of the Navy John L. Sullivan or Chief of Naval Operations admiral Louis E. Denfield, Sullivan resigns from office in protest.

April 26

Aviation: In another blow aimed at the Marine Corps, Secretary of Defense Louis Johnson declares he is transferring all marine aviation assets and personnel to the new U.S. Air Force.

April 28
POLITICS: In Washington, D.C., political wrangling intensifies over the Marine Corps after Carl Vinson, chairman of the House Armed Services Committee informs Secretary of Defense Louis Johnson that any changes to the National Security Act of 1947, including those respecting Marine Corps aviation, must meet first with congressional approval.

April 29
MARINES: At Shanghai, China, the 3rd Marines embark for the United States, leaving a sole rifle company in Tsingtao as the only Leathernecks on the Asian landmass.

May 1
MARINES: In light of prevailing realities in China, the 7th Marines, en route to Shanghai, are rerouted back to Pearl Harbor, Hawaii.

May 7
AVIATION: A special act of Congress makes retired five-star general Henry H. Arnold a permanent general of the U.S. Air Force; he remains the only officer so honored.

May 9
AVIATION: At Quantico, Virginia, the marine experimental helicopter squadron HMX-1 performs a simulated amphibious assault for members of Congress. Eight HRP-1s convey 56 marines and 75mm pack howitzers into two successful lifts.
• At Edwards Air Force Base, California, the Republic XF-91 Thunderceptor jet/rocket hybrid performs its first flight. Based roughly on the F-84 Thunderjet, this new design employs inverse-tapered swept wings; it does not enter production.

May 11
AVIATION: In Washington, D.C., President Harry S. Truman signs legislation to construct a guided-missile test range for the air force at Cape Canaveral, Florida. The actual range itself extends 3,000 miles out to sea.

May 12
DIPLOMACY: In East Germany, Soviet forces lift their ground blockade of Berlin, but airlift sorties continue to build up stockpiles of supplies for an emergency.

May 14
NAVAL: The *Salem* becomes the last all-gun cruiser in the U.S. Navy; like all *Des Moines*-class vessels, it is equipped with automatic 8-inch guns.

May 16
MARINES: The 9th Marines are assigned to the 2nd Marine Division at Camp Lejeune, North Carolina.
• At Tsingtao, China, Company C, 3rd Marines embarks for the United States, ending postwar occupation duties on the Asian landmass.

May 20–21
AVIATION: At Camp Lejeune, North Carolina, Marine experimental helicopter squadron HMX-1 lifts several infantry units ashore as part of Operation Packard III.

1949

May 21
AVIATION: Over Bridgeport, Connecticut, a Sikorsky S-52-1 flown by Captain H. D. Gaddis establishes a world altitude record 21,220 feet.

May 24–26
AVIATION: In New York City, the Institute of Aeronautical Sciences and the Royal Aeronautical Society convene their second International Conference of Aeronautics.

May 25
NAVAL: In Washington, D.C., Francis P. Matthews gains appointment as the 50th secretary of the navy.

May 26
NAVAL: Off Tsingtao, China, the cruiser *Manchester* sails off in anticipation of a Nationalist surrender there.

June 3
NAVAL: At Annapolis, Maryland, Wesley Brown is the first African-American cadet to graduate from the U.S. Naval Academy with an ensign's commission.

June 4
AVIATION: The streamlined Lockheed XF-90 strategic fighter successfully flies for the first time. It does not go into production, but, a decade later, it appears in the comic book *Black Hawk* as the protagonist's aircraft. Shortly afterward, it also appears in *Wonder Woman* comics as her invisible mount.

June 20
MILITARY: In Washington, D.C., Secretary of the Army Kenneth C. Royall is replaced by Gordon Gray.

June 29
MILITARY: Pursuant to a prior agreement, the United States removes the last of its X Corps from South Korea, while 472 military advisers remain in place. No sooner do they depart, however, than a series of hostile events takes place along the 38th parallel separating South and North Korea.

June 30
MILITARY: The 5th Regimental Combat Team is the last U.S. Army unit to depart South Korea at the end of American occupation. The only military presence are the 472 officers and men attached to the Korean Military Assistance Group (KMAG).

July 1
AVIATION: In California, the first F-94A Starfire, the first American jet fitted with an afterburner, is flown for the first time.
MEDICAL: Major General Malcom C. Grow is appointed first surgeon general of the Air Force and the U.S. Air Force Medical Service is also established.
MILITARY: In light of Philippine independence, the army disbands its elite Philippine Scouts after 48 years of distinguished service.
MARINES: In light of budgetary cuts, the Fleet Marine Force plans to reduces its number of battalions from 11 to eight, and aviation squadrons from 23 to 12.

1949

July 3
AVIATION: The B-29 *Enola Gay,* which dropped the atomic bomb on Hiroshima, Japan and helped to end World War II, is donated to the Smithsonian Institution and stored at Park Ridge, Illinois.

August 1
NAVAL: In the western Pacific, the Seventh Fleet is reestablished as the navy's forward-deployed force, ostensibly to keep an eye on Red China and its threats to invade Taiwan.

August 8
AVIATION: Over Edwards Air Force Base, California, a Bell X-1 flown by Major Frank K. Everest reaches a record 71,902 feet, the highest altitude attained by a first generation research aircraft.

August 9
AVIATION: Over South Carolina, Lieutenant J. L. Fruin, flying an F2H Banshee jet fighter belonging to VF-171, suffers from engine trouble and punches out at 500 miles per hour. He is the first American jet aviator to use an ejection seat in the line of duty.
•   The Soviet Union, aided and abetted by an efficient spy ring at Alamogordo, New Mexico, during World War II, detonates its first atomic bomb at Semipalatinsk. It is a virtual copy of the "Fat Boy" weapon that destroyed Nagasaki, Japan, five years earlier.

August 10
MILITARY: The National Security Act is amended by President Harry S. Truman, which establishes the new Department of Defense (DoD) to replace the National Military Establishment. It also grants subcabinet status to the secretaries of the army, navy, and air force, who thus lose their executive status and become subordinate branches within the department. The Joint Chiefs of Staff is also enlarged from 100 to 210 officers while the Marine Corps mission, originally spelled out in 1947, is left unaltered.

August 11
MARINES: In the Middle East, Brigadier General William R. Riley becomes chief of staff of the UN Palestine Truce Mission to oversee the shaky peace between Israel and its resentful Arab neighbors.

August 16
MILITARY: General Omar Bradley is appointed the first chairman of the Joint Chiefs of Staff (JCS). General Joseph Lawton succeeds him as chief of staff.

August 25
AVIATION: Over Edwards Air Force Base, California, a Bell X-1 flown by Major Frank K. Everest experiences drastic decompression at 69,000 feet, and he becomes the first pilot saved by a T-1 pressure suit; he is able to land safely.

August 26
NAVAL: In the Greenland Sea, the submarine *Cochino* suffers a battery explosion while submerged and is forced to surface. Before a second explosion sinks the

vessel, its crew safely transfers to the submarine *Cusk* nearby; one civilian and six sailors are killed.

August 31
GENERAL: The Grand Army of the Republic holds it 83rd encampment in Indianapolis, Indiana, and is attended by six of the surviving 16 Civil War veterans.

September
AVIATION: A Sikorsky S-52 helicopter, the first such machine fitted with metal rotor blades, also becomes the first helicopter to be successfully looped in flight.

September 8
MARINES: Annie E. Graham makes history by becoming the first African-American female to enlist in the Marine Corps.

September 9
MARINES: Consistent with new desegregation laws, the Montford Point Camp reserved for African-American marines closes down and all personnel are integrated into training platoons at Camp Lejeune, North Carolina.

September 24
AVIATION: At Inglewood, California, the prototype T-28 flies for the first time. It enters the service as the T-28A Trojan and serves as a basic trainer and an attack plane through the Vietnam War years.

September 30
AVIATION: The Berlin airlift, America's first victory of the cold war, officially concludes today. More than 277,000 flights have been flown by U.S. Air Force, U.S. Navy, Royal Air Force, and Commonwealth aircraft, which delivered 2.34 million tons of food, coal, and supplies. Air force pilots are responsible for 1.78 million tons of that total.

October 1
AVIATION: At Cape Canaveral, Florida, Major General W. L. Richardson takes charge of the new Long Range Proving Ground.
DIPLOMACY: In Beijing, China, Chairman Mao Zedong declares the founding of the People's Republic of China; remaining Nationalist forces still on the Asian continent flee to Taiwan offshore.
NAVAL: The navy establishes the Military Sea Transportation Service, which encompasses both army and navy cargo ships. It is controlled by the secretary of the navy.
MARINES: The J-series tables of organization are replaced and historic regiments are restored to their true numerical sequence. The 1st Marine Division acts first, converting the 1st, 6th, and 7th Marines into the headquarters, 1st Battalion and 2nd Battalion, 5th Marines.

October 5
POLITICS: In Washington, D.C., Congressman Carl Vinson, chairman of the House Ways and Means Committee, conducts hearings relative to complaints by navy and marine authorities that the sea services are being neglected. The seemingly arbitrary cancellation of the supercarrier *United States* is cited as the most glaring example. With shrinking defense appropriations also comes renewed

1949

naval opposition to the air force's new B-36 intercontinental bomber. Several high-ranking naval officers, headed by Admiral Arthur W. Radford, testify to that effect before Congress.

October 11
AVIATION: In Washington, D.C., assistance director of Marine Corps Aviation, Brigadier General Vernon A. Megee, alerts the House Armed Services Committee that the air force is neglecting its close air support mission to the army and marines.

October 14
AVIATION: The Chase Aircraft Company XC-123 assault transport prototype flies for the first time. It enters service as the Fairchild C-123 Provider and performs yeoman work during the Vietnam War.

October 17
NAVAL: In Washington, D.C., Chief of Naval Operations Louis E. Denfeld defies instructions from the secretary of defense and secretary of the navy, and vociferously speaks out against the air force B-36 Peacekeeper program. He is consequently removed from office as of November 1. However, this "Revolt of the Admirals" induces Congress to preserve traditional roles for the U.S. Navy and Marine Corps in the standing military establishment.

MARINES: Commandant Clifton B. Cates declares before Congress that the Marine Corps is being made irrelevant despite provisions of the National Security Act of 1947 to the contrary. He also maintains that, because the marines lack representation on the Joint Chiefs of Staff, their budgets are being drastically cut.

October 21
MARINES: In Washington, D.C., Secretary of Defense Louis Johnson assures leaders of the Marine Corps that their service is secure. However, rumors abound that Secretary of the Navy John L. Sullivan resigned from office because of his vocal opposition to abolishing the corps.

October 25–26
MARINES: Off Hawaii, the navy and Marine Corps stage their largest ever amphibious assault exercises by "liberating" the islands from an aggressor.

October 27
AVIATION: In Washington, D.C., Congress passes the Unitary Wind Tunnel Act to construct several advanced wind tunnels at test facilities nationwide. A further $100 million is earmarked for the new Arnold Engineering Development Center in Tullahoma, Tennessee.

October 30
MARINES: In line with the latest spate of defense expenditure reductions, plan are made to reduce existing marine battalions to two rifle companies of two platoons each.

November 2
NAVAL: In Washington, D.C., Admiral Forrest P. Sherman is appointed the 12th chief of naval operations to replace the defiant Louis Denfeld; he is the youngest officer to hold this position.

1949

November 5
AVIATION: At El Toro, California, marine aviators begin jet training in a Lockheed TO-1, a two-seater version of the famous F-80 "Shooting Star."

November 10
AVIATION: At Stratford, Connecticut, the Sikorsky YH-19A Chickasaw helicopter performs its maiden flight. This somewhat bulbous craft is the first such machine with an unobstructed cabin, as the engine is mounted in the nose.

November 18
AVIATION: The giant Douglas C-74 Globemaster I named *The Champ* flies non-stop from Mobile, Alabama, to RAF Marham, United Kingdom, while carrying 103 passengers and crew. It is the first aircraft to make a transatlantic crossing with more than 100 people onboard.
MARINES: The Marine Corps formally embraces President Harry S. Truman's executive order banning racial discrimination against African Americans and other minorities. Henceforth, unit assignments must be made without regard to race.

November 29
AVIATION: The prototype Douglas YC-124 performs its maiden flight. It enters service as the C-124 Globemaster II, better known to passengers as "Old Shakey" and sees extensive service with the Military Air Transport Service (MATS) and the Strategic Air Command (SAC).

December
AVIATION: At Langley, Virginia, NACA engineers reach a technical milestone by creating the first, continuous, transonic flow of air in their eight-foot-high speed tunnel.

December 2
AVIATION: At Holloman Air Development Center, New Mexico, the new Aerobee research rocket (RTV-A-1a) is successfully fired.

December 5
AVIATION: The air force diverts $50 million from other projects and begins constructing a chain of radar stations across the northern Alaskan frontier for the purpose of detecting incoming Soviet bombers. The recent testing of a Soviet atomic bomb makes this all the more imperative.

December 22
AVIATION: The North American YF-84D all-weather interceptor completes its maiden flight. It enters service as the F-86D, or Sabre Dog, conspicuous with its redesigned radome nose cone.

December 25
AVIATION: The air force reveals the existence of the new ceramic called Stupalith, which expands and contracts when heated and cooled and can withstand 2,000 degree temperatures. It is utilized as insulation around jet and rocket engines.

December 28
AVIATION: Amid much public hoopla, the air force ends a two-year old investigation of "flying saucers" at Wright Patterson Air Force Base, Ohio, concluding that they do not exist.

1949

December 29
AVIATION: In California, an F-51 Mustang flown by noted aviatrix Jacqueline Cochran establishes an international speed record of 436.995 miles per hour over a 500-kilometer course.

1950

January
MILITARY: Army personnel declines to 593,167–10 divisions–in light of drastic budget cuts; the force is also hobbled by a lack of large-scale, live-fire exercises and by decreases in new weapons development.

January 9
MARINES: The latest round of military budget cuts will reduce Marine Corps personnel by an additional 10,000 men to 74,396.

January 14
AVIATION: Off Miami, Florida, aviation units from the air force, navy, and marines stage their first unified aerial maneuvers.

January 15
AVIATION: In Sonoma, California, General of the Air Force Henry H. Arnold dies. He was a major architect of American air power with a career spanning the Wright brothers' pioneering efforts to the dawn of jet aviation and rockets.

January 17
NAVAL: Off Hampton Roads, Virginia, the battleship *Missouri* runs aground, resulting in court-martials for its captain, operations officer, and combat information officer.

January 18
AVIATION: The Lockheed YF-94C prototype completes its maiden flight; this is the first air force interceptor armed solely with air-to-air rockets.

January 23
AVIATION: To separate research operations from logistics and procurement activities of the Air Materiel Command, the Air Force Research and Development Command is established at Wright-Patterson Field, Ohio. It is subsequently redesignated the Research and Development Command.

January 31
TECHNOLOGY: President Harry S. Truman, forewarned that the Soviets are already developing a "super bomb," orders the military and scientific communities to begin work on constructing a new thermonuclear weapon, or hydrogen bomb.

February 12
NAVAL: The navy officially designates the Sixth Task Fleet and Seventh Task Fleet the Sixth and Seventh Fleets, respectively.

February 14
DIPLOMACY: The Soviet Union and the People's Republic of China conclude a treaty of alliance and mutual assistance. For all intents and purposes, this is a pact between two scorpions in a bottle but it frightens the United States and the West.

February 25–March 11
MARINES: At Vieques Island, Puerto Rico, all four U.S. services participate in POR-TEX, the largest peacetime amphibious-airborne maneuver since World War II. It involves 800,000 men, 160 vessels, and 700 aircraft; seven people die in accidents.

March 1
AVIATION: Following a protracted development to wrinkle out the bugs, the first B-47A Stratojet is delivered to the air force for testing. The A-model is used strictly for training flight and ground personnel.
MARINES: In Washington, D.C., a report is issued by the House Armed Services Committee, which argues that the Commandant of the Marine Corps should be admitted as a full partner to the Joint Chiefs of Staff. It also calls for more joint training and expanded wartime roles for naval aviation.

March 10
MARINES: At Quantico, Virginia, the new Marine Corps Development Center and the Marine Corps Educational Center are formed from the older Marine Corps Schools in order to place added focus on new equipment and doctrines along with better educational and training programs.

March 15
AVIATION: The Department of Defense allocates exclusive responsibility for developing strategic guided missiles, ICBMs, to the U.S. Air Force.

March 16–April 5
NAVAL: The submarine *Pickerel* performs a record underwater voyage between Hong Kong and Pearl Harbor, Hawaii, by remaining submerged for 21 days and covering 5,194 nautical miles.

March 22
AVIATION: At RAF Marham, England, the United States hands over the first four of 70 Boeing B-29 Superfortress bombers to the Royal Air Force. Once employed by the British, they receive the designation of Washington.

April 8
AVIATION: Soviet La-7 fighters attack and shoot down a navy Consolidated PB4Y-2 Privateer as it performed an electronic reconnaissance mission over the Baltic Sea near the Latvian coastline; the entire crew of 10 perishes.

April 12
MILITARY: In Washington, D.C., Frank Pace is appointed the third secretary of the army.

April 18
AVIATION: The air force declares that its anticipated procurement of 1,250 modern aircraft this year will set the taxpayers back $1.2 billion.

April 21
AVIATION: A North American AJ-1 Savage, the first naval attack craft capable of delivering atomic weapons, is successfully launched from the deck of the carrier *Coral Sea* for the first time. This aircraft is also unique in being powered by two propeller-driven engines and one jet engine in the tail section.

1950

April 24
AVIATION: In Washington, D.C., Thomas K. Finletter gains appointment as the secretary of the air force.

April 28
NAVAL: At Annapolis, Maryland, Vice Admiral Harry W. Hill is appointed the 36th superintendent of the U.S. Naval Academy.

May 5
AVIATION: At Hawthorne, California, the futuristic YRB-49A Flying Wing, which sports two additional J-35 engines in wing-mounted pods, performs its maiden flight. This spectacular-looking reconnaissance machine does not enter production.
MILITARY: In Washington, D.C., the Articles of War, long the judicial regulations for the U.S. armed forces, are replaced by the new Uniform Code of Military Justice.

May 9
MARINES: In China, the Communists release two marine airmen held since October 1948 when their airplane crash-landed in Manchuria.

May 10
TECHNOLOGY: In Washington, D.C., President Harry S. Truman signs legislation creating the National Science Foundation.

May 12
AVIATION: At Edwards Air Force Base, California, the first Bell X-1 rocket plane makes a final flight before being turned over to the Smithsonian Institution for display purposes.

June 1
AVIATION: The air force is ordered to organize the Ground Observer Corps to serve as an adjunct of the overall civil air raid warning system.

June 3
AVIATION: The Republic YF-96A, a swept-wing version of the venerable F-84 Thunderjet, makes its initial flight. It enters the service as the F-84F Thunderstreak.

June 9
AVIATION: In Washington, D.C., Secretary Louis Johnson, citing budgetary restrictions, announces that military aircraft will not be participating in this year's National Air Races.

June 15
AVIATION: At Quantico, Virginia, Marine Corps helicopters and infantry stage a mock aerial assault for President Harry S. Truman. The service seeks to convince him that they deserve a bigger slice of the Defense Department's shrinking pie.

June 25
AVIATION: The Korean War commences as Russian-flown Yak-9 fighters strafe Kimpo Air Base, South Korea. Consequently, Major General Earle E. Partridge, commanding the Fifth Air Force in Japan, places his forces on high alert.
DIPLOMACY: In New York, the UN Security Council passes a resolution condemning the Communist invasion of South Korea.

MILITARY: Prevailing winds of the cold war suddenly blow hotter when 135,000 men of the North Korean People's Army (NKPA), backed by 150 Soviet-built tanks, roll south of the 38th parallel and invade South Korea. Communist forces have been both trained and equipped by the Soviet Union, and the aggression unfolds with the apparent acquiescence of Soviet leader Joseph Stalin and Chinese leader Mao Zedong. For the United States, this is the first military challenge of the cold war.

June 26
AVIATION: Air Force F-82 Twin Mustangs of the 68th Fighter All-Weather Squadron provide top cover for evacuation activities at Inchon, South Korea, as thousands of foreign nationals flee the Communist onslaught.
MILITARY: President Harry S. Truman immediately authorizes U.S. Navy and U.S. Air Force units in Japan to begin direct military support of South Korean forces below the 38th parallel.
NAVAL: The destroyers *Mansfield* and *De Haven* are on hand at Inchon, South Korea, to assist in the evacuation of 700 foreign nationals caught up in fighting between North and South Koreans.

June 27
AVIATION: Over Seoul, South Korea, an F-82 Twin Mustang, flown by Lieutenant William Hudson and Lieutenant Carl S. Fraser, shoots down a Soviet-made Yak-11 fighter of the North Korean air force. This is the first American aerial victory of the war and is soon joined by seven others—the highest tally scored on a single day in 1950.
• B-26 Invaders of the Fifth Air Force commence launching air strikes against North Korean infantry and tank columns; poor weather negates most of their actions. Meanwhile, RF-80s deploy at Itazuke, Japan, to provide badly needed aerial reconnaissance.
• The 374th Troop Carrier Wing deploys C-46s, C-147s, and C-54s to Suwon Air Field, South Korea, in order to evacuate hundreds of foreign nationals to Japan.
DIPLOMACY: In New York, the UN Security Council passes a second resolution condemning Communist aggression in South Korea and recommends that UN members so inclined contribute military forces to help repel it.
MILITARY: In Washington, D.C., President Harry S. Truman authorizes General Douglas MacArthur, as commander in chief, Far East, to commit air and naval forces against Communist aggression in South Korea.
• At Suwon, South Korea, Brigadier General John H. Church arrives as part of the General Headquarters, Advance Command and Liaison Group, to assess military conditions on the Korean Peninsula. He subsequently notified General Douglas MacArthur, commander in chief, U.S. Far East Command, that American troops are necessary to drive out the invaders.

June 28
AVIATION: As North Korean troops occupy Kimpo Air Base near Seoul, South Korea, B-26 Invaders of the 3rd Bombardment Group continue hammering away at them, sometimes as far north as the 38th parallel. They are joined by other

Invaders from the same unit, who commence their first offensive daylight missions of the war by striking Heijo Air Field near Pyongyang, North Korea.
• The first jet reconnaissance mission is flown by Lieutenant Bryce Poe in an RF-80.
MILITARY: Tanks and infantry of the North Korean People's Army capture the South Korean capital of Seoul. Soldiers of the Republic of Korea (ROK) resist tenaciously but, being lightly equipped as a constabulary, they are completely outclassed by their heavily armed, Soviet-equipped opponents.

June 29
AVIATION: In South Korea, F-82s drop napalm for the first time while five North Korean fighters are shot down in the vicinity of Suwon. A force of B-29s bombing targets near Seoul shoots down a Communist aircraft, marking the first bomber gunner victory of the war.
• At Yokota, Japan, aircraft of the 8th Tactical Reconnaissance Squadron (TRS) commence flying photographic sorties over South Korea.
MILITARY: At Suwon, South Korea, five soldiers of the 507th Antiaircraft Artillery Battalion become the nation's first casualties of the Korean War.
NAVAL: Off Samchok, Korea, the light cruiser *Juneau* bombards shore installations in the first example of naval gunfire in the Korean War.

June 30
AVIATION: General Douglas MacArthur is authorized by President Harry S. Truman to employ air force fighters and bombers to destroy targets in Communist North Korea as well as in South Korea.
• In Japan, the Fifth Air Force is bolstered by the arrival of No. 77 Squadron, Royal Australian Air Force (RAAF).
MILITARY: President Harry S. Truman orders the deployment of U.S. ground forces to South Korea and he also signs a bill extending the military draft for another year while Reserve and National Guard personnel are subject to call up and 21 months of service. The closest American forces, the Eighth Army in Japan, are in poor shape after five years of occupation duty, and they lack heavy tanks and other essential equipment.
• North Korean columns cross the Han River below Seoul, South Korea, and threaten the airfield at Suwon. Far East Air Forces (FEAF) orders an immediate evacuation of that field and transfers its assets to Pusan on the east side of the peninsula.
NAVAL: President Harry S. Truman orders a naval blockade of the Korean coastline.
MARINES: At the onset of hostilities in Korea, marine manpower levels are only 7,254 officers and 67,025 enlisted men. Fortunately, the Marine Corps can dip into a very large pool of trained reservists to buttress all ranks.

July 1
AVIATION: With the fall of Suwon Air Field, Seoul, to the Communists, the 374th Troop Carrier Wing (TCW) airlifts advanced echelons of the 24th Infantry Division from Japan to Pusan, South Korea.
MILITARY: Army troops from the 1st Battalion, 21st Regiment, 24th Infantry Division, designated Task Force Smith, cross from Japan and deploy in South Korea.

1950

U.N.C. Commander General of the Army Douglas MacArthur (right) at the frontlines in Suwon, Korea, with Lieutenant General Matthew B. Ridgway (third from right) *(Library of Congress)*

They are commanded by Lieutenant Colonel Charles B. Smith, who takes up defensive positions at Osan. The remainder of the division is expected to join them in days under Major General William F. Dean.

NAVAL: The Military Transportation Service begins shipping the main body of the 24th Infantry Division from Japan to Pusan, South Korea.

July 2

NAVAL: The light cruisers *Juneau* and HMS *Jamaica* and the frigate HMS *Black Swan* are attacked by three North Korean patrol boats; the Communist vessels are all sunk without damage to the UN ships. This is also the sole purely naval action of the war involving an American warship.

MARINES: General Douglas MacArthur requests the immediate dispatch of a Marine Corps regimental combat team to Korea, so Fleet Marine Force Pacific (FMFPAC) issues embarkation orders to the 1st Marine Division.

July 3

AVIATION: Over Pyongyang, North Korea, navy F9F Panthers from VF-51 shoot down two Yak-9 fighters, the first jet aerial victories of the Korean War.

• Because large, heavy Douglas C-54 Sky Masters damage the thin airfields at Pusan, South Korea, the work of troop transport falls upon smaller C-46s and C-47s.

NAVAL: Task Force 77 under Vice Admiral Arthur D. Struble orders the carrier *Valley Forge,* then the only American carrier available in the western Pacific, and the British carrier *Triumph* to launch the first naval aviation strikes of the Korean War.

MARINES: In Washington, D.C., the Joint Chiefs of Staff agree to General Douglas MacArthur's request for a Marine Corps Regimental Combat team and accompanying aircraft.

July 4

DIPLOMACY: In Washington, D.C., President Harry S. Truman declares the coasts of North Korea to be under a naval blockade.

MILITARY: In Tokyo, Japan, the staff of General Douglas MacArthur begins planning for a major amphibious assault upon the western Korean port of Inchon. The plan is initially scrubbed as overly ambitious but it is resurrected two months later under the title Operation Chromite.

July 5

AVIATION: The 1st Marine Aviation Wing absorbs men and equipment of Marine Air Group 33 under Brigadier General Thomas J. Cushman.

MILITARY: In South Korea, the Battle of Osan unfolds as the men of Task Force Smith are attacked in strength by the North Korean 4th Division. Though outnumbered, the Americans destroy four T-34 tanks and delay the enemy advance by seven hours. Task Force Smith loses 181 dead, wounded, and missing.

July 6

AVIATION: The Harmon International Aviation Awards Committee votes General James H. Doolittle "Aviator of the Decade" while Jacqueline Cochran is named "Outstanding Aviatrix." Vice Admiral Charles E. Rosenthal also becomes the top aeronaut (lighter-than-air pilot).

• Nine Fifth Air Force B-29s make their first strategic bomb run of the war by striking at the Rising Sun Oil Refinery at Wonsan and various chemical facilities in Hungnam, North Korea.

July 6–12

MILITARY: At Pyongtaek, South Korea, the 34th Infantry tangles with advancing North Korean forces and wages a desperate rearguard action that delays the Communist advance for several hours. The 21st Infantry performs similar work at Chochiwan before being forced to retreat. A number of American soldiers taken prisoner are subsequently bound and executed by Communist forces, who also shoot thousands of South Korean civilians.

July 7

AVIATION: Headquarters Marine Corps directs that flight and ground personnel of the experimental helicopter squadron HMX-1 be transferred to observation squadron VMO-6, so that the 1st Provisional Marine Brigade can possess a helicopter detachment.

MARINES: At Camp Pendleton, California, the 1st Provisional Marine Brigade is cobbled together under the command of Brigadier General Edward A. Craig. It consists of the entire 5th Marines and the forward echelon of the 1st Marine Air Wing (1st MAW). Presently, its three battalions consist of only six rifle companies and other platoons are hurriedly added to bring the units up to strength.

1950

July 7–8
MILITARY: In New York, the United Nations Security Council asks the United States to serve as its executive agent for hostilities in South Korea through the aegis of a UN Command (UNC).

July 8
MILITARY: General Douglas MacArthur is appointed supreme commander of United Nations forces in Korea and head of the United Nations Command (UNC) by President Harry S. Truman.
• At Yokota, Japan, Major General Emmett "Rosie" O'Donnell takes charge of Far East Air Forces Bomber Command (Provisional), which now directs B-29 operations against North Korea.

July 9
AVIATION: In South Korea, air force forward air controllers fling L-5G and L-17 liaison craft into directing close support missions for F-80 Shooting Star fighter bombers.
NAVAL: Commander Michael J. Luosey is placed in command of all South Korean naval assets.

July 10
AVIATION: In South Korea, a T-6 Texan trainer employed on a "Mosquito" mission, calls down an F-80 close support strike on a column of North Korean tanks, which is destroyed.
• A North Korean column is caught in the open near Pyongtaek, South Korea, and destroyed by F-80s, F-82s, and B-26s. Dozens of vehicles go up in flames.
MILITARY: Advanced elements of the 24th Infantry Division begin debarking at Pusan, South Korea, under Major General William F. Dean.
• In light of the mounting military crisis on the Korean Peninsula, General Douglas MacArthur requests additional reinforcements, including an entire marine division with air support.

July 11
NAVAL: In a bold attack, Commander W. B. Porter of the light cruiser *Juneau* goes ashore with 10 sailors and marines to blow up a railroad tunnel at Rashin, North Korea.

July 12
AVIATION: The first shipment of 58 3.5-inch bazookas capable of knocking out Soviet-made T-34 tanks arrives from the United States onboard four Military Air Service Transport Service (MATS) aircraft.
• Over South Korea, North Korean fighters manage to down a B-29, a B-26, and an L-4, the first Communist aerial victories in this conflict.
MILITARY: In Tokyo, Japan, General Douglas MacArthur orders Lieutenant General Walton H. Walker to take control of all U.S. ground forces in Korea.
MARINES: The first elements of the 1st Provisional Marine Brigade ship out from California and head for Korea.

July 13
AVIATION: A force of 49 B-29s from the 22nd and 92nd Bombardment Groups strikes marshaling yards and an oil refinery at Wonsan, North Korea. These units had arrived from the United States only six days previously.

MILITARY: At Taegu, South Korea, Lieutenant General Walton H. Walker, head of the Eighth Army, establishes his headquarters and assumes control of all U.S. forces on the peninsula.

July 14

AVIATION: Eager to be closer to the scene of action to preserve fuel, the 35th Tactical Interceptor Group deploys at Pohang, South Korea, while the 6132d Tactical Air Control Squadron also arrives at Taegu.

July 14–26

MILITARY: Along the Kum River, South Korea, the badly outgunned 24th Infantry Division wages an ill-fated struggle to stop superior North Korean forces from crossing. Fighting focuses on the city of Taejon, an important communications hub and Major General William F. Dean joins his men, bazooka in hand, in destroying an enemy tank in the streets. At length the Americans give way and fall back in disorder; Dean is separated from his men and is taken captive on August 25. However, this gallant stand allows General Walton H. Walker to set up a defensive perimeter along the Naktong River outside Pusan.

July 15

AVIATION: F-51 Mustangs belonging to the 51st Fighter Squadron (FS) at Taegu, South Korea, commence flying their first sorties.

MARINES: Orders are issued from Fleet Marine Force Pacific (FMFPAC) that the 1st Marine Division is going to be expanded to full strength. Two air transport squadrons are also dispatched to Korea to support airlift orations.

July 16

MILITARY: The U.S. Eighth Army assumes control of all Republic of Korea (ROK) military forces.

July 18

AVIATION: Task Force 77 launches carrier air strikes against Wonsan, North Korea, hitting railroad yards, factories, and an oil refinery.

MILITARY: Advanced elements of the 1st Cavalry Division under Major General Hobart R. Gay debark at Pohang, South Korea.

NAVAL: Amphibious Group 1 under Rear Admiral James H. Doyle transports men and equipment of the 1st Cavalry Division from Japan to Pohang, South Korea.

July 19

AVIATION: At Kangmyong-ni, North Korea, an AD Skyraider flown by Ensign Donald E. Stevens of VA-55 hits a truck while on a strafing run; he is naval aviation's first fatality in this conflict.

• Over Taejon, South Korea, Fifth Air Force F-80s shoot down three Communist Yak fighters, this month's highest tally.

• Determined to acquire air superiority over the enemy, a strike by seven F-80s of the 8th Fighter Bomber Group (FBG) destroys 15 North Korean aircraft on a field near Pyongyang.

MARINES: In Washington, D.C., President Harry S. Truman signs legislation activating the Organized Marine Corps Reserve.

July 20

AVIATION: In Japan, Major General Otto P. Weyland arrives to serve as Far East Air Forces (FEAF) vice commander for operations.

Dean, William F.   (1899–1981)
Army general

William F. Dean was born in Carlyle, Illinois, on August 1, 1899, and he applied, but failed, to gain entrance into the Military Academy, West Point. He nonetheless took Reserve Officer Candidate (ROTC) training at the University of California, Berkeley, and was commissioned a second lieutenant in 1922. An excellent soldier, he rose rapidly through the ranks and attended the Command and General Staff School, the Army Industrial College, and the Army War College before being assigned as assistant secretary to the War Department general staff. Dean rose to brigadier general in 1943 and began soliciting for a combat command. The following year, he became commander of the 44th Infantry Division and was assigned to General Alexander M. Patch's Seventh Army. He participated in Operation Anvil/Dragoon, the invasion of southern France in August 1944, and particularly distinguished himself in the captures of Strasbourg and Worms. His

subsequent actions in Austria also led to the surrender of 30,00 German troops. In consequence, Dean received a Distinguished Service Cross and gained a reputation as a leader who led from the front. He returned home to serve as assistant commandant of the War College and, in October 1947, Dean was appointed military governor of South Korea. He was reassigned to Japan the following year as commander of the 24th Infantry Division and was serving in this office when Communist North Korea attacked South Korea in an act of overt aggression.

No soon had the Korean War started than General Douglas MacArthur dispatched Dean's 24th Division to South Korea to halt the Communist onslaught. Unfortunately for the Americans, the North Koreans were hardened veterans of fighting the Japanese in World War II, and they were equipped with Soviet-built T-34 tanks, which were fast and well-armored. Dean's advance troops,

• Two Communist Yak-9s fall before the guns of Fifth Air Force F-80s, becoming the final aerial victories until November. The United Nations now enjoys virtual air superiority over the entire Korean Peninsula.

MILITARY: In Washington, D.C., President Harry S. Truman, fearing that all-out war with the Soviet Union might be inevitable, urges Congress to pass a $10 billion rearmament program.

• The Army Reorganization Act of 1950 is passed by Congress, which, among other changes, removes size limits on the Army General Staff, consolidates the field, coast, and antiaircraft artillery into a single artillery branch, merges tanks and mechanized cavalry into the armor branch, and recognizes a total of 14 specialist branches within the U.S. Army, namely, Chemical Corps, Corps of Engineers, Military Police Corps, Ordnance Corps, Quartermaster Corps, Transportation Corps, Adjutant General Corps, Finance Corps, Women's Army Corps, Army Medical Service, Chaplain Corps, Inspectors General, and Judge Advocate General Corps.

1950

Task Force Smith, were easily brushed aside in one battle. The Communists then began converging on the city of Taejon from the north and west. Dean was preparing to evacuate that city when General Walton H. Walker arrived and asked him to hold out at least two days while he consolidated his position around Pusan. Dean complied and pitched into the defense of Taejon, personally destroying a T-34 tank with a new 3.5-inch bazooka. He ordered a withdrawal two days later but became separated from his men and spent 36 days in the countryside avoiding roving columns of North Koreans. He was turned in to the Communists by a peasant on August 25, 1950, becoming the highest-ranking UN prisoner in captivity. Despite hardship and torture, Dean held up well to captivity until his release on September 4, 1953. At that time he was surprised to learn that he had won a Medal of Honor for his deeds at Taejon. After his repatriation, he served as deputy commander of the Sixth Army based at San Francisco, California. He

Major General William F. Dean, commander of the 24th Division during the Korean War. Dean won the Medal of Honor and was the highest-ranking officer to be held prisoner during the war. (*Center for the Study of the Korean War, Graceland University*)

retired in 1955 and died in nearby Berkeley on August 26, 1981, an unsung hero of the Korean War.

• With the fall of Taejon, South Korea, the 24th Infantry Division begins falling back to the southeast and the port of Pusan.

July 22
AVIATION: An emergency shipment of 145 air force F-51 Mustang fighters arrives in Japan aboard the carrier *Boxer*.
• At Taegu, South Korea, the 3rd Air Rescue Squadron deploys the first Sikorsky R-5 helicopter in the theater. Helicopters, though in their technical infancy, begin playing a very prominent role in this conflict.
MARINES: In Washington, D.C., Commandant Cates, determined to flesh out his skeletal formations, orders the formation of three rifle companies to bring the entire 1st Provisional Marine Brigade up to strength. Moreover, all ranks will ship immediately out of California on August 10, 1950.

July 24
AVIATION: At Taegu, South Korea, Eighth Army Headquarters is joined by Fifth Air Force in Korea headquarters to better coordinate missions and planning.

MILITARY: As the United Nations command solidifies, General Douglas MacArthur reaffirms General Walton S. Walker as ground commander, Eighth Army, Admiral C. Turner Joy as commander, Naval Forces, and General George E. Sratemeyer as commander, Far East Air Forces (FEAF).

July 25

AVIATION: In light of the desperate situation of the Eighth Army along the Pusan perimeter, General Walton H. Walker requests close air support from carrier aircraft. Supporting army units is something naval aviators are not accustomed to do and some technical awkwardness results.

NAVAL: Off San Francisco, California, the hospital ship *Benevolence* collides with the vessel SS *Mary Luckenbach* and sinks with the loss of 13 lives.

• The navy configures Task Force 96.5 to blockade the east coast of North Korea. Responsibility for the west coast falls upon British Commonwealth forces of Task Group 96.53 under Rear Admiral William G. Andrewes, RN.

MARINES: In Washington, D.C., the Joint Chiefs of Staff agree to General Douglas MacArthur's plea for a full marine division, but it will partly consist of the provisional brigade already en route to Korea. Commandant Cates also orders the 2nd Marine Division to depart Camp Lejeune, North Carolina, for Camp Pendleton, California, where they will help bring the 1st Marine Division up to full strength. Moreover, to scrape together every available marine, a 50 percent reduction in marine security forces at all naval installations is also undertaken.

July 25–27

MILITARY: At Chinju, South Korea, two battalions of the 29th Infantry Regiment are sent to reinforce a badly battered 19th Infantry; all are decimated in combat by the North Korean 6th Division. The 3rd Battalion, 29th infantry, loses 400 men, while the 1st Battalion sustains a further 200. The survivors are eventually reassigned as part of the 25th Infantry Division.

July 27

MILITARY: In Washington, D.C., President Harry S. Truman extends the enlistment period for all armed forces for 12 months; he also authorizes a draft of 50,000 men to report for training in September.

July 28

AVIATION: The first Grumman SA-16 Albatross, an outstanding air sea rescue aircraft, deploys in Japan for service off Korea's coastline.

MILITARY: The Military Police Corps is established as a permanent army unit by Congress.

July 29

MILITARY: At Pusan, South Korea, General Walton H. Walker, his back to the sea at Pusan, issues a "Stand or Die" order to the Eighth Army, declaring "There will be no Dunkirk, there will be no Bataan."

July 30

AVIATION: In another major raid, 47 Bomber Command B-29s strike the Chosin nitrate explosive factory near Hungnam, North Korea.

1950

Walker, Walton H. (1889–1950)
Army general

Walton Harris Walker was born in Belmont, Texas, on December 3, 1889, and, in 1909, he was admitted to the U.S. Military Academy. After graduating in 1912, Walker became an infantry lieutenant and, in 1918, he received two Silver Stars for bravery at the battles of Saint-Mihiel and Meuse-Argonne. A promising officer, he was allowed to attend the Infantry School, the Command and General Staff School, and the Artillery School before being billeted with the War Plans Division of the War Department in Washington, D.C., in 1936. Five years later he rose to temporary brigadier general commanding the 3rd Armored Brigade. In light of his excellent reputation for leadership, Walker took charge of the 3rd Armored Division during World War II, which was expanded into the XX Corps by 1944. With it, he blazed a trail across western Europe as part of General George S. Patton's Third Army, moving so fast that his force gained renown as the "Ghost Corps." He especially demonstrated his skill at handling units during the Battle of the Bulge, when Patton ordered his army to turn north on a 90-degree axis and flank the Germans from below. In April 1945, Walker's tanks smashed through the remaining Nazi defenses and liberated the infamous death camp at Buchenwald. Patton, who valued Walker as a no-nonsense fighter, promoted him to lieutenant general.

After the war, Walker held several administrative posts back in the United States until 1948, when he transferred to Japan as head of the Eighth Army. He did not get along well with the imperious general Douglas MacArthur, but he did work to restore his troops, having grown soft through occupation duty, back to combat efficiency. When the Korean War erupted in 1950, Walker's troops were ordered into combat and he established his first headquarters at Taegu. However, the Americans could not cope initially with the well-armed and ferociously disciplined North Koreans, who swept aside Task Force Smith and pushed General William F. Dean out of Taejon. Walker drew up his last-ditch perimeter around the port of Pusan, and he ordered his men to stand or die. Under his aggressive leadership, the Eighth Army withstood a constant pounding for six weeks and did not yield until MacArthur made his famous Inchon landing. As soon as the Communists retreated, Walton sprang at them like a tiger and captured the North Korean capital of Pyongyang on October 19, 1950. When MacArthur ordered all UN forces to advance to the Yalu River, Walker suspected a Chinese trap and proceeded cautiously. On November 25, a massive Communist attack drove the Eighth Army southward and destroyed the 2nd Division, then acting as a rearguard. Nonetheless, Walker managed to stabilize his line against tremendous odds and established new lines below the 38th parallel. He died in a traffic accident in Korea on December 23, 1950, a pugnacious combat commander. In recognition of his excellent service, the army christened its newest light tank the M-41 *Walker Bulldog*.

July 31

AVIATION: Marine Air Group 33 (MAG-33) arrives at Kobe, Japan, and occupies Itami Airfield as its initial base for operations.

• Secretary of Defense Louis Johnson authorizes the expansion of Marine Corps aviation units to 18 squadrons.

MARINES: In Washington, D.C., President Harry S. Truman authorizes expansion of the Marine Corps to a full two divisions of 23,500 men apiece.

July 31–August 1

MILITARY: At Pusan, South Korea, the Eighth Army is stiffened by the arrival of the 5th Regimental Combat Team, the 555th Field Artillery Battalion, and advanced elements of the 2nd Infantry Division under Major General Laurence B. Keiser. These forces have come from as far as Hawaii and Fort Lewis, Washington.

August 2

MILITARY: At Fort Bragg, North Carolina, Major General John B. Coulter assumes command of the newly activated I Corps; it is immediately ordered to ship out to Korea.

MARINES: Advanced elements of the 1st Provisional Marine Brigade under Brigadier General Edward A. Craig begin disembarking at Pusan in southeast South Korea.

August 2–3

AVIATION: The best airlift record of the Korean War happens when the 374th Troop Carrier Squadron delivers 150 tons of supplies from Ashiya, Japan, to Eighth Army units in South Korea in only 24 hours.

August 3

AVIATION: Over Chinju, South Korea, Marine Corps aviation debuts when F4U Corsairs of VMF-214 of Marine Air Group 33 (MAG-33) make rocket and bombing strikes against Communist forces for the first time. They are flying from the escort carrier *Sicily* to reduce flying time to the battlefield.

• Along the Korean coast, Grumman SA-16 Albatross amphibians begin flying rescue sorties; by war's end they have saved several thousand pilots and crew.

MILITARY: As part of the general mobilization scheme, 134 National Guard units are federalized and ordered to report for active duty.

• Outside Pusan, South Korea, the Eighth Army under General Walton H. Walker establishes its perimeter behind the Naktong River. The position, anchored on Pusan, runs 10 miles north and south, 50 miles east to west, and is garrisoned by the 1st Cavalry Division, the 2nd, 24th, and 25th Infantry Divisions, the 1st Provisional Marine Brigade, the 27th British Brigade, and eight Republic of Korea (ROK) divisions.

MARINES: As Marine units and reservists begin arriving at Camp Pendleton, California, orders go out to resurrect the 1st Marines under the legendary Colonel "Chesty" Puller. Its missing third rifle companies are transferred from the 5th Marines.

• With the bulk of the 1st Provisional Marine Brigade in place at Pusan, South Korea, they are ordered to position themselves along the Naktong River to the southwest corner of the evolving "Pusan Perimeter." Once in place, the Leathernecks will act as a "fire brigade," a mobile reserve tasked with closing off any Communist penetrations of UN lines.

August 4
AVIATION: In South Korea, HO3S-1 helicopters of VMO-6 begin executing reconnaissance missions and also perform the first aerial evacuations of wounded personnel.
• Far East Air Forces (FEAF) commences Interdiction Campaign No. 1 by dispatching B-29 bombers to raid key bridges in North Korea.
MILITARY: To flesh out the army's peacetime ranks, 62,000 reservists are recalled to the colors.

August 5
AVIATION: F4U Corsairs of VMF-214 launch from the escort carrier *Sicily* and perform bombing missions in the Inchon-Seoul region for the first time. Meanwhile, newly arrived VMF-323 departs from Itami Airfield, Japan, and lands on the escort carrier *Badoeng Strait* to commence air strikes on the Korean Peninsula.
• Near Hamchang, South Korea, an F-51D Mustang flown by Major Louis J. Sebille is damaged while strafing North Korean targets; rather than parachute, he dives directly into an enemy position, sacrificing himself. Sebille receives the first Medal of Honor ever given to a member of the U.S. Air Force.

August 5–19
MILITARY: The First Battle of the Naktong Bulge unfolds as North Korean forces begin probing the American perimeter near the 24th Infantry Division. That unit, assisted by the 1st Provisional Marine Brigade, and 2nd and 25th Infantry Divisions, drive the enemy off with 8,500 casualties and large amounts of equipment destroyed; UN losses amount to 1,800 killed, wounded, and missing.

August 7
MARINES: Headquarters Marine Corps alerts 80,000 individual reservists for call up to active-duty status.
• On this propitious date, the eighth anniversary of the Guadalcanal landings, the 1st Provisional Marine Brigade is ordered into combat to seize the town of Chinju, 25 miles to the west of their present position along the Naktong River. This puts them directly in the path of oncoming North Korean troops.

August 8
AVIATION: Near Chindong-ni, South Korea, a Marine Corps H03S-1 helicopter from VMO-6 makes the first nighttime evacuation of wounded troops.

August 10
AVIATION: The first two Reserve Air Force Units are called to active duty by the U.S. Air Force; they are gradually joined by a total of 25 such units.
MILITARY: At Fort Sheridan, Illinois, the Army IX Corps is activated and ordered to Korea under Major General Frank W. Milburn. Four National Guard divisions (28th, 40th, 43rd, and 45th Infantry Divisions) are called to active duty.
MARINES: At San Diego, California, the first elements of the 1st Marine Division begin embarking on ships for Korea.

August 11

AVIATION: The Fairchild XC-120 Packplane makes its maiden flight, cobbled together from C-119B Flying Boxcar wing and tail assemblies. It does not enter production.
• Using rockets and napalm, marine air units attack and destroy a North Korean convoy as it retreats down the road from Kosong, South Korea, destroying roughly 100 enemy vehicles.
• At Tachikawa Air Base, Japan, Fairchild C-119 Flying Boxcars begin transporting trucks and other utility vehicles to Taegu, South Korea.
MARINES: Along the "Pusan Perimeter," marine artillery scatters a North Korean motorized force in the town of Kosong, South Korea, which falls to the 1st Provisional Marine Brigade this evening.

August 12

MARINES: Marines and army troops no sooner begin a drive to capture Changchon, several miles south of Chinju, when Communist forces break the UN defensive lines along the Naktong River and the offensive is called off.

August 14

MARINES: As the "Pusan" perimeter's fire brigade (mobile reserve), the 1st Provisional Marine Brigade moves 75 miles by truck, train, and ship to the Naktong River bulge to secure UN defensive lines.

August 15–16

NAVAL: The high-speed transport *Bass* delivers several Underwater Demolition Teams (UDT) that raid the eastern coast of Korea at night, destroying several bridges and railroad tunnels.

August 16

AVIATION: Near Waegwan, South Korea, a force of 98 Fifth Air Force B-29s carpet bomb North Korean troop formations in a 30-square-mile area. This spoiling attack is the largest such aerial operation undertaken since D-Day in 1944.
MILITARY: In Japan, the X Corps is activated under Major General Edward M. Almond in anticipation of the upcoming Operation Chromite, an amphibious descent upon Inchon, South Korea. This consists of the 1st Marine Division and the 7th Infantry Division, and it is independent of the Eighth Army.
NAVAL: At Yonghae, South Korea, the encircled ROK 3rd Division is evacuated to safety by Task Element 96.51's four landing ships and the cruiser *Helena*.

August 17

MARINES: The 1st Provisional Marine Brigade counterattacks along the Naktong Bulge and drives the 4th North Korean Division back across the river with a loss of 34 guns; they are assisted by the army's 24th Infantry Division on their right flank.

August 18

MARINES: The Marine Corps reduces the minimum service contract from four to three years to spur enlistments. It also enlists recruits directly into the Volunteer Reserve for active duty, allowing enlistees to achieve reserve status once the war has ended.

- General Oliver P. Smith, commanding the 1st Marine Division, arrives in Japan for meetings with Eighth Army officials. He learns that his force will spearhead the forthcoming Inchon landings scheduled for September 15.
- In South Korea, the 5th Marines seize the Obong-ni Ridge as fleeing North Koreans are rocketed and napalmed by F4U Corsairs.

August 18–25

MILITARY: Outside Pusan, South Korea, North Korean forces try attacking through a series of narrow valleys dubbed the "Bowling Alley" by American forces. However, the 23rd and 27th Infantry Regiments easily hold their ground, inflicting an estimated 4,000 casualties on the Communists. American losses are minimal.

August 19

AVIATION: At Yongsan Bridgehead, American aircraft drive North Korean forces back across the Naktong River, thereby helping to end the battle for the Naktong Bulge.

MARINES: After a stiff fight, the 5th Marines eliminate all remaining North Koreans from the Naktong Bulge. The Pusan Perimeter is secured for the time being, although Communist attacks are developing elsewhere along the line.

August 20

MARINES: The 1st Provisional Marine Brigade resumes its role as the Eighth Army reserve, and it is billeted in the rear at Masan, South Korea, until needed again.

August 21

AVIATION: Over Pyongyang, North Korea, naval aviation units from the carriers *Valley Forge* and *Philippine Sea* establish a new operational record by completing 202 bombing sorties in one day. From this point forward, the air war over Korea intensifies exponentially.

August 22

AVIATION: In an ominous development, Chinese antiaircraft gunners across the Yalu River begin firing at RB-29 aircraft operating in North Korean airspace. This is the first-known instance of Chinese aggression against UN forces.

August 23

AVIATION: The air force drops guided Razon bombs against North Korean targets for the first time; results are limited with only one bridge west of Pyongyang being brought down.

MILITARY: In Tokyo, Japan, General Douglas MacArthur dramatically presents his case for an amphibious assault upon Inchon, on the west coast of South Korea, to sever Communist supply lines and possibly end the war. He convinces both Admiral Forrest P. Sherman, chief of naval operations, and General Joseph L. Collins, army chief of staff, to agree. The date for the Inchon invasion is fixed at September 15 by MacArthur himself.

August 25

AVIATION: To prevent a possible buildup of Communist air strength prior to the Inchon landings, Fifth Air Force is directed to maintain around-the-clock surveillance of all enemy airfields. It will be followed by air strikes, as necessary.

MILITARY: In Washington, D.C., President Harry S. Truman orders the army to take control of the railroad system during a period of labor unrest; they remain in charge until May 1952.

• The Japan Logistical Command is formed by the army to facilitate the flow of supplies to the Eighth Army in South Korea.

August 26

AVIATION: In Washington, D.C., Air Force Chief of Staff General Hoyt S. Vandenberg presents Smithsonian Institution officials with the first Bell X-1, the aircraft that first broke the sound barrier.

• At Ashiya, Japan, Major General William H. Tunner, the architect of the Berlin airlift, arrives to take charge of a new Combat Cargo Command (Provisional) based on the 1st Troop Carrier Task Force. On a related note, the Far East Air Force (FEAF) begins scraping together all available C-46 Commando transports within its jurisdiction in anticipation of a UN offensive the following September.

August 27

MARINES: In Washington, D.C., Representative Carl Vinson, chairman of the House Armed Services Committee, declares that the Marine Corps should consists for no less than four divisions and 26 squadrons.

• In Saigon, Vietnam, a dozen marines arrive to serve as U.S. embassy guards.

August 29

AVIATION: Marine experimental helicopter squadron HMX-1 begins experimenting with a 3.5-inch bazooka mounted on a Bell HTL-3 utility helicopter. However, the use of armed helicopters is still a decade off.

MARINES: Advanced echelons of the 1st Marine Division begin trickling into Japan. Once arrived, they immediately begin rehearsing for the upcoming landing at Inchon, South Korea.

August 31–September 9

AVIATION: As North Korean forces begin probing UN lines for a final, last-ditch offensive, aircraft of the Fifth Air Force hammer away at them incessantly with close air support.

• At Chinnampo, North Korea, the largest strategic mission of the month unfolds as 74 Bomber Command B-29s strike at mining facilities, metal industries, and marshaling yards.

MILITARY: North Korean forces launch their second attempt to penetrate the Naktong Bulge; some American positions are overrun but army and marine units counterattack, driving the Communists off with as many as 10,000 casualties.

September 1

MILITARY: In Washington, D.C., President Harry S. Truman unveils a plan to double the existing defense establishment from 1.5 million to 3 million.

MARINES: In Washington, D.C., Representative Gordon L. McDonough publishes a letter from President Harry S. Truman, in which the latter declares that the Marine Corps employs a propaganda program "that is almost equal to Stalin's." An uproar ensues along with demands for the president to apologize.

• As four North Korean divisions begin a second drive against the Naktong River and push the army's 2nd Infantry Division back, the 1st Provisional Marine

1950

Brigade is withdrawn from the Inchon operation and sent advancing in the direction of the fighting.

September 3
MARINES: The 1st Marine Division begins to combat load its ships in preparation for the Inchon landing, although their labors are complicated by heavy rains soaking their equipment and supplies.
• In South Korea, the 1st Provisional Marine Brigade counterattacks along the Naktong Bulge, first slowing, then stopping a concerted North Korean advance.

September 4
AVIATION: Navy Chance Vought F4U-4Bs of VF-53 intercept a Soviet Lend-Lease Douglas A-20 Havoc bomber west of the North Korean coast and shoot it down after the tail gunner fires on them.
• The first combat rescue mission behind enemy lines occurs when a Sikorsky R-5 helicopter flown by Lieutenant Paul W. Van Boven retrieves a downed UN pilot.

September 5
MARINES: In South Korea, the 1st Provisional Marine Brigade counterattacks and drives North Korean forces before them, partially restoring the Naktong Bulge. They stop just short of retaking Obong-ni Ridge, however, when orders arrive directing them to embark in preparation for a landing at Inchon.

September 6
MARINES: In Washington. D.C., President Harry S. Truman sends a letter of apology to Commandant Cates and one to the Marine Corps League, which will be read aloud during the latter's national convention.

September 9
AVIATION: Captain Leslie F. Brown, a marine exchange pilot with an air force squadron, flies the first jet combat mission of the Marine Corps at the controls of a Lockheed F-80 Shooting Star.
• North of Seoul, South Korea, B-29s of Bomber Command begin attacking rail-bound Communist reinforcements headed for Inchon while B-26s attack key supply routes and marshaling yards.

September 10
MARINES: The 1st Marine Division has embarked at Japan and is steaming toward Inchon on South Korea's northwestern coast.

September 12
MILITARY: In Washington, D.C., Secretary of Defense Louis Johnson resigns from office and is replaced by former general and secretary of state George C. Marshall.
NAVAL: Off Korea, blockading forces are reorganized under the title Task Force 95, although operations on the western coastline remain the responsibility of British Commonwealth forces.

September 13
MARINES: At Pusan, South Korea, the 1st Provisional Marine Brigade is deactivated once it embarks for Inchon and is reassigned to the 1st Marine Division.

1950

September 14
AVIATION: At Itami Field, Japan, the 1st Marine Air Wing Headquarters joins Marine Air Group 12 (MAG-12) as Marine Corps aviation assumes a more definite form in this theater.
NAVAL: At Samchok, South Korea, the newly arrived battleship *Missouri* lays down a heavy barrage of 50 16-inch shells that knock out a strategic bridge.

September 15
AVIATION: Fifth Air Force light and heavy bombers redouble their efforts in attacking North Korean positions outside Pusan, South Korea, to prepare for an expected UN breakout.
MILITARY: General Douglas MacArthur launches the audacious Operation Chromite at Inchon, South Korea, braving tricky tides and tough defenses to land the X Corps of Major General Edward M. Almond on the west coast of the peninsula. The attack succeeds brilliantly with few casualties on the American

Almond, Edward M.   (1892–1979)
Army general

Edward Mallory Almond was born in Luray, Virginia, on December 12, 1892, and he graduated from the Virginia Military Institute in 1915. The following year he was commissioned a lieutenant in the infantry and fought in France while commanding a machine gun company. After World War I, Almond returned to the United States where he attended the Infantry School, the Command and General Staff College, and the War College. He was promoted to brigadier general in March 1942 and, the following July, he received command of the 92nd Infantry Division, composed mainly of African Americans. He was personally selected for this command by Army chief of staff George C. Marshall, who was a good judge of his abilities as a leader. Almond transcended the awkwardness of being a white officer from the South commanding black troops, and he spent two years training them. Constantly exposed to the media and closely scrutinized by the public, Almond considered this assignment the most difficult of his long career. Nevertheless, his "Buffalo soldiers" performed poorly in grueling campaigns in the Serchio Valley in 1944, and along the German Gothic Line in 1945, although the famous 442nd Regimental Combat Team composed of Japanese Americans excelled. He returned home a highly decorated major general commanding the 2nd Infantry Division, but his reputation was tarnished by racism.

In 1946 Almond was ordered to Japan, where he served as deputy chief of staff to General Douglas MacArthur's Far East Command, and, by 1950, he had advanced to chief of staff, United Nations Command. Almond commanded the new X Corps during MacArthur's brilliant Inchon campaign, and he helped spearhead the recapture of side, and the 1st Marine Division, backed by the 7th Infantry Division under Major General David G. Barr, begins pressing inland toward the capital of Seoul. In a single stroke, the tide of war in Korea has turned decisively in the UN's favor.

NAVAL: General Douglas MacArthur stages one of the most brilliant amphibious operations in military history by storming ashore at Inchon, South Korea, and threatening North Korean supply lines. The actual operation is flawlessly performed by Amphibious Group One, Task Force 90, under Rear Admiral James H. Doyle. In the words of General MacArthur, "The navy and marines have never shone more brightly than this morning."

MARINES: At Inchon, South Korea, the 1st Marine Division under General Oliver P. Smith, consisting of the 1st and 5th Marines, lands and captures the city by nightfall. The attack is preceded by the 3rd Battalion, 5th Marines, who seize the island of Wolmi-do in the harbor, and clear it in only 45 minutes.

Seoul, South Korea, in September 1950. The X Corps then packed up and landed at Hungnam, North Korea, that October, as part of the overall UN advance to the Yalu River bordering China. An aggressive commander, Almond pushed his columns deep into the countryside, some might say recklessly, until November 25, when a massive Chinese counterattack forced UN forces to withdraw. Despite heavy losses and subzero weather, Almond kept his force intact and waged a fighting retreat back to Hungnam, where 105,000 men and all their equipment were safely evacuated. Thereafter the X Corps was anchored in east-central Korea on the UN line, which was gradually forced back to the 38th parallel. During the retreat from Chosin, Almond made exclusive use of Marine Corps helicopters to fly in supplies and fly out the wounded. He thereafter advocated similar units for the army. He also instituted studies for adopting tactical air support techniques, heretofore a Marine Corps specialty, into army doctrine. Made a lieutenant

Edward M. Almond observing the shelling of Inchon from the USS *Mt. McKinley* (U.S. Army)

general in February 1951, he rotated back to the United States in July to take charge of the Army War College. He died in Washington, D.C., on June 11, 1979, an aggressive but somewhat limited commander.

- At Inchon, Lieutenant Baldomero Lopez, a platoon leader in the 3rd Marines, covers a North Korean hand grenade with his body, dying in the explosion but saving the lives of his men. He wins a posthumous Medal of Honor.

September 15–18
AVIATION: The first wave of F-84E Thunderjets of the 27th Fighter Escort Wing depart Bergstrom Air Force Base, Texas, and begin their deployment in West Germany.

September 16
MILITARY: In concert with landing operations at Inchon, General Walton H. Walker orders the Eighth Army to break out of the Naktong Perimeter. North Korean forces, wary of being cut off, hastily retreat northward. The 3rd Infantry Division under Major General Robert H. Soule also arrives at Pusan and forms the new reserve.

September 17
AVIATION: Acting in concert with the Eighth Army, F-51 Mustangs and F-80 Shooting Stars from the Fifth Air Force harry retreating North Korean columns with massed napalm attacks, killing hundreds of Communist soldiers.
MARINES: The 3rd Battalion, 5th Marines under Colonel R. L. Murray overcome die-hard resistance and capture Kimpo Airfield, which places American forces halfway between Inchon and Seoul, South Korea.

September 18
AVIATION: A force of 42 B-29 bombers from the 92nd and 98th Bombardment Groups drop 1,600 500-pound bombs on Communist troop concentrations near Waegwan, South Korea. The confusion wrought allows the Eighth Army to better consolidate its position around the port of Pusan.
NAVAL: At Samchok, South Korea, the withdrawal of 725 South Korean troops to vessels offshore is covered by gunfire from the battleship *Missouri*, heavy cruiser *Helena*, and four destroyers.

September 19
AVIATION: Marine Air Group 33 (MAG-33) deploys at Kimpo Airfield, South Korea, bringing with it VMF-212 and VMF-312, and the night-fighting VMF (N)-542.
- In Japan, the Combat Cargo Command launches a force of 32 C-54 Skymasters carrying troops and equipment to Kimpo Airfield near Seoul, South Korea. This is the start of a major supply effort by airlift.
MILITARY: The Second Logistical Command is created to replace the Pusan Logistical Command for the purpose of supporting the Eighth Army. The Third Logistical Command also is established to support the X Corps.
- As the 1st Marine Division drives on Seoul, South Korea, its right flank is covered by the 7th Infantry Division. Hard fighting ensues with fanatical North Korean troops, who are slowly driven back.

September 20
AVIATION: At Kimpo Airfield, South Korea, transports of the Combat Cargo Command begin round-the-clock operations by using night-lighting equipment to illuminate the field.

1950

MILITARY: In Washington, D.C., Congress promotes General Omar N. Bradley to the rank of general of the army (five stars), the first so honored since the end of World War II and also the last. Bradley continues as chairman of the Joint Chiefs of Staff (JCS).

MARINES: Eight miles northwest of Seoul, South Korea, the 5th Marines cross the Han River and establish a bridgehead. Simultaneously, the 1st Marines launch an attack on the industrial suburb of Yongdungpo on the west bank of the Han River. Communist resistance remains fierce.

September 21

MILITARY: In Washington, D.C., Secretary of State George C. Marshall is formally appointed secretary of defense to replace outgoing Louis Johnson.

MARINES: At Inchon, South Korea, the 7th Marines come ashore to reinforce the 1st Marine Division.

September 22

AVIATION: Colonel David C. Schilling completes another nonstop jet fighter flight over the Atlantic by departing RAF Manston, England, and touching down at Limestone, Maine, after covering 3,300 miles in 10 hours, one minute. Schilling refueled three times in the air but his wingman, Lieutenant Colonel William D. Ritchie, ran out of fuel and was forced to ditch safely. Schilling receives the Harmon Trophy for his feat.

• In South Korea, a T-6 Mosquito aircraft flown by Lieutenant George W. Nelson drops surrender notes to 200 North Korean soldiers holed up at Kunsan and, upon further reflection, they lay down their arms and report to a designated hill for internment.

MARINES: After a stiff fight, Yongdungpo, South Korea, falls to the 1st Marines of Colonel Lewis B. "Chesty" Puller as the drive on Seoul continues.

September 23

AVIATION: At Pusan, Headquarters, Fifth Air Force in Korea begins relocating to Taegu to be closer to the front.

• An SB-17 is recorded as having made the first classified, special mission over North Korea.

September 24

MARINES: Near Seoul, South Korea, the 1st Marines finally link up with the 5th Marines under Colonel Chesty Puller and hoist the first American flag over the city's suburbs.

September 24–25

MILITARY: At Kimpo Airfield, Seoul, South Korea, the 187th Airborne Regimental Combat Team is flown in from Japan under Colonel Frank S. Bowen. This is the first parachute unit deployed in the war.

MARINES: Pushing inland, the 1st and 5th Marines launch a concerted effort to capture the remaining parts of Seoul, South Korea. Advancing out of the city that night, the 1st Marine Division stumbles into a heavy North Korean counterattack and drives it off with heavy losses.

Puller, Lewis B.   (1898–1971)
Marine Corps general

Lewis Burwell Puller was born in West Port, Virginia, on June 26, 1898, and he briefly attended the Virginia Military Academy before quitting to join the Marine Corps in 1918. World War I ended before he could ship overseas, so he spent several tours in Haiti and Nicaragua fighting bandits. Puller proved himself adept as a fighter and he won two Navy Crosses for bravery under fire. His aggressive patrolling netted several prisoners, which gained him the nickname of "El Tigre." The rebel leader Augusto Sandino found him so troublesome that he offered a price for Puller's head. His next stint of duty came with the famous "Horse Marines," which guarded the U.S. legation in Beijing, China. He came to respect and admire Chinese and Japanese soldiers for their discipline and endurance. In August 1941 Puller reported to Camp Lejeune, North Carolina, where he was one of the first marine officers to study jungle fighting techniques. This paid tremendous dividends during World War II when Puller, commanding the Seventh Marines on Guadalcanal, bloodily repulsed a Japanese night attack upon Henderson Field on October 24, 1942. Puller won his third Navy Cross, and, subsequently, he fought well at Cape Gloucester and Peleliu, winning his fourth Navy Cross. He then returned to the United States using his expertise to train new recruits.

The onset of the Korean War in 1950 saw Puller rejoin the 1st Marine Division and participate in General Douglas MacArthur's brilliant Inchon landing.

He then followed the UN advance into North Korea, where, in November 1950, the marines were suddenly cut off by thousands of Chinese troops. Puller again distinguished himself by directing the 1st Marine Regiment in the defense of Koto-ri, which allowed the Fifth and Seventh Marines to escape intact. He was virtually the last marine out of Koto-ri as the retreat continued, winning his fifth Navy Cross. Puller advanced to brigadier general in January 1951, and he spent several months as assistant divisional commander before transferring back home. He was billeted at Camp Pendleton, California, for several months and, in September 1953, he rose to major general commanding the 2nd Marine Division. He suffered a mild stroke and concluded 37 years of exceptional service by resigning from active duty in January 1955. Never one to skirt controversy, Puller testified favorably at the trial of Sergeant Matthew McKeon, charged with the reckless death of six recruits, in insisting that tough discipline and realistic training were essential to the Marine Corps. Puller, who went by the nickname "Chesty" on account of his habit of walking with his chest extended, died in Hampton, Virginia, on October 11, 1971. Such was his renown that the Marine Corps commandant, 43 generals, and 1,500 former and active-duty marines attended his funeral. A rugged disciplinarian who fought fearlessly and trained his men vigorously, Puller remains the most decorated officer in Marine Corps history.

September 25–29
NAVAL: The destroyer *Mansfield* and minesweeper *Magpie* strike mines in North Korean waters; the former is heavily damaged and the latter is sunk. The navy estimates that there are in excess of 3,500 mines in Communist waters, which poses serious problems for shipping.

September 26
AVIATION: Fighters and bombers of the Fifth Air Force continue supporting the UN counterattack with close support missions in the drive toward the 38th parallel.
• The first strategic bombing campaign against North Korea concludes after a force of 20 B-29s of the 22nd Bomb Group attack and destroy munitions factories in Haeju and a hydroelectric power plant near Hungnam.
MILITARY: The 7th Infantry Division (X Corps), pushing west, and the 1st Cavalry Division (Eighth Army), marching north, link up at Suwon, South Korea. Communist forces continue their pell-mell retreat back to North Korea and cease to exist as an organized force.
MARINES: Headquarters Marine Corps reports that the Organized Reserve is completely mobilized.
• Near Seoul, South Korea, the 7th Marines pitch into the fighting as they position themselves on the north flank of the 5th Marines.

September 27
AVIATION: With all of North Korea's strategic targets in ruins, the Joint Chiefs of Staff (JCS) order a halt to all strategic bombardment missions.
MILITARY: In a fateful move, President Harry S. Truman, acting upon the advice of the Joint Chiefs of Staff (JCS), orders UN forces north of the 38th parallel separating North and South Korea to destroy all remaining forces of the NKPA. This will facilitate unification of the country under UN auspices. However, this decision sparks a sharp reaction from the People's Republic of China, which has until now refrained from active intervention in the conflict.
MARINES: After a hard fight against fanatical North Korean resistance, the 1st Marine Division and the 7th Infantry Division recapture the South Korean capital of Seoul. A party from the 1st Marines raises the American flag over the U.S. consulate.

September 28
AVIATION: A group of eight mice, launched to 97,000 feet in a test balloon, are returned to Holloman Air Force Base, New Mexico, in perfect health.
POLITICS: In Seoul, South Korea, President Syngman Rhee is officially restored to power by General Douglas MacArthur.
• At Yotota, Japan, three RB-45C Tornados from Detachment A, 84th Bombardment Squadron, arrive from Hawaii. The world's most capable reconnaissance aircraft at present, their top-secret mission is delayed when special photographic equipment fails to arrive.

September 29
AVIATION: Over Holloman Air Force Base, New Mexico, Captain Richard V. Wheeler sets a record for parachuting when he jumps from an altitude of 42,449 feet.

MILITARY: Newly victorious South Korean troops arrive at the 38th parallel, where the war began four months earlier.

NAVAL: Off Chuksan, North Korea, the minesweeper *Magpie* strikes a mine and sinks, becoming the first U.S. Navy vessel lost in the Korean War.

October 1

NAVAL: The carrier *Leyte,* having sailed all the way from the Atlantic Fleet, joins the war effort off Korea.

MILITARY: General Douglas MacArthur calls upon North Korean premier Kim Il Sung to surrender his forces and prevent a useless effusion of blood. The summons goes unanswered.

MARINES: The town of Uijongbu is the target of a determined thrust by the 7th Marines, which captures it two days later.

POLITICS: Representative McDonough sells his insulting letter from President Harry S. Truman for $2,500, and he donates the proceeds to the Marine Corps League.

October 2

AVIATION: Over North Korea, B-29s of Bomber Command strike the training facilities at Nanam, destroying three-quarters of all buildings and impeding Communist reinforcements.

• At Taegu Air Base (T-2), South Korea, the 8th Tactical Reconnaissance Squadron deploys, becoming the first reconnaissance unit deployed on the peninsula.

October 4

AVIATION: Far East Air Forces (FEAF) is directed to assume tactical control of all land-based aircraft in Korea, including those belonging to the Marine Corps at Kimpo.

• The aerial war effort is bolstered by F-51s of South African Squadron No. 2, which is attached to the Far East Air Forces (FEAF).

October 5

MARINES: The 1st Marine Division, having been replaced by army units, returns to Inchon, South Korea, for immediate embarking. Its losses in the recent campaign amounted to 411 dead and 2,029 wounded.

October 6

AVIATION: At Edgewater Arsenal, Maryland, Piasecki HRP-1 from marine experimental helicopter squadron HMX-1 test drops a bomb from an altitude of 8,000 feet.

• Near Seoul, South Korea, the air force assumes control of Kimpo Airfield from the Marine Corps.

• The arsenal at Kan-ni, North Korea, is leveled by 18 Bomber Command B-29s. However, Far East Air Forces (FEAF) instructs that bombing of all bridges south of Pyongyang and Wonsan be halted, presumably to allow their use by counterattacking UN forces.

October 7

DIPLOMACY: The United Nations passes a resolution authorizing UN forces to enter North Korea for the purpose of establishing a unified and democratic regime in that country.

1950

October 8
AVIATION: The Fifth Air Force, headquartered in Tokyo, Japan, is given control of the 1st Marine Air Wing (1st MAW) and begins directing its operational sorties.
• Once Razon bombs are fitted with more reliable electronic equipment arrive, attacks with these radio-guided weapons resumes.

October 9
MILITARY: Near Kaesong, South Korea, the I Corps, Eighth Army, crosses the 38th parallel in force and begins working its way toward Pyongyang, North Korea, the Communist capital. The advance is spearheaded by the 1st Cavalry Division. General Douglas MacArthur issues a second summons to the North Korean government to surrender. Red China issues increasingly vocal warnings that it will not tolerate non-Korean units along its borders.

October 10
AVIATION: The Air National Guard mobilizes the first of 66 units and 45,000 men that will see service in the Korean War.
• In Europe, Lieutenant General Lauris Norstad is appointed commander of United States Air Forces Europe (USAFE).
NAVAL: Task Force 77 minesweepers begin clearing the harbor of Wonsan, North Korea, in preparation for landing the Army X Corps on October 20.

October 11
DIPLOMACY: General Douglas MacArthur calls on the North Korean government to surrender, which again goes unheeded.
• The government of the People's Republic of China sternly reiterates that it will not "stand idly by" as American forces advance toward its border with North Korea.

October 12
NAVAL: Off Wonsan, North Korea, the minesweepers *Pirate* and *Pledge* strike mines as they maneuver to avoid enemy shore fire and sink. It is estimated that the harbor is defended by 3,000 Soviet magnetic and acoustic mines.

October 15
AVIATION: VMF-312 and VMF (M)-513 of Marine Air Group 12 (MAG-12) are the first American aviation units to operate on North Korean soil when they begin operating from the airfield at Wonsan.
MILITARY: President Harry S. Truman and General Douglas MacArthur convene at Wake Island in the Pacific to discuss military strategy in Korea. At the time, MacArthur denies any further need for additional troops and also discounts any possibility of Soviet or Chinese intervention. Despite a good public showing, tension is mounting between the two leaders.
MARINES: At Inchon, South Korea, the 1st Marine Division embarks for an intended attack upon the North Korean port of Wonsan on the east coast of North Korea, unaware that it has already fallen to ROK forces.

October 14–17
MILITARY: At Pusan, South Korea, the 7th Infantry Division embarks on ships for immediate redeployment to the northeastern coast of the peninsula.

October 19
MILITARY: Pyongyang, the capital of Communist North Korea, falls to the 1st Cavalry Division and the 1st ROK Division.

October 20
AVIATION: The Fairchild C-119 Flying Boxcar makes its combat debut by dropping 4,000 paratroopers over Sukchon and Sunchon, North Korea, 30 miles north of the capital Pyongyang. This is also the first time that 105mm howitzers are successfully air-dropped to ground forces.
MILITARY: The 187th Airborne Regimental Combat Team makes the first parachute drop of the Korean War by landing at Sukchon and Sunchon, North Korea. The move fails to snare many retreating North Koreans, however.

October 21
MILITARY: In a move that is viewed as somewhat premature, General Douglas MacArthur publicly declares that the end of the war in Korea is at hand.

October 24
MILITARY: In a fateful move, General Douglas MacArthur removes all movement restrictions on UN forces, allowing them to advance up to the border with Red China.

October 25
AVIATION: Far East Air Forces suspend all B-29 operations for want of appropriate targets. However, all restrictions on close air support missions are lifted, allowing UN aircraft to fly up to the Chinese border.
• In Japan, Combat Cargo Command establishes a new daily record of 1,767 tons of equipment conveyed to South Korea.
MILITARY: North of Unsan, North Korea, ROK forces are attacked by the Chinese 50th Field Army for the first time. A Chinese prisoner taken by the Americans declares that large numbers of Chinese troops have already infiltrated into North Korea. Despite this alarming intelligence, General Douglas MacArthur allows the X Corps and the Eighth Army, divided by the Taebeck Mountains, to operate independently of each other.

October 26
AVIATION: Over North Korea, C-119 Flying Boxcars of the Combat Cargo Command drop 28 tons of food, supplies, and ammunition to UN troops cut off by Communist forces.
MILITARY: At this juncture of the war, the Army X Corps is tasked with assisting South Korean forces to eliminate Communist troops in northeastern Korea, while the Eighth Army does the same in northwest Korea. However, neither force operates in conjunction with the other and they are separated by a mountain range between them.

Private Seiju Nakandakarc and Private Ralph Saul operate a 3.5-mm bazooka on the frontlines of Korea, 1950. *(Library of Congress)*

1950

NAVAL: Two weeks of minesweeping at Wonsan Harbor, North Korea, results in advanced echelons of the 1st Marine Division landing there. The landing is five days behind schedule.

October 27
MARINES: As UN forces surge northward, the 5th Marines become responsible for controlling 50 square miles of terrain between the ports of Wonsan and Hungnam, North Korea. Meanwhile, the 1st Battalion, 1st Marines occupies the town of Kojo, 25 miles south of Wonsan. Tonight NKPA forces attack in force and are driven off; marine casualties are 27 killed and 47 injured.

October 28
AVIATION: F-84Es belonging to the 27th Fighter Escort Wing complete their deployment from Texas to bases in West Germany. This is the first mass transatlantic crossing by jet aircraft and wins the unit a Mackay Trophy.
MILITARY: In an ominous sign, ROK troops engage Chinese Communist forces (CCF) at Suding, North Korea, taking 16 prisoners. They talk freely and alert their captors that thousands of Chinese are in the vicinity.

October 29
MILITARY: At Iwon, North Korea, the 7th Infantry Division comes ashore unopposed and begins advancing north toward the Chinese border.

November 1
AVIATION: Russian-built and -manned MiG-15 jet fighters begin harassing UN aircraft from bases across the Yalu River in Manchuria.
MILITARY: The 21st Infantry Regiment, 24th Infantry Division, slogs into Chonggodo, North Korea, 18 miles south of the Yalu River separating Korea from China. It is the northernmost point the Eighth Army will reach during this war.

November 2
AVIATION: At Yokota, Japan, an RB-45C of Detachment A, 84th Bomb Squadron flies its first reconnaissance mission of the war.
MARINES: At Majon-ni, North Korea, Communist forces ambush a marine supply convoy, killing 25 and wounding 41.
• At Sudong, farther north, ROK forces in the area are relieved by the 7th Marines, which begin advancing along a narrow mountain road to the Chosin (Cangjin) Reservoir. Tonight, Chinese forces make several strong probes along their perimeter, but they are repulsed.

November 2–6
MILITARY: Near Unsan, North Korea, the 116th Chinese Division annihilates the 3rd Battalion, 8th Cavalry Regiment, 1st Cavalry Division as a warning to UN forces, then disappears back into the hills. The message goes unheeded at General Douglas MacArthur's headquarters.

November 2–20
NAVAL: UN minesweeping forces clear the harbor of Chinnampo, the port city of Pyongyang, North Korea, without casualties.

1950

November 3

MILITARY: At Wonsan, North Korea, the 3rd Infantry Division disembarks and begins marching northward.

November 4

AVIATION: Near Chongju, North Korea, B-26s fly close support missions for the Eighth Army, killing hundreds of enemy soldiers and allowing the Eighth Army to retreat.

November 4–6

MARINES: As the 7th Marines under Colonel Homer L. Litzenberger march up the Funchilin Pass, they stumble headlong into the Chinese 124th Division directly in their path. Three days of intense fighting fails to dislodge them, but the Communists finally withdraw on the evening of the 6th. Marine losses are 50 dead and 200 wounded; the Chinese are estimated to have lost at least 2,000 men.

November 5

AVIATION: A force of 21 B-29s from the 19th Bomb Group drops incendiaries on the North Korean city of Kanggaye, only 20 miles from the Chinese border, burning 65 percent of the urban center.

MILITARY: General Douglas MacArthur informs UN authorities of Chinese forces deployed in North Korea.

MARINES: On the road to Majon-ni, Company A, 1st Marines, under Captain Robert Barrow engages and destroys a North Korean roadblock, killing 51 of the enemy.

November 8

AVIATION: The world's first all jet dog fight breaks out over North Korea as American F-80 fighters tangle with Soviet MiG-15s; the Americans claim one kill by Lieutenant Russell J. Brown. However, the Russians have since disputed this claim, noting that the MiG-15 in question, though damaged, made it back to base.

• An armada of 70 Bomber Command B-29s drops 580 tons of fire bombs on Sinuiju, North Korea, astride the Chinese border. This is the largest incendiary raid of the war and occurs as other B-29s attack bridges spanning the Yalu River.

• Carrier aircraft of Task Force 77 are ordered to attack bridges across the Yalu River near Chongsonjin, North Korea; however, they are to strike only the Korean side of the structure.

November 9

AVIATION: Over North Korea, Lieutenant Commander William T. Amen, flying an F9F Panther with VF-111 from the carrier *Philippine Sea*, conducts the first naval jet-versus-jet combat in aviation history when he downs a MiG-15.

• B-29 tail gunner Airman Jarry J. LaVerne shoots down the first MiG-15 lost to a bomber. His own aircraft is nonetheless badly shot up and crash-lands back in Japan; five crewmen are killed.

MARINES: In Sweden, detachments from the cruiser *Columbus* and destroyer *Furse* attend ceremonies marking the funeral of King Gustav V.

November 10
AVIATION: Near the Yalu River, Russian-piloted MiG-15s, bedecked in North Korean colors, shoot down the first B-29 lost in the Korean War. The crew, belonging to the 307th Bombardment Group, survives the crash but are imprisoned.
MARINES: At the Washington Navy Yard, D.C., the Marine Corps celebrates its 175th anniversary by opening an exhibit of historical documents and artifacts.

November 15
MARINES: At Hagaru-ri, North Korea, the 7th Marines occupy the southern end of the Chosin Reservoir and the balance of the division trudges up to join it. Movement in this vicinity is restricted to a single road stretching along the mountains from the reservoir to Hungnam.

November 18
AVIATION: The 35th Fighter Interceptor Group (FIG) departs its airfield in South Korea and deploys near Hungnam, North Korea, becoming the first unit to fly from Communist soil.

November 19
AVIATION: A force of 50 B-26s unloads incendiary bombs on Musan, North Korea, destroying three-quarters of the military barracks there. This is the first mass attack by light bombers in the war and takes place on the Tumen River bordering Red China.

November 20
MARINES: In North Korea, the 1st Marine Division is joined by 41 independent commandos of the Royal Marines under Lieutenant Colonel Douglas B. Drysdale.

November 21
MILITARY: Disregarding Chinese warnings, United Nations forces continue advancing and reach the Yalu River bordering Manchuria. Elements of the 17th Infantry, 7th Infantry Division, march into Hyesanjin along the river and directly on the Chinese border.

November 22
AVIATION: The 2nd Helicopter Detachment, equipped with Bell H-13s, deploys in Korea as part of the 8055th Mobile Army Surgical Hospital (MASH); this is the army's first helicopter unit committed to combat operations in the war.

November 23
AVIATION: Fifth Air Force B-29s continue striking Communist supply and communication centers throughout North Korea and light bombers and fighters redouble their close support missions.
• Combat Cargo Command begins air dropping large quantities of ammunition to UN forces in North Korea to support their new offensive.
MARINES: The 1st Battalion, 1st Marines occupies the town of Chinhung-ni, on the main road just north of Sudong.

November 24
MILITARY: At Bamberg, Germany, the Headquarters, U.S. Army Constabulary, is deactivated and all of its constituent units rejoin their parent organizations as part of the U.S. Seventh Army.

1950

- In North Korea, as UN forces launch what they hope will be their final offensive of the war, General Douglas MacArthur assures reporters that it will "get the boys home by Christmas."

MARINES: As the 5th Marines move up the eastern side of the Chosin Reservoir, responsibility for protecting Koto-ri falls to the headquarters and 2nd Battalion, 1st Marines.

November 25–27

MILITARY: In North Korea, despite repeated warnings that went unheeded, the Chinese 13th Army Group, comprising 18 divisions and 300,000 men, stages a successful counteroffensive against the Eighth Army. Their nighttime assault, committed during bitterly cold weather, overruns the 2nd and 25th Infantry Divisions while several South Korean formations of the ROK II Corps are likewise destroyed. The Eighth Army begins an immediate withdrawal back down the peninsula to prevent encirclement and destruction.

MARINES: In North Korea, the 7th Marines advance to Yudan-ni west of the Chosin Reservoir, and they string out several company-sized outposts along the Toktong Pass. Meanwhile, the 5th Marines are relieved at the Chosin Reservoir by an army battalion, and they trudge up through Hagaru-ni toward Yudam-ni in freezing, subzero weather.

November 26

AVIATION: Bomber Command B-26s conduct their first night close support missions against Chinese forces pressing down upon the X Corps and Eighth Army in North Korea.

MARINES: Two companies of the 3rd Battalion, 1st Marines are assigned to hold Hagaru-ni, which serves as the divisional command post, supply dump, and airfield for the 1st Marine Division.

November 27

MILITARY: In North Korea, the X Corps launches an immediate offensive to take pressure off the battered Eighth Army. Meanwhile the Chinese 9th Army Group begins an offensive of its own in the Chosin Reservoir area. They manage to catch the 31st Regimental Combat Team under Colonel Allan D. MacLean and completely overrun it. MacLean is killed, his column is annihilated, and only 1,000 soldiers of the original 2,500 manage to make it to marine lines at Hagaru-ri by December 1. The majority of the survivors suffer from frostbite and are unable to fight further. However, their gallant stand upsets Chinese timetables and enables the marines to prepare defensive positions at Chosin.

MARINES: X Corps orders the 2nd Battalion, 5th Marines to attack west from Yudan-ni, but Chinese resistance proves insurmountable. The remainder of the regiment arrives later in the day and reinforces the 7th Marines in Yudan-ni. The Chinese launch four divisions after dark and in freezing temperatures below zero, but all marine positions ar Yudan-ni and the Toktong Pass hold fast and repel them.

November 28

AVIATION: Fifth Air Force B-26s, assisted by advanced radar equipment, begin dropping bombs within 1,000 yards of UN lines.

• The Combat Cargo Command begins airlifting wounded soldiers and marines out of North Korea while also delivering 1,600 tons of supplies to the surrounded 1st Marine Division at Chosin.

MILITARY: At Singalpajin, North Korea, elements of the 3rd Battalion, 32nd Infantry, 7th Infantry Division, become the second American unit to reach the Yalu River separating Korea from China.

MARINES: Near the Chosin Reservoir, General Oliver O. Smith halts the marine offensive west of Yudan-ni in favor of clearing the main supply route back to Hungnam, which is the only way out. The 1st Battalion, 7th Marines succeeds in rescuing Company C and brings it back into town. Tonight, massive Chinese forces again surge toward the Hagaru-ni perimeter, but again the 3rd Battalion, 1st Marines hold their ground and inflict severe losses upon their antagonists.

November 28–29

MILITARY: The Battle of Kunri, North Korea, unfolds as the 2nd Division forms the rearguard of the retreating Eighth Army. Proceeding south in a massive convoy, they are ambushed by thousands of Chinese and overrun, losing 5,000 killed, wounded, and captured; the 9th and 38th Infantries are nearly wiped out.

November 29

AVIATION: The Combat Cargo Command resorts to a maximum effort to keep the 1st Marine Division, trapped by overwhelming Chinese forces at Chosin, North Korea, adequately supplied by air. They are a major contributor to the division's survival against tremendous odds.

MARINES: Near Chosin, North Korea, the 1st Battalion, 1st Marines launches a spoiling attack against Chinese forces massing at Chinhung-ni as Task Force Drysdale (41 Commando, G Company, 3rd Battalion, 1st Marines, and an Army infantry company) escort a convoy of headquarters and other elements from Koto-ri to Hagaru-ni. Tonight, the Chinese stop and overrun the convoy, but they are repulsed at Koto-ri by the 2nd Battalion, 1st Marines.

• In the face of overpowering Chinese strength, X Corps commander Major General Edward M. Almond orders the 1st Marine Division to fall back to Hamhung.

November 30

AVIATION: To be closer to ground forces, Marine Air Group 12 (MAG-12) transfers its operations from Wosan, North Korea, to Yonpo Field, Hungnam.

MILITARY: In light of the deteriorating situation, Major General Edward M. Almond orders his X Corps (3rd and 7th Infantry Divisions, 1st Marine Division, and ROK I Corps) to fall back to the port of Hungnam for evacuation.

MARINES: The Chinese launch another mass attack against marines holding Haragu-ni, but they are again repulsed with heavy losses.

December 1

AVIATION: After Herculean efforts, the airstrip at Hagaru-ni is kept operational and the first C-47 lands, bringing supplies and evacuating the wounded.

MARINES: Near Chosin, North Korea, the 5th and 7th Marines fight their way from Yudam-ni and reach Hagaru-ni while the 1st Battalion, 7th Marines marches tonight to relieve Fox Company trapped at Toktong Pass.

December 2

MARINES: Near Chosin, North Korea, the rearguard of marines at Yudam-ni defeats a Chinese attempt to carry the position. Meanwhile, the 1st Battalion, 7th Marines links up with Fox Company in the Toktong Pass, which has lost half its men to nightly attacks.

December 3

MARINES: At Toktong Pass, North Korea, the 5th and 7th Marines fight their way to join the 1st Battalion, 7th Marines already there. By evening, the head of the column is trudging into Hagaru-ni. Despite 79 hours of continuous combat, the Chinese are determined to cut off and annihilate the marines, redoubling their efforts to prevent them from reaching the port of Hungnam.

December 4

AVIATION: The world's first jet bomber interception takes place when Russian-piloted MiG-15s shoot down an air force RB-45C Tornado reconnaissance aircraft over Sinuiju, along the Yalu River between Red China and North Korea; the crew of four is killed.

• While flying in support of marines at Chosin Reservoir, Ensign Jesse L. Brown's F4U Corsair is damaged and he crash-lands near Hagaru-ni. Brown is injured and pinned in the wreckage, so Lieutenant Thomas J. Hudner of carrier *Leyte*'s VF-31 deliberately crash-lands his Corsair nearby to assist, but he cannot cut him free from the wreckage. A helicopter arrives and evacuates Hudner before the position is overrun by Chinese and Brown, the navy's first African-American aviator, perishes horribly in subzero weather. For his attempted rescue of a squadron mate, Hudner wins the Medal of Honor; Brown receives a posthumous Distinguished Flying Cross.

MARINES: Remaining elements of the 5th and 7th Marines slog into Hagaru-ni with massed Chinese close behind, but, now united, the 1st Marine Division under Major General Oliver P. Smith prepares to fight its way back to the sea.

December 5

AVIATION: On a frozen airstrip at Hagaru-ni, North Korea, the Combat Cargo Command, aided by C-47s of the Royal Hellenic Air Force, has its most active day by flying 131 missions and evacuating 3,925 patients to Japan. This is the largest aeromedical airlift of the entire war.

MILITARY: As the Chinese juggernaut rolls down the Korean Peninsula, Pyongyang is abandoned by retreating United Nations forces; it had been occupied since October 19.

NAVAL: At Chinnampo, on the west coast of North Korea, U.S. and Commonwealth naval forces evacuate 7,700 American and South Korean forces.

December 6

AVIATION: The marine withdrawal from Hagaru-ni is covered by an average of 200 close support air strikes per day by air force, navy, and marine aircraft. To this end, a marine R5D transport is rigged as a aerial direction center, the first time a transport aircraft has been rigged for this purpose.

• F-84 Thunderjets of the 27th Fighter Escort Wing perform their first combat mission over North Korea, flying from airfields at Itazuke, Japan.

MARINES: Near Chosin, North Korea, General Oliver P. Smith orders his 1st Marine Division to attack down the single road from Hagaru-ni to the port of Hungnam. The Chinese resort to ambushes in daylight and, tonight, they launch a mass assault against marine positions on East Hill, being repulsed with losses.

Smith, Oliver P.   (1893–1977)
Marine Corps general

Oliver Prince Smith was born in Menard, Texas, on October 26, 1893, and he joined an ROTC chapter while attending the University of California, Berkeley. He was commissioned a second lieutenant in the army after graduating in 1916, but he transferred to the Marine Corps the following year. Thereafter Smith fulfilled the usual litany of overseas assignments, including stints in Haiti, Guam, and a two-year course at the École Supérieure in Paris, France. Smith subsequently taught amphibious tactics at the Marine Corps school in Quantico, Virginia, and, given his background as a religious, highly courteous individual, he acquired the nickname of "the Professor." When World War II broke out, Smith was serving as executive officer at Marine Corps headquarters, but he pushed for a combat position and, in March 1944, he assumed command of the Fifth Marines. He helped to plan and execute the successful campaigns at New Britain and Peleliu. His final wartime assignment was as deputy chief of staff to U.S. Army general Simon B. Buckner on Okinawa in April–June, 1945. After the war, Smith returned to Quantico, where he became fascinated with helicopter technology and urged its wholesale adoption by the Marine Corps.

Smith was serving as assistant commandant and chief of staff of the Marine Corps when the Korean War erupted in

General Oliver P. Smith (*U.S. Marine Corps*)

June 1950. He gained command of the 1st Marine Division and helped plan and execute the successful landing at Inchon under General Douglas MacArthur. After directing the recapture of Seoul, South Korea, in a stiff, month-long fight, Smith became part of General William M. Almond's X Corps and was directed to land on the eastern coast of North Korea. From here

(continues)

1950

(continued)

UN forces advanced to the Chinese border along the Yalu River, but Smith, anticipating a trap, ordered supplies stockpiled and airstrips constructed along his avenue of advance. During the massive Chinese attack of November 27, 1950, the 1st Marine Division managed to stand its ground at the Chosin Reservoir and, under Smith's enlightened generalship, fought its way 76 miles to safety. This retreat, conducted under howling, subzero weather in the face of eight Chinese divisions, became a legendary performance in the annals of warfare. Not only did Smith manage to bring off all his dead, his wounded, and his equipment, he also inflicted an estimated 25,000 casualties on superior Chinese forces, which failed to destroy him. The marines were evacuated at Hungnam and redeployed in South Korea as part of IX Corps, where, after an army general suffered a heart attack, Smith became the first Marine Corps general to lead a combined army-marine force in the field. In April 1951 he returned to the United States to assume control of Camp Pendleton, California, and, two years later, he advanced to lieutenant general. Smith died in Los Altos, California, on December 25, 1977, one of the greatest tactical minds in Marine Corps history.

December 7

AVIATION: In a bit of ingenuity, air force transports successfully parachute bridging sections to waiting marines below, and they reconstruct a fallen, 1,500-foot span over Funchilin Pass. This is the first bridge ever air-dropped in military history. Meanwhile, the close proximity of Chinese forces makes VMF-214 depart the airfield at Yonpo and return to the carrier *Sicily*.

• B-29s of Bomber Command strike Communist towns and troop concentrations near the Chosin Reservoir, North Korea, to assist marine and army units surrounded there. The troops fashion crude air strips wherever possible to permit transport craft to land supplies and remove the wounded.

MARINES: The rearguard of the 1st Marine Division reaches Koto-ri, while the vehicle column stretches out ahead of it for several miles.

December 8

AVIATION: To this date, the Combat Cargo Command has flown in 1,580 tons of food, ammunition, and supplies to the 1st Marine Division, including eight bridge spans. They have also airlifted 5,000 sick and injured marines to safety.

MARINES: Lead elements of the 1st Marine Division fight their way through Koto-ri as the entire force continues pushing south. Ahead of them, the 1st Battalion, 1st Marines clears Funchilin Pass of enemy troops, and engineers begin repairing a fallen span.

December 9

MILITARY: At Hungnam, North Korea, the X Corps is ordered to evacuate that port by General Douglas MacArthur and redeploy at Pusan, South Korea.

NAVAL: Vice Admiral Turner C. Joy, commander, U.S. Naval Force, Far East, instructs Rear Admiral James H. Doyle, Task Force 90, to evacuate the X Corps from Hungnam, North Korea.

December 10

AVIATION: At Yonpo Airfield, North Korea, VMF-311 deploys and flies the first Marine Corps jet missions while flying Grumman F9F Panthers.

NAVAL: Task Force 90 under Rear Admiral James H. Doyle commences evacuating UN forces and their equipment from Hungnam, North Korea. Over the next two weeks, 105,000 American and South Korean forces, 91,000 civilians, and 350,000 tons of supplies are safely transported before all Hungnam's harbor installations are destroyed by demolition charges.

MARINES: The front of the 1st Marine Division reaches Chihung-ni while its rearguard still holds its own at Koto-ri. However, several M-26 Pershing tanks are abandoned on the one-lane road after the lead vehicle suffers from locked brakes.

December 11

MARINES: The rearguard of the 1st Marine Division presses on into the safety of Hungnam, North Korea; they are ordered to embark on ships the following day. The perilous retreat from the Chosin Reservoir was a brilliantly conducted affair and a hallmark in Marine Corps history. Marine losses are 908 dead, 3,508 wounded, and 7,513 noncombat casualties, mostly frostbite and illness. Chinese casualties are estimated in excess of 40,000.

December 12

AVIATION: During the mass evacuation at Hungnam, North Korea, UN forces are covered by VMF-212 on the carrier *Bataan*, VMF-214 on the carrier *Sicily*, and VMF323 on the *Badoeng Strait*.

December 14

AVIATION: The first six-ton Tarzon radio-guided bombs are dropped on a tunnel near Huichon, North Korea, with mediocre results.

December 14–17

AVIATION: With Communist forces fast approaching Hamhung, North Korea, Combat Cargo Command stages a three-day evacuation from nearby Yonpo Airfield, removing 228 wounded, 3,891 passengers, and 20,088 tons of cargo in only 72 hours.

December 15

AVIATION: The air force ups the ante over North Korea as North American F-86A Sabre jet fighters begin combat operations.

MILITARY: General Walton H. Walker deploys his battered Eighth Army in new defensive lines along the Imjin River north of Seoul, and he awaits the Chinese onslaught.

MARINES: Final elements of the 1st Marine Division depart Hungnam, North Korea, leaving behind only the 1st Amphibious Tractor Battalion.

December 16

POLITICS: In light of the deteriorating situation in northeastern Asia, President Harry S. Truman declares a national emergency while Dwight D. Eisenhower quits his post as president of Columbia University and becomes head of NATO as supreme allied commander. A surprise attack by the Soviet Union on western Europe is greatly feared.

MARINES: The 1st Marine Division disembarks at Masan, in the same rest area employed by the 1st Provisional Marine Brigade during the Pusan Perimeter campaign. Several units are deployed in the countryside, scouring it for bandits and Communist guerrillas.

December 17
AVIATION: Over North Korea, the first swept-wing jet combat in aviation history results in Lieutenant Colonel Bruce H. Hinton downing a MiG-15 in his F-86A.

December 18
AVIATION: Patrol Squadron 892 (VP-892) becomes the first of many Naval Air Reserve squadrons to deploy in the Korean War.
MARINES: The 1st Marine Division is reassigned to the Eighth Army reserve.

December 19
MILITARY: General Dwight D. Eisenhower is approved as supreme commander of all Western European defense forces by the North Atlantic Council.

December 20
AVIATION: At Kimpo, South Korea, Operation Christmas Kidlift unfolds as 12 C-54s of the 61st Troop Carrier Group transport 800 Korean orphans to the safety of Cheju-do, an island off the coast.

December 23
DIPLOMACY: The United States enters a mutual defense pact with France, Vietnam, Cambodia, and Laos to provide indirect military assistance in the face of a mounting Communist insurgency throughout Indochina.
MILITARY: Near Uijongbu, South Korea, Lieutenant General Walton H. Walker dies in an unfortunate jeep accident. The Americans scramble for a new commander to replace him.

December 24
AVIATION: Navy jets and air force B-26s sweep in over Hungnam, North Korea, to cover the final departing UN forces there.
MARINES: At Hungnam, North Korea, the 1st Amphibious Tractor Battalion is the last UN unit to depart from that port. Over the past two weeks, over 105,000 troops of the X Corps and 91,000 civilians have been removed to safety.

December 25
MILITARY: Communist Chinese forces, flush with victory, cross the 38th parallel into South Korea.

December 26
MILITARY: Lieutenant General Matthew C. Ridgway is appointed commander of the Eighth Army in South Korea.

December 28
AVIATION: In Japan, Marine Corps R5D air transports ferry the first Bell HTL helicopters for use in Korea.

1950

December 29
AVIATION: In Korea, RF-51 Mustangs begin flying critical reconnaissance missions out of Taegu for the first time. Though slower than the RF-80 Shooting Star, they possess far greater range and loitering time over a target.
MILITARY: The outspoken general Douglas MacArthur publicly states that the United Nations ought to attack Communist installations in Manchuria, even with the use of atomic weapons. He also seeks a naval blockade of the Chinese coast and the employment of Nationalist Chinese troops. He informs the Joint Chiefs of Staff (JCS) that failure to abide by his demands will result in the loss of the entire Korean Peninsula to the Communists.

December 31
AVIATION: As the Chinese resume their offensive, Marine Corps aviation lends direct air support to units in the frontline while the majority of air force jets strike at enemy rear areas and supply lines.
MILITARY: Gleeful Chinese Communist forces, surprised by their easy success over UN forces, launch another offensive involving seven field armies and two North Korean corps in a bid to drive the Americans farther south. They are successful in routing the ROK 1st Division, prompting the allies to fall back from the 38th parallel to new lines 70 miles farther south.

1951

January
MILITARY: In light of recent events, the Army's size swells through draftees and volunteers to 1.5 million and 18 divisions.

January 1
AVIATION: The Air Defense Command is reestablished under Lieutenant General Ennis C. Whitehead.
• In light of the new Chinese offensive, the carrier *Bataan* and VMF-212 shift from Korea's east coast to provide air support along the west coast. Fifth Air Force fighters and bombers also turn out in force to help blunt Communist advances.

January 2
AVIATION: In South Korea, a C-47 transport drops flares to assist B-26s and F-82s making night attacks against Chinese positions.
MILITARY: In Washington, D.C., a supplemental defense appropriations bill is passed by Congress by adding $20 billion to the $14 billion already approved for the Department of Defense.

January 3
AVIATION: In Washington, D.C., the Joint Chiefs of Staff authorizes the Marine Corps to create an additional three aviation squadrons, bringing the total to 21.
• Over 60 Bomber Command B-29s strike targets in Pyongyang, North Korea, with over 650 tons of incendiary bombs with a similar-sized follow-up raid two days later.
• Desperate to assist the retreating Eighth Army, Far East Air Forces (FEAF) mount a record 958 combat sorties today.

MILITARY: With Chinese forces pressing hard upon the Han River east and west of Seoul, South Korea, the Eighth Army evacuates the capital and continues falling back to new lines farther south.

January 4–5
AVIATION: After the final American aircraft depart from Kimpo Airfield, South Korea, the runway is bombed and cratered to prevent its use by Communist air forces.
MILITARY: Advancing Communists capture Inchon and the Kimpo airport in South Korea, for the second time in six months, forcing UN forces to evacuate Seoul once again. Meanwhile, General Matthew B. Ridgway orders the Eighth Army and X Corps withdrawn to Line D, 50 miles below the 38th parallel. The Chinese willingly follow, all the while overextending their supply lines and exposing themselves to attacks from the air.

January 6
AVIATION: In Japan, the Combat Cargo Command finishes an extensive resupply division to the 2nd Infantry Division as it fights to hold off a determined Chinese advance.

January 7
AVIATION: All three carriers with Marine Corps squadron onboard are withdrawn from Korean waters; consequently, VMF-214, VMF-311, and VMF-323 end up back at Itami Airfield, Japan, for want of good operating conditions on the peninsula.

January 7–14
MILITARY: General Matthew B. Ridgway stabilizes X Corps and Eighth Army positions 50 miles south of the 38th parallel in a bid to receive–and crush–the latest Chinese offensive. However, the 2nd Infantry Division is forced to give ground and leaves a 20-mile salient on the UN's right flank, through which North Korean guerrillas pour through. Consequently, Ridgway directs the 1st Marine Division from the reserves to this threatened position.

January 10
AVIATION: In Tokyo, Japan, Brigadier General James E. Briggs arrives to take charge of Bomber Command. This reflects the Strategic Air Command's (SAC) policy of rotating commanders every six months to give them as much wartime experience as possible.
• Marine air transport squadrons VMR-152 and 352 begin airlifting thousands of replacements for the 1st Marine Division in South Korea.
MARINES: The 1st Marine Division begins moving north to the port city of Pohang on South Korea's eastern coast.

January 12
AVIATION: In a new tactic for heavy bombers, Fifth Air Force B-29s drop 500-pound bombs fused for airburst above the ground. The result is like a giant shotgun, showering Chinese formations with millions of metal shards.
DIPLOMACY: In New York, the UN cease-fire committee suggests ending the fighting in Korea. The Chinese, who are convinced that they are winning, express no interest at first.

January 13
AVIATION: A six-ton Tarzan guided bomb scores a direct hit on the bridge at Kanggye, North Korea, taking out 60 feet of the center span.

January 14
MILITARY: Attacking Chinese columns capture the city of Wonju, South Korea, marking their farthest advance down the peninsula.

January 15
AVIATION: At El Toro, California, the Marine Helicopter Squadron 161 (HMR-161) becomes the first such organization in the world.
MILITARY: In Washington, D.C., President Harry S. Truman asks Congress for another $14 billion defense budget supplement.

January 15–17
MILITARY: Throughout western South Korea, General Matthew B. Ridgway commits Operation Wolfhound, which unleashes 6,000 troops, tanks, and artillery to destroy nearby Chinese Communist units. The revived UN forces inflict 1,800 casualties over the next two days at a loss of three dead and seven injured.

January 16
AVIATION: The U.S. Air Force contracts with Convair to begin Project MS-1593, which is designed to acquire the nation's first intercontinental ballistic missile (ICBM) by the end of the decade. The end result is the Atlas missile.
•   Six B-36 Peacekeeper bombers from the Strategic Air Command (SAC) depart Bergstrom Air Force Base, Texas, and fly the entire 7,000 miles distance to RAF Lakenheath, England, without refueling.
•   In Korea, continuing teething problems with Grumman F9F Panthers leave VMF-121 grounded until the manufacturer can send technical representatives.
MILITARY: The 31st and 47th National Guard Divisions are federalized, but they both will remain stateside.

January 17
AVIATION: At Taegu, South Korea, a small force of F-86 Sabres deploys in order to be closer to the frontlines and cut down traveling time to targets. This is also the first time they are rigged to serve as fighter bombers in close support missions.
DIPLOMACY: Through intermediaries, the Chinese Communists formally reject the proposed United Nations cease-fire in Korea. They are placing great faith in their ongoing and upcoming offensives.

January 17–18
AVIATION: From bases in Japan, the Cargo Combat Command conducts 109 C-119 Flying Boxcar missions and airdrops over 550 tons of supplies to embattled UN forces in South Korea.

January 18
MARINES: The 1st Marine Division, having deployed over a 1,600-square mile area north and west of Pohang, South Korea, begins the arduous task of clearing out Communist guerrillas and keeping all supply routes to the frontlines open. Once regiments are assigned a zone of action, the hunt begins.

January 19
AVIATION: Determined to interrupt the flow of Communist supplies and rein- forcements into South Korea, Far East Air Forces initiates a comprehensive air interdiction campaign.

January 21
AVIATION: In several aerial battles against superior MiG-15s, an F-80 and an F-84 are lost in combat over North Korea. However, Lieutenant Colonel Wil- liam E. Bertram shoots down a Communist jet, marking the first victory for an F-84.
MARINES: The 1st Korean Marine Corps (KMC) regiment is assigned to the 1st Marine Division.

January 23
AVIATION: At Bofu Airfield, Japan, Marin Air Group 33 (MAG-33) and VMF- 312 begin flying sorties to South Korea; they are joined the next day by men and aircraft of the 1st Marine Air Wing (1st MAW).
• A swarm of 33 F-84s staging from Taegu, South Korea, strike Sinuiju, North Korea, which prompts a large MiG force to intercept them from across the Yalu River. A swirling, 30-minute melee ensues, but the Thunderjets manage to down three Communist jets.
• As Bomber Command B-29s strike airfields around Pyongyang, North Korea, 46 F-80s attack Communist antiaircraft defenses.

UN soldiers in Korea fought in all kinds of weather. *(Center for the Study of the Korean War, Graceland University)*

January 24–26
MARINES: Near Pohang, South Korea, North Korean guerrillas attack the command post of the 7th Marines, who pursue them over the next two days, killing 168 Communists.

January 25
AVIATION: In concert with Operation Thunderbolt, Combat Cargo Command dispatches 70 C-119 Flying Boxcars to airdrop 1,162 tons of supplies to sustain the UN offensive.
MILITARY: On the western flank of South Korea, Gen- eral Matthew B. Ridgway initiates Operation Thunder- bolt with the I and IX Corps to recapture Inchon and Suwon. The attack is slow and methodical, much like a meat grinder, and forces Chinese troops to take cover behind the Han River by February 20. To the east, the X Corps also conducts a similar operation entitled Roundup.

January 26
AVIATION: To better coordinate artillery and air strike spotting aircraft, a C-47 transport is outfitted with radio equipment and serves as an aerial tactical center in contact with all T-6 Mosquitos.

1951

January 29

AVIATION: Admiral Arthur D. Struble instructs carrier aviation of Task Force 77 to begin systematically destroying railway and bridge systems along the eastern coast of North Korea; Struble initially opposed the mission, feeling his aviators were better suited for flying close support.

January 31

AVIATION: The UN makes its first spy mission of the war when the 21st TCS drops an agent at Yonan, South Korea, behind enemy lines.

February 1

MILITARY: At Sinchon, South Korea, the 23rd Infantry Regiment and a French battalion attack and rout the Chinese 125th Division, inflicting 5,000 casualties for a loss of 225 dead and injured.

February 2

NAVAL: Off Wonsan Harbor, North Korea, the minesweeper *Partridge* strikes a mine and sinks with the loss of eight sailors; this is the last vessel of its class lost in Korea.

February 5–8

AVIATION: A force of eight AJ-1 Savages and three P2V Neptunes from VC-5 flies from Norfolk, Virginia, to Port Lyautey, French Morocco, there to be deployed on *Midway*-class carriers as atomic strike aircraft.

February 5–9

MILITARY: South of Seoul, South Korea, General Matthew B. Ridgway commences Operation Punch to seize the Hill 440 complex south of the city. Here the 25th Infantry Division, backed by artillery, tanks, and air power, seizes its objective and inflicts 4,200 casualties on Chinese forces at a cost of 70 killed and wounded.

February 8

AVIATION: Far East Air Forces (FEAF) launches a maximum effort to neutralize all Communist rail lines in northeastern North Korea.
• In Tokyo, Japan, Brigadier General John P. Henebry assumes command of the 315th Air Division to oversee all cargo-carrying operations into South Korea.

February 10

MILITARY: The army 24th Infantry Division seizes Inchon and Kimpo Airfield from the Chinese.

February 11

MILITARY: In central Korea, Chinese forces commence the Fourth Offensive in an attempt to destroy remaining UN forces. Two ROK divisions give way at the onset and the IX Corps is forced to withdraw from the middle of the UN lines.

February 11–13

MILITARY: As the 2nd Infantry Division withdraws through Hoengsong, South Korea, it is attacked by superior Chinese forces and suffers heavy losses. While two battalions of the 38th infantry are decimated and the 15th and 503rd Field Artillery Battalions lose many of their guns, a determined stand by the Dutch Battalion allows the Americans to withdraw safely to Wonju.

February 12
MARINES: Antiguerrilla operations at Pohang, South Korea, conclude with a loss of 36 dead and 148 wounded. The 1st Marine Division is ordered up to Chungju in support of Operation Killer to retake territory lost in the center of UN lines.

February 13
AVIATION: Operating from forward airstrips throughout South Korea, the 315th Air Division transports over 800 sick and wounded soldiers to hospitals at Taegu and Pusan.
• At K-3 airfield near Pohang, South Korea, Marine Air Group 33 (MAG-33) establishes a command post before ordering its squadrons in. Meanwhile, VMF-311 has restored its F9F Panther jets back to operating condition and resumes tactical support missions.

February 13–15
AVIATION: Braving strong winds and intense antiaircraft fire from the ground, 100 transports of the 315th Air Division (Combat Cargo Command) drop 420 tons of food, supplies, and ammunition to the defenders of Chipyong-ni.
MILITARY: The strategic Battle of Chipyong-ni unfolds as the 23rd U.S. Infantry under Colonel Paul Freeman, in concert with a French battalion and supporting armor and artillery units, defend their perimeter against superior Chinese forces. In two days of severe fighting UN forces lose 350 men killed, wounded, and missing, and they are completely cut off and surrounded, but they refuse to surrender. At length the defenders are rescued by the 5th Cavalry Regiment. China's failure to take Chipyong-ni indicates that its latest offensive is losing steam and it finally stalls by February 18.

February 14–17
MILITARY: At Wonju, South Korea, elements of the 2nd and 7th Infantry Divisions, 187th Airborne Regimental Combat Team, and several artillery detachments engage large numbers of Chinese infantry in a one-sided slaughter that becomes known as the "Wonju Shoot" owing to the vast amount of shells expended.

February 15–16
AVIATION: At Chipyong-ni, South Korea, H-5 helicopters of the 3rd Air Rescue Squadron ignore blinding snowstorms and 40-knot winds to deliver medical supplies to soldiers of the 2nd Infantry Division. They also evacuate 52 wounded men.

February 16
AVIATION: Army Cessna L-19 Bird Dogs begin their lengthy career as a forward artillery spotting aircraft, leaving Fifth Air Force pilots to attend to other missions.
NAVAL: With all UN forces safely evacuated, the navy institutes an 861-day blockade of Wonsan, North Korea, to deny its use to Communist forces. However, the nearby harbor remains a popular ditching area for damaged American aircraft, and helicopters continue rescuing pilots landing there throughout the war.

February 17–18
AVIATION: B-26 bombers fly the first Shoran mission of the war. Shoran is a navigational system employing ground beacon stations and an airborne radar receiver to insure precise navigation.

1951

February 21–24

MARINES: The 5th Marines are the first unit attacking from Wonju; their target is the town of Hoengsong and resistance is slight until the 23rd. Despite heavy rain and fighting, the objective falls on the 24th.

February 21–March 6

MILITARY: As a preliminary move to a major counteroffensive, General Matthew B. Ridgway initiates Operation Killer by ordering the IX and X Corps to clear out a large Chinese-held salient in UN lines. The operation takes two weeks and inflicts 10,000 Communist casualties.

February 23

AVIATION: Northeast of Seoul, South Korea, Bomber Command B-29s begin air strikes using MPQ-2 airborne radar. The first target is a highway bridge seven miles from the capital.

February 24

AVIATION: C-119 Flying Boxcars of the Combat Cargo Command air drop a record 333 tons of supplies to UN forces on the frontlines of Korea.

MARINES: After the army commander of IX Corps dies in a helicopter crash, he is temporarily succeeded by Major General Oliver P. Smith. Command of the 1st Marine Division consequently reverts to Colonel Chesty Puller, pending Smith's return.

March 1

AVIATION: The air force establishes Thule Air Base in Greenland, 690 miles north of the Arctic Circle, which serves as its northernmost operational base.

• After a force of 18 Bomber Command B-29s are unable to rendezvous with their F-80 fighter escort over North Korea, they are set upon by MiG-15s, which damage 10 aircraft; three of these make forced landings in South Korea.

• Operation Killer serves to highlight the air force's tendency toward centralizing control of all air missions, the vast majority of which fall upon rear-area targets. Consequently, requests made by the marines for close air support are largely ignored. Afterward, marine commanders confer with the Fifth Air Force commander, who authorizes additional marine aircraft, specializing in close support missions, to assist the 1st Marine Division.

MARINES: The 1st Marine Division fulfills its part of Operation Killer by advancing from Hoengsong and, overcoming all Chinese resistance, achieves its objectives three days later.

March 4

AVIATION: C-119 Flying Boxcars of Combat Cargo Command deliver a record 260 tons of supplies to the 1st Marine Division; this is the month's largest airdrop.

March 5

MARINES: General Oliver P. Smith is relieved from command of the IX Corps and he returns to the 1st Marine Division in time for Operation Ripper.

March 6

AVIATION: After a three-month hiatus, F-86 Sabres begin patrolling along the Yalu River again. There is no shortage of MiG opposition based across the river in Manchuria.

March 6–31
MILITARY: Sensing the time ripe, General Matthew B. Ridgway commences a broad offensive he calls Operation Ripper. Under a heavy artillery bombardment, the 25th and 7th Infantry Divisions cross the Han River against light opposition and recapture Seoul on March 14. The city is promptly occupied by the 3rd Infantry Division and ROK 6th Division as Ridgway's remaining forces continue pressing toward the 38th parallel. Despite Ripper's success, the State Department complains about the aggressive names given to Ridgway's offensives and insists they assume less menacing titles.

March 7
MARINES: During Operation Ripper, the goal of the 1st Marine Division is the town of Hongchon, north of Hoengsong. The Leathernecks push northward, encountering only slight resistance.

March 8
NAVAL: UN naval forces establish a tight blockade of the port of Songjin, North Korea.

March 12
AVIATION: Night fighting VMF (N)-542 departs Korea for the United States to transition to new Douglas F3D Skynights, an all-weather, night-fighting jet interceptor.

March 14
AVIATION: In yet another attempt to retard Communist supply efforts, B-26 bombers drop millions of tetrahedral tacks designed to puncture truck tires.
MILITARY: Republic of Korea troops (ROK) are allowed to recapture their capital of Seoul from the Communist Chinese and begin driving them back over the 38th parallel.
MARINES: As Operation Ripper concludes, marine forces capture the town of Hongchon, then begin fanning out northward into the hilly countryside.

March 14–19
NAVAL: In an impressive display of firepower, the battleship *Missouri* shells eight railroad bridges and seven highway bridges between Wonsan and Kyojo Wan, North Korea.

March 15
AVIATION: In a major development, a B-47 Stratojet bomber refuels in midair from a KC-97A tanker. This ability greatly extends the range of Strategic Command Aircraft (SAC) and puts targets in the Soviet Union within striking distance from wherever they are based.
• In Korea, Far East Air Forces (FEAF) fly a record 1,123 sorties of all kinds.
MILITARY: For a second time, victorious UN forces occupy the much battered capital of Seoul, South Korea, only now for good.
MARINES: North of Hongchon, the 1st and 7th Marines engage Chinese infantry in hilly terrain and flush them out in a close-quarters firepower and grenades fight.

1951

March 20
AVIATION: In England, the Strategic Air Command (SAC) 7th Air Division, which fields nuclear-armed B-47 Stratojets, establishes its headquarters at South Ruislip, outside London.

March 21
MILITARY: Secretary of Defense George C. Marshall announces American military strength at 2.9 million men and women, roughly twice the strength prior to the Korean War.

March 22–31
MILITARY: In concert with Operation Ripper, General Matthew Ridgway commences Operation Courageous against Chinese forces confronting the I Corps; not many enemy soldiers are killed, but UN forces push them and their North Korean allies north of the 38th parallel.

March 23
AVIATION: In South Korea, Operation Tomahawk, the largest-single airborne maneuver of the Korean War, commences as a fleet of 120 C-119s and C-46s convey the 187th Airborne Regimental Combat Team behind enemy lines at Munsan-ni, South Korea. They drop 3,400 men and 220 tons of supplies under the watchful gaze of 16 F-51s acting as escorts.
• In another major raid, 22 B-29s of the 19th and 307th Bomb Groups knock out two bridges in northwestern North Korea. A force of 45 F-86s Sabres provides an escort.
MILITARY: Near Munsan-ri, South Korea, the 187th Airborne Regimental Combat Team, reinforced by companies from the 2nd and 4th Rangers, makes the second and final airborne assault of the war in an attempt to cut off retreating Communist forces. However, the majority of enemy troops escape; one American is killed while 84 suffer jump-related injuries.

March 24
AVIATION: The air force deploys its first Sikorsky H-19 Chickasaw helicopters in South Korea. This versatile machine continues to serve with distinction for over a decade.
MILITARY: General Douglas MacArthur, buoyed by recent events, unilaterally demands that the Chinese surrender in Korea. Not only do they refuse, but the action also compromises a peace initiative tended by Washington to Beijing.

March 29
AVIATION: The carrier *Boxer* arrives in Korean waters bearing Carrier Air Group (CVG) 101, comprised solely of Naval Reserve units, and begins flying combat missions.
• With ice over the Yalu River beginning to thaw, Bomber Command B-29s begin striking at bridges to help cut off Communist supply efforts.

March 31
MILITARY: As Chinese resistance fades, army forces begin pushing north of the 38th parallel for the first time in four months.

1951

April 1
MARINES: At Camp Lejeune, North Carolina, Fleet Marine Force Atlantic organizes to provide support and combat units for any marine division involved in extended operations.

April 2
AVIATION: Major General David M. Schlatter is appointed to command the new Air Research and Development Command (ARDC).

• Navy F9F Panther jets of VF-191 perform their first mission as bombers when they bomb the bridge at Songjin, North Korea. This squadron, operating from the carrier *Princeton,* is composed mostly of pilots from the Blue Angels Flight Demonstration Team, which has been temporarily disbanded for the duration of the conflict.

April 3
AVIATION: The 3rd Air Rescue Squadron (ARS) deploys a service-test H-19 helicopter for the fist time as it rescues a downed F-51 pilot southeast of Pyongyang, North Korea, under heavy fire.

April 4
MILITARY: General Dwight D. Eisenhower selects Paris, France, as the new site for Supreme Headquarters, Allied Power in Europe (SHAPE).

April 5
MILITARY: General Douglas MacArthur, unhappy with President Harry S. Truman's intention to seek a negotiated truce with the Communist powers, unequivocally declares in a letter to Speaker of the House Joseph Martin that, "there is no substitute for victory."

• Operation Rugged unfolds as units of the 8th Army cross the 38th parallel en masse and establish lines Kansas and Utah; American losses are roughly 1,000 killed, wounded, and missing.

NAVAL: Hospital Corpsman Richard D. DeWert, attached to the 1st Marine Division, dashes through enemy fire four times to rescue wounded marines. Fatally wounded on his last foray, he receives a posthumous Medal of Honor.

April 6
AVIATION: In Washington, D.C., the Labor Department announces that an additional 100,000 workers are now toiling in aircraft factories around the nation.

April 7
AVIATION: Aerial defense of the Pusan-Pohang region is entrusted to men and aircraft of the 1st Marine Air Wing (1st MAW).

NAVAL: The cruiser *St. Paul* and two destroyers cover a landing by 251 men of the 41st Independent Commando, Royal Marines, as they destroy a bridge section near Chongjin, along North Korea's east coast.

April 8
MARINES: Shortly after resuming close air support for marine units, the Air Force Joint Operations Center begins diverting operations of the 1st Marine Air Wing (1st MAW) to other priorities.

April 9
AVIATION: Over Indio, California, an F-51 Mustang flown by aviatrix Jacqueline Cochran sets a new world speed record of 469.5 miles per hour over a 16-mile course. This is her fifth propeller-driven aircraft record.

April 10
MILITARY: In a search for additional manpower, the Department of Defense imposes the army's lower intelligence standards on the air force, navy, and marines. The three services are also authorized to accept draftees for the first time since World War II.

April 11
MILITARY: President Harry S. Truman, angered by General Douglas MacArthur's tactless public comment about his policies in Korea, relieves him as UN supreme commander, Far East, and appoints General Matthew B. Ridgway to succeed him. MacArthur was tactlessly adamant about expanding the war into Manchuria and possibly using atomic weapons against Communist China.

April 11–22
MILITARY: Operation Dauntless is launched as the 2nd, 24th, and 25th Infantry Divisions press northward into North Korea and enter the region known as the Iron Triangle against light opposition to establish Lines Utah and Wyoming.

April 12
AVIATION: Over Sinuiji, North Korea, a huge air battle erupts as a fleet of 46 B-29s bomb bridges over the Yalu River while escorted by 100 fighters. The Communists also scramble 100 MiG-15s in response. Three bombers are shot down and seven more are damaged. However, seven Communist jets are claimed by the bomber gunners while the F-86s down four more.

April 14
MILITARY: Lieutenant General James Van Fleet, formerly commander of the Second Army at Fort Meade, Maryland, is appointed the new commander of the Eighth Army.

April 15
MARINES: At Parris Island, South Carolina, the first Officer Candidate School is convened since World War II.

April 17
AVIATION: In North Korea, Warrant Officer Donald Nicholas wins a Distinguished Service Cross for leading a helicopter-borne special operations team to examine and recover technical information from a downed MiG-15 fighter.
MILITARY: In Washington, D.C., President Harry S. Truman, determined to alleviate pressing manpower shortages, signs an executive order extending all military enlistments by nine more months.

April 18
AVIATION: At Holloman Air Force Base, New Mexico, an Aerobee rocket is launched with a live monkey as a passenger. Sadly, the primate does not survive reentry back to Earth.

Ridgway, Matthew B.   (1895–1993)
Army general

Matthew Bunker Ridgway was born in Fort Monroe, Virginia, on March 3, 1895, the son of an army colonel. He graduated from West Point in 1917 but failed to secure a combat position in World War I, instead spending several months patrolling the Mexican border. Over the next two decades, Ridgway fulfilled a typical regimen of far-ranging appointments in China, Nicaragua, and the Philippines, and, in 1935, he was chosen to pass through the elite Army War College. He graduated two years later with distinction and found himself attached to the War Plans Division within the War Department as a lieutenant colonel. Following American entry into World War II, Ridgway rose to major general commanding the 82nd Infantry Division and supervised its conversion to a parachute unit. In July 1943 Ridgway spearheaded the invasion of Sicily with his 82nd Airborne Division, and he overcame a scattered landing to seize strategic points of that island until relieved. He enjoyed similar success at Salerno the following August and, in June 1944, he jumped with his men over Normandy, France, this time spearing heading Operation Overlord. Ridgway's command suffered nearly 50 percent losses but took all their strategic objectives and he subsequently assumed control of the 18th Airborne Corps of American, British, and Polish units. He spearheaded ill-fated Operation Market Garden against German forces in the Netherlands, becoming one of the few commanders to seize their objectives. In December 1944 Ridgway's paratroopers helped blunt the northern shoulder of the German offensive during the Battle of the Bulge in the Ardennes, Belgium. They crossed the Rhine River into Germany in 1945 and linked up with Soviet forces along the Elbe River in May. For his distinguished services, Ridgway gained temporary promotion to lieutenant general.

April 19

AVIATION: In Japan, the entire fleet of C-119 Flying Boxcars undergoes an upgrade and refurbishing before resuming combat operations.

POLITICS: An unrepentant general Douglas MacArthur, addressing a joint session of Congress, renews his call for use of atomic bombs and other weapons against the Chinese in Manchuria. He then declares, "Old soldiers never die, they just fade away." It is the passage of a national icon.

April 21

AVIATION: A Fairchild XC-123 is fitted with four J47 jet engines and becomes the first jet-powered transport aircraft, but it does not enter production.

• Marine Corps captain Philip C. DeLong of VMF-312 scores that service's first aerial victories of the war by downing two Russian-made Yak-9 fighters while wingman Lieutenant Harold D. Haight bags another. However, increasingly

★ ★ ★ ★ ★ ★ ★ ★ ★ ★ ★ ★ ★ ★

During the postwar period, Ridgway served with the Military Staff Committee of the United Nations from 1946 to 1948, and, in 1950, he was ordered to replace the late general Walton Walker as head of the Eighth Army in Korea. At that time UN forces were buckling under a huge Chinese surprise offensive, but Ridgway calmly reordered his lines, allowed the Communists to outstrip their supply lines below Seoul, then sharply counterattacked. Operations Killer and Ripper promptly drove Chinese forces back across the 38th parallel where the war began. Ridgway consented to cease-fire talks in July 1951. In May 1952 he was tapped to succeed General Dwight D. Eisenhower as commander of the North Atlantic Treaty Organization (NATO), and he supervised its enlargement from 12 to 80 divisions. The following year Eisenhower picked him to serve as army chief of staff in Washington, D.C., and he strongly urged the president not to get involved in French Indochina. Ridgway retired from active service in 1955,

Matthew Ridgway arrives at Haneda Air Force base. *(U.S. Army)*

and he died in Pittsburgh, Pennsylvania, on July 26, 1993. From the standpoint of strategy and tactics, he remains one of the most adept American military leaders of the 20th century.

effective Chinese antiaircraft defenses account for 16 Marine Corps aircraft this month, with nine pilots killed and one captured.

April 22
MILITARY: In light of extended military service in Korea, the army adopts a new troop rotation policy, which is based on a point system. Any soldiers accumulating 36 points in a combat zone will be returned to the United States and discharged from the service. However, officers complain that the relatively high turnover rate hurts unit cohesion due to the steady influx of new replacement personnel.

• Undaunted by massive losses, the Chinese Communists unleash their Fifth Offensive against the Eighth Army with 250,000 new troops. The Americans are forced back to a new defensive line north of Seoul, which is dubbed "No Name Line," to contain the Chinese, inflicting 70,000 casualties. UN losses are 1,900 killed, wounded, and missing.

MARINES: The 1st Marine Division, having advanced 45 miles since the inception of Operation Ripper, reaches the Hwachon Reservoir in concert with the 1st Korean Marine Corps regiment. This evening, however, the Chinese unleash their spring offensive, which routs the ROK 6th Division on their left flank. Fortunately, the 7th Marines hold firm while the remainder of the 1st Division refuses its left flank.

April 23
AVIATION: Aircraft of the Far East Air Forces conduct 340 close support sorties for UN forces, the highest daily tally achieved before 1953.
• At Suwon, South Korea, F-86 Sabre jet fighters begin deploying to cut down their flying time to "MiG Alley" astride the Yalu River.
• Reverting back to close air support missions, the 1st Marine Air Wing (1st MAW) flies 205 sorties along the frontlines; the 1st Marine Division is the object of no less than 42 of its sorties.
MARINES: The new Chinese offensive, having punched a few holes in UN lines, Eighth Army headquarters orders the 1st Marine Division to fall back and attempt to plug the leaks. Chinese forces also mount a strong attack against the 1st Battalion, 1st Marines along Horseshoe Hill and a fierce battle rages.

April 23–26
AVIATION: Aircraft of the Far East Air Forces fly over 1,000 combat sorties in to interdict enemy supplies and inflict heavy troop losses.

April 26
NAVAL: UN naval forces place Hungnam, North Korea, under blockade.

April 30
AVIATION: In Japan, bombers of the Fifth Air Force undertake 960 combat sorties for a new daily record.
MARINES: As UN forces cease their withdrawal, the 1st Marine Division repositions itself at Hongchon, where it had been deployed two months earlier.

May 1
AVIATION: In a very innovative sortie, eight navy AD Skyraiders from Attack Squadron VA-195 and Composite Squadron VC-35 strike the Hwachon Dam, North Korea, with torpedoes, scoring several hits and flooding the Han and Pukhan River valleys. To this day VA-195 (now VFA-195) goes by the nickname "Dambusters."

May 3
MILITARY: In another provocation, a military policeman from the 769th Military Police Battalion is killed by Soviet troops in Vienna, Austria.

May 5
MARINES: In Washington, D.C., the Senate votes to give the Marine Corps a 400,000-man ceiling and full membership in the Joint Chiefs of Staff, while the House of Representatives seeks a 300,000-man limit with JCS representation. The legislation fails when neither body can reach a compromise in conference; the entire effort is strenuously resisted by both the navy and the army.

May 9
AVIATION: Over Sinuiju, North Korea, now the temporary Communist capital, over 300 U.S. aircraft, including F4U Corsairs and F9F Panthers of the 1st

Marine Air Wing (1st MAW), strike important bridges spanning the Yalu River into China.

May 15

AVIATION: Marine Fighter Squadron VMF-121 is reequipped with Douglas AD Skyraiders, each capable of lugging 5,000 pounds of ordnance. They are accordingly redesignated VMA-121 (attack).

May 16

MILITARY: Switching fronts, the Chinese Communists mass 175,000 soldiers and hurl them down the center of UN lines by striking the X Corps, the ROK III Corps, and the right flank of the 8th Army. The Allies are driven back by sheer weight of numbers but gradually contain the attack with massed artillery and air power. Chinese losses are estimated at 90,000 while the Americans suffer 1,200 killed, wounded, and missing.

MARINES: Chinese Communist forces launch a large offensive against the 1st Marine Division near Hongchon, which is defeated. However, ROK formations to the east of the Marines are routed, creating a new 20-mile gap in UN lines.

May 16–26

AVIATION: For 10 uninterrupted days, the Combat Cargo Command airlifts an average 1,000 tons of supplies per day to embattled troops in South Korea.

May 17–22

AVIATION: B-29s of Bomber Command execute 94 close support missions for UN ground forces, many of them at night.

May 20

AVIATION: Over North Korea, Major James Jabara, 334th Fighter Interceptor Squadron, flames his fifth and sixth MiG-15s, becoming the first all-jet ace in aviation history.

• In Tokyo, Far East Air Forces commander Lieutenant General George E. Stratemeyer suffers a heart attack and is replaced the following day by Major General Earle E. Partridge. He is replaced at Fifth Air Force by Major General Edward J. Timberlake.

MILITARY: In several quick moves, Eighth Army reserves plug a 20-mile gap created recently by Chinese forces.

NAVAL: Off Wonsan, North Korea, the destroyer *Brinkley Bass* is struck from shore battery fire, which kills one sailor and wounds nine more. After maneuvering out of range of enemy cannon, the ship responds with counterbattery fire.

• The newly recommissioned battleship *New Jersey* enters the Korean War by shelling Communist positions at Kangsong, North Korea.

May 21

NAVAL: The battleship *New Jersey*, on its second day of action in Korea, is struck by shore battery fire that kills one sailor and wounds three more.

May 23

AVIATION: Determined to blunt the latest Chinese offensive, the Fifth Air Force commences Operation Strangle to interdict Communist supply lines running down the length of the Korean Peninsula. The region known as the "Iron Triangle" is

1951

assigned to the 1st Marine Air Wing (1st MAW), near Pyongyang, North Korea. Activity here costs them 20 aircraft over the next two months.

MARINES: As UN forces mount a sharp counterattack, the 1st Marine Division advances into the vicinity of the Hwachon Reservoir again, where opposition is light and many prisoners are taken.

May 27
AVIATION: The 1st Marine Air Wing (1st MAW), in order to be closer to the front lines, moves its F4U Corsairs from airfield K-46 to K-1 (Kimpo). Marine transport aircraft also drop flares in support of Marine night operations on the ground.

May 27–28
AVIATION: Psychological warfare flights by specially equipped C-47 transports armed with broadcast speakers convince over 4,000 Communist troops to surrender to the Army IX Corps. Interrogators learn that enemy morale is low, due mainly to incessant air attacks.

May 31
AVIATION: The Fifth Air Force commences Operation Strangle, its most ambitious aerial interdiction campaign of the war so far.

MILITARY: In Washington, D.C., traditional army-navy-marine-air force legal systems are all replaced by the new Uniform Code of Military Justice.

• The Eighth Army is pushing Chinese forces back across the front, having inflicted roughly 200,000 casualties since January. The Communists verge on collapse but President Harry S. Truman, fearful of an expanding conflict, rules out a second advance into North Korea.

June
AVIATION: At Edwards Air Force Base, California, the Air Force Flight Test Center (AFFTC) is officially opened.

June 1
AVIATION: In Tokyo, Japan, Major General Frank E. Everest is appointed commander of the Fifth Air Force.

• Aeromedical researcher Major John P. Strapp commences subjecting himself to a series of High-G (Earth gravity) experiments by being strapped to a series of rocket sleds. At one point, he survives the force of 48 "Gs," highlighting that the human body can endure far more physical stress than thought medically possible.

MARINES: At Camp Pendleton, California, the 3rd Marine Brigade is reestablished as part of the authorized buildup to four divisions and is centered around the 3rd Marines.

• The Marine Corps discharges 2,200 officers and men from the organized reserve back into civilian life.

June 3
AVIATION: After two C-119 Flying Boxcars are downed by friendly fire, the army and air force establish new identification procedures to accompany air drops.

June 3–12
MILITARY: General James A. Van Fleet commences Operation Piledriver, the last large UN offensive of the Korean War, in ordering the 8th Army back into

Van Fleet, James A. (1892–1992)
Army general

James Alward Van Fleet was born in Coytesville, New Jersey, on March 19, 1892, and he graduated from the U.S. Military Academy in 1915. He commanded a machine gun battalion at Meuse-Argonne in 1918, and returned home to teach military science at several universities. Van Fleet passed through the Infantry School in 1929 and was serving as colonel of the 8th Infantry when World War II erupted. It was not until June 6, 1944, when he landed at Utah Beach on D-Day, that Van Fleet first saw battle, but his rise through the ranks proved meteoric. He advanced to brigadier general commanding the 90th Division that fall, distinguished himself in the capture of Metz, gained promotion to major general in General George S. Patton's Third Army, and subsequently commanded the III Corps as it spearheaded the drive across Remagen bridgehead into Germany proper. Van Fleet returned home after the war, but, in 1948, he became lieutenant general and director of the Joint U.S. Military Advisory and Planning Group in Athens, Greece. He helped train the Greek army to successfully stamp out a Communist-inspired insurgency, which was completely routed by 1949. This was one of the West's earliest Cold War triumphs. Van Fleet subsequently returned home to command the Second U.S. Army until events in Asia summoned him abroad once more.

In April 1951, Van Fleet arrived in South Korea to replace General Matthew B. Ridgway as commander of the Eighth Army. His immediate task was to prepare his troops to brace for several Chinese offensives, which were heavily repulsed that spring, and then to drive the Communists back across the 38th parallel. Van Fleet's aggressive tactics inflicted 250,000 Chinese casualties, but Ridgway, fearing that a renewed drive into North Korea would prove too costly, ordered him to halt just north of the 38th parallel and dig in. The war then degenerated into a struggle of small units fighting and dying over various hills and positions along the UN lines. Van Fleet, amply supplied with artillery and air power, invariably inflicted greater losses than he sustained, but he remained frustrated by the concept of limited victory and pressed superiors for an all-out offensive. Meanwhile, he rose to full general in August 1951 and his small but successful offensives that fall were ended by superiors who wished to facilitate truce talks with Communist leaders. An angry Van Fleet reverted back to small-scale actions, backed by massive artillery fire, which expended so much ammunition that shortages resulted. Van Fleet was frustrated and greatly relieved when General Maxwell D. Taylor replaced him as head of the Eighth Army in February 1953, and he came home to resign from the army. Van Fleet harshly criticized the handling of the Korean War, but President Dwight D. Eisenhower nonetheless appointed him special ambassador to the Far East. He died on September 23, 1992, an aggressive military leader but too wedded to traditional notions of victory to flourish in the age of "limited war."

the Iron Triangle, just north of the 38th parallel. Heavy resistance is encountered and the Americans fail to take all their objectives. For the remainder of the war, the Iron Triangle remains something of a no-man's land, possessed by neither side.

June 5–September 20

AVIATION: Naval aviation attached to Task Force 77 begins participating in the Air Force's Operation Strangle to interdict Communist supply routes. They are soon joined by aircraft of the First Marine Air Wing, but the effort is deemed only marginally successful.

June 6

MARINES: Men of the 1st Marines begin a concerted drive to secure the Hwachon Reservoir, encountering stiff resistance from North Korean troops.

June 10

AVIATION: In Tokyo, Japan, Lieutenant General Otto P. Weyland arrives to serve as the commander of Far East Air Forces (FEAF).
• F4U Corsairs from VMF-214 and VMF-(N)-513 provide around-the-clock, close support missions for operations along the ridges of the Hwachon Reservoir.

MARINES: Six days of close-in fighting with bayonets and hand grenades end with the 1st Marines seizing the heights overlooking the Hwachon Reservoir, North Korea. The 1st Korean Marine Corps regiment and the 7th Marines have an equally hard go at it but at length stand triumphant over their section of the ridge line known as the "Punchbowl"—a huge, extinct volcanic crater.

June 11

AVIATION: At Edwards Air Force Base, California, a Douglass D-558 Phase II Skyrocket attains a world record speed of 1,200 miles per hour.

June 12

NAVAL: Off Hungnam, North Korea, the destroyer *Walker* strikes a mine, which kills 26 sailors and wounds 35. The vessel does not sink, however, and is eventually towed off and repaired.

June 14

NAVAL: Off Songjin, North Korea, Communist shore batteries strike the destroyer minesweeper *Thompson* with 14 hits, killing three sailors and wounding four more.

June 15

MARINES: Off Southern California, Fleet Marine Force Pacific (FMFPAC) stages Operation Lex, a large amphibious exercise.

June 16

MARINES: The 1st Marine Division, having secured a line from Hwachon Reservoir northeast to the Punchbowl, are ordered to dig in and consolidate their positions.

June 18

NAVAL: The NATO post of commander, Allied Command Southern Europe, is tended to Admiral Robert B. Carney.

June 19
MILITARY: In Washington, D.C., President Harry S. Truman signs the Universal Military Training and Service Act, which extends the national draft through July 1, 1955, and increases the length of service to two years. The draft age is also lowered to 18½ years. The act also endorses the concept of Universal Military Training (UMT) but it provides no funding or legal requirements to enforce it.

June 20
AVIATION: At Edwards Air Force Base, California, a Bell X-5, the first aircraft with variable-sweep (adjustable) wings is flown by test pilot Jean L. Ziegler.
• The Martin B-61 Matador guided surface-to-surface missile is launched for the first time.
MARINES: At Camp Lejeune, North Carolina, two mortar rounds fall short during a training exercise and strike a battalion command post; eight Marines are killed and 25 wounded.
• At Camp Pendleton, California, the 3rd Marines are formally activated as the nucleus of the new 3rd Marine Brigade.

June 23
DIPLOMACY: In New York, Soviet UN ambassador Jacob Malik suggests opening cease-fire negotiations in Korea, a good indication of how badly Communist forces there have fared of late.

June 25
AVIATION: At Tullahoma, Tennessee, President Harry S. Truman attends ceremonies marking the opening of the Arnold Engineering Development Center.
DIPLOMACY: In light of staggering losses suffered since January, the Chinese Communists also make known their desire for truce talks on Korea.

June 30
AVIATION: Over Seoul, South Korea, a Marine Corps Grumman F7F Tigercat from VMF-513 shoots down a North Korean PO-2 biplane during a nighttime nuisance raid; this is the first operational kill for the twin-engine Tigercat, the last and best piston-engined navy fighter.
MARINES: At this date, Marine Corps manpower levels have risen to 15,150 officers and 177,770 enlisted men—more than double from the year previous.

July 1
DIPLOMACY: North Korean leader Kim Il Sung and Chinese military leader Peng Teh-huai accept General Matthew Ridgway's invitation to attend cease-fire talks. In light of recent Communist losses, it is a face-saving expedient.
• In South Korea, Colonel Karl L. Polifka, the distinguished reconnaissance pilot, dies when his RF-51 Mustang is shot down near the frontlines. His parachute is snagged by the aircraft's tail after he jumps.

July 3
AVIATION: Over North Korea, a navy HO3S helicopter flown by Lieutenant John K. Koelsch is shot down while rescuing a badly burned marine aviator. The men evade capture for several days and are then seized and interned. Koelsch refuses

to aid the Communists and dies in captivity, winning posthumously a Medal of Honor.

July 4
AVIATION: An Air Force RB-45C Tornado jet reconnaissance bomber flown by Captain Stacy D. Naftel, having penetrated 500 miles into Manchuria on a top-secret overflight mission, is attacked by MiG-15 jet fighters, but nonetheless out-runs his antagonists.

July 6
AVIATION: Over North Korea, a KB-29M tanker belonging to the 43rd Air Refueling Squadron performs the first combat refueling mission when it gasses up four RF-80s during a reconnaissance mission over enemy territory.
MARINES: In Washington, D.C., President Harry S. Truman signs legislation extending the enlistments of 300,000 personnel by a full year before they are set to expire on July 1, 1952.

July 9–November 27
MILITARY: United Nations forces take to the counteroffensive in launching a pro-tracted campaign to further wear down Chinese units in their immediate front-lines. This entails some of the heaviest fighting of the war.

July 10
DIPLOMACY: With the Korean War effectively stalemated on the ground, the United States joins United Nations truce talks with the Communist powers at Kaesang at the 38th parallel, Korea. Vice Admiral Turner C. Joy is the principal UN negotiator during discussions, joined by Rear Admiral Arleigh A. Burke.
MARINES: In light of declining enlistments, the Marine Corps is forced to accept 7,000 draftees, the first admitted since World War II.

July 14
AVIATION: Across the United States, the civilian Ground Observer Corps begins an around-the-clock vigil looking for Communist aircraft in American skies.
• Unable to resolve problems associated with a muddy, dirt runway, Marine Air Group 12 (MAG-12) transfers its operations in Korea to airfield K-18, much closer to the 38th parallel.

July 15
MARINES: The 1st Marine Division is replaced in line by the 2nd Infantry Division and is reposted to the Eighth Army Reserve.

July 22
NAVAL: In Naples, Italy, Chief of Naval Operations admiral Forrest P. Sherman dies of a heart attack while on official business.

July 25
DIPLOMACY: At Kaesong, South Korea, truce talks between UN and Communist representatives result in an agenda for further discussions, including a prisoner exchange and a line of demarcation.

July 28
NAVAL: In a lightning raid, the cruiser *Los Angeles* slips into waters off the Ongjin Peninsula, North Korea, and shells several Communist positions with impunity.

July 30

AVIATION: Over Korea, a major air strike involving 91 F-80s, which suppresses antiaircraft defenses, and 354 marine and air force fighter bombers that strike Communist positions across the peninsula, is executed. The Joint Chiefs of Staff, however, not wishing to generate negative publicity during cease-fire talks, withholds information about the action.

July 31

NAVAL: In Washington, D.C., Dan A. Kimball, a former army pilot during World War II, becomes the 51st secretary of the navy.

August 11

NAVAL: Off Hodo-Pando, North Korea, minesweepers *Dextrous* and *Redstart* come under fire from shore batteries; *Dextrous* takes two direct hits that kill one sailor and wound three others.

August 15

AVIATION: The Douglass D-558 Phase II Skyrocket reaches a record altitude of 79,494 feet over Southern California.

August 16

NAVAL: In Washington, D.C., Admiral William M. Fechteler is appointed the 13th chief of naval operations.

August 17

AVIATION: At the National Air Races in Detroit, Michigan, an F-86E flown by Colonel Fred J. Ascani establishes a new world speed record by reaching 635.6 miles per hour over a 100-kilometer course; he wins the Mackay Trophy for his efforts.

August 18

AVIATION: The first jets-only Bendix Trophy transcontinental air race is won by an F-86A Sabre flown by Colonel Keith Compton, who flies from Muroc, California, to Detroit, Michigan, in three hours and 27 minutes. He narrowly edges out an F-84 and two B-45 Tornado jet bombers pitted against him.
• Fifth Air Force bombers and fighter bombers expand the mission of Operation Strangle to include railroads in North Korea.
• With a powerful typhoon threatening the Korean Peninsula, the 1st Marine Air Wing (1st MAW) relocates men and equipment to Japan over the next three days.

August 18–September 5

MILITARY: A region at the southwest apex of the Iron Triangle, known locally as Bloody Ridge, is the focus of incessant attacks by the 2nd Infantry Division, assisted by several ROK units. The position is taken at a loss of 2,700 UN casualties while Chinese losses are estimated at 15,000.

August 23

DIPLOMACY: Unable to achieve their goals, Communist negotiators break off truce talks at Kaesong, South Korea.

August 24

AVIATION: In Washington, D.C., air force chief of staff Hoyt S. Vandenberg declares that tests involving a new generation of smaller, tactical nuclear weapons have been completed in the previous February. Most of the new weapons developed will be deployed in Europe on Air Force F-84G Thunderjet and B-45A Tornado jet bombers.

August 24–25

AVIATION: In Korea, during a single night of anti-truck operations, Fifth Air Force B-26s claim to have destroyed over 800 vehicles as part of Operation Strangle.

August 25

AVIATION: Marshaling yards at Rashin, North Korea, are destroyed by a fleet of 35 Bomber Command B-29s under heavy U.S. navy jet escort. This attack takes place only 20 miles from the Soviet border, but no aircraft are lost.

• F2H Banshees and F9F Panthers from the carrier *Essex* escort air force B-29 bombers on a long-range strike against railyards in Rashin, North Korea, just south of the Soviet border.

August 27

MARINES: The 1st Marine Division redeploys into the line southeast of the Punch Bowl, North Korea, in anticipation of a new round of fighting.

August 28

AVIATION: The air force competition to construct the next generation of large transport aircraft is won by Lockheed's XC-130. It enters service as the C-130 Hercules, garners the reputation as one of the most rugged and dependable aircraft ever built, and is still in service today.

August 31–September 3

AVIATION: Marine helicopter squadron HMR-161 deploys in South Korea with 15 Sikorsky HRS-1s, each capable of hauling 1,500 pounds of cargo or an infantry squad.

MARINES: The 1st Marine Division launches an attack intending to seize a ridge running along the northeast rim of the Punch Bowl, North Korea. Three days later it falls through the combined efforts of the 7th Marines and the 1st KMC regiment.

September 5

AVIATION: Convair Aircraft contracts with the U.S. Air Force to construct a specially modified B-36 bomber capable of using a nuclear reactor as its power source. The aircraft flies in 1955 but the program is ultimately cancelled for a host of technical and environmental reasons.

September 7

AVIATION: The missile test ship *Norton Sound* successfully launches a Terrier antiaircraft missile, which strikes an F6F target drone.

DIPLOMACY: The United States becomes mired further into the problems of Southeast Asia, when it agrees to provide economic assistance to the French-controlled government of Vietnam, then in the throes of a Communist insurgency.

September 9

AVIATION: Over North Korea, a force of 28 F-86 Sabres is jumped by 70 Communist MiG-15s. Ignoring three-to-one odds, Captains Richard S. Becket and Ralph D.

Gibson each flame a MiG, raising the number of all-jet aces to three.

September 11–20
MARINES: Along the Punchbowl, North Korea, the 1st Marine Division prepares to storm another series of ridgelines. The 2nd Battalion, 7th Marines manages to infiltrate Chinese positions, which fall the following day, but cost the attackers 250 men. During the lull created by truce talks, the Chinese have strengthened their positions and can now field nearly as many howitzers and mortars as the Americans.

September 13
AVIATION: Near Cocoa, Florida, the air force establishes its first pilotless bomber squadron at the Missile Test Center.

The F-86 Sabre was the USAF's first swept-wing jet fighter. (*U.S. Air Force*)

• In a clear demonstration of their battlefield utility, helicopters of HMR-161 lift 10 tons of supplies to marines battling along the Punchbowl, and they evacuate 74 casualties.

MARINES: At the Punchbowl, North Korea, the 1st Marines renew their drive to capture the right half of the Communist-controlled ridgeline. The dug-in Chinese resist tenaciously.

September 13–October 15
MILITARY: Moving up from Bloody Ridge, the 2nd Infantry Division sets its sights on seizing Heartbreak Ridge in concert with several ROK formations and a French battalion. Fighting is fierce and the UN forces suffer 2,700 casualties before finally storming the ridge. The Chinese lose an estimated 25,000 men and UN artillery expends so many shells evicting them that it creates an ammunition shortage for the entire army. At one juncture, the 15th Field Artillery Battalion loosed 14,425 rounds in a single 24-hour period.

September 14
AVIATION: Over North Korea, a B-26 Invader flown by Captain John S. Walmsley, Jr., exhausts all of its munitions while attacking a train, then turns on its experimental wing searchlight to illuminate the target for other bombers. Walmsley is subsequently shot down and killed, but he receives a posthumous Medal of Honor.

September 16–17
MARINES: At Punchbowl Ridge, North Korea, the 5th Marines advance through the line to take strategic Hill 812.

September 17
MILITARY: In Washington, D.C., Robert A. Lovett gains appointment as the fourth secretary of defense.

September 20
AVIATION: For the first time, an Aerobee rocket flies to an altitude of 236,000 feet and returns with its cargo of one monkey and 11 mice alive and well.

MARINES: The 1st Marine Division concludes its offensive along the Punchbowl ridgelines and consolidates its position. The units, having replaced the ROK 11th Division, is now strung out for 23,000 yards (13 miles) in rugged terrain. This action marks the final U.S. drive of the war, which is now restricted to local offensives for territorial gain, reminiscent of trench fighting in World War I.

September 21

AVIATION: Helicopters of HMR-161 achieve another first by depositing 224 marines of the 2nd Battalion, 7th Marines on Hill 884 near the Punchbowl, North Korea. They achieve in four hours what would have taken infantrymen 15 hours to accomplish across difficult terrain.

September 23

AVIATION: The first production B-47B Startojet bomber is delivered to the 306th Bombardment Wing.
• Over North Korea, eight B-29s guided by Shoran navigation knock out the center span of the Sunchon rail bridge.

September 25

AVIATION: In a major clash over Suniju, North Korea, 36 F-86 Sabres and an estimated 100 MiG-15s clash in swirling, high-speed combat. The Sabres get the better of it this time, downing five Communist jets.

September 26

MILITARY: The Department of Defense releases plans to increase the number of women in the armed services. For the marines, current numbers of 63 officers and 2,187 enlisted are elevated to 100 and 2,900, respectively.

September 27

AVIATION: At the Punchbowl, North Korea, helicopters of HMR-161 rehearse moving a marine infantry company by air to any threatened position along the attenuated frontline. The move is accomplished in only two hours and 20 minutes.
• A service-test Douglas C-124 Globemaster II lands at Seoul, South Korea, and disgorges 30,000 pounds of aircraft parts as part of Operation Pelican.

September 28

AVIATION: In a mission lasting 14 hours and 15 minutes, an RF-80 reconnaissance fighter refuels in the air several times before concluding its record-breaking sortie.

September 29

MARINES: In Washington, D.C., President Harry S. Truman authorizes a rise in Marine Corps personnel to 211,000. The upcoming drafts for November and December are expected to bring in 19,900 of these.

September 30

AVIATION: In Tokyo, Japan, Brigadier General Joe W. Kelly gains appointment as the head of Bomber Command.
MARINES: Offensives in the Punchbowl region result in 2,416 casualties, the third-highest since December 1950 and June 1951.

TECHNOLOGY: Marines introduce the MPQ-14 radar system, which is designed to drop bombs based on radar guidance from the set.

October 1

MILITARY: In a major development, the Eighth Army integrates itself by disbanding the all-black 24th Infantry Regiment and 159th Field Artillery battalion and assigning the personnel to the 25th Infantry Division. The two units in question are replaced by the 14th Infantry and 69th Field Artillery Battalion.

MARINES: At Quantico, Virginia, Lieutenant General Franklin A. Hart is appointed the first president of the Joint Landing Force Board.

October 3

AVIATION: At Naval Air Station Key West, Florida, Helicopter Antisubmarine Squadron 1 (HS-1) introduces rotary-wing aircraft into the arena of submarine warfare for the first time.

October 3–9

MILITARY: Operation Commando unfolds as the I Corps commits five divisions to secure Lines Jamestown in the Old Baldy area. Success here costs the Americans 2,500 casualties, primarily among the 1st Cavalry Division.

October 11

AVIATION: It takes 156 sorties, but helicopters of HMR-161 make aviation history by completing the first battalion-sized troop lift. In effect, they relocate the 958 men of the 3rd Battalion, 7th Marines from a reserve position 17 miles in the rear, to the frontlines of the Punchbowl.

October 13

TECHNOLOGY: A handful of soldiers and marines in Korea are issued new bullet- and shrapnel-resistant flak jackets for testing under combat operations. Success leads later to mass production.

October 16

AVIATION: In various air battles over North Korea, a record nine MiG-15s are shot down by F-86 Sabres.

October 22

AVIATION: Off the Korean coast, SA-16 Albatrosses rescue 12 men from a downed B-29 bomber; this is the largest single number of men pulled out of the water of the entire war.

October 23

AVIATION: At MacDill Air Force Base, Florida, the first shipment of production model B-47Bs for the 306th Bombardment Wing is completed. This craft emerges as one of the most important jets in Strategic Air Command (SAC) history.

• One of the largest air battles over North Korea occurs as Communist jets attack B-29s and their F-84 Sabre escorts. Three bombers and a Thunderjet go down in flames while gunners manage to claim five MiG-15s.

October 25

AVIATION: Over North Korea, marine F4Us encounter MiG-15 jets; no damage is incurred by either side.

October 29
AVIATION: The carrier *Essex,* acting upon military intelligence, launches a strike with AD Skyraiders VF-54 against Communist Party headquarters at Kapsan, North Korea. Apparently, the raid kills over 500 Communists.

November 2
MILITARY: In Washington, D.C., the Department of Defense declares a large draft call of 60,000 men, from which 11,650 are slated for the Marine Corps.

November 4
AVIATION: Over Sinanju, North Korea, a clash between 34 F-86 Sabres and an estimated 60 MiG-15s results in two Communist aircraft downed and three damaged.
• Over North Korea, an F9F Panther flown by Captain William F. Guss of VMF-311 shoots down a Chinese MiG-15 jet fighter. This is the first Communist jet downed by a marine.

November 6
AVIATION: Soviet La-11 fighters intercept a U.S. navy weather reconnaissance P2V-3W Neptune patrol plane in the Sea of Japan off Vladivostok, shooting it down and killing the crew of 10.

November 9
AVIATION: A C-47 transport lands on the beaches of Paengnyong-do Island, North Korea, and rescues 11 members of a downed B-29 bomber that crashed there.

November 10
MARINES: At Quantico, Virginia, sculptor Felix de Weldon unveils his limestone rendition of the Iwo Jima flag-raising scene and it is displayed at the front gate of the base. This also serves as the basis for his much larger bronze version, which is located in Arlington, Virginia.

November 12
DIPLOMACY: UN-Communist peace negotiations are transferred from Kaesong, South Korea, to the village of Panmunjom, which lays in the middle of the new Demilitarized Zone (DMZ) on the 38th parallel.
MILITARY: General Matthew B. Ridgway orders a halt to offensive operations across Korea and substitutes a new policy of "active defense" whereby UN units will employ patrols, raids, and ambushes instead of simply remaining static. Any operations undertaken will also be supported by air power and ample artillery.

November 15
TECHNOLOGY: The 1st Marine Division distributes new thermal boots to all personnel. This footwear is designed to prevent frostbite by retaining body heat, which is caught by two layers of rubber insulation. The boots are heavy to walk in but are satisfactory for the kind of static warfare the Leathernecks now find themselves in.

November 16
AVIATION: Fifth Air Force bombers and fighter bombers begin another concerted air interdiction campaign against Communist supply routes, this time focusing upon rail lines through North Korea. Bridges, gun positions, supply buildings, and freight cars are also targeted when espied.

November 18
AVIATION: An Air Force C-47 transport accidentally strays into Romanian airspace while flying to Belgrade, Yugoslavia, and is shot down by MiG-15 jets; three crew members die, but one survives and is released.

November 21
NAVAL: Off Kojo, North Korea, the cruiser *Los Angeles* slips into bombardment position and shells enemy forces attacking the ROK I Corps; the Communists are driven back.

November 27
DIPLOMACY: Truce talks between UN and Communist negotiators yield little beyond an agreement to accept a line of demarcation roughly along existing lines of contact.

November 30
AVIATION: In another major air battle, F-86 Sabres intercept 44 Communist aircraft flying south to attack UN forces. The Americans shoot down 12 enemy aircraft and damage three more; Major George A. Davis becomes a double ace this day, in being distinct among contemporaries as an ace from World War II.

December 5–29
MILITARY: In South Korea, the 45th Infantry Division, a National Guard formation, replaces the 1st Cavalry Division in the frontlines as the latter rotates back to Japan as part of the Far East Command reserve.

December 8
MILITARY: The War Department announces a draft of 55,000 men, of which 14,000 are slated for the Marine Corps.

December 13
AVIATION: Over Sinanju, North Korea, a force of 29 F-86 Sabres tackles 75 MiG-15s, downing nine of them. Added to aerial victories elsewhere, UN aircraft claim a total of 13 victories this day.

December 27
AVIATION: In their biggest sortie of the month, Far East Air Forces (FEAF) mount 900 sorties aimed at destroying locomotives, railcars, buildings, vehicles, and gun positions–in sum, anything of use to the enemy.

December 31
MARINES: In Washington, D.C., General Lemuel C. Shepherd, Jr., gains appointment as the 20th commandant of the Marine Corps.
• The 1st Marine Division maintains its lines along the Punchbowl and restricts its activities to occasional trench raids; casualties for the month decline to only 171.

1952

January
MILITARY: In light of the ongoing Korean conflict, the army's size has expanded to 20 divisions and 1.5 million officers and men.

January 2

MARINES: In Washington, D.C., Commandant lieutenant general Lemuel C. Shepherd orders Headquarters Marine Corps to adopt a general staff system similar to that in the army (G1, G2, G3, G4) to replace the Division of Plans and Policies, although the Aviation and Personnel branches survive intact.

January 7

AVIATION: In Washington, D.C., the secretary of the air force announces plans for a 50 percent increase in combat strength. This entails enlarging the force to 143 wings and 1.2 million airmen.

• In another demonstration of helicopter versatility, HMR-161 completes Operation Mule Train by providing sufficient supplies to a frontline marine battalion for over a week.

MARINES: At Camp Pendleton, California, the 3rd Marine Brigade becomes the 3rd Marine Division, and is slated to contain the 3rd, 4th, 9th, and 12th Marines, with the latter formed as an artillery unit. However, at present, only the 3rd Marine is fully formed and deployed.

January 8–13

AVIATION: Exercise Snowfall unfolds as 100 aircraft of the 516th Troop Carrier Wing convey over 8,600 men from Fort Campbell, Kentucky, to Wheeler-Sack Airfield, New York. This is also the largest troop airlift to date.

January 11

NAVAL: Project Package and Project Detail are undertaken by the vessels of Task Force 95 and the aircraft of Task Force 77 in an attempt to disrupt Communist rail lines along the coast.

January 12

AVIATION: Over North Korea, having bombed shut the entrance to a train tunnel, F-84s systematically destroy a Communist supply train as it sits idled.

January 29

NAVAL: Landing Ship Tanks (LSTs) of Task Force 90 complete the evacuation of 20,000 South Korean civilians trapped on islands along the west coast of Korea.

January 30

NAVAL: The position of Supreme Allied Commander Atlantic within the NATO infrastructure is assigned to Vice Admiral Lynde D. McCormick.

January 31

AVIATION: At Camp Lejeune, California, helicopters of HMR-261 and HMR-262 perform Operation HELEX 1, during which the 1st Battalion, 8th Marines is airlifted from the escort carrier *Siboney* and transferred to shore in only four hours and 25 minutes.

MILITARY: In South Korea, the 40th Infantry Division, a National Guard unit, moves into the frontlines to replace the 25th Infantry Division, which heads to Japan. However, the 5th Infantry remains behind in concert with the 555th Field Artillery Battalion to act as an independent regimental combat team.

MARINES: In an expanded experiment, men of the 1st Marine Division are issued the first 500 flak jackets to be worn by those most exposed to enemy fire. The vests prove highly successful.

February 1
TECHNOLOGY: The air force employs its first Univac I, a high speed digital computer using primitive vacuum-tube electronics.

February 9
AVIATION: A force of 10 B-29s, bombing by radar-aiming devices, drop over 100 tons of 500-pound bombs on the Chongju rail bridge, nearly destroying it.

February 10
AVIATION: Along the Manchurian border, a flight of F-86E Sabres under Major George A. Davis engages a large force of MiG-15s. Davis shoots down two Communist jets, bringing his total to 14 kills. He is then shot down and killed while rescuing his wingman. Davis receives a posthumous Medal of Honor.
MARINES: The Eighth Army, in an attempt to lure enemy patrols forward and capture them, engages in a series of feigned retreats known as Operation Clam-Up. Marines are involved in several firefights but secure no captives.

February 11
AVIATION: The F4Us of VFM-312 depart Itami Airfield, Japan, and deploy onboard the escort carrier *Bairoko,* which then sails off to Korea's western coast. Shortly after, VMF-115 is assigned to Marine Air Wing 33 (MAG-33) at Pohang, South Korea.

February 19
NAVAL: Off Songjin, North Korea, the destroyer *Shelton,* the minesweeper *Endicott,* and the New Zealand frigate *Taupo* interrupt a Communist attack on Kil-chu and Myongchon Islands offshore. The enemy, who employ a force of 45 sampans crammed with troops, is completely defeated.
MARINES: A handful of North Korean sampans that manage to reach the island of Kil-chu, South Korea, are quickly mopped up by a detachment of South Korean marines under Lieutenant Joseph Bartos of the U.S. Marine Corps.

February 20
AVIATION: In light of mounting airport congestion in American cities, retired general James H. Doolittle is appointed to a presidential commission by President Harry S. Truman to seek solutions.

February 23
AVIATION: Off the California coast, helicopters of HMR-162 participate in LEX Baker One in concert with the 3rd Marines. This is the largest amphibious operation held since 1949 and serves as a major test of rotary aircraft in a troop-carrying role.

March
AVIATION: Ongoing studies by the new Rocket Engine Advancement Program (REAP) suggest better thrust would be achieved by changing the standard arrangement of liquid oxygen and hydrocarbon fuel combinations. These changes come in time to power the new Atlas intercontinental ballistic missiles.

March 1
AVIATION: After a spate of hard landings, helicopters of HMR-161 are grounded pending the arrival of redesigned tail pylons.

March 3
AVIATION: The Fifth Air Force commences Operation Saturate, its latest all-out interdiction of Communist supply lines in North Korea.

March 11
AVIATION: Over North Korea, Fifth Air Force fighter bombers unload 150 tons of bombs and 33,000 gallons of napalm on a four-square-mile supply storage and troop training facility. This proves to be one of the most effective napalm attacks of the war.
MARINES: By this date the Marine Corps has accepted 73,340 draftees, but Headquarters Marine Corps declares that, because voluntary enlistment quotas are being met, none will be accepted after June 30.

March 12
MARINES: The Eighth Army alerts the 1st Marine Division that it will be shifting its position from the east-central front to farther west along the line.

March 17
MARINES: At Camp Pendleton, California, the 9th and 12th Marines are reactivated as part of the new 3rd Marine Division.
• The 1st Marine Division, with the 1st KMC Regiment in tow, begins marching 140 miles west to new positions along the UN line.

March 19
AVIATION: North American test flies its new F-86F-25 Sabre, which features modified leading edges for better control at high altitude. Prior to its deployment, MiG-15s enjoy better performance higher up.

March 22
MARINES: To achieve its three division/three air–wing authorized strength, the Marine Corps activates six battalions and a new air group along the West Coast.

March 25
AVIATION: In concert with Operation Saturate, Fifth Air Force bombers and fighter bombers execute 959 interdiction sorties between Sinanju and Chongju, North Korea. Railroads and highways are the main target.
MARINES: The 1st Marine Division assumes new positions astride the traditional invasion route toward Seoul, South Korea, as part of the I Corps. Their new front covers 32 miles, but it is effectively hemmed in on either flank by the Han and Imjin Rivers.

March 30
AVIATION: Night fighting VMF (N)-513 redeploys from the east coast of South Korea to K-8 airfield (Kunsan), placing it 100 miles below the capital of Seoul.

April 1
AVIATION: The air force drops its former army enlisted grades of private first class, corporal, and buck sergeant to airman third, second, and first class.
• Over North Korea, a flight of F-86 Sabres downs 10 MiG-15s for the loss of one. Colonel Francis "Gabby" Gabreski claims one Communist jet and becomes the eighth American ace of the war.

MARINES: Above Seoul, South Korea, Chinese forces single out and launch a heavy attack on the 1st Korean Marine Corps Regiment, and they are handily repulsed.

April 5
AVIATION: Helicopters of HMR-161 perform Operation Pronto in concert with the 2nd Battalion, 7th Marines, which simulates a reserve force being rushed in to counterattack enemy landings along the coast.

April 10
AVIATION: In Tokyo, Japan, Brigadier General Chester E. McCarty assumes command of the 315th Air Division for the remainder of the war.

April 12
AVIATION: Over Seattle, Washington, Boeing's eight-jet YB-52 jet bomber prototype flies for the first time. It becomes the first all-jet intercontinental heavy bomber and a mainstay of Strategic Air Command (SAC) operations; over half a century later, B-52s are still a mainstay of air force bombardment forces.

April 15
MARINES: At an isolated outpost in the 1st Marine Division area, Easy Company, 2nd Battalion, 5th Marines defeats a Chinese attempt to storm their position, losing 11 killed and 25 wounded to an enemy loss of 70 men. To save the useless effusion of blood in static warfare, the division orders its outposts abandoned at night and uses them only during daylight hours.

April 17
MILITARY: In Washington, D.C., President Harry S. Truman signs Executive Order 10345 to extend enlistments for another nine months.

April 18
AVIATION: At Carswell Air Force Base, Texas, the Convair YB-60 jet bomber flies for the first time. Essentially a swept-wing, jet-powered version of the B-36, it loses to the YB-52 for an air force contract.

April 21
NAVAL: Off the Korean coast, a turret explosion onboard the cruiser *St. Paul* kills 30 sailors.

April 24
AVIATION: The first aerial engagement of the year occurs when Communist MiGs attack two marine photo reconnaissance jets; no damage is incurred.

April 26
AVIATION: Helicopters of HMR-161 are grounded for three weeks pending the replacement of defective tail rotor shafts.
NAVAL: The destroyer *Hobson* accidentally collides with the carrier *Wasp* in the mid-Atlantic and sinks with a loss of 176 men. This is the navy's worst operational accident since World War II.

April 27
MILITARY: The United States formally terminates its occupation of Japan after civilian authority is restored. However, the Americans retain basing rights on

the mainland and administration of the Ryukyu Islands also remains under U.S. jurisdiction.

April 28
MILITARY: General Matthew Ridgway is tapped to serve as the new supreme commander of NATO forces in Europe after General Dwight D. Eisenhower retires.
NAVAL: The navy decides to adopt steam catapult systems invented by the Royal Navy for eventual use on American carriers.

April 29–30
AVIATION: During this two-day period, the 315th Air Division loses a C-47, a C-119, and a C-46 through crashes, with a loss of 16 lives. This is the division's biggest single loss of life for the first half of the year.

April 30
AVIATION: Over North Korea, F9F Panthers of VMF-311 engage eight Communist MiG-15s, damaging one.

May 1
MARINES: At Yucca Flats, Nevada, Exercise Desert Rock IV unfolds as 2,000 men from the 3rd Marine Division are stationed in trenches just 2,000 yards from an atomic bomb blast. Immediately afterward, the marines move in and conduct simulated military maneuvers near the drop zone.

May 2
MARINES: In Boston, Massachusetts, Red Sox star and Marine Reserve captain Ted Williams reports for duty following activation. He is subsequently an F9F

A Panther jet that failed its carrier landing burns off the side of the carrier. *(Center for the Study of the Korean War, Graceland University)*

1952

Panther pilot with VMF-311. In New York, Jerry Coleman of the New York Yankees also returns to duty and flies 63 missions in his F4U Corsair.

May 3

AVIATION: A ski-equipped air force C-47 flown by Lieutenant Colonel William Benedict and Joseph Fletcher makes the first successful landing at the North Pole.

May 7

AVIATION: A test B-29 launches the Lockheed X-7 air-launched ramjet for the first time. Success results in the design of the new Bomarc missile program.

May 7–June 10

MILITARY: On Koje-do Island, South Korea, Chinese and North Korean prisoners stage a mass uprising, seizing Brigadier General Francis Dodd, the camp commander. The impasse continues until June 10, when the 187th Regimental Combat Team is sent in to restore order, killing 150 captives; one American dies in the fighting.

May 8

AVIATION: A Communist supply depot located 40 miles southwest of Pyongyang, North Korea, is struck by 465 sorties by Fifth Air Force fighter bombers. This is the largest one-day interdiction sortie of the war so far and destroys over 200 buildings, shelters, revetments, vehicles, and gun positions. However, the first F-86 lost to ground fire goes down while flying a dive-bombing mission.

MILITARY: The new, 75-ton atomic cannon is under development, according to Secretary of the Army Frank Pace.

NAVAL: The Fleet Air Gunnery Unit is established to provide more realistic aerial gunnery training for Pacific Fleet aircraft squadrons.

May 9

MARINES: In the 1st Marine Division area, the 1st Battalion, 5th Marines raids a former outpost now occupied by Chinese. They suffer seven dead and 66 wounded but Communist losses are believed to be even higher.

May 12

DIPLOMACY: General Mark W. Clark replaces General Matthew Ridgway as supreme commander of United Nations forces in the Far East and is also directed to begin peace negotiations with the Communists there.

May 16–17

AVIATION: In Japan, C-199s, C-54s, and C-46s convey the 187th Airborne Regimental Combat Team to Koje-do, South Korea, to help put down a prisoner-of-war insurrection.

May 19

AVIATION: In Tokyo, Japan, the Fifth Air Force relaxes restrictions on close air support missions to allow marine aviators to hone their skills along the front occupied by the 1st Marine Division.

MILITARY: At Panmunjom, Korea, Major General William K. Harrison, Jr., deputy commander of the Eighth Army, gains appointment as the senior UN negotiator. One of his first acts is to declare a recess when the Chinese and North Koreans begin reciting propaganda speeches.

May 22

AVIATION: Fifth Air Force fighter bombers and light bombers conduct 500 sorties against industrial targets southwest of Pyongyang, North Korea, completely destroying several arms-making facilities.

May 26

AVIATION: In Japan, the 315th Air Division receives its first Douglas C-124 Globemaster IIs to replace their aging C-54s.

May 29

AVIATION: A force of 12 F-84 Thunderjets complete a strike mission in northernmost North Korea, then refuel en route home to Itazuke, Japan, as part of Operation Rightside.

May 30

AVIATION: In Tokyo, Japan, Lieutenant General Glenn O. Barcus assumes command of the Fifth Air Force.

June 1

MILITARY: In Washington, D.C., General Dwight D. Eisenhower confers with President Harry S. Truman over the state of NATO and its defenses in Western Europe.

June 7

AVIATION: Over North Korea, Lieutenant Jon W. Andre of VMF (N)-513 shoots down a North Korean Yak-9 fighter; added to his four Japanese kills achieved in World War II, he becomes another Marine Corps ace.

• Operation Hightide unfolds as a force of 35 F-84 Thunderjets takes off from Japan, refuel from KB-29Ms in the air, then strikes at targets deep in North Korea. Aerial refueling is fast becoming a standard air force practice.

June 10

AVIATION: Off the Korean coast, helicopters of HMR-161 participate in MARLEX-1 and amphibious operations held in conjunction with the 1st Marine Division's reserve elements. This is subsequently adopted as a standard, large-unit exercise.

June 10–11

AVIATION: Three B-29s bombers are lost to searchlights, flak, and MiG interceptors during a night attack against the rail bridge at Kwaksan, North Korea, which prompts the Fifth Air Force to begin revising its electronic countermeasures program.

June 11

MILITARY: At Fort Bragg, North Carolina, the 10th Special Forces Group is activated; this is the army's first, formal Special Forces outfit.

June 13

AVIATION: Russian MiG-15 fighters intercept an air force RB-29 Superfortress reconnaissance aircraft in international waters over the Sea of Japan, shooting it down and killing the crew of 10.

June 14

MILITARY: In Korea, the Chinese launch a heavy attack on a position known as Old Baldy, which is defended by the 2nd and 45th Infantry Divisions. For the remainder of the war, this position changes hands several times at considerable loss to both sides.

NAVAL: President Harry S. Truman attends keel-laying ceremonies for the *Nautilus,* the world's first atomic-powered submarine, at the Electric Boat Company, Groton, Connecticut.

June 15

AVIATION: U.S. Air Force lieutenant James F. Low, only six months out of flight school, becomes the latest F-86 Sabre ace.

June 23–24

AVIATION: Hydroelectric plants at Suiho, Chosen, Fusen, and Kyosen, North Korea, are the target of multiple attacks by air force, navy, and marine aircraft. This marks a shift in Fifth Air Force priorities away from cutting supply lines and back to hitting strategic targets. Over 1,200 sorties are flown, making this the largest single air strike since World War II.

• The Suiho raid is accompanied by 35 AD Skyraiders and a like number of F9F Panthers from the carriers *Boxer, Philippine Sea,* and *Princeton.*

June 24

AVIATION: Aircraft of the Far East Air Forces (FEAF) complete over 1,000 sorties, the highest daily total for the month.

MARINES: In the 1st Marine Division area, the Chinese mount several mortar-supported attacks on daylight outposts of the 2nd Battalion, 5th Marines, and are roundly repulsed.

June 28

MARINES: In Washington, D.C., Congress passes the Armed Force Reserve Act of 1952. Hereafter, the Marine Corps Reserve is restructured into a Ready Reserve, a Standby Reserve, and the Retired Reserve. A Reserve Policy Board is also created to advise the secretary of the navy.

June 30

AVIATION: In an attempt to reduce the number of aircraft lost to enemy antiaircraft fire, the 11th Marines publishes a procedure for suppressing losses with artillery fire while close air supports are being executed. These SEAD (suppression of enemy air defenses) tactics result in an immediate drop in aerial losses.

MARINES: In Washington, D.C., President Harry S. Truman signs the Douglas-Mansfield Act, which authorizes a three-division, three-wing organization for the Marine Corps with a 400,000-man peacetime ceiling to quell fears of the corps becoming a second land army. Equally important, the commandant is now allowed to attend Joint Chiefs of Staff meetings in a limited capacity and vote on matters considered essential to the Marine Corps. The Marine Corps also now exists as a separate service within the Navy Department.

July 1

AVIATION: The air force makes public its new F-94C Starfire interceptor, the first jet fighter armed solely with unguided air-to-air rockets.

NAVAL: At Dam Neck, Virginia, the Naval Guided Missile School is founded while at Naval Air Station Jacksonville, Florida, the Naval Air Guided Missile School

(Advanced) is also founded. Missile technology plays an increasingly vital role in naval armaments.

July 3

AVIATION: The first of the huge C-124 Globemaster II transports touches down in South Korea.

• A record 22 million propaganda leaflets are dropped over North Korea by C-47s this month.

MARINES: In the 1st Marine Division area, G Company, 3rd Battalion, 7th Marines launches a night raid against Hill 159, only to find it defended by a Chinese battalion; they suffer 44 casualties before withdrawing.

July 4

AVIATION: A major air battle unfolds over North Korea as MiG-15s attempt to penetrate a fighter screen of F-86s and shoot down incoming bombers. However, the Sabres have a field day in downing 13 Communist jets for a loss of two of their own.

July 4–17

AVIATION: A force of 58 F-84Gs under Colonel David C. Schilling makes the first massed transpacific flight by departing Turner Air Force Base, Georgia, and landing at Yokota Air Base, Japan. A total of 10,895 miles are covered through seven ground stops and two inflight refuelings.

July 6

MARINES: In another heavy night action along the 1st Marine Division area, the 1st Battalion, 7th Marines raids Hill 159 for the second time, losing 102 casualties.

July 9

MILITARY: The Armed Forces Reserve Act of 1952 is passed by Congress to overhaul the army's reserve components. Consequently, the Officers' Reserve Corps and the Enlisted Reserve Corps are eliminated in favor of the new Organized Reserve Corps of the Army Reserve.

July 10

AVIATION: The 315th Air Division begins airlifting the entire 474th Fighter Bomber Wing from Misawa, Japan, to Kusan, South Korea. This constitutes the largest unit transported by air to date.

July 11–12

AVIATION: A combined force of air force, navy, and marine aircraft, assisted by units from Britain and Australia, attack marshaling yards and industrial targets in Pyongyang, North Korea, as part of Operation Pressure Pump. This represents the largest single air strike of the war and results in the North Korean Ministry of Industry being completely flattened.

July 13–31

AVIATION: Two air force H-19 helicopters, christened *Hopalong* and *Whirl O Way* conduct the first transatlantic helicopter flight by flying from Westover, Massachusetts, to Prestwick, Scotland, after five refueling stops.

July 14
AVIATION: To enhance the nationwide air-defense effort, the Ground Observer Corps initiates its 24-hour per day Skywatch program to scan the skies for possible Soviet intruders.
NAVAL: At Norfolk, Virginia, the keel of the navy's first supercarrier, the *Forrestal*, is laid at the Newport News Shipbuilding and Dry Dock Company.

July 16
MILITARY: Congress passes the Korean War G.I. Bill of Rights, which confers educational benefits, loan guarantees, and similar perquisites for veterans.

July 19
AVIATION: The air force declares success in flying balloons at controlled constant stratospheric altitudes for up to three days.

July 27–28
AVIATION: Task Force 77 launches carrier aircraft that strike the lead and zinc mill at Sindok and the magnesite plant at Kilchu, North Korea.

July 29
AVIATION: An air force RB-45C Tornado jet reconnaissance bomber flown by Majors Louis H. Carrington, Frederick W. Shook, and Captain Wallace D. Yancey travels nonstop from Elmendorf Air Force Base, Alaska, to Yokota Air Base, Japan, for the first time. They cover the entire 3,640 miles in nine hours and 50 minutes, winning the Mackay Trophy.

July 30–31
AVIATION: Over North Korea, a force of 60 Bomber Command B-29s obliterates the Oriental Light Metals Company located only four miles from the Yalu River. The attack, made at night, suffers no losses despite search lights, flak, and MiGs.

August 3
AVIATION: The Fifth Air Force, harassed by Eighth Army complaints that the 1st Marine Division receives more close air support than their units, terminates the program allowing marine pilots to rehearse close air support missions with other marine units. Marine aviators are unhappy with the decision.

August 4
NAVAL: In Annapolis, Maryland, Vice Admiral Turner C. Joy gains appointment as the 37th superintendent of the U.S. Naval Academy.

August 6
AVIATION: In the final major air battle of the month, a force of 34 F-86s are attacked by 52 MiG-15s, and they bring down six of their antagonists without loss.
• Marine Air Group 33 (MAG-33) flies a record daily number of 141 sorties.
NAVAL: Off the Korean coast, a fire onboard the carrier *Boxer* kills eight sailors but does not necessitate that vessel's withdrawal from combat operations.

August 8
AVIATION: Fifth Air Force fighter bombers conduct 285 close support sorties, this month's highest daily total. Tonight, specially rigged B-265 fly three voice broadcast psychological warfare sorties over enemy positions.

August 9
MARINES: In South Korea, the Marine Corps reverses its policy and resumes permanently occupying outposts at night. Tonight, the Chinese attack and seize outpost Siberia and the 1st Marines win it back and lose it twice more by daybreak. Their losses are 17 dead and 243 wounded.

August 11–15
MARINES: The Combat Duty Pay Act is enacted, allowing increased compensation for personnel serving in combat zones.
• This evening the 1st Marines return to outpost Siberia by seizing Bunker Hill, which commands the latter position. The Chinese make repeated and costly attempts to regain both and are finally driven off after four days of fighting. American loses are 38 killed and 268 wounded to a Chinese tally estimated in excess of 3,200.

August 13
NAVAL: In Korea, U.S. Navy corpsman John E. Kilmer rushes through enemy force to treat wounded marines and shields one Leatherneck from enemy gunfire, which kills him; he wins a posthumous Medal of Honor.

August 19
AVIATION: During Operation Ripple, helicopters of HM-161 deploy a battery of 4.5-rockets into firing position, they then remove it to safety before the enemy can mount effective counterbattery fire.

August 20
AVIATION: At Changpyng-ni, North Korea, Marine warplanes participate in a mass strike against Communist supply areas.

August 22
MILITARY: Not to be outdone, the army orders 25,000 copies of the Marine Corps flak vests for its soldiers.

August 22–23
AVIATION: Over the frontlines in South Korea, three C-47s fly 60-minute voice broadcasts to accentuate the UN's growing emphasis on psychological warfare.

August 28
AVIATION: At Hungnam, North Korea, an explosive-laden F6F drone controlled by Guided Missile Unit 90 (*Boxer*) damages a railroad bridge.

August 29
AVIATION: At the behest of the U.S. State Department, Far East Air Forces (FEAF) mount a major aerial attack against Pyongyang, North Korea, in one of the biggest concerted air strikes of the war. They do so in response to the arrival of Chinese foreign minister Chou Enlai in Moscow, so a show of strength seemed appropriate. Only three UN aircraft are lost in 1,400 air-to-ground sorties.

August 30
NAVAL: Off Hungnam, North Korea, the ocean tug *Sarsi* strikes a mine and sinks; this is the final navy vessel lost in the Korean War.

1952

Gunners of the U.S. Fifth Air Force in Korea, September 1952 *(National Archives and Records Administration)*

September 1
AVIATION: Task Force 77 aircraft strike at the oil refinery at Aoji, North Korea, only eight miles from the Soviet border. This is also the largest single carrier raid of the Korean War.
NAVAL: In the North Atlantic, Operation Mainbrace, NATO's first large-scale maneuver, is undertaken. Present are the carriers *Midway* and *Franklin D. Roosevelt,* and the battleship *Wisconsin.*

September 1–2
AVIATION: During MARLEX VII, helicopters of HM-161 operate off the escort carrier *Sicily* and transport the 1st Battalion, 7th Marines to objectives ashore.

September 2
AVIATION: In a setback for marine aviation, Douglas A3D-2 Skynight jet night fighters are restricted from combat operations after a series of engine explosions.
MARINES: At Camp Pendleton, California, the 4th Marines are activated and begin filling its battalions. This becomes the final unit for the 3rd Marine Division.

September 3
AVIATION: At Inyokern, California, the first test-firing of a heat-seeking air-to-air Sidewinder missile is conducted by the Naval Ordnance Test Station. The Sidewinder becomes a standard naval weapon over the next four decades.

September 3–4
AVIATION: Bomber Command B-29s fly 52 sorties, all but two against hydroelectric power plants at Chosin, North Korea,.

September 4
AVIATION: UN aircraft mount a major fighter bomber attack along the Manchurian border to provoke a Communist response. An estimated 90 MiG-15s tangle with the F-86 escorts, losing 13 jets in exchange for four Sabres. Major Frederick Blesse downs his fifth Communist jet to become the latest American ace.

September 4–6
MARINES: In the 1st Marine Division area, the Chinese make several strong attacks to capture Bunker Hill and Outpost Bruce, but they are rebuffed over the next two evenings.

September 5
NAVAL: In a Communist night attack against the 1st Marine Division, Hospital Corpsman Third Class Edward C. Benford rushes to the assistance of wounded Leathernecks under fire, grabs two enemy grenades, then charges into a group of oncoming Chinese; Benford and several enemy troops are killed in the explosion that follows. He wins a posthumous Medal of Honor.

September 9
AVIATION: At Sakchu, North Korea, the military academy is attacked by a force of 45 F-84s, who are in turn attacked by MiG-15s. Three Thunderjets are shot down while escorting F-86 Sabres claim five Communists jets.

September 10
AVIATION: Over North Korea, a marine F4U Corsair flown by Captain Jessie G. Folmar of VMA-312 becomes the first American propeller fighter to shoot down a Communist MiG-15 jet and after eight of them pounce on him and his wingman. Folmer himself is also shot down and rescued at sea.
•   At K-2 airfield, South Korea, a flight of six F9F Panthers from VMF-115, attempting to land during foggy weather, crashes headlong into a mountainside.

September 15
AVIATION: In South Korea, Composite Squadron 1 (VMC-1) is created to perform electronic countermeasure missions in support of aerial operations.

September 16
AVIATION: Night-flying B-26s conduct 110 interdiction and attack sorties over North Korea, destroying over 100 enemy vehicles.
NAVAL: Several miles off Wonsan, North Korea, the destroyer *Barton* strikes a mine, which kills five sailors onboard.

September 19
AVIATION: A force of 32 Bomber Command B-29s attacks Communist barracks and supply areas southwest of Hamhung, North Korea. This is the first B-29 raid in almost 11 months and is preceded by an RB-45C flight for acquiring prestrike reconnaissance.

1952

September 21
AVIATION: Over Pukchong, North Korea, an F-86 flown by Captain Robinson Risner flames two MiG-15s, making him the latest American jet ace.

September 28
AVIATION: Marine Major Alexander J. Gillis, performing exchange duty with an air force squadron, bags two Communist MiG-15s over the Yellow Sea before he is himself shot down and rescued.

September 30
AVIATION: The Bell GAM-63 Rascal, an air-launched air-to-surface missile, is launched for the first time. Though capable of carrying an atomic warhead, the Rascal does not proceed beyond the experimental stage.

October 1
AVIATION: After this date navy and marine aircraft begin de-emphasizing supply interdiction missions in favor of more traditional, close support sorties.

October 2
MARINES: In the 1st Marine Division area, the Chinese successfully storm into Outposts Warsaw and Seattle. The marines counterattack at dawn and retake the former, but not the latter; losses are 13 dead and 88 wounded.

October 4
AVIATION: In Tokyo, Japan, Brigadier General William P. Fisher assumes control of Bomber Command.

October 6–7
MARINES: In the 1st Marine Division area, the 7th Marines have a second go at recapturing Outpost Seattle and fail, losing a further 12 dead and 44 wounded. Adding insult to injury, the Chinese attack and seize Outposts Detroit and Frisco the same evening. The marines counterattack at dawn and retake Frisco, but ultimately they abandon this exposed position. Total losses in this front-line squabble are 32 dead marines and 128 wounded.

October 7
AVIATION: Soviet La-11 fighters intercept an air force RB-29 Superfortress reconnaissance bomber over the Kurile Islands and shoot it down, killing the crew of eight.

October 8
AVIATION: A force of 10 B-29s conducts a rare daylight raid over Kowon, North Korea, in conjunction with 12 F2H-2 Banshee carrier-based navy fighters. This proves the second and last time navy fighters cover air force bombers.
DIPLOMACY: At Panmunjom, South Korea, peace talks deadlock over the issue of prisoner-of-war repatriation. The Communists insist that all their captives be returned to them, whether they are willing to return or not.

October 9
NAVAL: Along the 38th parallel, South Korea, Admiral Joseph J. Clark directs Seventh Fleet aircraft strikes that go well beyond the range of UN artillery. Such attacks are popularly deemed "Cherokee strikes" owing to Clark's Native-American ances-

try, and they prove extremely popular with Eighth Army commanders. These operations occupy half the carrier aviation for the remainder of the war.

October 13

AVIATION: Over Seoul, South Korea, Communist PO-2 biplanes begin nocturnal harassment raids after nearly a year. The troops refer to them as "Bedcheck Charlies."

October 14–November 5

MILITARY: In Korea, General James A. Van Fleet responds to a Chinese attack on White Horse Hill by ordering the 7th Infantry Division to capture Triangle Hill. The attack is spearheaded by the 31st Infantry, backed by 16 field artillery battalions and waves of air force fighter bombers, but they fail to take the hill after 12 days of fierce combat. The 7th Division suffers 2,000 casualties to an estimated Chinese loss of 19,000 by the time General Mark W. Clark cancels the operation.

October 15

AVIATION: An air force RB-47 Stratojet reconnaissance jet makes a deep penetration of the Chutotsky Peninsula from Alaska and the pictures taken confirm that the Soviets are, in fact, building Arctic bomber bases from which they could strike targets in North America. The mission was personally authorized by President Harry S. Truman.

October 20

AVIATION: At Edwards Air Force Base, California, the futuristic Douglas X-3 Stiletto flies for the first time with test pilot William Bridgeman at the controls. It provides useful information about titanium construction and short-span, low-aspect wings in high-speed flight.

October 24–28

MARINES: In the 1st Marine Division area, massed Chinese artillery begin the heaviest bombardment marines will face during the Korean War. Over 34,000 shells rain down on the position known as the Hook, followed by a determined infantry assault. At one point Lieutenant Sherrod E. Skinner, Jr., jumps on a grenade tossed into his bunker to shield fellow marines from the explosion; he wins a posthumous Medal of Honor. The 7th Marines scrape together a handful of troops to counterattack, whereupon Lieutenant George O'Brien, badly wounded, jumps into a trench and kills three Chinese in hand-to-hand combat, then refuses to be evacuated. He also receives a Medal of Honor for bravery under fire. The Hook is recaptured after four days of intense combat and a tally of 70 dead Marines, 435 wounded, and 39 missing. The Chinese leave 369 bodies on the ground and sustain an estimated 1,000 more wounded. Hereafter, the marines resort to digging deeper trenches and employing better barbed wire.

October 28

AVIATION: The twin-jet XA3D-1 Skywarrior, the largest aircraft to operate off a carrier deck, performs its maiden flight. Popularly known as "the Whale" on account of sheer size, Skywarriors remain in service through the 1980s, performing nuclear strike, reconnaissance, electronics, and aerial refueling missions.

1952

October 30
AVIATION: Helicopters of HM-161 perform a record 365 medical evacuations this month while the 1st Marine Aviation Wing (1st MAW) achieves 3,765 sorties, its second highest monthly total.

October 31
AVIATION: At Eniwetok, Marshall Islands, the United States explodes "Mike Shot," its first thermonuclear, or hydrogen, bomb. The weapon has a yield of 10 million tons of TNT, and is more than 1,000 times more powerful than the atomic device that destroyed Hiroshima, Japan, in 1945.

November 1
AVIATION: Off the Naval Air Test Center, Point Magu, California, the missile testing vessel *Norton Sound* fires a Regulus I Missile for the first time.
• In South Korea, VMF (N)-513 resumes operations following repairs and engine upgrades to their Douglas F3D-2 Skyknights. In light of mounting resistance from MiG-15 fighters, they are now tasked with escorting air force B-29s during nighttime raids.

November 3
AVIATION: Over North Korea, an F3D-2 Skyknight flown by Major William T. Stratton and Master Sergeant Han C. Hoglind of VMF (N)-513 scores the first nocturnal kill of a jet fighter by downing a Soviet-built Yak-15.

November 4
POLITICS: Former general Dwight D. Eisenhower is elected president of the United States as a Republican. He is the first professional military officer to occupy the White House since Ulysses S. Grant in 1868. One of his first acts as president-elect is to visit the troops in Korea.

November 8
AVIATION: Over North Korea, Captain Oliver R. Davis and Warrant Officer Dramus F. Fessler of VMF (N)-513 score the nighttime kill of a MiG-15 with their squadron.

November 10
AVIATION: In Japan, the 315th Air Division passes another milestone by evacuating its 250,000th patient from South Korea.

November 12–13
AVIATION: A force of six B-29s from the 98th Bomb Group attack four repaired spans in Pyongyang, North Korea, bringing them down again.

November 15
AVIATION: A C-119 Flying Boxcar belonging to the 315th Air Division crashes in Japan, killing 40 passengers.

November 18
AVIATION: As Task Force 77 launches air strikes against North Korean installations 90 miles south of Vladivostok, Soviet Union, the Russians dispatch seven MiG-15 fighters toward the fleet. They are intercepted by F9F Panthers from VF-781, which down two of the enemy jets while damaging a third.

1952

President-elect Dwight D. Eisenhower inspects the living quarters of troops of the ROK's Capital Division, December 4, 1952. (*Dwight D. Eisenhower Library and Museum*)

November 19

AVIATION: Over the Salton Sea, California, an F-86D flown by Captain J. Slade Nash sets a new world record of 698.5 miles per hour over a three-kilometer course.
• The North American XLR-43-NA-3 becomes the first American rocket engine to develop over 100,000 pounds of thrust in a test firing.

November 22

AVIATION: Over South Korea, an F-80 flown by Major Charles J. Loring, Jr., deliberately crashes into Communist infantry positions along Sniper Ridge after being hit by ground fire. His sacrifice spares the lives of many UN troops and he receives a posthumous Medal of Honor.

November 26

AVIATION: The Northrop Snark, an early turbojet-powered cruise missile with intercontinental range, is successfully tested from a zero-launch ground launcher for the first time. It enters into service as the B-62 following a prolonged and troubled development.

December 2–5

POLITICS: In South Korea, President-elect Dwight D. Eisenhower tours the frontlines and also confers with President Syngman Rhee.

December 3

MARINES: The 1st Marine Division command post is visited by President-elect Dwight D. Eisenhower and JCS chairman Omar N. Bradley.

December 4

AVIATION: The prototype Grumman XS2F-1 flies for the first time; it enters service as the Tracker and is the first carrier-based aircraft specifically designed for antisubmarine warfare.

December 9

DIPLOMACY: In light of overwhelming Soviet tactical superiority in conventional weapons, the United Nations adopts Strategy 14/1, predicated on defending Western Europe with American nuclear weapons.

December 11

AVIATION: At Kunsan Airfield, South Korea, a fully loaded B-26 bomber catches fire and explodes, wrecking three nearby Invaders and damaging six F-84s on the tarmac.

December 16

AVIATION: The Tactical Air Command activates its first helicopter squadron, which is equipped with bulky but reliable Sikorsky H-16s.

December 17

AVIATION: Above the Suiho Reservoir, North Korea, a pair of roaming F-86s espy a Soviet-built Illyushin Il-28 Beagle jet bomber escorted by MiG fighters. They attack and drive them back across the Yalu River.

1953

JANUARY: Army personnel levels remain at 1.5 million, which are shunted into 20 divisions.

January 5
MARINES: In a test of alternative tables of organization, the 3rd Battalion, 4th Marines adds a fourth rifle company while the 4th Battalion, 4th Marines is raised.

January 9
MARINES: In Washington, D.C., President Harry S. Truman requests $46 billion in defense spending in his 1954 fiscal budget.

January 12–16
AVIATION: Operational testing commences with the new angle-deck carrier *Antietam*. Six types of aircraft and various wind conditions are employed, along with day and night conditions. Adoption of the angle deck on modern classes of carriers increases sorties and greatly reduces the accident rate.

January 17–18
AVIATION: Over Pyongyang, North Korea, a force of 11 B-29s drops 2,000-pound bombs on an underground radio station. Several direct hits are scored, although the radio station remains intact and keeps on broadcasting.

January 18
AVIATION: Off Swatow, China, a P2V Neptune of VP-22 is shot down by Communist antiaircraft fire. Eleven survivors of 13 men on board are rescued by a Coast Guard PBM Mariner, which crashes in heavy seas while attempting to lift off. It falls upon the destroyer *Halsey Powell* to rescue 10 men from the water; eleven navy and Coast Guard personnel perish.

January 19
AVIATION: At Kaneohe Bay, Oahu, Hawaii, the Marine Corps 1st Provisional Air-Ground Task Force is formed.

January 20
MILITARY: In Washington, D.C., Dwight D. Eisenhower is inaugurated as the 34th president and commander in chief of the armed forces.

January 22
AVIATION: In Korea, the air force retires that last of its venerable F-51 Mustangs prior to transitioning to F-86 Sabres; this marks the final use of propeller-driven fighters in this war.

January 24
AVIATION: Over North Korea, Captain Dolphin D. Overton III scores five kills in only five days, the shortest period of any air force pilot for becoming an ace.

January 28
AVIATION: Off Cape Cod, Massachusetts, the former battleship turned missile test vessel *Mississippi* fires a new Terrier surface-to-air missile for the first time.

January 28
NAVAL: In Washington, D.C., Charles E. Wilson becomes the fifth secretary of defense.

January 28–29
AVIATION: Over Sariwon, North Korea, a B-29 is shot down, becoming the last aircraft of its type lost in the Korean War.

January 30
AVIATION: At Seattle, Washington, the B-47E flies its maiden flight and becomes the major production model with over 1,300 bomber versions constructed, along with 255 RB-47E reconnaissance aircraft.
• A B-29 from the 307th Bomb Wing is jumped by 10 Communist fighters and so damaged that it is forced to make an emergency landing in South Korea.
• Over the Yellow Sea east of Pyongyang. North Korea, a Tupelov Tu-2 bomber is intercepted by an F-86 fighter and shot down. This is also the first Tu-2 encountered since November 1951.

February 2–20
MILITARY: The Netherlands suffers from massive flooding and army troops are called in as part of a large relief operation.

February 3
MARINES: In the 1st Marine Division area, the 1st Battalion, 5th Marines, raids Hills 51 and 51A and inflicts an estimated 400 Chinese casualties. American losses are 41 dead and 91 wounded.

February 4
AVIATION: In Washington, D.C., Harold E. Talbott gains appointment as the new secretary of the air force.
MILITARY: In Washington, D.C., Robert Ten Broeck Stevens is appointed the fourth secretary of the army.
NAVAL: Former Texas attorney Robert B. Anderson becomes the 52nd secretary of the navy.

February 8
MEDICAL: The American Medical Association recognizes Aviation Medicine as a medical specialty, the first branch to originate solely from military practice and research.

February 9–10
AVIATION: Task Force 77 launches carrier air strikes against transportation networks from Wonsan through Songjin and Chongjin, North Korea.

February 10
MILITARY: In Korea, General James A. Van Fleet is replaced by Lieutenant General Maxwell D. Taylor as commander of the Eighth Army.

February 12
AVIATION: Off Pusan Harbor, South Korea, HMR-161 suffers its first casualties when an HRS-1 helicopter crashes into the sea.

February 13
AVIATION: At the Naval Missile Test Center, Point Mugu, California, the Sparrow radar-guided missile is launched for the first time under its own guidance. This weapon sees active service over the next three decades as a standard anti-aircraft missile.

1953

February 14

AVIATION: At Edwards Air Force Base, California, the Bell X-1A is launched on its first successful test glide with pilot Jean Ziegler at the controls. This is an enlarged version of the original X-1, possessing a revised cockpit and greater fuel loads.

February 15

AVIATION: Over North Korea, a force of 22 F-84 Thunderjets strikes the Suiho hydroelectric power plant with 1,000-pound bombs while their F-86 Sabre escort tangles with 30 MiG-15s. The facility is knocked out for several months.

February 16

AVIATION: Captain Joseph C. McConnell, Jr., bags his fifth MiG-15, becoming an ace.
• After a large air raid, Captain Ted Williams, the Red Six slugger, crash-lands his damaged F9F Panther and walks away unscathed.

February 18–19

AVIATION: South of the Suiho Reservoir, four F-86s pounce on a formation of 48 MiG-15s, downing two. Two more MiG-s crash after maneuvering violently and entering into uncontrollable flat spins. Captain Manuel Fernandez, who bags his fifth Communist jet, also becomes an ace.
• A force of 500 fighter bombers attacks a tank and infantry school southwest of Pyongyang, North Korea, obliterating 243 buildings.
• Over North Korea, Marine Corps colonel Robert Shaw, commander of Marine Air Group 22 (MAG-22), leads a total of 208 marine and air force aircraft against military targets around Pyongyang. This is the largest air raid conducted by a marine officer.

February 25

MARINES: In the 1st Marine Division area, the 2nd Battalion, 5th Marines stages a large raid against Chinese-held Outpost Detroit.

March 1

AVIATION: The 138th Fighter-Interceptor Squadron at Syracuse, New York, and the 104th Fighter-Bomber Squadron at Hayward California, are tapped to commence the Air Defense Command's (ADC) runway alert program. This is the first step in exposing Air National Guard units to the new "total force" concept training for all air force components.

March 1–5

AVIATION: Task Force 77 launches carrier strikes against the hydroelectric plant at Chosen, North Korea, and they hit it again four days later.

March 5

AVIATION: Today Fifth Air Force fighters and fighter bombers perform 700 sorties. One of these involves an attack by 16 F-84 Thunderjets against an industrial park only 60 miles south of the Soviet border.
MILITARY: In Moscow, Soviet Union, Communist dictator Joseph Stalin dies, removing a dogged obstacle to peace in Korea.

1953

March 6
NAVAL: The World War II submarine *Tunny* is recommissioned and undergoes modifications to carry the Regulus I surface-to-surface missile.

March 10
AVIATION: Two air force F-84G fighter bombers accidentally stray into Czechoslovakian airspace from West Germany and are attacked by MiG-15 fighters; one American plane crashes and the pilot is eventually released.

March 13
AVIATION: Carrier aircraft from Task Force 77 launch a destructive raid against the industrial areas of Chongjin, North Korea.

March 14
AVIATION: Over newly bombed sites in North Korea, air force combat crews drop leaflets that tauntingly ask: "Where is the Communist Air Force?" in order to provoke an aerial confrontation.

MARINES: In the 1st Marine Division sector, the Chinese launch several company-sized attacks against Outposts Hedy and Esther but elements of the 1st Marines repel them.

March 21–22
AVIATION: At Yongmi-dong, North Korea, Operation Spring Thaw unfolds as Fifth Air Force B-26s knock down two spans across a river and damage a third.

March 23–25
MILITARY: After an artillery and mortar bombardment, Chinese Communist forces capture the hill known as Old Baldy. The 31st Infantry Regiment, supported by the Colombian Battalion, is ordered to recapture it, but they fail to overcome stout defenses. Moreover, General Maxwell D. Taylor, who views the hill as unessential to UN defenses, cancels further operations against it.

March 25–30
AVIATION: The 1st Marine Air Wing is allowed by Fifth Air Force headquarters to provide emergency close support during the attempt to take back the Vegas Cities outposts; 100 sorties are flown on March 28 alone.

MARINES: In the 1st Marine Division area, the Chinese launch a large attack against the Nevada Cities complex defended by the 5th Marines. Outposts Vegas and Reno are quickly taken from defending platoons, but Carson manages to hold out. The 5th Marines launch a counterattack over the next five days and manage to liberate only Outpost Vegas. American losses are 214 dead and 801 wounded to a Chinese tally estimated at 2,300.

March 26–27
NAVAL: Hospital Corpsman Francis C. Hammond, serving with the 1st Marine Division, ignore serious wounds as he crawls along the ground under fire to treat injured Leathernecks. He is killed supervising the evacuation of casualties, winning a posthumous Medal of Honor.

March 27
AVIATION: In a surprising turn of events, two MiG-15s equipped with drop tanks fly to within 38 miles of the 38th parallel and attack several RF-80s and Australia Meteor jets.

NAVAL: In a stiff action with Chinese troops, Hospital Corpsman Third Class William R. Charette performs bravely under fire, shielding a wounded marine from grenades with his own body, and donating his body vest to another. He wins a Medal of Honor.

March 31

AVIATION: After performing yeoman work for two-and-a-half years, the air force retires the last of its Lockheed F-80 Shooting Stars from front-line service.

April 7

AVIATION: The Atomic Energy Commission reveals that it will study radioactive clouds generated by atomic tests by flying Lockheed QF-80 drones directly into them. These are controlled by other aircraft using Sperry radio equipment.

April 12

AVIATION: Over the Yellow Sea west of North Korea a MiG-15 and an F-86 flown by Captain Joseph C. McConnell shoot each other down; this is McConnell's eighth kill and he is rescued by an H-19 helicopter.

• Discussions between the 1st Marine Division and the 1st Marine Air Wing (1st MAW) result in the use of searchlights to illuminate targets for close air support at night; the tactic proves successful.

April 13

AVIATION: Over North Korea, the F-86F Sabre performs its first combat mission; this new model equals or exceeds MiG-15 fighters at high altitudes for the first time.

April 17

AVIATION: Marine Air Groups 12 and 33 jointly execute 262 sorties in one 24-hour period while the 39 pilots of VMF-115 rack up 114 sorties and drop 120 tons of bombs.

April 18

MARINES: At Yucca Flats, Nevada, Operation Desert Rock IV involves the participation of 2,200 marines in the wake of a nuclear exercise. After the blast subsides, four helicopter squadrons of Marine Air Group 16 (MAG-16) airlift troops to within 1,000 yards of the blast site. The employment of 39 helicopters also makes this the largest such operation in the United States to date.

April 20–May 3

MILITARY: Operation Little Switch commences as the UN repatriates 6,670 Communist captives while the Chinese return 684 prisoners, including 149 Americans.

MARINES: Off the California coast, the 3rd Marine Division participates in PACPHIBEX II, which involves helicopters, simulated atomic strikes, and a full-scale landing on Coronado Island off San Diego. The exercise continues through May 10.

April 26–27

AVIATION: Over North Korea, Project Moola commences as B-29s begin dropping leaflets encouraging MiG pilots to defect south with their aircraft in order to collect a $1 million reward.

North Korean prisoners of war released under Operation Little Switch march into Compound #13 for processing and repatriation. *(Center for the Study of the Korean War, Graceland University)*

April 29

MARINES: Colonel Katharine Towle, director of Women Marines, becomes the first female line officer to retire from military service; she is replaced by Lieutenant Colonel Julia E. Hamblet.

April 30

MARINES: In Washington, D.C., President Dwight D. Eisenhower submits a defense plan to Congress that enlarges the secretary of defense's power.

May 1–4

MARINES: The 1st Marine Division is being replaced on the frontline by the Army's 25th Infantry Division. The only unit retained is the 1st Tank Battalion, which provides artillery support for the soldiers. The bulk of the marines serve as the I Corps reserve at Camp Casey, 15 miles farther back.

May 13

AVIATION: Over Pyongyang, North Korea, a force of 59 F-84 Thunderjets makes their first attacks on irrigation dams north of the city. The target is destroyed by four waves of aircraft and the ensuing flood ruins five square miles of rice crop, five bridges, a highway, and also closes the Sunan airfield.

MARINES: In South Korea, the 5th Marines are tapped to take part in an amphibious training exercise, and the remaining regiments also take their place in turn.

May 16

AVIATION: Over Chasan, North Korea, waves of 90 F-84 Thunderjets destroy the irrigation dam there, flooding the area, spoiling rice, and destroying three railroad bridges.

May 18

AVIATION: Over North Korea, Captain Joseph C. McConnell, Jr., bags three more MiG-15s to become the highest-scoring American ace of the war with 16 kills.

• Over Edwards Air Force Base, California, aviatrix Jacqueline Cochran is the first woman to break the sound barrier while flying a North American F-86E Sabre at 652.3 miles per hour over a 100-kilometer course. This is also a new world speed record, one of many established by Cochran.

May 25

AVIATION: The North American YF-100, the first American fighter capable of sustained supersonic flight, debuts at Edwards Air Force Base, California, with test pilot George Welsh at the controls. It enters the service at the F-100 Super Sabre, of which 2,300 are built.

1953

MILITARY: At Fort Sill, Oklahoma, the army announces that it has successfully tested the 280mm new atomic cannon in Nevada. The projectile flies 10,000 meters and detonates 160 meters above the ground with a force of 15 kilotons; while impressive, this remains the only nuclear artillery shell ever fired by army forces.

May 25–29
AVIATION: Over South Korea, VFM-121, 212, and 323 fly several close support missions from the 25th Infantry Division as it battles renewed Chinese attacks along the Nevada Cities complex.

MARINES: The 11th Marines and the 1st Tank Battalion support the 25th Infantry Division in its struggle to maintain the Nevada Cities complex; the position is ultimately abandoned on the 29th.

May 27
AVIATION: The Air Force Historical Foundation is established to preserve and disseminate the story of American military aviation.

May 29–June 10
AVIATION: On the escort carrier *Bairoka*, VMA-332 begins arriving from the United States to replace VMA-312.

May 31
AVIATION: In Tokyo, Japan, Lieutenant General Samuel E. Anderson gains appointment as commander of the Fifth Air Force.

June 8
AVIATION: Over Luke Air Force Base, Arizona, highly decorated F-84s of the 3600th Air Demonstration Flight make their unofficial debut; they become better known as the U.S. Air Force Thunderbirds.

June 10
MILITARY: In South Korea, the Chinese launch a heavy assault against Outpost Harry, defended by troops of the 74th Infantry Division. In heavy fighting, the 15th Infantry Regiment and 5th Regimental Combat Team repel their antagonists, inflicting an estimated 4,200 casualties at a cost of 550 killed, wounded, and missing. This is also one of the last major Communist attacks of the war.

June 10–18
AVIATION: Aircraft of the 1st Marine Air Wing (1st MAW) perform close support missions for ROK troops defending the center of the UN line, including a one-day record of 283 sorties flown on June 15.

June 11
AVIATION: A force of 13 F-84 Thunderjets strike at targets along the Manchurian border; this is also the deepest raid flown into enemy territory and completely disrupts a Communist runway.

NAVAL: By this date, the navy has evacuated 19,425 Korean civilians from offshore islands along the peninsula's western coast and north of the 38th parallel.

June 13–18
AVIATION: Over North Korea, a joint strike by Fifth Air Force F-84s, Bomber Command B-29s, and Navy F4Us destroys the irrigation dams at Toksan and

Kusong. However, because the Communists had expected to be attacked and previously lowered water levels behind the dam, the raid does not cause extensive damage to the countryside.

June 15
AVIATION: In Tokyo, Japan, Brigadier General Richard H. Carmichael takes charge of Bomber Command.
• The carrier *Princeton* launches a record 184 sorties against enemy targets in a single day.

June 16
AVIATION: Fighter bombers and light bombers of the Fifth Air Force conduct 1,834 sorties over North Korea; half of these are close support missions in the Pukhan Valley.

June 18
AVIATION: An air force C-124 Globemaster II transport crashes near Tokyo, Japan, killing 129 servicemen; this is the most serious aviation accident to date.

June 21
AVIATION: Over Cheyenne, Wyoming, the U.S. Air Force Thunderbirds make their official first performance before enthralled onlookers.

June 24–20
AVIATION: As Chinese Communists resume their offensive against ROK troops, aircraft of the 1st Marine Air Wing (1st MAW) break their own sortie record by flying 301 close support missions on June 30.

June 30
AVIATION: In Washington, D.C., General Nathan F. Twining gains appointment as the new air force chief of staff.
• Over North Korea, F-86 fighter sweeps bring down a record total of 16 MiG-15s. Obviously, the Russian veterans have withdrawn from combat and the Americans are now facing poorly trained Chinese and North Korean pilots.
MARINES: At this point in the war, Marine Corps strength is 18,731 officers and 230,488 enlisted.

July 6
MARINES: The 1st Marine Division is ordered back to its former position along the west flank of the Eighth Army line.

July 6–10
MILITARY: In North Korea, the Battle of Pork Chop Hill takes place as the Chinese stage a large attack to seize it. Men of the 7th Infantry Division are subsequently sent in to take it back, supported by massive artillery fire, but they fail after trying four days. At this juncture, General Maxwell D. Taylor, who regards the position as unimportant, orders the struggle abandoned. American losses are 232 killed, 805 wounded, and nine missing; the Chinese are estimated to have suffered around 6,500 casualties.

July 7–8
MARINES: In the 1st Marine Division area, Chinese forces launch a major attack against Outposts Berlin and East Berlin as marines are arriving to relieve Turkish

forces defending them. Marines and Turks hold Berlin and recapture East Berlin in a subsequent counterattack. Additional Chinese are repelled during the night. The 7th Marines suffer 21 killed and 140 wounded.

Twining, Nathan F. (1897–1982)
Air Force general

Nathan Farragut Twining was born in Monroe, Wisconsin, and raised in Oregon. He joined the National Guard at 16 before attending the U.S. Military Academy during World War I. Afterward, he completed routine assignments in Germany and at home, and, in 1923, he became an air power enthusiast and received his wings at Brook Field, Texas. Over the next 15 years Twining held down a succession of staff and command positions in the expanding Army Air Corps and, in 1938, he reported to Washington, D.C., to serve on the general staff. Twining rose to colonel at the Pentagon but sought a combat command. In July 1942 he became a brigadier general assigned to the Southwest Pacific. He helped coordinate a concerted air strategy that destroyed Japanese air power over Bougainville and Rabaul, winning a commendation from Admiral William F. Halsey. In November 1943 he transferred to Italy as head of the Fifteenth Air Force and again distinguished himself by orchestrating a prolonged bombardment campaign against German-held oil refineries at Ploesti, Romania. In May 1945 Twining transferred back to the Pacific to replace General Curtis E. LeMay as head of the Twentieth Air Force in the Marianas. He supervised the fire bombing of major Japanese cities and, that August, his aircraft dropped atomic bombs on Hiroshima and Nagasaki. An obscure lieutenant colonel when it began, Twining ended the war with a temporary rank of lieutenant general.

During the ensuing cold war period, Twining was called on to fulfill major administration positions with the Air Materiel Command and the Alaska Defense Command, and, in 1948, he gained appointment as vice chief of staff in the newly independent U.S. Air Force. In 1953 President Dwight D. Eisenhower appointed him to succeed General Hoyt S. Vandenberg as U.S. Air Force chief of staff. Twining did much to accommodate Eisenhower's "New Look" strategy by acquiring large numbers of jet bombers and laying the groundwork for the first intercontinental ballistic missiles. Stridently anticommunist, in 1956 Twining became the first American general to tour Soviet aviation facilities since World War II and he came back warning the nation about an impending "bomber gap." In response, Eisenhower appointed him chairman of the Joint Chiefs of Staff in 1957, whereupon he pushed for the Atlas and Jupiter missiles, the XB-70 jet bomber, and the navy's Polaris submarine. However, other generals questioned his overreliance on nuclear weapons. In September 1960, Twining resigned from the Joint Chiefs. Thereafter he held several positions in corporate management, published the book *Neither Liberty nor Safety* in 1964, and unsuccessfully ran for the U.S. Senate from New Hampshire that same year. Twining died at Lackland Air Force Base, Texas, on March 29, 1982, one of the most highly respected and influential military officials of the early cold war period.

July 11
AVIATION: Over North Korea, Major John F. Bolt, flying as an exchange pilot with the 51st Fighter Interceptor Squadron (FIS), becomes the first and only Marine Corps jet ace after downing his fifth and sixth MiG-15s.
DIPLOMACY: In South Korea, President Syngman Rhee agrees to the terms of a cease-fire with the Communists; he receives promises of a mutual security pact with the United States in exchange.

July 13–20
MILITARY: In Korea, Chinese forces stage their final offensive of the war by attacking in strength along the Kumsong River. The six divisions committed engage the 2nd, 3rd, 40th and 45th Infantry Divisions, backed by the 187th Airborne Regimental Combat Team and massed artillery. They are repelled with a loss estimated at several thousand men. American casualties total 243 dead, 768 wounded, and 88 missing.

July 15
AVIATION: Over North Korea, Major James Jabara downs his fifteenth Mig-15 to become the world's second triple jet ace.
• The submarine *Tunny* test launches a Regulus I surface-to-surface missile at sea for the first time.

July 16
AVIATION: An F-86D Sabre flown by Lieutenant William Barnes pushes the absolute flight speed record to 715.7 miles per hour in level flight. He does so by breaking an early record also achieved by the F-86D.
• Lieutenant Guy P. Bordelon, Jr., of VC-3, shoots down a North Korean PO-2 biplane ("Bedcheck Charlie") at night in his F4U-5N Corsair; this is also his fifth kill, rendering him the navy's only ace of the Korean War.

July 17
AVIATION: Near Milton, Florida, a marine Fairchild C-119 Flying Boxcar crashes, killing four crewmen and 38 NROTC midshipmen.

July 19
DIPLOMACY: At Panmunjom, South Korea, armistice negotiators convene their final session. Technical negotiators subsequently hammer out the actual cease-fire details.
MARINES: In the 1st Marine Division area, a Chinese battalion captures Outposts Berlin and East Berlin, wiping out the two platoons guarding them. Consequently, the marines adopt a defense-in-depth strategy of multiple lines rather than simply isolated outposts to their immediate front.

July 20
AVIATION: Over Middle River, Maryland, the first Martin B-57A Canberra light jet bomber flies for the first time. This is an American copy of the famous English Electric aircraft built under license, and it is the first non-American aircraft to begin service with the U.S. Air Force.
• Over North Korea, Marine Corps major Thomas M. Sellers bags two MiG-15s while flying in an air force squadron, but he is then shot down and killed.

July 21–22
AVIATION: A force of 18 Bomber Command B-29s flies their final mission of the war by striking at Uiju Airfield, North Korea.

July 22
AVIATION: Over North Korea, Marine Major John H. Glenn shoots down his third MiG-15 in 10 days while flying as an exchange officer in an air force squadron.
• In a final aerial confrontation over North Korea, three F-86Es attack four MiG-15s, whereupon Lieutenant Sam P. Young shoots down a final Communist fighter.

July 24–27
MARINES: In the 1st Marine Division area, two Chinese battalions attack the hill dubbed Boulder City, while other units lunge at Outposts Esther and Dagmar. The defending marines easily repel the attackers. The Chinese attack again over the next two nights without success. Marine losses are 43 dead and 316 wounded; Communist losses are estimated as much higher.

July 25
MARINES: In Washington, D.C., President Dwight D. Eisenhower orders the 3rd Marine Division and Marine Air Group 11 (MAG-11) to deploy to Japan as part of a ready amphibious force in the region.

July 27
AVIATION: Shortly after the Korean armistice takes effect, an air force F-86 Sabre jet fighter flown by Captain Ralph S. Parr, Jr., encounters a Soviet Il-12 transport over Kanggye, North Korea, and shoots it down, killing all 21 passengers. Apparently, these were high-ranking Chinese and Soviet military personnel and their loss sparks a retaliatory response from the Russians off Vladivostok. Parr, for his part, becomes the last double ace of the war.
• On this, the final day of hostilities, Task Force 77 launches air strikes that destroy or damage 23 railroad cars, 11 bridges, a tunnel, and nine highway bridges.
• Just 24 minutes before the cease-fire takes effect at midnight, a B-26 crew flies the final close support mission of the Korean War in a radar-directed bomb strike. Ironically, Invader aircraft had also flown the very first bomber raid three years previously.
• Over North Korea, a Fifth Air Force RB-26 conducts the final reconnaissance mission of the war.
DIPLOMACY: After two years of negotiations, UN and Communist representatives conclude an armistice at Panmunjom to go into effect at 10 o'clock (2200) tonight. Lieutenant General William K. Harrison signs the document for the United Nations. The lines as they are presently occupied are preserved with a 4,000-yard demilitarized zone between them. The U.S. Army has suffered 29,856 dead or missing and 77,596 wounded with the 2nd Infantry Division hardest hit of all (7,094 killed, 16,575 wounded). The marines have sustained 4,262 dead and 26,038 wounded. Chinese and North Korean casualties are estimated as high as 1.2 million while an estimated 2 million Korean civilians are believed to have been killed.

July 28
AVIATION: A Boeing B-47 Stratojet establishes a new transatlantic speed record by crossing from Limestone, Maine, to Fairford, England, averaging 618 miles per hour. It completes its mission in only four hours and 43 minutes.
MARINES: The 1st Marine Division is reorganized, with one regiment deployed on the forward line while the rest are farther back to provide in-depth defense.

July 29
AVIATION: The air force releases its official tally for the three-year air war over Korea: Far East Air Forces claim 839 MiG-15s shot down, with another 154 probables, and 919 damaged over the course of 37 months. In exchange, the UN lost 110 aircraft in aerial combat, 677 to antiaircraft fire, and 213 to accidents and other causes.
• An air force RB-50 Superfortress reconnaissance aircraft flying from Yokota Air Base, Japan, is shot down by Soviet MiG-15 jet interceptors off the coast of Vladivostok, Siberia. One man from the 17-man crew survives and is rescued. The attack is most likely in retribution for the earlier downing of an IL-2 transport over North Korea.
MILITARY: In Washington, D.C., Congress passes a $34 billion defense budget for fiscal year 1954.

August 3
AVIATION: At Cape Canaveral, Florida, the Missile Test Center successfully launches a Redstone missile for the first time. This is the first such ballistic weapon designed to carry a tactical nuclear warhead.

August 5–December 23
MILITARY: At Panmunjom, Korea, Operation Big Switch unfolds as the Communists repatriate 12,773 UN prisoners in exchange for 75,823 Chinese and North Koreans. Of these 157 are marines–27 having died in captivity. Twenty-three Americans voluntarily decide to remain in Communist hands.

August 6
AVIATION: Operation Big Switch continues as 800 former prisoners of war are flown back to the United States by the Military Air Transport Service (MATS).
MARINES: The standard tour in Korea for marines is extended from 11 months to 14.

August 7
MARINES: Staff Sergeant Barbara O. Barnwell saves a fellow marine from drowning and wins the first Navy-Marine Corps Medal for Heroism given to a female.

August 12
AVIATION: The experimental ship *Mississippi* test launches a fully operative Terrier antiaircraft missile, which downs an F6F target drone.
TECHNOLOGY: In another ominous cold war development, the United States loses its monopoly on thermonuclear weapons when the Soviet Union explodes its first hydrogen bomb.

August 13
AVIATION: Marine Air Group 16 (MAG-16), a helicopter transport group flying Sikorsky HRS-2s, arrives in Japan.

MARINES: At Camp Pendleton, California, headquarters, 3rd Marine Division, ships out for Japan.

August 14–19
MARINES: In the Mediterranean, the Sixth Fleet sends in marines to assist earthquake survivors in the Greek Ionian Isles.

August 16
AVIATION: VMR-253, a transport squadron operating the first squadron of Fairchild R4Q Packets, arrives at Atsugi, Japan.
MILITARY: In Washington, D.C., General Matthew B. Ridgway is appointed the new army chief of staff to replace outgoing General Joseph L. Collins. Ridgway considers this assignment the toughest job he has ever held.

August 17
NAVAL: In Washington, D.C., Admiral Robert B. Carney gains appointment as the 14th chief of naval operations.

August 20
AVIATION: At the White Sands Proving Ground, New Mexico, the army successfully launches a Redstone missile, which is capable of lobbing a nuclear warhead over 200 miles.
• Two separate F-84G units of the 40th Air Division fly en masse from the United States to overseas bases in a clear demonstration of the Strategic Air Command's (SAC) long-range deployment abilities. The 31st Strategic Fighter Wing lifts off from Albany, Georgia, and wings its way nonstop to Nouasseur Air Base, Morocco. Aircraft assigned to the 508th Strategic Fighter Wing also travel nonstop from Albany to RAF Lakenheath, England. The feat earns the 40th Air Division a Mackay Trophy for most significant flight of the year.

August 25
AVIATION: In a return to the "parasite fighter" concept first espoused with dirigibles in the 1930s, a modified RF-84F successfully attaches itself to a B-36 bomber using the new Fighter Conveyor (FICON) system. The air force touts the aging B-36 as a "flying aircraft carrier," although the concept never proves practical.

August 31
AVIATION: Marine Corps lieutenant colonel Marion E. Carl sets a world altitude record of 15 miles while flying the Douglas D-558-2 *Skyrocket.*

September 1
AVIATION: The first jet-to-jet aerial refueling occurs when a B-47 Stratojet hooks up with a KB-47 jet deploying a hose and drogue system. As a rule, propeller-driven tankers are too slow for most jet bombers to refuel with a margin of safety.

September 2
NAVAL: Plans are announced to retrofit and upgrade all *Midway*-class aircraft carriers with new angle decks and steam catapults.

September 4
DIPLOMACY: General William Dean, captured in the early days of the Korean conflict, is released by North Korean authorities at Panmunjon, Korea.

September 6
MILITARY: By this date the repatriation of all willing prisoners of war is completed.

September 10
AVIATION: At Atsugi, Japan, Marine Air Group 11 (MAG-11) deploys three squadrons, all equipped with Grumman F9F Panthers.

September 11
AVIATION: Over China Lake, California, an AIM-9 infrared-guided Sidewinder missile successfully intercepts and destroys an airborne F6F drone.

September 21
AVIATION: At Kimpo Airfield in Seoul, South Korea, air traffic controllers are taken aback when a Communist MiG-15 jet fighter touches down and taxis in. The defecting pilot, Lieutenant Noh Kum Suk, is not aware of Operation Moola, which encouraged such action, but he nonetheless receives $100,000 and political asylum in the United States. The aircraft in question is subsequently disassembled and flown to Okinawa for flight tests; it ultimately ends up on display at the Air Force Museum in Dayton, Ohio.

October 1
AVIATION: At McClellan Air Force Base, California, Lockheed delivers its first RC-121 Super Constellation to the 4701st Early Warning Radar Squadron, Air Force Defense Command. The aircraft displays a conspicuous radar dome on its backside and is intended to serve as a distant early warning aircraft. It is a forerunner of present-day AWACS aircraft.

October 3
AVIATION: Over Muroc, California, Lieutenant Commander James F. Verdin pilots a Douglas F4D Skyray to a new world speed record of 752.943 miles per hour.

October 14
AVIATION: The North American X-10 (B-64) Navaho ramjet-powered, surface-to-surface, guided missile is successfully test flown for the first time.

October 16
NAVAL: The carrier *Leyte* suffers from a catapult explosion and fire while docked at Boston Navy Yard, Massachusetts, killing 32 sailors and injuring five civilian workers.

October 23
AVIATION: The Piasecki YH-16 twin rotor helicopter prototype is flown for the first time.

October 24
AVIATION: Over Edwards Air Force Base, California, the delta-wing Convair XF-102 flies for the first time, being the first jet fighter designed to be armed solely with air-to-air missiles. However, it fails to break the speed barrier and is subject to extensive redesign under the new "area rule." This gives it a pinched fuselage to cut down wind resistance; only then does it enter service as the F-102 Delta Dart.

1953

October 30
MILITARY: National Security Directive No. 162 is adopted by the government as national defense policy. It fully reflects President Dwight D. Eisenhower's "New Look," which emphasizes strategic (nuclear) warfare at the expense of conventional arms.

October 31
AVIATION: In Washington, D.C., the Strategic Missiles Evaluation Committee is formed under the aegis of the secretary of the air force. It is eventually headed by distinguished mathematician John von Neumann.

November 6
AVIATION: A B-47 Stratojet departs Limestone Air Force Base, Maine, and sets a new transatlantic crossing record by touching down at RAF Brize Norton, England, in four hours and 57 minutes.

November 20
AVIATION: A Douglas D-558-2 Skyrocket flown by A. Scott Crossfield becomes the first manned vehicle to break Mach 2 by reaching 1,328 miles per hour. This particular vehicle remains in service until 1957 and is on permanent display at the National Air and Space Museum, Washington, D.C.

November 30
MARINES: Marine Corps strength reaches 251,770, its maximum strength during the Korean War period.

December 10
DIPLOMACY: Former general and now Secretary of State George C. Marshall receives a Nobel Peace Prize for his efforts at rebuilding Europe's shattered economic structure. He is the first professional soldier so honored.

December 12
AVIATION: Over Edwards Air Force Base, California, Major Charles E. "Chuck" Yeager flies the Bell X-1A to 1,612 miles per hour, or 2½ times the speed of sound, at an altitude of 70,000 feet. However, he loses control of the craft, which spirals down to 25,000 feet before he can recover and successfully land. Yeager wins the Harmon Trophy for his efforts.

December 26
MILITARY: The United States announces the withdrawal of two infantry divisions from the Korean Peninsula.

1954

January
MILITARY: With the Korean War over, army personnel levels have declined slightly to 1.4 million officers and men while the six National Guard divisions called into federal service have gradually reverted back to state control.

January 4
NAVAL: In a major development, the carrier *Leyte* begins serving as the first anti-submarine warfare (ASW) carrier. This is an integrated concept employing carrier

aircraft, destroyers, and attack submarines in concert to thwart the rising menace posed by Soviet submersibles.

January 10
AVIATION: In Washington, D.C., the Air Force Strategic Missile Evaluation Committee (or Teapot Committee) reports great strides in reducing the size and weight of nuclear warheads. The committee strongly recommends that a group be formed to expedite the speedy development of practical intercontinental ballistic missiles (ICBMs).

January 15
MARINES: In South Korea, the 3rd Battalion, 4th Marines act as guards on vessels conveying 14,500 Chinese captives who desire Taiwanese citizenship.

January 21
NAVAL: The *Nautilus,* the world's first nuclear-powered submarine, is launched at Groton, Connecticut.
MARINE: Off Inchon, South Korea, a ship strikes a landing craft crammed with marines; 27 drown along with two navy corpsmen.

January 27
AVIATION: An air force RB-45C Tornado reconnaissance bomber is jumped by North Korean MiG-15 fighters over the Yellow Sea and is rescued by a flight of F-86 Sabres; one MiG is shot down.

February 15
AVIATION: In Washington, D.C., President Dwight D. Eisenhower signs a bill to begin construction of a series of early warning radar sites across the Arctic Circle called the Distant Early Warning (DEW) Line.

February 28
AVIATION: The Lockheed XF-104, the world first jet capable of sustained speeds in excess of Mach 2, performs high-speed taxi tests for the first time.

March 1
TECHNOLOGY: In the Marshall Islands, Pacific Ocean, American technicians detonate a new thermonuclear (hydrogen) weapon with a 15 megaton yield.

March 5
AVIATION: At Edwards Air Force Base, California, test pilot Tony LaVier flies the new XF-104 prototype for the first time. This machine, nicknamed "the missile with a man in it," is the brainchild of famous aircraft designer Clarence Kelly Johnson of Lockheed's noted "Skunk works." It enter the service as the F-104 Starfighter.

March 16
AVIATION: In Washington, D.C., the fact that the United States possesses a viable thermonuclear weapon that can be delivered anywhere in the world is announced by Representative W. Sterling Cole, chairman of the Atomic Energy Committee (AEC).

April 1
AVIATION: In Washington, D.C., President Dwight D. Eisenhower signs legislation creating the U.S. Air Force Academy. The first classes are to take place at

Lowry Air Force Base in Denver until construction of a separate facility can be completed.

• The air force takes delivery of its first Convair C-131A transport aircraft. This is the military version of the Model 240 airliner.

• At Fort Bragg, North Carolina, the army activates its first formal Helicopter Battalion under Major Robert Kolb. It consists of three helicopter companies and one maintenance company.

April 8

AVIATION: At the Pentagon, Washington, D.C., the office of the Air Force Assistant Chief of Staff for Guided Missiles is created. The quest for intercontinental ballistic missiles is a project of increasing concern to national security in light of the world political situation.

April 13

AVIATION: Pilots of VMF-324 ferry their fighters from the light carrier *Saipan* to Touraine Airfield, Vietnam, where the aircraft are turned over to the French. The equipment is needed for battling a mounting Communist insurgency.

May 3

NAVAL: In Washington, D.C., Charles S. Thomas gains appointment as the 53rd secretary of the navy.

May 7

DIPLOMACY: In the wake of the Communist victory over France at Dien Bien Phu, negotiators from the Viet Minh, the United States, Communist China, and France convene a meeting at Geneva, Switzerland, to hammer out cease-fire terms.

May 25

AVIATION: The heyday of dirigibles has passed, but ZPG-2 under Commander Marion H. Eppes sets a new record flight for the type by remaining aloft eight days and eight hours.

May 26

NAVAL: At Newport, Rhode Island, a catapult explosion on board the vessel *Bennington* kills 103 sailors and injures another 201.

May 27

NAVAL: Chief of Naval Operations Charles S. Thomas, eager to extend the usefulness of World War II straight deck carriers, authorizes the addition of angled flight decks and closed hurricane bows to all *Essex*-class vessels in service.

May 30

AVIATION: At Fort Meade, Maryland, the army activates its first Nike Ajax surface-to-air missile site. For the rest of the decade, this system will be deployed around the nation to defend major cities, industrial centers, and military facilities from aerial attack.

June 1

AVIATION: The army deploys eight artillery batteries armed with Honest John ballistic missiles, its first tactical nuclear weapon delivery system.

• The *Hancock* tests the first steam-powered catapult installed on a carrier by successfully launching a Grumman S2F Tracker aircraft.

June 4
AVIATION: Over Edwards Air Force Base, California, a Bell X-1A rocket airplane flown by Major Arthur Murray reaches a record altitude of 90,000 feet.

June 7–July 1
MARINES: Off Guatemala, the amphibious assault vessel *Mellette* prepares to evacuate American citizens as the pro-Communist government there is overthrown in a CIA-inspired coup. The 2nd Battalion, 8th Marines remains on station, if needed, until July 1.

June 18
AVIATION: The Martin B-57B Canberra, the first interdiction version of this noted aircraft, makes its maiden flight. It differs from the A model by replacing the British-inspired "bowl" canopy with a more traditional "teardrop-shaped" structure.

June 21
AVIATION: Three B-47 Stratojets commanded by Major General Walter C. Sweeney, 22nd Bombardment Wing, fly nonstop from March Air Force Base, California, to Yokota Air Base, Japan, with two inflight refuelings. They cover 6,700 miles in 15 hours; the Strategic Air Command (SAC) is beginning to flex its aerial muscles.

June 22
AVIATION: The diminutive Douglas XA4D-1 light bomber makes its successful maiden flight. This versatile craft enters service as the A-4 Skyhawk (or "Scooter') and serves with distinction in Vietnam and elsewhere.
MARINES: In Washington, D.C., President Dwight D. Eisenhower signs an executive order adopting an official seal for the U.S. Marine Corps.

June 24
AVIATION: In Washington, D.C., Secretary of the Air Force Harold E. Talbott announces that the new U.S. Air Force Academy will be located on 15,000 acres in Colorado Springs, Colorado.

June 26–July 17
AVIATION: In Vietnam, Operation Wounded Warrior unfolds as the 315th Air Division and the Military Air Transport Service (MATS) begins transporting 500 wounded French soldiers back to France. Their route takes them first to Japan and then across the United States before reaching home.

June 28
AVIATION: The Douglas RB-66 Destroyer reconnaissance aircraft performs its maiden flight. This sleek-looking machine is based on the navy A3D Sky Warrior and performs distinguished service throughout the Vietnam conflict.

June 30
MARINES: The post–Korean War strength of the Marine Corps begins dipping to 18,593 officers and 205,275 men.

July 1
AVIATION: Brigadier General Bernard A. Schriever gains appointment as head of the new Western Development Division, tasked with facilitating creation of the

first intercontinental ballistic missiles (ICBMs). Schriever's first priority is accelerating the deployment of the forthcoming Atlas missile.

July 12

MARINES: In Japan, the 3rd Marine Division is placed on alert for a possible transfer to Vietnam to help the French military, but President Dwight D. Eisenhower has no intention of getting involved with Southeast Asian affairs.

July 15

AVIATION: In Seattle, Washington, the prototype Boeing KC-135 aerial tanker jet performs its maiden flight. In order to relieve jet-powered strategic bombers from the dangerous practice of refueling behind slower propeller-driven tankers, several hundred KC-135s are ordered; they receive the appropriate moniker Stratotanker.

July 21

DIPLOMACY: In Geneva, Switzerland, peace negotiators debating the fate of Vietnam agree to a Communist zone established above the 17th parallel (North Vietnam) and a non-Communist zone to the south (South Vietnam). The two regions are never meant to be sovereign states, even though the North is ruled by the Viet Minh and the South by the French-installed Bao Dai regime. The United States, wishing to contain the growth of communism in Southeast Asia, begins offering military assistance to the Bao Dai government.

July 26

AVIATION: Lieutenant General Hubert R. Harmon becomes the first superintendent of the new U.S. Air Force Academy.
• Off Hainan Island, China, a pair of Douglas AD-1 Skyraiders, searching for a British Cathay airliner downed by the Communists two days earlier, are attacked by a pair of Communist La-7 fighters. The navy planes promptly flame both of their antagonists.

August 2

MARINES: In Vietnam, Lieutenant Colonel Victor J. Croizat is the first marine assigned to work with the U.S. Military Assistance Advisory Group (MAAG).

August 5

AVIATION: The first production of the eight-jet B-52 A bomber flies for the first time. Unlike the prototype, which featured a fighter-type "teardrop" canopy, production models house pilot and co-pilot side-by-side in a cockpit cabin. Possessing much greater range and payload than the B-47 Stratojet, it quickly becomes the backbone of the Strategic Air Command (SAC).

August 6–7

AVIATION: The 38th Air Division conducts two impressive demonstrations of long-range strategic flying when two B-47s from the 308th Bombardment Wing fly from Hunter Air Force Base, Georgia, and complete a 10,000-mile round trip flight to French Morocco and back. Concurrently, two additional B-47s from the 308th depart Hunter and conduct a simulated bomb run over Morocco, then land there. For its efforts, the 38th Air Division receives a Mackay Trophy.

August 11

DIPLOMACY: Red Chinese foreign minister Chou En-lai insists that Nationalist-held Taiwan will be "liberated" by Communists forces.

August 12
NAVAL: At Annapolis, Maryland, Rear Admiral Walter F. Boone is appointed the 38th superintendent of the U.S. Naval Academy.

August 16
NAVAL: At Haiphong, North Vietnam, the navy commences Operation Passage to Freedom, which eventually relocates 293,002 civilians and 17,846 Vietnamese soldiers to South Vietnam who decline to live under communism by May 1955. This is done in accordance with the Geneva accords ending the French Indochina War.

August 17
DIPLOMACY: President Dwight D. Eisenhower, reacting to Chinese Communist threats to attack Taiwan, declares that any Communist invasion of that island "would have to run over the 7th Fleet."

August 23
AVIATION: The prototype Lockheed YC-130 transport completes its maiden flight.

August 26
AVIATION: Over Edwards Air Force Base, California, a Bell X-1A flown by Major Arthur Murray reaches a record 90,440 feet, where, the pilot reports, the curvature of the Earth is visible.

September 1
AVIATION: The Continental Air Defense Command is established at Colorado Springs, Colorado, under General Benjamin W. Chidlaw.

September 3
MILITARY: Communist Chinese forces on the mainland shell National Chinese positions on Quemoy Island, killing army advisers Lieutenant Colonels Alfred Medendorp and Frank Lynn.

September 4
AVIATION: Off the coast of Siberia, Soviet MiG-15 fighters accost a navy P2V-5 Neptune patrol aircraft of VP-19 and shoot it down, killing one crew member. Nine others are rescued by Coast Guard aircraft.

September 8
DIPLOMACY: The Southeast Asia Treaty Organization (SEATO), a collective defensive alliance, is established among the United States, Australia, France, Great Britain, the Philippines, and Thailand. It differs from NATO, however, establishing neither an allied army nor an integrated command.

September 13
NAVAL: In Washington, D.C., President Dwight D. Eisenhower directs the Seventh Fleet to logistically support Chinese Nationalist forces on the islands of Quemoy and Matsu.

September 27
AVIATION: At George Air Force Base, California, the first North American F-100A Super Sabres achieve operational status. This is the first air force fighter to routinely exceed the speed of sound in level flight.

September 29
AVIATION: The prototype, twin-engined McDonnell-Douglas XF-101, an enlarged version of the earlier XF-88, completes its maiden flight. It enters service as the F-101 Voodoo and performs as both an interceptor and a reconnaissance craft.

September 30
NAVAL: The *Nautilus*, the world's first nuclear-powered submarine and the navy's first nuclear-powered vessel, is commissioned into service at Groton, Connecticut.

October 4
AVIATION: At Coronado Beach, California, the giant, turboprop-powered Convair R3Y-2 Tradewind flying boat lands a detachment of marines ashore for the first time.

October 8
AVIATION: Over Edwards Air Force Base, California, the Bell X-1B research rocket plane makes its maiden flight with Major Arthur Murray at the controls.

October 9
AVIATION: In Washington, D.C., Congress adds an additional $500 million to accelerate development and production of the Atlas intercontinental ballistic missile.

October 12
AVIATION: At Wichita, Kansas, Cessna unveils its XT-37 side-by-side trainer; it enters production as the T-37 "Tweety Bird" and also serves as a light attack craft.

October 13
AVIATION: Congress agrees to fund development of the Convair XB-58, a four-engined, delta-winged jet bomber destined to be the first supersonic aircraft of its class.
MARINES: In South Vietnam, the Bao Dai administration orders the creation of a Marine Corps of 1,137 men.

October 17
AVIATION: A Sikorsky XH-39 helicopter piloted by U.S. Army warrant officer Billy Wester reaches a record altitude of 24,500 feet.

October 18–19
AVIATION: In Washington, D.C., the Air Force Scientific Advisory Board assembles an ad hoc committee under Dr. Theodore von Karman to ponder the possibilities of using atomic power for missile propulsion. At this juncture, the board can recommend only additional study of the concept so as not to fall behind the Soviets.

October 24
DIPLOMACY: President Dwight D. Eisenhower alerts the new South Vietnamese premier Ngo Dinh Diem that the United States will provide military assistance directly through his government, instead of through the French.

October 27
AVIATION: Another racial barrier falls as Benjamin O. Davis, Jr., becomes the first African-American brigadier general in the U.S. Air Force. During World War II he commanded the famous "Tuskegee Airmen."

November 1
AVIATION: After a long and distinguished service career in both the Army Air Force and the U.S. Air Force, the venerable Boeing B-29 is retired from active service.

November 2
AVIATION: At San Diego, California, the radical Convair XFY-1 Pogo vertical takeoff fighter is tested with test pilot James F. Coleman at the controls. The device takes off like a helicopter, flies like a normal aircraft for 21 minutes, then lands backward on its launching pad without incident. Coleman wins a Harmon Trophy for his efforts.

November 7
AVIATION: An Air Force RB-29 Superfortress reconnaissance aircraft is attacked by Soviet MiG-15s near Hokkaido, northern Japan, and shot down. One crew member dies.

November 10
MARINES: At the Marine Corps War Memorial, Arlington, Virginia, sculptor Felix de Weldon dedicates his bronze statute of the Iwo Jima flag raising; this is perhaps the most iconic representation of the Marine Corps.

November 17–19
AVIATION: England's notoriously bad weather was never more manifest than when Colonel David A. Burchinal flies his B-47 Stratojet for 47 hours and 35 minutes–refueling in midair nine times–while waiting for safe landing conditions to appear!

December
MARINES: In some administrative fine-tuning, the ranks of first sergeant and sergeant major are reestablished, although below master sergeant in seniority. All three grades receive the same pay.

December 7
AVIATION: At Edwards Air Force Base, California, a Navaho X-10 guided missile arrives successfully using an automated approach and landing system.

December 10
AVIATION: Colonel John P. Stapp, a glutton for punishment, rides a rocket sled to 632 miles per hour. This is the equivalent of ejecting from a jet plane at 35,000 feet at Mach 1.7, yet he survives without serious injuries.

December 11
NAVAL: The giant angle-deck carrier *Forrestal,* weighing in at 59,650 tons, is launched at Newport News, Virginia.

December 20
AVIATION: The first production Convair F-102A Delta Dagger performs its maiden flight; this is the first air force fighter armed solely with guided missiles.

The USS *Nautilus* (SS-571), the navy's first atomic-powered submarine, on its initial sea trials *(Library of Congress)*

MARINES: In Washington, D.C., the secretary of defense declares that the 1st Marine Division will depart South Korea and be replaced by an army infantry division; the marines will head back to Camp Pendleton, California.

December 23
AVIATION: The search for a new, hypersonic research aircraft begins once representatives from the air force, navy, and NACA, sign a joint memorandum to begin development. The end result is the famous X-15 rocket-powered airplane.

1955

January
MILITARY: Demobilization continues in the army, reducing overall manpower levels to 1.1 million officers and men in 19 divisions.

January 19
NAVAL: The nuclear-powered submarine *Nautilus* under Commander Eugene P. Wilkinson slips out of Groton, Connecticut, and heads into blue water for sea trials. The vessel heralds a new age in submarine capabilities for the reactors powering it possess virtually unlimited range.

January 20
DIPLOMACY: The governments of the United States, Great Britain, and France conclude an agreement with South Vietnam to assist modernization of its military forces.

January 26–May 6
MARINES: At Camp Lejeune, North Carolina, the 2nd Marine Division begins a series of amphibious exercises named TRAEX 2-55, which will also take them on simulated raids against guided-missile launching sites.

January 29
MILITARY: Congress approves a resolution allowing an immediate troop mobilization by President Dwight D. Eisenhower should Chinese Communists attack Taiwan.

February 1
MILITARY: General John E. Dahlquist is appointed the first commander of the U.S. Army Continental Army Command (CONARC), which is tasked with supervising military matters within the United States. It replaces the older Army Field Forces.

February 3
MARINES: In Japan, the 3rd Engineering Battalion begins shifting men and equipment to its future home on the U.S.-administered island of Okinawa; in time, the entire 3rd Marine Division is stationed there.

February 4
MARINES: At Kaneohe Bay, Oahu, Hawaii, the 4th Marines arrive from Japan; this is to be their new duty station.

February 5
AVIATION: An air force RB-45C Tornado jet reconnaissance bomber is attacked by North Korean MiG-15s over the Yellow Sea and is rescued by an escort of F-86 Sabres, who shoot down two MiGs.

February 6
NAVAL: At the Tachen Islands, China, the Seventh Fleet under Vice Admiral Alfred M. Pride begins the evacuation of 29,000 Nationalists soldiers and civilians to Taiwan. To prevent any interference from the Red Chinese air force, the maneuver is amply covered by carrier aviation.

February 12
MARINES: In South Vietnam, no sooner do the French relinquish control of Vietnamese armed forces than the United States steps in and begins training them through the Military Advisory Assistance Group (MAAG).

February 19
DIPLOMACY: The SEATO alliance extends its protective umbrella to Laos, Cambodia, and South Vietnam in an attempt to deter Communist aggression there.

February 26
AVIATION: Over California, test pilot George Smith is forced to eject from his F-100 Super Sabre at 600 miles per hour. He is knocked unconscious by the force of 64 "Gs" upon ejecting, and he falls until he awakens and parachutes into the Pacific; he is picked up by a fishing boat with serious injuries but eventually resumes flight testing. Smith's experience typifies what jet pilots face during a high-speed egress.
MILITARY: Professor Cecil F. Powell of England estimates that the United States has stockpiled 4,000 atomic bombs while the Soviet Union possesses 1,000.

March 1
AVIATION: In Washington, D.C., Trevor Gardner is appointed the first secretary of the air force for research and development.
•   At Otis Air Force Base, Massachusetts, the new RC-121D Super Constellation airborne early warning radar plane begins operating along the east coast of the United States.

1955

March 6
AVIATION: In Washington, D.C., U.S. Air Force chief of staff general Nathan F. Twining announces that the Atlas, Navaho, and Snark programs are being accelerated in light of Soviet advances in missile technology.

March 17–18
MARINES: Along the Demilitarized Zone (DMZ), South Korea, the 1st Marine Division has been completely supplanted by the army's 24th Infantry Division.

March 25
AVIATION: The Chance Vought XF8U-1 prototype carrier fighter exceeds Mach 1 on its maiden flight and eventually goes into service as the F8U Crusader, an outstanding fighter and reconnaissance platform of the Vietnam War.

April 6
AVIATION: Over Yucca Flats, Nevada, a B-36 launches a nuclear-tipped missile, which climbs to 42,000 feet before detonating; this is the highest altitude that a nuclear device has ever been exploded.

April 17
AVIATION: Soviet MiG-15 jets intercept and shoot down an air force RB-47E Stratojet reconnaissance airplane near Kamchatka, killing the crew of three.

April 21
AVIATION: The new Aerobee-Hi rocket is launched for the first time and reaches an altitude of 123 miles while carrying a 200-pound cargo.

May 2
AVIATION: The Western Development Division's suggestion to begin constructing a second and larger type of intercontinental ballistic missile is approved by air force authorities; this is the genesis of the Titan missile program.

May 5–July 27
MILITARY: The United States concludes its military occupation of West Germany following the election of a civilian government. Germany is also granted NATO membership. The city of Berlin, replete with an American, French, and British garrison, remains deep behind Soviet/East German lines.

May 10
AVIATION: The air force accepts its final Douglas C-124 Globemaster II transport; a total of 448 have been constructed and deployed.
• At Schenectady, New York, a B-45 jet bomber takes off with a GE XJ-79 jet engine buried in its bomb bay for testing purposes. The J-79 design goes on to power several air force aircraft.

May 20
NAVAL: U.S. naval vessels, assisted by contingents of marines, assist in the removal of an additional 300,000 anti-Communist refugees from North Vietnam to new homes in the south.

May 31
AVIATION: After five years of service in the Far East, Marine Air Group 33 (MAG-33) returns to El Toro, California.

June 1
MARINES: The 9th Marines transfer from Japan to new bases on Okinawa, which is still administered by the U.S. military.

June 11
AVIATION: At Wright-Patterson Air Force Base, Ohio, an F-80C jet constructed almost entirely from magnesium is flown to test its strength and weight under flying conditions.
• The prototype Atlas rocket is test fired for the first time.

June 16
MILITARY: The Selective Service Act is extended by the House of Representatives to June 30, 1959.

June 20
MARINES: In Washington, D.C., a proposal by the House of Representatives to slash marine manpower from 215,000 to 193,000 is defeated in the Senate.

June 22
AVIATION: Soviet MiG-15 jet fighters shoot up a P2V-5 Neptune patrol plane from VP-9 in the Bering Sea, injuring seven of 11 crew members. Fortunately, the aircraft makes a forced landing on St. Lawrence Island without further damage.

June 29
AVIATION: At Castle Air Force Base, California, the 93rd Bombardment Wing receives its first operational, eight-jet B-52 Stratofortress. They remain an important part of the air force inventory to present times.

June 30
MILITARY: In Washington, D.C., General Maxwell D. Taylor gains appointment as the 20th chief of staff, U.S. Army, to replace outgoing General Matthew D. Ridgway. Like Ridgway, Taylor finds himself conflicted by President Dwight D. Eisenhower's policy of emphasizing nuclear weapons ("massive retaliation") at the expense of conventional forces and flexible military responses.

July 1
AVIATION: In light of the rapidly approaching dawn of space flight, the air force resumes testing on the problems of weightlessness. One result is the use of parabolic flight profiles for aircraft, which produce momentary weightlessness while descending. To those participating in such flights, the aircraft are jocularly known as "Vomit Comets."
• At Kaneohe Bay, Oahu, Hawaii, the 1st Provisional Marines Air Ground Task Force is cobbled together from the 4th Marines Marine Air Group 13 (MAG-13).

July 7
DIPLOMACY: Communist China signs an agreement with North Vietnam to provide economic assistance.

July 11
AVIATION: The first class of 306 cadets reports to the U.S. Air Force Academy at Lowry Air Force Base, Denver, Colorado, until more permanent facilities at Colorado Springs are constructed.

1955

Taylor, Maxwell D.   (1901–1987)
Army general

Maxwell Davenport Taylor was born in Keytesville, Missouri, on August 26, 1901, and he gained admittance into the U.S. Military Academy in 1918. He graduated fourth in his class four years later, and he enjoyed a far-ranging career over the next two decades, including stints as military attaché in China and Japan. Shortly after World War II broke out, Taylor joined the 82nd Airborne Division as General Matthew B. Ridgway's chief of staff. He fought with the division in North Africa and Sicily and, in September 1943, Taylor performed one of the most daring clandestine missions of the war by entering Rome in a truck to see if the city could be seized by paratroopers. Several hours in the city convinced him that German defenses were far too strong, so he secretly telegraphed General Dwight D. Eisenhower to halt an impending attack. For this display of courage, Taylor received a Silver Star and served as part of the Allied Control Commission in occupied Italy. The following year he reported to England as a major general commanding the 101st Airborne Division. In this capacity, on June 6, 1944, Taylor was the first American general to reach occupied France by dropping over Normandy. He accompanied his division in campaigns in the Netherlands and also fought in final phases of the Battle of the Bulge in December 1944. On May 7, 1945, Taylor rounded out a superb military career by capturing Berchtesgaden in Bavaria, which served as Adolf Hitler's mountain retreat.

After the war Taylor held several important posts and commanded UN forces during the last six months of the Korean War. In 1955 President Eisenhower appointed him chief of staff of the army, but his tenure proved an unhappy one. Taylor strongly disagreed with Eisenhower's "New Look" program, which forsook conventional forces in favor of nuclear arms. In concert with Ridgway and General James M. Gavin, Taylor advocated a more flexible response to the threat of communism. He was consequently eased into retirement in July 1959 and, the following year, he published *The Uncertain Trumpet*, a scathing appraisal of Eisenhower's defense policies. This brought him to the attention of President John F. Kennedy in 1961, who appointed him chairman of the Joint Chiefs of Staff shortly before the Cuban missile crisis. Taylor was subsequently dispatched to South Vietnam to evaluate conditions there, and while he supported giving the regime weapons and assistance to fight a Communist-backed insurgency, he predicated such aid on carrying out meaningful reforms. Taylor left Saigon in 1965 to serve as President Lyndon B. Johnson's special military adviser, and he also served as head of the Foreign Intelligence Advisory Board, which oversaw the American military buildup in Southeast Asia. In that position he became the architect of early American involvement in Vietnam. Taylor resigned from the military in 1970 and resumed his publishing activities. He died in Washington, D.C., on April 19, 1987, one of the most influential soldier-statesmen of the 20th century.

July 18
DIPLOMACY: Not to be outdone by its fast-rising rival, the Soviet Union also concludes an economic aid agreement with North Vietnam.

July 20
AVIATION: An NB-36H Peacekeeper aircraft carrying a nuclear reactor is flown for the first time, although the reactor itself remains inert.

July 21
MILITARY: In Washington, D.C., Wilber M. Bruckner, the general counsel for the Department of Defense, gains appointment as the fifth secretary of the army.
NAVAL: The *Sea Wolf,* the world's second atomic-powered submarine, is launched at Groton, Connecticut.

July 26
MILITARY: Congress passes a bill calling for U.S. military reserves to be expanded from 800,000 to 2.9 million by 1960.

August 1
AVIATION: Lockheed F-80s and T-33 aircraft are used as aerial simulation programs in the first zero-gravity research flights.

August 4
AVIATION: Over a secured airfield at Groom Lake, Nevada, the top-secret U-2 high-altitude reconnaissance aircraft prototype flies for the first time.
• The crew of the special operations B-29 Stardust 40 gain their freedom after being held in Red China since January 13, 1953. They had been incarcerated longer than any other prisoners of the Korean War.

August 8
AVIATION: Over Edwards Air Force Base, California, the Bell X-1A rocket plane explodes in the belly of its B-29 mothership and is ejected; test pilot Joseph A. Walker is rescued beforehand and survives unhurt.

August 10
AVIATION: The 3rd Marine Aviation Wing (3rd MAW) begins transferring its aerial assets from Miami, Florida, to El Toro, California.

August 13
MARINES: In Washington, D.C., President Dwight D. Eisenhower signs an executive order mandating that the army and marines begin enlisting personnel under the new Armed Forces Reserve Act of 1955. This stipulates that all new reservist personnel must undergo a six-month period of active duty training before being released into the Reserves. Consequently, reservists receive the same intensity of training as the regular forces they supplement in wartime.

August 17
MILITARY: The U.S. Army, ever conscious of public relations, creates the Civil Affairs/Military Government Branch as part of the Army Reserve. In 1959 it is subsequently renamed the Civil Affairs Branch.

Burke, Arleigh A.   (1901–1996)
Admiral

Arleigh Albert Burke was born in Boulder, Colorado, on October 19, 1901, and he passed through the U.S. Naval Academy in 1919 within the top third of his class. He fulfilled the usual tour of routine duties on land and sea over the next two decades while receiving graduate degrees in chemical engineering and becoming a noted weapons expert. In 1937 Burke became executive officer onboard the destroyer *Craven*, commencing his long association with "Tin Cans." Two years later he commanded his own vessel, the *Mugford*, trained it to a razor's edge, and won the Coveted Destroyer Gunnery Trophy for 1939. After World War II broke out he appealed for a combat command and, in March 1943, he took charge of Destroyer Squadron 23 commanding the *Waller*. Within days, he sank a Japanese destroyer in the Solomon Islands, rose to captain, then assumed control of Destroyer Squadron 23. In the Battles of Empress Augusta Bay and Cape St. George, Burke's well-aimed torpedoes sank several more Japanese destroyers without loss. Admiral William F. Halsey even christened him "Thirty-One Knot Burke" on account of his high-speed tactics. In March 1944 Burke transferred to the staff of Vice Admiral Marc A. Mitscher's Task Force 58, where he helped plan and coordinate some of the largest naval encounters of the Pacific war. Off Okinawa in April 1945, repeated kamikaze strikes forced Burke to change his flagship three times and, after the war,

he served as director of research at the Bureau of Ordnance in Washington, D.C.

The postwar years were a period of fiscal entrenchment for the military, and, in 1948, he had emerged as a leading opponent of the air force's new B-36 intercontinental bomber. His vocal opposition caused President Harry S. Truman to delete Burke's name from the list of potential flag officers, but, in July 1950, Truman reversed himself and promoted him to rear admiral. Burke performed distinguished service in Korea, and, in 1955, President Dwight D. Eisenhower appointed him—at age 53—the youngest-ever chief of naval operations, bypassing 97 other officers with more seniority. In this office, Burke helped the navy redefine itself and its mission in an age of limited conflict and nuclear weapons by promoting nuclear-powered submarines, the Polaris ballistic missile, and the angle-deck *Forrestal*-class carriers. He also orchestrated a far-ranging series of activities from handling the Quemoy-Matsu crisis off China to marine landings in Lebanon. His success as CNO may be gauged from the fact that he served three terms, longer than another other incumbent, before retiring from active service in 1961. The navy paid him a distinct homage by naming one of their most powerful group warships, the Arleigh Burke class (DDG-51) guided-missile destroyers in his honor while he was still alive. Burke died in Washington, D.C., on January 1, 1996, one of the navy's most far-sighted and accomplished senior officers.

Naval: In Washington, D.C. Admiral Arleigh A. Burke, a noted destroyerman of World War II, gains appointment as the 15th chief of naval operations.

August 18
Aviation: In the wake of Hurricane Diane, helicopters from HMR-161 and HMX-1 perform emergency relief work in battered areas of Connecticut and Pennsylvania.

August 20
Aviation: Over Edwards Air Force Base, California, a North American F-100 Super Sabre jet flown by Colonel Horace A. Hanes, director of the Air Force Flight Test Center, achieves a world speed record of 822 miles per hour in a production aircraft. For achieving the first high speed record set at high altitude, Hanes wins the Mackay Trophy.

August 22–24
Aviation: The carrier *Bennington* tests the new mirror landing system with pilots of Experimental Squadron VX-3. Highly successful, these replace the old hand-held paddle system and become standard features on all U.S. carriers.

September 8
Marines: Command of Fleet Marine Force Pacific (FMFPAC) passes to Lieutenant General William O. Brice, the first aviator so appointed since General Roy S. Geiger.

September 10
Marines: The dictum "Every Marine is a rifleman" is soundly underscored when a team of marksmen sweeps the National Trophy Rifle Matches, including the National Trophy, the Pershing Trophy, the Daniel Boone Trophy, the Rattlesnake Trophy, and the Infantry Trophy.

September 13
Aviation: In Washington, D.C., President Dwight D. Eisenhower orders the Department of Defense to begin work on a ballistic missile with a range of 1,500 miles, one capable of being launched from either land or sea.

September 16–30
Marines: In Hawaii, the 3rd Battalion, 4th Marines and helicopters of HMR-161 conduct training exercises simulating counterguerrilla, mountain, and night fighting operations.

September 20
Marines: Near Santa Barbara, California, 600 marines from the 2nd Infantry Training Regiment at Camp Pendleton are rushed to the Los Padres National Forest as fire fighters.

October 1
Naval: At Newport News, Virginia, the *Forrestal*, the navy's largest carrier, is commissioned into active service. This is also the first of a class of six "super" carriers, each weighing 59,630 tons and specifically designed to handle jet aircraft operations.

October 2–13
Aviation: Aircraft and helicopters of the 2nd Marine Air Wing (2nd MAW) fly to Tampico, Mexico, to provide relief aid in the wake of heavy flooding.

October 5

AVIATION: The air force contracts with Boeing to procure 29 KC-135 tankers, the first of 700 it will acquire in 88 models. It grants bombers of the Strategic Air Command (SAC) virtually unlimited range to reach hostile targets.

October 6

AVIATION: In Washington, D.C., the Department of Defense reveals a contract with the Glenn L. Martin Company to construct a rocket vehicle capable of putting a small satellite into Earth orbit. General Electric is also contracted to construct the actual rocket motor.

MILITARY: Edward L. T. Lyon, an anesthetist, is the first male commissioned into the Army Nurse Corps.

October 20

AVIATION: At Biggs Air Force Base, Texas, the 97th Bombardment Wing retires its last propeller-driven B-50D Superfortress. The age of jet bombardment is at hand.

October 22

AVIATION: Over Edwards Air Force Base, California, The Republic XF-105 prototype flies successfully for the first time and breaks the sound barrier during its maiden flight. It enters service at the F-105 Thunderchief, or "Thud," and accrues a distinguished career during the Vietnam War.

October 26

DIPLOMACY: In South Vietnam, Ngo Dinh Diem declares himself elected president of the new Republic of Vietnam; the move does nothing to deter North Vietnamese Communists under Ho Chi Minh from planning its ultimate subjugation.

November 1

MILITARY: Lieutenant General Samuel T. Williams is appointed head of the new Military Assistance Advisory Group Vietnam (MAAG-Vietnam). This body is tasked with supply arms and advice to the new government of South Vietnam.

NAVAL: At the Philadelphia Navy Yard, Pennsylvania, the new guided-missile cruiser *Boston* is commissioned. This is the first vessel of its kind in the world and capable of firing Terrier antiaircraft missiles from two automated launchers.

November 2

EXPLORING: Admiral Richard E. Byrd is appointed director of all Antarctic research by President Dwight D. Eisenhower.

November 7–18

MARINES: At Camp Pendleton, California, the 1st Marine Division and the 3rd Marine Air Wing (3rd MAW) participate in the PACTRAEX 56L fleet training exercise; opposition forces are provided by the Fleet Marine Force Pacific.

November 8–14

AVIATION: With guided ballistic missile programs pronounced the nation's top military priority, the Joint Army-Navy Missile Committee implements streamlined procedures to accelerate their procurement. The first intermediate-range ballistic missile (IRBM) to emerge is the Jupiter.

November 17
NAVAL: In Washington, D.C., the Special Projects Office is established by the secretary of the navy to oversee the development of new ballistic missiles and their shipboard launching systems. It is commanded by Rear Admiral William F. Raborn, Jr.

November 18
AVIATION: Over Edwards Air Force Base, California, the streamlined Bell X-2 research rocket plane successfully completes its first flight once dropped from an EB-50A. It reaches 627 miles per hour with Colonel Frank Everest at the controls.
MARINES: At Belleau Wood, France, Commandant Lemuel C. Shepherd dedicates a memorial to the 4th Marine Brigade that so distinguished itself here in 1918.

November 28
AVIATION: In Washington, D.C., the secretary of the navy establishes 1965 as the target date to acquire functional, solid-fuel ballistic missiles for a new class of submarines designed to carry and launch them.

December 2
MARINES: In Jacksonville, North Carolina, marines are dispatched from Camp Lejeune to assist fire fighters in extinguishing a major fire in the downtown district.

December 10
AVIATION: The Ryan X-13 Vertijet flies for the first time as a conventional aircraft; it is designed to rise vertically off the ground using its jet engine.

December 13
MARINES: The new Landing Force Bulletin Number 17 announces that, very soon, advanced echelons of an invading amphibious force will be transported entirely by helicopters.

December 25–27
MARINES: In Northern California, helicopters of HMR-152 and 352 are dispatched from El Toro to provide relief and medical supplies to flood victims.

December 31
MARINES: In Washington, D.C., General Randolph M. Pate is appointed the 21st Marine Corps Commandant to replace retiring general Lemuel C. Shepherd.

1956

January 1
AVIATION: The Strategic Air Command (SAC) accepts its 1,000th Boeing B-47 Stratojet, now the mainstay of its bomber fleet.

January 10
NAVAL: At New London, Connecticut, the U.S. Navy establishes its first school for nuclear propulsion.

January 17
AVIATION: In Washington, D.C., the Department of Defense reveals that its semi-automated ground environment (SAGE) has been activated. This is an automated,

electronic air defense system employing telephone lines to transmit information to large computers housed at combat centers.

January 31

MARINES: On Halawa Heights, Oahu, Hawaii, Headquarters, Fleet Marine Force Pacific (FMFPAC) opens its new headquarters at Camp H. M. Smith.

February 1

MILITARY: The U.S. Army initiates its Army Ballistic Missile Agency at the Redstone Arsenal, Huntsville, Alabama, for the purpose of developing the new Thor and Jupiter intermediate-range ballistic missiles. However, in light of public safety concerns, Secretary of Defense Charles Wilson restricts the range of all testing to only 200 miles.

February 17

AVIATION: At Edwards Air Force Base, California, the first production Lockheed F-104 Starfighter completes its maiden flight.

March 9

AVIATION: Over Seattle, Washington, the first B-52C jet bomber performs its maiden flight; it differs from earlier models in possessing large underwing fuel tanks.

March 12

AVIATION: Attack squadron VA-83, flying Chance Vought F7U Cutlass fighters on the carrier *Intrepid,* becomes the first missile-equipped navy squadron. These aircraft are equipped with early versions of the Sparrow radar-guided, air-to-air missile.

March 16

NAVAL: In Annapolis, Maryland, Rear Admiral W. R. Smedberg III gains appointment as the 39th superintendent of the U.S. Naval Academy.

March 28

AVIATION: Airman D. F. Smith establishes a record, of sorts, in remaining sealed in the air force space cabin simulator for 24 hours.

April 8

MILITARY: During a night exercise in a swamp, six recruits from Platoon 71, Company A, 3rd Recruit Training Battalion, drown in Ribbon Creek near Parris Island, South Carolina. Staff Sergeant Matthew C. McKeon is charged with negligent homicide.

April 23

AVIATION: The prototype Douglas XC-133 flies for the first time. This very large aircraft enters service as the C-133 Cargomaster, of which 50 are built over the ensuing two years to air transport ballistic missiles.

May 1

MARINES: In response to the recent recruit fatalities at Ribbon Creek, Commandant General Randolph M. Pate orders that training commands at Parris Island, South Carolina, and Camp Pendleton, California, be separated from base commands and assigned to brigadier generals. The new Inspector General of Recruit Training is also established.

May 7
AVIATION: On the Georges Bank, 100 miles off the Cape Cod coast, Massachusetts, the air force activates its "Texas Tower" early warning radar platform.

May 14–18
MARINES: At Twenty-Nine Palms, California, Marines from Camp Pendleton conduct military exercises involving simulated atomic weapons.

May 21
AVIATION: Operation Redwing takes places as a B-52 bomber commanded by Major David Crichlow test drops the first air-delivered hydrogen bomb over Bikini Atoll; the weapon is released from an altitude of 50,000 feet.

May 22
NAVAL: In Washington, D.C., the secretary of the navy and the commandant, Marine Corps sign a five-year plan to construct five helicopter landing ships (LPH). They are to be built by converting existing escort carriers to that role.

May 31
AVIATION: At Turner Air Force Base, Georgia, the 4080th Strategic Reconnaissance Wing receives its first, high-altitude RB-57D Canberra jet.

June 4
AVIATION: Over Seattle, Washington, the new B-52D jet bomber performs its maiden flight. It becomes a major production variant.

June 4–December 1
MARINES: At Quantico, Virginia, the Organization and Composition Board convenes to consider organizational changes within the Fleet Marine Force (FMF).

June 12
MILITARY: In a ceremony at Independence Hall, Philadelphia, presided over by President Dwight D. Eisenhower, the U.S. Army adopts its first official flag in 181 years.

June 22
AVIATION: The Air Force Reserve commences Operation Sixteen Tons in the Caribbean; this is the first sustained cargo exercise ever conducted by these forces.

July 4
AVIATION: The secret Lockheed U-2 spy plane begins the first overflight of Soviet territory by photographing Minsk, Leningrad, and the Baltic region before returning to its base at Wiesbaden, West Germany.

July 5
AVIATION: The 1st Marine Aviation Wing (1st MAW) relocates permanently from Korea to Japan.

July 15
AVIATION: At Torrejón, Spain, the Sixteenth Air Force is activated.

July 18
AVIATION: At Renton, Washington, the final Boeing KC-97G aerial tanker is constructed.

1956

The TR-1 is an advanced, modern version of the famous U-2 "Dragon Lady"
(*National Archives*)

July 20
NAVAL: The *Thetis Bay* is commissioned into active service; this is the navy's first amphibious assault ship, although it never engages in any landings prior to being decommissioned in 1964. It was formerly an escort carrier and can carry 20 Sikorsky HRS helicopters along with a battalion of marines.

July 23
AVIATION: Over Edwards Air Force Base, California, the Bell X-2 rocket plane flown by Lieutenant Colonel Frank K. Everest reaches at altitude of 75,000 feet at 1,900 miles per hour. This is a new world speed record.

August 2
MILITARY: Albert Woolson, the oldest surviving Union soldier of the Civil War, dies at the age of 109. He had served as a drummer boy in the 1st Minnesota Heavy Artillery.

August 4
MARINES: At Parris Island, South Carolina, Staff Sergeant Matthew C. McKeon is convicted of negligent homicide for the death of six recruits during night maneuvers at Ribbon Creek.

August 14
MILITARY: Over Fort Rucker, Alabama, the army conducts its first aerial refueling between an H-21 helicopter and a fixed wing aircraft.

August 21
AVIATION: Over the Naval Ordnance Test Station, China Lake, California, an F8U Crusader piloted by Commander Robert W. Windsor establishes a new national speed record of 1,015.428 miles per hour. Crusaders are the first jet aircraft to routinely operate at such high rates of speed.

August 22
AVIATION: A Japan-based Martin P4M-1Q Mercator of VQ-1 is attacked by Chinese fighters 32 miles off the coast of Wenchow and shot down with a loss of all 16 crewmen.

August 23–24
AVIATION: An Army H-21 Chickasaw helicopter with a crew of five men conducts the first transcontinental flight for this type of aircraft by flying nonstop from San Diego, California, to Washington, D.C., and covering 2,610 miles in 37 hours.

August 27
AVIATION: At Edwards Air Force Base, California, the first static engine test of the new Thor rocket is run by the Flight Test Center.

August 31
AVIATION: At Renton, Washington, the first production model Boeing KC-135 aerial tanker performs its maiden flight.

September 7
AVIATION: Over Edwards Air Force Base, California, the Bell X-2 rocket research aircraft flown by Captain Iven C. Kincheloe reaches an altitude of 126,000 feet. This is the first manned flight exceeding the 100,000 foot-mark and earns Kincheloe the Mackay Trophy.

September 15
AVIATION: At Hahn Air Base, Germany, the 701st Tactical Missile Wing (TMW) is activated as part of the Twelfth Air Force. This is the first such unit in the air force and will be equipped with Matador tactical missiles.

September 20
AVIATION: At Cape Canaveral, Florida, the first Jupiter C, three-stage missile, is successfully launched. It reaches 680 miles in altitude and splashes down 3,300 miles away.

September 21
MILITARY: At Fort Campbell, Kentucky, the 101st Airborne Division becomes the first unit to adopt the new Pentomic structure. This replaces the traditional triangular organization of three regiments with five battle groups, each slightly larger than a battalion. Although all infantry and airborne divisions adopt this scheme, there are no changes made to current armor formations.

September 27
AVIATION: Over Edwards Air Force Base, California, a Bell X-2 flown by Captain Milburn G. Apt manages to exceed Mach 3.2-2,094 miles per hour–then loses control; Apt is killed after crashing.

October 11
AVIATION: Over the Atlantic, a Douglas R6D Skymaster of VR-6 crashes, killing all 59 passengers and crewmen onboard.

October 23
MILITARY: The brutal Soviet response to the Hungarian uprising results in the 6th Armored Cavalry Regiment being placed on alert along the West German–East German border.

October 26
AVIATION: At Fort Worth, Texas, the prototype Bell XH-40 helicopter performs its maiden flight. It enters into production as the UH-1 Iroquois and renders exceptional service during the Vietnam War.

1956

October 29
NAVAL: In response to the Suez Crisis in Egypt, the Sixth Fleet begins evacuating 2,213 people from the Sinai Peninsula, Israel, and Syria.
MARINES: At Port Lyautey, Morocco, a company from the 2nd Battalion, 2nd Marines is flown in to reinforce the Naval Air Station there during increasing tensions between Moroccans and French authorities.

October 30
MARINES: In the wake of the latest round of fighting between Egyptians and Israelis, the 3rd Battalion, 2nd Marines is reinforced and placed on alert for possible landings in the eastern Mediterranean.

October 31
AVIATION: Lieutenant Commander Conrad Shinn lands his Douglas R4D Skytrain at the South Pole, becoming the first to visit that area since 1912, when British Royal Navy captain Robert F. Scott arrived. Among the passengers are Rear Admiral G. J. Dufek, commander of Naval Support Force Antarctic, and seven of his officers.

November 1
NAVAL: In Alexandria, Egypt, vessels of the Sixth Fleet and marines help evacuate 1,500 Americans and other foreign nationals; at this time British and French forces are attacking Egypt in retaliation for its nationalization of the Suez Canal.

November 6
AVIATION: At Cape Canaveral, Florida, a Navaho ramjet missile is launched for the first time and breaks up 30 seconds into its flight.

November 11
AVIATION: At Fort Worth, Texas, the Convair XB-58, the world's first supersonic jet bomber, is flown for the first time and eventually goes into production as the B-58 Hustler. It incorporates the "area rule," giving it a pinched-in fuselage, making such high-speed flight possible.
MARINES: On Okinawa, the 3rd Battalion, 3rd Marines sails for Port Lyautey, Morocco, to bolster American facilities there during heightened tensions caused by the ongoing Suez Crisis. A cease-fire takes place while they are en route and the marines are diverted to a goodwill tour of Asia.

November 16
AVIATION: Parts of Camp Cooke, California, are transferred to the air force by the Department of Defense. This is the future site of Vandenberg Air Force Base and the nation's first intercontinental ballistic missile base.

November 26
AVIATION: In Washington, D.C., Secretary of Defense Charles E. Wilson assigns operational jurisdiction over all long-range missiles to the air force. Within four years, this authority will have to be shared, however, once the navy perfects its Polaris submarine-launched missiles.

November 30
AVIATION: The jet-propelled Martin TM-61 Matador becomes operational, being the first tactical guided missile deployed by the U.S. Air Force. It possesses a speed of 650 miles per hour and can reach an altitude of 35,000 feet.

1956

December 1
MILITARY: In a sign of the times, the army deactivates its last mules and carrier pigeons for transport and communication purposes, respectively.

December 3
AVIATION: The navy receives permission to withdraw from the liquid-fueled Jupiter missile project in seeking to concentrate its efforts on the new Polaris, solid-fuel ballistic missile program. This weapon is designed specifically for use in submarines.

NAVAL: The destroyer *Gyatt* becomes the first vessel of its class to be equipped with Terrier antiaircraft missiles. This vessel is also fitted with a Denny-Brown stabilization system, including two 45-square-foot retractable fins fitted amidships below the waterline. This device greatly reduces pitching and rolling in heavy seas.

December 8
AVIATION: The Special Projects Office receives authorization to begin development of the navy's first generation of solid-fuel guided missiles for use in ballistic submarines. They emerge in 1960 as the Polaris.

December 9
AVIATION: The 463rd Troop Carrier Wing receives its first C-130 Hercules transport aircraft. A wonderfully versatile aircraft, it can carry a 25-ton cargo or 92 fully equipped troops over 2,500 miles, as well as operate off primitive 4,000-foot airstrips.

December 11
AVIATION: In light of the failed Hungarian revolt, the Military Transport Service (MATS) commences Operation Safe Haven to transport 10,000 refugees from West Germany to the United States. The entire operation lasts seven months.

December 18
AVIATION: Unable to compromise between the competing Jupiter and Polaris ballistic missile programs, the Joint Army-Navy Missile Committee disbands.

December 19
AVIATION: The Special Projects Office under Admiral William F. Raborn is accorded the highest priority in designing and constructing the new Polaris, submarine-launched, ballistic missile.

December 21
AVIATION: At the Air Research and Development Command, Dayton, Ohio, Major Arnold I. Beck endures conditions equivalent to those at 198,770 feet in a simulated altitude chamber.

December 26
AVIATION: Over Edwards Air Force Base, California, the Convair YF-106 performs its maiden flight. It enters service as the F-106 Delta Dagger and serves as a supersonic bomber interceptor over the next three decades.

December 31
AVIATION: HMR squadrons are redesignated Marine Light Helicopter Squadrons HMR (L) as larger, "medium" helicopters are slated to be deployed soon.

1957

January
AVIATION: The Marine Corps's first Douglas A-4 Skyhawk light jet bombers are assigned to VMA-224; these render exceptional service during the Vietnam War years.

January 7
MARINES: In Washington, D.C., the Organization and Composition Board (or Hogaboom Board) makes its final recommendations to Commandant General Randolph M. Pate. They include adding a fourth rifle company to each infantry battalion, transferring the tank battalion to the Fleet Marine Force, and adding a battalion of 45 Ontos antitank tracked vehicles (each mounting six 105mm recoilless rifles). A new M-series table of organization, meant to facilitate helicopter transportability of a division, is also advocated. The commandant concurs with the suggestions and most are implemented by the fall of 1958.

January 12
AVIATION: At New River, North Carolina, the first Marine Corps medium helicopter squadron is formed. HMR(M)-461 is equipped with new Sikorsky HR2S-1 (CH-37) helicopters capable of carrying 23 marines or 8,000 pounds of cargo at 100 knots. This is also the largest helicopter in American service.

January 16–18
AVIATION: The B-52 *Lucky Lady II,* commanded by Major General Archie J. Olds, 93rd Bombardment Wing, makes the first around-the-world flight by a jet aircraft. The aircraft covers 24,325 miles in 45 hours, 19 minutes, and requires three aerial refuelings. Consequently, the crewmen all receive the Distinguished Flying Cross while their unit is awarded a Mackay Trophy. Operation Power Flite also demonstrates to the Soviets that the U.S. Air Force can deploy its assets quickly to any point on the globe.

January 25
AVIATION: The first test launch of the air force's Thor intermediate-range ballistic missile ends in failure; the first successful launch occurs in August.

January 28
MILITARY: Secretary of Defense Charles E. Wilson addresses the House Armed Services Committee and declares that the National Guard harbored draft dodgers throughout the Korean War.

February 1
MARINES: In Southern California, the Twenty-Nine Palms desert facility is configured as a Marine Corps base.

February 8
AVIATION: Chief of Naval Operations Admiral Arleigh Burke, unwilling to brook further delays, reiterates a January 1965 deadline for deploying solid-fuel, submarine-based missiles with a 1,500-mile range.

February 13
AVIATION: The Marine Corps receives its first Sikorsky HUS-1 utility helicopters, capable for hauling 12 marines or 6,000 pounds of cargo at 90 knots.

February 14
MARINES: In the Pacific, the 3rd Marine and helicopter squadron HMR-162 are positioned 550 miles north of Sumatra, Indonesia, in case a violent rebellion against the government requires the evacuation of American citizens.

February 18
AVIATION: At Harvard University, Cambridge, Massachusetts, the Aviation Health and Safety Center receives $250,000 from the Guggenheim Foundation.

March 4–15
AVIATION: The airship ZPG-2 under Commander Jack R. Hunt makes a record endurance flight by flying from the United States to the African coast and back in 264 hours.

March 10
AVIATION: The NACA Lewis Laboratory commences research on an ion engine for use in outer space. This entails emitting ions, or charged particles, as exhaust, which reach 30 kilometers per second and theoretically can propel a vehicle through the vacuum of space.

March 17
AVIATION: At Cape Canaveral, Florida, the Navy launches its first satellite, *Vanguard*, weighing in at three and-a-half pounds.
• In the Philippines, Marine helicopters of HMR(L)-162 assist in search and rescue operations after the aircraft carrying President Ramon Magsaysay crashes while on a flight from Cebu to Manila.

March 21
AVIATION: A Douglas A3D Skywarrior piloted by Commander Dale Cox establishes an east-to-west continental speed record followed by a west-to-east one between New York and Los Angeles, California, and back.

March 27
AVIATION: The McDonnell F-101B Voodoo, a two-seater version of the fighter interceptor, performs its maiden flight.

March 30
NAVAL: The *Seawolf*, America's second nuclear-powered submarine, is commissioned at Groton, Connecticut.

April 1
AVIATION: In order to concentrate on its bombing functions, the Strategic Air Command (SAC) begins turning over the first of its seven fighter wings to the Tactical Air Command (TAC).
NAVAL: In Washington, D.C., Thomas G. Gates gains appointment as the 54th secretary of the navy.

April 11
AVIATION: The Ryan X-13 Vertijet vertical takeoff and landing (VTOL) aircraft flies for the first time in its intended mode by rising straight off the ground, flying in level flight, and then landing vertically.

April 19
AVIATION: At Cape Canaveral, Florida, the Douglas Thor (SM-75) intermediate-range ballistic missile (IRBM) is successfully launched but ends up being destroyed by the range safety officer in midflight.

April 29
MILITARY: At Fort Belvoir, Virginia, the army's first nuclear reactor is dedicated by Secretary of the Army William M. Bruckner. This device, SM1, becomes the first American reactor providing power to an electrical grid.

May 1
MILITARY: The M1 semi-automatic rifle, which has been a standard-issue weapon since 1939, is replaced by the M14 automatic/semi-automatic rifle. This new weapon dispenses with traditional .30-caliber bullets and is chambered to fire the standard NATO 7.62mm round.

May 6
AVIATION: In Washington, D.C., William M. Holaday becomes Department of Defense special assistant for guided missiles.

May 15–July 5
MARINES: At Desert Rock, Nevada, the 4th Provisional Marine Brigades participate in Operation Plumbbob, an atomic exercise.

May 16
NAVAL: The world's third nuclear-powered submarine, the *Skate*, is launched at Groton, Connecticut.

May 23
MARINES: Sergeant Major Wilbur Bestwick becomes the first sergeant major of the Marine Corps and serves as the commandant's senior enlisted adviser.

May 31
AVIATION: At Cape Canaveral, Florida, the army-developed Jupiter intermediate-range ballistic missile (IRBM) makes its first successful test flight of 1,500 miles at an altitude of 300 miles.

June 1
MARINES: At Rota, Spain, as a sign of increasing commitments to the Mediterranean region, a Marine Barracks is established.

June 2
AVIATION: Over Minnesota, the balloon *Man High 1* flown by Captain Joseph W. Kittinger reaches an altitude of 96,000 feet for two hours and establishes a new world record for lighter-than-air aircraft. This is also the first solo balloon flight to reach the stratosphere

June 11
AVIATION: At Laughlin, Texas, the 4080th Strategic Reconnaissance Wing receives its first operational U-2 spyplane. It is capable of flying 10-hour missions at extremely high altitude.

June 19
MARINES: At Camp Pendleton, California, the 1st Force Reconnaissance Company is created from the older 1st Amphibious Reconnaissance Company.

1957

June 28
AVIATION: At Castle Air Force Base, California, the 93rd Refueling Squadron receives its first operational Boeing KC-135 Stratotanker. Because it is capable of high-speed flight, refueling large jet bombers can be accomplished with less time and greater safety.

June 30
MARINES: At this juncture, Marine Corps manpower stands at 17,434 officers and 183,427 enlisted men.

July 1
AVIATION: In Washington, D.C., General Thomas D. White is appointed the air force chief of staff.
• At Cook (Vandenberg) Air Force Base, California, the 704th Strategic Missile Wing (SMW), armed with Northrop Snark missiles, becomes the first intercontinental ballistic missile wing.
• In Tokyo, Japan, the Far East Air Forces (FEAF) is redesignated the Pacific Air Command (PACAF) and its headquarters are transferred to Hickham Air Force Base, Hawaii.

July 10
AVIATION: The super-sleek and futuristic Convair B-58 Hustler is unveiled to the public for the first time.

July 13
AVIATION: In Washington, D.C., President Dwight D. Eisenhower becomes the first chief executive to fly in a helicopter, an air force Bell UH-13J.
• Marine Corps major John H. Glenn sets a new transcontinental speed record of three hours, 23 minutes, eight seconds flying in a Chance Vought F8U Crusader from Los Alamitos, California, to Floyd Bennet Field, New York; he averages 760 miles per hour.
MILITARY: Secretary of Defense Charles E. Wilson announces his intention to cut the armed forces by 100,000 men by year's end.

July 19
AVIATION: Over Yucca Flats, Nevada, a nuclear-tipped Douglas MB-1 Genie missile is fired for the first time by an F-89J Scorpion. This weapon is intended to break up or destroy Soviet bomber formations attacking the United States.

July 31
AVIATION: The chain of distant early warning (DEW) radars strung across the Arctic Circle becomes operational and is christened the DEW Line.

August 1
AVIATION: The United States and Canada formally establish the North American Air Defense Command (NORAD) with joint responsibilities for air-defense missions.

August 12
AVIATION: On the carrier *Antietam*, Lieutenant Commander Don Walker makes the first "hands-off" landing on a flight deck in an F3D Skyknight, relying solely upon the automated landing system installed on that vessel.

1957

Marines: In Washington, D.C., the secretary of the navy orders a reduction in Marine Corps personnel to 175,000 men and women of all ranks. Budget constraints also impose similar cutbacks on the navy.

August 15

Military: In Washington, D.C., General Nathan F. Twining gains appointment as the chairman of the Joint Chiefs of Staff (JCS); he is the first air force officer so honored.

August 19–20

Aviation: Over Crosby, Minnesota, Major David G. Simon sets a new balloon altitude record of 101,486 feet in *Man High II,* which places him on the very edge of space. His flight lasts 32 hours and terminates at Elm Lake, South Dakota.

August 20

Aviation: At Morehead City, North Carolina, helicopters of HMR(L)-261 and HMR(L)-262 accompany the 6th Marines on a deployment with the Sixth Fleet. This is the first time helicopters have been committed to vessels afloat.

September 3

Aviation: The *Study of the Feasibility of a Hypersonic Research Plane* is prepared by NACA for the air force.

September 4

Aviation: The Lockheed CL-329 performs its maiden flight; it enters the service with the Military Air Transport Service (MATS) as the C-140 Jetsar for testing navigation aids and communication equipment.

September 20

Aviation: In Washington, D.C., U.S. Air Force chief of staff Thomas D. White reveals the existence of radar units capable of detecting incoming ICBMs up to 3,000 miles away.
• At Cape Canaveral, Florida, a Thor intermediate-range ballistic missile (IRBM) is successfully launched.

September 22

Marines: At Saros, Turkey, the 6th Marines, Marine Air Group 26 (MAG-26), VMF-312, and the 2nd Amphibious Reconnaissance Company conduct landing exercises.

September 24

Military: In Little Rock, Arkansas, National Guard Troops and units of the 101st Airborne Division are ordered by President Dwight D. Eisenhower to assist desegregation efforts at the city's Central High School.

October 1

Aviation: At Cape Canaveral, Florida, air force technicians test fire a Northrop Snark missile for the first time.

October 4

Aviation: The Soviets launch *Sputnik I,* Earth's first artificial satellite, and the launch resonates throughout the United States like a technological Pearl Harbor. The new Space Age has arrived and the U.S. government responds by calling for

☆ ☆ ☆ ☆ ☆ ☆ ☆ ☆ ☆ ☆ ☆ ☆ ☆ ☆

Glenn, John H. (1921–)

Marine Corps officer, astronaut

John Herschel Glenn, Jr. was born in Cambridge, Ohio, on July 18, 1921, the son of a plumber. He was raised in nearby New Concord and attended Muskingum College to study chemical engineering, but left before graduating to undergo naval aviation training for service in World War II. By March 1943 Glenn was commissioned a lieutenant in the Marine Corps Reserve and flew F4U Corsairs with VMO-155 in the Pacific; he completed 59 missions, winning two Distinguished Flying Crosses and 10 Air Medals. After the war, he rose to captain and returned to the United States to serve as a flight instructor. In 1952 Glenn was sent to Korea to fly F9F Panthers with VMF-311, although toward the end of that conflict he served as an exchange pilot with the U.S. Air Force, switched to F-86 Sabres, and downed two MiG-15s. Glenn consequently received two additional Distinguished Flying Crosses and eight more air medals. He then rose to major in 1953 and was assigned to the navy's Patuxent River test school as a test pilot. As a test pilot, he completed the first supersonic, transcontinental flight in an F8U Crusader on July 16, 1957, crossing the country in only three hours, 23 minutes. He won his fifth Distinguished Flying Cross, became a lieutenant colonel, and then gained entry into Project Mercury, which aimed to put an American in orbit. Glenn trained intensely for three years and, on February 20, 1963, he piloted his *Friendship 7* space capsule for three orbits around the globe at an altitude of 185 miles and for a distance of 81,000 miles. Glenn became a national hero and received ticker-tape parades in both New York and Washington, D.C.

It was President John F. Kennedy who is believed to have convinced Glenn to run for public office. Glenn resigned from the astronaut program in 1964 and declared his candidacy for the U.S. Senate seat in Ohio, but his campaign was sidelined by a severe per-

greater concentration on science and mathematics courses in the public school system.

October 9
NAVAL: In Washington, D.C., Neil H. McElroy gains appointment as the sixth secretary of defense.

October 11
AVIATION: At Cape Canaveral, Florida, the second successful launching of a Thor intermediate-range ballistic missile is accomplished. The vehicle travels 2,000 miles down range and splashes into the Atlantic Ocean.

October 16
AVIATION: The air force launches an Aerobee research rocket to an altitude of 35 miles, whereupon its nose cone separates and coasts a further 54 miles into the atmosphere. At that juncture, the shaped charges it carries forces pellets into

sonal injury. He worked as a business executive until 1970, when he lost a Democratic primary for the Senate to Howard Metzenbaum. It was not until 1974 that Glenn was elected to office as Ohio's junior senator, and he served on the Foreign Relations and Governmental Affairs Committees. Glenn was a moderate Democrat, conservative on defense matters and liberal on labor and social issues. In 1984 he declared his candidacy for the presidency but he was defeated by the leading contender, Vice President Walter Mondale. He subsequently gained reelection to Congress in 1992. Glenn was launched into space a second time on October 29, 1998, 35 years after his initial flight, as a member of the crew of the space shuttle *Discovery*. Although his flight was dismissed in political circles as a public relations stunt, the 77-year-old Glenn, the oldest person ever to fly in space, performed useful service researching the effects of weightlessness on the aged. He retired from public life in 1998 with little fanfare although earlier, in 1989, actor Ed Harris portrayed him in the popular movie *The Right Stuff*. He currently

Colonel John H. Glenn, Jr. (USMC) (*U.S. Marine Corps*)

holds an adjunct professorship at Ohio State University in the Department of Political Science.

space at speeds of 33,000 per hour, well past escape velocity for Earth's gravity. These are the first man-made objects in outer space.

MARINES: At Valencia, Spain, helicopters of HMR(L)-262, flying from the carrier *Lake Champlain*, assist flood victims and deliver medical supplies.

October 22

AVIATION: At Eniwetok, Operation Far Side unfolds as a four-stage rocket is carried aloft by a large balloon to 100,000 feet, launches at high altitude, and reaches 2,700 miles into outer space. This is an attempt by the Air Force Office of Scientific Research to collect data on cosmic rays from 4,000 miles up.

October 24

AVIATION: A new proposal is submitted by the Air Force Research and Development Command, which calls for a hypersonic glide rocket weapon system designated WS464L. This is the genesis of the Dyna-Soar vehicle.

November 13
AVIATION: U.S. Air Force Vice Chief of Staff general Curtis E. LeMay establishes two flight records while piloting a KC-135 Stratotanker. The first is a nonstop distance record of 6,350 miles flown between Westover Air Force Base, Massachusetts, to Buenos Aires, Argentina. The second is between Buenos Aires and Washington, D.C., a 5,200-mile trip covered in 11 hours and five minutes. LeMay is awarded the Distinguished Flying Cross after landing.

November 21
AVIATION: U.S. Air Force authorities select Francis E. Warren Air Force Base, Wyoming, as the site of the first intercontinental ballistic missile (ICBM) base. Said missiles are to be housed underground in silos until launched.
• Retired general James H. Doolittle assembles a special committee on space technology for NACA.

November 25
AVIATION: Noted nuclear physicist Dr. Edward Teller testifies before the Senate Preparedness Committee that strengthening nuclear-armed jet bomber forces is presently the best deterrent against Soviet attack.

November 27
AVIATION: In Washington, D.C., the government elects to proceed with production of the Thor and Jupiter intermediate-range ballistic missiles (IRBM). Responsibility for operating weapons will be the exclusive domain of the air force.
• Operation Sun Run unfolds as three RF101C Voodoos of the 363rd Tactical Reconnaissance Wing establish three transcontinental speed records. They achieve this through careful planning and refueling from KC-135 tankers at high altitude.

November 29
AVIATION: In Washington, D.C., U.S. Air Force Chief of Staff Thomas D. White assigns control of all Thor and Jupiter missiles to the Strategic Air Command (SAC), along with the 1st Missile Division. The Air Force Depot at San Bernadino, California, will also support continuing missile programs.

December
AVIATION: The first Marine Corps F8U Crusader jet fighters are delivered to VMF (AW)-122.

December 1
MARINES: At Headquarters Marine Corps, duties of the assistant commandant and chief of staff are divided into two sections headed up by their own lieutenant general.

December 6
SCIENCE: The navy's *Vanguard*, America's first space rocket, explodes humiliatingly on its launching pad at Cape Canaveral, Florida.

December 9
AVIATION: In Washington, D.C., Secretary of Defense Neil H. McElroy accelerates the deadline for deploying new Polaris submarine-launched ballistic missiles

to 1960. The new class of vessel intended to carry them have also been designed and are awaiting construction.

December 12
AVIATION: Major Adrian E. Drew sets a new jet speed record of 1,207.6 miles per hour while flying a McDonnell F-101A Voodoo jet fighter over the Mojave Desert, California.

December 15
AVIATION: At Patrick Air Force Base, Florida, the air force activates the 556th Strategic Missile Squadron; it is the first unit armed with Northrop Snark (SM-62) missiles.

December 17
MILITARY: A prototype of the Atlas intercontinental ballistic missile (ICBM) is successfully tested by the air force and splashes 500 miles down range.

December 18
MARINES: At Okinawa, the 3rd Marines and helicopters of HMR(L)-162 sail for Indonesia in the event that continuing civil violence against the government requires evacuating American citizens.

December 19
AVIATION: The air force successfully tests a Thor intermediate-range ballistic missile; this is also the first fully guided flight employing its own inertial guidance system.

December 23
AVIATION: The air force contracts with North American aviation to construct a supersonic, intercontinental jet bomber; this is the genesis of the XB-40 Valkyrie.
NAVAL: The nuclear-powered submarine *Skate* is commissioned. It is the first such vessel in this class of new warship.

December 24
AVIATION: An air force RB-57D Canberra conducting a top-secret reconnaissance spy flight is intercepted over the Black Sea by Soviet fighters and shot down.

December 26
AVIATION: Helicopters of HMR(L)-162, stored on the carrier *Princeton*, are diverted to Ceylon to assist victims of recent flooding.

December 28
AVIATION: A Cessna YH-41 helicopter reaches a record altitude of 30,335 feet.

December 31
MARINES: At Iwakuni, Japan, the Naval Air Station is transformed into a Marine Corps base.

1958

January
MILITARY: Lieutenant James M. Gavin, angered by what he deems President Dwight D. Eisenhower's neglect of the army through his nuclear-oriented "New Look" policy, resigns from the service on the cusp of being promoted to full general.

Furthermore, he articulates his critique of American military weakness in the book *War and Peace in the Space Age.*

NAVAL: Construction of the first three Polaris fleet ballistic submarines commences. The first vessel, *George Washington,* was originally a *Scorpion*-class nuclear-powered attack submarine, which was cut in half with a 130-foot long midsection for carrying missiles.

January 1–15

AVIATION: At Cooke (Vandenberg) Air Force Base, California, the 672nd Strategic Missile Squadron begins training to handle and deploy the Thor intermediate-range ballistic missile (IRBM).

January 3

AVIATION: Two squadrons of intermediate-range ballistic missiles (IRBM) are formed by the Strategic Air Command (SAC) as part of air force nuclear deterrence under General Curtis E. LeMay.

Gavin, James M.   (1907–1990)

Army general

James Maurice Gavin was born in Brooklyn, New York, on March 22, 1907, and he enlisted as a private in April 1924. Intent upon making a career in of the military, he passed entrance exams to the U.S. Military Academy at West Point, and he was commissioned a second lieutenant in 1929. Gavin, an excellent soldier, capably performed routine duties over the next decade, although his career changed dramatically in 1940 when he decided to become a paratrooper. After attending the new jump school at Fort Benning, Georgia, he became a colonel of the 505th Parachute Infantry Regiment, 82nd Airborne Division, by 1942. Gavin jumped with his units into hazardous locations over Sicily and Anzio in Italy and Normandy, France, and invariably distinguished himself in combat. At one point, Gavin seized a bazooka and destroyed a German tank at point-blank range to demonstrate the relative weakness of American antitank weapons. In light of his splendid combat reputation, the aggressive, hard-hitting Gavin replaced Major General Matthew Ridgway as commander of the 82nd Airborne in August 1944, aged but 37 years. Gavin went on to further distinguish himself during the failed Operation Market Garden in the Netherlands, then helped spearhead the final drive in Germany itself. Under his command, the 82nd Airborne emerged as one of the nation's premier fighting units and, in May 1945, it was selected to lead the four-mile-long victory parade through New York City.

After the war, Gavin accepted several high-level command positions in Western Europe, and, in 1954, he served as chief of staff to the Joint Chiefs of Staff in Washington, D.C. In March 1955 he became the youngest lieutenant general in American history and served as chief of research and development for new mobile forces, including helicopters. However, Gavin

January 7
MILITARY: President Dwight D. Eisenhower asks the Democratic majority in Congress for $1.3 billion dollars for missile and air defense research.

January 15
AVIATION: The 475th Air Defense Missile Wing is activated to develop and train with the new Bomarc supersonic intercept missile; this guided, supersonic weapon possesses a range of 450 nautical miles.

January 16
MARINES: At Camp Hansen, Okinawa, the 3rd Antitank Battalion is the first unit to receive the new Ontos vehicles.

January 21
MARINES: A spate of civil violence brought on by the overthrow of dictator Pérez Jiménez in Venezuela leads to a company of marines deployed on the cruiser *Des Moines,* which hovers off the coast for a week.

grew disillusioned with President Dwight D. Eisenhower's "New Look" policy, which emphasized nuclear arms at the expense of conventional forces. This approach, or so he believed, restricted the United States to using nuclear weapons in an age of mounting guerrilla warfare. Gavin was slated for promotion to full general in 1958 but, rather than uphold a policy he opposed, he resigned from the army and published the book *War and Peace in the Space Age* to protest administration strategy. He held several high-level corporate positions until 1962, when President John F. Kennedy appointed him ambassador to France. He also became a vocal critic of America's increasing involvement in Vietnam. He promulgated the "enclave plan," which would have restricted American forces to the defense of a few key regions while negotiating a political settlement with the Communists. Gavin continued penning various treatises on national defense until his death in Baltimore, Maryland, on February 23, 1990. The wiry, athletic general,

Major General James M. Gavin *(U.S. Army Military History Institute)*

known to the troops as "Slim Jim," was the most celebrated paratroop commander of his day.

1958

January 25
Marines: In Japan, construction of Camp Futema begins to house Marine Air Group 16 (MAG-16), presently deployed at Oppama.

January 28
Marines: At Vieques, Puerto Rico, the amphibious exercise PHIBTRAEX 1-58 commences and lasts through March 17.

January 29
Aviation: In Washington, D.C., the Department of Defense announces its intention to create the National Pacific Missile Range at Point Magu, California. This facility will serve as part of the Naval Air Missile Test range already extant.

January 31
Aviation: At Cape Canaveral, Florida, the army successfully launches *Explorer I,* the nation's first satellite, on top a Jupiter C launch vehicle. The device is only 80 inches long, six inches in diameter, and 30.8 pounds in weight.

February 1
Aviation: At Francis E. Warren Air Force Base, Wyoming, the 706th Strategic Missile Wing, armed with new Atlas missiles, is activated by the Strategic Air Command (SAC).

February 4
Naval: At Newport News, Virginia, the keel of the *Enterprise,* the world's first nuclear-powered aircraft carrier, is laid.

February 7
Aviation: In Washington, D.C., the Defense Department founds the Advanced Research Projects Agency (ARPA) to better promote and coordinate space exploration.

February 8
Aviation: In order to provide a viable, early warning system against ballistic missile attacks, the air force contracts with the RCA Corporation to manage all existing communications facilities such as the DEW Line and the SAGE system.

February 11
Marines: In the Philippines, Marine units conduct amphibious exercise PHIBLEX 58M, which lasts until March 13.

February 14
Marines: In Pennsylvania, the onset of blizzard conditions results in the 6th Truck Company deploying from Scranton and assisting motorists stranded along the Pennsylvania Turnpike.

February 18
Aviation: At Tullahoma, Tennessee, air force scientists at the Arnold Research Development Center create a wind tunnel airflow of 32,400 miles per hour lasting for one-tenth of a second.

February 27
Aviation: With the tactical shortcomings of liquid-fueled rockets glaringly apparent, a plan to build a 5,000-mile-range solid fuel ballistic weapon is approved

by Missile Director William M. Holaday. This is the genesis of the Minuteman missile.

February 28
SCIENCE: A Thor/Agena rocket lifts *Discoverer 1,* the world's first photo reconnaissance satellite, into orbit.

March 4
AVIATION: Secretary of the Air Force James H. Douglas revokes the court-martial verdict against General William "Billy" Mitchell rendered 37 years earlier, declaring that his beliefs in air power have been vindicated.

March 5
NAVAL: The nuclear submarine *Skate* crosses the Atlantic Ocean in only eight days, 11 hours, before berthing at Plymouth, England.

March 7
NAVAL: The *Grayback,* the navy's first nuclear ballistic missile submarine, is commissioned. It had been designed from the onset to carry a complement of Regulus II nuclear-tipped missiles that are launched while surfaced. However, the concept is quickly abandoned in favor of the new Polaris firing vessels.

March 9
MARINES: In light of continuing violence in Indonesia, ships of the Seventh Fleet are bolstered by the arrival of Company C, 1st Battalion, 3rd Marines, VMA-332, and helicopters of HMR(L)-163 offshore.

March 17
AVIATION: America's second satellite, *Vanguard I,* is successfully launched at Cape Canaveral, Florida by the navy and enters a wider orbit than any man-made device thus far. It is only 6.4 inches in diameter and weighs 3.25 pounds yet it reveals that planet Earth has a slight pear shape to it.

March 21
AVIATION: At Holloman Air Force Base, New Mexico, a two-stage rocket sled is fired that accelerates to 2,700 miles per hour.

March 23
AVIATION: Off Los Angeles, the navy successfully conducts an underwater launch test of their new Polaris ballistic missile. These weapons are designed to be fired from submerged nuclear submarines.

March 26
AVIATION: An F-100D Super Sabre, fitted with an Astrodyne rocket motor, is launched for a rail system for the first time. This is an attempt to get jet fighters airborne in as little time as possible.

March 27
AVIATION: A plan is conceived by Advanced Research Projects Agency (ARPA) to carry three lunar probes aloft through a Thor-Vanguard launching system. The actual work is to be done by the Air Force Ballistic Missile Division.

1958

April 2
AVIATION: In Washington, D.C., President Dwight D. Eisenhower signs legislation creating the National Aeronautics and Space Administration (NASA), which incorporates NACA and numerous civilian and military projects related to outer space.

April 5
AVIATION: At Cape Canaveral, Florida, an Atlas intercontinental ballistic missile is launched 600 miles downrange and strikes its designated impact area.

April 8
AVIATION: An air force KC-135 Stratotanker, flying between Tokyo, Japan, and Lajes Field, Azores, covers the 10,288 miles while establishing a nonstop, unrefueled jet flight record.

April 16
MILITARY: Dr. Edward Teller warns a Senate subcommittee that the United States imperils millions of its own citizens in a nuclear war with the Soviet Union should it halt its own atomic testing.

April 20
MARINES: In northern Oahu, Hawaii, the 4th Marines begin three days of intense counterguerrilla warfare instruction at the Kahuku Training Area.

April 23
MILITARY: Strong winds at Fort Campbell, Kentucky, result in the deaths of five paratroopers during a practice drop.
MARINES: The first helicopter squadrons assigned to the Marine Corps Reserve are created on the orders of Commandant Randolph M. Pate.

April 25
MARINES: In Hyde County, North Carolina, Company M, 3rd Battalion, 2nd Marines deploys to help fight forest fires.

April 28
AVIATION: A B-47 Stratojet from the 341st Bombardment Wing experiences a serious inflight explosion, prompting the pilot and navigator to eject successfully. However, co-pilot James E. Obenauf notices that a fourth crew member is unconscious and unable to egress, so he fights to keep the weaving bomber under control and makes a safe landing at Dyess Air Force Base, Texas. Obenauf wins a Distinguished Flying Cross for his heroism.

May 1
AVIATION: Sensors onboard the *Explorer I* satellite reveal the existence of an intense radioactive band around the Earth at an altitude of between 600 to 8,000 miles above ground level. It is christened the Van Allen Radiation Belt in honor of the scientist who designed the sensors, Dr. James Van Allen.
MARINES: In the Mediterranean, the 2nd Battalion, 2nd Marines and helicopters of HMR(L)-262 deploy with the Sixth Fleet as its landing force.
POLITICS: The Coast Guard intercepts four antinuclear protestors as they depart Honolulu for testing grounds at Eniwetok in the Pacific.

May 7

AVIATION: A Lockheed F-104 Starfighter flown by Major Howard Johnson reaches a record altitude of 91,249 feet, quite a feat for an air-breathing aircraft.

May 12

AVIATION: At Colorado Springs, Colorado, the new North American Air Defense Command (NORAD) is commissioned for the purpose of protecting the United States and Canada from Communist missile and bomber attacks. It is jointly staffed by American and Canadian personnel.

DIPLOMACY: The United States and Canada agree to jointly man the North American Defense Command (NORAD) for their mutual defense against Soviet bombers and missiles.

NAVAL: The Defense Department doubles the size of the U.S. Sixth Fleet in the Mediterranean.

May 13

MARINES: A naval task force containing the 1st Battalion, 6th Marines and Marine Air Groups 26 and 35 deploy off Venezuela during riots occasioned by the state visit of Vice President Richard M. Nixon.

May 14

MARINES: Mounting political instability in Lebanon necessitates that the 1st Battalion, 8th Marines be withheld on the Sixth Fleet to reinforce the newly arriving 2nd Battalion, 2nd Marines.

May 16

AVIATION: Captain Walter W. Irwin sets a new jet speed record of 1,404.2 miles per hour while flying his Lockheed F-104 Starfighter over Edwards Air Force Base, California.

May 24

AVIATION: The Bell X-14 vertical flight research plane makes its debut and transitions from vertical liftoff to horizontal flight in 30 seconds. It is also the only open-cockpit X-plane and is eventually transferred to NASA.

• At Holoman Air Force Base, New Mexico, Captain E. L. Breeding is strapped to a rocket sled and accelerated up to 83 "Gs" without injury.

May 27

AVIATION: At St. Louis, Missouri, the McDonnell-Douglas XF4H-1 prototype flies for the first time; it eventually enters service as the Phantom II, a legendary fighter plane.

• At Eglin Air Force Base, Florida, the 335th Tactical Fighter Squadron begins deploying the first Republic F-105B Thunderchiefs.

May 28

NAVAL: The new guided-missile cruiser *Galveston* is commissioned, being the first vessel equipped with Talos antiaircraft missiles.

• Off Pearl Harbor, Hawaii, the destroyer escort *Silverstein* collides with the submarine *Stickleback* once the latter loses power and hurriedly surfaces. It gradually sinks but the crew is saved.

May 30
MILITARY: Ceremonies are conducted at the Tomb of the Unknown Soldier at Arlington National Ceremony, Virginia, for soldiers killed in World War II and Korea.

June 3
AVIATION: It is revealed that the forthcoming X-15 hypersonic research aircraft will employ an inertial guidance system, similar to those used in ballistic missiles, to control its pitch attitude while reentering the atmosphere.

June 4
AVIATION: At Cape Canaveral, Florida, a Thor intermediate-range ballistic missile is launched for the first time from a tactical launcher.

June 8
AVIATION: An army helicopter makes a forced emergency landing in East Germany and its nine-man crew is taken into custody.

June 16
AVIATION: The air force contracts with Martin to build its new Dyna-Soar boost-glide orbital spacecraft while Boeing becomes a major parts subcontractor.

June 27
AVIATION: Air force pilot Colonel Harry Burrell establishes a world speed record by flying from New York to London in only five hours and 27 minutes in a Boeing KC-135 tanker jet. His average speed is 630.2 miles per hour.
• An air force Fairchild C-119 Flying Boxcar accidentally strays into Armenian airspace while on a routine mission to Iran, and it is shot down by Soviet fighters; the crew of nine survives and is repatriated.
• At Cape Canaveral, Florida. The 556th Strategic Missile Squadron fires off its first Snark intercontinental cruise missile.
NAVAL: At Annapolis, Maryland, Rear Admiral Charles L. Melson gains appointment as superintendent of the U.S. Naval Academy.
MARINES: In Cuba, a group of marines and sailors are kidnaped by revolutionaries under Raúl Castro, brother of rebel leader Fidel Castro; all are released on July 18.

June 30
AVIATION: Space flight has become such a research priority that NACA declares that fully 50 percent of its efforts are taken up by missiles and other forms of space vehicles.

July 1
NAVAL: Submarine Squadron 14 becomes the navy's first Fleet Ballistic Missile Submarine Squadron, which forms an important part of America's nuclear deterrence during the cold war.

July 9
AVIATION: At Cape Canaveral, Florida, a mouse is launched in the nose cone of a Thor-Able reentry test vehicle, which flies 6,000 miles downrange and lands near the Ascension Islands.

1958

July 12
MARINES: At Camp Pendleton, California, 1,500 marines of the 1st Marine Division are deployed in that state's Cleveland National Forest to fight forest fires.

July 14
DIPLOMACY: In Beirut, Lebanon, President Camille Chamoun appeals to the United States for assistance to combat rising Syrian interference and prevent a possible civil war between Lebanese Christians and Muslims. Accordingly, President Dwight D. Eisenhower orders several marine battalions in the Mediterranean to land and assist.

July 14–15
AVIATION: Operation Blue Bat unfolds as the Tactical Air Command (TAC) transports 2,000 army troops from West Germany to Beirut, Lebanon, at the behest of the president there.

July 15–18
MARINES: The Sixth Fleet under Admiral James J. Holloway, Jr., disembarks marines from the 2nd, 6th, and 8th Regiments at various control points along the Lebanese coast.

July 19
DIPLOMACY: Nine captured members of an American helicopter crew are released to the International Red Cross by the East German government.
MILITARY: In Lebanon, Task Force 201, consisting of the 187th Battle Group, 24th Infantry Division, lands in support of marines conducting Operation Blue Bat to prevent an outbreak of civil war there.

July 26
AVIATION: Over Edwards Air Force Base, California, Captain Iven C. Kincheloe dies when his F-104 Starfighter crashes in the desert.

August 1
AVIATION: Over Johnson Island in the Pacific, the air force launches and detonates a nuclear-armed anti-ICBM missile to test its capacity for destroying incoming enemy missiles.

August 2
AVIATION: For the first time, the air force launches an Atlas missile with a full-power profile for both its sustainer and its booster rocket engines.

August 3
NAVAL: The nuclear submarine *Nautilus* under Commander William R. Anderson makes the first submerged crossing of the North Pole under 50-foot thick sheets of ice over a period of 96 hours. It becomes the first vessel of any kind to reach the North Pole.

August 6
AVIATION: The Rocketdyne Division of North American contracts with the air force to develop a rocket engine with one-million pounds of thrust.
MILITARY: President Dwight D. Eisenhower signs the Defense Reorganization Act that gives the secretary of defense more administrative control over the Departments of the Army, Navy, and Air Force.

1958

August 11
NAVAL: At the North Pole, the nuclear-powered submarine *Skate* under Commander James F. Calvert is the first vessel of its kind to surface and break the ice with its conning tower. It then submerges and resurfaces on August 17.

August 13
MILITARY: A force of U.S. Marines is withdrawn from Lebanon following the restoration of stability.

August 14
MARINES: In the wake of peaceful elections and declining tensions, the 2nd Battalion, 2nd Marines is ordered to embark back to the Sixth Fleet.

August 19
AVIATION: In Washington, D.C., Dr. T. Keith Glennan gains appointment as the first head of the National Aeronautics and Space Agency (NASA)
• The Lockheed XP3V-1 makes its maiden flight; it enters into service as the P-3 Orion patrol plane and it is still in service today.
• At the Naval Ordnance Test Station, China Lake, California, a Tartar surface-to-air missile successfully tacks and destroys an F6F Target drone.

August 21
AVIATION: In Washington, D.C., the venerable National Advisory Committee for Aeronautics (NACA) holds its final meeting before being incorporated into NASA. Retired general James H. Doolittle presides over the ceremonies.

August 23
AVIATION: In Washington, D.C., Congress creates the new Federation Aviation Administration (FAA) charged with establishing civilian and military air control procedures, as well as locating airports and missile sites. Retired U.S. Air Force general Elwood Quesada is appointed its first president.
NAVAL: Once Communist Chinese forces begin bombarding the Nationalist-held islands of Matsu and Quemoy off its coast, President Dwight D. Eisenhower orders the Seventh Fleet to begin shuttling supplies to the 100,000-man garrison there. All six carriers are present in the waters surrounding Taiwan as a deterrent to attack.
MARINES: In Scotland, revelers at the annual Edinburgh Tattoo are serenaded by music from the Marine Corps Drum and Bugle Corps, the Marine Corps Recruit Depot Parris Island Band, and a ceremonial troop.

August 25
AVIATION: Navy commander Forrest S. Petersen flies the rocket-powered X-15 high-speed research aircraft for the first time. Currently, he is the only naval aviator working for the National Aeronautics and Space Administration (NASA).

August 28
AVIATION: At Cape Canaveral, Florida, an Atlas intercontinental ballistic missile is launched, which flies accurately for 3,000 miles down range under the influence of its radio-command guidance system.

September 2
AVIATION: An air force C-130C Hercules electronic intelligence-gathering (ELINT) aircraft is shot down by Soviet MiG-17s after it strays into Armenian airspace near Yerevan, killing the crew of 17.
MARINES: At Camp Pendleton, California, units of the 1st, 5th, and 7th Marines, and Marine Air Groups 33 and 36 participate in amphibious exercise PHIBLEX 2-59, which keeps them occupied through September 14.

September 3–9
AVIATION: Recent Chinese threats made against Taiwan result in Operation Xray Tango, during which by a composite force of F-100 Super Sabres, F-101 Voodoos, B-57 Canberras, and C-130 Hercules aircraft are readily deployed there by the Tactical Air Command (TAC). The swift and competent transfer of all these aircraft over a short period of time results in a Mackay Trophy.

September 8
AVIATION: During the latest crisis between Communist China and Taiwan, wherein the latter begins an artillery barrage of the Nationalist-held islands of Quemoy and Matsu, Marine Air Group 11 (MAG-11) deploys from Japan to Taiwan to bolster nationalist air defenses.

September 9
AVIATION: A Boeing EB-50 airplane launches a Lockheed X-7 pilotless ramjet aircraft that reaches Mach 4 in level flight.

September 10
MARINES: North of Beirut, Lebanon, a small detachment of marines and army troops in boats and helicopters conducts a joint amphibious exercise.

September 15
AVIATION: An F8U Crusader flown by Lieutenant William P. Lawrence hits speeds of 1,200 miles per hour in level flight; he becomes the first naval aviator to fly twice the speed of sound.

September 16
AVIATION: The North American NA-246 jet transport prototype performs its maiden flight; it enters the service as the T-39 Sabreliner for purposes of transport, cargo carrying, and radar training.

September 19
AVIATION: The Kaman twin-rotor H-43A Huskie helicopter flies for the first time. The air force acquires 18 as firefighting and crash recovery machines with the Tactical Air Command. In light of their side-by-side intermeshing rotors, they acquire the name "Eggbeaters."

September 22
NAVAL: The nuclear-powered submarine *Skate* sets a new underwater endurance record by remaining submerged for 31 days while circumnavigating the polar ice cap.

September 24
AVIATION: In Washington, D.C., the National Aeronautics and Space Administration (NASA) holds its first senior staff meeting.

• At Cape Canaveral, Florida, a Bomarc missile is fired at an incoming target drone flying at 48,000 feet and 1,000 miles per hour. The Bomarc, remotely controlled from Kingston, New York, successfully destroys the target 75 miles away over the Atlantic.

October 1
AVIATION: In Washington, D.C., the National Aeronautics and Space Administration (NASA) officially begins tackling the thorny problems associated with manned spaceflight and nonmilitary scientific space projects.

October 6
NAVAL: The nuclear-powered submarine *Seawolf* sets an endurance record by operating while submerged for 60 days.

October 11–13
AVIATION: The air force launches the *Pioneer I* lunar probe vehicle, which rises to an altitude of 80,000 miles before falling back to Earth.

October 13
AVIATION: Aircraft belonging to VMF-212 and 214 fly the entire 4,800 miles from Hawaii to Japan without incident. This is the first squadron strength transpacific flight by either navy or marine fighters.

October 18
MARINES: The American deployment in Lebanon ends once the 2nd Battalion, 6th Marines and its headquarters embark on Sixth Fleet vessels offshore.

October 24
AVIATION: At Nicara, Cuba, the transport *Kliensmith* evacuates 56 American citizens fleeing Fidel Castro's revolution, now drawing to a successful conclusion.

October 25
MILITARY: The last remaining American forces are withdrawn from Lebanese soil.

October 26
AVIATION: At Travis Air Force Base, California, the new Boeing B-52G model performs its maiden flight. This particular version is also designed to carry two AGM-28 Hound Dog nuclear-tipped missiles under its wings.

November 1
AVIATION: The Kaman H-43B performs its maiden flight; the air force acquires several hundred of these useful craft and deploys them around the world.

November 8
AVIATION: At Cape Canaveral, the air force tries and fails to launch a lunar probe for the third time. In this instance, the third stage of the rocket fails to ignite and *Pioneer 2* falls back into the atmosphere and burns up. Given pressing priorities in other missile-related fields, the air force abandons moon shots.

November 10
AVIATION: At Norfolk, Virginia, the carrier *Boxer* hosts the first marine aviation detachment permanently assigned to a navy vessel. It is there to supply and service marine helicopters operating from the flight deck.

November 28
AVIATION: The air force launches an operational Atlas missile that flies 6,300 miles down range and lands near its assigned target.

December 2
MARINES: Near Malibu, California, 650 men of the 2nd Infantry Training Regiment deploy to combat forest fires.

December 3
AVIATION: In Washington, D.C., President Dwight D. Eisenhower directs that the Jet Propulsion Laboratory (JPL) in Pasadena, California, be transferred to the National Aeronautics and Space Administration (NASA).

December 6
MARINES: Near Pungo Lake, North Carolina, a party of marines from the 3rd Battalion, 6th Marines is tapped to fight a forest fire.

December 12
AVIATION: In Washington, D.C., the secretary of the navy cancels the Regulus II missile program in light of more capable Polaris missiles then under development. Like its predecessor, the Regulus II can be launched only from a submarine while it is surfaced.

December 14
MARINES: Near San Juan Capistrano, California, 700 marines of the 2nd Infantry Training Regiment are assigned to combat forest fires.

December 16
AVIATION: At the new Pacific Missile Test Range, California, Air Force technicians test-fire a Thor missile. Simultaneously, another Thor missile is launched from Cape Canaveral, Florida.
•   A Douglas C-133 Cargomaster of the Military Air Transport Service (MATS) sets an official payload record by hauling 117,900 pounds up to 10,000 feet.

December 18–19
AVIATION: Project Score unfolds as an Atlas rocket carries the first communications satellite into low Earth orbit; the following day a taped message from President Dwight D. Eisenhower sending the nation Christmas greetings is broadcast around the world. Ike's is the first human voice to come from space.

December 23
AVIATION: At Cape Canaveral, Florida, the Atlas-C missile is successfully tested for the first time.

1959

January
MILITARY: In light of President Dwight D. Eisenhower's emphasis on nuclear weapons, the army is allowed to decline in strength to 861,964 officers and men in 16 divisions, the lowest it has been since before the outbreak of the Korean War.

January 1

DIPLOMACY: In Cuba, the government of dictator Fulgencio Batista is driven from power by rebels under Fidel Castro; for the time being, naval and marine facilities at Guantánamo Bay are placed on alert.

MARINES: The Marine Corps overhauls its enlisted rank structure as follows: private, private first class, lance corporal, corporal, sergeant, staff sergeant, gunnery sergeant, and first or master sergeant. The last two ranks are reserved for technical specialists while first sergeant and sergeant major remain leadership positions.

January 4

AVIATION: In California, both Vandenberg Air Force Base and the Pacific Missile Range are declared operational for testing purposes.

January 10

AVIATION: In Yuma, Arizona, Vincent Air Force Base is transferred to the Marine Corps and serves as an auxiliary airfield for El Toro, California.

January 15

AVIATION: The integration of missile and bomber units begins after the Strategic Air Command (SAC) orders the 703rd and 706th Strategic Missile Wings transferred from the 1st Missile Division to the Fifteenth Air Force.

January 21

AVIATION: An army Jupiter intermediate-range ballistic missile (IRMB) successfully reaches its designated target 1,700 miles downrange. It eventually becomes an air force weapon.

February

NAVAL: The navy declares its intention to scrap 43 obsolete warships, including the pre-World War II battleships and Pearl Harbor survivors *California, Colorado, Maryland,* and *Tennessee.*

February 1

AVIATION: Across the Canadian Arctic, the United States formally transfers control of the Distant Early Warning (DEW) Line over to the Royal Canadian Air Force.

February 6

AVIATION: The air force successfully tests the Titan I intercontinental ballistic missile for the first time. This is a two-stage, liquid-fueled rocket with a range of 5,500 miles and among the largest weapons of its class. It is stored in underground silos and has to be raised to the surface in order to be launched.

February 12

AVIATION: With the retirement of the last B-36 Peacekeeper, the Strategic Air Command (SAC) becomes an all-jet deterrent force.

MARINES: On Vieques Island, Puerto Rico, the Marine Corps training base is named in honor of PFC Fernando Luis Garcia, a Medal of Honor recipient.

February 17

AVIATION: In Cambridge, Massachusetts, Dr. J. Allen Hynek of the Smithsonian Astrophysical Observatory declares that the air force should take an active and objective role during all UFO investigations.

February 19
AVIATION: At Holloman Air Force Base, New Mexico, a two-stage rocket sled reaches 3,090 miles per hour, four times the speed of sound.

February 28
AVIATION: At Vandenberg Air Force Base, California, a Thor-Hustler rocket system successfully hoists the *Discoverer 1* satellite into a polar orbit for the first time. This trajectory allows a satellite to cover the entire planet due to the Earth's rotation.

March 10
AVIATION: A B-29 carries the first X-15 hypersonic research airplane aloft during its first captive flight. Test pilot A. Scott Crossfield makes several instrument check flights in preparation for a real test drop.

March 11
AVIATION: The Sikorsky XHSS-2 antisubmarine helicopter successfully performs its maiden flight; it enters service as the Sea King.

March 17
MARINES: At Camp Pendleton, California, the 1st Battalion, 1st Marines embarks on a one-year tour of duty on Okinawa as part of the 3rd Marine Division. This pilot program gradually rotates several battalions to that island over the next few years.

April 2
AVIATION: From a field of 110 applicants, the National Aeronautics and Space Administration selects seven astronauts for its ambitious Mercury program.

April 5
MILITARY: The Naval Research Laboratory reports a 300 percent increase in radioactive air samples over the East Coast of the United States, signifying that the Soviet Union has been conducting above-ground nuclear tests.

April 6
AVIATION: The seven Project Mercury astronauts chosen by NASA are introduced to the public for the first time amidst national celebration: Alan B. Shepard (Navy), Virgil I. Grissom (Air Force), John H. Glenn (Marines), Malcolm Scott Carpenter (Navy), Walter M. Schirra (Navy), L. Gordon Cooper (Air Force), and Donald K. Slayton (Air Force).
• The Northrop YT-38 prototype performs its maiden flight; it enters service as the T-38 Talon jet trainer, which is still in service today.

April 13
SCIENCE: The military research satellite *Discoverer 2* is launched into orbit from Vandenberg Air Force Base, California.

April 18
MARINES: Off the South Korean coast, the 3rd Marines, Marine Air Group 12 (MAG-12) and the Korean Marine Corps conduct an amphibious training exercise that lasts through May 9.

April 20
AVIATION: At Cape Canaveral, Florida, the prototype Polaris submarine-launched ballistic missile makes a successful maiden flight.

April 23
AVIATION: Over the Atlantic Missile Range, Eglin Air Force Base, Florida, the GAM-77 Hound Dog supersonic, air-to-surface nuclear-tipped missile is launched from a B-52 bomber for the first time.

April 25
AVIATION: Attack Squadron VA-16 deploys on the carrier *Lexington*, being the first navy squadron equipped with Bullpup air-to-ground missiles.

April 27
AVIATION: NACA, which was founded in 1915, published its 44th and final annual report to Congress. The historical sections are written by James H. Doolittle and Jerome C. Hunsaker, previously heads of that agency.

April 28
AVIATION: Douglas Aircraft contracts with the National Aeronautics and Space Administration (NASA) to design and build a three-stage, Thor-Vanguard type rocket called the Delta.

May 1
AVIATION: At Woomera, Australia, the Smithsonian Optical Tracking Station successfully photographs the *Vanguard 1* satellite at a range of 2,500 miles above the Earth's surface.

May 4
AVIATION: Two Marine A-4 Skyhawk jets fly nonstop from Argentia, Newfoundland, to Rota, Spain, a total of 2,270 miles, for the first time.

May 6
AVIATION: The air force declares its Jupiter intermediate-range ballistic missile operational. On a recent test flight, one Jupiter landed near its assigned target 1,500 miles downrange.

May 8
MARINES: In Camden County, North Carolina, men from the 8th Marines are utilized to put out forest fires.

May 12
AVIATION: At Andrews Air Force Base, Maryland, the 1298th Air Transport Squadron accepts delivery of three Boeing VC-137a executive transports (Model 707s).
• A Thor missile is launched, which carries a GE Mark 2 nose cone that photographs the Earth from a range of 300 miles.

May 15
AVIATION: Air Research and Development Center commander general Bernard A. Schriever displays the first reentry vehicle recovered from an intercontinental missile flight.

1959

May 18

MARINES: At Camp Pendleton, California, the 1st Marine Expeditionary Force, consisting of the 1st Marine Division and the 3rd Marine Air Wing (3rd MAW) undergo amphibious maneuvers.

• In British North Borneo, the 89th Marines, Marine Air Group 16 (MAG-16), and helicopters of HMR(L)-362 conduct amphibious exercises.

May 19

MARINES: In light of tensions arising from Communist threats to blockade the city of Berlin, the 1st Battalion, 2nd Infantry and helicopters of HMR(L)-262 are alerted for possible deployment there; they are ordered to stand down on June 4.

May 22

CIVIL: Benjamin O. Davis, Jr., becomes the first African-American major general in the U.S. Air Force.

May 25

AVIATION: The first Convair F-106 Delta Daggers are delivered to the Air Defense Command, where they serve 30 years. They gradually replace the F-102 Delta Darts already in service.

May 28

AVIATION: Two monkeys named Able and Miss Baker are placed in the nose cone of a Jupiter rocket, launched to an altitude of 300 miles, then parachuted back into the ocean and recovered. The medical data recovered helps advance the state of human space travel.

June 1

MARINES: In South Vietnam, the Vietnamese Marine Corps adds a third battalion to its organization, which now boasts 3,000 men.

June 2

MARINES: The 2nd Battalion, 6th Marines departs Morehead City, North Carolina, for the newly opened St. Lawrence Seaway and Great Lakes region, where it will perform amphibious landings for public viewing.

June 3

AVIATION: At Colorado Springs, Colorado, the Air Force Academy graduates its first class of 207 cadets as newly commissioned officers.

June 8

AVIATION: Over the Mohave Desert, a B-52 carrier aircraft releases the X-15 hypersonic research airplane on its first nonpowered flight. Test pilot A. Scott Crossfield guides the craft from 38,000 feet to a successful landing. This exceptional aircraft is designed to operate along the edge of space at 4,000 miles per hour.

NAVAL: In Washington, D.C., William B. Franke gains appointment as the 55th secretary of the navy.

June 9

NAVAL: The nuclear-powered submarine *George Washington* is launched at Groton, Connecticut, being the first submarine to carry nuclear-tipped Polaris ballistic missiles.

Davis, Benjamin O.   (1912–2002)
Air Force general

Benjamin Oliver Davis, Jr., was born in Washington, D.C., the son of Lieutenant Benjamin O. Davis, Sr., an African-American army officer. Raised in a military environment, he acquired leadership traits from his father and graduated from the nearly all-white Central High School in Cleveland, Ohio, as president of his class. Davis subsequently attended Case Western University and the University of Chicago, but he found the lure of military service irresistible. In 1932 he gained appointment to the U.S. Military Academy, West Point, and graduated four years later 35th in his class of 276. However, options for African Americans in the military proved limited and Davis was completely shut out from flying, his main interest. He subsequently taught military science at the famous Tuskegee Institute, Alabama, until 1940, when political pressure forced the Army Air Force to accept minority pilots. Davis passed through the flying program established at Tuskegee,

commanding the first class, and gained his wings in March 1942. He then rose to lieutenant colonel of the all-black 99th Pursuit Squadron, but high-level discrimination kept them out of combat. It was not until April 1943 that Davis and his men were deployed to North Africa, and they fought well there, in Italy, and in the Balkans. The following year Davis rose to colonel commanding the all-black 322nd Fighter Group, the famous "Red tails," which he led competently through 60 missions. So adept were his pilots at performing escort missions that, in two years of combat, the 322nd lost fewer bombers to German aircraft than any fighter group. After the war Davis repaired back to Godman Field, Kentucky, where he commanded the racially troubled 477th Composite Group, and he succeeded in calming the tense situation due to his evenhandedness and leadership abilities.

In 1947 the new U.S. Air Force was born and the following year President

June 16
AVIATION: Over the Sea of Japan near Korea, a Martin P4M Mercator from VQ-1 is attacked and damaged by a pair of MiG fighters; it is forced to make an emergency landing in Japan.

June 19
AVIATION: At Naval Air Station Lakehurst, New Jersey, the ZPG-3W, the world's largest nonrigid airship, is delivered to the navy.

June 20
MARINES: At Gufo di Bomba, Libya, the 3rd Battalion, 2nd Marines train with British Royal Marine Commandos during week-long landing exercises.

June 23
AVIATION: In Tullahoma, Tennessee, the Arnold Engineering Development Center accepts operational and design requirements for a large space test facility to test weapons in space.

☆ ☆ ☆ ☆ ☆ ☆ ☆ ☆ ☆ ☆ ☆ ☆ ☆ ☆

Harry S. Truman, bowing to the inevitable, ordered all branches of the military completely desegregated. Davis, for his part, attended the Air War College in 1949 and served in the Pentagon as deputy of operations in the Fighter Branch. In 1954 he made history by becoming the U.S. Air Force's first black brigadier general, and, in 1959, he rose to become the first African-American major general in that service. By 1965 he had risen to become the first black lieutenant general of any service. He concluded his lengthy career as deputy commander of the U.S. Strike Force at McDill Air Force Base, Florida. Davis retired from active duty in 1970 and then held several high-ranking posts within the government, including assistant secretary of the Transportation Department. However, owing to bitter memories of discrimination he encountered at West Point, Davis did not return to that institution until 1987, over 50 years after his graduation. He also published his memoirs in 1991 and, in 1998, he became the first African American to hold

General Benjamin O. Davis, Jr. *(U.S. Air Force)*

the honorary rank of general. Davis, a consummate military leader, died in Arlington, Virginia, on July 4, 2002.

July 1

AVIATION: At Jackass Flats, Nevada, the *Kiwi I,* the first experimental nuclear reactor designed for space flight, undergoes initial testing.

MILITARY: In Washington, D.C., Vice Chief of Staff Lyman L. Lemnitzer replaces outgoing General Maxwell Taylor as the 21st army chief of staff.

July 8

MILITARY: In a foretaste of things to come, Vietcong rockets kill U.S. Army advisers Major Dale Buis and Master Sergeant Chester Ovnard at Bienhoa, South Vietnam.

July 11

AVIATION: At Pensacola, Florida, shortages in the number of military pilots being commissioned forces the Marine Corps to resume its participation in the aviation cadet program there.

July 13
MARINES: The 1st Reconnaissance Battalion is ordered to undertake a 175-mile foot march from Death Valley, California, to Mount Whitney. In sum, they have to traverse the lowest point in the United States to the highest.

July 24
AVIATION: In the waters off Antiqua, a Thor rocket nose cone is recovered with film coverage of the inflight nose-cone separation.

July 30
AVIATION: The Northrop Y5-5A, a light-weight fighter based on the T-38 Talon, flies for the first time and even breaks the speed barrier. It is subsequently redesignated the F-5 Freedom Fighter.
MARINES: In North Carolina, the 3rd Battalion, 8th Marines, VMA-225, and helicopters of HMR(L)-262 depart to serve with the Sixth Fleet as its Mediterranean landing force.

August 7
AVIATION: A pair of F-100 Super Sabres become the first jet fighters to fly over the North Pole.
• In space, the *Explorer 6* satellite transmits the first televised images back to Earth, along with an intercontinental message relayed from Major Robert G. Mathis, U.S. Air Force.

August 24
AVIATION: During the flight of an Atlas C rocket, cameras in its nose cone photograph one-sixth of the Earth's surface from an altitude of 700 miles. The nose cone is subsequently recovered and demonstrates that space photography has military reconnaissance potential.

August 28
MARINES: Sergeant Major Francis D. Bauber becomes the second sergeant major of the Marine Corps.

August 29
AVIATION: In California, the Lockheed Aircraft Company signs onto Project Oxcart to design and develop a high-speed, high-altitude photo-reconnaissance aircraft. Such a machine will be managed for the Central Intelligence Agency (CIA) by the U.S. Air Force. This is the origin of the Lockheed SR-71 Blackbird.

September 1
AVIATION: At Vandenberg Air Force Base, California, the Strategic Air Command assumes control of all Atlas intercontinental ballistic missile (ICBM) operations.

September 2
AVIATION: In Washington, D.C., noted scientist Theodor von Kármán is tasked with heading an international committee that will help create an International Academy on Astronautics.

September 5
MARINES: On Okinawa, the 3rd Marine Expeditionary Force, consisting of the 9th Marines and Marine Air Group 16 (MAG-16), sails to join the Seventh Fleet as its first landing force in the western Pacific.

September 9

AVIATION: At Vandenberg Air Force Base, California, the air force test-fires an Atlas missile, which flies 4,300 miles downrange at a speed of 16,000 miles per hour. Consequently, the Atlas weapon system is declared to be operational by General Thomas S. Power.

September 17

AVIATION: The X-15 hypersonic research aircraft makes its first powered drop from a B-52 bomber with A. Scott Crossfield at the controls. In this initial flight, Crossfield reaches Mach 2.11 at an altitude of 53,000 feet.

September 21

NAVAL: The submarine *Barbero*, equipped with nuclear-capable Regulus I missiles, makes the cold war's first deterrent patrol in the North Pacific.

October 1

MEDICAL: At Brooks, Air Force Base, Texas, the U.S. Air Force Aerospace Medical Center is activated to consolidate a number of similar aerospace facilities.

October 2

AVIATION: General Donald N. Yates, currently commander of the Air Force Missile Test Center, becomes the Department of Defense representative for NASA's Project Mercury.

October 6

AVIATION: At Cape Canaveral, Florida, the air force launches an Atlas and Thor missile to their full flight range in this latest test.

NAVAL: At Nagoya, Japan, the carrier *Kearsarge* provides medicine and disaster relief to survivors of a recent typhoon. Ultimately, 6,000 people are evacuated from the city while 200,000 pounds of medicine and food are transferred ashore.

October 13

AVIATION: A B-47 bomber launches an air-launched ballistic missile dubbed Bold Orion, which reaches an altitude of 160 miles.

October 16

MILITARY: Former general George C. Marshall, a major architect of victory in World War II, dies at Walter Reed Army Hospital, Maryland.

October 28–December 19

AVIATION: The Air Force Thunderbirds conduct a precision flying demonstration throughout the Far East. Their goodwill tour culminates in receipt of a Mackay Trophy.

October 31

AVIATION: An Atlas intercontinental ballistic missile, armed with a nuclear warhead, becomes the first such weapon placed on military alert status. It is now fully armed and capable of delivering its warhead to distant targets.

November 2

MARINES: In Alaska, the 1st Battalion, 9th Marines, Company H, 2nd Battalion, 9th Marines, and the 1st Force Reconnaissance Company engage in winter exercises that last through December.

1959

November 3
AVIATION: A Douglas C-133 Cargomaster lifts an Atlas missile to its designated silo. This large aircraft had been expressly designed for that purpose.

November 5
MARINES: In California, 200 men of the 5th Marines are tapped to help fight fires in the Cleveland National Forest.

November 7
AVIATION: The air force places the *Discovery VII* satellite in a polar orbit but, unfortunately, its camera capsule cannot be recovered for examination.

November 10
NAVAL: The nuclear submarine *Triton,* which is also the world's largest submersible, is launched at Groton, Connecticut.

November 16
AVIATION: Captain Joseph W. Kittinger is carried aloft to 76,400 feet by the balloon *Excelsior I,* then he jumps and makes a record parachute fall.
MILITARY: President Dwight D. Eisenhower places a defense budget request for $41 billion and declares there would be no immediate reductions in U.S. troop strengths abroad.

November 17
AVIATION: In Washington, D.C., all satellite and space vehicle programs are transferred from the Advanced Research Projects Agency (ARPA) to the military service enjoying "primary interest" in each. For the air force, they assume control of Projects Discoverer, Midas, and Samos.

November 20
MARINES: Camp Pendleton, California, deploys 300 marines to fight fires in the Las Pulgas and Alysso Canyons.
• In North Carolina, the 4th Provisional Marine Force departs Camp Lejeune for deployment in Cuba during a period of rising tensions with the regime of Fidel Castro.

November 30
MARINES: The first element of marines from Camp Lejeune, North Carolina, deploys at Guantánamo, Cuba, to bolster local defenses there.

December 1
DIPLOMACY: By the Antarctic Treaty, the United States, Soviet Union, and 10 other nations agree not to conduct any kind of military activity near the South Pole.
NAVAL: In Washington, D.C., the Bureau of Naval Weapons is created by merging the Bureau of Aeronautics with the Bureau of Ordnance.

December 2
MILITARY: In Washington, D.C., Thomas S. Gates gains appointment as the seventh secretary of defense.

December 3–7
AVIATION: FJ-4 Furys flown by pilots of Marine Air Group 13 (MAG-13) fly nonstop from Hawaii to California. This is the first such flight by single-engine naval fighters.

1959

December 6
AVIATION: A McDonnell-Douglas F4H-1 Phantom II jet piloted by Commander Larry E. Flint zooms upward to 98,560 feet, breaking no less than 12 speed, altitude, and time-to-climb marks.

December 8
AVIATION: In Washington, D.C., Major General Don R. Ostrander departs the Advanced Research Projects Agency (ARPA) and becomes head of the Office of Launch Vehicle Programs for the National Aeronautics and Space Administration (NASA).

December 9
AVIATION: A Kaman H-43B helicopter reaches a new rotary-wing altitude record of 29,846 feet.
• Over Akron, Ohio, a Goodyear balloon equipped with a radar camera reaches 100,000 feet in altitude, takes a picture, then safely descends.

December 11
AVIATION: The balloon *Excelsior 2* flies to 74,400 feet, at which point Captain Joseph Kittinger jumps and freefalls for 55,000 feet—another record.
• Brigadier General J. H. Moore, piloting a Republic F-105B Thunderchief, reaches a speed of 1,216.5 miles per hour over a 100-kilometer course.

December 14
AVIATION: Over Edwards Air Force Base, an F-104C piloted by Captain Joseph B. Jordan flies to a record 103,389 feet, the first time that an air-breathing machine has exceeded the 100,000-foot mark.

December 15
AVIATION: At Edwards Air Force Base, California, Major Joseph W. Rogers sets an absolute speed record by flying a Convair F-106A Delta Dart at an average speed of 1,525.95 miles per hour.

December 30
NAVAL: The *George Washington*, the first nuclear-powered, ballistic missile submarine in the world, is commissioned at Groton, Connecticut. Hereafter, nuclear-powered ballistic missile submarines form an important part of America's nuclear-armed "Triad," along with strategic jet bombers and intercontinental ballistic missiles (ICBMs).

December 31
MARINES: In Washington, D.C., Lieutenant General David M. Shoup is appointed the 22nd commandant of the Marine Corps. In 1943 Shoup received a Medal of Honor for bravery at Tarawa.
• Ongoing cuts in Marine Corps manpower levels have reduced the number of battalions available from 27 to 21.

1960

January
MILITARY: Army strength levels off at 873,078 but the number of active divisions declines to 15.

• Former U.S. Army chief of staff general Maxwell Taylor strongly critiques American military policy in his book *Uncertain Trumpet*. He criticizes America's growing overreliance on nuclear weapons and argues for a more conventional, "flexible response."

NAVAL: During Project Nekton this month, Lieutenant Don Walsh and civilian Jacques Piccard take the bathyscaph *Trieste* to depths of 35,800 feet off the coast of Mauritania.

January 2
MARINES: On Okinawa, the Marine Corps Air Facility Futema is commissioned and begins operations.

January 20
MARINES: At Bridgeport, California, 1st Battalion, 5th Marines commences SNOWFLEX II-60 at the Cold Weather Training Center, which lasts until February 11.

January 21
AVIATION: Off Wallops Island, Virginia, helicopters of Marine Air Group 21 (MAG-21) help recover a Mercury space capsule from an early unmanned test flight.

January 25
AVIATION: At the White Sands Missile Range, New Mexico, an army Hawk missile successfully downs an Honest John ballistic missile for the first time. The Hawk is specifically designed to down low-flying aircraft.

January 30
AVIATION: The Central Intelligence Agency (CIA) orders 12 of Lockheed's super-secret A-12 jets for high-speed, high-altitude reconnaissance work. Funding for this "Black" project is immediately approved.

MARINES: At Vieques, Puerto Rico, the 8th Provisional Marine Brigade tests new aerial/amphibious delivery techniques with helicopters from the carrier *Boxer*.

February 3
MARINES: In Washington, D.C., Commandant David M. Shoup declares that, due to the success of the four-year enlistment program, it is possible to reactivate two of the recently disbanded infantry battalions.

February 9
AVIATION: At Bedford, Massachusetts, the air force initiates the National Space Surveillance Control Center (SPACETRACK) to keep an eye on the mounting number of man-made objects circling the planet.

February 10–12
AVIATION: In light of rising tensions with the Castro regime, fighter craft from VMF-122 and 312 are deployed at Naval Air Station Leeward Point, Cuba.

February 17
SCIENCE: The Defense Department conducts a feasibility study on the possible use of underground seismic stations to detect underground nuclear testing.

1960

February 23
MILITARY: Missouri senator Stuart A. Symington declares that the American people are being misled by the present administration and that a profound "missile gap" exists between the United States and the Soviet Union, favoring the latter.

February 24
AVIATION: At Cape Canaveral, a Titan intercontinental ballistic missile flies downrange for 5,000 miles, its longest flight thus far.

February 25
AVIATION: A collision between a navy R6D Liftmaster and a Brazilian airliner over Rio de Janeiro takes the lives of 35 sailors and 26 Brazilians; three sailors survive.
• At the White Sands Missile Range, New Mexico, the Army successfully test launches its new Pershing tactical ballistic missile, which is solid fuel–propelled, nuclear capable, and designed to replace the earlier Redstone.

March 1
AVIATION: At Beaufort, South Carolina, the auxiliary air station is upgraded to a Marine Corps Air Station.
MARINES: At Port Lyautey, Morocco, marines are utilized to provide relief to earthquake victims at Agadir.

March 4
MARINES: The army chief of staff presents Commandant David M. Shoup with a new M14 automatic rifle, which will replace the famous M1 Garand from World War II.

March 7–April 10
MARINES: Off Taiwan, the 3rd Marine Division, 1st Marine Brigade, 1st Marine Air Wing (1st MAW), the Seventh Fleet all perform large-scale military exercises with the Nationalist Chinese Navy and Marine Corps. This involves the first helicopter lift of Nationalist troops and the first construction of a Short Expeditionary Landing Field (SELF).

March 14–30
MARINES: At Twenty-Nine Palms, California, the bulk of the 5th Marines begins a 150-mile training march through the desert.

April 1
AVIATION: At Cape Canaveral, a Thor-Able rocket lifts TIROS 1, the first American weather satellite, into orbit. Equipped with a television and an infrared detection system, it takes 22,952 images of Earth's cloud formations during the course of over 1,300 orbits.

April 13
AVIATION: At Cape Canaveral, Florida, the navy launches *Transit 1B*, its first navigational satellite.

April 14
NAVAL: A Polaris missile, destined to carry nuclear warheads while onboard submarines, is successfully test-fired off San Clemente Island, California.

April 19
AVIATION: The Grumman YA2F-1 makes its successful maiden flight; it enters service as the A-6 Intruder all-weather bomber.

April 20
MILITARY: The new M-60 Patton tank, sporting a large 105mm cannon, enters production and begins replacing the earlier M-48 tank. Continually modified, it will see front-line service over the next 30 years.

May 1
AVIATION: A Lockheed U-2 reconnaissance aircraft piloted by Captain Gary Francis Powers is shot down by an SA-2 missile over Sverdlovsk in the Soviet Union. Ironically, the radar proximity fuse employed by the Soviet missile had been designed by the United States during World War II and supplied to the Soviets by the Rosenberg spy ring.

May 2
AVIATION: At Twenty-Nine Palms, California, the marines activate the 1st Light Antiaircraft Missile Battalion (LAAM) as part of the Fleet Marine Force. This is also the first marine unit to employ Hawk (homing all the way killer) missiles.

May 5
DIPLOMACY: The South Vietnamese government requests that the United States double the current number of military advisers to 685 and the Americans comply.

May 6
NAVAL: In the San Nicholas Channel off Cuba, the submarine *Sea Poacher* is fired upon by the Cuban cutter *Oriente*.

May 9
DIPLOMACY: The Eisenhower administration declares an end to all U-2 over-flights such as the one recently downed by the Soviets over Russia.

May 10
NAVAL: The nuclear-powered *Triton* under Commander Edward L. Beach, then the world's largest submarine, completes the first undersea transit around the world by covering 41,419 miles in only 84 days. The vessel subsequently receives a Presidential Unit Citation.

May 19
AVIATION: The X-15 hypersonic research aircraft, piloted by Major Robert M. White, reaches an altitude of 107,000 feet.

May 20
AVIATION: The military potential of intercontinental ballistic missiles is underscored when an Atlas missile launched from Cape Canaveral, Florida, reaches an apogee of 1,000 miles and splashes down off the tip of Africa, 9,000 miles distant.

May 23
AVIATION: Operation Amigos unfolds as air force transports begin a massive relief effort for earthquake victims in Chile. Over the ensuing month, over 1,000 tons of supplies are carried across 4,500 miles to their destination.

May 24
MILITARY: A top-secret *Midas 2* satellite weighing 5,000 pounds is launched from Cape Canaveral, Florida, to serve as an early warning system against Soviet missile attacks. It is the first to contain infrared detection sensors.

June 6
MARINES: Off the South Korean coast, the 9th Provisional Marine Brigade engages in amphibious exercises, which includes a 4,600-men airborne assault conveyed by helicopters.

June 10
DIPLOMACY: In Tokyo, a stone-throwing band of ultranationalists forces Ambassador Douglas MacArthur II to escape on a marine helicopter.
MARINES: In the Caribbean, the 2nd Marine Expeditionary Brigade (including battalions from the 2nd, 6th, and 8th Marines), VFM-225, and the Provisional Marine Air Group 30 begin an extensive series of training exercises.

June 22
NAVAL: At Annapolis, Maryland, Rear Admiral John F. Davidson gains appointment as the 41st superintendent of the U.S. Naval Academy.

June 25
AVIATION: The Aerospace Corporation is established by the air force, which is a nonprofit civilian group to oversee engineering, research, and development of projects related to missile and space programs.

June 28
AVIATION: In Washington, D.C., the late rocket pioneer Dr. Robert W. Goddard receives a posthumous Langley Medal from the Smithsonian Institution.

June 30
MARINES: The Department of the Pacific headquarters and the Marine Barracks at the Naval Ammunition Depot, Bremerton, Washington, are both deactivated.
• At this date, Marine Corps manpower totals 16,203 officers and 145,418 enlisted men.

July 1
AVIATION: At Norfolk, Virginia, Fleet Marine Force Atlantic consolidates both its headquarters and Air headquarters in the same building, at considerable savings to the corps.
• Soviet MiG-17 jet fighters shoot down an unarmed American ERB-47H aircraft in international airspace over the Barents Sea, killing four crew members and capturing two. The survivors are released on January 25, 1961.

July 8
AVIATION: At Jackass Flats, Nevada, the second part of Project Rover commences as the second experimental reactor, *Kiwi-A Prime,* is tested at full power as a possible nuclear rocket motor.
• When civil and ethnic unrest results in rioting throughout the Democratic Republic of the Congo, Operation New Tape commences to evacuate American citizens and foreign nationals from the trouble zone. The operation lasts four years and also flies in UN peacekeepers.

July 9
MARINES: Company L, 3rd Battalion, 2nd Marines and helicopters from HMR(L)-261 are dispatched from the carrier *Wasp* to serve as UN peacekeepers in newly independent Congo.

July 11
DIPLOMACY: The Soviet Union claims that the American RB-47 it shot down in international airspace was actually flying in Soviet airspace.

July 14
AVIATION: Over 100 C-130 and C-124 transport aircraft conduct Operation Safari, which airlifts some 38,000 UN peacekeepers at various places on the African continent.

July 17
AVIATION: To test the effect of prolonged cosmic ray exposure on living organisms, an NASA balloon goes aloft to 130,000 while carrying 12 live mice. They remain subject to such exposure for 12 hours, then return safely.

July 19
NAVAL: Off Long Beach, California, the destroyers *Ammen* and *Collett* collide during maneuvers; the former is beyond repair and loses 11 dead and 20 injured. The former is so heavily damaged that it is scrapped.

July 20
NAVAL: Off Cape Canaveral, Florida, the fleet ballistic missile submarine *George Washington* successfully test-fires two Polaris A-1 missiles, which fly downrange for 1,150 miles. This is also the first test launch from a submerged vessel.

August 1
AVIATION: At Carswell Air Force Base, Texas, the 43rd Bombardment Wing accepts delivery of its first Convair B-58 Hustler. This delta-wing giant is also the first strategic bomber capable of sustained supersonic flight and is capable of being refueled in midflight.

August 4
AVIATION: Civilian test pilot Joseph A. Walker flies the experimental X-15 rocket plane to a record speed of 2,196 miles per hour.

August 10–11
NAVAL: Navy frogmen recover a 300-pound payload from outer space, which had been ejected from orbit by the *Discoverer XIII* military reconnaissance satellite. This is the first object from space to be retrieved; however, it could not be retrieved by helicopter as planned for it fell outside its designated landing zone.

August 12
AVIATION: A North American X-15 hypersonic research plane is piloted to a record 136,500 feet by Major Robert White.

August 13
MARINES: In Washington, D.C., Commandant David M. Shoup reveals plans to reactivate the rest of the six battalions that were demobilized due to budget cuts in 1959.

1960

August 14
MARINES: On Okinawa, the 2nd Battalion, 5th Marines, embarks with the amphibious assault ships to serve as the landing force of the Seventh Fleet. Plans are enacted to continually rotate battalions in this capacity to hone their proficiencies.

August 15
MARINES: In light of increasing tensions with the Castro regime in Cuba, the 8th Marine Expeditionary Force (3rd Battalion, 8th Marines, VMA-331, VMF-122, HMR(L)-261, and HMR(M)-461 arrives in the Caribbean in the event of hostilities.

August 16
AVIATION: The *Excelsior III* balloon carries Captain Joseph W. Kittinger, Jr., to an altitude of 102,800 feet, whereupon he makes a record-breaking jump of 17 miles in free fall and reaches a speed of 614 miles per hour during the next four minutes and 17 seconds. Kittinger fell 84,700 feet, which remains the highest parachute jump on record.

August 18
AVIATION: At Vandenberg Air Force Base, California, the air force launches the satellite *Discovery XIV* into a polar orbit.

August 19
AVIATION: Off Honolulu, Hawaii, a Fairchild C-119 Flying Boxcar flown by Captain Harold F. Mitchell successfully snares a 300-pound KH-1 Corona 13 capsule in midair for the first time; the item had been ejected from space by the *Discoverer XIV* reconnaissance satellite. Consequently the 6593rd Test Squadron (Special) wins the Mackay Trophy.
•   In Moscow, Soviet Union, U-2 pilot Francis Gary Powers is sentenced by a State Court to 10 years of "deprivation of freedom."

August 22–24
MARINES: At Twenty-Nine Palms, California, Operation Charger is conducted by 13 ground units and 9 squadrons from the reserves, along with the 1st Marine Division, force troops, and the 1st Marine Air Wing (1st MAW). This is also the largest reserve exercise ever held.

August 26
AVIATION: Construction of the world's largest radar begins at Arecibo, Puerto Rico, under air force supervision. This device is capable of sending signals out as far as Venus, Mars, and Jupiter.

August 30
AVIATION: At F. E. Warren Air Force Base, Wyoming, the 564th Strategic Missile Squadron becomes the first fully operational ICBM unit; it boasts a strength of six nuclear-tipped Atlas missiles.

September 5
AVIATION: A McDonnell Douglas F4H Phantom II jet flown by Lieutenant Colonel Thomas H. Miller blazes a new world speed air record of 1,218.78 miles per hour.

F-4 Phantom (U.S. Air Force)

September 10
AVIATION: All commercial air operations cease for six hours as NORAD conducts Operation Sky Shield, which entails military aircraft flying defensive maneuvers across the entire United States.
NAVAL: The navy commissions the Charles F. Adams, the first guided-missile destroyer designed that way from the "keel up." It is also the first of 23 such 4,500-ton warships in its class.

September 11
MARINES: At Quantico, Virginia, the Marine Corps Museum is officially opened.
• Camp Lejeune, North Carolina, is heavily damaged by Hurricane Donna and sustains $500,000 in damages.

September 14
AVIATION: Jets of VMF-122 take up stations at Roosevelt Roads, Puerto Rico, while supporting the 8th Marine Expeditionary Unit. They remain in place until June 1961.

September 15
AVIATION: At Brooks Air Force Base, Texas, U.S. Air Force captain W. D. Habluetzel and Lieutenant J. S. Hargreaves undergo a simulated moon flight by remaining in a space cabin simulator over the next 30 days. The test is conducted by the School for Aviation Medicine located on the base.

September 17
NAVAL: The new helicopter carrier Iwo Jima is launched; this is the first vessel designed to operate helicopters from the keel up. Moreover, it can carry up to 2,000 marines and an entire squadron of helicopters to convey them ashore.

September 21
AVIATION: The first nuclear-capable F-105D Thunderchiefs are deployed by the Tactical Air Command at Nellis Air Force Base, Nevada.

1960

October 1
AVIATION: At Thule, Greenland, the first Ballistic Missile Early Warning System (BMEWS) becomes operational. This station is to provide the Strategic Air Command (SAC) with sufficient warning of an enemy attack for it to get its jet bombers off the ground.
MILITARY: In Washington, D.C., General George Decker is appointed the 22nd army chief of staff, replacing outgoing General Lynam L. Lemnitzer, who is advancing to chairman, Joint Chiefs of Staff.

October 6
MARINES: Tours of Fleet Marine Force units in the Far East are reduced from 15 months to 13.

October 12
AVIATION: Over El Centro, California, an air force C-130 parachutes a record 41,470 pounds of heavy equipment airdrop.
MARINES: On Okinawa, the 1st Force Reconnaissance Company begins the rotation process through that island.

October 21
AVIATION: The Grumman W2F-1 prototype flies successfully for the first time; it enters the service as the E-2 Hawkeye, which is still employed today.

November 1
DIPLOMACY: In London, England, Prime Minister Harold Macmillan declares his government's intention to allow Polaris submarines to berth at Holy Loch, Scotland.

November 12
AVIATION: At Vandenberg Air Force Base, California, the launch of the *Discovery XVII* satellite employs a restartable rocket motor for the first time.

November 14
AVIATION: A capsule ejected from the *Discovery 17* satellite is successfully retrieved in midair by a C-119 Flying Boxcar. The capsule carries a letter from General Thomas D. White, U.S. Air Force chief of staff, to the secretary of defense.

November 15
NAVAL: At Charleston, South Carolina, the nuclear-powered ballistic submarine *George Washington* departs on its first deterrence cruise. It is armed with 16 Polaris A-1 nuclear-tipped missiles, each with a range of 1,200 miles.
MARINES: At Camp Lejeune, North Carolina, the 24th Expeditionary Unit is activated; it consists of an infantry battalion, a light helicopter squadron, and an attack squadron.

November 19
NAVAL: At the Brooklyn Navy Yard, New York, a fire breaks out onboard the carrier *Constellation*. The vessel sustains $75 million in damages while 50 workers are killed and 150 are injured.

November 23
AVIATION: A Thor-Delta rocket launches the *TIROS II* weather satellite; this is also the 14th successful launch of a U.S. space vehicle for 1960.

1960

November 30
MARINES: Company G, 2nd Battalion, 6th Marine and helicopters of HMR(L)-264 are dispatched to Africa on a goodwill tour.

December 1
AVIATION: The Jet Propulsion Laboratory (JPL) in Pasadena, California, receives a detailed scale map of the lunar landing site selected by the National Aeronautics and Space Administration.

December 3
AVIATION: During a nighttime refueling exercise at Vandenberg Air Force Base, California, a Titan missile explodes in its silo.

December 10
AVIATION: A C-119 Flying Boxcar piloted by Captain Gene Jones snares a capsule ejected from the *Discovery XVIII* satellite at an altitude of 14,000 feet. This carried sample human tissues onboard to check the effects of space radiation.

December 13
AVIATION: Over Edwards Air Force Base, California, a North American A3-J Vigilante jet bomber piloted by navy commander Leroy A. Heath achieves a new altitude record of 91,540.8 feet.

December 14
AVIATION: A B-52 Stratofortress from the 5th Strategic Bombardment Wing, Travis Air Force Base, Texas, flies 10,079 miles in 19 hours and 44 minutes, establishing a new, unrefueled distance record for jet aircraft.

December 15
MARINES: By adopting the new Landing Party Manual, the Marine Corps abolishes the World War II–era, eight-man squad as a basic tactical unit.

December 16
AVIATION: At Vandenberg Air Force Base, California, an Atlas-D missile mounting A Mark 3 reentry nose cone flies 4,384 miles downrange to Eniwetok. This is also the first missile fired by the Strategic Air Command (SAC).

December 19
AVIATION: At Cape Canaveral, Florida, a Redstone rocket booster is launched carrying an unmanned space capsule as part of Project Mercury. The capsule flies 235 miles downrange at 4,200 miles per hour and reaches an altitude of 135 miles. After splashdown in the ocean by parachute, it is quickly recovered by helicopters.

December 20
POLITICS: In Hanoi, North Vietnam, Ho Chi Minh organizes the National Liberation Front of South Vietnam, or Viet Cong. Its purpose is to drive out all foreign military advisers and overthrow the current South Vietnamese regime.

December 22
MILITARY: A Polaris intermediate-range ballistic missile (IRBM) is successfully launched by the nuclear ballistic submarine *Robert E. Lee.*

1960

December 23
AVIATION: The first Chance Vought F8U-2N Crusaders in Marine Corps service are handed over to VMF-334.

1961

January
MILITARY: Only four months in office, U.S. Army chief of staff general George Decker confronts rising concerns about Southeast Asia as a Communist insurgency in Laos mounts. At this time there are also 800 military personnel serving in South Vietnam as part of the Military Assistance Advisory Group (MAAG).

January 1
MARINES: In Okinawa, the 3rd Marine Division imposes a new designation system for the units that are constantly rotating through it. Now, newly arrived units must adopt the designation of the unit they replace, which, critics claim, undercuts traditional, identified unit histories.

January 3
DIPLOMACY: In Washington, D.C., President Dwight D. Eisenhower formally severs diplomatic ties with the Communist regime of Fidel Castro in Cuba. He also warns that American facilities at Guantánamo Bay will be defended by force, if need be.

January 12
NAVY: In Washington, D.C., President Dwight D. Eisenhower submits a proposal for fiscal year 1962 for a U.S. Navy of 817 ships and 625,000 personnel, and a three air wing, three division Marine Corps of 175,000 men.

January 13
AVIATION: Major H. J. Deutschendorf flies a B-58 Hustler through six world speed records; it averages 1,200.2 miles per hour while carrying a 4,408 payload.

January 18
MARINES: Bertha L. Peters is the first female marine to reach the esteemed rank of sergeant major.

January 20
MILITARY: President John F. Kennedy appoints Robert S. McNamara to be the eighth secretary of defense.
NAVAL: In Washington, D.C., John B. Connally, Jr., gains appointment as the 56th secretary of the navy.
MARINES: In Orange County, California, a force of 400 marines from Camp Pendleton arrive to help put out brush fires.
• At Matadi, Congo, a famine relief force is helicoptered in from the landing ship LSD-34.

January 22
AVIATION: The air force selects the new Titan II rocket to launch the Dyna-Soar project into space.

January 24
MILITARY: In Washington, D.C., Elvis J. Stahr is appointed the sixth secretary of the army.

January 28
MILITARY: Newly inaugurated President John F. Kennedy approves a $28.4 million "counterinsurgency" plan to thwart growing Communist infiltration and sabotage in South Vietnam. The funds will be used to increase the size of the Army of the Republic of South Vietnam (ARVN) to 170,000 men.

January 31
AVIATION: In the Mediterranean, VMA-225, the first marine squadron equipped with Douglas A4D-2N Skyhawks, joins the Sixth Fleet onboard the carrier *Shangri-La*.
• At Holoman Air Base, New Mexico, an Army Redstone rocket booster launches a chimpanzee named Ham into orbit while inside a Mercury space capsule. The test proves that the capsule's life support systems work and Ham endures the 18-minute, 420-mile ride without ill effects.
• At Cape Canaveral, Florida, the new LGM-130 Minuteman, a three-stage, solid-propellant missile, is successfully launched and flies downrange 4,600 miles to its target area. Missiles of this sort are intended to replace the more dangerous, liquid-fuel variety.
• At Point Arguello, California, an Atlas-Agena rocket places the 4,100-pound *Samos II* photographic satellite into orbit.
MARINES: By this date, active duty women marines total 124 officers and 1,486 enlisted.

February 1
AVIATION: At Matadi, Congo, helicopters of HMR(L)-264 evacuate UN peacekeepers to the safety of the *Hermitage* offshore. They are subsequently landed at Conakry, Guinea, a week later.
• At Cape Canaveral, Florida, a Minuteman I intercontinental ballistic missile (ICBM) is launched for the first time under its own internal guidance. The vehicle travels downrange for 4,600 miles and hits its designated target area.
• At Thule, Greenland, the ballistic missile early warning system is declared operational by the North American Air Defense Command. It is designed to detect a Soviet missile attack and give the United States ample time to respond militarily.
MILITARY: In Washington, D.C., President John F. Kennedy revokes restrictions on the number of dependents that can accompany military personnel overseas.

February 3
AVIATION: The ambitious Looking Glass program is initiated by the Strategic Air Command (SAC). This entails EC-135 aircraft, specially outfitted with communication equipment, to act as airborne command posts 24 hours a day. While aloft they are in constant touch with the Joint Chiefs of Staff, SAC air bases, and any SAC aircraft. This program is designed to lessen the impact of a surprise Soviet missile strike upon air force command centers.

February 6
AVIATION: At Vieques Island, Puerto Rico, a F4D-1 Skyray piloted by Lieutenant Colonel W. D. Patterson lands on the Short Expeditionary Landing Field (SELF) for the first time.

February 13
AVIATION: An F-100 Super Sabre fires a GAM-83B Bullpup missile for the first time. This is an adaptation of the navy weapon of the same name and it can be either fitted with a nuclear warhead or guided by the pilot through use of a miniature joystick.

March 1
AVIATION: Lockheed GV-1 Hercules tanker aircraft are delivered to Marine Corps VMR-352, which is the first inflight refueling squadron in that service.
MARINES: Headquarters Marine Corps adds the Marine Corps Emergency Actions Center to its G-3 division.

March 6
AVIATION: At Wichita, Kansas, the first B-52H bomber flies. This version is unique in mounting eight turbo-fan engines and is capable of firing GAM-87A Skybolt nuclear missiles.

March 7
AVIATION: An X-15 hypersonic research aircraft piloted by Major Robert M. White reaches 2,905 miles per hour and White is the first human being to fly faster than Mach 4.
• The GAM-72A Quail diversionary missile is authorized for use on B-52 bombers by the Strategic Air Command (SAC). This device makes a false radar impression of the size of a B-52 bomber to confuse Soviet ground defenses.

March 17
AVIATION: At Randolph Air Force Base, Texas, the Training Air Command accepts deliveries of the first Northrop T-38 Talon supersonic jet trainers.

April
MILITARY: To thwart potential Communist gains, the Military Assistance Advisory Group–Laos (MAAG-Laos) is formed under Lieutenant Colonel Arthur D. Simons. This consists of 430 soldiers divided into 48 mobile "White Star" training teams.

April 1
AVIATION: In a reorganization move, the Air Materiel Command is designated the Air Force Logistics Command while the Air Research and Development Command is redesignated the Air Force Systems Command.

April 3
MARINES: In Southern California, Operation Greenlight involves 50,000 personnel, 150 vessels, and 300 U.S. Navy and Marine Corps aircraft. The maneuver runs through June 8.

April 12
AVIATION: In a second shock to the American scientific community after the launch of *Sputnik,* the Soviets successfully launch Yuri Gagarin into space and

return him safely to Earth. Public and political pressure begins building to launch an American into space.

April 14
AVIATION: At Hurlburt Field, Florida, the 4400th Combat Crew Training Squadron becomes the air force's first special operations unit since the Korean War.
MARINES: In Borneo, the 5th Marine Expeditionary Brigade (9th Marines and helicopters of HMR(L)-162) conducts a SEATO exercise through May 4.

April 17
AVIATION: At Vernalis, California, a constant-altitude balloon is launched, which remains in place for nine days at 70,000 feet while carrying a 49-pound payload.

April 17–20
AVIATION: During the ill-fated Bay of Pigs invasion launched by President John F. Kennedy against the Communist regime of Fidel Castro, six jets from the carrier *Essex* are launched to protect a force of CIA-flown B-26 light bombers. However, the B-26s arrive over their target before the escort does, and two are downed by Cuban aircraft.
MARINES: During fighting associated with the Bay of Pigs invasion, facilities at Guantánamo Bay are placed on heightened alert.

April 18
MARINES: In North Carolina, Company F, 2nd Battalion, 2nd Marines, and helicopters of HMR(L)-262 are dispatched to Africa on a goodwill tour entitled Operation Solant Amity II.

April 19
AVIATION: In closing phases of the Bay of Pigs "invasion," four Alabama Air National Guard crewmen are killed when two B-26s are downed while conducting special operations.

April 21
AVIATION: An X-15 hypersonic research plane flown by Captain Robert M. White reaches 3,074 miles per hour at 105,000 feet; he is the first pilot to exceed 3,000 miles per hour.

April 26–29
MILITARY: In Washington, D.C., Deputy Secretary of Defense Roswell L. Gilpatric promulgates a scheme to send 3,200 military advisers and 400 Special Forces into Laos to thwart a growing Communist insurgency instigated by North Vietnam. He does so at a time when President John F. Kennedy and the National Security Council ponder how to handle what they view as deliberate Communist aggression.

April 27–30
MARINES: At Porto Scudo, Sardinia, the 16th Marine Expeditionary Brigade is involved in an amphibious exercise.

April 29
NAVAL: At Camden, New Jersey, the *Kitty Hawk,* the first missile-armed aircraft carrier, is commissioned.

1961

May

MARINES: In Washington, D.C., the Headquarters Marine Corps Reorganization Board is appointed by Commandant Shoup and includes Lieutenant General Robert H. Pepper, Major General Alpha M. Bowser, and Colonel Norman Anderson. They are to report their findings and recommendations by August 1.

• In Vietnam, the On the Job Training (OJT) program is begun by the Marine Corps, which rotates 20 junior officers and senior NCOs to Southeast Asia to observe ongoing counterinsurgency operations.

May 2

AVIATION: A B-58 Hustler named *Fire Fly* makes a record transatlantic flight between New York and Paris, France, in three hours and 56 minutes.

May 3

AVIATION: At Vandenberg Air Force Base, California, a Titan I missile is launched aboveground from a "hard silo" lift launcher for the first time.

May 3–5

MARINES: At Zambales Beach, Luzon, Philippines, the 2nd Battalion, 12th Marines engages in live-fire artillery exercises.

May 4

AVIATION: Over the Gulf of Mexico, Project Stratolab unfolds as navy commander Malcolm D. Ross and marine lieutenant commander Victor A. Prather set a new balloon altitude record by climbing to 113,740 feet. Prather, unfortunately, drowns when he falls from the recovery helicopter.

May 5

AVIATION: At Cape Canaveral, Florida, navy commander Alan B. Shepard, Jr., is the first American to complete a 15-minute suborbital flight of 300 miles downrange at a height of 116.5 miles in a Mercury capsule named *Freedom 7.* He and his craft are secured in the ocean by a helicopter from HMR(L)-262, which transports them to the carrier *Lake Champlain.*

MILITARY: In Washington, D.C., President John F. Kennedy begins pondering the use of American forces to help South Vietnam counter a rising Communist insurgency.

May 11

MILITARY: In Washington, D.C., National Security Action Memorandum No. 52 is issued by President John F. Kennedy to explore ways of increasing the army's counterinsurgency abilities. He also authorizes deployment of 400 Special Forces to Laos, with a further 100 military advisers sent to South Vietnam. This is the beginning of a military and political quagmire that no one could have anticipated.

May 15

MARINES: Off Southeast Asia, the Seventh Fleet is bolstered by the arrival of the 3rd Battalion, 9th Battalion and helicopters of HMR (L)-162, which serve as its landing force.

May 20

MARINES: At Marmaris, Turkey, the 3rd Battalion, 6th Marines and helicopters of HMR (L)-262 provide relief and medical assistance to earthquake victims.

1961

May 25
MARINES: In Washington, D.C., President John F. Kennedy seeks funding from Congress to enlarge the Marine Corps from 175,000 men to 190,000.

May 26
AVIATION: A Convair B-58 Hustler supersonic bomber under Major William R. Payne of the 43rd Bombardment Wing makes a record flight of only three hours and 19 minutes from New York City to Paris, France. This flight, made to commemorate the 34th anniversary of Charles A. Lindbergh's transatlantic crossing, earns the crew a Mackay Trophy.

June 1
AVIATION: At Kincheloe Air Force Base, Michigan, the air force activates its first Bomarc-B pilotless interceptor base.

June 3
AVIATION: At Paris, France, the B-58 Hustler named *Fire Fly* stalls and crashes during an air show, killing its crew of three.

June 9
AVIATION: The Military Air Transport Service (MATS) accepts delivery of its first Boeing C-135 Stratolifter, marking the modernization of the piston-driven transport fleet with jet aircraft.
MILITARY: President Ngo Dinh Diem requests military assistance from President John F. Kennedy to increase his army by an additional 100,000 men to 275,000. Kennedy only consents to fund an additional 30,000-man build up, but he also holds back on sending the necessary advisers to train them.

June 12
MARINES: In Washington, D.C., President John F. Kennedy orders that the U.S. flag be flown 24 hours a day at the Marine Corps Memorial in Arlington, Virginia.
• Off Southeast Asia, the 1st Battalion, 3rd Marines joins the Seventh Fleet to act as its special landing force.

June 15
MARINES: In the Caribbean, the 8th Marine Expeditionary Force (1st Battalion, 8th Marines, Marine Air Group 20, VMA-242, and helicopters of HMR(L)-262 are deployed on standby alert. Until August 1, they practice counterinsurgency and riot control exercises.

June 23
AVIATION: An X-15 hypersonic research aircraft flown by Major Robert M. White reaches 3,603 miles per hour; White is the first man to exceed Mach 5 in level flight.

June 30
AVIATION: In Washington, D.C., General Curtis E. LeMay gains appointment as the chief of staff, U.S. Air Force.
MARINES: At this juncture, marine manpower levels are 16,132 officers and 160,777 enlisted men.

1961

July

AVIATION: In a sign of growing competence and confidence, the Strategic Air Command (SAC) places 50 percent of all its airborne nuclear assets on 15-minute ground-launch alert.

July 1

AVIATION: The North American Defense Command initiates a cataloging effort to log all man-made space objects with a specially designed tracking system.
•   The Air Force Communications Service (AFCS) begins maintenance of communications and air traffic control at U.S. Air Force installations across the globe.

July 3

GENERAL: Aging and ailing, former general Douglas MacArthur pays a final visit to his beloved Philippines, receiving an affectionate welcome by an estimated 2 million Filipinos.

July 8

MILITARY: In light of a possible confrontation with the Soviet Union over Berlin, President John F. Kennedy orders a complete reappraisal of American military strength.

July 15

AVIATION: A *Midas 3* satellite is launched onboard an Agena Rocket with a restartable second stage, which boosts it into a polar orbit nearly 1,850 miles above the surface.

July 21

SPACE: At Cape Canaveral, Florida, Air Force Captain Virgil I. "Gus" Grissom becomes America's second man in space by zooming 188 miles in a suborbital flight while commanding the Mercury capsule *Liberty Bell 7*. His flight attains an altitude of 118 miles and speeds of up to 5,310 mile per hour. Grissom consequently wins the first-ever General Thomas D. White USAF Space Trophy for his efforts.

July 25

MILITARY: Determined to display his resolve to the Soviet Union, President John F. Kennedy asks Congress for $3.5 billion for defense and additional troops for the Reserve.

August

MARINES: An unexpected increase in voluntary enlistments, coupled with a strong response from reservists flocking to the colors, means that the Marine Corps will reach its assign strength of 190,000 men six months earlier than expected.

August 1

AVIATION: In response to the Berlin Wall crisis, five U.S. Air Force Reserve C-124 units and over 15,000 reservists are mobilized for active duty.
•   On Okinawa, helicopters of HMR(L)-362 begin a transplacement rotation alongside infantry units.
NAVAL: In Washington, D.C., Admiral George W. Anderson becomes the 16th chief of naval operations.

LeMay, Curtis E. (1906–1990)
Air Force general

Curtis Emerson LeMay was born in Columbus, Ohio, on November 15, 1906, and he attended Ohio State University ROTC after failing to secure an appointment to the U.S. Military Academy. LeMay was commissioned in the artillery on June 14, 1928, but, inspired by the feats of Charles Lindbergh, he volunteered for flight training. LeMay won his wings at March Field, California, in October 1929 and spent six years touring with fighter squadrons. The turning point in his career came in 1937 when he transferred to bombers at Langley Field, Virginia, and demonstrated his prowess as a navigator by intercepting the Italian liner *Rex* at sea in 1938. After the United States entered World War II, LeMay was promoted to colonel commanding the 305th Bombardment Squadron and deployed to England, where he proved himself tactically innovative. In August 1943 he personally led the first shuttle bombing run from England to North Africa and in March 1944, at the age

of 37, he became the youngest major general since Ulysses S. Grant. That summer he transferred to China to command the XX Bomber Command flying new B-29 Superfortresses and commenced the first large raids on the Japanese homeland. When these proved inadequate due to range considerations, LeMay transferred to the XXI Bomber Command on Guam, much closer to his target, and he orchestrated a devastating firebomb campaign against Japanese cities. His low-altitude raid against Tokyo on March 9, 1945, burned out 16 square miles of the city and inflicted over 100,000 casualties. In August 1945 LeMay transferred again to the staff of General Carl A. Spaatz, where he helped plan the final atomic bomb missions over Hiroshima and Nagasaki.

LeMay came home after the war and, as deputy chief of research and development, he helped develop and deploy the first American jet bombers. In 1948 he was called upon to break the Soviet land block-

MARINES: Responding to increasing tension with the Soviet Union, Congress votes to authorize the president to call up 250,000 reservists for up to one year.

August 2

DIPLOMACY: In a major policy decision, President John F. Kennedy declares that the United States will do everything in its power to help South Vietnam in its struggle against communism. This marks the beginning of a doomed 15-year effort.

August 8

AVIATION: At Cape Canaveral, Florida, the Atlas F intercontinental ballistic missile is successfully tested. This weapon is also designed for long-term storage of volatile liquid fuels that can be placed in hardened silos. It also enjoys a significantly shorter launch sequence than earlier models.

1961

ade of Berlin, which he countered with Operation Vittles, the famous Berlin airlift, forcing the Russians to relent. However, his biggest challenge came that same year when he advanced to lead the Strategic Air Command (SAC), which he transformed from a dispirited force with a handful of obsolete bombers to a thoroughly elite atomic strike force of nearly 2,000 jets. By the time he left in 1957 to serve as vice chief of staff, U.S. Air Force, SAC was a modern, well-equipped nuclear deterrent force, second to none. In June 1961 President John F. Kennedy appointed him chief of staff of the U.S. Air Force, although in this office he clashed repeatedly with the missile-oriented defense secretary, Robert MacNamara. He was also vociferous in his support for the unpopular war in Vietnam, and felt that President Lyndon B. Johnson was not doing enough. LeMay then concluded 47 years of distinguished service by resigning in 1965 and, three years later, he ran as the vice presidential candidate with Alabama governor George Wallace.

General Curtis E. LeMay *(Library of Congress)*

He died in San Bernadino, California, on October 1, 1990, the foremost aerial strategist of the cold war years.

August 10
MARINES: Off Southeast Asia, the 2nd Battalion, 3rd Marines and helicopters of HMR(L)-261 join the Seventh Fleet as its landing force.

August 13
DIPLOMACY: In a monumental blunder, Soviet premier Nikita Khrushchev orders a concrete wall constructed between East and West Berlin to cut off a steady stream of refugees fleeing communism. The obstacle, reviled as the "Berlin Wall," becomes symbolic of Soviet political oppression throughout the world.

August 24
AVIATION: Noted aviatrix Jacqueline Cochran flies her Northrop T-38 talon to a new women's speed record of 844.2 miles per hour.

August 26
NAVAL: The landing assault ship *Iwo Jima* is commissioned; it is the first vessel capable of launching marines from landing craft and helicopters.

August 30
AVIATION: Operation Stair Step commences as the first of 216 Air National Guard fighters begin deploying across the Atlantic to bases in Europe.
MARINES: Over Camp Horno, California, 31 marines of the 1st Force Reconnaissance Company make their first nighttime jump from a GV-1 Hercules transport aircraft.

September 6
MARINES: In North Carolina, the 500 marines participating in Operation Solant Amity II return from Africa, having visited 17 ports and covered 30,191 miles.

September 8
AVIATION: Aviatrix Jacqueline Cochran flies her T-38 Talon over a 1,000-kilometer closed speed course at 639.4 miles per hour, a new women's speed record.

September 10
NAVAL: The nuclear-powered cruiser *Long Beach* is commissioned as the only vessel of its class in the world. It is also the first warship armed entirely with missiles.

September 12
MARINES: Victims of Hurricane Carla in Texas and Louisiana are assisted by 400 marines from the 2nd Marine Division and Marine Air Group 26 (MAG-26).

September 13
AVIATION: The new global Mercury tracking network is used to observe the orbit of an unmanned Mercury space capsule for the first time. This successful launch also demonstrates to air force authorities that the Atlas rocket is an ideal vehicle for lifting a man into space.

September 14
MARINES: In North Carolina, Company F, 2nd Battalion, 6th Marines, embarks on Solant Amity II, another African goodwill tour.

September 15
AVIATION: Jacqueline Cochran sets another women's closed course distance record in a T-38 by flying 1,346.5 miles.

September 19
AVIATION: At Eglin Air Force Base, Florida, a Bomarc B pilotless interceptor is launched toward a Regulus II supersonic target drone. The Bomarc, remotely controlled from Gunther Air Force Base, Alabama, executes a 180-degree turn in pursuit of its quarry and destroys it at an altitude of seven miles and 250 miles downrange.

October
MARINES: For the first time, enlisted marines serve as voting members on the board that chooses individuals for promotion to gunnery sergeant.

1961

October 1
AVIATION: The ongoing Berlin Wall crisis results in Operation Stairstep, during which 18,500 members of the Air National Guard are called to active service while several units are deployed to Europe to support the regular air force there.

October 11
AVIATION: An X-15 hypersonic research aircraft flown by Major Robert M. White reaches an altitude of 217,000 feet; White is the first man to exceed the 200,000 foot mark.

October 12
AVIATION: Jacqueline Cochran flies her Northrop T-38 Talon to 56,712 feet, establishing a new women's altitude record.

October 18
AVIATION: An air force Kaman H-43B helicopter reaches a new altitude record of 32,840 feet.
MILITARY: In Saigon, South Vietnam, former U.S. Army chief of staff general Maxwell D. Taylor is assured by President Ngo Dinh Diem that the presence of American military troops is not required. However, he does appeal for continuing military aid and advisers.

October 20
AVIATION: In South Vietnam, an air force RF-101C Voodoo jet aircraft begins flying tactical reconnaissance missions at the behest of the South Vietnamese army.

October 23
AVIATION: In the Atlantic, the fleet ballistic submarine *Ethan Allen* completes the first submerged launching of a new A-2 Polaris missile. This new version features an increased range of 1,500 miles.

November 1
MILITARY: The Central Intelligence Agency (CIA) founds the Civilian Irregular Defense Group (CIDG) to organize indigenous mountain peoples (Montagnards) into anticommunist paramilitary forces. Total authorized strength is 530 men, including many Special Forces.

November 1–3
MILITARY: General Maxwell D. Taylor recommends to President John F. Kennedy that a "U.S. military task force" of 6,000 to 8,000 men be dispatched to South Vietnam to help combat the mounting Communist insurgency there. The president dismisses the project.

November 1–17
MARINES: In British Honduras, marines and helicopters of HMR(L)-264 assist recent victims of Hurricane Hattie.

November 9
AVIATION: An X-15 hypersonic research aircraft flown by Major Robert M. White hits speeds of over 4,000 miles per hour at an altitude of 101,600 feet. Thus,

on the X-15's 45th successful flight, it becomes the first manned craft to reach Mach 6.

• In South Vietnam, an Air Commando detachment called Farm Gate begins cobbling together a fleet of AT-28 Trojans, Douglas C-47s, and B-26 Invaders for the South Vietnamese air force.

November 15
AVIATION: In Saigon, South Vietnam, the 2nd Advanced Echelon, Thirteenth Air Force, is formally activated. The U.S. Air Force is now formally committed to the war in Southeast Asia. Operation Farm Gate also commences as teams from the 4400th Combat Crew Training Squadron deploy with special operations aircraft.

November 16
MILITARY: In Washington, D.C., President John F. Kennedy, after reading a report by General Maxwell D. Taylor, increases the number of military advisers to the Republic of South Vietnam.

November 17
AVIATION: At Cape Canaveral, Florida, a solid-propelled Minuteman missile is launched from a silo for the first time and sails to its target area 3,000 miles downrange.

November 18
MARINES: In the Dominican Republic, a navy task force carrying marines positions itself off the coast in the event of civil strife occasioned by the overthrow of its ruling dictator, General Rafael Trujillo.

November 21
AVIATION: At Cape Canaveral, Florida, the 6555th Aerospace Test Wing launches a Titan ICBM that carries a nose cone used in Nike-Zeus antimissile tests.

November 22
AVIATION: A McDonnell-Douglas F-4 Phantom II jet fighter establishes a new air speed record of 1,606 miles per hour.

• The air force launches an Atlas-Agena B launch booster carrying a highly secret *Samos* reconnaissance satellite.

November 25
NAVAL: At Newport News, Virginia, the nuclear-powered aircraft carrier *Enterprise* is commissioned. It is also the largest warship constructed to date, being 1,123 feet in length and possessing a flight deck covering four and a half acres and a gross weight of 85,320 tons.

November 28
AVIATION: The navy formally approves the antisubmarine rocket system (ASROC), the first of its kind in the world.

November 29
AVIATION: At Cape Canaveral, Florida, a Mercury capsule is launched while carrying two chimpanzees as passengers. They complete two orbits and then return safely to Earth.

1961

November 30
AVIATION: The navy decides to eliminate lighter-than-air craft, which it has employed since the days of World War I.

December 1
AVIATION: At Malmstrom Air Force Base, Montana, the 10th Strategic Missile Squadron becomes the first Minuteman-equipped unit to be activated.

December 5
AVIATION: A McDonnell-Douglas F-4 Phantom II jet sets a new sustained altitude record of 66,443 feet; air force F-102 Delta Darts also intercept a Soviet Tu-16 Badger jet bomber attempting to penetrate Alaskan air space and turn it back.

December 11
AVIATION: The first shipment of 33 Vertol H-21C Shawnee helicopters and 400 crewmen arrives in Saigon, South Vietnam, onboard the transport vessel *Core*. Their mission is to ferry South Vietnamese forces to battle zones; they are also the first American combat troops in Southeast Asia.

December 15
AVIATION: With the completion of the 21st and final control center at Sioux City, Iowa, the North American Air Defense Command (NORAD), the SAGE system, becomes operational.

December 26
MILITARY: Viet Cong capture Army Specialist George Fryett as he rides his bicycle in Saigon, South Vietnam. He is the first American prisoner of the war, although the Communists, perplexed by this foreigner, release him the following June.

December 31
MILITARY: The tally of army casualties in Southeast Asia amounts to 14 killed and wounded.

1962

January
AVIATION: In Europe, the air force disbands the Skyblazers, its first jet display team, which had been performing before enthralled spectators since 1948.
MILITARY: Presently, there are 3,200 American personnel in South Vietnam of which 2,100 are army troops, which is a fourfold increase from only two months previously.
MARINES: In South Vietnam, Detachment A, 1st Radio Company, Fleet Marine Force, arrives to assist an army communications unit.

January 1
NAVAL: The navy creates the first Sea Air Land (SEAL) teams in response to President John F. Kennedy's penchant for unconventional warfare and counterinsurgency operations. The first cadre are drawn from existing Underwater Demolition Teams (UDT), which were first created during World War II.
MARINES: In South Vietnam, the Vietnamese Marine Corps is enlarged to over 6,000 rank and file.

January 4
NAVAL: In Washington, D.C., Fred Korth gains appointment as the 57th secretary of the navy.

January 7
AVIATION: At Tan Son Nhut Air Base, Saigon, South Vietnam, a detachment of specially equipped Fairchild C-123 Providers deploys to participate in Operation Trail Dust. This ambitious deforestation program is designed to deny Communist units their jungle cover through the spraying of herbicides. The air force contribution to this project, dubbed Ranch Hand, lasts nine years to the day and performs its last mission on January 7, 1971.

January 9
MARINES: At Camp Pendleton, California, the 5th Marines, elements of the 1st Marine Division, and the 3rd Marine Air Group (3rd MAW) rehearse a four-day counterinsurgency exercise. This training appears increasingly relevant, considering the course of events in Southeast Asia.

January 10–11
AVIATION: An air force Boeing B-52H jet bomber flown by Major Clyde P. Evely flies nonstop from Okinawa, Japan, to Madrid, Spain, in 22 hours and 10 minutes, covering 12,532 miles. This is a new record for unrefueled flight distance.
MILITARY: To calm tensions along the Berlin Wall, the American government removes its tanks from that sector of Berlin. The Soviets reciprocate two days later.

January 13
AVIATION: Near Saigon, South Vietnam, air force C-123 Providers begin Ranch Hand operations by spraying deforesting agents along suspected Communist jungle strongholds.

January 15
AVIATION: A force of 18 F4U-2N Crusader jet fighters from VMF-451 crosses the Pacific to Hawaii nonstop while refueling from tanker squadrons VMR-153, 253, and 352. This is also the first mass crossing of the Pacific by an active jet squadron.

January 20
MILITARY: In a major move, men and officers of the Military Advisory and Assistance Group (MAAG) are ordered by the commander in chief, Pacific, to accompany into the field South Vietnamese units they are training. Shortly after, they are authorized by President John F. Kennedy to return fire if attacked.

January 29
AVIATION: At Cape Canaveral, the last of 47 test firings of the Titan I missile occurs; there were only three complete failures.

February 1
AVIATION: Marine helicopter squadrons receive new designations with HMR(L)s becoming medium helicopter squadrons (HMM), HMR(M) squadrons becoming HMH, while fixed-wing transport and tanker squadrons become aerial refueler transport squadrons (VMGR).

1962

February 2
AVIATION: Over South Vietnam, a C-123 Provider performing defoliant missions crashes into the jungle during a training exercise. Captain Fergus C. Groves, Captain Robert D. Larsen, and Staff Sergeant Milo B. Coghill are the first air force fatalities in Southeast Asia.

February 4
AVIATION: South of Saigon, South Vietnam, Vietcong ground fire brings down the first army H-21C Shawnee helicopter as it ferries ARVN troops into battle. The crew of four is killed; this is also the first helicopter lost in Southeast Asia.

February 5
AVIATION: A Sikorsky SH3A turbine-powered helicopter flown by Marine captain L. K. Keck and Navy lieutenant R. W. Crafton achieves a world speed record of 210.6 miles per hour.

February 8
AVIATION: At Lakehurst, New Jersey, an A-4 Skyhawk jet is launched at only 1,000 feet by the new XRE-1 Cataport (portable catapult). When combined with portable arresting gear, the new Short Afield for Tactical Support (SATS) system will allow aircraft to operate from primitive expeditionary airfields.
MILITARY: In the latest sign of growing American involvement, the new Military Assistance Command, Vietnam (MACV) is created under Major General Paul D. Harkins for funneling advisers and supplies into South Vietnam. This unit complements the preexisting Military Advisory Assistance Group (MAAG), which continues as an independent entity under the commander in chief, Pacific (CINCPAC), for another two years.

February 10
DIPLOMACY: In Berlin, the Soviet Union releases Gary Francis Powers, whose U-2 spy plane was shot down over Russia in May 1960, in return for Soviet spy Rudolf Abel. He served one and a half years of a 10-year sentence.

February 20
AVIATION: Marine Corps lieutenant colonel John H. Glenn, Jr., becomes the first American to successfully orbit the Earth three times in his Mercury capsule named *Friendship 7.* He remains in space for five hours at a speed of 17,400 miles per hour at an altitude of 162 miles before a heat shield malfunction forces him to return early.

March 5
AVIATION: A B-58 Hustler flown by Captain Robert G. Sowers, 43rd Bombardment Wing, makes three speed records while flying round-trip and cross-country from New York to Los Angeles and back in four hours, 41 minutes, 11 seconds at an average speed of 1,044.5 miles per hour. The crew wins both Mackay and Bendix trophies.

March 8
MARINES: Along the Outer Banks, North Carolina, helicopters of HMM-263 render emergency relief assistance after one of the most violent storms to hit the area.

March 15
MILITARY: The first official campaign streamer of the Vietnam conflict, the Vietnam Advisory Campaign, begins today.

March 16
SCIENCE: The 100-foot tall, multiengined Titan 2 ICBM missile is launched and tested for the first time from Cape Canaveral, Florida, and flies downrange as far as Ascension Island in the South Atlantic.

March 21
AVIATION: The high-speed ejection capsule of the B-58 Hustler is tested when a live bear is strapped inside and then shot out at 35,000 feet while traveling at 870 miles per hour. The animal survives the seven-minute parachute descent without harm.

March 22
AVIATION: Reports of unidentified aircraft flying over South Vietnam prompts the deployment of four F-102 Delta Daggers to Tan Son Nhut Air Base, Saigon. The aircraft arrive from their deployment station at Clark Air Base, Philippines.
MILITARY: The Strategic Hamlet program, also known as Operation Sunrise, begins in Binh Dong province, South Vietnam, as American advisers help construct and fortify a new village to deny the Viet Cong access to the local population. However, this forced relocation causes intense resentment as many villagers do not want to move.

March 23
MILITARY: The first battalion-sized American unit to arrive in South Vietnam is the 39th Signal Battalion; it is in charge of all communication and support for the U.S. Army Support Group, Vietnam.

April 3
MILITARY: The Defense Department orders the full racial integration of military reserves and National Guard units.

April 4
AVIATION: A McDonnell Douglas F-4 Phantom II jet sets several time-to-climb records, becoming the first aircraft in history to simultaneously hold world records for high speed, sustained altitude, and climbing speed.
MARINES: Near Jacksonville, North Carolina, around 400 marines are dispatched to assist fire fighters.

April 9
MARINES: At the Soc Trang airstrip, Mekong Delta, South Vietnam, Marine Task Force Unit 79.3.5 (Shufly detachment) are flown in by transport aircraft. Their mission is to assist Vietnamese combat units with helicopter transport.

April 12
MARINES: Amphibious transport vessels of the Seventh Fleet land marines ashore in Thailand to support an independence movement there.

April 14
MARINES: At Onslow Beach, North Carolina, marines participate in LANTPHIBEX 1-61 while observed by President John F. Kennedy.

1962

April 15
MARINES: At Soc Trang airstrip, Mekong Delta, South Vietnam, helicopters of HMM-362 depart the carrier *Princeton* and deploy ashore to assist Vietnamese combat units.

April 18
AVIATION: At Lowry Air Force Base. Colorado, the Strategic Air Command (SAC) activates the 724th Strategic Missile Squadron, armed with nine nuclear-tipped Titan I missiles. They are also deployed in hardened underground silos designed to survive a Soviet first strike. The unit attains operational alert two days later.

April 19
AVIATION: An experimental Skybolt missile, an early form of cruise missile, is test-fired from a B-52 jet bomber over Cape Canaveral, but it falls short of its intended target.

April 22
AVIATION: Noted aviatrix Jacqueline Cochran flies a Lockheed Jetstar named *Scarlet O'Hara* across the Atlantic. Not only is Cochran the first woman to do so, but she also breaks 68 flight records in the process.
• In Lien Phong Province, Mekong Delta, South Vietnam, a force of 29 helicopters from HMM-362 airlifts a battalion of ARVN soldiers from the 7th Division into combat against the Viet Cong.

April 23
AVIATION: Helicopters of marine HMM-362 provide tactical assault airlift to units of the South Vietnamese marines.

April 26
AVIATION: The prototype Lockheed A-12 high-speed aircraft flies for the first time with company test pilot Lou Schalk at the controls. This aircraft is the precursor of the famous SR-71 Blackbird.

April 27
AVIATION: At Eglin Air Force Base, the Special Air Warfare Center is established.

May 2
MILITARY: The Pentagon and the Central Intelligence Agency agree to form a joint National Reconnaissance Office (NRO) to better manage spy satellite programs.

May 4
AVIATION: The top-secret Lockheed A-12 performs its maiden flight and reaches Mach 1.1 for the first time.

May 6
NAVAL: The nuclear missile submarine *Ethan Allen* successfully conducts a live Polaris missile test, which explodes downrange near Christmas Island. This is the first test of an American ballistic missile armed with a live warhead.

May 9
AVIATION: On the Ca Mau Peninsula, South Vietnam, eight marine helicopters are pot-shot at by Viet Cong small arms fire and damaged.

May 12

MARINES: Alarmed by the recent gains by Communist insurgents in Laos, the State Department authorizes the deployment of 5,000 marines to Thailand to enhance the latter's security.

MEDICAL: In Tuy Hoa, South Vietnam, the first Medevac operation is performed by the 57th Medical Detachment. This is also the first helicopter evacuation unit in the theater. By war's end in 1975, units such as this will have evacuated 900,000 American and allied casualties from a battlefield environment.

May 18

AVIATION: At Udorn Airfield, Thailand, a squadron of 20 A-4 Skyhawks arrives from the Philippines.

MARINES: In response to possible Communist aggression, the 3rd Marine Expeditionary Brigade begins deploying troops in Thailand. The Seventh Fleet also disgorges its landing force (3rd Battalion, 9th Marines and helicopters of HMM-261) at Bangkok.

May 20

MILITARY: In Washington, D.C., Cyrus W. Vance is named secretary of the army.

May 24

AVIATION: Lieutenant Commander Malcolm Scott Carpenter becomes the second American blasted into space and he completes three orbits in his Mercury capsule named *Aurora 7.*

June 16

MILITARY: Two U.S. Army officers, acting as advisers, are killed in a Viet Cong ambush north of Saigon.

June 19

AVIATION: The Dyna-Soar reentry vehicle receives the official designation of X-20. It is destined to be carried aloft by the huge Titan II rocket.

June 26

NAVAL: At Charleston Navy Base, South Carolina, the fleet ballistic submarine *Ethan Allen* conducts the first deterrent cruise while armed with new Polaris A-2 missiles.

June 29

AVIATION: At Cape Canaveral, Florida, the first military crew launches a Minuteman missile from an underground silo. The weapon flies to a target area 2,300 miles away.

• At El Toro, California, VMF(AW)-314 becomes the first marine squadron to receive F4H Phantom II jet fighters.

MARINES: Sergeant Major Thomas J. McHugh becomes the third sergeant major of the Marine Corps.

June 30

MARINES: On the cusp of intervention in Southeast Asia, Marine Corps manpower levels stand at 16,861 officers and 174,101 enlisted men.

1962

July 1
MILITARY: In Washington, D.C., General Orders 58 creates the new Army Intelligence and Security Branch; in 1967 it is redesignated the Military Intelligence Branch.

MARINES: In a major move, the new 4th Marine Division and the 4th Marine Air Wing (4th MAW) are created entirely from reserve components. This is a complete departure from the previous organization, which relied entirely upon battalions and squadrons. Those units newly reestablished include the 23rd, 24th, and 25th Marines, the 14th Marines (artillery), and Marine Air Groups 41, 43, and 46.
•   In light of ongoing negotiations in Laos, 1,000 men of the 3rd Marine Expeditionary Brigade depart Thailand and return to vessels of the Seventh Fleet.

July 5
MILITARY: In Washington, D.C., Cyrus R. Vance is sworn in as the seventh secretary of the army.

July 9
AVIATION: Operation Dominic unfolds 248 miles above the Pacific Missile Range as a nuclear-tipped missile, launched from Johnson Island in the Pacific, is detonated 200 miles up in the atmosphere. This is the highest-ever thermonuclear explosion and its electromagnetic pulse is felt at Oahu, Hawaii, 800 miles away.

July 17
AVIATION: An X-15 hypersonic research aircraft piloted by Major Robert M. White sets a new world altitude of 58.7 miles at a speed of 3,748 miles per hour. Having briefly glided through the vacuum of space at 300,000 feet, White also becomes the first test pilot to win astronaut wings in an airplane.

July 18
AVIATION: The growing utility of helicopters as a battlefield weapon is clearly demonstrated today when ARVN troops are airlifted into battle by a fleet of 18 marine, 12 army, and 11 Vietnamese air force helicopters.

July 19
AVIATION: Over the Pacific, a Nike-Zeus antimissile missile launches from Kwajalein Atoll and intercepts an Atlas missile nose cone previously launched from Vandenberg Air Force Base, California. This marks the first time that a missile has been intercepted by a specifically designed antimissile missile.

July 25
AVIATION: The army activates the Utility Tactical Transport Squadron, unique in also being the first armed helicopter unit.

July 27
MARINES: Laos having declared its neutrality, the last of 5,000 marines begins withdrawing from Thailand.

August 1
AVIATION: At Vandenberg Air Force Base, California, the first launch of an Atlas F missile takes place successfully and flies toward its target area in the Marshall Islands some 5,000 miles downrange.

MILITARY: Congress passes a military appropriations bill for $48.1 billion.

August 7
AVIATION: At Cape Canaveral, Florida, the first A-3 Polaris ballistic missile is launched; this vastly improved version has a range of 2,500 miles.

August 9
AVIATION: At Cape Canaveral, Florida, a demonstration of multiple countdown capability is staged when two Atlas D missiles are launched in quick succession.

August 17
NAVAL: At Seattle, Washington, the navy launches its first experimental, high-speed hydrofoil named the *Long Point.*

August 18
NAVAL: At Annapolis, Maryland, Rear Admiral Charles C. Kirkpatrick gains appointment as the 42nd superintendent of the U.S. Naval Academy.

August 22
NAVAL: The successful rendezvous of two American nuclear submarines beneath the North Pole's ice caps is announced by President John F. Kennedy.

August 31
AVIATION: At Naval Air Station Lakehurst, New Jersey, the navy's last airship makes its final flight before all lighter-than-air operations cease.

September 4
MARINES: The Shufly force and its helicopters (HMM-362 having replaced HMM-163) are deployed at Da Nang, South Vietnam, in the I Corps tactical zone.

September 8–20
NAVAL: The *Raleigh,* the first in a class of amphibious transport docks, is commissioned.

September 14
AVIATION: The National Aeronautics and Space Administration (NASA) reveals the next nine astronauts chosen for the space program. The air force officers are Major Frank Borman, Captain James A. McDivitt, Captain Edward H. White, and Captain Thomas P. Stafford. A civilian NASA pilot among them, Neil A. Armstrong, becomes the first man to walk on the moon in 1969.

September 18
AVIATION: At Edwards Air Force Base, a B-58 Hustler flown by Major Fitzhugh L. Fulton carries an 11,000-pound payload at an altitude of 85,360 feet; this record remains unbroken.

September 21
MILITARY: At Fort Bragg, North Carolina, the 5th Special Force Group, 1st Special Forces, is activated. President John F. Kennedy takes a keen interest in their counterinsurgency capabilities.

September 30–1 October
MILITARY: In Oxford, Mississippi, the Mississippi National Guard is federalized by President John F. Kennedy and sent to restore order after integration-related riots break out at the University of Mississippi.

1962

October 1
MILITARY: In Washington, D.C., General Earle G. Wheeler becomes the 23rd chief of staff of the army.

October 3
AVIATION: At Cape Canaveral, Florida, Commander Walter M. Schirra completes six orbits around the Earth in 10 hours and 46 minutes while piloting his Mercury capsule *Sigma 7.*

October 6
MILITARY: The army removes its last Special Forces White Team from Laos. That nation had declared its neutrality four months earlier.
NAVAL: The navy commissions the *Bainbridge,* the world's first nuclear-powered guided missile frigate.
MARINES: In South Vietnam, the marines sustain their first fatalities when a helicopter of HMM-362 (Shufly force) crashes, killing five marines and two navy corpsmen.

October 12
MILITARY: In a move of iconic significance, President John F. Kennedy approves a request by Brigadier General William P. Yarborough to allow Special Forces to wear green berets as part of their standard uniform.

October 14
AVIATION: In a startling revelation, a U-2 flown by Major Steve Heyser from the 4080th Strategic Reconnaissance Wing photographs Soviet medium-range ballistic missiles on the island of Cuba. Viewed as a direct threat to American security, it marks the start of the Cuban missile crisis.

October 15
AVIATION: At Naval Air Station Jacksonville, Florida, the RF-8A Crusaders of Light Photoreconnaissance Squadron 62 (VFP-62) begin assisting air force units with intelligence-gathering flights over Communist Cuba.

October 16
MILITARY: In Washington, D.C., President John F. Kennedy is shown incontrovertible evidence of Soviet missiles and IL-28 Beagle jet bombers through U-2 photographs. He consults with the Executive Committee of the National Security Council to draft an appropriate response. Kennedy rejects a recommendation from the Joint Chiefs of Staff for surgical air strikes because they cannot guarantee that all missiles sites and bombers would be disabled in the first strike. He settles upon a more flexible approach by imposing a quarantine, a peacetime naval blockade, of Cuba.

October 18
AVIATION: The air force mobilizes eight Reserve troop-carrier wings and six aerial port squadrons in response to the Cuban missile crisis.

October 19
MILITARY: Marine units begin receiving alert orders following the discovery of Soviet offensive nuclear missiles on Cuba. The first unit to depart is the

1962

Wheeler, Earle G.   (1908–1975)
Army general

Earl Gilmore Wheeler was born in Washington, D.C., on January 13, 1908, and he graduated from the U.S. Military Academy in 1932. A competent officer, he passed through the Infantry School in 1937 and the Command and General Staff College in 1941, and, by the end of World War II, he was a colonel in the 63rd Infantry Division. Wheeler campaigned in Europe throughout 1945 and returned home to successfully fill a number of significant positions, including intelligence officer with the Joint Chiefs of Staff, director of plans for the Office of the Deputy Chief of Staff for Military Operations, and director of the Joint Staff of the Department of Defense. Wheeler became a protégé of General Maxwell D. Taylor and agreed with him on many fundamentals of his new "flexible response" strategy. He was also an extremely cordial, low-key individual, much given to the notion of civilian authority over the military. In October 1962, with Taylor's urging, President John F. Kennedy appointed him the new army chief of staff. Wheeler's deference to Secretary of Defense Robert S. McNamara, his willingness to part with other senior military leaders and endorse the nuclear test ban treaty, and his overall reputation as a "team player" culminated in his appointment as chairman of the Joint Chiefs of Staff in July 1964. Given his reputation for intelligence and military acumen, much was expected of him.

Wheeler was certainly a smooth and loyal operative, but his six-year tenure in office proved stormy owing to the expanding American role in the Vietnam War. As President Lyndon B. Johnson ordered more and more American troops into that theater, Wheeler pressed him to declare a national emergency and mobilize the Reserves to maintain army manpower levels elsewhere, but the president refused. Wheeler also expressed public support for Johnson's and McNamara's "gradualist"

2nd Battalion, 1st Marines, which leaves El Toro, California, on the following day.
• In Tay Ninh Province, South Vietnam, a force of 5,000 ARVN soldiers are ferried by helicopters to battle Viet Cong forces northwest of Saigon.

October 21
MARINES: To increase pressure on the Soviet and Cuban governments, advanced echelons of the 1st and 2nd Marine Divisions begin arriving at Guantánamo Bay, Cuba, to bolster the garrison there.

October 22
AVIATION: In light of ongoing tensions with the Soviet Union over Cuba, all aircraft and missiles of the Strategic Air Command (SAC) are placed on 24-hour alert. To underscore American determination, B-52 bombers take up orbital positions outside of Soviet airspace where they are clearly observed by radar.

approach to military escalation, but he opposed it privately as did the Joint Chiefs of Staff. The downturn in developments in the war nearly alienated Johnson from his senior military leaders, but Wheeler remained unwilling to confront civilian authority and American strategy remained unchanged. The politically disastrous Tet Offensive in January 1968 was exploited by Wheeler, who sought to have General William C. Westmoreland request 200,000 additional troops by mobilizing the Reserves and National Guard. Once again, Johnson refused. Wheeler enjoyed a closer rapport with President Richard M. Nixon, who took Wheeler's advice and bombed Communist sanctuaries in Laos and Cambodia, but, by then the war was lost. Wheeler suffered a second heart attack in July 1970 and resigned from active duty. He died in Frederick, Maryland, on December 18, 1975, generally regarded as a highly intelligent and competent military leader, but one whose deference to political authority and whose nonconfrontational style

Earle Wheeler, former secretary of the U.S. Army *(Department of Defense)*

insured that the disastrous strategy devised by civilians and imposed on the military throughout the Vietnam War prevailed.

MILITARY: From Washington, D.C., President John F. Kennedy addresses the nation on television about his imposition of a naval quarantine of Cuba, as of October 24. After that date, no Soviet vessels will be allowed to approach the island and will be turned back at sea, by force if necessary.
• In light of growing tensions over Soviet nuclear missiles in Cuba, President John F. Kennedy orders two Hawk and one Nike-Hercules missile batteries into southern Florida; similar units will remain on active alert there until 1979.
MARINES: In San Diego, California, the 5th Marine Expeditionary Brigade–11,000 strong–prepares to sail for service in the Caribbean.

October 24–November 30
NAVAL: Because Soviet offensive weapons are arriving by ship in Cuba, President John F. Kennedy takes the unprecedented step of ordering the navy to quarantine that island and search all Russian vessels approaching Cuban water. The mission

falls upon Task Force 136 under Vice Admiral Alfred G. Ward, whose force consists of the antisubmarine carrier *Essex,* assisted by two heavy cruisers and support ships. Simultaneously, Task Force 135 is created under Rear Admiral John T. Hayward to help defend American bases at Guantánamo Bay. This consists of two carrier battle groups centered upon the *Enterprise* and *Independence* as backup. The Cuban missile crisis is edging the world to the brink of nuclear war.

October 23
DIPLOMACY: In New York, the United Nations Security Council convenes to consider a charge by the United States that the Soviet Union is threatening world peace. The Organization of American States also vote 19–0 to authorize force to impose the quarantine on Cuba.

October 24
NAVAL: With the naval quarantine of Cuba in effect, upward of 25 Soviet vessels headed for that island halt, then turn around.

October 25
AVIATION: RB-47 Stratojets and KC-97 tankers of the Strategic Air Command (SAC) assist the navy in detecting and tracking Soviet vessels headed for Cuba.
NAVAL: The destroyer *Gearing* accosts the Soviet tanker *Bucharest* at sea and searches it for offensive weapons; none are found and the ship is allowed to continue.

October 26
DIPLOMACY: In Washington, D.C., President John F. Kennedy receives a letter from Soviet premier Nikita Khrushchev stating that he placed missiles in Cuba only to deter the United States from invading. Moreover, he is willing to remove them if the Americans end the blockade and pledge not to attack the Castro regime.
NAVAL: Destroyers *Joseph P. Kennedy* and *John R. Pierce* halt the Soviet chartered Lebanese freighter SS *Marucla* at sea and allow it to continue once its cargo is inspected.

October 27
AVIATION: A U-2 reconnaissance craft flown by Major Rudolph Anderson, Jr., of the 4080th Strategic Reconnaissance Wing is shot down by Soviet missiles over Cuba; Anderson is killed and wins a posthumous Medal of Honor.
• At Malmstrom Air Force Base, Montana, the 10th Strategic Missile Squadron places its 10 Minuteman I missiles on operational alert for the first time.

October 28
DIPLOMACY: Under intense pressure, the Soviet government agrees to remove all offensive nuclear missiles from Cuba. In return, the United States will not attack that island and will also remove its intermediate-range missiles from Turkey. Concerning the latter, given their obsolete, liquid-fuel technology, the Americans were intending to scrap them anyway.
MARINES: As the 5th Marine Expeditionary Brigade sails from San Diego, California, the 2nd Marine Division and elements of Marine Air Groups 14, 24, 26, 31, and 32 deploy at Key West, Florida, for an anticipated invasion of Cuba.

October 28
Diplomacy: In Moscow, Premier Khrushchev informs the American government that he is ordering all offensive Soviet weapons in Cuba withdrawn within 30 days. This declaration diffuses the crisis.

October 29
Aviation: Continuing reconnaissance flights by air force RF-101 Voodoos reveal that Soviet missiles in Cuba are being dismantled.
Naval: The United States temporarily lifts its blockade of Cuba to allow UN Secretary-General U Thant passage to confer with Communist dictator Fidel Castro.

November 2
Aviation: In the wake of the Chinese/India border clash, Operation Long Skip is authorized by President John F. Kennedy to airlift military supplies and equipment to Calcutta. In this instance the Military Air Transport Service (MATS) relies on its new C-135 jet transports and conveys 1,000 tons of military cargo in only two weeks.
•   Marine lieutenant colonel John H. Glenn receives the first Cunningham Trophy for outstanding marine pilot of the year. It is presented by the Marine Aviation Force Veterans Association.

November 8
Military: In Washington, D.C., Department of Defense officials certify that all Soviet missile launchers in Cuba have been disassembled.

November 13
Marines: In Hawaii, 400 men of the 3rd Battalion, 4th Marines are airlifted to Guam to provide relief measures in the wake of a violent typhoon.

November 20
Naval: In light of the Soviet decision to remove all offensive bombers and missiles from Cuba, the naval quarantine is suspended by President John F. Kennedy.

November 24
Aviation: Both Grumman and General Dynamics are contracted by the Department of Defense to construct the prototype Tactical Fighter Experimental (TFX), an advanced design with variable-sweep wings, twin engines, and a 20,000 payload capacity at Mach 2.5. It emerges as the controversial F-111, popularly known as the Aardvark because of its peculiarly long nose.

November 30
Marines: Marine units activated for service during the Cuban missile crisis are ordered to stand down and begin returning to their home stations.

December 5
Aviation: At Cape Canaveral, Florida, the last Atlas missile is test-fired, at which point the program concludes. Of 151 launches, only 108 are judged successful.

December 13–14
Aviation: Project Stargazer takes place over New Mexico as a specially equipped balloon piloted by Captain Joseph A. Kittinger, Jr., and astronomer William C.

White rises to 82,000. They remain in place for 18 hours and use the gondola-mounted telescope for the closest-ever observation of the stars.

December 22
AVIATION: On Kwajalein Island, the air force fires a Nike-Zeus antimissile missile and an incoming Atlas launched from Vandenberg Air Force Base, California. The test proves that the Nike-Zeus can discriminate between a target and its attendant decoys.

December 27
AVIATION: The air force orders six Lockheed SR-71 high-speed reconnaissance aircraft; they are derived from the A-12 version already under construction.

1963

January
MILITARY: American troop strength in South Vietnam stands at 7,900 soldiers and advisers. To date, army aviation units have performed 50,000 sorties on behalf of ARVN, nearly half of them during combat operations.

January 2
AVIATION: At Ap Bac, South Vietnam, U.S. aircraft participating in Operation Burning Arrow bomb suspected Viet Cong sites for an hour. Subsequently, Piasecki H-21 helicopters follow up by landing South Vietnamese troops and supplies in the area.

January 7
AVIATION: At Fort Benning, Georgia, moves are underway to create an experimental Air Assault Division under Brigadier General Harry O. Kinnard. It will consist of eight battalions in three brigades, two assault helicopter battalions, a company of light observation helicopters and several companies of Bell UH-1B gunships armed with M60 machine guns and rocket pods. By 1965 it is ready for deployment to South Vietnam as the 1st Air Cavalry Division.

February 1
AVIATION: The American Rocket Society (1930) and the Institute of Aerospace Sciences (1932) are combined to form the new American Institute of Aeronautics and Astronautics.

February 6
AVIATION: At Cape Canaveral, the 655th Aerospace Test Wing launches a Titan II for the first time.
MARINES: In Washington, D.C., President John F. Kennedy invokes Theodore Roosevelt's 1908 orders that marine officers serving in the capital should complete a 50-mile hike within 20 hours of marching over three days. Twenty officers at Camp Lejeune, North Carolina, take up the president's challenge.

February 13
MARINES: At Camp Lejeune, North Carolina, a force of 53 marines board the ship *Spiegal Grove* on a 14-week goodwill tour of Africa entitled Solant Amity IV.

February 21
AVIATION: Two Cuban-based military jets attack the American fishing boat *Ala* as it drifts in international waters 60 miles north of Cuba.

February 24
MILITARY: In South Vietnam, an American soldier is killed after Viet Cong ground fire downs three H-21 helicopters. Hereafter, all army soldiers are authorized to shoot back in their own defense. The gloves are coming off.

March 1
AVIATION: At Cape Canaveral, Florida, the air force successfully tests an advanced ballistic reentry system for the first time.

March 13
AVIATION: Two large Soviet reconnaissance aircraft apparently flew over Alaskan territory and three days later the United States files a formal protest.

April 10
NAVAL: In the North Atlantic, 240 miles east of Cape Cod, Massachusetts, a tragic accident claims the nuclear-powered submarine *Thresher* under Lieutenant Commander John W. Harvey and 129 crew members during a test dive. The vessel was apparently at a test depth of 1,300 feet when its reactor shut down and its auxiliary engines could not halt its descent.

April 11
MILITARY: In Saigon, South Vietnam, 100 soldiers from the 25th Infantry Division arrive to serve as door gunners on army H-21 Shawnee helicopters.

April 12
AVIATION: Noted aviatrix Jacqueline Cochran sets a new women's world speed record of 1,273.2 miles per hour in a Lockheed F-104 Starfighter.

April 13
AVIATION: In Vietnam, marine transport helicopters are escorted by army UH-1B helicopter gunships for the first time.

April 23
NAVAL: The submarine *Lafayette* is commissioned, the first of a new class of ballistic missile vessels.

April 30
DIPLOMACY: In Haiti, the government requests that the marine training mission be withdrawn.

May 1
AVIATION: Over Edwards Air Force Base, California, aviatrix Jacqueline Cochran makes another women's world record by passing through a 100-kilometer course at 1,203.7 miles per hour.

May 4
MARINES: During a period of political unrest in Haiti, the 2nd, Battalion, 2nd Marines, while training in the Caribbean, positions itself off that embattled country if needed.

1963

Cochran, Jacqueline   (1906–1980)
Air Force officer

Jacqueline Cochran was born in Pensacola, Florida, and orphaned at an early age. Raised by relatives, she endured a hardscrabble existence by toiling in the cotton fields until finding success as a beautician. In 1932, while on a business trip to New York City, she met and married millionaire Floyd Odlum, who convinced her to take flying lessons. Barely literate, she passed her flying exam orally in 1934 and the following year became the first woman to compete in the Bendix Continental Air Race. In 1938 she was approached by flamboyant aircraft designer Alexander P. De Seversky to fly his specially modified fighter craft, and that year Cochran became the first woman to win the Bendix Trophy. She later garnered no less than six prestigious Harmon trophies for being the most distinguished aviator of the year. Following the outbreak of World War II,

Cochran approached Army Air Force head Henry H. Arnold to push for female pilots, and, in 1941, he allowed her to ferry a bomber to England for the first time. Once America joined the war, Arnold appointed

Jackie Cochran in the cockpit of a Canadair F-86 with Chuck Yeager (*U.S. Air Force*)

May 7
AVIATION: In South Vietnam, an air force RB-57E participates in Operation Patricia Lynn by performing a high-altitude reconnaissance mission.

May 9
MILITARY: A highly classified air force satellite is launched from Point Arguello, California, containing 400 million copper hairs that are released in orbit to form a reflective cloud for relaying radio signals across the United States.

May 15–16
AVIATION: At Cape Canaveral, Florida, the Mercury Space Capsule *Faith 7* blasts into orbit carrying U.S. Air Force major L. Gordon Cooper. He remains in space for 34 hours and 19 minutes while completing 22 orbits before returning safely to Earth. Cooper is the first American astronaut to remain in space for more than one day and his mission also concludes Project Mercury.

Cochran head of the new Women's Air Force Service Pilots (WASPs) with a rank of lieutenant colonel. In this post she oversaw more than 1,000 women pilots who flew more than 60 million miles while ferrying aircraft abroad, and who sustained 38 fatalities. The WASPs were disbanded in December 1944 and women would not be allowed to fly military aircraft again for the next three decades. In 1945 Cochran became the first woman to land an aircraft in Japan and was present during surrender ceremonies on the battleship *Missouri* in Tokyo Harbor. She was also the first civilian to receive the Distinguished Service Medal and was honored by the governments of France, Spain, Turkey, China, and Thailand.

After the war, Cochran remained a lieutenant colonel in the Air Force Reserve and eagerly sought to become part of the new jet age. Mentored by her friend and test pilot Chuck Yeager, she became the first woman to break the sound barrier fly-ing an F-86 Sabrejet in May 1953. Three years later she became the first woman president of the Federation Aeronautique International, and, in 1962, she became the first woman to pilot a jet aircraft across the Atlantic. Cochran next set the woman's world speed record flying an F-104 Starfighter at speeds of 1,424 miles per hour in 1964. Cochran retired from the military as a full colonel in 1969, and, two years later, she became the first woman inducted into the U.S. Aviation Hall of Fame. Cochran also pushed Congress to recognize the WASPs as military veterans, which it finally did in 1977. Through all this Cochran also found the time to run a successful cosmetics company, serve as a director of Northwest Airlines, and twice be nominated as businesswoman of the year. Cochran died in Indio, California, on August 9, 1980, having set over 200 flying records, most of which still stand, and forever laying to rest the gender barrier in aviation.

May 24

AVIATION: At Wendover, Utah, a top-secret Lockheed A-12 crashes for the first time.

May 27

AVIATION: At St. Louis, Missouri, the first F-4C Phantom II performs its maiden flight; nearly 600 are acquired by the Tactical Air Command (TAC).

June 8

AVIATION: At Davis Monthan Air Force Base, the 570th Strategic Missile Squadron is the first operational Titan II unit in the Strategic Air Command (SAC).

June 15–24

MARINES: Off Pohang, South Korea, the 11th Marine Expeditionary Brigade and elements of the Korean Marine Corps (KMC) conduct joint amphibious operations.

June 17
AVIATION: The prototype Sikorsky CH-3C helicopter performs its maiden flight; it is unique in possessing a hydraulic rear ramp.

July 1
MILITARY: In Southeast Asia, the CIA CIDG program to recruit indigenous tribesmen as anticommunist allies falls under the purview of the 5th Special Forces Group.

July 20
AVIATION: The Lockheed A-12 flies for the first time over Mach 3.

July 20–21
AVIATION: In South Vietnam, a C-47 transport flown by Captain Warren P. Tomsett rescues a group of wounded South Vietnamese soldiers near the Cambodian border. They then land at Lon Noc under Viet Cong fire and fly the injured men back to Bien Hoa Air Base. Their efforts culminate in a Mackay Trophy.

July 25
DIPLOMACY: Negotiations between the United States, Great Britain, and the Soviet Union culminate in the Partial Test Ban Treaty, which outlaws aboveground, outer space, or underwater testing of nuclear weapons.

July 26
AVIATION: *Syncon 2* becomes the first satellite placed in a geosynchronous orbit, which remains fixed over a specific position on Earth.

August 1
AVIATION: An air force rocket booster launches the *Mariner 2* satellite; a year later it completes a journey of 540 million miles to become the first man-made object to orbit the Sun.
•   Marine all-weather attack squadrons are redesignated fighter attack squadrons. They are now called MFA-314, 513, and 531, and are equipped with McDonnell-Douglas F4H Phantom II jets.
NAVAL: In Washington, D.C., Admiral David L. McDonald gains appointment as the 17th chief of naval operations.

August 7
AVIATION: At Groom Lake, Nevada, the Lockheed YF-12A high-speed interceptor performs its maiden flight with test pilot James Eastham at the controls.

August 22
AVIATION: An X-15 hypersonic research airplane flown by test pilot Joe Walker reaches an altitude of 354,200 feet (67 miles) while cruising at 4,159 miles per hour. This is the highest altitude ever reached during the program.

August 30
MILITARY: In Tay Ninh Province, northwest of Saigon, South Vietnam, Viet Cong ground fire downs an H-21 Shawnee helicopter, killing two Americans and injuring three others.

October 7
MARINES: At Bridgeport, California, the new Mountain Warfare Training Center is created from the previous Cold Weather Training Center.

1963

October 10
AVIATION: All seven of the original Mercury astronauts receive the Collier Trophy for their accomplishments.

October 16
MILITARY: To preclude any secret violations of the nuclear test ban treaty, two top-secret detection satellites (Project Vela Hotel) are launched from Cape Canaveral, Florida. They assume 7,000-mile orbits at opposite poles of the Earth to obtain the widest possible coverage.
• During Operation Greased Lightning, a B-58 Hustler flies from Tokyo, Japan, to RAF Greenham Common, England, in eight hours and 35 minutes This is a new record for the 8,028-mile distance.

October 22
AVIATION: The Cessna YAT-37D, an armed version of the T-27 trainer, flies for the first time. This craft will see extensive service over South Vietnam.
• In a startling display of military airlift, the entire 2nd Armored Division transfers from Fort Hood, Texas, to Germany in only 65 hours. This is the first time an entire armored formation has been moved in such fashion.
MARINES: At Port-au-Prince, Haiti, helicopters of HMM-162 arrive on the *Thetis Bay* to bring food and medical supplies to hurricane ravaged areas of that nation.

October 25
NAVAL: The nation of Haiti, reeling from the effects of Hurricane Flora, is assisted by humanitarian supplies provided by several navy ships, which deliver 375 tons of supplies, food, and medicine.

October 26
AVIATION: The fleet ballistic submarine *Andrew Jackson* conducts the first submerged test firing of a Polaris A-3 missile. This latest variant weighs two tons more than its predecessors and has a range of 2,500 miles.

November 1–2
DIPLOMACY: In Saigon, South Vietnam, the government of Ngo Dinh Diem is overthrown by a military coup; President Diem is killed. The ensuing political instability impedes American efforts to assist the country fight a Communist insurgency.
MILITARY: In Southeast Asia, the CIA turns over its border surveillance program to the 5th Special Forces Group. By the following summer, border camps have been erected along strategic infiltration routes.

November 4
DIPLOMACY: Soviet troops obstruct a U.S. military convoy headed for Berlin, but it is allowed to proceed after protests are lodged.

November 15
MILITARY: In South Vietnam, MACV declares that 1,000 of the 16,575 American military personnel present will be gradually withdrawn owing to progress made by the Vietnamese armed forces.

November 22
MILITARY: President Lyndon B. Johnson is sworn in as president and commander in chief following the assassination of John F. Kennedy. At the time, Johnson, who

has been deliberately kept out of Kennedy's inner circle, knows little about his predecessor's plans for Southeast Asia.

November 24

POLITICS: In Washington, D.C., President Lyndon B. Johnson declares his support for continued military support for South Vietnam in its struggle against Communist aggression.

November 29

AVIATION: In Washington, D.C., President Lyndon B. Johnson signs an executive order renaming Cape Canaveral, Florida, Cape Kennedy.

NAVAL: In Washington, D.C., Paul H. Nitze gains appointment as the 58th secretary of the navy.

December 3

MILITARY: In South Vietnam, the first 100 American military advisers slated for removal depart.

December 4

AVIATION: The navy makes public its plans to develop a rocket-powered, nuclear-tipped guided missile capable of destroying enemy submarines at long range. Entitled SUBROC, it is designed to be fired from a conventional torpedo tube.

December 10

AVIATION: In Washington, D.C., Secretary of Defense Robert S. McNamara signs legislation to produce the Manned Orbiting Laboratory for the air force.

• Over Edwards Air Force Base, California, a rocket-augmented NF-104A Starfighter flown by Colonel Chuck Yeager reaches 90,000 feet and then stalls in a flat spin. Yeager falls to 10,000 feet before he is able to eject safely with minor injuries.

• The X-20 Dyna-Soar program is cancelled without ever reaching the prototype stage.

December 17

AVIATION: At Dobbins Air Force Base, Georgia, the Lockheed C-141 Starlifter performs its maiden flight. This will be the first all-jet transport aircraft obtained by the air force and is capable of hauling 123 fully armed troops or 70,000 pounds of cargo.

December 31

AVIATION: In Washington, D.C., President Lyndon B. Johnson authorizes U-2s of the 4028th Strategic Reconnaissance Squadron to deploy in South Vietnam. They will join the 100 or so air force aircraft already there.

MARINES: In Washington, D.C., General Wallace M. Greene becomes the 32nd commandant of the Marine Corps.

1964

January

MILITARY: Presently, there are 10,100 army personnel in South Vietnam; of these 489 have become casualties with 45 killed in action.

January 11
NAVAL: In Annapolis, Maryland, Rear Admiral Charles S. Minter gains appointment as the 43rd superintendent of the U.S. Naval Academy.

January 13
NAVAL: In the Indian Ocean off Africa, a spate of revolutionary violence on the island of Zanzibar forces the destroyer *Manley* to evacuate 55 American citizens.

January 16
MILITARY: In Washington, D.C., the Joint Chiefs of Staff approve creation of the MACV Studies and Observation Group (SOG), a highly classified operation employing Special Forces and intended for secret operations in Vietnam, Cambodia, and Laos. Special teams of South Vietnamese operatives are also being instructed for clandestine work inside of Communist North Vietnam.

January 24
AVIATION: An air force T-39 Sabreliner, on a routine training mission, strays into East German airspace and is shot down over Thuringia; the crew of three is killed.

January 28
MILITARY: In Washington, D.C., Stephen Ailes becomes the eighth secretary of the army. He becomes responsible for dispatching the first combat units to South Vietnam.

February 1
NAVAL: Vice Admiral Hyman G. Rickover, assistant chief of the Bureau of Ships for Nuclear Propulsion and director of atomic reactors in the Atomic Energy Commission, remains in service at the request of President Lyndon B. Johnson. Rickover is at the mandatory retirement age of 64, but he subsequently obtains biennial extensions for the next decade and a half.

February 3
MILITARY: In an ominous development, Viet Cong sappers attack an army advisory compound and kill an American soldier. This marks the first time that soldiers have been targeted within their own facilities.

February 6
NAVAL: After Communist authorities on Cuba cut off fresh water supplies to the navy base at Guantánamo, the United States responds by constructing its own saltwater conversion plants to make it self-sufficient.

February 29
AVIATION: President Lyndon B. Johnson announces at a press conference that the Lockheed A-11 (a fighter version of the famous SR-71 reconnaissance jet) is capable of operating at speeds in excess of Mach 3, or 2,000 miles per hour, at altitudes of 70,000 feet. However, it does not enter production.

March 3
MARINES: On Taiwan, the VII Marine Expeditionary Force (elements of the 1st and 3rd Marine Divisions, the 1st Marine Brigade, and the 1st Marine Air Group) conduct joint amphibious exercises with Nationalist Chinese forces.

1964

March 10

AVIATION: Soviet jets shoot down an unarmed Douglas RB-66 Destroyer reconnaissance jet after it strays into East German airspace near Gardelegen; the crew of three is detained and then released.

March 23

MARINES: In light of current events in Southeast Asia, the 1st Marines conduct a 12-day counterinsurgency exercise at Camp Pendleton, California.

March 28–April 17

AVIATION: In the wake of a devastating earthquake/tidal wave at Anchorage, Alaska, Operation Helping Hand is launched as air force cargo planes fly in 1,800 tons of supplies over the next three weeks.

April

MARINES: On Okinawa, the 1st and 3rd Battalions, 12th Marines, have their mortar companies equipped with the new M98 107mm mortar. The device is dubbed the "Howtar" because of its howitzer-like wheeled mount.

April 8

AVIATION: At Cape Canaveral, Florida, an air force Titan II launch rocket carries an unmanned Gemini space capsule into orbit for the first time.

April 9–15

MILITARY: In the Mekong Delta, South Vietnam, Viet Cong attacks kill 250 ARVN soldiers and militiamen, along with four American advisers.

April 21

AVIATION: In an important benchmark, the number of intercontinental ballistic missiles in the Strategic Air Command (SAC) equals the number of manned bombers it operates for the first time. From this point forward, faster ICBMs begin to exceed manned bombers in importance from the standpoint of nuclear deterrence.

April 27

AVIATION: In northern II Corps, South Vietnam, helicopters of HMM-364 transport Vietnamese troops throughout Operation Sure Wind.

May 11

AVIATION: Aviatrix Jacqueline Cochran sets a new women's speed record by flying a Lockheed F-104G Starfighter at 1,429.3 miles per hour over a 15–25 kilometer course.
• At Palmdale, California, North American rolls out its futuristic XB-70 Valkyrie supersonic bomber, capable of flying to targets from 70,000 feet and three times the speed of sound. It is also a huge bombing platform, being 185 feet long with a 105-foot wingspan.

May 13

NAVAL: The first nuclear-powered task group, consisting of the carrier *Enterprise*, the cruiser *Long Beach*, and the frigate *Bainbridge*, forms in the Mediterranean as part of the Sixth Fleet.

1964

Rickover, Hyman G.   (1900–1986)
Admiral

Hyman George Rickover was born in Makow, Poland, on January 27, 1900, a son of Russian Jews. He immigrated to the United States at the age of six and helped support his family by working as a messenger. An excellent student, in 1918 he gained admission to the U.S. Naval Academy and weathered four years of anti-Semitism by studying in his room. Rickover graduated in 1922 and performed a number of routine land and naval assignments before receiving a master's degree in electrical engineering from Columbia University in 1929. His reputation as a problem-solver then landed him a position as head of the electrical division with the Bureau of Ships in Washington, D.C. In this post he oversaw the development and installation of modern electrical systems on warships. However, the turning point in his career occurred in 1946 when he was one of a handful of officers chosen to study at the Manhattan Engineering District at Oak Ridge, Tennessee. Here Rickover was fully exposed to the new science of atomic energy and he began crusading for its application to sea power. The problem was that the tradition-bound naval bureaucracy scoffed at the notion of nuclear energy for anything but weapons. Fortunately for the navy, he proved himself a skilled political fighter with influential friends in Congress.

In 1947 Rickover maneuvered himself into serving as both chief of the nuclear power division at the Bureau of Ships and head of the naval reactor branch of the Atomic Energy Commission. Moreover, he had a direct hand in designing and building all the essential components, which, when tested, worked perfectly. These efforts culminated in March 1953 when the *Nautilus,* the world's first atomic-powered submarine, was launched. It was a brilliant technological accomplishment coming only a decade after the first atomic reaction, but Rickover made plenty of enemies in the process. He was passed over for promotion twice in 1951 and 1952, until Congress pressured the navy to make him an admiral in July 1953. Admiral Rickover pushed hard for a fleet of nuclear-powered surface vessels, and, in the early 1960s, the carrier *Enterprise,* the guided-missile cruiser *Long Beach,* and the frigate *Bainbridge* all demonstrated the viability of nuclear propulsion for warships. To say that he controlled the navy's atomic program is an understatement; Rickover not only held final authority over the most minute design changes, but he also rigorously grilled and handpicked all officers serving on nuclear submarines at sea. Rickover was considered so indispensable that he was retained on active duty after the mandatory retirement age of 65 and, in 1973, he advanced in rank to full admiral. Rickover retired in January 1982 after six decades of conscientious service to the nation. He died in Washington, D.C., on July 8, 1986, one of the most contentious and truly visionary figures in American naval history. The nuclear submarines he championed in the 1940s have since become standard equipment in all major navies of the world. He was truly "father of the nuclear navy."

May 15

MILITARY: In a consolidation move, MACV absorbs the MAAG, and also receives increased manpower and expanded responsibilities for training and arming the ARVN.

• Leaping Lena, a CIA-run covert reconnaissance project, is turned over to MACV under the new code name Project Delta. It requires U.S. Special Forces to train several companies of their South Vietnamese counterparts for intelligence-gathering missions anywhere in the country. The project is maintained until July 1970 and collects useful information on 70 North Vietnamese units and infiltration routes.

May 18

AVIATION: The first RF-4C Phantom II reconnaissance jet performs its maiden flight. This craft serves as the tactical reconnaissance workhorse of the Vietnam War.

May 20

MARINES: A threshold is crossed after Marine Advisory Team One under Major Alfred M. Gray arrives in South Vietnam, consisting of 30 radio operators and 76 men from Company G, 2nd Battalion, 3rd Marines. This is the first marine combat unit sent to Southeast Asia and it is tasked with providing radio support to ARVN forces.

June 1–20

MARINES: In Norway, 300 miles above the Arctic Circle, Company I, 3rd Battalion, 6th Marines participates in Northern Express, a NATO cold-weather exercise.

June 4

MARINES: On Mindoro, Philippines, the SEATO Exercise Ligta unfolds with marines from the United States and troops from Australia, Great Britain, New Zealand, and the Philippines. Exercises include large amphibious and airborne assaults.

June 6

AVIATION: Over the Plaine des Jarres, Laos, an RF-8A Crusader of VFP-63 (*Kitty Hawk*) flown by Lieutenant Charles F. Klusmann is shot down by the Pathet Lao and he ejects into the jungle; he is held captive until escaping on September 1 and receives a Distinguished Flying Cross. Klusmann is part of a reconnaissance effort known as "Team Yankee."

June 7

AVIATION: Over Laos, an F8U Crusader flown by Commander Doyle W. Lynn of VF-111 (*Kitty Hawk*) is shot down; Doyle ejects and is rescued by a helicopter.

June 9

AVIATION: Eight F-100 Super Sabres, refueled in midair by KC-135 Stratotankers, bomb Pathet Lao Communist gun emplacements for the first time.

June 20

MILITARY: In Saigon, South Vietnam, General William C. Westmoreland succeeds to the head of MACV.

1964

June 21
AVIATION: In South Vietnam, HMM-364 turns over all its helicopters to the Vietnamese air force, which is forming its first squadron. Its role in Shufly Force is also assumed by HMM-162.

June 28
AVIATION: VMFA-531 arrives in the Far East after flying from Cherry Point, North Carolina, and crossing the Pacific after stops at Hawaii and Wake Island.
•   At Cape Canaveral, Florida, the *Ranger 7* space probe is launched on a lunar trajectory. It is tasked with taking photographs of the moon's surface before crashing northwest of the Sea of Clouds.

July 1
AVIATION: At Santa Ana, California, marine helicopter squadron HMM-164 is activated and also becomes the first such unit equipped with new, twin-rotor Boeing CH-46 Skyknights.

July 3
MILITARY: In Washington, D.C., General Harold K. Johnson gains appointment as the 24th chief of staff of the army.

July 4
MILITARY: At Polei Krong, South Vietnam, a strong Viet Cong detachment overruns a Special Forces camp, killing 51 ARVN soldiers and wounding two American advisers.

July 6
AVIATION: Marine helicopters of HMM-162 participate in the relief of the Special Forces camp at Nam Dong.
MILITARY: At Nam Dong, Central Highlands, South Vietnam, a Viet Cong battalion attempts to storm a Special Forces camp but is repelled by Captain Roger A. Donlon and 11 men of Detachment A-726.

July 17
MARINES: On Tiger Tooth Mountain, South Vietnam, Marine Advisory Team One repels a Viet Cong attack on its perimeter.

July 24
AVIATION: In Washington, D.C., President Lyndon B. Johnson reveals the existence of the RS-71 high-speed reconnaissance aircraft. He inadvertently refers to it as the "SR-71" and the moniker sticks.

July 27
MILITARY: In light of mounting Communist activity throughout South Vietnam, the United States announces the deployment of 5,000 additional combat troops.

July 30
NAVAL: At Guantánamo Bay, Cuba, the navy dedicates a new freshwater plant; the base is no longer dependent upon Cuban water sources.

July 31–October 3
NAVAL: At Gibraltar, Task Force 1, consisting of the carrier *Enterprise,* the cruiser *Long Beach,* and the guided-missile frigate *Bainbridge,* all nuclear-powered,

Westmoreland, William C.   (1914–2005)
Army general

William Childs Westmoreland was born in Spartanburg, South Carolina, on March 26, 1914, the son of a banker. He graduated from the U.S. Military Academy in 1936 and was assigned routine garrison duties in Hawaii prior to World War II. Once the United States entered the conflict, Westmoreland transferred to the European theater where he performed capably in North Africa, Sicily, and France from 1943 to 1944. Westmoreland advanced to colonel in July 1944 and served as a staff officer in the drive toward Germany, and afterward commanded the 60th Infantry during a stint of occupation duty. He returned home after the war to take paratroop training at Fort Bragg, North Carolina, and subsequently attended the Command and General Staff College at Fort Leavenworth, Kansas. After the Korean War broke out in 1950 he pressed superiors for a command and subsequently led the 187th Airborne Regimental Combat Team into action. This was the only paratroop formation committed to combat during that conflict and Westmoreland led it with distinction. After serving several years as secretary to U.S. Army chief of staff general Maxwell Taylor, Westmoreland became the army's youngest major general in 1956, and, two years later, he took charge of the elite 101st Airborne Division. In July 1960 President Dwight D. Eisenhower appointed him superintendent of West Point, where he remained three years before leaving to command the 18th Airborne Corps at Fort Bragg. The turning point in Westmoreland's career came in 1964 when President Lyndon B. Johnson appointed him head of the U.S. Military Assistance Program in South Vietnam, one of the most daunting challenges ever faced by any American general of the 20th century.

South Vietnam was then being heavily infiltrated by guerrilla units commanded by

embark on an around-the-world cruise without refueling. Operation Sea Orbit is completed in only 64 days after they dock at Charleston, South Carolina, on October 1.

August 1
MARINES: At Quantico, Virginia, the Marine Corps School Senior Course is redesignated the Marine Corps Command and Staff College, and the Junior Course becomes the Amphibious Warfare School.

August 2
NAVAL: The destroyer *Maddox* under Captain Herbert L. Ogier, patrolling the Gulf of Tonkin 30 miles off of North Vietnam, is attacked in international waters by three Communist patrol boats, one of which is sunk by return fire.

August 4
NAVAL: In the Gulf of Tonkin off North Vietnam, the destroyers *Maddox* and *Turner Joy* report being attacked by several Communist torpedo boats, which

1964

Communist North Vietnam, and Westmoreland successfully pressed for an increase in American manpower from 20,000 to half a million by 1968. With such a force at his disposal, he orchestrated an intense campaign of "search-and-destroy" missions in the jungles to root out the insurgents and their supply bases, and the forces inflicted heavy losses on enemy units when cornered. Though bloodied, however, the Communists were far from defeated, and, in January 1968, they launched their surprise Tet Offensive. Westmoreland quickly countered this attack and defeated it with severe losses, but many Americans now felt that the war was unwinnable. Prior to this event, Westmoreland had been sending back optimistic progress reports and he took the blame for failing to crush his adversaries. In June 1968 he was succeeded by General Creighton Abrams and returned home to serve as chief of staff of the army. He served in this post until his retirement in July 1972. In 1982 he won

Secretary of Defense Robert S. McNamara and General Westmoreland talk with Gen. Thi, I Corps Commander, July 1965. *(National Archives)*

a bitter lawsuit against the CBS network over its assertion that he had lied about known enemy troop strengths. Westmoreland died in Charleston, South Carolina, on July 18, 2005, a talented but luckless commander.

they repel with gunfire. This is a major escalation of hostilities between the two nations and provides President Lyndon B. Johnson with a convenient pretext for expanding American military involvement in Southeast Asia.

August 5
AVIATION: Acting upon the orders of President Lyndon B. Johnson, Operation Pierce Arrow commences as aircraft from the carriers *Ticonderoga* and *Constellation* attack petroleum assets and naval facilities at Vinh, Phuc Loi, Loc, Chao, Hongay, and Quang Khe, North Vietnam. The *Constellation* loses two aircraft: Lieutenant Richard A. Sather dies when his A-1H Skyraider is downed by antiaircraft defenses; Lieutenant Everett Alvarez becomes the first American captive of the Vietnam War after his A-4 Skyhawk is shot down; he remains a prisoner for nine years until February 1973.
• The air force begins a mass redeployment of B-57s, F-100s, F-102s, RF-101s, and F-105s to Southeast Asia for participation in the Vietnam War.

1964

August 7
POLITICS: In a major abrogation of its oversight responsibilities, Congress overwhelmingly approves the Gulf of Tonkin Resolution, which grants President Lyndon B. Johnson unlimited authority to expand the conflict in South Vietnam.

August 14
AVIATION: At Vandenberg, California, the Atlas/Agena D booster rocket is flight tested for the first time.

August 17
MARINES: At Camp Pendleton, California, the Edson Range opens as a replacement for Camp Calvin B. Matthews, which is closing due to urban encroachment from nearby San Diego.

September 1
AVIATION: At the General Electric Space Center, Valley Forge, Pennsylvania, Air Force Captains Albert R. Crews and Richard E. Lawler finish a two-week "mission" onboard a simulated space cabin. NASA officials now believe humans can perform numerous tasks in space for longer periods of time than previously expected.

September 11
AVIATION: The air force retires two squadrons of Atlas liquid-fueled intercontinental ballistic missiles in favor of more versatile Minuteman I solid-fuel rockets. Over 100 more Atlas missiles are destined to be decommissioned as more Minuteman missiles are deployed.

September 13
MARINES: In South Vietnam, Marine Advisory Team One is disbanded and departs the theater.

September 17
MILITARY: President Lyndon B. Johnson announces that two antimissile systems, based upon existing Nike-Zeus and Thor rockets, are under development. Apparently, these employ radar that can see "over the horizon" by following the curvature of the Earth.

September 18
NAVAL: Nighttime jitters continue in the Gulf of Tonkin as the destroyers *Morton* and *Parsons* fire on radar contacts believed to be North Vietnamese torpedo boats. Neither vessel sustains damage.

September 21
AVIATION: At Palmdale, California, the huge North American XB-70 Valkyrie, an experimental supersonic bomber, passes its maiden flight. This is a six-engined giant intended to fly at supersonic speeds. However, because of recent strides in surface-to-air missile technology, such aerial tactics are obsolete and it never enters production.
MILITARY: In Darlac, Central Highlands, South Vietnam, allied Montagnard tribesmen rebel against South Vietnamese troops in their vicinity, killing 34 and taking several American advisers hostage. Special Forces are rushed in to prevent a general massacre of South Vietnamese prisoners and calm is restored.

September 28
NAVAL: At Charleston, South Carolina, the fleet ballistic submarine *Daniel Webster* embarks on its first deterrent cruise while armed with the new Polaris A-3 missiles.

October 1
MILITARY: In South Vietnam, the 5th Special Forces Group deploys and establishes its headquarters. However, because many field teams are undermanned, the tour of duty is extended from six months to 12.

October 13
MILITARY: The army declares its decision to dispatch a third helicopter company to work with ARVN forces in the Mekong Delta, South Vietnam.

October 26
MARINES: In Spain, Exercise Steel Pike I unfolds as 22,000 marines train with 2,000 Spanish marines.

November 1
AVIATION: In another major escalation, Viet Cong sappers sneak past the perimeter of the U.S. air base at Bien Hoa, South Vietnam, and fire mortars; five B-57s Canberras are destroyed and 15 more are damaged while four Americans are killed and 72 wounded. Four Douglas A-1 Skyraiders belonging to the South Vietnamese air force are also gutted.

November 10
AVIATION: The first A-12 reconnaissance sortie takes place over the island of Cuba.

November 17
AVIATION: Operation Dragon Rouge unfolds as C-130 Hercules transports of the 464th Troop Carrier Wing deliver French paratroopers and help rescues hostages held in Zaire. After returning nearly 2,000 hostages to France, the unit receives a Mackay Trophy.
• Marine helicopters from HMM-365 and 162 assist victims of recent flooding in central South Vietnam.

November 26
MARINES: In Cairo, Egypt, a mob protesting U.S. policies in Zaire attacks the U.S. embassy and part of the Marine Guard facility is burned.

December 4
MILITARY: At Binh Gia, southeast of Saigon, South Vietnam, Viet Cong units attack and defeat ARVN forces until three battalions of marines and airborne troops are helicoptered in. The Communists withdraw, but only after 500 South Vietnamese and five American advisers are killed.

December 6
NAVAL: At Guantánamo Bay, Cuba, the navy completes the last of three saltwater conversion plants, making the base independent of any outside water source. The Communist regime of Fidel Castro had cut off the flow of fresh water the previous February 6.

December 10
AVIATION: A Titan II booster hoists a 3,700-pound satellite into orbit using new "Transtage" technology. This entails placing the entire third stage of the rocket into orbit, then launching the payload into an even farther orbit.
• Over Quang Tin and Bihn Dinh Provinces, South Vietnam, air force A-1 Skyraiders deliver punishing blows to Viet Cong units caught in the open. Rocket and cannon fire inflicts several hundred casualties.

December 14
AVIATION: In Southeast Asia, Operation Barrel Roll commences as air force armed reconnaissance aircraft begin flying missions over northern Laos; the project is maintained until the following April.

December 15
AVIATION: In South Vietnam, an AC-47 flown by Captain Jack Harvey, equipped with side-firing Gatling guns, performs the first aerial gunship mission of the Vietnam War. Such aircraft also receive the nickname "Spooky."

December 17
MILITARY: Special Forces captain Roger A. Donlon becomes the first American soldier to receive the Medal of Honor for fighting in South Vietnam, and the first so honored since the Korean War.

December 21
AVIATION: At Fort Worth, Texas, the revolutionary General Dynamics YF-111A successfully flies for the first time; this is the first American military aircraft incorporating a variable geometry (swing) wing.

December 22
AVIATION: The SR-71A flies a one-hour mission, during which time it easily reaches 1,000 miles per hour.
• In Washington, D.C., President Lyndon B. Johnson approves funding for development of a new, large jet transport, the C-5A Galaxy. This new aircraft will be capable of carrying 345 fully armed troops or 250,000 pounds of cargo over 6,500 miles at speeds of 550 miles per hour.

December 22–January 22
AVIATION: Severe flooding in Oregon and northern California leads to Operation Biglift, during which air force transports carry 1,500 tons of humanitarian relief to victims.

December 23
MILITARY: In An Xuyen Province, South Vietnam, U.S. troops use CS riot gas in an attempt to free prisoners held by the Viet Cong. The mission turns up empty, although, hereafter, MACV policy allows soldiers to employ gas in self-defense when attacked.

December 24
MILITARY: In Saigon, South Vietnam, a Viet Cong bomb demolishes the Bachelor Officer's Club, killing two Americans and wounded 51.

1964

December 26
NAVAL: At Guam, the fleet ballistic submarine *Daniel Boone* embarks on the first A-3 Polaris deterrent cruise of Pacific waters.

December 31
MILITARY: At this juncture, the United States has deployed 23,000 servicemen from all four branches in South Vietnam.

1965

January
AVIATION: The Bell Corporation begins manufacturing the AH-1 Cobra, the world's first helicopter gunship. This is a complete departure from existing helicopter designs for it is slim, agile, and heavily armed with machine guns and rockets.
MILITARY: Army personnel in South Vietnam totals 14,700 officers and men. More important, because MACV is aware that North Vietnamese troops have begun infiltrating down the Ho Chi Minh Trail into South Vietnam, the cry goes out for additional manpower to stop them. Since fighting began in 1961, the United States has suffered 1,300 dead and 6,100 wounded in South Vietnam.

January 1
AVIATION: At Beale Air Force Base, California, the 4200th Strategic Reconnaissance Wing is activated. It is the first unit equipped with SR-71 Blackbirds.

January 6
AVIATION: Flight testing continues with the General Dynamics F-111A swing-wing fighter bomber. Early trials of the variable-geometry wing at 470 miles per hour reveal no ill effects to the flight profile.

January 12
AVIATION: An Atlas rocket booster launches the Aerospace Research Satellite into a westward orbit for the first time. This device is used to measure radiation and micrometeorites while in orbit.

January 18
AVIATION: In Washington, D.C., President Lyndon B. Johnson informs Congress of his intention to acquire a short-range attack missile to be carried by B-52s and F-111s. This nuclear-tipped, standoff weapon will have a range of at least 50 miles.

February 1
AVIATION: In Washington, D.C., General John P. McConnell gains appointment as U.S. Air Force chief of staff.
MARINES: At Fort Drum, New York, the 1st Battalion, 8th Marines, VMGR-252, and helicopters of HMM-265 participate in Operation Snowflex-65. For marines, this is the largest cold-weather exercise on the East Coast in four decades.

February 4
AVIATION: A Titan IIIC solid-fuel rocket booster is fired for the first time in a two-minute test, and develops 25 percent greater thrust than anticipated—1.25 million pounds.

• A Bomarc supersonic drone is successfully intercepted by Air Defense Command pilots. The target was cruising at 1,500 miles per hour at an altitude of 50,000 feet.

February 6
MILITARY: A Viet Cong raid on Camp Holloway at Pleiku, South Vietnam, results in eight Americans killed and 126 wounded. President Lyndon B. Johnson expands aerial bombardment of North Vietnam in retaliation.

February 7–11
AVIATION: The navy executes Operation Flaming Dart 1, during which the carriers *Hancock, Coral Sea,* and *Ranger* launch air strikes against military barracks at Dong Hoi, North Vietnam. The move comes in response to an earlier Viet Cong attack against American installation at Pleiku, South Vietnam; one aircraft is shot down.

February 8
AVIATION: As part of Operation Flaming Dart, air force F-100 Super Sabres fly top cover for South Vietnamese aircraft making bombing strikes over North Vietnam. This is the first time air force aircraft have ventured so far north.

MARINES: In light of recent Communist attacks on American units, President Lyndon B. Johnson orders the 1st Light Anti-Aircraft Missile (LAAM) Battalion to deploy at Dan Nang, South Vietnam.

February 10
MILITARY: At Qui Nhon, Vietnam, an American enlisted men's barracks is blown up by Viet Cong sappers, 23 soldiers die and 21 are wounded.

February 11
AVIATION: In retaliation for the recent attack on Americans in Qui Nhon, South Vietnam, the carriers *Hancock, Coral Sea,* and *Ranger* unleash Operation Flaming Dart II against military barracks at Chan Hoa, North Vietnam. The *Coral Sea* loses an F-8 Crusader.

February 12–March 9
MARINES: At Camp Pendleton, California, Operation Silver Lance is the largest amphibious operation held since World War II and involves 25,000 marines and 20,000 sailors.

February 17
MARINES: In Da Nang, South Vietnam, a company of the 7th Engineer Battalion is deployed.

February 18
AVIATION: In South Vietnam, the air force begins a long regimen of tactical air strikes against Communist ground targets when B-57s and F-100s unload bombs near An Khe.

February 22–26
MARINES: In South Vietnam, MACV commander General Westmoreland requests two battalions of marines for the defense of the coastal city of Danang. Former general Maxwell D. Taylor, now ambassador to South Vietnam, cautions against

the move, feeling that it will give the impression that the Americans are coming to fight the war for the South Vietnamese. After much deliberation, however, the Joint Chiefs of Staff agree to the move, which constitutes the first phase of a general American buildup.

March 1
AVIATION: At Ellsworth Air Force Base, South Dakota, the first launch of an operational Minuteman I missile transpires.

March 2
AVIATION: President Lyndon B. Johnson, determined to awe the North Vietnamese into submission, authorizes Operation Rolling Thunder, a sustained aerial offensive against Communist military and economic targets. The strategy lasts until October 31, 1968, but its gradual escalation, allowing the North Vietnamese to adjust accordingly, fails to break the enemy's resolve to resist.
• An air force F-100 Super Sabre flown by Lieutenant Hayden J. Lockhart is shot down over North Vietnam on the first day of Operation Rolling Thunder. After evading capture for a week, he is imprisoned and remains a POW for the next eight years.

March 5
AVIATION: At Fort Worth, Texas, the General Dynamics F-111 prototype completes its first supersonic flight.

March 8
NAVAL: At Da Nang, South Vietnam, the amphibious transport dock *Vancouver*, the amphibious force flagship *Mount McKinley*, the attack transport *Henrico*, and the attack cargo ship *Union* land the 9th Marine Expeditionary Brigade ashore.

MARINES: The 9th Marine Expeditionary Brigade under Brigadier General Frederick J. Karch, totaling 3,500 men, lands at Da Nang, South Vietnam, This is the first American combat unit assigned here although its mission is to protect airfield facilities only. They join 23,000 military personnel already deployed, although the bulk of these troops serve in advisory capacities only.

March 9
MARINES: At Da Nang, South Vietnam, helicopters of HMM-162 and 163, and the 1st Light Antiaircraft Missile Battalion (LAAM), are assigned to the 9th Marine Expeditionary Brigade. All three are incorporated into Marine Air Group 16 (MAG-16).

March 11
NAVAL: Operation Market Time takes place as navy vessels and patrol aircraft of the Seventh Fleet are detailed to begin tracking and searching all coastal traffic for Communist arms smugglers. In time, Task Force 71 is created to coordinate all such endeavors and, by November, some 6,000 junks have been boarded and searched.

March 15
AVIATION: Aircraft from the carrier *Hancock* strike at the Phu Qui ammunition dump, 100 miles south of Hanoi; one aircraft and its pilot are lost.

March 21

MILITARY: To prevent the outbreak of hostilities, President Lyndon B. Johnson federalizes the Alabama National Guard and then deploys 2,200 army troops to protect 25,000 civil rights marchers en route from Selma to Montgomery.

March 23

AVIATION: At Patrick Air Force Base, Florida, Project Gemini commences as Lieutenant Colonel Virgil I. Grissom and Lieutenant Commander John W. Young are successfully launched in the *Gemini 3* capsule for three orbits around the Earth. This is the space flight in which the orbit was deliberately modified. Grissom is also the first American astronaut to return to space.

March 24

MILITARY: In Saigon, South Vietnam, the 716th Military Police Battalion is the first army unit to arrive following the decision to build up American forces. The country is also divided into four tactical zones for combat and administrative purposes.

March 26

AVIATION: A force of 40 aircraft from the carriers *Hancock* and *Coral Sea* attack four radar sites across North Vietnam; two are shot down but the pilots are rescued.

March 29

MARINES: In Saigon, South Vietnam, a bomb explodes outside the U.S. embassy, at which point the Marine Security Guard detachment restores order and security in that compound.

March 30

AVIATION: In the wake of civil unrest on the island of Cyprus, air force C-124 Providers transport 3,000 Danish peacekeepers and 76 tons of cargo to restore the peace.

April

AVIATION: From this month to the end of the Vietnam War, carriers on Yankee Station in the South China Sea begin launching daily raids of up to 100 aircraft against targets in North Vietnam, especially military bases, transportation networks, and power stations.

April 1

MARINES: At Da Nang, South Vietnam, the 9th Marine Expeditionary Brigade receives authorization to engage Viet Cong and North Vietnamese forces in their vicinity.

April 2–5

MILITARY: In the Mekong Delta, South Vietnam, heavy skirmishing with Viet Cong units takes the lives of six American advisers.

April 3

AVIATION: The air force, cognizant that the Communists are using a jungle route called the Ho Chi Minh Trail to infiltrate men and supplies into South Vietnam, commences Operation Steel Tiger to interdict them. This operation persists for the remainder of the war.

- South of Hanoi, North Vietnam, carrier aircraft from the *Hancock* and *Coral Sea* destroy the Dong Phuong Highway bridge. American pilots also mark the first visual observations of enemy MiG aircraft in the distance.

April 3–4
AVIATION: Over North Vietnam, Air Force F-105 Thunderchiefs severely damage the Thanh Hoa Bridge but are unable to drop any spans. Two F-105s are claimed by heavy antiaircraft fire.

April 9
AVIATION: South of Hainan Island, China, four navy F-4 Phantom IIs escorting an air raid into North Vietnam are attacked by four MiG-17s whose nationality is not determined. One F-4 is apparently lost.

April 10
AVIATION: Marine jets of VFMA-531 deploy directly onto the airfield at Da Nang, South Vietnam. This is the first appearance of Marine Corps aviation in the war.
MARINES: At Da Nang, South Vietnam, the 9th Marine Expeditionary Brigade is reinforced by the 2nd Battalion, 3rd Marines while its accompanying helicopters deploy at Phu Bai, 50 miles to the north.

April 12
MARINES: At Da Nang, South Vietnam, headquarters of the 3rd Marines arrive as the command element of various battalions.

April 13
AVIATION: Marine jets of VMFA-531 conduct their first combat mission in South Vietnam.

April 14
MARINES: At Da Nang, South Vietnam, the 3rd Battalion, 4th Marines is landed and marches inland. American combat strength at this juncture is 8,000 troops.

April 15
AVIATION: Aircraft from the carriers *Midway* and *Coral Sea* are joined by land-based army and marine counterparts in bombing suspected Viet Cong positions in South Vietnam. This is the first air strike to involve men and machines from all three services.
- The *Coral Sea* and *Midway* launch 10 aircraft, which perform the first reconnaissance missions over North Vietnam.

April 16
AVIATION: At Da Nang, South Vietnam, Marine Composite Reconnaissance Squadron 1 (VMCJ-1) deploys. It is equipped with updated but venerable Douglas EF-10B Skyknights.

April 20
AVIATION: At Lincoln, Nebraska, a milestone in American missile history is reached as the last of the liquid-fueled Atlas F intercontinental ballistic missiles of the 551st Strategic Missile Squadron are retired from operational status and placed in storage until used as launch vehicles for satellites. This completes the

1965

phaseout of the first generation of ICBMs. Hereafter, the U.S. Air Force depends almost entirely on solid-fueled rockets such as the Minuteman.

MARINES: At Da Nang, South Vietnam, the 9th Marine Expeditionary Brigade numbers 8,600 men and MACV commander General William C. Westmoreland orders them to conduct aggressive patrolling in the area. They are also instructed to prepare to act as a mobile reserve force.

April 22

AVIATION: A company of the 1st Battalion, 3rd Marines conducts the first helicopter assault in Marine Corps history by reinforcing a patrol outside Da Nang, South Vietnam.

MARINES: Outside Da Nang, South Vietnam, a patrol of the 9th Marine Expeditionary Brigade engages in the first firefight with Viet Cong forces, killing one enemy and sustaining one wounded.

April 23

AVIATION: At Travis Air Force Base, California, the first operational Lockheed C-141 Starlifter arrives. This four-engine jet becomes the backbone of the Military Air Transport Service (MATS).

April 26

MILITARY: Secretary of Defense Robert S. McNamara estimates that the total cost for supporting the burgeoning war effort in South Vietnam will cost $1.5 billion annually.

April 27

AVIATION: An air force ERB-47H Stratojet is attacked by North Korean MiG-17s over the Sea of Japan, suffers damage, yet lands safely in Japan.

NAVAL: In light of civil unrest in the Dominican Republic, the amphibious assault ship *Boxer* lands marines ashore and also evacuates 556 American citizens.

April 28

MILITARY: Elements of the 82nd Airborne Division and some Special Forces units are deployed to the Dominican Republic to restore order following a military coup and the onset of civil war. Once a provisional government is installed in September, the Americans are withdrawn.

MARINES: At Santo Domingo, Dominican Republic, parts of the 3rd Battalion, 6th Marines are landed to provide protection to the U.S. embassy during a period of political turmoil.

April 29–30

AVIATION: At Pope Air Force Base, North Carolina, Air Force C-130s and C-124s commence Operation Power Pack by flying in 17,000 tons of supplies to the strife-torn Dominican Republic. The flights are made by aircraft belonging to the U.S. Air Force, Air Force Reserve, and National Guard.

MARINES: At Santo Domingo, Dominican Republic, U.S. Marines strength rises to 1,600 with the arrival of other units, all of which are being organized into the 4th Marine Expeditionary Brigade.

April 30

MARINES: In Santo Domingo, Dominican Republic, two marines from the 3rd Battalion, 6th Marines are killed during street fighting to restore order in the city.

May 1

AVIATION: In a very good day for Colonel Robert L. Stephens, he flies the YF-12A at 2,070 miles per hour, breaking eight speed and altitude records in the process. Stephens and the SR-71 Test Force consequently win the Mackay Trophy.

May 2

AVIATION: The air force deploys an Oklahoma National Guard C-97 flying command post to facilitate transport services to the Dominican Republic. MATS eventually flies in 4,547 tons of supplies and 5,436 passengers as part of the mission.

MARINES: Men of the 4th Marine Expeditionary Brigade begin deploying in the Dominican Republic to help restore order; there are presently over 5,500 marines in the country. However, street fighting results in one marine death and three marines wounded.

May 3

MARINES: In the Dominican Republic, marines from the *Newport News* are landed to assist the 3rd Battalion, 6th Marines.

May 3–12

MILITARY: At Bien Hoa, northeast of Saigon, South Vietnam, the 173rd Airborne Brigade flies in from Okinawa and deploys. It is the first army combat unit to arrive in theater, and consists of 3,500 men, including the 3rd Battalion, 319th Artillery, also the first of its kind to arrive.

May 7

MARINES: In the I Corps zone, South Vietnam, III Marine Amphibious Force under Lieutenant General Lewis W. Walt replaces the 9th Marine Expeditionary Brigade while 3rd Marine Division headquarters assumes command for most ground units. The term expeditionary is dropped following a request by General William C. Westmoreland to remove the stigma attached to the French Expeditionary Force of a decade earlier.

• At Chu Lai, South Vietnam, the 3rd Marine Amphibious Brigade lands at Chu Lai, 50 miles south of Da Nang to construct a marine airfield. They are accompanied by several SeaBees construction engineers to complete the task.

May 9

MILITARY: The State Department announces that American troop strength in South Vietnam stands at 42,200.

May 10

AVIATION: Off the California coast, the tank-landing vessel *Tioga County* test-fires the first Seaspar antiaircraft missile. This weapon is subsequently renamed the Sea Sparrow, being based largely on the aircraft-carried Sparrow missile.

MILITARY: In Phuoc Long Province, South Vietnam, two Viet Cong regiments attack and overrun a base at Song Be, killing 48 South Vietnamese and five American advisers.

May 11

AVIATION: Headquarters, 1st Marine Air Wing (1st MAW) arrives at Da Nang to assume control of marine squadrons.

1965

MILITARY: In the Dominican Republic, elements of the 82nd Airborne Division begin arriving, bringing total American manpower on that island to 5,000 army and 6,000 marines. Political order, however, remains elusive.

MARINES: Near Da Nang, South Vietnam, men of the 2nd Battalion, 3rd Marines clear Viet Cong from the village of Le My and begin civic action programs to win over the population.

May 12

MARINES: At Chu Lai, South Vietnam, the 3rd Marine Amphibious Brigade disbands with the arrival of the 3rd Battalion, 3rd Marines, and control of the forces passes to the III Marine Amphibian Force. A total of 17,500 marines are present in country.

May 12–18

AVIATION: The air force is ordered by President Lyndon B. Johnson to suspend bombing of North Vietnam for the next six days in the hopes of prodding the Communist leadership into negotiating an end to the fighting; the gesture fails to evoke a response.

May 16

NAVAL: The navy establishes the single-carrier Dixie Station, 100 miles southeast of Cam Ranh Bay, South Vietnam, from which air strikes can be launched in support of ground forces. Within 15 months, once air strength ashore builds up, the station is abolished.

May 20

NAVAL: Destroyers of the Seventh Fleet provide the first naval gunfire support missions of the Vietnam War by attacking suspected enemy positions along the coast of South Vietnam.

May 22

AVIATION: Air force F-105 Thunderchiefs bomb north of the 20th parallel for the first time by striking North Vietnamese army barracks.

May 25

MARINES: In the Dominican Republic, U.S. mediation leads to a truce between various factions and marine units begin departing to vessels offshore.

May 26–June 6

MILITARY: Once the Organization of American States arranges a cease-fire in the Dominican Republic, army troops and marines begin withdrawing from that island.

June 1

AVIATION: At Chu Lai, South Vietnam, A-4 Skyhawks of VMA-225 deploy on the new SATS field completed there, the first time this concept has been used under combat conditions. The squadron also runs its first air strikes the same day.

June 3

MARINES: In Washington, D.C., President Lyndon B. Johnson orders the remaining 2,100 marines in the Dominican Republic withdrawn from the island. Casualties during this operation came to nine dead and 30 wounded.

Walt, Lewis W. (1913–1989)
Marine Corps general

Lewis William Walt was born near Harveyville, Kansas and attended Colorado State University. After graduating in 1936 Walt was commissioned second lieutenant in the Marine Corps and the following year he served as a platoon leader in Shanghai, China, guarding the International Settlement there. After World War II commenced, Walt joined the First Marine Raider Battalion and, in August 1942, he won his first Silver Star by fighting at Tulagi. Walt next fought on Guadalcanal, where he was wounded and won a Navy Cross defending Aogiri Ridge, subsequently named Walt Ridge in his honor. As a lieutenant colonel, Walt commanded the Fifth Marines in severe actions at New Britain and Peleliu, being wounded again. Walt remained in the service after the war and, in November 1952, he resumed command of the Fifth Marines in Korea and also served as chief of staff in the 1st Marine Division. He fought in the mountains of western Korea until August 1953, then returned home to receive the Legion of Merit and Bronze Star for outstanding service there. Walt rose to brigadier general in 1961 and major general in 1965. That year he faced his most daunting assignment as head of the III Marine Amphibious Force, then part of America's growing military involvement in the Vietnam War.

For a headstrong combat officer like Walt, his assignment in the I Corps tactical zone bordering Communist North Vietnam was vexing in the extreme. He differed with the large unit, search-and-destroy strategy of General William C. Westmoreland and felt that American interests were best served by small unit actions backed by an extensive rural pacification program. He originated the Combined Action Platoon program, which dispersed marine units in villages to help train local militias to defend themselves against the Viet Cong. Some progress was made, but after 1966 the North Vietnamese Army (NVA) began moving bigger units across the demilitarized zone, forcing Walt to respond in kind. The result was a higher casualty count on both sides, but no real military solution. Leaders in Washington also felt that his approach to winning hearts and minds was too slow to produce viable results. Walt departed Vietnam in June 1967, angered by the lack of progress, his disputes with Westmoreland, sagging public support for the war, and the refusal of political leaders in Washington, D.C., to allow the marines to attack Communist sanctuaries in neighboring Laos and Cambodia. Nonetheless, in light of his sterling reputation, he was appointed assistant commandant of the Marine Corps in 1968 and advanced to four-star rank a year later. Walt retired from active duty in February 1971, although not before roundly criticizing Congress for its lack of leadership, public schools for their ineffectiveness, and parents for not correctly teaching children. He also published his memoir, *Strange War, Strange Strategy* (1970), which excoriated American conduct of the Vietnam War. Walt died in Gulfport, Mississippi, on March 26, 1989, an accomplished and outspoken Marine Corps leader.

June 3–7

AVIATION: The *Gemini 4* space capsule blasts into space with U.S. Air Force majors Edward H. White and James A. McDivitt onboard. They set a new endurance record for U.S. astronauts by completing 63 Earth orbits in 97 hours. White also becomes the first American to perform a space walk outside his capsule, propelled by a gas-jet propulsion unit, for 23 minutes.

June 4

MARINES: In I Corps, South Vietnam, the III Marine Amphibious Force and 3rd Marine Division are to be commanded by Major General Lewis W. Walt.
• In a sign of escalating conflict, marines wage several company-sized engagements near Da Nang and Phu Bai, which costs them two dead and 10 wounded. They report killing 70 Communist troops.

June 7

MILITARY: In Saigon, General William C. Westmoreland requests an additional 44 battalions to counter the increasing number of North Vietnamese troops infiltrating down the Ho Chi Minh Trail. He hopes that such a show of force will convince Communist leaders that they cannot possibly win the war.

June 9

MILITARY: At Cam Ranh Bay, South Vietnam, the army 35th Engineer Group lands and begins developing it into a major port facility.

June 9–12

MILITARY: In Phuoc Long Province, South Vietnam, an estimated force of 1,500 Viet Cong attacks a Special Forces camp at Dong Xoai in the northern III Corps. The defenders, consisting of Montagnards and 24 Special Forces advisers, manage to repulse four heavy attacks before they can be evacuated by helicopter. Eight Americans die in action; executive officer Lieutenant Charles Q. Williams wins a Medal of Honor.

June 10

NAVAL: At Dong Xoai, South Vietnam, Seabee Team 1104 is attacked by superior Viet Cong forces and Construction Mechanic Third Class Marvin G. Shields, already wounded, volunteers to knock out a Communist machine-gun emplacement. He succeeds and is wounded a second time, then is fatally hit while returning to American lines. Shields receives a posthumous Medal of Honor.

June 12

NAVAL: At Annapolis, Maryland, Rear Admiral Draper L. Kaufman gains appointment as the 44th superintendent of the U.S. Naval Academy.

June 17

AVIATION: Over North Vietnam, two F-4B Phantom II jets from VF-21 (*Midway*) engage four North Vietnamese MiG-17s fighters and down two with Sidewinder missiles. These are the first confirmed aerial kills of the war.

June 18

AVIATION: An air force Titan III booster rocket, which generates 2.5 million pounds of thrust, hoists a 10.5-ton payload into Earth orbit. This is presently the most powerful launch rocket in use anywhere and consists of a liquid-fueled center rocket and two solid-fuel, trap-on boosters.

• Massed B-52 bombing raids (Arc Light missions) are carried out against suspected Viet Cong emplacements and concentrations only 30 miles north of Saigon, South Vietnam. A total of 28 aircraft complete the mission after flying in from Guam. This is the first time these massive bombers, designed for nuclear warfare, are impressed into a tactical role.

June 20
AVIATION: Over North Vietnam, four AD-1 Skyraiders from the carrier *Midway* are attacked by four MiG-17s; 20mm cannon fire from one of the Spads downs a MiG.

June 25
AVIATION: At El Toro, California, a military transport plane crashes after takeoff. A total of 79 marines are killed.

June 26
MILITARY: In Washington, D.C., the government allows General William C. Westmoreland permission to commit American forces to combat whenever he deems necessary. This move spells the end of the former, defense-minded enclave strategy and a new offensive phase of the war commences.

June 29
AVIATION: At Edwards Air Force Base, test pilot Joseph Engle, who flies the hypersonic X-15 research rocket, becomes the youngest pilot to earn his astronaut's wings.

June 30
AVIATION: At F. E. Warren Air Force Base, Wyoming, the 800th Minuteman I missile is activated by the Strategic Air Command (SAC). This is also the final example of this particular model acquired.

MARINES: At this stage in the Vietnam War, marine manpower totals 17,258 officers and 172,995 enlisted men. Of 50,000 American military personnel engaged in South Vietnam, marines account for 18,156, over one-third.

July 1
MARINES: At Da Nang, South Vietnam, Viet Cong sappers covered by a mortar barrage slip past the perimeter and damage six air force aircraft.

• In Qui Hon, South Vietnam, the Special Landing Force (3rd Battalion, 7th Marine and helicopters of HMM-163) are landed to protect an important logistics base in II Corps tactical zone.

July 2
MILITARY: In Washington, D.C., Stanley R. Resor is sworn in as the ninth secretary of the army. During his tenure, the first large overseas deployment of American combat troops occurs, as well as their initial withdrawal.

July 8
AVIATION: The former NASA communication and weather satellites *Syncom 2* and *Syncom 3* are taken over by the Air Force Satellite Control Facility upon orders from the Department of Defense.

1965

July 10
AVIATION: Over North Vietnam, a pair of F-4C Phantom IIs from the 45th Tactical Fighter Squadron shoots down two Communist MiG-17 jets, the first air force aerial victories of this war. The crews in question are pilots Thomas S. Roberts and Kenneth E. Holcomb and weapons officers Ronald C. Anderson and Arthur C. Clark.

July 14
MARINES: At Dong Ha, South Vietnam, units of the 3rd Marine Division move to an airfield just south of the Demilitarized Zone (DMZ) and bridges crossing the Cua Viet River into North Vietnam.

July 16
AVIATION: The prototype YOV-10A counterinsurgency (COIN) aircraft flies for the first time. It enters the U.S. Air Force and Marine Corps inventories as the OV10 Bronco.
MARINES: Sergeant Major Herbert J. Sweet becomes the fourth Sergeant major of the Marine Corps.

July 20–August 1
NAVAL: Coast Guard Division 1, boasting 17 82-foot vessels, arrives off of South Vietnam. They are tasked with monitoring coastal traffic to interdict weapons being smuggled to the Viet Cong.

July 24
AVIATION: Over North Vietnam, surface-to-air missiles down an air force F-4C Phantom II jet; this is the first American aircraft downed by SAMs in combat.
MILITARY: The Pentagon points to great advances in battlefield medicine and treatment, as the ratio of wounded to dead soldiers in combat is five-to-one, the highest of any American conflict.

July 26
MILITARY: President Lyndon B. Johnson, determined to stop Communist attacks in South Vietnam, announces an increase in military manpower from 75,000 to 125,000. The military draft will also be doubled from 17,000 to 35,000 young men per month.

July 28
MILITARY: In Washington, D.C., President Lyndon B. Johnson addresses the nation, informing the public that he is dispatching the 1st Cavalry Division and other units to South Vietnam. This move boosts American military strength in the region to 125,000.

July 29
MILITARY: The 1st Brigade, 101st Airborne Division under Colonel Joseph D. Mitchell deploys to II Corps, where it is to garrison the coastal province of Phu Yen. General William C. Westmoreland and Ambassador Maxwell D. Taylor, both former commanders, are on hand to greet them.

August 1
NAVAL: Along the coast of South Vietnam, Operation Market Time gives way to Task Force 115 under Rear Admiral Norvell G. Ward, Military Advisory Command, Vietnam (MACV).

1965

MARINES: At Phu Bai, South Vietnam, the Combined Action Program commences with units of the 3rd Battalion, 4th Marines. This entails a "Combined Action Platoon" of marines being assigned to local Vietnamese militia units for the purpose of protecting a specific village from Communist coercion.

August 2–11

MILITARY: At Duc Co, Central Highlands, South Vietnam, a Viet Cong force estimated at 3,000 attacks a Special Forces camp for several days until it is succored by the 173rd Airborne Brigade.

August 3

MILITARY: In Saigon, Army Military Police units deploy the first sentry dogs in the Vietnam War. No less than 2,200 dogs are used for scouting, sentry work, and mine detection by war's end.

MARINES: In the village of Can Ne, South Vietnam, marines are filmed burning huts by a CBS film crew; the footage, once aired, occasions public controversy.

August 5

AVIATION: The huge Saturn V booster rocket is ignited for a 2.5 minute static burn, during which it releases the equivalent of 7.5 million pounds of thrust. This same test vehicle is presently on display at the Kennedy Space Center.

August 7

AVIATION: At Grand Forks Air Force Base, North Dakota, the first Minuteman II missile is eased into its hardened silo.

A marine from 1st Battalion, 3rd Marine, escorts a Vietcong suspect. (*National Archives*)

August 10
MARINES: The Marine Corps is authorized to add three new infantry battalions, expanding manpower levels to 223,100.

August 11
AVIATION: Over North Vietnam, an A-4 Skyhawk from VA-23 (*Midway*) becomes the first navy jet shot down by a North Vietnamese surface-to-air missile (SAM).
• In South Vietnam, marine aircraft drop cluster bomb units (CBU) during a tactical sortie. These are particularly devastating in antipersonnel roles, although unexploded bomblets pose a hazard to civilians.

August 13
AVIATION: The dangers of attacking a heavily defended region like North Vietnam is underscored today when an A-1 Skyraider, two A-4 Skyhawks, and two F-8 Crusaders from the carriers *Midway* and *Coral Sea* are lost in combat.

August 14
NAVAL: In Washington, D.C., the Navy Department announces that all navy and marine enlistments will be involuntarily expanded by four months to facilitate personnel requirements.

August 15
MARINES: At Chu Lai, South Vietnam, the 7th Marine headquarters and the 1st Battalion, 7th Marines are deployed as the 3rd Battalion, 9th Marines rotates back to Okinawa.

August 18–24
NAVAL: On the Van Tuong Peninsula, 14 miles south of Chu Lai, South Vietnam, Operation Starlite commences as the amphibious ship *Iwo Jima* lands marines in defense of the city while the cruiser *Galveston,* accompanied by two destroyers, provides close support fire.
MARINES: Near Van Tuong, south of Chu Lai, South Vietnam, III Marine Amphibious Force commences Operation Starlite, the first regimental-sized operation since the Korean War. Elements of the 7th Marines either helicopter in or land on the shoreline and engage several Viet Cong units in firefights. The Communists are overpowered, leaving 623 bodies on the ground and several hundred sealed off in caves and bunkers; marine losses are 51 killed and 203 wounded. This is also the biggest land engagement fought by Americans since the Korean War.

August 21–29
AVIATION: At Cape Canaveral, Florida, the *Gemini V* space capsule roars aloft with Lieutenant Colonel L. Gordon Cooper and Commander Charles "Pete" Conrad; they successfully fly an eight-day mission and complete a record-breaking 120 Earth orbits.

August 28
NAVAL: Off La Jolla, California, an experiment is conducted to test the capacity of humans to live in confined spaces simulating space flight. To that end a 10-man group, including astronaut commander Malcolm Scott Carpenter, enter the *Sealab II* structure some 200 feet below the surface. While three teams of

volunteers rotate through every 15 days, Carpenter remains on the bottom for an entire month without ill effects.

September 1
MARINES: To increase the flow of manpower to the front without enlarging the instructor cadre, recruit training is decreased from 12 to eight weeks.

September 1–October 27
MARINES: In the I Corps tactical zone, the 9th Marines commence Operation Golden Fleece, a series of cordons and patrols intended to deny Viet Cong units access to the local rice harvest. All similar operations conducted by the III Marine Amphibious Force will bear the same title.

September 2
AVIATION: Marine Air Group 36 (MAG-36) begins deploying in South Vietnam with four helicopter squadrons and an observation squadron.

September 7
MARINES: Headquarters Marine Corps announces that, despite an influx of volunteer recruits, they will have to resort to a draft come January to meet their authorized manpower levels.

September 7–10
MARINES: South of Van Tuong, South Vietnam, the 7th Marines disperse Viet Cong concentrations along the Batangan Peninsula, killing 163 Communists.

September 8
AVIATION: Hurricane Betsey is photographed intensely by four U.S. Air Force–launched *Tiros* satellites, becoming the first large storm so studied.

September 11
MILITARY: At An Khe, South Vietnam, advanced elements of the 1st Cavalry (Airmobile) Division establish their headquarters in the central II Corps. This is a new formation sent to test the theory of vertical envelopment with helicopters and represents a quantum leap in terms of troop mobility.

September 15–21
AVIATION: After the newest India-Pakistan war erupts, the air force commences Operation Nice Way to evacuate 1,000 citizens and foreign nationals.

September 20
MILITARY: In Washington, D.C., the Joint Chiefs of Staff authorize Project Shining Brass, which entails highly classified cross-border operations into Laos for the purpose of gathering military intelligence along the Ho Chi Minh Trail and performing sabotage. The teams involved usually consist of three Special Forces troops and nine Montagnard tribesmen. Over 1,200 missions are performed through 1970.

September 25–26
MARINES: South of Qui Nhon, South Vietnam, the Seventh Fleet Special Landing Force (SLF) employs helicopters and landing craft to strike at Viet Cong positions along the coast. Operation Dagger Thrust is the first of several amphibious raids by the SLF.

1965

September 27
AVIATION: The Vought A-7 Corsair II light attack jets debut over the skies of North Vietnam, seeing distinguished service over the next three decades.

October 1
AVIATION: The air force assembles its first heavy-repair civil-engineering squadron, or Red Horse units, which provide a quick-response civil engineering force in national emergencies.

October 2
MILITARY: At Bien Hoa, South Vietnam, the 1st Infantry Division ("Big Red One") deploys in the northern part of III Corps to guard against Communist infiltration.

October 5
MILITARY: In Washington, D.C., President Lyndon B. Johnson authorizes the use of tear gas in an effort to smoke out Viet Cong units from their underground lairs.

October 10–14
AVIATION: Over Edwards Air Force Base, California, the XB-70 Valkyrie bomber hits 2,000 miles per hour while cruising at 70,000 feet.
MILITARY: Near An Khe, Central Highlands, South Vietnam, the 1st Cavalry Division performs its first airmobile operation by deploying en masse against Communist troop concentrations. The elusive enemy manages to escape intact but the Americans do manage to reopen a highway from the coast to Pleiku.

October 15
AVIATION: At Maxwell Air Force Base, Alabama, the Air University Institute of Technology graduates its first class of 16 missile combat officers, who receive master's degrees in rocket science.
NAVAL: To facilitate supply measures, the U.S. Naval Support Activity Da Nang is founded. It is organized under the Commander, Service Force, Pacific Fleet, to support the naval war effort.

October 17
AVIATION: An A-6 Intruder and four A-4 Skyhawks from the carrier *Independence* successfully attack and knock out a North Vietnamese mobile surface-to-air missile site at Kep, northeast of Hanoi.

October 18
AVIATION: The 107th Tactical Fighter Group (New York ANG) is the first Air National Guard unit deployed to the Pacific for joint service exercises.

October 19–27
MILITARY: At Lei Me, Central Highlands, South Vietnam, Viet Cong forces attack a Special Forces camp for over a week until it is relieved by ARVN troops. The 1st Cavalry Division subsequently lands men west of the camp to cut off the retreat of Communist soldiers before they reach Cambodia.

October 23
AVIATION: In South Vietnam, the 4503rd Tactical Fighter Squadron arrives with the first 12 Northrop F-5E Freedom Fighters deployed in that theater. This aircraft, designed for the export market, is here to conduct combat evaluation tests.

1965

October 26
NAVAL: Off the Vietnam coast, the destroyer *Turner Joy* suffers from a powder charge detonation, which kills three sailors and injures three more.

October 28
AVIATION: At Da Nang, South Vietnam, Viet Cong sappers manage to get onto the airfield, destroying two jets and 19 helicopters.

October 31
AVIATION: The 447th Strategic Missile Squadron at Grand Forks Air Force Base, North Dakota, deploys the first 10 Minuteman II intercontinental ballistic missiles (ICBMs). This version is larger and more accurate than its predecessor, but still squeezes into the same silo.
NAVAL: As Operation Market Time unfolds in South Vietnam the first PCFs, or swift boats, make their successful debut. These are aluminum-hulled craft, 50 feet in length, and armed with three .50-caliber machine guns and an 81mm mortar, and they are manned by one officer and four enlisted men. Their success in an estuary environment eventually gives rise to the so-called Brown Water Navy.

November 1
AVIATION: In Washington, D.C., Colonel Jeanne M. Holm gains appointment as director of the Women of the Air Force (WAF).

November 3
MARINES: In a search-and-destroy operation near Chu Lai, South Vietnam, correspondent Dickie Chapelle is killed by a booby-trapped mortar round while accompanying marines into the field.

November 14–20
AVIATION: For the first time in the war, giant B-52 bombers are called in to assist ground troops during the Battle of Ia Drang, South Vietnam.
MILITARY: In Pleiku Province, South Vietnam, the Battle of Landing Zone X-Ray unfolds between U.S. and Viet Cong forces. The 1st Cavalry Division is deployed deep inside enemy territory in an attempt to secure control of the Cambodian border. No sooner does the 1st Battalion, 7th Cavalry, under Lieutenant Colonel Harold G. Moore land at position "X-Ray" than they are hotly engaged by 2,000 North Vietnamese of the 33rd and 66th Regiments. A platoon from Company D is cut off and surrounded for 24 hours before being rescued. At length the Americans pour in the 2nd Battalion, 7th Cavalry, followed by the 2nd Battalion, 5th Cavalry. This infusion of strength proves too much for the Communists, who break and run for their sanctuary in Cambodia. In this first major engagement of the Vietnam War, the Americans lose 240 killed and 470 wounded while Communist losses are estimated at around 2,000.

November 15
MILITARY: At Nha Trang, South Vietnam, the Field Force, Vietnam (FFV) is created as a provisional headquarters for the II Corps Zone. It is adopted to avoid confusion with South Vietnamese corps headquarters operating in the same zone.

1965

November 17
MILITARY: The 1st Cavalry Division, intent on cutting off Viet Cong and North Vietnamese Army (NVA) units fleeing toward Cambodia, deploys the 2nd Battalion, 7th Cavalry at Ia Drang two miles to the northeast of Landing Zone X-Ray. Marching en route to Landing Zone Albany, they are ambushed by strong Communist forces and nearly overrun until being rescued by the 1st Battalion, 5th Cavalry. The Americans lose 276 men to an estimated Viet Cong loss of 400.

November 17–18
AVIATION: In the Que Son Valley, a force of 30 UH-34 helicopters from Marine Air Groups 16 and 36 transport two ARVN battalions to recapture the village of Hiep Duc, which was recently seized by the Viet Cong. One marine dies in combat while 17 helicopters are damaged by ground fire.

November 26
NAVAL: The carrier *Enterprise* and the guided-missile frigate *Bainbridge* arrive off Vietnam, being the first nuclear-powered vessels committed to the war zone.

November 27–December
MILITARY: In the final months of the year, American troop strength in South Vietnam is built up from 15,000 to 116,800 officers and men. These men are now engaged in direct combat operations and have sustained 898 killed in action. The Defense Department informs General William C. Westmoreland that his active strategy of seeking out and destroying the enemy over so vast a country will require an additional 400,000 men.

December 2
AVIATION: Off Vietnam, the nuclear-powered carrier *Enterprise* launches 118 sorties against Viet Cong positions in South Vietnam.

December 3
AVIATION: In Washington, D.C., the secretary of defense announces that the air force is developing a reconnaissance version of the General Dynamics F-111.
MARINES: The draft for the upcoming month of January is set at 8,980 men and represents the first use of draftees by the Marine Corps since the Korean War.

December 4
AVIATION: At Cape Kennedy, Florida, the *Gemini VII* space capsule is launched into orbit with U.S. Navy commander James A. Lovell and U.S. Air Force lieutenant commander Frank Borman.

December 7
AVIATION: At Vandenberg Air Force Base, California, a Strategic Air Command (SAC) crew launches a Minuteman II missile from its silo for the first time. The projectile flies 4,000 miles downrange toward its target area.
NAVAL: In the South China Sea, the carrier *Kitty Hawk* suffers from a fire in its machinery room that kills two sailors and injures an additional 28.

December 8
AVIATION: In Washington, D.C., Secretary of Defense Robert S. McNamara declares that the air force will begin phasing out all older B-52 Stratofortresses

and all of its B-58 Hustlers. The latter, while impressive, were overly expensive to operate owing to very high fuel consumption rates.

December 8–29
MARINES: Between Chu Lai and Da Nang, South Vietnam, the 2nd Battalion, 7th Marines, 3rd Battalion, 3rd Marines, and 2nd Battalion, 1st Marines conduct an intense sweep backed by artillery and four B-52 bomb strikes. The Viet Cong lose 407 dead and 33 captured while Marine casualties amount to 51 killed and 256 wounded.

December 10
AVIATION: In Washington, D.C., Secretary of Defense Robert S. McNamara declares that the air force is developing a strategic bomber version of its F-111 to be known as the FB-111.

December 14
AVIATION: An air force RB-57F Canberra reconnaissance aircraft crashes near Odessa on the Black Sea, but authorities believe the crew died due to an oxygen system malfunction and not Soviet action.

December 15
AVIATION: In Earth orbit, the *Gemini 7* space capsule piloted by Commander James A. Lovell and Lieutenant Colonel Frank Borman successfully docks with *Gemini 8* flown by Captain Walter M. Schirra and Major Thomas P. Stafford. Lovell and Borman go on to establish a 14-day record in space that endures for the next five years.

December 18
NAVAL: In the Mekong Delta, South Vietnam, Task Force 116, also known as the U.S. Navy River Patrol Force or "Brown Water Navy," is established to root out Viet Cong units in the vicinity. The activities they engage in on various deltas and waterways fall under the rubric of Operation Game Warden.

December 22
AVIATION: North of Hanoi, North Vietnam, the first Wild Weasel (flak suppression) attack unfolds as Air Force F-100F Wild Weasels destroy a Fan Song radar site while F-105 Thunderchiefs demolish an SA-2 missile battery.
• Aircraft from the carriers *Enterprise, Kitty Hawk,* and *Ticonderoga* attack the thermal power plant at Uong Bi, North Vietnam, for the first time; two aircraft are downed in this, the first naval air raid against a purely industrial target.
MILITARY: In a goodwill gesture, MACV institutes a 30-hour truce over Christmas; American and South Vietnamese units will fire only if attacked.

December 23–January 23
AVIATION: At Hickham Air Force Base, Hawaii, Operation Blue Light unfolds as air force transports begin conveying the 3rd Infantry Division to Pleiku, South Vietnam. The entire process takes a month and is the largest maneuver of its kind ever attempted. In addition to 3,000 soldiers, 4,600 tons of equipment are also delivered.

1965

December 24
AVIATION: In Washington, D.C., President Lyndon B. Johnson orders a second halt to air strikes against North Vietnam in the hope of spurring peace talks.

December 31
MARINES: Although not quite a quagmire yet, of 181,000 U.S. military personnel present in South Vietnam, Marines account for 39,092. Since March 8 of this year, 342 marines have died, 2,047 have been wounded, and 18 are missing in action. They claim to have killed 2,627 Viet Cong in return.

1966

January
MILITARY: As the number of American ground forces increases, so does the strength of the Viet Cong and North Vietnamese Army (NVA). The nature of the war also begins changing from a guerrilla conflict to one hinging upon conventional, stand-up engagements. However, the Americans place increasing stress on advisory efforts in an attempt to get ARVN forces to shoulder their share of the fighting.

January 1
AVIATION: The airlift units of the U.S. Air Force are redesignated: hereafter the Military Airlift Transport Service (MATS) is known as the Military Airlift Command (MAC). The Air Rescue Service is renamed the Aerospace Rescue and Recovery Service (ARRS). Concurrently, the Eastern Air Transport Force and the Western Air Transport Force become the Twenty-First and Twenty-Second Air Forces, respectively.
• To assist the Military Airlift Command (MAC) in South Vietnam, Air National Guard (ANG) transport units begin flying 75 sorties per month to that region.
• At Tullahoma, Tennessee, a large rocket facility is constructed at the Arnold Engineering Development Center.

January 3–15
MARINES: Commandant General Greene spends several days touring marine facilities in the Western Pacific, including Vietnam.

January 7
AVIATION: At Beale Air Force Base, California, the first operational SR-71 Blackbird is delivered.

January 15
MARINES: In Guantánamo Bay, Cuba, the 2nd Battalion, 8th Marines arrives at the naval base to serve as the ground defense force.

January 17
AVIATION: Potential disaster strikes as a B-52 jet bomber laden with nuclear weapons collides with a KC-135 tanker off Palomares, Spain, killing seven of 11 airmen onboard. Three of the bombs fall on land and a fourth is eventually salvaged from 2,500 feet of water.

January 20
MARINES: In Washington, D.C., President Lyndon B. Johnson asks Congress for funds to maintain a fourth active-duty division of the Marine Corps.

January 22
AVIATION: Operation Blue Light concludes, during which 3,000 troops and 4,600 tons of equipment have been conveyed by the Military Airlift Command (MAC) from Hawaii to Pleiku, South Vietnam.

January 28–February 17
NAVAL: Near Quang Ngai City and Tam Ky, South Vietnam, the Seventh Fleet Amphibious Ready Group commences Operation Double Eagle I, the largest amphibious landing of the war to date. The landings go off well but the Viet Cong manage to evade most serious contact.
MARINES: Marines of Task Force Delta (4th Marine headquarters, 2nd Battalion, 9th Marines, 2nd Battalion, 3rd Marines, and 2nd Battalion, 4th Marines) conduct an extensive amphibious operation in southern Quang Ngai Province. In stiff fighting, the marines kill 312 Viet Cong and capture 19 while losing 24 dead and 156 wounded.

January 28–March 6
MILITARY: In Binh Dinh Province, South Vietnam, the 3rd Brigade, 1st Cavalry Division under Colonel Hal Moore commences Operation Masher, the war's first "search-and-destroy" mission, in concert with ARVN and Republic of South Korea (ROK) formations. These troops invade the Communist stronghold on the Bong Son Plain against light resistance, and the operation ends with indifferent results. Communist losses are estimated at 1,300 dead, but they quickly reclaim most of the lost territory once the Americans depart.

January 31
AVIATION: In Washington, D.C., President Lyndon B. Johnson orders the aerial bombing of North Vietnam resumed after a 37-day cease-fire after the Communist regime of Ho Chi Minh rejects any notion of "peace talks."

February 1
MEDICAL: At Cam Ranh Bay, South Vietnam, the air force opens a 200-bed hospital facility.

February 14
NAVAL: In the Gulf of Thailand off South Vietnam, *PCF-4* becomes the first swift boat lost in action when it strikes a mine that kills four of six crewmen.

February 16
MEDICAL: At Chu Lai, South Vietnam, the hospital ship *Repose* arrives to provide services.

February 20
NAVAL: At Yerba Linda Island, San Francisco, Fleet Admiral Chester W. Nimitz dies at the age of 81; he is the last U.S. Navy five-start admiral.

February 21
AVIATION: American aircraft resume their attacks against North Vietnam by striking the former French military base at Dien Bien Phu.

February 22
MILITARY: A force of 20,000 American, South Vietnamese, and South Korean troops conduct Operation White Wing to ferret out Viet Cong troops and supply concentrations in Quang Ngai Province.

February 23
MARINES: In Vietnam, the 1st Marine Division headquarters and the 11th Marines begin deploying for combat operations.

February 24
AVIATION: At Vandenberg Air Force Base, California, a Strategic Air Command (SAC) missile crew from the 341st Strategic Missile Wing makes the first Minuteman salvo launch over the Pacific.

February 26
NAVAL: At Vung Tau, South Vietnam, nine newly arrived Coast Guard cutters are organized into Coast Guard Division 13. This brings the total number of cutters in Southeast Asia to 26.

March 1
MARINES: At Camp Pendleton, California, the reactivated 26th Marines become the lead element of the new 5th Marine Division.
• On Okinawa, the 9th Marine Amphibious Brigade is activated to take charge of all marine units throughout the western Pacific that are not in South Vietnam.

March 2
MILITARY: Secretary of Defense Robert S. McNamara declares that American troop strength in Vietnam has reached 215,000 and that another 20,000 are en route.

March 4
AVIATION: Over North Vietnam, three Communist MiG-17 fighters tangle briefly with a flight of F-4C Phantom II fighters, then break off the engagement and return to their airfields.

March 4–7
MARINES: In South Vietnam, Operation Utah commences as helicopters from Marine Air Group 11 (MAG-11) transport the 1st ARVN Airborne Battalion into combat under heavy fire as the 2nd Battalion, 7th Marines, 3rd Battalion, 1st Marines, and 2nd Battalion, 4th Marines pitch into a nearby North Vietnamese Army (NVA) regiment. The Communists are severely drubbed, losing 600 men; Marine casualties total 98 dead and 278 wounded; the ARVN sustains 30 dead and 120 wounded.

March 7
AVIATION: In France, after President Charles de Gaulle announces his decision to withdraw from the North Atlantic Treaty Organization (NATO), several units operating there as part of United States Air Force Europe (USAFE) are obliged to relocate elsewhere.
MARINES: In Washington, D.C., Secretary of Defense Robert S. McNamara seeks to increase the Marine Corps to 278,184 men, a force larger than during the Korean War.

1966

March 8
AVIATION: In South Vietnam, HMM-164 deploys with the first Boeing CH-46 Seaknights to see service in the country.

March 8–17
MARINES: Winter Express unfolds above Norway's Arctic Circle, with the 3rd Battalion, 6th Marines participating in NATO's largest ever cold-weather exercise.

March 10
AVIATION: At an abandoned airstrip in the A Shau Valley, an A-1E Skyraider flown by Major Bernard F. Fisher, 1st Air Commando, lands under enemy fire to rescue downed major Dafford W. Myers. Fisher becomes the first air force officer awarded the new "Air Force Medal of Honor," which was redesigned in 1963.
MILITARY: In the I Corps zone, a popular Vietnamese general is dismissed by his government and a wave of political unrest sweeps the country. The turmoil hinders a successful prosecution of the war for several months.

March 15
MARINES: In I Corps zone, the Force Logistics Command (1st and 3rd Service Battalions) is created by the III Marine Amphibious Force to supply marine units campaigning in country.

March 16
AVIATION: In the A Shau Valley, marine helicopters of HMM-163 and VMO-2 rescue the survivors of a Special Force camp overrun by the Viet Cong; antiaircraft fire results in several losses.
MILITARY: Viet Cong troops overrun a Special Forces camp in the A Shau Valley after a 72-hour siege, killing or wounding 200 Americans and South Vietnamese. This is the last of three such camps previously established in the valley, which is of great strategic importance to the Communists.

March 16–17
AVIATION: The *Gemini 8* space capsule flown by astronauts Neil A. Armstrong and David Scott experience, uncontrollable rolling due to a faulty thruster and cut short their flight. Upon splashing down in the Pacific Ocean, they are rescued by an air force helicopter, the first time that service has been involved in the Gemini project.

March 20–25
MARINES: Northwest of Quang Ngai, Operation Texas commences as the 3rd Battalion, 7th Marines, 2nd Battalion, 4th Marines, and 3rd Battalion, 1st Marines, assisted by an ARVN regiment, attack two entrenched Communist regiments. The marines, strongly supported by air and artillery elements, kill 283 enemy troops while suffering 99 dead and 212 wounded.

March 26–April 6
NAVAL: Thirty-five miles south of Saigon, South Vietnam, the Seventh Fleet Amphibious Ready Group lands U.S. and South Vietnamese marines in a fruitless search for Viet Cong units. This is also the first large amphibious operation executed in the Mekong Delta.

1966

MARINES: Near Saigon, South Vietnam, marines stage their first ground action near the capital when the 1st Battalion, 5th Marines sweeps Viet Cong units from the Mekong River delta region, southeast of the city.

March 28
AVIATION: Over the White Sands Missile Range, New Mexico, the first successful midair catch of an air-launched, air-recoverable rocket is made by the Air Force Special Weapons Center.

MILITARY: At Cu Chi, South Vietnam, the famed 25th Infantry Division ("Tropic Lightning") deploys northwest of Saigon to block a well-known Communist infiltration route across the Cambodian border.

March 29
AVIATION: At Naval Air Station Pensacola, Florida, Ensign Gale Ann Gordon becomes the first woman to solo in a navy airplane. She does so as part of her training in aviation experimental psychology.

MARINES: At Chu Lai, South Vietnam, the 1st Marine Division begins to formally operate in the country. This is the first time since World War II that two divisions of marines are in combat together.

March 31
AVIATION: The Strategic Air Command (SAC) completes phasing out all its B-47 Stratojets in favor of B-52 Stratofortresses. This early, swept-wing bomber joined the Strategic Air Command (SAC) in 1951.

NAVAL: In an unusual disciplinary move, Lieutenant Commander Marcus A. Arnheiter is relieved from commanding the destroyer picket *Vance* off South Vietnam. Arnheiter ascribes his dismissal to the disloyalty of junior officers and congressional hearings. Lawsuits persist for several years thereafter.

April 1
AVIATION: In Saigon, South Vietnam, the Seventh Air Force under Lieutenant General Joseph H. Moore becomes a subcommand of the Pacific Air Forces (PACAF).

NAVAL: Rear Admiral Norvell G. Ward is appointed head of the new U.S. Naval Forces Vietnam, which is responsible for all naval forces in the South Vietnamese theater of operations.

April 5
AVIATION: The Air Force Avionics Laboratory conducts the first successful voice communications test utilizing aircraft, satellite, and ground equipment simultaneously.

MARINES: At Camp Pendleton, California, the 5th Marine Division continues taking shape as the 13th Marines are activated as its artillery unit.

April 6
AVIATION: In Vietnam, the army transfers all its tactical lift aircraft to the air force, which now operates a fleet of Canadian-made DeHaviland C-7A Caribous and C-8A Buffalos.

April 7
AVIATION: Off Palomares, Spain, navy divers retrieve an H-bomb lost when a B-52 and a KC-135 collided in midair earlier in the year.

April 10
NAVAL: Along South Vietnamese waterways, Operation Game Warden is strengthened by the arrival of two 31-foot-long, water jet-propelled river patrol boats (PBRs).

April 11–12
AVIATION: In a pitched battle 35 miles east of Saigon, South Vietnam, Airman 1st Class William H. Pitsenbarger, 38th Aerospace Rescue and Recovery Squadron, elects to remain and fight with army troops rather than expose his crew mates and helicopter while picking him up. Pitsenbarger fights bravely and dies in combat, winning a posthumous Medal of Honor.
MILITARY: Major General William E. DuPuy moves his 1st Infantry Division into the heart of Viet Cong territory in III Corps. However, a company of the 2nd Battalion, 16th Infantry, is ambushed and surrounded by Viet Cong units 40 miles east of Saigon and cut to ribbons, losing 35 dead and 71 wounded.

April 12
AVIATION: Giant B-52 bombers are used against targets in North Vietnam for the first time, striking at supply lines running through the Mu Gia Pass, 85 miles north of the Demilitarized Zone (DMZ).

April 17
NAVAL: The heavy cruiser *Canberra*, operating off Vietnam, becomes the first U.S. Navy warship to relay an operational message via the *Syncom 3* communications satellite to the Naval Communications Station, Honolulu, Hawaii, 4,000 miles distant.

April 17–June 9
MILITARY: In the Rung Sat Special Zone, southeast of Saigon, South Vietnam, the 1st Battalion, 18th Infantry enters a swamp-entangled morass seeking Communist hideouts. However, Operation Lexington III concludes without any major engagements and the elusive guerrillas escape.

April 21–23
MARINES: The 7th Marines, sweeping northwest of Quang Ngai, kill over 150 Communist forces.

April 25
AVIATION: At Grand Forks Air Force Base, the 447th Strategic Missile Squadron becomes the first operational Strategic Air Command (SAC) unit to deploy 50 Minuteman II intercontinental ballistic missiles.

April 26
AVIATION: Over Hanoi, North Vietnam, an air force F-4C Phantom II flown by Major Paul Gilmore and Lieutenant William T. Smith brings down the first Communist MiG-21 with a Sidewinder missile. At the time they were escorting a flight of F-105 Thunderchiefs on a bombing run.

May
AVIATION: In the Mekong Delta, South Vietnam, five UH-1 helicopters ("Hueys") are outfitted with experimental night-vision cameras as an aid to night combat

1966

and navigation. Though not entirely successful, the experiment accelerates the development and deployment of more sophisticated devices by 1969.

May 1

NAVAL: In Washington, D.C., the Navy Department completely overhauls its entrenched bureau system, some of which has been in effect since 1842. Henceforth, the Bureau of Naval Personnel and the Bureau of Naval Medicine are placed directly under the chief of naval operations. Also, the Bureaus of Weapons, Yards and Docks, and Supplies and Accounts are restructured into six system commands under the chief of naval materiel.

May 3

AVIATION: At Edwards Air Force Base, California, the first test of a Fulton Recovery System, or "air snatch" of a man standing on the ground, is successfully completed.

May 5

AVIATION: Air Force A-1E Skyraiders are ordered to bomb targets in North Vietnam for the first time.

May 9

NAVAL: Ten River patrol boats (RPBs) are ordered up the Bassac River into the Mekong Delta, South Vietnam, for the first time. They are tasked with interdicting

Troops of the 173rd Airborne Brigade dash to helicopters under heavy fire during an operation 30 miles north of Saigon, May 1966. *(Texas Tech University Vietnam Archive)*

weapons smuggling to Viet Cong units. Within a year the Mekong River Patrol Group has expanded to include 80 boats, three helicopters, and several SEAL units.

• Three new patrol air-cushion vehicles (PACV) enter Operation Market Time while patrolling the Bassac River of the Mekong Delta, South Vietnam, for Viet Cong units. While capable of 50 knots and heavily armed, PACVs are too troublesome to maintain in this difficult environment.

May 10–July 30

MILITARY: In the Central Highlands of South Vietnam, the 3rd Brigade, 25th Infantry Division, and the 2nd Brigade, 1st Cavalry Division, are committed to a series of sweeps entitled Paul Revere I through IV.

May 11

NAVAL: Off South Vietnam, the escort ship *Brister,* the minesweeper *Vireo,* and the Coast Guard patrol ship *Point Gray* attack and sink a 120-foot North Vietnamese freighter attempting to run supplies to Viet Cong units.

MARINES: At Chu Lai, South Vietnam, jet aircraft are launched for the first time from a land-based catapult when four A-4 Skyhawks take off. With this equipment, their standard runway roll of 8,000 feet is reduced to just 1,400 feet.

May 12

AVIATION: At the Pacific Missile Range at Point Mugu, California, the advanced and highly sophisticated Phoenix missile is test-fired for the first time. Within a decade it is the standard armament of new Grumman F-14 Tomcat fighters.

May 17

MARINES: At New Orleans, Louisiana, Jesuit High School sponsors the first marine-oriented junior naval ROTC program.

May 21

MARINES: At Guantánamo Bay, Cuba, a marine sentry shoots a Cuban soldier attempting to infiltrate the base.

May 22

NAVAL: The swift boat *PCF-41,* while patrolling the Dinh River in the Rung Sat Special Zone, South Vietnam, is fired upon by a 57mm recoilless rifle and sunk.

May 23

AVIATION: Over the Tonkin Gulf, North Vietnam, a Talos missile fired from the nuclear-powered cruiser *Long Beach* downs a Communist MiG at extreme range. This is the first successful kill by the Talos system.

May 25

AVIATION: In South Vietnam, the 1st Aviation Brigade is activated by the army to better manage and control the huge influx of helicopters and light observation aircraft deploying throughout the country. By 1970 they will be servicing 3,500 helicopters and 600 fixed-wing aircraft.

MARINES: At Guantánamo Bay, Cuba, marines drive off five Cuban soldiers who had scaled the fence and infiltrated the naval base.

May 30–31
AVIATION: Nearly 300 American warplanes strike targets in North Vietnam, including an important arsenal, in their heaviest raid yet.

June 1
MARINES: At Camp Pendleton, California, 5th Marine headquarters and two battalions of the 27th Marines are activated. Meanwhile, the 1st Battalion, 27th Infantry is also activated at Kaneohe, Hawaii, within the 1st Marine Brigade.

June 2
AVIATION: The lunar exploration vehicle *Surveyor 1* lands safely on the moon and sends televised images of the surrounding surface back to Earth. These are then relayed around the world by the *Early Bird* satellite.

June 2–13
MILITARY: In Bien Long Province, South Vietnam, the 1st Infantry Division begins Operation El Paso II to destroy Viet Cong units lurking north and west of Saigon. Heavy fighting develops near the Cambodian border by the time the operation concludes; for a loss of 200 dead and wounded, the Americans inflict nearly 1,000 casualties on the Communists.

June 2–20
MILITARY: Near Dak To, Konum Province, General Willard Pearson commits his 101st Airborne Division to Operation Hawthorne. In its course, Lieutenant Colonel David Hackworth's 1st Battalion, 327th Infantry, defeats a force of Viet Cong besieging a Special Forces camp. The Communists are also reinforced and begin attacking the intruders, badly mauling one of Hackworth's companies. Both sides continue pouring in troops and at length the North Vietnamese are forced to withdraw with heavy losses.

June 3–6
AVIATION: As Lieutenant Colonel Thomas P. Stafford pilots the *Gemini 9* spacecraft on orbit around the Earth, Lieutenant Commander Eugene A. Cernan is the second American astronaut to walk in space. However, problems with their Agena Target Docking Adapter result in a shortened mission.

June 7
MILITARY: In Kontum Province, South Vietnam, Company C, 2nd Battalion, 503rd Infantry is besieged by superior numbers of Viet Cong and nearly overrun until Captain William Carpenter calls down a napalm strike on his own position. The Communists are driven back while the Americans hold their ground with a loss of six dead and 25 injured.

June 8
AVIATION: The massive XB-70 Valkyrie prototype is destroyed when an escorting F-104N Starfighter is suddenly drawn in by powerful wingtip vortices and collides with it, knocking off its tail. Major Carl Cross is unable to eject from the spinning bomber and dies in the crash.

June 11
MILITARY: Secretary of Defense Robert McNamara declares U.S. troop strength in South Vietnam at 285,000 men, with total fatalities since the year began at 2,100.

June 12

AVIATION: Commander Harold L. Marr, flying an F-8 Crusader off the carrier *Hancock*, downs a MiG-17 over North Vietnam with a Sidewinder heat-seeking missile. This is also the first confirmed kill by Crusader aircraft, which acquire the nickname "MiG Masters."

June 16

AVIATION: Over Than Hoa, North Vietnam, aircraft from the carrier *Hancock* commence a sustain campaigned to destroy the petroleum facilities located there. Similar facilities at Hanoi and Haiphong are likewise struck.

• An Air Force Titan IIIC launch rockets hurls seven experimental communications satellites into orbit 18,000 miles above the equator. Tests demonstrate the viability of a global communications system for the military.

June 18–27

MARINES: In the II Corps zone, the Seventh Fleet Special Landing Force (3rd Battalion, 5th Marines) storms ashore in Phu Yen Province during Operation Deckhouse I. Three more landings are made under the same designation in 1966.

June 20

NAVAL: Along the Mekong Delta, South Vietnam, Coast Guard cutters *Point League* and *Point Slocum* intercept a 120-foot steel trawler near the Co Chien River, drive it ashore, and burn it. The vessel was carrying 120 tons of munitions for local Viet Cong units.

June 25–July 2

MARINES: Helicopter assaults bring the 2nd Battalion, 4th Marines and 3rd Battalion, 1st Marines into combat northwest of the ancient capital of Hue, South Vietnam. They suffer 23 dead and 58 wounded but recover 82 Viet Cong bodies on the ground.

June 26

MARINES: In South Vietnam, Sergeant James S. Dodson and Lance Corporal Walter Eckes, prisoners of the Viet Cong since the previous May, escape and make their way to friendly lines.

June 29

AVIATION: The American government, reacting to increasing infiltration of men and materiel from North Vietnam to the South, now allow the bombing of targets on the outskirts of Hanoi and the port of Haiphong, especially its oil storage facilities. To that end, 46 jets from the carriers *Constellation* and *Ranger* sweep and destroy several petroleum installations.

June 30

MARINES: At this point in the war, marine manpower levels are 20,512 officers and 241,204 enlisted men.

July 1

AVIATION: At Tan Son Nhut Air Base, South Vietnam, General William W. Momyer is appointed commander of the Seventh Air Force.

NAVAL: Off Haiphong, North Vietnam, three Communist torpedo boats attack the frigate *Coontz* and the destroyer *Rogers,* and are all torpedo boats are sunk through a combination of gunfire and carrier aircraft.

• To keep the Long Tau River channel south of Saigon, South Vietnam, free of mines, 12 57-foot minesweepers of Mine Squadron 11 are organized into Detachment Alpha.

July 4–14

MARINES: In the An Hoa area south of Da Nang, South Vietnam, several battalions of the 9th Marines sweep through and engage the resident Viet Cong battalion. By the time the operation concludes, the marines kill 380 Communists at a cost of 24 dead and 172 wounded.

July 6

AVIATION: According to Radio Hanoi, American prisoners have been paraded through the city and subjected to taunts by North Vietnamese onlookers.

July 7–August 3

AVIATION: In support of Operation Hastings in the I Corps tactical area, marine helicopters fly 10,000 sorties in support of ground forces while attack aircraft perform another 1,677.

MARINES: In Quang Tri Province, South Vietnam, directly below the Demilitarized Zone (DMZ), Operation Hastings, the largest single marine endeavor to date, commences when five battalions belonging to the 1st, 3rd, 4th, and 5th Marines tackle the North Vietnamese 324B Division, which had infiltrated across the border. In the fighting, reconnaissance units operating deep behind enemy lines call in air and artillery strikes under the code name "Stingray," and they prove highly effective. By the time fighting ceases, 700 Communists are dead while the marines sustain 126 killed and 448 wounded.

July 9

AVIATION: The General Dynamics F-111 swing-wing fighter hits 1,800 miles per hour for the first time.

July 11

MILITARY: Sergeant Major William O. Woodridge, a highly decorated, 25-year veteran of two wars, is sworn in as the first sergeant major of the army.

July 13

AVIATION: Over North Vietnam, five MiG-17s are downed by air force F-4 Phantom IIs while a sixth falls to a Navy F-4 from the carrier *Constellation.* This brings the total of enemy aircraft destroyed to 15.

July 16

NAVAL: In Quang Tri Province, South Vietnam, the Seventh Fleet Amphibious Ready Force lands marines during opening phases of Operation Deck House II.

July 18–21

AVIATION: The *Gemini 10* space capsule, piloted by Commander John W. Young and Major Michael Collins, completes 43 Earth orbits and also successfully docks with the Athena space vehicle.

July 20
AVIATION: Over southern North Vietnam, the Seventh Air Force commences Operation Tally Ho against military targets there. They are assisted by men and aircraft of the 1st Marine Air Wing (1st MAW), which contributes several sorties.

July 21
AVIATION: In the I Corps tactical zone, South Vietnam, all Boeing CH-46 Sky-knight helicopters are grounded until better air and fuel filters can be retrofitted to handle the intense dust present during operating conditions.

July 30
AVIATION: American warplanes bomb Communist units and strong points in the Demilitarized Zone (DMZ) separating North and South Vietnam.

August 3
AVIATION: Aircraft from the carrier *Constellation* attack oil facilities at Haiphong, North Vietnam. The Soviet Union claims that its merchant ship *Medyn* was struck by bullets fired by the jets.

August 3–September 13
MARINES: In the I Corps tactical zone, the III Marine Amphibious Force commences a reconnaissance effort named Operation Prairie and employs "Stingray" tactics to halt the infiltration of two North Vietnamese divisions into Quang Tri Province.

August 4
MILITARY: The call goes out for a monthly draft of 46,200 men, the highest inducted since the Korean War.

August 6
AVIATION: At Williams Air Force Base, Arizona, civilian scientists-astronauts Owen K. Garriot, Edward G. Gibson, and Harrison H. Schmitt all receive their air force pilot wings.
NAVAL: The *Asheville*, part of a new class of small patrol vessels, or PGMs, is commissioned. In time, PGMs play a vital role in naval operations throughout Southeast Asia.

August 6–22
MARINES: In Quang Nam and Quang Tri Provinces, South Vietnam, the 5th Marines and South Vietnamese forces begin Operation Colorado by sweeping through the Que Son Valley in a search-and-destroy effort, killing 170 Communists. Consequently, the 2nd North Vietnamese Division withdraws from the region.

August 18
MARINES: On the Batangan Peninsula, south of Chu Lai, South Vietnam, the 2nd Korean Marine Brigade deploys for combat operations in the I Corps tactical zone.

August 20–29
MARINES: In Quang Nam Province, South Vietnam, Operation Allegheny commences as a battalion of the 3rd Marines sweeps the region, killing an additional 117 Viet Cong.

1966

August 22
NAVAL: Operation Deckhouse II unfolds as the amphibious assault ship *Iwo Jima* lands marines 100 miles east of Saigon, South Vietnam. There they are to join U.S. and South Vietnamese paratroopers in rooting out local Viet Cong units.

August 23
NAVAL: The freighter SS *Baton Rouge* strikes a mine in the Long Tau Channel 20 miles east of Saigon, South Vietnam; it suffers seven dead and is beached in consequence. This particular vessel had been chartered by the Military Sea Transport Service (MSTS).

August 25
AVIATION: At Sheppard Air Force Base, Texas, the first class of 212 German air force student pilots arrives for training similar to that obtained by U.S. pilots. The clear skies of Texas are also a welcome change from the overcast clime of their homeland.

August 26
AVIATION: Today air force and navy aircraft fly a record 156 missions over North Vietnam without losing a single plane.

Bell UH-1B Iroquois (Huey) gunship flying with Navy Light Attack Helicopter Squadron 4 (HAL-4) in support of navy riverine operations in South Vietnam. *(San Diego Aerospace Museum)*

MILITARY: Northwest of Saigon, Vietnam, the 196th Infantry Brigade (Light) is rushed into position.

August 29

AVIATION: In the wake of a massive earthquake that devastates large portions of Turkey, air force transports begin conveying 50 tons of medical supplies, water purifying systems, and medical personnel to the afflicted regions.
• In Haiphong Harbor, North Vietnam, several Chinese torpedo boats fire upon A-6 Intruders and A-4 Skyhawks from the carrier *Constellation* and are sunk in consequence. The Red Chinese government protests that these vessels were actually unarmed merchant ships.

August 30

AVIATION: Naval aviators begin flying UH-1B "Huey" helicopters acquired from the army in support of Operation Game Warden. Their success culminates in the founding of Helicopter Attack (Light) Squadron 3 (HAL-3), a highly decorated navy squadron from this conflict.

September 3

AVIATION: Soviet-supplied MiG-21 jet fighters begin appearing at North Vietnamese airfields for the first time but, strangely, they remain off limits to U.S. aircraft.

September 4

MARINES: In the Thang Binh District, Que Son Valley, two companies of the 1st Battalion, 5th Marines are involved in a stiff firefight. At length they are reinforced by the 3rd Battalion, 5th Marines, who are helicoptered in. Father Vincent Capodanno, the beloved "Grunt Chaplain," is among them, and he sacrifices his life under fire to save several wounded marines. The navy padre wins a Medal of Honor.

September 6

MARINES: Headquarters, Marine Corps requests women marines for service in the Western Pacific. By spring, more than 100 are stationed in Japan, Okinawa, and South Vietnam.

September 8

MILITARY: At Bien Hoa, South Vietnam, the 11th Armored Cavalry ("Blackhorse") deploys as an independent tactical unit. Equipped with numerous tanks, helicopters, and flamethrower units, it is tasked with securing the U.S. embassy and escorting convoys along dangerous roads.

September 11

AVIATION: Air force and navy aircraft fly a record 171 missions over North Vietnam without losing a single plane.

NAVAL: As Operation Game Warden continues along the Co Chien River, South Vietnam, Viet Cong forces fire upon two river patrol boats, killing one sailor; this is the operation's first fatality.

September 12–15

AVIATION: In space, the *Gemini 11* space capsule piloted by Lieutenant Commander Richard Gordon and Commander Charles C. Conrad completes 44 orbits, a space walk, and a docking with an Athena space vehicle. They are recovered by the helicopter assault ship *Guam* in the Atlantic after 71 hours in space.

September 13

MARINES: Just south of the Demilitarized Zone (DMZ), I Corps tactical zone, the Seventh Fleet Special Landing Force (SLF) embarks on Operation Deckhouse in support of ongoing Operation Prairie by landing along the coastline. Over the next 12 days over 200 Communists are killed at a cost of 36 marines killed and 167 wounded.

September 13–February 12, 1967

MILITARY: In Binh Dinh Province, South Vietnam, the 1st Cavalry Division unleashes Operation Thayer in deploying 120 helicopters and five battalions in its biggest maneuver to date. These units invade the Viet Cong stronghold in the Kim Son Valley, but most Communist units slip away and escape intact.

A UH-1D helicopter from the 336th Aviation Company sprays a defoliation agent on the jungle in the Mekong Delta. *(National Archives)*

September 14–November 3
MILITARY: Northwest of Saigon, South Vietnam, the 196th Infantry Brigade begins patrolling in concert with Operation Attleboro. Light resistance is encountered.

September 15
NAVAL: Operation Deckhouse IV unfolds as the Seventh Fleet Amphibious Ready Group deposits marines in Quang Tri Province, South Vietnam.

September 16
AVIATION: Off the Pratas Reef southeast of Hong Kong, helicopters from the carrier *Oriskany* rescue 44 sailors from the sinking merchant vessel *August Moon.*
MARINES: In the I Corps tactical zone, several companies of the 1st Battalion, 4th Marines are ambushed while approaching the Nui Cay Tre ridge line and an intense bush fight erupts that also draws in the 3rd Battalion, 4th Marines and the 2nd Battalion, 7th Marines. The struggle continues until October 4.

September 17–27
MARINES: In Quang Nai Province, South Vietnam, Operation Golden Fleece 7-1 commences when a battalion of the 7th Marines kills 244 Viet Cong while protecting the local rice harvest.

September 20
AVIATION: Over Edwards Air Force Base, California, the NASA X-24 "lifting body" is successfully demonstrated by Lieutenant Colonel Donald M. Sorlie, who reaches 400 miles per hour in a three-and-a-half minute descent. This is the first such aircraft ever flown by an air force officer, which is dropped from 45,000 feet by a B-52.

September 22
NAVAL: On the Long Tau River, South Vietnam, two minesweeping vessels are bombarded by Viet Cong recoilless rifle fire; *MSB 15* is struck in the pilot house, losing one dead and 11 wounded.

September 23
MILITARY: In an attempt to cut off Communist infiltration into South Vietnam, American aircraft began a concerted aerial defoliation program by spraying jungles south of the DMZ.

September 25
MILITARY: At Pleiku, Central Highlands, South Vietnam, the 4th Infantry Division arrives and deploys one of its armored units to the southern reaches of III Corps near Saigon.

September 29
AVIATION: At Khe San, South Vietnam, the 1st Battalion, 3rd Marines and an artillery battery of the 13th Marines are airlifted in place by marine KC-130 transports. This base is in supporting distance of a Special Forces camp known locally as the Rockpile.
NAVAL: The amphibious vessels *Boxer, Rankin, Plymouth Rock, Ruchmankin,* and *Suffolk County* assist victims of Hurricane Inez in Haiti and the Dominican Republic.

October 6
MARINES: In the I Corps tactical zone, the 3rd Marine Division assumes responsibility for Quang Tri and Thua Thien Provinces, the northernmost regions of South Vietnam, while the 1st Marine Division occupies Quang Nam, Quang Tin, and Quang Ngai farther south.

October 7
AVIATION: Given mounting public anxiety over UFO sightings, the air force chooses the University of Colorado to help conduct independent investigations of such phenomena.

October 9
AVIATION: Navy aircraft score two kills over North Vietnam when an A-1 Skyraider from the carrier *Intrepid* downs a MiG-21 over the Phy Ly Bridge, Hanoi, while an F-8 Crusader from the *Oriskany* bags another.

October 13–14
AVIATION: A force of 173 American warplanes launch the heaviest strike on North Vietnam to date; the U.S. government announces that a total of 403 warplanes have been downed by enemy fire since February 7, 1965.

October 14–16
MARINES: In Tampico, Mexico, Marines airlifts assist victims of Hurricane Inez.

October 17
AVIATION: Pressed for trained personnel in South Vietnam, the Marine Corps defers the resignations and retirements of 500 pilots and maintenance officers.

October 25
NAVAL: Off the coast of North Vietnam, Operation Sea Dragon unfolds as warships of the Seventh Fleet, ranging from battleships to destroyers, begin bombarding Communist coastal batteries, radar installations, and transportation routes. They also begin directly attacking enemy coastal shipping, sinking 230 small vessels by month's end. This activity is designed to dovetail with the ongoing air campaign over North Vietnam.

October 26
NAVAL: In the Gulf of Tonkin, a flare locker fire onboard the carrier *Oriskany* kills 43 sailors and injures 16. This is the first of three destructive conflagrations onboard carriers in this conflict.

October 31
AVIATION: The air force contracts with the Boeing Company to develop and manufacture the AGM-65 Maverick missile. This is a short-range, television-guided weapon to be carried by FB-111 and B-52 jet bombers.
NAVAL: On the Mekong River, patrol boats *PBT-105* and *PBR-107* sink or seize 57 Viet Cong junks and sampans in a three-hour action. During the fracas, Boatswain's Mate First Class James E. Williams orders his boat's searchlights turned on to assist the gunners and arriving helicopters, despite exposing himself to greater danger. He wins a Medal of Honor.
• On the Tau River, the minesweeper *MSB-54* strikes a mine and sinks with the loss of two sailors. This is the first vessel of its class lost in combat.

1966

November 1
AVIATION: At Da Nang, South Vietnam, VMA(AW)-242 deploys with the first marine A-6 Intruder jet bombers in the theater.
MARINES: In California, four marines die during fire fighting efforts along the Piedro de Lumbre Canyon.

November 2
MILITARY: Along the Demilitarized Zone (DMZ), South Korea, North Koreans ambush a patrol of the 23rd Infantry, 2nd Infantry Division, killing six Americans.

November 3
MILITARY: Northwest of Saigon, South Vietnam, the 1st Battalion, 27th Infantry under Major Guy S. Meloy encounters a Viet Cong division near Dau Tieng. The Americans successfully defend themselves over the next 30 hours, heavily repulsing six major assaults.

November 4
NAVAL: In the South China Sea, a fire in the oil and hydraulic storage area onboard the carrier *Franklin D. Roosevelt* results in the deaths of seven sailors, with a further four injured.

November 6–25
MILITARY: In the Central Highlands, South Vietnam, II Field Force commander Lieutenant General Jonathan O. Seaman expands Operation Attleboro into the first multidivisional endeavor of the war effort. The 1st Infantry Division and a brigade from the 25th Infantry Division sweep their assigned area clean of Viet Cong forces, sending them reeling toward the Cambodian border. For a loss of 155 dead and 494 wounded, the Americans kill 300 Communists and take several large weapon caches. General William C. Westmoreland is also convinced that the Viet Cong, normally elusive, will stand and fight to protect their base areas. These regions are the next object for expanded "search-and-destroy" operations.

November 9
AVIATION: The General Dynamics F-111 passes an important hurtle by flying at the speed of sound for 15 minutes at an altitude of less than 1,000 feet. This is a major test of its terrain-following internal guidance system, the first such system anywhere in the world.

November 11–15
AVIATION: The *Gemini 12* space capsule, piloted by Commander James A. Lovell and Lieutenant Colonel Edwin E. Aldrin, Jr., completes 59 Earth orbits, a space walk, and a successful docking with an Athena space craft. This is also the last flight of the Gemini Project.

November 14
AVIATION: At McCurdo Sound, Antarctica, a C-141 Starlifter flown by Captain Howard Geddes, 86th Military Airlift Squadron, having traversed 2,200 miles from Christchurch, New Zealand, successfully touches down on the ice.

1966

November 15
AVIATION: At Tuy Hoa, South Vietnam, the air force constructs its first base, finishing it 45 days ahead of schedule.

November 18
NAVAL: The destroyers *John R. Craig* and *Hamner* shell and destroy a Communist radar facility two miles north of the Demilitarized Zone (DMZ).

November 23
NAVAL: Off the coast of North Vietnam, ongoing Operation Sea Dragon scores a striking success when the destroyers *Mullany* and *Warrington* engage a Communist convoy of 60 barges laden with supplies and sink or damage 47.

December 2
MILITARY: Along the road near Suoi Cat, South Vietnam, the Viet Cong 275th Regiment ambushes the 1st Squadron, 11th Armored Cavalry. The "Blackhorses" respond with concentrated artillery and tank canister rounds that rout the enemy with heavy losses.

December 5
NAVAL: Northeast of Dong Hoi, North Vietnam, Communist shore batteries shell the destroyer *Ingersoll,* scoring several near misses.

December 10
MILITARY: To throw an even tighter security cordon around Saigon, South Vietnam, the 199th Light Infantry Brigade arrives and deploys to III Corps. For the rest of its tour, this unit remains in close proximity to the capital.

December 11
NAVAL: In the Mekong River, South Vietnam, two PBR patrol boats engage a Viet Cong force of 40 sampans along a canal, sinking 28 and killing nine enemy soldiers.

December 14
AVIATION: During a nighttime air strike in South Vietnam, Colonel Albert R. Howarth displays extreme courage and ingenuity under enemy fire; he is awarded the Mackay Trophy.

December 16
MILITARY: At Bear Cat, South Vietnam, the 9th Infantry Division arrives and deploys in the Southern III Corps area. Within weeks it is drawn into fighting along the Mekong Delta and its 2nd Brigade joins the Mobile Riverine Force, the first amphibious force employed by the U.S. Army since the Civil War.

December 23
NAVAL: Three miles north of Dong Hoi, North Vietnam, Communist shore batteries bombard and strike the destroyer *O'Brien* twice, killing two sailors and wounding four.
MARINES: In the I Corps area, III Marine Amphibious Force reaches a strength of 67,789 men (18 infantry battalions, eight artillery battalions, two tank battalions, 11 fixed-wing squadrons, and 10 helicopter squadrons). This year marine losses totaled 1,692 killed and 10,270 injured.

1966

December 24–January 31
Aviation: In a goodwill gesture, President Lyndon B. Johnson orders a one-month Christmas cease-fire in order to promote peace talks; Communist leaders in Hanoi do not reciprocate.

December 27
Military: In the Lim Som Valley, South Vietnam, Company C, 1st Battalion, 12th Cavalry, is attacked by the North Vietnamese 22nd Regiment at landing Zone Bird. The Americans are nearly overrun until nearby Battery B, 2nd Battalion, 19th Artillery fires new "Beehive" antipersonnel rounds point-blank into enemy ranks.

1967

January
Military: Of the 485,000 U.S. forces in South Vietnam, no less than 239,400 are U.S. Army troops. General William C. Westmoreland, buoyed by the influx of manpower, wishes to do more than simply stabilize the situation and declares 1967 the "year of the offensive."

January 1–April 5
Military: In Pleiku Province, Central Highlands, South Vietnam, the 4th Infantry Division under Major General William R. Peers begins screening operations to prevent North Vietnamese infiltration into the region. By the time his offensive ends, no less than 11 engagements have been fought and won by his troops.

January 2
Aviation: Over the Red River valley, North Vietnam, F-4C Phantom IIs under Colonel Robin Olds of the 8th Tactical Fighter Wing, fly a mission profile identical to F-105 Thunderchiefs fighter bombers to lure MiG-21 interceptors to them. Operation Bolo works perfectly and seven Communist jets are shot down in only 12 minutes. This is a single-day aerial record; among the victors was Colonel Olds, who bagged a MiG and became the only U.S. Air Force ace to score kills in both World War II and Korea.

January 5
Military: The State Department admits that, to date, 5,008 Americans have been killed in South Vietnam, and 30,093 wounded in the year 1966. Total casualties since January 1961 are even higher; 6,664 dead, and 37,738 injured. Presently 380,000 American troops are slogging around Southeast Asia, the majority of them combat troops.

January 8
Aviation: At Marble Mountain, South Vietnam, marine HMH-463 introduces the first Sikorsky CH-53A Sea Stallion heavy lift helicopters, each capable of lifting up to 12,000 pounds in outside configurations.

January 8–26
Military: Northwest of Saigon, South Vietnam, a force of 16,000 army troops, backed by 14,000 South Vietnamese, commence "Operation Cedar Falls" against Viet Cong positions and encampments in a region known as the Iron Triangle. Elements of the 175th Airborne Brigade, the 1st and 25th Infantry Divisions, and

South Vietnamese forces sweep through the region, but the Viet Cong wisely decide not to stand and fight. It results in 750 Communist dead and 280 captured plus large caches of weapons and supplies, but no knockout blow. The Americans lose 72 soldiers killed in action.

January 12
MILITARY: In Gia Dinh Province, South Vietnam, General William C. Westmoreland commences Operation Fairfax to shore up the defenses of Saigon. The 199th Infantry Brigade and the South Vietnamese 5th Ranger Group commence a year-long pacification program that eliminates much of the threat, but Communist guerrillas remain a persistent problem.

January 13
NAVAL: In Washington, D.C., Master Chief Gunner's Mate Delbert D. Black becomes the navy's senior enlisted adviser, who counsels the chief of naval operations on matters pertaining to enlisted personnel. In time, the position is renamed master chief petty officer of the navy (MCPON).

January 16
MILITARY: Determined to halt Communist infiltration along the Demilitarized Zone (DMZ), MACV orders the construction of a fortified line along the northern border of South Vietnam.

MARINES: In light of intensifying ground combat, the Marine Corps resumes the practice of granting battlefield commissions to enlisted men who demonstrate exceptional leadership qualities under fire.

• At Vieques Island, Puerto Rico, the 10th Marines deploy for month-long live-fire exercises with the 6th and 8th Marines, the 2nd Field Artillery Group, and the 2nd Marine Air Wing (2nd MAW).

January 17
MARINES: At Camp Pendleton, California, the 28th Marines is created as part of the rapidly developing 5th Marine Division.

January 18
AVIATION: At Cape Kennedy, Florida, a Titan IIIC launch vehicle carries eight Department of Defense communications satellites into orbit at one throw.

January 26–April 7
MARINES: In southern Quang Tri Province, South Vietnam, the 7th Marines conducts search-and-destroy missions against Viet Cong units within its grasp. For a loss of 69 marines killed and 556 wounded, the Communists leave behind 383 dead.

January 27
AVIATION: At Cape Kennedy, Florida, a fire onboard the sealed *Apollo 1* space capsule kills three astronauts: Lieutenant Commander Roger B. Chaffee (USN), and Lieutenant Colonel Gus Grissom and Lieutenant Colonel Ed White (both USAF). The accident results in safety modifications to subsequent Apollo spacecraft.

January 31
MARINES: In the I Corps tactical zone, Operation Prairie concludes with a loss of 239 marines dead and 1,214 wounded in return for Communist losses of 1,397 killed.

1967

February 1–March 18
MARINES: In the I Corps tactical zone, the 3rd Marine Division commences Operation Prairie II with one battalion sweeping along the upper part of Quang Tri Province along the Demilitarized Zone (DMZ), while two other battalion stand by in supporting roles. The marines claim 693 Vietnamese dead for the loss of 93 marines killed in action and 483 wounded.

February 4
NAVAL: On the Co Chien River, South Vietnam, the *PBR-113* is set afire by a Viet Cong grenade; damaged beyond repair, it is eventually salvaged for parts.

February 6
AVIATION: The Space Command Center, North American Aerospace Defense Command, is relocated into the very heart of Cheyenne Mountain, Colorado. This hardened, underground facility, protected by millions of tons of solid rock, is impervious to all but a direct hit by a nuclear weapon.

February 8–12
MILITARY: Tet, the Vietnamese New Year, occasions a four-day cease-fire punctuated by small violations, but also a lack of major fighting. However, the Communists use the pause in the fighting to shift 25,000 tons of supplies down the Ho Chi Minh Trail.

February 10
MARINES: At Quantico, Virginia, the Marine Security Guard Battalion is created to train and administer embassy guard detachments around the globe.

February 11–January 21, 1968
MILITARY: In Binh Dinh Province, South Vietnam, Operation Pershing begins as the 1st Cavalry Division unleashes its three brigades in a year-long sweep of the region. They are joined by the South Korean Capital Division and the ARVN 22nd Division; an estimated 9,000 Vietcong are killed.

February 12
MILITARY: Along the Demilitarized Zone (DMZ), South Korea, North Koreans again ambush a patrol of the 23rd Infantry, killing an American soldier.

February 12–22
MARINES: In Quang Nam Province, South Vietnam, the 1st Marine Division begins Operation Stone with a search-and-destroy mission of Go Noi Island; 400 Communists are slain and 74 captured at a price of nine dead and 76 wounded.

February 13
MILITARY: In Long An Province, South Vietnam, Operation Enterprise unfolds as the 3rd Brigade, 9th Infantry Division begins a year-long pacification program to clear out resident Viet Cong units.
MARINES: In the United States, marines begin training with the new, lighter Colt M16 rifle, which is intended to replace the larger, heavier M14. While lethal at close range, the first models acquire a reputation for jamming under combat conditions.

U.S. troops examine drugs and equipment found in an underground Vietcong hospital in War Zone during Operation Junction City, 1967. *(Texas Tech University Vietnam Archive)*

February 14

MILITARY: In Long Khanh Province, South Vietnam, the 11th Armored Cavalry commences Operation Kittyhawk, designed to keep the highways north of Saigon free from enemy interference. The operation lasts a little over a year and is generally successful.

February 15

NAVAL: On the waterways leading to Saigon, Vietnam, *MSB-45* strikes a mine and sinks while *MSB-49* is damaged by enemy shore fire. One sailor is killed and 16 are wounded.

February 16

NAVAL: In the Rung Sat Special Zone, South Vietnam, River Assault Flotilla 1 cooperates with troops of the 9th Infantry Division while rooting out local Viet Cong units.

February 16–March 3

MARINES: At the southern tip of Quang Ngai Province, South Vietnam, the Special Landing Force (1st Battalion, 4th Marines and helicopters of HMM-363) commences operation Deckhouse IV. They are assisted by Stingray reconnaissance units behind enemy lines, whose air and artillery strikes kill about 280 Viet Cong. Overall, resistance is light and marines sustain seven killed and 111 wounded.

February 21

MARINES: In Hue, South Vietnam, a Viet Cong mine kills writer Bernard B. Fall while he accompanies a marine patrol north of the city.

February 22

AVIATION: Operation Junction City unfolds as a force of 23 C-130 Hercules transports inserts the 173rd Airborne Brigade along the Cambodian border.

MILITARY: In War Zone C near the Cambodian border, the 2nd Brigade, 173rd Airborne Brigade, performs the first and only airborne operation of the Vietnam War. Operation Junction City drops 778 parachutists near Katum in an attempt to halt Communist infiltration movements there.

February 22–May 14

MILITARY: Northwest of Saigon, General William C. Westmoreland commits the second corps-sized operation when Operation Junction City deploys 22 battalions tasked with clearing enemy formations from base areas around the city.

February 24

AVIATION: Near Dalat, South Vietnam, a Cessna O-1A Bird Dog flown by Captain Hilliard A. Wilbanks, 21st Tactical Air Support Squadron, single-handedly engages approaching Viet Cong forces that are threatening a body of South Vietnamese rangers. He is mortally wounded and shot down on his last pass, winning a post-humous Medal of Honor.

February 25–March 18

MARINES: In the I Corps tactical zone, Operation Prairie II escalates once III Marine Amphibious Force obtains permission to fire artillery across the Demilitarized Zone (DMZ) into North Vietnam. The North Vietnamese army responds in kind; by the time all action ceases, 694 Communists have been killed and 20 taken prisoner. Marine losses are 93 killed and 483 wounded.

February 26

AVIATION: The mouths of the Song Ca and Song Giang Rivers, North Vietnam, are mined by A-6 Intruders off the carrier *Enterprise* in an attempt to stop the flow of enemy supplies. This is also the first aerial mining mission of the Vietnam War.

NAVAL: Off Thanh Hoa, North Vietnam, the cruiser *Canberra* and destroyers *Benner* and *Joseph Strauss* bombard Communist installations along the shoreline. This is the first offensive use of naval gunfire without enemy provocation.

February 27

MARINES: In Da Nang, South Vietnam, Viet Cong forces employ large 122mm Soviet-made rockets for the first time against the airfield; 11 men are killed, 97 are wounded, and 18 parked aircraft are damaged. A further 72 Vietnamese civilians are wounded.

February 28

NAVAL: In the Mekong Delta, South Vietnam, the Mobile Riverine Force, or Task Force 117, employs armored river gunboats to flush out Viet Cong units along the riverbanks.

March 6

NAVAL: While *PBR-124* is patrolling along the banks of the Mekong River, a Viet Cong soldier throws a hand grenade that lands on its deck. Seaman David G. Ouellet suddenly dashes from his machine gun mount and places himself between his captain and the blast, dying instantly. He wins a posthumous Medal of Honor.

March 7

NAVAL: The personnel ceilings for the Women Accepted for Voluntary Emergency Service (WAVES) rise to 600 commissioned and 6,000 enlisted, a 20 percent increase.

March 9–11

NAVAL: Near Vinh Binh, North Vietnam, the heavy cruiser *Canberra* and destroyers *Ingersoll* and *Keppler* shell and destroy several coastal batteries; on the 11th, *Keppler* is struck once, but without casualties.

March 10

AVIATION: Over North Vietnam, air force F-105 Thunderchiefs and F-4C Phantom IIs strike the Thai Nguyen steel factory; this is also the first air raid launched from Ubon, Thailand.

- Today Captain Merlyn H. Dethlefsen ignores damage to his F-105 Thunderchief inflicted by a missile strike and repeatedly attacks Communist gun emplacements so that accompanying fighter bombers can attack the Thai Nguyen steel plant. He wins a Medal of Honor for bravery under fire.
- Two MiG-17s fall before the cannon of Captain Max Brestel, flying an F-105 Thunderchief of the 355th Tactical Fighter Squadron. He is the first air force pilot to claim dual victories during a single sortie.

March 11
AVIATION: The Canal des Rapides bridges outside of Hanoi, North Vietnam, are struck by air force fighter bombers.
- Navy aircraft from the carrier *Oriskany* deploy new Walleye, television-guided glide bombs to attack the Sam Son military barracks, North Vietnam, thereby introducing precision-guided munitions into the war.
NAVAL: The destroyer *Keppler,* operating off Vinh, North Vietnam, is struck by an enemy shore battery in its forward mount; six sailors are injured.

March 14
NAVAL: Off South Vietnam, the picket escort ship *Brister* and the Coast Guard cutter *Point Ellis* corner a North Vietnamese trawler attempting to land supplies and drive it aground. They had been alerted of its presence by an orbiting P-2 Neptune on Market Time patrol.

March 15
AVIATION: The large Sikorsky HH-53B helicopter performs its maiden flight; it becomes the largest such machine in the air force inventory. It is assigned to Aerospace Rescue and Recovery Squadron operations (ARRS).

March 16
MARINES: Outside Khe Sanh, South Viet Nam, Viet Cong units ambush several marine platoon-sized patrols, killing 19 and wounding 59; only 11 Communists are found dead on the field.

March 17
NAVAL: Off the coast of North Vietnam, the destroyer *Stoddard,* while rescuing a downed pilot from the water, is struck by fire from enemy shore batteries. The vessel uses counterbattery fire to silence its antagonist and then sails off.

March 18
MARINES: In Saigon, South Vietnam, Master Sergeant Barbara J. Dulinsky is the first woman marine to deploy to Vietnam as part of MACV headquarters.

March 19–April 19
MARINES: In the I Corps tactical zone, Operation Prairie II unfolds as the 3rd Marine Division commits five infantry battalions and four artillery battalions to search-and-destroy efforts in Dong Ha and Cam Lo, South Vietnam. By the time the operation winds down 252 Communists have been killed at a cost of 55 dead and 529 wounded.

March 19–20
MILITARY: Near Bau Bang village, northwest of Saigon, South Vietnam, two Viet Cong battalions strike at the 3rd Squadron, 5th Cavalry, but they are repelled in a successful night action.

March 20
NAVAL: Just south of the Demilitarized Zone (DMZ), South Vietnam, the Seventh Fleet's Special Landing Force goes ashore as part of Operation Beacon Hill I. The amphibious ships *Monticello, Ogden,* and *Princeton* are all involved.

March 20–April 1
MARINES: Northeast of Dong Ha in the I Corps tactical zone, the Special Landing Force (1st Battalion, 4th Marines) stages an amphibious landing and sweeps along through the region near the coastline. The marines claim 334 North Vietnamese regulars killed at a cost of 29 dead and 230 wounded.

March 21
AVIATION: At Anderson Air Force Base, Guam, President Lyndon B. Johnson decorates 12 Strategic Air Command (SAC) crewmen for B-52 and KC-135 operations over Southeast Asia.
MILITARY: In response to Operation Junction City, large Viet Cong forces attack Firebase Gold near Suoi Tre, South Vietnam, and are badly repulsed by concentrated artillery fire.

March 22
AVIATION: B-52 jet bombers begin arriving at U Tapao, Thailand, to prevent overcrowding at Anderson Air Base, Guam. However, use of this base obviates the need for aerial tankers during bombing missions.

March 22–25
MARINES: In Quang Nam Province, South Vietnam, Operation Newcastle accounts for 188 dead Viet Cong.

March 25
AVIATION: At Eielson Air Force Base, Alaska, the 6th Strategic Wing begins operating as a strategic reconnaissance unit and operates a variety of RC-135 aircraft.

April 1
MILITARY: At Firebase George, northwest of Saigon, South Vietnam, the 1st battalion, 26th Infantry under Lieutenant Colonel Alexander M. Haig repels a determined Viet Cong night attack. By this date, Operation Junction City has succeeded at clearing out major Communist concentrations from the Saigon area.
NAVAL: The navy commissions the *Will Rogers,* the last of its 26 Polaris-armed ballistic missile submarines.
• The cruiser *Providence,* accompanied by four destroyers, unleashes the single-largest shore bombardment of the Vietnam War by hitting coastal targets in North Vietnam.
• The Coast Guard, having spent the last 177 years as part of the Treasury Department, is transferred to the Department of Transportation.

April 3
AVIATION: Paul W. Airey is appointed the first chief master sergeant of the U.S. Air Force; as such, he will advise senior leadership on issues concerning enlisted personnel.

April 8
AVIATION: In Puerto Rico, air force C-141 Starlifters participate in Exercise Clove Hitch III, dropping paratroopers for the first time. This large maneuver

involves over 21,000 U.S. Air Force, U.S. Army, U.S. Navy, and Marine Corps personnel.

April 9–14
AVIATION: Air force C-130 transports of the 315th Air Division begin the largest tactical unit deployment of the Vietnam War by flying 3,500 men of the 196th Light Infantry Brigade and 4,000 tons of equipment from Tay Ninh to Chu Lai, South Vietnam.

April 10
AVIATION: At U Tapao, Thailand, B-52s begin conducting their first air raids against targets in South Vietnam.
MEDICAL: The hospital ship *Sanctuary* is the second vessel of its class to perform medical service off Vietnam.

April 12
MILITARY: In Binh Dinh Province, South Vietnam, a division-sized provisional unit labeled Task Force Oregon deploys in the southern I Corps near Chu Lai to bolster the 1st Cavalry's ongoing operations.
MARINES: In Washington, D.C., Commandant Greene testifies before Congress that the III Marine Amphibious Force requires an additional 40,000 men to successfully fulfill its mission.

April 15
MARINES: Along the Demilitarized Zone (DMZ), South Vietnam, MACV instructs III Marine Amphibious Force to commence building a barrier line just below the border of North Vietnam.

April 19
AVIATION: Over North Vietnam, Major Leo K. Thorsness, 357th Tactical Fighter Squadron, attacks and destroys a missile site and then remains in the area to help discourage MiG-17s from attacking incoming fighter bombers. During this time he refuels twice over Thailand, dodges heavy antiaircraft fire, and shoots down two MIG-17s. He consequently receives a Medal of Honor for his actions. Thorsness is shot down and captured on March 4, 1973.

April 20
AVIATION: Aircraft from the carriers *Kitty Hawk* and *Ticonderoga* strike power plants only one mile from the center of downtown Haiphong, North Vietnam, the closest they have ever come.

April 20–May 31
MARINES: In the I Corps tactical zone, the 3rd Marine Division commences Operation Prairie IV with new search-and-destroy missions in the vicinity of Dong Ha and Cam Lo. The result is 489 Communist dead and nine captured at a cost of 164 marines killed and 999 wounded.
• At Chu Lai, South Vietnam, marines in the southern I Corps tactical zone are replaced by an army brigade, and they are redeployed along the Demilitarized Zone (DMZ) to staunch the flow of Communist infiltration from North Vietnam.

1967

April 21–May 12
NAVAL: Operation Beacon Star unfolds as the Seventh Fleet drops the Special Landing Force in Thua Thien Province, South Vietnam, to engage any Viet Cong units lurking there. They kill an estimated 764 Communist troops.

April 22–May 17
MARINES: South of Da Nang, South Vietnam, three marine battalions joined by a similar-sized South Vietnamese force begin combat sweeps through the region to eliminate resident Viet Cong units. For a loss of 110 marines dead and 473 wounded, 865 Communists are killed while 173 are captured.

April 24
AVIATION: The carriers *Bon Homme Richard* and *Kitty Hawk* launch jets, which strike enemy airfields at Kep, North Vietnam, for the first time. Concurrently, the air force attacks another base at Hoa Lac, 19 miles to the west. The navy claims two MiG-17s shot down as they attempt to take off.

April 24–May 13
AVIATION: Jets of the 1st Marine Air Wing (1st MAW) fly 1,100 close support missions for marines in close combat near Khe Sahn, South Vietnam.
MARINES: Near Khe Sanh, South Vietnam, Company B, 1st Battalion, 9th Marines engages Communist forces on Hill 861 and they are gradually reinforced by two battalions of the 3rd Marines. This force attacks two North Vietnamese regiments in fortified positions on Hills 861, 881, and 881 South, and intense fighting lasts through May 13. During the struggle, supporting artillery units fire 25,000 rounds. For a cost of 155 marines dead and 425 wounded, 940 Communists are killed.

April 26
AVIATION: The MiG airfields at Kep and Hoa Lac, North Vietnam, become subject to aerial attacks, but those airfields closer to Hanoi remain off limits.
• During his latest Iron Hand mission to Haiphong, North Vietnam, Lieutenant Commander Michael J. Escotin of VA-192 (*Ticonderoga*) is severely damaged by antiaircraft fire, yet continues attacking a SAM battery before crashing and being killed. He receives a posthumous Medal of Honor.

April 27
NAVAL: Rear Admiral Kenneth L. Veth succeeds Rear Admiral Norvell G. Ward as commander of U.S. naval forces, Vietnam.

April 28
AVIATION: At Ramstein Air Base, West Germany, Operation Creek Party unfolds as Air National Guard KC-97L tankers begin refueling operations as part of a voluntary support effort. This also marks the first time that the ANG has served overseas in an extended capacity.
• A Titan IIIC launch booster sends five *Vela* satellites into orbit for the purpose of monitoring nuclear testing worldwide, especially in China.

April 28–May 12
MARINES: In the Que Son Valley, South Vietnam, Special Landing Force Alpha (1st Battalion, 3rd Marines, and helicopters of HMM-263) conducts Operation

Beaver Cage, an intense search-and-destroy mission against Viet Cong units positioned there. They account for 181 Communists killed and 66 captured at a cost of 55 dead marines and 151 wounded.

April 29

AVIATION: The Military Airlift Command (MAC) wins the 1966 Daedalian Flight Safety Award for a record fifth time.

MILITARY: Along the Demilitarized Zone, South Korea, men of the 2nd Division extract a measure of revenge by ambushing North Korean infiltrators, killing one soldier.

May 1

AVIATION: Aircraft from the carriers *Bon Homme Richard* and *Kitty Hawk* make a second attack on the air base at Kep, North Vietnam, shooting down two MiG-17s and destroying four on the ground.

May 8

MARINES: This being the 13th anniversary of the Communist victory at Dien Bien Phu, North Vietnamese army units attack the marine base at Con Thien, just below the Demilitarized Zone (DMZ). The 1st Battalion, 4th Marines, responds in kind, killing 197 Communists and capturing eight in exchange for 44 dead and 110 wounded.

May 9

MILITARY: In South Vietnam, the Civilian Operations and Revolutionary Development Support (CORDS) is created to support existing pacification efforts. Although a civilian-run agency, 95 percent of its 6,464 advisers are from the army. It is also quite effective at recruiting and enlarging local militias, which mushroom to 475,000 men within one year.

May 11–August 2

MILITARY: In the southern I Corps region, Task Force Oregon is committed to Operation Malheur I to seek out and destroy Communist units in its vicinity. At the end of three months they account for 869 Viet Cong killed, but at the price of 9,000 forcibly evacuated civilians. The extensive use of artillery to reduce suspected targets also leads to widespread devastation.

May 13

AVIATION: Jets of the 8th Tactical Fighter Wing, flying out of Ubon Royal Thai Air Base, Thailand, shoot down another seven MiGs in various aerial engagements for a second time.

May 13–July 16

MARINES: At Khe Sanh, I Corps tactical zone, the newly arrived 26th Marines commit Operation Crockett, a spoiling attack intended to keep the North Vietnamese from building up forces in the region. Marines account for 206 Communist dead while sustaining 52 dead and 255 wounded.

May 15

NAVAL: Three 311-foot long Coast Guard cutters, *Barataria, Bering Strait,* and *Gresham,* arrive off South Vietnam. Each carries a crew of 150 men and, collectively, they double the number of Coast Guardsmen in Southeast Asia.

1967

May 18–26

AVIATION: As part of Operation Rolling Thunder, the Seventh Air Force's strategic bombing campaign against North Vietnam, VMA(AW)-242 flies several sorties north of the DMZ in support.

MARINES: Along the Demilitarized Zone (DMZ), marines launch three concurrent sweeps through the area to clear it of Communist forces. Special Landing Force Alpha (1st Battalion, 3rd Marines and helicopters of HMM-263) lands along the coastline and pushes inland under the code name Beau Charger. Simultaneously, battalions of the 4th, 9th, and 26th Marines move into the area of Con Thien as code name Hickory while SLF Bravo lands northeast of that village under the code name Belt Tight. Fighting is intense: 447 Communists are killed at a cost of 142 marines dead and 896 wounded.

MILITARY: In Kontum Province, Central Highlands, South Vietnam, the 4th Infantry Division commits itself to Operations Sam Houston and Francis Marion while engaging two regiments of North Vietnamese regulars. They account for more than 2,000 enemy dead but are worn out by multiple engagements over the next nine days. Consequently, I Field Force commander Lieutenant General Stanley R. Larsen requests MACV to transfer the 173rd Airborne Brigade to the vicinity as reinforcements.

May 19

AVIATION: The carrier *Bon Homme Richard* launches A-4 Skyhawks, which attack a thermal power plant one mile from downtown Hanoi. Escorting F-8 Crusaders also manage to down four MiG-17s in aerial combat.

Marines from 5th Regiment fire at the enemy near the DMZ, May 1967. (*National Archives*)

May 20–28
MARINES: In Quang Tri Province, South Vietnam, two battalions of the 3rd Marine Division sweep the region, killing 445 Communist troops.

May 22
MILITARY: At Camp Greaves, just below the Demilitarized Zone (DMZ), South Korea, Communist infiltrators blow up an American barracks, killing several soldiers.
• Along the Cambodian border, American and Vietnamese Special Forces embark on Operation Daniel Boone, a highly classified border-crossing operation to gather intelligence, take prisoners, and commit sabotage where possible. In the course of four years, 1,825 such missions are launched.

May 25–June 6
MARINES: In Quang Nam and Quang Tin Provinces, I Corps tactical zone, Operation Union II commences as the 5th Marines and 1st Ranger Group (ARVN) commence a search-and-destroy mission through the region. At its conclusion, 701 Communists have been slain in exchange for 110 dead Marines and 241 wounded.

May 27
NAVAL: At Camden, New Jersey, the navy commissions its second nuclear-powered guided-missile frigate, the *Truxtun*.

May 31
AVIATION: Over the Gulf of Tonkin, a KC-135 Stratotanker flown by Major John H. Casteel, 902nd Air Refueling Squadron, makes an emergency refueling of navy fighters low on fuel and saves six of them. For their efforts, Casteel and his crew receive the Mackay Trophy.
• The first A-12 high-speed reconnaissance mission over North Vietnam is flown by CIA pilot Mel Vojvodicha and transpires in three hours and 40 minutes.

May 31
MARINES: Elements of the 3rd Marine Division sweep again through Quang Tri Province, South Vietnam, during Operation Prairie IV, killing 489 Viet Cong; marines losses are 164 dead and 999 wounded.
• Lieutenant General Lewis W. Walt is replaced by Lieutenant Robert E. Cushman as the head of III Marine Amphibious Force.

May 31–June 1
AVIATION: A pair of air force Sikorsky HH-53Es make the first nonstop transatlantic helicopter crossing in time for the Paris air show. They do so in retracing the original flight of Charles A. Lindbergh and complete their sojourn in 30 hours and 46 minutes with nine aerial refuelings.

June 1
AVIATION: The air force transfers 20 Northrop F-5 Freedom Fighters to the South Vietnamese air force to serve as their first jet aircraft.

1967

June 1–July 14
MARINES: In Quang Tri Province, South Vietnam, the 30th Marines, 3rd Marine Division, conduct Operations Cimarron and Buffalo to uproot any lingering Communist influence in the region; 1,290 Viet Cong are reported killed.

June 2
DIPLOMACY: The Soviet Union protests that the merchant vessel *Turkestan* was attacked at Cam Pha, North Vietnam, by American aircraft, killing one sailor and wounding others.

June 5
MARINES: In Qunag Nam and Quang Tri Provinces, South Vietnam, the 5th Marines conduct a final drive through the region, killing 701 enemy soldiers.

June 5–11
AVIATION: When the Six-Day War breaks out between Israel and her Arab neighbors, 1,300 American citizens in Libya are evacuated to Wheelus Air Force Base for their own protection.

June 8
NAVAL: Israeli warplanes mistakenly bomb the intelligence-gathering vessel *Liberty* in international waters north of the Sinai Peninsula, killing 34 sailors and wounding 171. Lieutenant Commander William L. McGonagle, though severely wounded, refuses to quit the bridge until his vessel is out of harm's way, and he wins a Medal of Honor. The government of Israel also promptly apologizes for the action.

June 9
AVIATION: The first Cessna O-2A Skymaster, a twin-boomed, twin-engine forward air control aircraft (FAC) deploys in South Vietnam.

June 17
MILITARY: In the Central Highlands, South Vietnam, the 3rd Brigade, 1st Cavalry Division, and the 173rd Airborne Brigade commence Operation Greeley to preempt any North Vietnamese attacks against Dak To.

June 23
AVIATION: Over Camp Lejeune, North Carolina, a collision between two troop-carrying helicopters results in the death of 20 marines.

June 25
NAVAL: Off the Ca Mau Peninsula, South Vietnam, patrol boat *PCF-97* is hit by Viet Cong recoilless rifle fire and sinks; one sailor is wounded.

June 30
DIPLOMACY: The Soviet Union protests that the merchant vessel *Mikhail Frunze* has been struck by bombs during an American raid on Haiphong, North Vietnam, the day previous.
MARINES: At this point in the war, Marine Corps manpower levels are 23,592 officers and 261,677 enlisted men.

1967

July 1

AVIATION: A Titan IIIC launch vehicle places six satellites in near-synchronous orbit as part of the Initial Defense Communications Satellite Program (IDSCSP); at this date, there are already 18 such satellites deployed.

•   At Maxwell Air Force Base, Alabama, the headquarters, Civil Air Patrol, completes its relocation from Ellington Air Force Base, Texas.

NAVAL: In Washington, D.C., the new U.S. Naval Intelligence Command is established under the direction of the director of naval intelligence.

July 2–14

MILITARY: In the I Corps tactical zone, South Vietnam, the 1st Battalion, 9th Marines commences Operation Buffalo with a sweep of the Con Thien area as Special Landing Force Alpha (1st Battalion, 3rd Marines), Special Landing Force Bravo (2nd Battalion, 9th Marines) and the 3rd Battalion, 9th Marines, move in as reinforcements. Communist resistance is fierce, as usual, but at the operation's conclusion 1,301 enemy soldiers have been killed. Marine losses are 113 dead and 290 wounded.

July 7

MARINES: In light of a pressing need for more infantry captains, the Marine Corps drops its two-year time-in-grade requirement for promoting first lieutenants to one year.

July 11

AVIATION: The air force publicly unveils its X-24A wingless lifting body, a rocket-powered vehicle destined for research in atmospheric reentry studies.

July 13

AVIATION: Distinguished Flying Crosses are awarded to 18 astronauts from the U.S. Air Force, U.S. Navy, and Marine Corps for their participation in the Mercury and Gemini space programs.

July 14

NAVAL: Coast Guard vessels performing Operation Market Time accost a steel-hulled trawler that ignores warning shots and is driven ashore at Cape Batangan, South Vietnam. It is found to have been carrying several tons of arms and stores to the Viet Cong.

July 15

MILITARY: At Da Nang, South Vietnam, Viet Cong gunners unleash 50 122mm rockets against aviation facilities. Eight Americans are killed, 175 wounded, and 42 parked aircraft destroyed or damaged.

July 16–October 31

MARINES: In the region of Dong Ha and Cam Lo, South Vietnam. Operation Kingfisher commences as the 3rd and 9th Marines engage in a series of search-and-destroy missions to root out Viet Cong and North Vietnamese units. The marines sustain 340 dead and 1,461 wounded in exchange for 1,117 Communists killed.

July 21

AVIATION: Over North Vietnam, F8U Crusaders from VF-24 and VF-211 (*Bon Homme Richard*) engage and shoot down three MiG-17s in aerial combat near the oil facility at Ta Xa. Air crews from this carrier now claim nine MiGs in all.

1967

July 24

AVIATION: North of Hanoi, North Vietnam, Marine Corps jets strike at the Thai Nguyen power plant facility.

July 29

NAVAL: In the Gulf of Tonkin, the supercarrier *Forrestal* is swept by a fire after a Zuni rocket prematurely ignites and causes a series of explosions on the flight deck. The ensuing conflagration kills 134 sailors and injures 62 and also destroys 21 jet aircraft. Through herculean efforts on the part of its crew, the *Forrestal* returns to operational status in only five days.

July 30

AVIATION: At Fort Worth, Texas, the General Dynamics FB-111A makes its maiden flight; this is a strategic bomber version of the fighter.

July 31

MARINES: At Camp Pendleton, California, regular and reserve Marine Corps units conduct Exercise Golden Slipper to test how well the two elements can be integrated under combat conditions. This is also one of the largest landing exercises held in the area.

August

MILITARY: Army bulldozers, fitted with the new, 4,000-pound Rome plow, begin clearing Route 13 north of Lai Khe, South Vietnam. The Americans clear the jungle back a distance of 200 yards on either side of the road, denying the enemy cover, and the road is declared open by November 1.

August 1

NAVAL: In Washington, D.C., Admiral Thomas H. Moorer gains appointment as the 18th chief of naval operations.
• The navy announces its decision to reactivate the *Iowa*-class battleship *New Jersey*, whose 16-inch guns would prove useful off the coast of Vietnam.

MARINES: At this date, the number of marines committed to combat operations in Southeast Asia tops 78,000.

August 9

MILITARY: In the Central Highlands, South Vietnam, army units return to the Song Re River valley to clear out a concentration of Communist forces. The 2nd Battalion, 8th Cavalry, deploys Company A under Captain Raymond K. Bluhm at Landing Zone (LZ) Pat, where it is immediately taken under enemy fire. Though badly outnumbered, Bluhm calls in helicopter gunships and artillery support as he attacks up the ridge, causing the enemy to flee. Success results in a Valorous Unit Award to the regiment while A Company's guidon also receives a streamer.

August 10

AVIATION: In Washington, D.C., Congress trims $172 million from the navy F-111B carrier aircraft program upon the understanding that it is too large for carrier operations. Only the air force acquires this aircraft in any quantity.
• South of Hanoi, North Vietnam, F-4 Phantoms from the carrier *Constellation* down two MiG-21s over a truck park they were defending.

MILITARY: Below the Demilitarized Zone (DMZ) in South Korea, Communist infiltrators attack a party of the 13th Engineers, killing three Americans.

1967

Moorer, Thomas H.   (1912–2004)
Admiral

Thomas Hinman Moorer was born in Mount Willing, Alabama, on February 9, 1912, and he graduated from the U.S. Naval Academy in 1933. After three years of sea duty he qualified to become a naval aviator and was assigned to Patrol Squadron 22 at the time of Pearl Harbor in 1941. The following February his PBY was shot down off northern Australia and the ship that rescued him was subsequently torpedoed. Moorer then transferred to England as an observer and he commanded Bombing Squadron 132 at Key West, Florida, before receiving his final billet during the war with air staff of the Atlantic Fleet. Immediately after the war, Moorer remained in Japan as part of the strategic bombing survey, then undertook a final stint at sea with the carrier *Midway* (1948–49). Thereafter he concentrated on carrier air operations and ordnance development for many years. Moorer also continued climbing up the ranks, reaching captain in 1951, rear admiral in 1957, and vice admiral in 1962. He returned to the Pacific, commanding the Seventh Fleet just as the United States began its involvement in Southeast Asia. On June 26, 1967, Moorer rose to full admiral and commander in chief of the Pacific Fleet and, in that post, he emerged as a vocal proponent of that conflict.

As commander, Moorer strongly supported the use of air power to dissuade Communist North Vietnam from helping insurgents in South Vietnam. To that end, he began dispatching reconnaissance aircraft over Laos and the Ho Chi Minh Trail to gather military intelligence. In August 1964, following an alleged Communist patrol boat attack on the destroyers *Maddox* and *Turner Joy,* Moorer was instrumental in persuading President Lyndon B. Johnson to launch retaliatory air strikes against North Vietnam. He transferred as commander of the Atlantic Fleet in April 1965, but not before committing naval units to patrol the coast of South Vietnam to interdict Communist supplies arriving by sea. He also helped orchestrate the first systematic bombing campaigns of North Vietnam and Laos while openly criticizing Secretary of Defense Robert S. McNamara's attempt to micromanage the air campaign from Washington. In 1967 Moorer advanced to chief of naval operations. He assumed a central role in the ongoing Vietnam War. He advocated mining North Vietnamese harbors and called for a slowdown in the pace of the American withdrawal from Southeast Asia, and he also supported the American incursion into Cambodia. During the Communist Easter offensive of April 1972, Moorer called for mining Haiphong Harbor, which was eventually done. He capped his career in July 1970 when President Richard M. Nixon appointed him chief of naval operations. Moorer resigned from active duty in July 1974 and died at Bethesda Maryland on February 5, 2004, an outspoken hawk throughout the Vietnam War. To the end, he believed that the United States should have invaded North Vietnam.

August 11
AVIATION: Over Hanoi, North Vietnam, F-105 Thunderchiefs from the 355th and 388th Tactical Wings manage to drop several spans of the Paul Doumer Bridge.

August 13–16
AVIATION: Recent flooding in Fairbanks, Alaska, results in a major airlift of humanitarian supplies and equipment by the U.S. Air Force, the Alaska Air National Guard, and the Alaska Air Command.

August 19
AVIATION: In South Vietnam, a Marine UH-1 Huey helicopter gunship flown by Captain Stephen W. Pless swoops in to rescue four American soldiers on a beach where they are being attacked by larger Viet Cong forces. While escaping, the overloaded machine strikes the water four times before becoming airborne. Pless consequently wins a Medal of Honor while his three crewmen receive Navy Crosses.

August 21
AVIATION: Air force officials estimates that 80 surface-to-air missiles have been fired at American warplanes this day, the largest total ever recorded.

August 24–September 4
AVIATION: In the latest goodwill gesture, President Lyndon B. Johnson orders another halt in air attacks against North Vietnam, eliciting no response from the Communist regime.

August 26
AVIATION: Over North Vietnam, an F-100 flown by Major George E. Day is shot down. Day ejects, evades capture for several days, and then is caught and tortured. Escaping again, he is shot and recaptured. For repeated displays of bravery during a harrowing captivity, he receives a Medal of Honor.

August 28
AVIATION: The Lockheed U-2R, a highly improved version, flies for the first time. Only a dozen are constructed with six going to the air force and six to the Central Intelligence Agency (CIA).
MARINES: At Dong Ha, South Vietnam, Communist artillery and rockets strike aviation facilities at Marble Mountain, killing 10 marines and damaging 49 parked aircraft.

August 30
AVIATION: The air assets of Task Force 77 on Yankee Station, Gulf of Tonkin, are ordered to isolate the port of Haiphong, North Vietnam, by cutting various links. The strategy commences with an attack by jets from the *Oriskany,* which strike four major bridges leading into the city.
MARINES: At Phu Bai, South Vietnam, Viet Cong mortars attack aviation facilities, wounding 57 marines and damaging 18 helicopters.

September–December
AVIATION: The marines ground all their Boeing CH-46 Skyknight helicopters after several accidents point to structural failures in the aft motor pylon. They do not resume combat operations again until December.

September 1
AVIATION: The first Bell AH-1G Cobra helicopter gunships deploy in Vietnam for service acceptance trials. Fast and heavily armed with rockets and minigun pods, they impress army evaluators and a further 838 craft are ordered.
NAVAL: In Washington, D.C., Paul R. Ignatius gains appointment as the 59th secretary of the navy.

September 1–October 4
MARINES: The garrison at Con Thien, south of the DMZ, weathers another harrowing siege until concentrated American fire power forces the Viet Cong to withdraw their artillery.

September 3
AVIATION: At Dong Ha, South Vietnam, a Viet Cong artillery barrage strikes the aviation facility, igniting the ammunition dump and fuel farm; 17 helicopters belonging to HMM-361 are also heavily damaged.
POLITICS: General elections held in South Vietnam make General Nguyen Van Thieu the new president; he holds power until April 1975.

September 4–5
MARINES: In the Que Son Basin, South Vietnam, the 5th Marines conducts Operation Swift, a search-and-destroy effort that kills 571 Communists; marine losses total 127 dead and 352 wounded.

September 9
AVIATION: For displaying extreme bravery under fire while rescuing a downed airman, Sergeant Duane D. Hackney becomes the first living enlisted man to receive the Air Force Cross.

September 11
MILITARY: In the southern I Corps tactical zone, Task Force Oregon launches Operation Wheeler, a major search-and-destroy effort.

September 18
MILITARY: Secretary Robert F. McNamara announces plans to develop and deploy a functional antiballistic missile system designed around the Nike X and Spartan missile systems. Its purpose is to thwart an attack from Communist China, which has developed its own atomic weapons.
MARINES: Throughout South Vietnam, intense monsoon rains and flooding near the Demilitarized Zone (DMZ) takes 10 marine lives and complicate supply efforts there.

September 25
MILITARY: As Operation Wheeler unfolds in the southern I Corps tactical zone, Task Force Oregon is reinforced by the 11th Infantry Brigade and the forthcoming 198th Infantry Brigade (Light). The entire force is then redesignated the 23rd Infantry Division (Americal) under Major General Samuel W. Koster.

MARINES: At Con Tien, I Corps tactical zone, marines endure one of the heaviest Communist bombardments of the entire war when 1,000 artillery rounds strike their facilities. Two Marines are killed while 202 are injured.

September 28
NAVAL: On the Mekong River, South Vietnam, Viet Cong rocket fire sinks a navy PBR with a loss of two killed and four wounded.

October 3
AVIATION: A North American X-15 hypersonic research plane piloted by Major William J. Knight reaches a record-breaking 4,534 miles per hour at an altitude of 102,100 feet. At the time this was the absolute world speed record for a non-orbiting manned aircraft.
• In light of the overreliance on air-to-air missiles, whose reliability under combat conditions has proven spotty, the first McDonnell Douglas F-4E Phantom II armed with a 20mm Vulcan gatling gun is delivered to the air force for evaluation.

October 4
MARINES: In Quang Tin and Quang Ngai Provinces, South Vietnam, additional marine units are dispatched to the Demilitarized Zone (DMZ) and are replaced by a brigade of the Army's 1st Cavalry Air Division.

October 5
AVIATION: In Florida, astronaut and Marine Corps major William C. Williams dies after his T-38 jet trainer crashes.

October 7
MILITARY: Along the Imjim River, South Korea, a patrol boat belonging to the 2nd Infantry Division is attacked by Communist infiltrators.

October 10
AVIATION: The Outer Space Treaty is signed by President Lyndon B. Johnson to prevent the militarization of space. It also includes provisions for the rescuing of stranded astronauts and prohibits any nation from claiming the moon or planets.

October 14
MILITARY: The United States charges North Vietnam with mistreatment of its prisoners in violation of the Geneva Convention.

October 16
AVIATION: At Nellis Air Force Base, Nevada, the first operational F-111A supersonic tactical fighter is delivered, This highly advanced machine, fitted with variable swept wings and nighttime terrain-following radar, is capable of missions under all weather conditions. It flew using radar guidance all the way from Fort Worth, Texas.

October 21
MILITARY: The new 198th Brigade (Light) arrives in South Vietnam from Fort Hood Texas, and is assigned to the new 23rd (American) Infantry Division in the I Corps.

October 25
Aviation: During Operation Rolling Thunder, marine, navy, and air force jets participate in a joint-service attack upon Phuc Yen airfield, North Vietnam; 10 MiG fighters are destroyed on the ground while the 69th MiG is downed by air force fighters.

October 26
Aviation: South of Hanoi, North Vietnam, a navy F-4 Phantom from the carrier *Constellation* downs a MiG-21.
Military: As a warning to peace protestors, Lewis Hershey, director of the Selective Service, informs college students that their educational deferment will be cancelled if they interfere with military recruiting.

October 27
Marines: In response to civil rights pressure, the Department of Defense releases a plan to double the number of African-American officers in the Marine Corps. It presently stands at 155, or less than 1 percent.

October 30
Aviation: Over North Vietnam, Communist forces fire six SA-2 missiles at a Lockheed A-12 aircraft during a reconnaissance mission. Afterward, a small missile fragment is found in the lower-wing fillet area.
• A flight of two F-4 Phantom IIs from the carrier *Constellation* engage four MiG-17s 35 miles northeast of Hanoi, North Vietnam; one MiG is downed by an air-to-air missile.

October 30–November 4
Military: A Special Forces camp at Loc Ninh on the Cambodian border resists a determined Viet Cong siege, assisted by artillery and air strikes.

October 31
Naval: At Mare Island, California, the navy decommissions the *Currituck*, its last remaining seaplane tender.

November 1
Marines: At Da Nang, South Vietnam, Vice President Hubert Humphrey arrives to award the 3rd Marine Division with a presidential Unit Citation for its performance and sacrifices along the Demilitarized Zone (DMZ).

November 1–January 28, 1968
Marines: In the I Corps zone, the 9th Marines embark on Operation Lancaster by conducting search-and-destroy missions in the vicinity of Camp Carroll, South Vietnam.

November 1–February 28, 1968
Marines: In the I Corps tactical zone, the 3rd Marine Division commences Operation Kentucky over the next four months; casualties are 520 American dead and 3,079 wounded for 3,281 Viet Cong killed in action.

November 3–December 1
Military: In Kontum Province, Central Highlands, South Vietnam, Viet Cong forces prepare to storm a Special Forces camp at Dak To. However, a spoiling attack is launched by the 4th Infantry Division's 3rd Battalion, 12th Infantry, that drives enemy forces off the top of Hill 1338. Units from the 173rd Airborne Brigade and the 1st Cavalry Division take up the pursuit as far as the Cambodian border.

1967

Hershey, Lewis B.   (1893–1977)
Army general

Lewis Blaine Hershey was born in Steuben County, Indiana, on September 12, 1893, and he joined the National Guard in 1911. He served in Europe without seeing combat during World War I, but nonetheless won a regular army commission in 1920. Hershey handled his affairs capably and, despite a polo accident that blinded him in one eye, he attended the Command and General Staff College in 1933. The turning point in his career came in 1936 when he was assigned to the Joint Army and Navy Selective Service Committee, a group of officers tasked with planning wartime mobilization in the event of hostilities. Hershey soon demonstrated that he knew more about manpower policy than any of his contemporaries and he played a central role in drafting the Selective Service and Training Act, passed by Congress in September 1940. The following year President Franklin D. Roosevelt appointed him director of the Selective Service, a position he was to hold for the next three decades. It fell upon Hershey to draft sufficient manpower to meet America's military needs during wartime while leaving sufficiently qualified young men available to work in the factories. To this end he was responsible for establishing a system of education-based deferments, alternative duty for conscientious objectors, and assistance in employment for returning veterans.

Hershey handled all his tasks with aplomb and tact, and the draft process unfolded smoothly. In light of his performance he became a major general in April 1942, despite his lack of combat experience. After the war, Hershey advocated maintaining a peacetime draft, but he was initially overruled by President Harry S. Truman. However, the expanding nature of the new cold war necessitated restarting the Selective Service in 1947, and Hershey was reinstalled as director. After the Korean War the draft continued but, due to declines in the demand for manpower, Hershey again resorted to broad-based exemptions for college students. The public mood, unfortunately, began turning against the draft in the 1960s as the unpopularity of the Vietnam War soared. In fact, Hershey and the draft became synonymous as symbols of government oppression, and students began burning their draft cards. Hershey, upon the urging of President Lyndon B. Johnson, recommended to local draft boards that deferments for protestors be revoked. Moreover, he opposed all attempts to remove the autonomy of local draft boards, which rendered him something of a political liability in 1968. It fell upon newly elected president Richard M. Nixon, who determined that an all-volunteer force was best for the nation, to remove him from Selective Service, promote him to full general, and name him a presidential adviser. The army retired Hershey in April 1973, ending 53 years of devoted service to the nation. He died in Angola, Indiana, on May 20, 1977, having orchestrated a mobilization campaign that inducted tens of millions of young men across three wars.

November 5
AVIATION: At Naval Air Station North Island, California (San Diego), a Martin SP-5B Marlin seaplane of VP- 40 makes the final operational flight of a navy seaplane. Such aircraft have been in operation since 1911.

November 5–December 9, 1968
MARINES: An extended search-and-destroy mission east of Gio Linh, South Vietnam, by the 3rd Marine Division, the Army 196th Light Infantry Brigade, and the 1st Brigade, 5th Infantry Division, accounts for 3,495 Communist dead. American losses are 395 dead and 1,680 wounded.

November 6
MARINES: Near An Hoa, South Vietnam, a sweep conducted by the 2nd Battalion, 5th Marines through Antenna Valley accounts for 72 dead Communists at the price of 37 marines killed and 122 wounded.

November 8
MILITARY: In Washington, D.C., President Lyndon B. Johnson signs legislation granting women equal opportunities for promotion throughout the U.S. military.

November 9
AVIATION: During a clandestine rescue mission to extract an army reconnaissance team from Laos, an HH-3E Jolly Green Giant helicopter flown by Captain Gerald O. Young, 37th Aerospace Rescue and Recovery Squadron is shot down. Rather than expose other helicopters to danger, he evacuates his wounded crewmen into the jungle and evades capture for 17 hours until he is finally able to call in his own rescue. Young consequently receives a Medal of Honor for bravery under fire. He is also the first Air Force Academy graduate so honored.
• A F-4C Phantom II jet flown by Captain Lance P. Sijan is shot down over North Vietnam, but he ejects and manages to evade capture for six weeks. Captured and severely tortured, Sijan escapes again but is caught and contracts pneumonia while imprisoned. He dies on January 21, 1968, and wins a posthumous Medal of Honor.

November 11
MILITARY: In the southern I Corps tactical zone, South Vietnam, the 1st Cavalry Divisions commence Operation Wallowa in concert with Task Force Oregon to crush the North Vietnamese 2nd Division, then lurking in the Que Son Valley. Enemy forces are decimated but not destroyed, and they filter back in once the Americans depart.

November 13–30
MARINES: West of An Hoa, South Vietnam, Operations Foster and Badger Hunt commence as the 3rd Battalion, 7th Marines and the 2nd Battalion, 3rd Marines engage in search-and-destroy operations; 125 Communists are killed at a cost of 21 marines dead and 137 wounded.

November 14
AVIATION: Northeast of Hue, South Vietnam, the UH-1E helicopter bearing Major General Bruno H. Hochmuth, commander of the 3rd Marine Division, crashes, killing him.

November 15
AVIATION: An X-15 hypersonic research aircraft flown by Major Michael J. Adams enters a Mach 5 spin and breaks up at 65,000 feet. Adams is killed in consequence

and receives astronaut wings posthumously. He is also the first fatality since the X-15 program commenced in 1959.

November 17–December 29
AVIATION: At Fort Campbell, Kentucky, Operation Eagle Thrust commences as C-133 and C-141 transports airlift 10,536 paratroopers and 5,118 tons of equipment (including 37 helicopters) to Bien Hoa Air Field, South Vietnam. This constitutes the largest and longest aerial movement of troops in the war.

November 19
MILITARY: At Bien Hoa, South Vietnam, the two remaining brigades of the 101st Airborne Division ("Screaming Eagles") are deployed while the 1st Brigade remains in the II Corps region. The entire unit is reunited in the I Corps as of April 1968.

November 19–22
MILITARY: Despite surging American forces in Kontum Province, the North Vietnamese position a regiment atop Hill 875 to serve as a rearguard. On this day the 2nd Battalion, 503rd Infantry, arrives to drive them off and does so after heavy fighting. The Americans are reinforced by the 4th Battalion, 503rd Infantry, at which point the Communists flee the area, having lost over 1,000 men. American losses are 115.

December 4
NAVAL: In Dinh Tuong Province, 66 miles south of Saigon, South Vietnam, the Mobile Riverine Force accounts for 235 Viet Cong dead.

December 8
AVIATION: An F-104 Starfighter jet crashes at Edwards Air Force Base, California, killing Major Robert H. Lawrence, Jr., the nation's first African-American astronaut selected to fly in space.
MILITARY: In Tay Ninh Province, northwest of Saigon, South Vietnam, the 25th Infantry Division commences Operation Yellowstone while the 1st Infantry Division sorties into the Iron Triangle, Binh Duong Province, in a concerted effort to preempt enemy troop concentrations from launching an offensive. The Americans gradually account for 5,000 Communists killed well into the new year.

December 13
MARINES: At Khe Sanh, South Vietnam, increased Viet Cong activity leads dispatch of the 3rd Battalion, 26th Marines to reinforce the garrison.

December 14
AVIATION: Over North Vietnam, Four navy F-4 Phantom IIs from the carrier *Oriskany* square off against four MiG-21s; one Communist jet is sent down in flames.

December 17
AVIATION: Over North Vietnam, Marine Captain Doyle D. Baker, flying as an exchange officer with an air force squadron, shoots down a Communist MiG-17 while escorting a bomb run. He is the first marine pilot to score a victory in this conflict.

1967

December 19
MILITARY: In the I Corps tactical zone, the 11th Infantry Brigade deploys as part of the Americal Division. This is presently the largest American formation in South Vietnam, with an assigned strength of 20,000 men.

December 26
AVIATION: Operation Rolling Thunder continues over North Vietnam as marine jets strike at targets near Hanoi and Dong Hoi.

December 29
AVIATION: At Offutt Air Force Base, Nebraska, the final RB-47H sorties occur when the 55th Strategic Reconnaissance Wing retires its last remaining Stratojet.

December 31
MILITARY: By year's end, no less than 9,378 American soldiers have been killed in action; to this must be added an additional 6,782 combat-related deaths between 1961 and 1966. Overall strength of combined U.S. military personnel tops 478,000.
• Along the Demilitarized Zone (DMZ) separating North and South Vietnam, work on the so-called McNamara Line, a strongpoint barrier system, has consumed 757,000 man-days over the past 12 months.
MARINES: In Washington, D.C., General Leonard F. Chapman is appointed the 24th commandant of the Marine Corps to replace General Greene.
• At this date, 81,249 marines are serving in South Vietnam, of which 3,461 have been killed and 25,525 have been wounded in 1967.

1968

January
MILITARY: The army has deployed 100 infantry and mechanized battalions, along with 54 artillery battalions, in South Vietnam, representing an aggregate of 331,098 officers and men.

January 1
AVIATION: The Aerospace Defense Command (ADC) is the new designation for the Air Defense Command.
• The Office of the Air Force Reserve becomes part of the Air Staff and functions as a policy planning center for Reserve operations.

January 1–15
AVIATION: Carrier aviation has one of its worst weeks as five jets are lost over North Vietnam during this period.

January 3
MARINES: In the I Corps tactical zone, Commandant General Leonard F. Chapman embarks on an inspection tour of marine units and their facilities.

January 5
AVIATION: The T-41 Mescalero Light Plane joins the Flying Program at the U.S. Air Force Academy.

January 6

AVIATION: In Chu Lai, South Vietnam, Major Patrick H. Brady flies his helicopter in and out of a hot landing zone to rescue wounded soldiers of the 198th Infantry Brigade. For evacuating 39 men under heavy fire to safety he receives a Medal of Honor.

MARINES: General William C. Westmoreland initiates Operation Niagara, which employs heavy air and artillery strikes to break up Communist troop concentrations around Khe Sanh, South Vietnam.

January 8

AVIATION: In South Vietnam, a CH-53 Sea Stallion troop helicopter crashes, killing 36 marines.

January 11

AVIATION: In Nevada, a marine transport aircraft from Quantico, Virginia, crashes, killing 19 marines.

January 12

AVIATION: Tactical air units are hereafter directed to carry with them all the essentials needed for operating at bare bases sporting only runways, taxiways, parking areas, and a water source.

January 15–18

DIPLOMACY: In Washington, D.C., President Lyndon B. Johnson suspends air attacks near Haiphong, North Vietnam, to stimulate interest in peace talks.

January 16

AVIATION: On Sicily, Italy, transports from the United States Air Force Europe (USAFE) and the Military Airlift Command (MAC) fly in humanitarian aid to assist earthquake victims.

DIPLOMACY: North Vietnamese officials spurn an offer of peace talks with the United States until all aerial bombing ceases.

MARINES: At Guantánamo Bay, Cuba, the 2nd Battalion, 28th Marines deploys as the permanent garrison. Henceforth, new units will no longer arrive and depart every 90 days, but will instead be rotated through the unit itself.

• The marine outpost at Khe Sanh, I Corps tactical zone, is reinforced by the 2nd Battalion, 26th Marines; the entire regiment is now present with the garrison.

January 19

MARINES: Near Khe Sanh, I Corps tactical zone, a marine patrol encounters strong enemy forces near Hill 881 North and is obliged to withdraw. This signals the beginning of the Communist siege there.

January 20

MARINES: At Khe Sanh, I Corps tactical zone, Company I, 3rd Battalion, 26th Marines attacks Hill 881 North and begins clearing it of Communist forces. However, the operation ceases and the company withdraws back inside the perimeter after a captured North Vietnamese lieutenant informs his captors that a major assault is brewing over the next several days.

1968

January 21

AVIATION: An eight-jet B-52 jet bomber belonging to the Strategic Air Command (SAC) explodes over North Star Bay, Greenland, spilling its four hydrogen bombs into the ocean. No radiation leaks occur, although one of the seven crew members dies in the ensuing crash.

• Waves of B-52s are employed throughout the siege of Khe Sanh, South Vietnam, which relentlessly carpet Viet Cong and North Vietnamese army troop concentrations around the Marine Corps perimeter.

NAVAL: During the protracted siege of Khe Sanh, South Vietnam, Naval Construction Battalion Unit 301, Detail Bravo, indelibly contributes to the defense of that place, winning a Presidential Unit Citation.

MARINES: In light of new intelligence pointing to some kind of Communist offensive, General William C. Westmoreland orders Marines to stop working on the McNamara Line barrier system along the Demilitarized Zone (DMZ).

• Near Camp Carroll, I Corps zone, the 4th Marines commence Operation Lancaster II to clear the region of Communist forces lurking nearby. The 3rd Marines at Quang Tri perform Operation Osceola for identical reasons.

• At Khe Sanh, I Corps zone, a Communist night assault upon Hill 861 is repulsed by Company K, 3rd Battalion, 26th Marines. North Vietnamese artillery units also begin raining shells and rockets on the marine position over the next 77 days. By this time they are surrounded by the 15–20,000 men of the North Vietnamese 324B and 325C Divisions. The NVA also cuts off Route 9, isolating the garrison. Khe Sanh itself is occupied by 3,500 men of Colonel David E. Lownd's 26th Marines.

January 22

AVIATION: At Thule, Greenland, A B-52G crashes while making an emergency landing, cracking several of its four nuclear weapons open. Several months of cleanup are required before radiation levels are returned to normal.

NAVAL: The intelligence-gathering vessel *Pueblo* is boarded and captured by North Korean forces in the Sea of Japan. The vessel's only defensive weapons, two .50-caliber machine guns, are fast frozen beneath tarpaulins on the bridge. The 83-man crew under Lieutenant Commander Lloyd Bucher, accused of violating the 12-mile territorial limit, is carried off into captivity for 11 months; one sailor, Duane Hodges, is killed in action.

MARINES: At Khe Sanh, I Corps area the garrison is stiffened by the arrival of the 1st Battalion, 9th Marines and two batteries of 105mm howitzers.

January 22–29

MILITARY: Along the Demilitarized Zone (DMZ), South Korea, North Korean infiltrators make harassing attacks against several outposts manned by the 2nd Infantry Division.

January 25

NAVAL: In response to the seizure of the *Pueblo,* the aircraft carrier *Enterprise* is dispatched to the Sea of Japan in a show of force. However, President Lyndon B. Johnson, with his hands effectively tied in Vietnam, does not want to risk a second Asian conflict.

1968

ARVN soldier fires at Vietcong positions in Cholon during the 1968 Tet Offensive fighting in Saigon. *(Texas Tech University Vietnam Archive)*

January 26
AVIATION: In light of tensions arising from the capture of the navy vessel *Pueblo,* an A-12 high-speed reconnaissance aircraft performs a mission over North Korea. Air National Guard and Air Force Reserve elements are also called into active duty status as a precaution.

January 27
MARINES: Despite a seven-day truce that begins the Tet holiday, the ARVN 37th Ranger Battalion joins the garrison at Khe Sanh, in the I Corps zone.

January 30–31
MILITARY: Although MACV has suspected a Communist buildup and a brewing offensive for some time, they are not able to predict when. It occurs at midnight on Tet, the Vietnamese New Year, and strikes at 36 provincial and 64 district capitals. In Saigon, a Communist sapper team even breaches the walls of the U.S. embassy before they are stopped by military police. American losses for the first nine days of the offensive total 546 dead and 6,000 wounded while Communist casualties are estimated as much higher, around 20,000. The offensive ends in a costly defeat for the Communists, but a corner has been turned in public opinion and the American public begins turning against continued American involvement.

February 1
AVIATION: During the assault on Hue, South Vietnam, helicopters of HMM-165 provide airlift for South Vietnamese forces attacking the Citadel.

1968

MARINES: In Hue, South Vietnam, the 1st Battalion, 1st Marines and 2nd Battalion, 5th Marine maneuver to retake the city back from Communist forces. Their immediate objective is to storm the area south of the Perfume River while the ARVN 1st Division attacks the Citadel on the north bank of the river.

February 2–24
MILITARY: In the III Corps tactical zone, South Vietnam, the old imperial capital of Hue, is the site of intense battling by army troops and marines to wrest it back from the Viet Cong. Elements of the 2nd Brigade, 101st Airborne Division are involved south of the city while the 7th and 12th Cavalry Regiments sweep in from the north and west. After an intense struggle, Communist supply lines are closed down and the city is retaken. Before departing, the Viet Cong line up and execute 5,000 political opponents in the war's single biggest atrocity.

February 3
AVIATION: In Tullahoma, Tennessee, air force engineers at the Arnold Engineering Development Center photograph high-velocity aircraft and missile models with a laser beam. This is the first time a laser has been utilized as a light source.

February 5
MARINES: At Khe Sanh, I Corps zone, marines rely upon ground sensors to detect the approach of enemy units and disrupt their concentration with an artillery barrage. Meanwhile, Company E, 2nd Battalion, 26th Marines successfully defends Hill 861A from a North Vietnamese attack.

February 6
MARINES: In Hue, South Vietnam, savage house-to-house fighting results in marines retaking the provincial headquarters, whereupon the Communist flag is taken down and the Stars and Stripes are run up.
• Aviation facilities at Da Nang suffer from another round of artillery and rocket bombardments, but marines defeat several attempt by sappers to penetrate the base.

February 7
MILITARY: The Special Forces camp at Lang Vei, near Khe Sanh, is overrun by North Vietnamese army troops employing Soviet-made PT-76 tanks for the first time.

February 8
MARINES: In a sharp firefight, Company A, 1st Battalion, 9th Marines defeats a Communist attack on one of its outposts.

February 10
MARINES: In Hue, South Vietnam, the 1st Battalion, 1st Marines and 2nd Battalion, 5th Marines complete mopping-up operations along the south bank of the Perfume River. The first phase of the city's reconquest costs the marines 38 dead and 320 wounded. Communist losses are estimated at over 1,000. Reinforcements also arrive in the form of the 1st Battalion, 5th Marines.

February 13
MARINES: In Hue, South Vietnam, the 1st Battalion, 5th Marines begins its assault on the Communist-held Citadel and they are joined in due course by two battalions of South Vietnamese marines.

February 14
AVIATION: Transports of the Military Airlift Command (MAC) begin conveying elements of the 82nd Airborne Division and 3,000 marines to bases in Southeast Asia. The Continental Air Command also activates Air Force Reserve units to assist the MAC in more routine missions for the time being.

February 17
MARINES: At Camp Pendleton, California, the 27th Marines and the 2nd Battalion, 13th Marines are dispatched as reinforcements to help fight the Tet Offensive.

February 18
MILITARY: At Chu Lai, South Vietnam, the 3rd Brigade, 82nd Airborne Division, deploys to reinforce I Corps while attached to the 101st Airborne Division.

February 24
AVIATION: The 1st Marine Aviation Wing (1st MAW), in an attempt to cut down on high helicopter losses to enemy ground fire, originates the concept of the "Super Gaggle." This involves up to one KC-130 tanker aircraft and eight or more CH-46 helicopters carrying sling-loads beneath their bellies, and backed by the firepower of four A-4 Skyhawks and hour UH-1 Huey helicopter gunships. The overall missions are coordinated by a TA-4 two-seater Skyhawk, with the back seat officer acting as director. Thus arranged, the attack planes would strafe and drop napalm along the sides of the flight path, then helicopters would swoop in and deliver their cargoes.

February 25
MARINES: In Hue, South Vietnam, the 1st Battalion, 5th Marines wipes out all final resistance at the Citadel, completing their reconquest of the city. Marine losses total 142 dead and 1,100 wounded to a Communist tally estimated between 1,000 and 5,000 killed, wounded, and missing.

February 27
AVIATION: The Ho Chi Minh Trail in Vietnam is attacked by AC-130A Hercules gunships for the first time.
• At Khe Sanh, I Corps tactical zone, Communist ground fire claims a CH-46 helicopter, killing 22 marine passengers.

February 28
AVIATION: At Tinker Air Force Base Oklahoma, the last C-141 Starlifter is delivered; a total of 284 have been acquired.
MARINES: At Khe Sanh, I Corps tactical zone, as two North Vietnamese battalions begin probing the sector held by the 37th Ranger Battalion, they are struck by heavy concentrations of artillery and air strikes before they can attack in force.

February 29
AVIATION: In light of new public laws removing restrictions from female promotions in the military, Colonels Jeanne Holm and Helen O'Day are made permanent colonels. Holm, for her part, continues as director of women in the air force while O'Day is billeted with the air force chief of staff.

- Transports of the Air Force Southern Command begin delivering humanitarian aid to flood victims in Bolivia.

February 29–March 2
NAVAL: Three North Vietnamese trawlers crammed with weapons and supplies for the Viet Cong are intercepted by Coast Guard vessels and sunk.

March 1
MILITARY: In Washington, D.C., Clark Clifford succeeds Robert F. McNamara as the ninth secretary of defense.

March 2
MILITARY: North of Tan San Nhut, South Vietnam, Company C, 4th Battalion, 9th Infantry (Manchu) stumbles into a heavy ambush and is nearly annihilated in minutes. American losses are 49 dead and 29 wounded and Specialist 4 Nicholas J. Cutinha wins a posthumous Medal of Honor for heroism under fire. This is one of the worst American setbacks of the entire war.

March 6
AVIATION: At Khe Sanh, South Vietnam, ground fire shoots down a Fairchild C-12 Provider transport plane, killing 43 marines and five crewmen.

March 10
MARINES: The Seventh Air Force assumes control of the 1st Marine Aviation Wing (1st MAW) to provide all tactical aviation with a single, guiding hand.

March 11
MILITARY: Having contained the Communist Tet Offensive, General William C. Westmoreland is determined to seize the strategic initiative by ordering II Field Force under Lieutenant General Frederick C. Weyand into action along the III Corps front. The first sweep, involving the 1st, 9th, and 25th Infantry Divisions, clears out numerous pockets of enemy troops, killing 2,658 Communists for a cost of 105 American and 193 dead South Vietnamese. A second consecutive sweep near Saigon kills an additional 3,542 enemy troops, clearing the Saigon region of Viet Cong.

March 13
GENERAL: An accidental U.S. Army nerve gas leak from the Dugway Proving Grounds, Utah, results in the deaths of 6,400 sheep.

March 16
MILITARY: In Quang Ngai province, South Vietnam, Company C, 1st Battalion, 20th infantry under Captain Ernest Medina occupies the village of My Lai. The Americans come under sniper fire and take several casualties from mines, at which point the 1st Platoon under Lieutenant William L. Calley goes on a rampage, killing men, women, and children. The killing continues until Warrant Officer Hugh Thompson steps in between Calley and the fleeing civilians. My Lai subsequently serves as a rallying point for the vocal antiwar movement around the globe.

March 19
AVIATION: At England Air Force Base, Louisiana, the first class of 12 South Vietnamese pilots begins training to operate Cessna A-37 Dragonflies.

March 22

AVIATION: The Marine Aviation Cadet program, which enables noncollege graduates to gain their wings, is terminated.

MILITARY: General William C. Westmoreland is appointed army chief of staff by President Lyndon B. Johnson, although he does receive a replacement in South Vietnam for the next three months.

March 25

AVIATION: At Norton Air Force Base, California, the 944th Military Airlift Group (Associate) is activated as the first Air Force Reserve unit assigned to fly and maintain aircraft assigned to an associated regular unit.

• Operation Combat Lancer commences as General Dynamics F-111s are committed to bombing raids over North Vietnam for the first time. By carrying highly sophisticated terrain-following radar (TFR), they can strike the more mountainous regions that were heretofore untouchable.

March 27

MILITARY: Along the Demilitarized Zone (DMZ), South Korea, a patrol from the 2nd Division turns the tables on a group of North Korean infiltrators, killing three.

March 30

MARINES: At Khe Sanh, I Corps tactical zone, Company B, 1st Battalion, 9th Marines launches a dawn attack against enemy trenches and bunkers, inflicting heavy losses. At this juncture the Viet Cong and North Vietnamese army abandon the siege and begin drawing back into the jungle. The successful defense of Khe Sanh costs the marines 208 dead and 1,668 wounded. Communist losses are 1,602 confirmed dead with total estimates running as high as 10,000.

March 31

AVIATION: President Lyndon B. Johnson, having declared that he will not seek reelection to the presidency, also declares a partial bombing halt of North Vietnam, above the 20th parallel, in an attempt to spur peace talks.

April 1

MARINES: The 1st Marine Division, acting in conjunction with the 1st Air Cavalry Division, commences Operation Pegasus to open a ground link to the garrison at Khe Sanh.

April 1–15

MILITARY: As a large force of marines is besieged at Khe Sanh near the Laotian border, the 1st Cavalry under Major General John J. Tolson is ordered to relieve them. Operation Pegasus commences with 20,000 American troops, the 26th Marines, and ARVN allies in a concerted drive against two North Vietnamese divisions. Tolson's fast and hard-hitting attacks scatter all opposition and Khe Sanh is relieved by April 15.

April 3

DIPLOMACY: Radio Hanoi announces that its government is willing to discuss conditions for holding peace talks with the United States.

1968

April 5
MILITARY: In the wake of inner-city riots caused by the assassination of civil rights leader Dr. Martin Luther King, Jr., army units and National Guard troops are called in to restore order.
MARINES: Detachments from Quantico, Virginia, and the Washington Barracks are ordered onto the street to restore order in Washington, D.C., following the assassination of civil rights leader Dr. Martin Luther King, Jr.

April 6
NAVAL: The battleship *New Jersey* is recommissioned and heads for service in Southeast Asia.

April 10
AVIATION: At Kadena Air Base, Okinawa, the 9th Strategic Reconnaissance Wing begins flying SR-71 missions over North Vietnam.
• The navy bids farewell to its propeller-driven Douglas A-1 Skyraiders, the first models of which joined the fleet in 1945.

April 14
MILITARY: Elements of the 1st Air Cavalry Division establish contact with the defenders of Khe Sanh, I Corps zone during Operation Pegasus/Lam Som 207, formally ending the siege. Marines losses are 208 dead and 1,668 wounded. The North Vietnamese are calculated to have lost 10,000 men killed, wounded, and missing in this failed attempt to repeat their victory of Dien Bien Phu over the French.

April 15
MARINES: In Quang Tri Province, South Vietnam, the 3rd Marine Division conducts Operation Scotland, a major search-and-destroy mission, that kills 3,034 Communists for a loss of 463 dead and 2,553 wounded.

April 16
AVIATION: At Quang Tri Province, South Vietnam, Marine Air Group 39 (MAG-39) arrives as part of the 1st Marine Air Wing (1st MAW).

April 18
MARINES: At Khe Sanh, I Corps tactical zone, the 1st Marines arrive to relieve the exhausted 26th Marines, who are subsequently redeployed to Dong Ha and Camp Carroll to rest and refit.

April 19–May 17
MILITARY: General William C. Westmoreland determines to shut down the major infiltration route through the A Shau Valley through Operation Delaware. The 1st Cavalry Division commits the 1st and 5th Battalions, 7th Cavalry into an air assault that loses 10 helicopters to severe antiaircraft fire. The survivors begin working their way southward.

April 21
MILITARY: Along the Demilitarized Zone (DMZ), South Korea, a company from the 31st Infantry conducts a fire-fight with a similar-sized unit of North Korean infiltrators.

April 24–May 3
MILITARY: In the A Shau Valley, South Vietnam, the 1st Brigade, 1st Cavalry Division under Colonel John E. Stannard, air assaults into the southern entrance of the valley, meeting stiff resistance, but the Americans carve out a logistics foothold that can supply additional sorties farther up the valley.

April 28
AVIATION: At La Toma, Ecuador, C-130 transports of the Air Force Southern Command convey 92,000 pounds of food to assist victims of drought.

April 29–May 17
MILITARY: In the A Shau Valley, South Vietnam, men of the 101st Airborne Division and some ARVN troops engage in several firefights, but within two weeks most enemy units have deserted the area, leaving behind valuable caches of food, supplies, and weapons.

April 30–May 3
MARINES: At Dai Do, South Vietnam, the 2nd Battalion, 4th Marines attacks entrenched North Vietnamese units dug in along the Cua Vier River. The marines prevail after stiff fighting with losses of 81 dead and 300 wounded; enemy casualties are estimated to exceed 500.

May 3
AVIATION: At Buckley Air National Guard Base, Colorado, the 120th Tactical Fighter Squadron is activated and begins deploying to South Vietnam. This is also the first Air National Guard (ANG) unit called to active duty in the war.
DIPLOMACY: Radio Hanoi announces that the government agrees to preliminary peace talks in Paris, France.
NAVAL: In Norfolk, Virginia, headquarters of the new Naval Safety Center is founded.

May 4–August 23
MARINES: South of Da Nang, South Vietnam, the 7th Marines begin Operation Allen Brook to root out Communist units lurking there. By the time the maneuver ends, 1,017 Communists are accounted for while the marines lose 172 dead and 1,124 wounded.

May 5
MILITARY: Communist units stage a miniature Tet Offensive by striking 199 towns and cities with rocket and mortar fire.

May 11–12
AVIATION: At Kham Duc, South Vietnam, air force C-130s and C-124s race in under heavy enemy fire to evacuate American Special Forces and South Vietnamese troops. Eight aircraft are lost, including one C-130 that is hit by a mortar round and explodes, killing 150 people. Air force personnel involved win four Air Force Crosses and Lieutenant Colonel Daryl D. Cole also receives the Mackay Trophy for his efforts.
• At Kham Duc, South Vietnam, a C-123 Provider piloted by Lieutenant Colonel Joe M. Jackson braves intense Communist ground fire to land and rescue a three-man Combat Control Team; he wins a Medal of Honor for his actions.

1968

MILITARY: The sole remaining Special Forces camp in I Corps, Kham Duc, Quang Tin Province, South Vietnam, is attacked by a strong force of North Vietnamese regulars. The 1,500 defenders, including elements of the 196th Infantry Brigade and South Vietnamese irregulars, are evacuated by helicopter before it falls. American losses are 24 killed, 112 wounded, and 26 missing in action.

May 13
AVIATION: In light of the Tet Offensive, President Lyndon B. Johnson mobilizes 22,000 military reservists, including 1,333 members of the Air National Guard. Seven Air Force Reserve units are also called up.
DIPLOMACY: In Paris, France, peace talks between the United States, South Vietnam, and North Vietnam begin.

May 16
AVIATION: Military Airlift Command (MAC) transports begin carrying 88.5 tons of food to flood victims in Ethiopia.
NAVAL: In Quang Tri Province, South Vietnam, Hospital Corpsman Third Class Donald E. Ballard is treating a wounded marine when an Viet Cong grenade lands nearby. Ballard selflessly throws himself upon it to shield his comrade, but it fails to explode. He win a Medal of Honor for bravery under fire.

May 17
MILITARY: In Thua Thien Province, South Vietnam, Operation Nevada Eagle unfolds as the 101st Airborne Division sweeps through the mountains of central I Corps. It is undertaken to keep the road network open and protect the rice harvest. The Communists dodge the offensive, preferring to snipe at helicopters.

May 18–October 23
MARINES: In Quang Nam Province, Operation Mameluke Thrust unfolds as the 1st Marine Division conducts extensive search-and-destroy missions west and south of Da Nang. It concludes with marine losses of 269 dead and 1,730 wounded and estimated Communist casualties of 2,728.

June 5
NAVAL: The nuclear attack submarine *Scorpion* under Commander Francis A. Slattery is reported missing off the Azores with its crew of 99 officers and men. The official navy report blames the accident on a systems malfunction while diving. On October 30, the oceanographic research vessel *Mizar* locates the wreckage 10,000 feet below the surface and 400 miles southwest of the Azores. It has since been deduced that this vessel was deliberately sunk by a Soviet submarine in retaliation for the accidental ramming and sinking of one of their missile-carrying submersibles in the Pacific six months earlier. This remains a major cold war coverup.

May 21–30
MARINES: At Dong Ha, I Corps zone, a North Vietnamese division presses on through the Demilitarized Zone (DMZ) in an attempt to infiltrate. The 3rd and 9th Marines counter by tackling them head-on, and sending them back across the

border with 770 dead and 61 captured. Marine and ARVN losses are 112 dead and 446 wounded.

May 22
AVIATION: The 1st Marine Aviation Wing deploys its first North American/Rockwell OV-10A Broncos, a light observation craft that can be rigged for COIN (counterinsurgency) purposes.

May 25
AVIATION: The Grumman EA-6B Prowler prototype makes its maiden flight; it enters service as a carrier-based electronic countermeasure aircraft, which is still active service today.

May 28
MARINES: In Khe Sanh, I Corps tactical zone, skirmishing in the immediate region continues as a North Vietnamese army force attempts to capture a hill along Route 9. They are driven back with a loss of 230 men; marine casualties are 13 dead and 44 wounded.

June 1
AVIATION: Over Go Noi Island, Operation Allen Brook commences as nine C-130s drop 31,000 gallons of gasoline in an attempt to burn away the island's intense jungle foliage.

June 10
MILITARY: General Creighton W. Abrams replaces General William C. Westmoreland as commander of U.S. forces in South Vietnam, a move reflecting dissatisfaction with the latter's conduct of the war.
NAVAL: The South Vietnamese navy assumes responsibility for minesweeping operations along the Long Tau River channel to Saigon. To that end, the U.S. Navy turns over 14 riverine warfare vessels to their allies.

June 13
AVIATION: At Cape Kennedy, Florida, a Titan IIIC launch booster carries eight military communications satellites into space to augment the first Defense Satellite Communications System.

June 16
AVIATION: Off the South Vietnamese coast, air force aircraft accidentally bomb the cruiser *Boston* and the Australian missile destroyer *Hobart*; they manage to sink patrol boat *PCF-19*.

June 17
AVIATION: At Long Beach, California, the first McDonnell Douglas C-9 Nightingale aeromedical evacuation aircraft is unveiled to the public.

June 19
AVIATION: A quick-drying cement that hardens in only 30 minutes is field-tested in South Vietnam. Developed by the Aero Propulsion Laboratory at Wright-Patterson Air Force Base, Ohio, it is intended for helicopter landing pads.
• Over North Vietnam, a UH-2 Seasprite helicopter piloted by Lieutenant Clyde E. Lassen braves enemy fire and dense foliage to rescue the downed crew of a

Abrams, Creighton W.   (1914–1974)
Army general

Creighton Williams Abrams was born in Springfield, Massachusetts, on September 15, 1914, and he passed through the U.S. Military Academy in 1940 with an undistinguished record. He served briefly in the cavalry before transferring to the newly created Armor Force as part of the embryonic 4th Armored Division. He rose to major in 1942 and subsequently commanded the 37th Tank Battalion throughout World War II. He distinguished himself during General George S. Patton's dash across northern France in 1944, wearing out seven tanks in the process. He capped his wartime career by breaking through German siege lines in the Battle of the Bulge and relieving the 101st Airborne Division at Bastogne. Abrams consequently received two Distinguished Service Crosses and two Silver Stars. After the war he was one of a handful of promising officers selected to attend the Command and General Staff School at Fort Leavenworth, and throughout the Korean War he served as chief of staff with the I, X, and XI Corps. He rose to brigadier general in 1956 and major general in charge of the 3rd Armored Division in 1960. He faced off against Soviet armor during the tense Berlin crisis of 1962. Later that year he faced a crisis of a different sort when he was directed to quell civil unrest arising from the admission of African-American James Meredith to the University of Mississippi. He also handled integration problems at Birmingham, Alabama, with similar success and received accolades from Secretary of the

Army Cyrus Vance and U.S. attorney general Robert F. Kennedy.

In 1967 Abrams fulfilled his most daunting task, that of commanding the U.S. Military Assistance Command, Vietnam (MACV), where he trained and equipped thousands of South Vietnamese soldiers for their struggle with Communist North Vietnam. In February 1968 Abrams also orchestrated the recapture of Hue from the Viet Cong during the infamous Tet Offensive, and, the following July, he succeeded General William C. Westmoreland as supreme commander in Vietnam. Abrams introduced a shift from search-and-destroy missions to aggressive small unit operations, while also accelerating the process of Vietnamization to compel the South Vietnamese to fight their own war. Having addressed military concerns, Abrams turned to nation-building pacification programs, which were designed to enhance the educational, medical, transportation, and agricultural systems of South Vietnam. He oversaw the reduction of American forces until July 1972, before reporting back to Washington, D.C., as the new army chief of staff. Abrams then began a remedial program to shake the military free of drug use and racial problems, and also oversaw the transition from draftees to an all-volunteer force. Abrams died in Washington, D.C., on September 4, 1974, a highly talented combat commander and military administrator. In light of his sterling contributions, the army christened its latest, turbine-powered tank the M-1 tank Abrams.

Phantom II jet. Disregarding the danger, he fires flares and turns on his lights to find the airmen, rescue them, and reaches his vessel with only five minutes of fuel remaining. Lassen wins a Medal of Honor.

June 23
MILITARY: As of this day, the conflict in Vietnam has become America's longest-running war.

June 26
AVIATION: Over North Vietnam, three F-8 Crusaders from the carrier *Bon Homme Richard* tangle with two MiG-21s; one Communist jet is downed by an air-to-air missile.
DIPLOMACY: The island of Iwo Jima, Japan, which figured so prominently in Marine Corps legacy, is returned to Japanese civilian control.

June 27
MARINES: At Khe Sanh, I Corps tactical zone, the marines begin dismantling their defenses in preparation for abandoning the base. New operational plans are afoot for the northern reaches of I Corps.

June 30
AVIATION: Lockheed rolls out its mammoth C-5A *Galaxy* for its initial flight; it is then the world's largest airplane. The Military Airlift Command (MAC) eventually obtains 81 of the giant craft.
MARINES: At this stage of the war, marine manpower levels are 24,555 officers and 282,697 enlisted men.

July 1–7
MILITARY: Operation Thor commences as combined air force, artillery, and naval surface units hammer away at targets in Cap Mui Lay, North Vietnam, just over the Demilitarized Zone (DMZ). Its purpose is to destroy or silence Communist long-range artillery units in the region.

July 3
MILITARY: In Washington, D.C., General William C. Westmoreland takes over as the 25th army chief of staff while General Creighton W. Abrams succeeds him as head of MACV in South Vietnam.

July 5
MARINES: In the I Corps tactical zone, the base at Khe Sanh is abandoned by the marines who so desperately defended it.

July 6
AVIATION: The Marine Corps begins operating North American OV-10 Broncos at Da Nang, South Vietnam.

July 9
NAVAL: On the Co Chen River, South Vietnam, the army-navy Mobile Riverine Force commences operations against Viet Cong units in the region. This is the only tributary of the Mekong River that has not been patrolled before.

1968

July 12
AVIATION: At Patuxent Naval Air Station, Maryland, the last Martin P-5 Marlin seaplane is dropped from the inventory. Flying boats were among the first aircraft operated by the navy and predate World War I.

July 20
MILITARY: Along the Demilitarized Zone (DMZ), South Korea, patrols from the 2nd and 7th Infantry Divisions are fired upon by North Koreans on the other side; no casualties are reported.

NAVAL: In Annapolis, Maryland, Rear Admiral James F. Calvert gains appointment as the 46th superintendent of the Naval Academy.

July 22
AVIATION: Commander Samuel R. Chessman, VA-195, carrier *Ticonderoga,* flies a record 306 missions over North Vietnam. The previous record holder, Commander Charles Hathaway of the same squadron, flew 305 as of April 1967.

July 25
MILITARY: At Fort Carson, Colorado, the 1st Brigade, 5th Infantry Division (Mechanized) is activated prior to being dispatched to Quang Tri, South Vietnam. Once there it is intended to patrol the Demilitarized Zone (DMZ) separating North and South Vietnam.

July 28
NAVAL: In Quang Nam Province, South Vietnam, Hospital Corpsman Third Class Wayne M. Caron assists several wounded marines while under heavy fire. While crawling to assist his third patient, he is struck by enemy fire and killed; he wins a posthumous Medal of Honor.

July 29
AVIATION: Northwest of Vinh, North Vietnam, four F-8 Crusaders from the carrier *Bon Homme Richard* engage four MiG-17s in a twisting, five-minute dogfight; one Communist jet is downed.

NAVAL: In an attempt to throttle ongoing Communist supply and infiltration efforts, Operation Game Warden is enlarged to cover the entire Mekong Delta region, from the South China Sea to Cambodia.

July 31
AVIATION: The Air Force Southern Command dispatches two UH-1F helicopters to Costa Rica during an eruption by Mount Arenal.

August 1
AVIATION: At Robbins Air Force Base, Georgia, the Continental Air Command disbands and is replaced by the Headquarters, Air Force Reserves. Meanwhile, the Air Force Reserve Personnel Center becomes a separate operating agency at Denver, Colorado.

• Transports of the Air Force Southern Command convey 13,000 pounds of relief supplies to San José, Costa Rica, in the wake of Mount Arenal's recent eruption.

• In Saigon, South Vietnam, General George S. Brown gains appointment as head of the Seventh Air Force.

August 5

MILITARY: Along the Demilitarized Zone (DMZ), South Korea, North Koreans fire upon a patrol from the 38th Infantry.

August 8

AVIATION: In Turkey, two Air Force medics die when their helicopter crashes while performing rescue operations.

• At Long Beach, California, the first C-9 Nightingale medivac aircraft performs its maiden flight.

August 16

AVIATION: At Cape Kennedy, Florida, the first Minuteman III intercontinental ballistic missile (ICBM) is test- launched for the first time. This version is capable of carrying three, independently targeted reentry vehicles.

August 17

NAVAL: The navy commissions the *Dolphin,* its sole diesel-electric, deep-diving, research submarine. Crammed with modern electronics, this vessel performs missions as varied as acoustic deep water and littoral research, ocean bottom surveys, weapon launches, sensor trials, and engineering evaluations. The technically multifaceted *Dolphin* remains in commission today.

August 21–15

AVIATION: In northeastern Nicaragua, an air force UH-1F helicopter rescues 260 flood victims while also bringing in 52,000 pounds of food and relief supplies.

August 25

AVIATION: In South Vietnam, the air force begins a 90-day evaluation of the North American/Rockwell OV-10 Bronco as a forward air controller aircraft.

August 28

MILITARY: In Chicago, Illinois, U.S. Army and National Guard troops are called in to quell street violence arising from the Democratic National Convention taking place there.

August 29

MILITARY: At Long Binh, South Vietnam, inmates at the U.S. Army, Vietnam, Installation Stockade riot, beating several guards before order can be restored. This facility is known to house some of the most violent criminals in the military.

August 29–September 9

MARINES: At Da Nang, South Vietnam, Operation Sussex Bay unfolds as the 5th and 7th Marines deploy to scour the region for Communist forces who have attacked the airfield recently. The campaign ends with an estimated 2,000 North Vietnamese and Viet Cong dead.

September 1

AVIATION: Near Quang Binh Province, South Vietnam, an A-1H Skyraider flown by Lieutenant Colonel William A. Jones, 602nd Special Operations Squadron, swoops in and lands to rescue a downed air force pilot while under heavy Communist fire. Jones is severely wounded but his heroic actions result in a Medal of Honor.

MILITARY: Brigadier General Frederic M. Davison becomes the first African-American general to command a combat brigade when he assumes control of the 199th Infantry Brigade. He replaces Brigadier General Franklin M. Davis.

September 5
MARINES: Military operations in the I Corps zone cease for two days following the onset of Typhoon Bess, whose driving rains wash out many defensive positions.

September 10
MARINES: The 27th Marines are the first unit to depart Vietnam for Camp Pendleton, California, on a nonrotational basis.

September 13
MILITARY: Major General Keith L. Ware, 1st Infantry Division, is killed in a helicopter crash and is succeeded by Major General Orwin C. Talbot.

September 16
MARINES: In the I Corps tactical zone, the command headquarters of the 2nd Battalion, 26th Marines are suddenly struck by an accurate Communist mortar barrage that kills 22 marines and wounds 146.

September 18
NAVAL: In Quang Tin Province, South Vietnam, a slashing attack by *PCF-21* destroys 44 Viet Cong junks and sampans.

September 19
AVIATION: Northwest of Vinh, North Vietnam, an F-8 Crusader from the carrier *Intrepid* downs a MiG-21; this is the navy's 29th kill and the last accredited to an F-8.

U.S. battleship *New Jersey* off the coast of Vietnam *(Texas Tech University Vietnam Archive)*

MILITARY: Along the Demilitarized Zone (DMZ), South Korea, a detachment of North Korean infiltrators is ambushed and wiped out by American troops.

September 25
MILITARY: In Tay Ninh Province, South Vietnam, artillery attached to the 25th Infantry Division, armed with new motion-detection equipment, begins firing shells in an attempt to interdict North Vietnamese infiltration movements. As the war continues, harassment and interdiction missions constitute half of all artillery fired and 70 percent of ammunition expended.

September 26
AVIATION: The LTV A-7D Corsair II fighter bomber performs its maiden flight.

September 29
NAVAL: Off the I Corps tactical zone, South Vietnam, the newly refurbished and recommissioned battleship *New Jersey* unleashes its nine 16-inch guns against Communist targets northwest of Con Thien near the Demilitarized Zone (DMZ).
• Vice Admiral Elmo R. Zumwalt replaces Rear Admiral Kenneth L. Veth as commander, U.S. Naval Forces, Vietnam.

September 30
MILITARY: In Vietnam, Special Forces personnel reach an all-time high of 3,542 officers and men deployed.

October 1
MARINES: More than 8,000 enlisted marines have become officers since the battlefield commission program was initiated in June 1965.

October 3
MARINES: In Washington, D.C., the Department of Defense declares that the Marine Corps is slated to receive 2,500 men of the 17,500 who will be drafted in December. This is the first time since May that the marines have accepted draftees.

October 5
MILITARY: At this point in the war, American military personnel totals 540,000 from all four services; 84,000 of these are marines.

October 6–19
MARINES: In Thuong Duc, South Vietnam, a Special Forces camp is relieved by a thrust by the 7th Marines, which kills 202 Communists. Marine losses are 28 dead and 143 wounded.
• Near An Hoa, South Vietnam, Operation Maui Peak unfolds as battalions of the 1st Marine Division, assisted by the ARVN 51st Regiment, sweep the region clean of Communist forces, killing 350 enemy troops.

October 11–22
AVIATION: At Cape Kennedy, Florida, a Saturn 1B launch vehicle launches the *Apollo 7* space capsule into orbit for the first time. Among the three astronauts is an air force officer, Major Donn F. Eisele.

1968

MILITARY: Along the Demilitarized Zone (DMZ), South Korea, a patrol from the 2nd Infantry Division ambushes a detachment of Communist infiltrators, killing two.

October 15

NAVAL: The new SEALORDS program (Southeast Asia Lake, Ocean, River, and Delta Strategy), as envisioned by Admiral Elmo R. Zumwalt. Jr., commences in an attempt to cut all Communist supply lines from Cambodia. This requires the participation of army, navy, and South Vietnamese units and is considered the start of the "Brown Water Navy."

October 23–December 6

MARINES: South of Da Nang, South Vietnam, Operation Henderson Hill commences as the 5th Marines begins a series of search-and-destroy missions. They account for 700 enemy dead at a cost of 35 killed and 272 wounded.

October 27–November 9

MILITARY: In light of upcoming troop reductions, General Creighton W. Abrams shifts the 1st Cavalry Division from I Corps to III Corps in Saigon, where it will screen the border to prevent enemy infiltration of the capital region. To accomplish this, air force C-130s fly 437 sorties and transport 11,550 troops and 4,000 tons of cargo while navy vessels convey a further 4,370 men and 16,600 tons of cargo.

October 29

NAVAL: In the Cua-Lon-Bo De River region, South Vietnam, a force of 242 Viet Cong watercraft and 167 structures are destroyed by navy patrol boats, South Vietnamese A-1 Skyraiders, the landing ship *Washoe County*, and the Coast Guard cutter *Wachusett*. The Americans suffer five wounded.

October 31

AVIATION: Operation Rolling Thunder, the first prolonged aerial bombardment campaign against North Vietnam, concludes. A day later, President Lyndon B. Johnson suspends all air attacks on North Vietnam to promote peace talks.

November 1

AVIATION: Operation Commando Hunt, a prolonged bombardment campaign of suspected Communist positions in Laos, begins and runs until March 30, 1972.

November 1–30

NAVAL: In a month of routine work, the battleship *New Jersey*'s 16-inch guns destroy 182 enemy bunkers, 15 cave complexes, nine sampans, and 800 other structures.

November 16

AVIATION: In Quang Ngai Province, South Vietnam, a UH-1H helicopter crashes, injuring Major General Charles M. Gettys. He is dragged to safety by Major Colin Powell, who himself has suffered a broken ankle.

November 19

MILITARY: Snipers attached to the 9th Infantry Division score their first confirmed kill. The program had been initiated by Major General Julian J. Ewell the previous June and one of his men, Sergeant Adelbert F. Waldron, ends the war with 109 kills and two Distinguished Service Crosses.

November 20–December 9
MARINES: Below Da Nang, South Vietnam, the 1st Marines embark on Operation Meade River to cordon off and pacify the area known as Dodge City. This is a 36-square-mile farming area and ultimately consumes the energies of seven marine battalions. For a loss of 108 marine dead and 510 wounded, 1,023 Communists are slain and 123 taken prisoner.

November 23
MARINES: In the I Corps zone, the search-and-destroy mission entitled Operation Lancaster II concludes with marine losses of 359 dead and 2,101 wounded. An estimated 1,800 Communists troops have been killed.

November 26
AVIATION: Near Duc Co, South Vietnam, a UH-1F Huey helicopter piloted by Lieutenant James O. Fleming, 20th Special Operations Squadron, makes a dangerous and daring rescue mission under fire. Fleming successfully retrieves a six-man Studies and Observations Group (SOG) team, earning a Medal of Honor for bravery in combat.

December 1
MILITARY: In the northern Mekong Delta, South Vietnam, the 9th Infantry Division commences Operation Speedy Express to halt Viet Cong infiltration. This entails using air mobility to land troops in the vicinity of enemy sightings as quickly as possible. The Americans lose 267 men and claim 10,899 killed, but only 748 weapons are captured.

December 6
NAVAL: Operation Giant Slingshot unfolds as navy patrol boats begin scouting up the Vam Co Dong and Vam Co Tay Rivers west of Saigon, South Vietnam, to cut Communist supplies infiltrating from the Parrot's Beak region of Cambodia. Within a year they account for 1,894 Communist dead and 517 tons of supplies.

December 7–March 8, 1969
MARINES: West of An Hoa, South Vietnam, Operation Taylor Common commences. The 1st Marine Division conducts an extensive search-and-destroy sweep through the region, killing 1,398 enemy troops. Marine losses are 151 dead and 1,324 wounded.

December 9
MARINES: In northeast Quang Tri Province, Operation Napoleon/Saline concludes as the 3rd Marines end a 13-month long search-and-destroy operation. Marine losses are 395 dead and 2,135 wounded to an enemy tally of 3,495 killed.

December 21–27
AVIATION: At Cape Kennedy, Florida, the three-man *Apollo 8* spacecraft under Navy Commander James A. Lovell leaves Earth orbit, accompanied by U.S. Air

1968

Force colonels Frank Borman and William Anders. This is the first time that a manned space vehicle slips from Earth orbit, circles the moon, and safely returns.

December 23
NAVAL: In An Xuyen Province, South Vietnam, four patrol boats, backed by army helicopters, sink 167 Viet Cong sampans and also destroy 125 structures and eight bunkers.
• In North Korea, Commander Lloyd Bucher and 82 crewmen of the *Pueblo* are released after being held in captivity for 11 months.

December 28
MARINES: In the I Corps tactical zone, the marines abandon Camp Carroll, which served as an important combat base for the past two years.

December 31
AVIATION: During the year, the 1st Marine Air Wing (1st MAW) flew 47,436 combat missions, the majority in close support, and 639,194 helicopter sorties.
MARINES: In the course of this pivotal year, the III Marine Amphibious Force is thought to have inflicted 31,691 casualties on North Vietnamese and Viet Cong units for a loss of 4,634 dead and 28,319 wounded.

1969

JANUARY: Army troop strength peaks at 359,800 officers and men, but politically motivated troop withdrawals begin under the aegis of President Richard M. Nixon. Hereafter, the Americans place increasing reliance on "Vietnamization" to make the Army of the Republic of South Vietnam (ARVN) shoulder a greater burden of fighting.

January 1
AVIATION: The 71st Special Operations Squadron, flying AC-119 Shadow gunships, begins flying in South Vietnam. This is also the first Air Force Reserve unit committed to combat operations.

January 1–August 31
MILITARY: In the Mekong Delta, South Vietnam, Operation Rice Farmer is launched by the 9th Infantry Division to ferret out local Viet Cong operatives and units; by the time it ends, the Americans claim 1,861 Communists killed.

January 3
AVIATION: At Naval Air Station North Island, California, the navy founds Attack Squadron Light 4 (VAL-4), equipped with OV-10 Bronco counterinsurgency aircraft. They will be deployed in concert with river patrol craft.

January 7
AVIATION: The air force accepts delivery of its 1,000th Northrop T-38 Talon jet trainer.

January 9
AVIATION: The National Aeronautics and Space Administration (NASA) announces that the first team of men to land on the moon will be civilian Neil

Armstrong, U.S. Air Force colonel Edwin E. Aldrin, and U.S. Air Force lieutenant colonel Michael Collins.

January 13–July 21
MILITARY: In Quang Ngai Province, South Vietnam, two Americal Division battalions and two Marine Corps battalions advance into the Batangan Peninsula to clear out any remaining Viet Cong and weapons caches. By the time it concludes, army losses to mines and booby traps are 56 dead and 268 wounded.

NAVAL: On the Batangan Peninsula, South Vietnam, the Seventh Ready Group conducts its largest amphibious assault to date by landing marines and soldiers ashore to root out Viet Cong units in the region. The movement is backed by the firepower of the newly recommissioned battleship *New Jersey*.

MARINES: Operation Bold Mariner unfolds as 2,500 marines of the Seventh Fleet Amphibious Force come ashore on the Batangan Peninsula, 10 miles south of Quang Ngan City.

January 14
NAVAL: At Pearl Harbor, Hawaii, a fire and explosions sweep the nuclear-powered carrier *Enterprise* after a rocket accidentally ignites on the flight deck, killing 28 sailors and injuring 65.

January 22
MILITARY: In Washington, D.C., Melvin R. Laird gains appointment as the 10th secretary of defense.

MARINES: In the A Shau Valley, Quang Tri Province, South Vietnam, the 9th Marines under Colonel Robert H. Barrow are helicoptered in to commence Operation Dewey Canyon, supported by heavy artillery fire. This is a major search-and-destroy mission that accounts for 1,600 enemy dead.

January 23
MILITARY: Along the Demilitarized Zone (DMZ), South Korea, outposts belonging to the 2nd Infantry Division are attacked by North Korean infiltrators, but each is repulsed.

January 25
DIPLOMACY: In Paris, France, representatives from the United States, South Vietnam, and North Vietnam begin formal peace negotiations.

January 31
NAVAL: In Washington, D.C., John H. Chaffee gains appointment as the 60th secretary of the navy.

February 1
NAVAL: In the Mekong Delta, South Vietnam, the U.S. Navy hands over 25 river gunboats to the South Vietnamese navy, who are now entrusted with riverine security for the region.

MARINES: At Yuma, Arizona, the 5th Light Antiaircraft Missile Battalion (LAAM) is disbanded after the 2nd LAAM Battalion rotates back from Southeast Asia.

February 4
AVIATION: Impressive but hopelessly out of date, the remaining XB-70 Valkyrie is flown from Edwards Air Force Base, California, to Wright-Patterson Air Force Base, Ohio, where it is put on permanent display at the National Museum of the U.S. Air Force.

February 9
AVIATION: In a major development for military communications, a Titan IIIC launches the TACSAT 1 satellite into geosynchronous Earth orbit. Its purpose is to relay signals between land, sea, or airborne unit in any tactical station.

February 15
MILITARY: The army's newest light tank, the M551 Sheridan, deploys in South Vietnam for the first time with the 3rd Squadron, 4th Cavalry. It is armed with a 152mm main gun/rocket launcher and designed as a lighter alternative to the heavier M-48 Patton tanks already in service.

February 24
AVIATION: Over Bien Hoa Province, South Vietnam, an AC-47 "Spooky" gunship of the 3rd Special Operations Squadron is struck by a mortar round that ignites an onboard magnesium flare. Airman First Class John L. Levitow, the aircraft loadmaster, throws himself on the flare and tosses it outside. On November 8, 2000, Levitow is the only enlisted man awarded a Medal of Honor in this conflict when a previous award for the deed is upgraded.

February 28
MARINES: In the triangular region of Cam Lo, Dong Ha, and Con Thien, the 3rd Marine Division ends Operation Kentucky, a search and cordon operation that killed an estimated 3,921 Communist troops. Marine losses since the operation began on November 1, 1967, are 52 dead and 3,079 wounded.
• The 3rd Division also terminates Operation Scotland II, a search-and-destroy endeavor in the vicinity of Khe San, which began on April 14, 1968. For the loss of 461 dead and 2,555 wounded, the marines killed 3,311 Communist troops.

March
MARINES: At Headquarters Marine Corps, plans are made to create a law enforcement branch to oversee training and other facets related to military police functions.

March 1–April 14
MILITARY: In Kontum Province, South Vietnam, Operation Wayne Gray, an aggressive patrolling by the 4th Infantry Division, results in 608 dead Communist soldiers.

March 1–May 8
MILITARY: In the A Shau Valley, Central Highlands, South Vietnam, the 101st Airborne Division moves in to cut a vital infiltration route and encounters stiff resistance. Nonetheless, by May the paratroopers have driven out the defenders and uncovered several large caches of weapons and supplies.

1969

March 2

POLITICS: Village elections transpire throughout South Vietnam without serious interference from Communist forces.

March 3

AVIATION: The Marine Corps unveils their new Sikorsky CH-53D Sea Stallion, a heavy lift helicopter that performs yeoman work for the rest of the war.

March 3–13

AVIATION: At Cape Kennedy, the *Apollo 9* space capsule is shot into orbit with Colonels James A. McDivitt and David R. Scott and civilian Russell L. Schweickart on board. During this mission, the Lunar Extension Module (LEM) is detached and maneuvered in space for the first time.

March 4

MILITARY: The Department of Defense announces regular shipments of nerve gas by rail, and an annual budget of $350 a year on such exotic weaponry.

March 5

NAVAL: The carrier *Ticonderoga* becomes the first carrier to begin a fifth tour of duty at Yankee Station in the Gulf of Tonkin.

March 9

MARINES: Southwest of An Hoa, South Vietnam, the marines conclude Operation Taylor Common, which began on December 7, 1967, as a search-and-destroy mission. They killed an estimated 1,398 Communist troops and captured 610, while losing 156 dead and 1,327 wounded.

March 10

MARINES: In Washington, D.C., Secretary of Defense Melvin Laird admits some aspects of Operation Dewey Canyon involved crossing the border into Laos.

March 13

MILITARY: Along the Demilitarized Zone (DMZ), South Korea, North Korean infiltrators attack army working parties repairing the southern fence, but they are repulsed without doing any harm.

March 14

MILITARY: President Richard M. Nixon announces his plans to substitute the earlier "Sentinel" antiballistic missile system (ABM) with the more advanced "Safeguard" plan, which is designed to stop an incoming attack from either Communist China or the Soviet Union.

NAVAL: In Nha Trang Bay, South Vietnam, a SEAL team assault an island used by the Viet Cong as a supply base. Lieutenant Joseph R. Kerrey is wounded by an enemy grenade, but he nonetheless manages the operations, calls in fire support, and leads his team to safety. He wins a Medal of Honor.

March 15

MARINES: At this point in the war, only 5.4 percent of Marine Corps volunteers are high school graduates, who also make up 71.5 percent of draftees. At least 1,071 enlisted marines hold college degrees.

1969

March 15–May 2
MARINES: Six miles south of Khe Sanh, South Vietnam, the 3rd Marines, 3rd Marine Division begin a major search-and-destroy operation, which kills 157 Viet Cong, secures 52 suspects, and seizes 465 weapons. Marine losses are 17 dead and 104 wounded.

March 18
AVIATION: At Vandenberg Air Force Base, California, three satellites are launched, which contain 17 experiments related to the Orbiting Vehicle Program. This is undertaken under the aegis of the Office of Aerospace Research.
• In an attempt to break North Vietnamese and Communist Khmer Rouge strength in Cambodia, Air Force B-52s begin flying a protracted series of secret bombing missions under the code names Breakfast, Lunch, Dinner, and Snack. These so-called Menu operations continue without interruption until May 1970.

March 18–April 2
MILITARY: In the II Corps, South Vietnam, Operation Atlas Wedge is conducted by the 1st Division and the 11th Cavalry to interdict traffic along Highway 13 near the Michelin plantation. The 11th Cavalry under Colonel George S. Patton, Jr. is closely engaged, killing more than 400 North Vietnamese at a cost of 20 killed and 100 wounded.
MARINES: In the A Shau Valley, South Vietnam, the 9th Marines conclude Operation Dewey Canyon after killing 1,617 Communist troops. This is also the largest haul of captured equipment during the war, amounting to two 122mm howitzers, 66 trucks, 14 bulldozers, and several million rounds of ammunition.

March 19
NAVAL: In Quang Nam Province, South Vietnam, Hospital Corpsman Second Class David R. Ray administers to wounded marines while attached to a howitzer battery. He selflessly covers one wounded Leatherneck with his own body to shield him from a grenade explosion, sacrificing himself; Ray wins a posthumous Medal of Honor.

March 25
AVIATION: Navy Light Attack Squadron 4 (VAL-4), flying new OV-10A Broncos, are assigned to support the River Patrol Force while based at Vung Tau and Binh Thuy, South Vietnam.

March 26
MARINES: In the I Corps tactical zone, Lieutenant General Herman Nickerson, Jr., is appointed the new commander of III Marine Amphibious Force. His predecessor, General Cushman, is appointed deputy director of the Central Intelligence Agency (CIA).

March 27
NAVAL: Near Phan Thiet, II Corps tactical zone, the battleship *New Jersey* destroys or damages 72 enemy bunkers in a single day's work.

March 30
MARINES: In the I Corps tactical zone, marine engineers and naval construction personnel erect the so-called Liberty bridge across the wide Thu Bon River.

March 31
NAVAL: The battleship *New Jersey* concludes a productive six month's tour off Vietnam and departs on leave.

March 31–May 29
MARINES: Southwest of Da Nang, South Vietnam, Operation Oklahoma Hills commences as the 7th Marines begin a major search-and-destroy operation. The Viet Cong lose 596 dead to a marine tally of 53 killed and 482 wounded.

April
AVIATION: In Vietnam, VMO-2 becomes the first Marine helicopter squadron equipped with Bell AH-1G attack helicopters. These are the first such machines in the Marine Corps arsenal.

April 3
MILITARY: Combat deaths in Vietnam stand at 33,641, slightly higher than the toll extracted by the Korean War (33,629).

April 4–10
AVIATION: At Holloman Air Force Base, New Mexico, the 49th Tactical Fighter Wing begins transferring its 72 F-4D Phantom IIs to Spangdahlem Air Base, West Germany, which they accomplish with 504 aerial refuelings. This smooth and trouble-free redeployment garners the unit a Mackay Trophy.

April 7–20
MARINES: Near An Hoa, the 5th Marines conduct Operation Muskogee Meadows to secure the yearly rice harvest from Communist interference. They kill 162 enemy troops in exchange for 16 marines dead and 121 wounded.

April 11
AVIATION: At Vandenberg Air Force Base, California, a Strategic Air Command (SAC) missile crew launches an operation Minuteman III intercontinental ballistic missile (ICBM) for the first time.

April 14
AVIATION: North Korean jets shoot down an unarmed EC-121M Warning Star electronic surveillance aircraft from Fleet Air Reconnaissance Squadron 1 over the Sea of Japan, killing all 31 crew members. The navy begins assembling Task Force 71, which includes four carriers, as a show of force in the Yellow Sea.

April 17
AVIATION: At Edwards Air Force Base, California, a B-52 carries the X-24A gliding body, piloted by Major Jerauld Gentry, on its first glide test. This is undertaken to test the possibility of reusable and maneuverable space craft for reentry purposes; the outgrowth of this effort is the space shuttle.
MARINES: In a major upgrade, the marines in South Vietnam deploy their first 175mm self-propelled howitzers to replace their older 155mm models.

April 18
NAVAL: The carrier *Bon Homme Richard* commences its fifth tour of duty at Yankee Station in the Gulf of Tonkin.

1969

April 20–26
NAVAL: Task Force 71 sails under the command of Rear Admiral Malcolm W. Cagle as a show of force in the Sea of Japan. The sailing comes in response to North Korea's destruction of a navy EC-121 aircraft six days earlier and it is deactivated shortly afterward. The Communists are apparently unimpressed.

April 22
MARINES: In Washington, D.C., the Senate passes legislation mandating four-star rank for future assistant commandants of the Marine Corps provided that manpower levels are in excess of 200,000 men.

April 24
AVIATION: Eight-engined B-52 jet bombers unload their heaviest concentration of ordnance to date by dropping 3,000 tons of ordnance on Communist positions along the Cambodian border.

April 25
MARINES: At Vieques, Puerto Rico, American and Brazilian marines train in an amphibious landing, the largest joint maneuver between the two nations since World War II.

April 27
MARINES: At Da Nang, South Vietnam, a grassfire ignites an ammunition storehouse, igniting it. In the ensuing inferno, 38,000 tons of ammunition and 20,000 drums of fuel are consumed; one marine is killed fighting the fire.

Helicopters of the 170th and 189th Helicopter Assault Companies await the loading of troops in the Central Highlands, April 1969. *(National Archives)*

1969

April 30
MILITARY: The combined U.S. military presence in South Vietnam levels off at 543,482, its highest numerical strength with army troops numbering 365,600 officers and men.

May 2
MARINES: South of Khe Sanh, I Corps tactical zone, the 3rd Marines conclude Operation Maine Crag to sweep the region free of North Vietnamese units. Begun on March 15, it accounts for 157 enemy dead in exchange for 21 marines killed and 134 wounded.

May 3
NAVAL: At Groton, Connecticut, the *Triton,* the first submarine to circumnavigate the globe while submerged, and also the largest nuclear-powered submarine constructed to date, is decommissioned.

May 5–20
MARINES: South of Da Nang, South Vietnam, Operation Daring Rebel unfolds as the Marine Battalion Landing Team (1st Battalion, 26th Marines), assisted by Vietnamese and South Korean forces, lands on the coast and sweeps the region all the way to Barrier Island. The Viet Cong lose 105 dead at a cost of two marines killed and 51 wounded.

May 6
MILITARY: Landing Zone Carolyn, War Zone C, astride the Cambodian border is attacked on two fronts by superior North Vietnamese forces. The 442 defenders, consisting of Company C, 2nd Battalion, 8th Cavalry, Battery A, 2nd Battalion, 19th Artillery, and Battery B, 1st Battalion, 21st Artillery, fight back desperately and call in support from AH-1G Cobra helicopter gunships. At length the Communists draw off, leaving 172 dead on the ground; American losses total 10 killed and 80 injured.
NAVAL: Secretary of the Navy John Chaffee overrules a naval court of inquiry and orders none of the newly freed members of the *Pueblo* to face disciplinary action. Commander Lloyd M. Bucher is thus spared the ignominy of a court-martial.
MARINES: Today is the fourth anniversary of III Marine Amphibious Force, presently occupying the I Corps region of South Vietnam. It currently commands the 1st and 3rd Marine Divisions, the Army XXIV Corps headquarters, the American Division, and the 1st Brigade of the 5th Infantry Division. The last time the marines fielded such a large force was the Tenth Army on Okinawa during World War II.

May 8
MARINES: In the northwest reaches of Quang Tri Province, South Vietnam, Operation Purple Martin unfolds as the 4th Marines sweep the area free of North Vietnamese forces. For a loss of 79 dead and 268 wounded, the marines account for 252 Communists.

May 9–12
MARINES: Northwest of An Hoa, South Vietnam, the 5th Marines embark on Arizona Territory, a search-and-destroy mission, which accounts for 230 Communist troops killed.

1969

May 10–June 7

MILITARY: General Creighton Abrams orders another sortie into the A Shau Valley, Central Highlands, South Vietnam, under the guise of Operation Apache Snow. The 3rd Battalion, 187th Infantry, 101st Airborne Division under Lieutenant Colonel Weldon Honeycutt engages two North Vietnamese battalion on Ap Bia Mountain–soon to be dubbed Hamburger Hill–and drives them off after a bloody, 10-day struggle. At length the paratroopers are joined by the 1st Battalion, 501st Infantry and the 2nd Battalion, 506th Infantry, plus a South Vietnamese battalion, and the Communists slink off in the direction of Laos. Victory costs Americans 56 dead and 300 wounded, a toll so steep that the entire action is investigated by Congress.

May 14

AVIATION: In Ecuador, Operation Combat Mosquito commences as two C-141 Starlifters arrive with 50 tons of insecticide, which is then sprayed over affected regions by two UC-123s. Within a month mosquito problems have been eradicated.

May 15

NAVAL: In a major accident at the San Francisco Bay Naval Shipyard, the nuclear submarine *Guitarro,* then under construction, accidentally sinks in 35 feet of water. A subsequent report by the Special House Armed Service Committee found shipyard workers guilty of "culpable neglect."

May 16

NAVAL: The Coast Guard cutters *Point Garnet* and *Point League* are the first such vessels transferred over to the South Vietnamese navy.

May 16–August 13

MILITARY: In Quang Tin Province, South Vietnam, Operation Lamar Plain commences as elements of the 101st Airborne Division and the Americal Division run a sweep through southern I Corps to root out any lingering Communist presence; 542 dead enemy soldiers are claimed.

May 18–26

AVIATION: At Cape Kennedy, Florida, *Apollo 10,* piloted by Captain John W. Young, Commander Eugene Cernan, and Colonel Thomas P. Stafford, blasts into Earth orbit and circles the moon; the lunar landing module (LEM) also detaches and makes a trial descent to within 5.5 miles of the surface before recoupling and returning home safely.

May 21

AVIATION: A giant Lockheed C-5A Galaxy lifts off with a gross weight of 728,100 pounds, achieving a new world record.

May 29

MARINES: South of Da Nang, South Vietnam, Operation Oklahoma Hills commences as the 7th Marines conduct search-and-destroy operations that kill 596 enemy troops over the next two months. Marine losses are 53 dead and 487 wounded.

1969

June 1

MILITARY: A series of joint operations entitled Dong Tien ("Progress Together") is enacted on a broad scale between U.S. and ARVN units in an attempt to hone the tactical proficiencies of the latter. This instruction continues until the last army units are withdrawn.

NAVAL: As an indication of the progress of Vietnamization, the South Vietnamese navy assumes control of all patrolling operations in the Fourth Coastal Zone, which stretches into the Gulf of Siam and the South China Sea.

June 2

NAVAL: In the South China Sea, the destroyer *Frank E. Evans* is rammed and sunk by the Australian carrier *Melbourne* during Southeast Asia Treaty Organization (SEATO) maneuvers, killing 74 sailors. The destroyer captain and his deck officer are court-martialed and reprimanded.

MARINES: In Washington, D.C., General Lewis W. Walt becomes the first assistant commandant of the Marine Corps with a four-star rank. This marks the first time in history that both senior marines wear four stars.

June 4

AVIATION: The Air Force Thunderbirds demonstration squadron begins performing with their new F-4C Phantom II jets. They dazzle the crowd at the U.S. Air Force Academy graduating ceremony.

June 5

AVIATION: In light of the lack of progress in commencing peace negotiations, air force aircraft begin striking targets in North Vietnam for the first time since November 1968. The Communists have put this eight-month lapse to good use by strengthening their antiaircraft defenses and expanding their infiltration routes through Laos and Cambodia into South Vietnam.

June 5–7

MILITARY: At Firebase Crook, South Vietnam, the garrison is alerted by seismic detectors that a large enemy force is massing nearby, apparently getting ready to strike. Over the next two nights, two companies of the 3rd Battalion, 22nd Infantry, handily repel the attackers with deadly beehive rounds fired at point-blank range. The Americans suffer one killed and seven injured.

June 7–12

MARINES: Near An Hoa, South Vietnam, Operation Arizona Territory continues as the 1st Battalion, 5th Marines, destroys a North Vietnamese command group, killing over 300 enemy soldiers.

June 8

DIPLOMACY: On Midway Island, President Richard M. Nixon declares that the United States will withdraw 25,000 troops from Southeast Asia no later than August 31. He is conferring with South Vietnamese president Nguyen Van Thieu. American military strength at the time is 540,000 men and women.

MILITARY: At Chu Lai, Vietnam, Lieutenant Sharon A. Lane is the first army nurse killed in action when a Communist missile strikes the 312th Evacuation Hospital; she receives a posthumous Bronze Star. By war's end 7,465 women will have served in Vietnam, the vast majority as nurses; a total of eight die from various causes.

June 10
AVIATION: In Washington, D.C., Secretary of the Air Force R. C. Seamans, Jr., presents X-15 No. 1 to the Smithsonian Institution.

June 15
NAVAL: On the Ong Muong Canal, South Vietnam, a naval patrol led by Lieutenant Thomas G. Kelley runs into problems when one of its craft develops engine trouble during a Viet Cong attack. Kelley interposes his own craft between the stricken vessel and the enemy's fire, suffers serves injuries, but carries the operation through to completion. Kelley receives a Medal of Honor for bravery under fire.

MARINES: In South Vietnam, the 1st Amphibious Tractor Battalion packs up and departs for a new billet on Okinawa.

June 19
MILITARY: The Defense Department announces its decision to develop and procure multiple independently targeted reentry vehicles (MIRVs) in order to pack more nuclear warheads on existing missile stocks.

June 20
MILITARY: After Special Forces troops murder a Vietnamese informant on suspicion that he is a double agent, Colonel Robert B. Rheault, commanding the 5th Special Forces Group, is relieved of command by General Creighton W. Abrams on July 21. He is succeeded by Colonel Alexander Lemberes.

June 23
MARINES: Southeast of Khe Sanh, I Corps tactical area, Operation Cedar Falls commences as the 9th Marines begin a concentrated search-and-destroy mission of the region. Over the next three weeks, 120 Communist troops are slain at a cost of 24 marine dead and 137 wounded.

June 30
MARINES: At this juncture, Marine Corps personnel levels reach 25,698 officers and 284,073 enlisted ranks–the highest totals since the end of World War II. Presently, 84,000 marines are in South Vietnam. This probably accounts for the fact that reenlistment rates among volunteers and draftees are at their lowest level since before the war began.

July 1
AVIATION: By this date, the U.S. Air Force Air Rescue and Recovery Service (ARRS) has retrieved its 2,500th downed pilot from Southeast Asia.

MILITARY: Starting today, the Department of Defense begins using Social Security numbers as identification numbers, replacing the numerical system that has been in place since World War I.

NAVAL: The U.S. Navy presently operates 886 vessels of varying sizes; their average age is 17 years.

July 8–August 31

AVIATION: Air Force C-141 Starlifters transport 25,000 troops from South Vietnam to McChord Air Force Base, Washington, as part of the first wave of troop withdrawals.

MILITARY: The army's personnel drawdown from Vietnam commences with Increment I, or Operation Keystone Eagle, which removes two brigades of the 9th infantry Division, totaling 15,700 officers and men. The 3rd Brigade remains behind as part of the Saigon garrison for the time being.

July 9

MARINES: Southwest of Khe Sanh, I Corps area, Operation Utah Mesa, a joint army-marine operation, which began on June 12, concludes with 309 Communist soldiers killed. The marines have lost 19 dead and 91 wounded while army casualties are put at 94.

July 10

AVIATION: In the Gulf of Thailand, OV-10A Broncos of the River Patrol Force attack and sink six Viet Cong boats off Kien Giang Province.

July 14

MARINES: As part of the overall drawdown of U.S. forces in South Vietnam, the 9th Marines are embarked on ships for redeployment on Okinawa.

July 16

AVIATION: At Cape Kennedy, Florida, a Saturn V rocket launcher hurls the *Apollo II* space capsule out from Earth orbit and into a lunar trajectory. This is the first attempt to place human beings on the moon.

MARINES: In the I Corps zone, the 3rd Marines concludes Operation Virginia Ridge, a search-and-destroy mission near an area known as the "Rockpile." Since May 1, the marines have killed 560 Communist troops while losing 108 dead and 490 wounded.

• Northeast of Khe Sanh, I Corps tactical zone, Operation Herkimer Mountain ceases after the 4th Marines complete sweeps that had begun on May 1. Their losses are 25 dead and 219 wounded to an enemy tally of 137 slain.

July 17

AVIATION: Responsibility for resupplying the T-3 research station on Fletcher's Ice Island is assumed by the Alaskan Air Command.

July 19

AVIATION: The Air Force Southern Command dispatches transports to carry food supplies and other materials to assist a cease-fire in the Honduras–El Salvador border war.

July 20

AVIATION: The *Apollo II* lunar orbiter safely lands on the moon's surface, at which point Astronaut Neil Armstrong, a former naval aviator, becomes the first man to walk on an extraterrestrial body. "That's one small step for [a] man, one giant leap for mankind," he declares. He is soon after joined by Edwin E. "Buzz" Aldrin, and the two complete a total of two hours and 32 minutes walking on the moon.

MARINES: Racial groups battle at Camp Lejeune, North Carolina, resulting in the death of one marine.

July 24
AVIATION: Marine helicopter squadron HMX-1 conveys President Richard M. Nixon to the carrier *Forrestal*, where he greets the returning *Apollo 11* astronauts in person. The three astronauts also returned with 50 pounds of lunar rocks and soil samples.

July 31
MARINES: Sergeant Major Joseph W. Daily becomes the fifth sergeant major of the Marine Corps.

August 1
AVIATION: In Washington, D.C., General John D. Ryan is appointed the U.S. Air Force Chief of Staff.
• Donald L. Harlow was made the new chief master sergeant of the U.S. Air Force.
MARINES: Brigadier General Duane L. Faw and Colonel Ralph K. Culver join seven navy officers and three civilians to form the new Navy Court of Military Review. They do so in accordance with the Military Justice Act of 1968.

August 5
NAVAL: The North Vietnamese, five years after taking their first prisoners, release three American pilots held captive, Captain Wesley L. Rumble, Lieutenant Robert F. Frishman, and Seaman Douglas B. Hegdahl, who were washed overboard from the cruiser *Canberra*. The men report the use of torture and abuse at the hands of their captors.

August 13
AVIATION: At Marble Mountain, South Vietnam, helicopters of HMM-165 fly off to the amphibious assault vessel *Valley Forge*, becoming the first unit of the 1st Marine Aviation Wing (1st MAW) to depart the country. Concurrently, the 1st Light Antiaircraft Missile Battalion (LAAM) departs Da Nang for new billets at Twenty-Nine Palms, California.

August 17
MILITARY: Near the Demilitarized Zone (DMZ), South Korea, a helicopter from the 59th Aviation Company accidentally strays into North Korea and is shot down; three Americans are taken prisoner.

August 18
AVIATION: In South Vietnam, marine helicopter squadron HMM-362 is ordered back home. It is also the last unit to be operating the venerable Sikorsky UH-34D and are scheduled to be reequipped with brand-new CH-53 Sea Stallions.

August 19–September 16
AVIATION: Once Hurricane Camille devastates large tracts of southern Mississippi, six types of air force transports begin ferrying 6,000 tons of supplies in one of the largest major humanitarian relief efforts of its kind.

Armstrong, Neil A. (1930–)

Navy officer, astronaut

Neil Alden Armstrong was born near Wapakoneta, Ohio, the son of a state bureaucrat. He developed an interest in flying at an early age and received his pilot's license at the age of 16. Armstrong subsequently entered Purdue University on a U.S. Navy scholarship in 1947, where he studied aeronautical engineering. However, he was called to active duty in 1949 and became qualified as a jet pilot at the Pensacola Naval Air Station, Florida, and, in 1950, he was the youngest officer flying with Fighter Squadron VF-51. Armstrong completed 78 combat missions piloting Grumman F9F Panthers in Korea, where he was shot down once and received three Air Medals. After the war he returned to Purdue to complete his degree and subsequently found work as a test pilot with the National Advisory Committee for Aeronautics (NACA) in Cleveland, Ohio. Shortly afterward, Armstrong transferred to Edwards Air Force

(continues)

Neil Armstrong with the X-15 aircraft *(NASA)*

(continued)

Base, California, where he tested some of the latest jets and research craft available. They included the North American X-15, a highly experimental rocket-propelled airplane, in which he set a world speed record of 207,500 feet at a speed of 6,615 miles per hour in 1961. But, despite this close proximity to space, Armstrong displayed no real interest in the ongoing astronaut program. Instead, he chose to pilot the new DynaSoar craft that was expected to leave the atmosphere, glide through space, then return like a conventional aircraft following reentry. However, once this program was cancelled by the government in 1962, Armstrong belatedly joined the next group of astronauts in training, hailed in the press as the "New Nine," which followed the original "Mercury Seven."

Armstrong successfully completed his space training and, on September 20, 1965, he rocketed into orbit commanding the *Gemini 8* craft with pilot David Scott. His technical expertise saved the mission when their capsule began mysteriously tumbling due to a faulty maneuvering thruster, which he promptly disconnected, and he brought the ship safely home within one mile of the anticipated landing zone. Armstrong's cool demeanor and technical expertise made him the natural choice to command the *Apollo 11* moon mission, destined to land the first human being on a celestial body. On July 16, 1969, accompanied by astronauts Buzz Aldrin and Michael Collins, Armstrong launched from Cape Kennedy, Florida, and four days later he successfully guided his Lunar Excursion Module (LEM) named *Eagle* to the lunar surface. "That's one small step for [a] man, one giant leap for mankind," he exclaimed upon taking man's first footsteps on the moon. He and the crew of *Apollo 11* returned safely to Earth on July 24, 1969, where they were fêted as national heroes and toured the globe. Armstrong retired from active duty soon after and spent several years as a top NASA administrator until 1971, when he joined the faculty of the University of Cincinnati. Armstrong, the first man on the moon, currently lives in retirement in Lebanon, Ohio.

August 21
NAVAL: In Washington, D.C., Secretary of Defense Melvin R. Laird declares that $3 billion will be removed from defense spending in fiscal year 1970, forcing the navy to deactivate more than 100 vessels, including the battleship *New Jersey*.

August 25
AVIATION: The Lockheed C-5A Galaxy is refueled aerially for the first time by Military Airlift Command (MAC) crews.

August 27
MILITARY: In South Vietnam, General Creighton W. Abrams orders that the CIDG program be terminated. This places thousands of Montagnard soldiers under direct South Vietnamese control in the form of 38 light infantry battalions.

September 3
POLITICS: Ho Chi Minh, the driving force behind North Vietnam's Communist-inspired unification with South Vietnam, dies in Hanoi.

September 5
MILITARY: At Fort Benning, Georgia, Lieutenant William Calley is charged with murder in conjunction with events at the My Lai Massacre on March 16, 1968. His ensuing court-martial is politically charged and serves as a rallying point for opposing viewpoints on the war.

September 16
MILITARY: In Washington, D.C., President Richard M. Nixon declares that an additional 35,000 troops will be removed from Vietnam no later than December 15, including 5,200 sailors and 18,500 marines.

September 17
MARINES: It is decided that 1,400 men of the October draft are slated to serve with the Marine Corps; this year 11,878 draftees have been accepted.

September 18–December 15
MILITARY: The army conducts Increment II (Keystone Cardinal) of the phased withdrawal from Vietnam by removing the 3rd Brigade, 82nd Airborne Division, back home.
MARINES: MACV declares that the bulk of marine forces withdrawn from South Vietnam will come mainly from the 3rd Marine Division. Moreover, marines with time still left on their tour will be transferred to other units that are remaining behind.

September 21
MARINES: In Washington, D.C., Secretary of Defense Melvin Laird declares that the 5th Marine Division is slated for deactivation with the exception of the 26th Marines, then deployed in South Vietnam.

September 27
MARINES: Southwest of Con Thien, I Corps tactical zone, Operation Idaho Canyon concludes after the 3rd Marines finish a search-and-destroy effort that has been ongoing since July 17. They accounted for 565 Communists killed at a cost of 95 dead and 450 wounded.

September 29
MARINES: Headquarters Marine Corps announces a 20,300-man reduction in its active duty roster.

October 1
MARINES: As the Marine Corps readjusts to a peacetime establishment, reenlistment standards are tightened, especially with regard to disciplinary behavior.

October 5
AVIATION: A Cuban defector effortlessly flies his MiG-17 past U.S. aerial defenses and lands at Homestead Air Force Base, Miami, Florida. President Richard M. Nixon was there onboard Air Force One when it happened.

October 8–14

AVIATION: At Wheelus Air Force Base, Libya, the air force dispatches three HH-53 helicopters from the 58th Aerospace Rescue and Recovery Squadron to aid in relief efforts for flood victims in nearby Tunisia; over 2,400 people are rescued from rising waters.

October 10

NAVAL: The navy hands over 80 river patrol boats (RPBs) to the South Vietnamese navy in the largest transfer of assets to date. Since June 1968 the total number of vessels transferred is 229.

MARINES: In an attempt to continue attracting recruits, unaccompanied tours in Japan and Okinawa are reduced from 13 months to 12.

October 15

MARINES: With the exception of divisional headquarters, the entire 5th Marine Division is deactivated.

October 18

MILITARY: Along the Demilitarized Zone (DMZ), South Korea, a jeep from the 7th Division is ambushed by North Koreans; four Americans are killed.

October 26

NAVAL: The carrier *Coral Sea* begins its fifth tour on Yankee Station in the Gulf of Tonkin.

October 27

NAVAL: The navy commissions *NR-1,* its first deep-water submersible designed expressly for working under the crushing pressures of oceanic depths.

October 29

AVIATION: The Strategic Air Command (SAC) declares the phaseout of all B-58 Hustler strategic bombers; this speedy craft first entered the U.S. Air Force inventory in August 1960.

November 6

AVIATION: At Holloman Air Force Base, New Mexico, a 34-cubic foot balloon towering 1,000-feet tall is launched with a record 13,000-pound payload. This is the largest craft of its type ever constructed.

MILITARY: Congress passes a military appropriations bill that includes funding for the Safeguard ABM system.

November 7

MARINES: In the Dodge City and Go Noi Island areas below Da Nang, South Vietnam, the 1st Marine Division concludes Operation Pipestone Canyon, which has been underway since May 26. The marines kill 488 Communist troops at a cost of 54 killed and 540 wounded.

• Final elements of the 3rd Marine Division embark and sail for their new home on Okinawa.

• On Okinawa, the I Marine Expeditionary Force is created to command all Fleet Marine Force units on that island and Japan.

1969

Soldiers carry a wounded comrade through a swampy area in Vietnam, 1969.
(National Archives)

November 11–15
MILITARY: In Washington, D.C., U.S. Army and National Guard units are braced for possible unrest as the capital braces for two large antiwar protests.

November 14–24
AVIATION: The *Apollo 12* space capsule, which features the all-navy crew of Commanders Charles C. Conrad and Richard F. Gordon, and Lieutenant Commander Alan Bean, makes a second successful landing on the moon, remaining on the surface for seven and a half hours.

November 19
MILITARY: Congress, at the behest of President Richard M. Nixon, changes the draft into a lottery system based on birth dates, effective December 1.

November 25
MILITARY: President Richard M. Nixon orders American germ warfare stockpiles destroyed in an attempt to induce a similar gesture from the Soviet Union. He also asks the Senate to approve a 1925 Geneva Protocol prohibiting both biological and chemical warfare and declares that the United States will never deploy such weapons first.

November 26
MILITARY: President Richard M. Nixon signs legislation establishing a lottery for the selective service, based on birth days, which commences on December 1.

1969

November 29
NAVAL: In the Mekong Delta, South Vietnam, the navy turns over My Tho naval base to the Vietnamese navy. This is the first such facility transferred.

December 1
MILITARY: A new draft lottery commences in selecting 19 year olds for military service based upon their birthday. It replaces the earlier blanket military obligation in an attempt to quell antiwar sentiments.

December 15
MILITARY: In Washington, D.C., President Richard M. Nixon announces that American troop strength in Vietnam will be cut to 434,000 by April, representing a total withdrawal of 110,000 combat soldiers since he took office.

December 17
AVIATION: The air force terminates Project Blue Book, dealing with investigating unidentified flying objects. It concludes that phenomena such as alien spacecraft simply do not exist.
NAVAL: At Bremerton, Washington, the refurbished battleship *New Jersey* is decommissioned and returned to mothballs at the Naval Inactive Ship Maintenance Facility.

December 18
AVIATION: At the Air Force Missile Development Center, air crews begin testing the television-guided Maverick (AGM-65) surface-to-ground missile. This is the first aerial weapon capable of tracking targets in motion on the ground.

December 23
AVIATION: The air force declares McDonnell Douglas as prime contractor for the new F-15 air superiority fighter. This high-performance aircraft is capable of 920 miles per hour with a ferry range of 3,450 nautical miles.

December 30
NAVAL: A navy river patrol boat (RPB) catches a body of Viet Cong crossing the Saigon River and attacks, killing 27 Communists at no loss to themselves.

December 31
AVIATION: The 1st Marine Aviation Wing (1st MAW) continues performing yeoman work in 1969 with fixed-wing sorties and 547,965 helicopter missions flown. Losses are 44 helicopters, 34 fixed-wing aircraft, 92 marines killed, 514 wounded, and 20 missing.
MARINES: From a total strength of 201,675, no less than 54,559 marines are still serving in Vietnam. In 1969 they suffered 2,258 dead and 16,567 wounded.

1970

January
MILITARY: Total army strength in South Vietnam is 330,300, with 6,710 killed in action during the previous 12 months.

January 1
NAVAL: On the Saigon River, navy and South Vietnamese riverine vessels battle Viet Cong swimmers attempting to capture a sunken Vietnamese river boat. They kill 12 enemy soldiers and subsequently salvage the disabled craft.

January 2
MILITARY: The Department of Defense reveals that 1,403 military personnel have deserted since July 1, 1966.

January 5
AVIATION: At Fortuna Air Force Station, North Dakota, the Backup Intercept Control (BUIC) III radar is activated with the 80th Air Defense Group, Aerospace Defense Command. This is designed to back up the existing SAGE system and relay information regarding air threats to North America.

January 6
MARINES: In the Que Son Valley, South Vietnam, Fire Support Base Ross is attacked by mortar fire and sappers attempting to break in, but men of the 1st Battalion, 7th Marines drive them off with 39 dead left on the ground. Marine losses are 13 dead and 63 wounded.

January 8
MARINES: In the I Corps tactical zone, South Vietnam, III Marine Amphibious Force institutes the new Combined Unit Pacification Program, whereby rifle squads deployed to villages receive no special training and, moreover, they remain attached to the parent formations.

January 9
AVIATION: In Tay Ninh Province, South Vietnam, a Sealords patrol engages a battalion-sized enemy force and calls in air support. Navy helicopter gunships and OV-10A Broncos sweep in and attack, killing 32 Viet Cong.

January 10
AVIATION: At Kirtland Air Force Base, New Mexico, air force engineers devise a portable water treatment plant capable of filtering 4,000 gallons of drinking water per day from sewage.

January 16
AVIATION: At Grissom Air Force Base, Indiana, the last operational B-58 Hustlers depart for Davis Monthan Air Force Base, Arizona, for decommissioning.

January 17
AVIATION: In New Orleans, Louisiana, Reserve transports airlift crews of carpenters and painters to assist repair efforts in the wake of Hurricane Camille.

January 18–25
MARINES: At Camp Drum, New York, the 2nd Reconnaissance Battalion initiates Operation Snowfer for cold weather training.

January 19
MARINES: In the Caribbean, naval and marine elements from Brazil, Canada, Colombia, the Netherlands, the United Kingdom, and the United States participate in Operation Springboard. This is a three-month training exercise involving 110 vessels and 260 aircraft. It is initially based at San Juan, Puerto Rico.

January 19–23
MARINES: On Okinawa, the Military Employees Labor Union strikes for five days with a major confrontation and has little effect on the flow of Marine Corps activities there.

1970

January 24
MARINES: As more marines are pulled from Southeast Asia, the Marine Corps begins extending the training period of recruits from eight to nine weeks.

January 27
AVIATION: To further assist the South Vietnamese air force master the intricacies of aviation maintenance and repair, the Air Training Command deploys the first element of its 64-man training team.

January 28
MILITARY: The Department of Defense announces a third wave of withdrawals from South Vietnam involving 50,000 military personnel from all four branches, including 12,900 marines. All are to depart no later than April 19.
NAVAL: Near Vung Tau, III Corps tactical zone, the destroyer *Mansfield* provides supporting fire for the 1st Australian Task Force.

January 30
AVIATION: The air force turns over operational control of the *Skynet* satellite to English operators; this vehicle had been placed in orbit by the Space and Missile Systems Organization on January 8.

January 31
MILITARY: This month, military analysts deduce that North Vietnamese truck and other traffic along the infamous Ho Chi Minh Trail has actually increased 10 times over what it had been the past fall.

February 1
MARINES: Headquarters Marine Corps reveals its expanded early-out program for Vietnam veterans in the ranks. Applying here can release individuals from active service by as much as 14 months earlier than stipulated in enlistment contracts.

February 1–April 15
MILITARY: Operation Keystone Bluejay removes the 1st Infantry Division from the III Corps and the 3rd Brigade, 4th Infantry Division departs soon afterward.

February 3
AVIATION: At Yokota Air Base, Japan, helicopters of the 36th Aerospace Rescue and Recovery Squadron (ARRS) swing into action by rescuing 44 seamen from the sinking commercial vessels *Antonious Demades* and *California Maru*.

February 14
NAVAL: The Coast Guard turns over three 82-foot cutters to the South Vietnamese navy.

February 17
AVIATION: Communist troop concentrations and supply dumps in northern Laos are struck by B-52 bombers for the first time; the public is not made aware of this activity until March 6.
MILITARY: In Washington, D.C., President Richard M. Nixon declares that the process of Vietnamization, namely, turning over the bulk of combat operations to South Vietnamese units, is proceeding on schedule.

1970

February 18
AVIATION: An HL-10 experimental lifting body flown by Major Peter C. Hoag is released by a B-52 bomber and glides at Mach 1.86 to an altitude of 65,000 feet.

February 19
MARINES: On Mount Suribachi, Iwo Jima, representatives from the United States and Japan attend a combined ceremony marking the 25th anniversary of the bloody battle. The Marine Corps is represented by Major General William K. Jones, commander of the 3rd Marine Division.

February 23
MARINES: To effectively end the draft and enhance the success of an all-volunteer military, the Gates Commission recommends pay increases for all ranks and other reforms. It is hoped that the draft, a source of considerable resentment among the nation's youth, will be ended by June 30, 1971.

February 24–27
AVIATION: A Tactical Employment conference is sponsored by the Marine Corps to evaluate the best methods of employing the new Hawker Siddeley AV-8A Harrier. This is a radical new jet aircraft that can rise vertically off the ground like a helicopter, then fly like a conventional jet.

February 27
AVIATION: Pratt and Whitney is selected by the Department of Defense to manufacture new engines for the air force F-15 Eagle and the navy F-14B Tomcat.
• At Edwards Air Force Base, California, the F-111E prototype is delivered for flight testing.

February 28
NAVAL: At Da Nang, South Vietnam, the navy turns over 11 swift boats to the Vietnamese navy, which is now responsible for patrolling the waters of all five northern provinces.

March 4
MILITARY: Secretary of Defense Melvin R. Laird announces that 371 military bases are to be closed down in an economizing move that will save the taxpayers $914 million.

March 7
NAVAL: In the IV Corps tactical zone, the South Vietnamese navy takes charge of Operation Tran Hung Dao I to interdict the infiltration of enemy supplies and personnel from Cambodia.

March 9
MARINES: In the I Corps tactical zone, South Vietnam, III Marine Amphibious Force surrenders tactical control of most of its remaining units to the Army XXIV Corps, which now constitutes the majority of units in the region. However, III MAF still controls the 1st Marine Division and the 1st Marine Air Wing (1st MAW) to preserve its traditional air-to-ground links.

- Lieutenant General Keith B. McCutcheon succeeds to command of the III MAF.

March 13
MARINES: Marine Corps basic school is extended from 21 weeks to 26.

March 14
MILITARY: At Fort Benning, Georgia, Lieutenant General William Peers files a preliminary report on the My Lai massacre. The Army Judge Advocate General, mindful that the statute of limitations runs out on the next day, files charges against 11 officers, including Major General Samuel W. Koster, American Division. The charge is subsequently dismissed.
MEDICAL: At Da Nang, the hospital ship *Repose* departs South Vietnam after four years of continuous service.

March 15
AVIATION: Work on the automatic voice network to connect all U.S. military bases by telephone is finished. This system is known as "Autovon."

March 16
NAVAL: At Da Nang, South Vietnam, the navy transfers four support ships and two more Coast Guard cutters to the South Vietnamese navy.

March 18
MILITARY: Air Force B-52s begin a protracted series of strikes against Communist troop concentrations and supply dumps in Cambodia. Over the next eight weeks they deliver 120,000 tons of ordnance in 4,300 sorties.
- In southern I Corps, American Division commander Major General Lloyd B. Ramsey is injured after his helicopter crashes during a survey mission. His replacement is Major General Albert E. Milloy.
POLITICS: In Cambodia, the leftist regime of Prince Sihanouk is overthrown by General Lon Nol, a staunch anticommunist who solicits aid from the administration of President Richard M. Nixon.

March 19
AVIATION: Over Edwards Air Force Base, California, the HL-10 lifting body performs its first powered flight with Major Jerauld R. Gentry at the controls.

March 20
AVIATION: At Cape Kennedy, Florida, a Thors-Delta rocket booster places the first two NATO communications satellites into orbit.

March 23
MILITARY: In New York City, U.S. Army National Guard troops are sent in to quell a labor dispute and restore order.
MARINES: Marine Reserve units are activated by President Richard M. Nixon for the purpose of assisting the U.S. Postal Department during a labor strike.

March 24
AVIATION: At Tyndall Air Force Base, Florida, a Bomarc B guided missile is launched for the first time using the new BUIC (Backup Intercept Control) III computerized command and control equipment.

March 25

MARINES: In Brooklyn, New York, 300 Marine Corps Reservists are assigned to assist at the main post office, although the labor situation is resolved the following day.

March 28

AVIATION: Over Thanh Hoa, North Vietnam, an F-4 Phantom II from the *Constellation* downs a MiG-21; this is the navy's first aerial victory in 16 months.

March 28–April 3

NAVAL: Off Rach Gia, IV Corps tactical zone, South Vietnam, the destroyer *Orleck* provides close supporting fire to the South Vietnamese 21st Infantry Division going ashore, destroying 44 enemy structures. At length it is joined by destroyers of the Seventh Fleet and Coast Guard cutters *Chase* and *Dallas,* and proceeds to destroy a further 48 bunkers and 28 sampans.

March 30

AVIATION: Transport aircraft are dispatched by the U.S. Air Force Europe (USAFE) to bring medical and relief supplies to victims of a destructive earthquake at Gediz, Turkey.

March 31

AVIATION: The final operation Mace tactical missiles are placed in storage at Davis Monthan Air Force Base, Arizona, for possible use as a subsonic target drone.

April 1

AVIATION: The Strategic Air Command (SAC) reorganizes and redistributes its post–nuclear attack command-and-control system at Offutt Air Force Base, Nebraska, Grissom Air Force Base, Indiana, and Ellsworth Air Force Base, North Dakota.

MILITARY: In Tay Ninh Province, South Vietnam, Firebase Illingsworth—only three miles from the Cambodian border—is attacked by a Viet Cong regiment. The garrison under Lieutenant Colonel Michael J. Conrad's 2nd Battalion, 8th Cavalry, and several field batteries, fights off their antagonists. The Communists leave 75 dead on the ground before departing; American casualties are 24 killed and 54 wounded.

• In Binh Tuy Province, South Vietnam, Brigadier General William R. Bond, commander, 199th Infantry Brigade, is killed by enemy fire while accompanying a resupply convoy. He is succeeded by Colonel Joseph E. Collins.

MARINES: At Camp Pendleton, California, training responsibility for all Marine Corps Reserve ground forces is handed off to headquarters, 4th Marine Division. Such instruction was formerly reserved for the senior officer of each Marine Corps district.

April 2

MARINES: In South Vietnam, the level of marines present dips to 43,600.

April 10

AVIATION: In South Vietnam, Project Pacer Bravo continues as the Air Training Command finishes the transfer of 872 training personnel to support the South Vietnamese air force modernization program.

1970

• Marine Lieutenant Larry Parsons, a helicopter pilot shot down near the Laotian border and believed to be killed, miraculously walks out of the jungle and back to friendly lines after 20 days in the jungle.

April 11

AVIATION: The 146th Tactical Airlift Wing, California Air National Guard, becomes the first unit of its kind transferred to the Tactical Air Command (TAC).

• Transports from the Air Force Southern Command begin flying in food and humanitarian relief to victims of recent flooding in Costa Rica and Panama.

April 11–17

AVIATION: The *Apollo 13* space capsule, piloted by Captain James A. Lovell, Jr., experiences an onboard fuel tank explosion only 56 hours into its moon mission. Engineers from the National Aeronautics and Space Administration (NASA) assist the astronauts to remain alive, and they pilot their crippled ship safely back to Earth six days later.

April 14

AVIATION: At Hill Air Force Base, Utah, a Minuteman III intercontinental ballistic missile (ICBM) is loaded onboard a C-141 Starlifter and flown to Minot Air Force Base, North Dakota. This is the first time a Minuteman III has been relocated by air.

MARINES: At Yang Po Ri, South Korea, the 11th Marine Expeditionary Brigade is slated to participate in Exercise Golden Dragon with the South Korean Marine Corps.

April 16

DIPLOMACY: In Vienna, Austria, the Strategic Arms Limitation Talks (SALT) commence between the United States and the Soviet Union. Talks are undertaken in an attempt to limit the size of nuclear arsenals, and reduce the chances of an accidental war.

April 17

AVIATION: At Minot Air Force Base, South Dakota, the 741st Strategic Missile Squadron places the first operational Minuteman III in its silo; the entire unit becomes operational by the end of the year.

April 20

DIPLOMACY: In Washington, D.C., President Richard M. Nixon accelerates the trend of Vietnamization by announcing the withdrawal of 150,000 from Southeast Asia by year's end. American deaths in combat now average 25 per week, down from 280 in 1968.

April 22

MARINES: A military mutiny on the island of Trinidad results in 2,000 marines being mobilized and sent to the area as a precaution in the event the evacuation of American civilians becomes necessary.

April 23–28

MARINES: At San Juan, Puerto Rico, the 3rd Battalion, 2nd Marines and helicopters of HMM-261 depart for possible service on the island of Trinidad. However, they soon after stand down and resume normal operations.

April 26
MILITARY: In the II Corps tactical area, Lieutenant General Michael S. Davidson alerts the 1st Cavalry Division that they must be prepared to invade the Fishhook region of Cambodia within 72 hours. This region is headquarters for the Communist Central Office for South Vietnam (COSVN) and responsible for all Viet Cong operations in the southern parts of the country.

April 27
MARINES: No Marine Corps casualties are reported this day, a first for 1970.

April 29–June 30
MILITARY: President Richard M. Nixon authorizes American forces to attack six Communist sanctuaries in Cambodia; while much damage is incurred by the enemy, most simply slip deeper into the interior to escape and wait for the storm to pass.
• South Vietnamese forces, backed by American air power and some Army units, commence Operation Toan Thang 42 ("Total Victory") with an advance into the Parrot's Beak region of Cambodia.
MARINES: A handful of marine advisers assist the South Vietnamese Marine Corps during its invasion of Cambodia.

April 30
MARINES: At Naval Air Station Quonset Point, Rhode Island, some battalions of the 6th and 8th Marines are placed on alert to assist authorities to quell civil unrest in New Haven, Connecticut, but they are not deployed.
• At Camp Pendleton, California, the 26th Marines and the 1st Battalion, 13th Marines are deactivated.

May 1
MILITARY: American forces begin their Cambodian incursion by advancing into the so-called Fishhook region. Operation Rockcrusher is spearheaded by the 1st Cavalry Division under Brigadier General Robert M. Shoemaker, assisted by the 11th Armored Cavalry and 5,000 South Vietnamese troops. Opposition is light and the town of Snoul is captured easily.
MARINES: Albert Schoepper becomes the first director of the Marine Corps Band to reach the rank of colonel in the 172-year history of that organization.

May 3–4
MILITARY: The 1st Squadron, 9th Cavalry, forges ahead of the 1st Cavalry Division and uncovers an enemy supply dump spanning nearly a square mile in length. Communist forces melt into the jungle before them.

May 4
AVIATION: At RAF Station Marham, England, four B-52 bombers from the Strategic Air Command compete in the Royal Air Force Strike Command bombing and navigation competition, winning the coveted Blue Steel Trophy.
MILITARY: At Kent State University, Ohio, National Guard troops fire upon rioting student demonstrators, killing four and wounding nine. In light of the deaths, antiwar protests are noticeably smaller and better behaved.

May 4–16
MILITARY: In the III Corps tactical area, the 4th Division under Major General Glen D. Walker and the 22nd South Vietnamese Division commence Operation Binh Tay ("Tame the West") by crossing the border into Cambodia. The force intends to wipe out enemy bases within their reach, although resistance throughout their advance is light. Thick jungles and foreboding terrain notwithstanding, a North Vietnamese hospital complex is overrun and the Americans withdraw.

May 5
AVIATION: At colleges across the country, Air Reserve Officer Training Corps (AFROTC) is opened to women candidates for the first time.
NAVAL: Along the Vam Go Dong and Van Vo Nay Rivers north of Saigon, South Vietnam, Vietnamese riverine forces take control of Operation Giant Slingshot, a patrolling action run by the Americans since December 1968. In that time, the river boats had fought in 1,200 actions and killed an estimated 2,400 Viet Cong.

May 6–8
NAVAL: A force of 40 navy patrol craft enters Cambodia by way of the Kham Span River and are attacked by Viet Cong forces 65 miles northwest of Saigon, South Vietnam. Two days later an additional 100 patrol craft sail up the Mekong River and enter that supposedly neutral nation. However, their penetration is limited to 2.17 miles.

May 6–14
MILITARY: West of Tay Ninh Province, South Vietnam, the 1st and 3rd Brigades, 25th Infantry Division push farther into Cambodia and enter the region known as the Dog's Head. Meanwhile, the 3rd Brigade, 9th Division, strikes at the Parrot's Beak.

May 8
AVIATION: During an attack against the Ho Chi Minh Trail, Vietnam, an AC-119K Shadow gunship piloted by Captain Alan D. Milacek loses 15 feet of right wing to enemy ground fire. Milacek continues destroying enemy trucks then gingerly nurses his crippled airplane back to base, winning a Mackay Trophy.

May 9–24
MILITARY: In the Mekong Delta, South Vietnam, the Vietnamese 9th and 21st Divisions scour the river banks for Viet Cong units and open up a river path to Phnom Penh, Cambodia. They are assisted by a large body of American advisers.

May 10
MARINES: In Washington, D.C., the 6th Marines are placed on alert in the event of civil unrest arising from a large antiwar demonstration. Other formations at Quantico, Virginia, are also activated.

May 12
NAVAL: Navy and South Vietnamese navy vessels form a blockade of the Cambodian coast reaching from the South Vietnam border to the city of Sihanoukville.

1970

This is a concerted attempt to throttle Communist supply routes from extending from that region.

May 14
MARINES: Along the North Carolina coast, the 3rd Marine Division participates in Exotic Dancer III, a three-week combined-service operation involving 60,000 men.

May 28
MILITARY: The army, stung by its handling of the My Lai massacre, issues Regulation 350-216 regarding the issue of war crimes, illegal orders, and the responsibility of individual soldiers under such circumstances.

May 31
MARINES: A severe earthquake in Peru, South America, prompts the dispatch of the helicopter assault ship *Guam,* which carries a company of the 1st Battalion, 2nd Marines and helicopters of HHM-365. They spend 11 days providing emergency relief to the victims.

June 2
AVIATION: After earthquakes devastate large sections of Peru, a large humanitarian mission is mounted by the U.S. Air Force Southern Command. Transports deliver 750 tons of supplies and 3,000 passengers while lifting out 500 medical patients. All this is accomplished from rudimentary airstrips 1,500 miles from home base.

June 5
AVIATION: The air force selects North American Rockwell to build its next generation of strategic bombers, the B-1A, while General Electric is chosen to design and build the engines. This aircraft is intended to replace the aging fleet of Boeing B-52s, although the latter displays remarkable longevity as a combat aircraft.

June 6
AVIATION: The first operational C-5A Galaxy transport is delivered to the Military Airlift Command (MAC). It is personally accepted by General Jack J. Catton, who presides over ceremonies.

June 11
MILITARY: History is made when Colonel Anna M. Hayes, chief of the Army Nurse Corps, and Colonel Elizabeth P. Hoisington, director of WAC, become the army's first female brigadier generals.
MARINES: Throughout South Vietnam, Communist forces launch their biggest offensive since Tet, aimed largely at Marine Corp Combined Action Program units in villages of the I Corps tactical zone. Many civilians are killed in consequence.

June 15
MILITARY: The U.S. Supreme Court decides the case of *Welsh v. United States,* ruling that conscientious objector status on moral—not religious—grounds is constitutional.

June 18
AVIATION: The Blue Angels precision flying demonstration team is joined by a Marine Corps KC-130 tanker aircraft.

1970

June 19
AVIATION: At Minot Air Force Base, North Dakota, the first Minuteman III intercontinental ballistic missiles (ICBMs) are declared operational.

June 22
AVIATION: At Chanute Air Force Base, Illinois, the Base Engineer Emergency Force (BEEF) is deployed to nearby Crescent City to restore the water system following a devastating series of explosions and fires.

June 23
NAVAL: The navy turns over an additional 273 river patrol boats to the South Vietnamese navy, raising the total number to 525. The remaining 125 still operated by the Americans are slated for eventual transfer in December.

June 24
POLITICS: In Washington, D.C., the Senate votes to repeal the 1964 Gulf of Tonkin Resolution, 81 to 10. This act gave the chief executive unbridled authority to deploy military units in a war zone.

June 25
MARINES: The Marine Barracks at Argentia, Newfoundland, founded in 1941, is formally deactivated.

June 30
MILITARY: The Cambodian incursion, which involves 30,000 American and 48,000 South Vietnamese troops, draws to a close as the forces withdraw. American losses are 338 dead and 1,525 wounded while the Vietnamese lose 638 dead and 4,009 wounded. The Communists are believed to have lost over 11,000 dead and 2,328 captured, along with mounds of equipment and supplies.
MARINES: Manpower levels in the Marine Corps have declined to 24,941 officers and 234,796 enlisted men.
• The first six months of 1970 result in the 1st Marine Division engaging in relatively few major clashes with Communist units in the field. Nonetheless, marines have accounted for 3,955 of the enemy at a cost of 283 dead and 2,537 wounded.

July 1
NAVAL: In Washington, D.C., Admiral Elmo R. Zumwalt, Jr., is appointed the new chief of naval operations. He is both the youngest officer promoted to four stars and also the youngest to occupy that office. In time, Zumwalt also becomes one of the most controversial reformers in navy history.

July 1–23
MILITARY: In Thua Thien Province, South Vietnam, Firebase Ripcord, west of Hue, is attacked by superior numbers of North Vietnamese. The defenders, consisting of two companies of the 2nd Battalion, 506th infantry, and the 2nd Battalion, 319th Artillery, stand their ground until July 18 when a helicopter crash ignites the base ammunition dump. At this juncture, Major General John J. Hennessy, 101st Airborne Division, decides to evacuate the firebase altogether, which is successfully accomplished by airlift while under heavy fire. American losses are 61 dead and 325 wounded.

July 1–December 31

MILITARY: Increments IV and V of the army drawdown are implemented, resulting in the removal of brigades from the 4th, 9th, and 25th Infantry Divisions, a total of 57,000 men.

July 3

MARINES: South of Quang Tri City, South Vietnam, militia units, backed by Marine Combined Action Program units, helicopter gunships, and artillery support, drive off North Vietnamese forces from several villages. Enemy losses amount to 135 dead, while the militia loses only 16 killed and six missing.

July 5

AVIATION: The air force contracts with the Boeing Company to design and construct its first airborne warning and control systems (AWACS) aircraft. These sophisticated machines will serve as aerial combat direction centers within the Aerospace Defense Command.

July 7

MILITARY: Major George W. Casey, newly appointed commander of the 1st Cavalry Division, dies when his helicopter crashes, and he is replaced by Major General George W. Putnam.

July 9

MARINES: During this fourth round of troop withdrawals, a total of 17,021 marines are ordered stateside. They include the 7th Marines, Marine Air Group 13 (MAG-13), and several squadrons.

July 14

AVIATION: C-5A Galaxies undergo their first transpacific flight of 21,500 miles by landing at Hickham Air Force Base, Hawaii, Andersen Air Base, Guam, Clark Air Base, Philippines, and Kadena Air Base, Okinawa.

July 15–27

AVIATION: As 5,000 ARVN troops sweep the region west of Da Nang for Communist units, they are transported on marine helicopters and assisted by marine advisers.
MARINES: West of Da Nang, South Vietnam, the 5th Marines commence Operation Barren Green to protect the local corn harvest from Communist interference. They manage to kill 18 enemy soldiers and burn 10,000 pounds of grain.

July 16–August 24

MARINES: Southwest of Da Nang, South Vietnam, the 7th Marines conduct Operation Pickens Forest to drive out Communist unit and confiscate their food caches. By the time the operation ends, the marines have killed 99 Communists soldiers at a price of four dead and 51 wounded.

July 20

AVIATION: The Compass Link photo relays system developed by the Electronics Systems Division, Hanscom Air Field, Massachusetts, is adopted by the Air Force Communications Service. This novel system employs three ground stations and two satellites, which speedily transmit film from Southeast Asia to the Pentagon through electronic signals and laser beams. This is a precursor to "real time" military intelligence.

Zumwalt, Elmo R.   (1920–2000)
Admiral

Elmo Russell Zumwalt was born in San Francisco, California, on November 29, 1920, and he graduated from the U.S. Naval Academy in 1943. He saw service in World War II onboard destroyers and won a Bronze Star for gallantry during the Battle of Leyte Gulf. Zumwalt commanded a destroyer during the Korean War, advanced to captain, and attended the National War College before serving as senior aide to Secretary of the Navy Paul Nitze. He made history in July 1965 by becoming the navy's youngest rear admiral at the age of 44. Three years later his career took a dramatic turn when he was appointed commander of all U.S. naval forces in Southeast Asia with a rank of vice admiral. Zumwalt determined that the navy should have a higher profile in that conflict, which he achieved through creation of the so-called Brown Water Navy. This was an extensive force of swift boats, light ships, and hovercraft that patrolled the innumerable waterways of the Mekong Delta to interdict Viet Cong supplies and movement. More controversial was the use of the Defoliant Agent Orange, which was used to strip away the thick jungle coverage used by the enemy. By 1969 Zumwalt's efforts had greatly impeded Communist infiltration in the region but, that same year, the process of Vietnamization began and Zumwalt's responsibilities were turned over to the South Vietnamese navy.

In July 1970 Zumwalt again made history when President Richard M. Nixon appointed him chief of naval operations; at 49, he remains the youngest officer to hold that post. Acting upon his Vietnam experiences and a disastrous decline in enlistment rates, Zumwalt began the most controversial phase of his career. He began issuing a series of 120 "Z-grams," which granted permission for beards, relaxed clothing standards, and dispensed with numerous traditional duties. The Navy also abolished all vestiges of discrimination against

July 22
NAVAL: In a sign of mounting Vietnamization, a class of 60 South Vietnamese naval officers graduates from the Officer Candidate School, Newport, Rhode Island. They are to be commissioned into active service once home.

July 31
AVIATION: At Keesler Air Force Base, Mississippi, the first class of Vietnamese exchange pilots graduates from the pilot training program. Their presence here is also part of the ongoing Vietnamization process.

August
AVIATION: In Washington, D.C., Secretary of Defense Melvin Laird advances the Total Force Concept for all armed services to bring Regular, Reserve, and National Guard elements into a closer, more efficient relationship, especially with respect to planning and budgeting functions.

★ ★ ★ ★ ★ ★ ★ ★ ★ ★ ★ ★ ★ ★ ★

minorities, and women were allowed to sail onboard ships at sea. Zumwalt faced an even greater challenge posed by the Soviet navy, which was undergoing a dramatic expansion and modernization. In light of tight, Congressional budgeting, he adopted the "High-Low" strategy of mothballing marginally obsolete vessels and investing the savings in numerous, smaller vessels. Defense critics protested as the number of commissioned vessels dropped from 769 to 512, but Zumwalt insisted this was the most cost-effective way to counter the Soviet threat. He retired from the navy in July 1974 and waged an unsuccessful bid to become U.S. senator from West Virginia. Zumwalt also published a noted memoir entitled *On Watch* (1976), in which he criticized attempts to achieve détente with the Soviet Union through arms control agreements. Sadly, Zumwalt's own son, who had been exposed to Agent Orange in Vietnam, died from cancer in 1988. Zumwalt died in Durham, North Carolina, on January 2, 2000, possibly the most controversial reformer in U.S. navy history.

Elmo Zumwalt receives a Distinguished Service Medal. (*U.S. Army*)

August 1
NAVAL: The Military Sea Transportation Service is redesignated the Military Sealift Command, although it remains under the control of the navy.

August 3
AVIATION: Off Cape Canaveral, Florida, the ballistic missile submarine *James Madison* conducts the first submerged test launch of the Poseidon C-3 missile. This new weapon features greater range than the Polaris missiles it is intending to replace, and it also carries multiple warheads.

August 6
DIPLOMACY: The United States and Spain conclude a five-year agreement that allows the Americans to use four Spanish military bases in exchange for assisting in continuing modernization of Spanish military forces.

August 8–13
MARINES: At Quantico, Virginia, 12 of 17 scheduled events from the 9th Annual Interservice Rifle Championships are won by marine marksmen.

August 17
MARINES: At Camp Pendleton, California, the 4th Marine Division, the 4th Marine Air Group (4th MAW), and 10,000 reservists wage Exercise Hugh Desert over the next two weeks.

August 20
MILITARY: As a sign of mounting disciplinary problems, the Department of Defense estimates that around 30 percent of U.S. military personnel have experimented with marijuana or other illegal drugs.

August 21
MILITARY: In Washington, D.C., Secretary of Defense Melvin Laird introduces the Total Force Concept for the armed services, whereby the Reserves and National Guard are to be the first recourse for augmenting active forces, rather than relying on a draft.

August 22
MARINES: At Camp Perry, Ohio, marine marksmen and team shooters win 20 out of 24 matches at the National Rifle and Pistol Championships. This is also the first time that the marines win the National Trophy Rifle and the National Trophy Pistol matches.

August 24
AVIATION: Two Air Force HH-53 helicopters make the first nonstop transpacific crossing by arriving at Da Nang Air Base, South Vietnam. They had originally departed from Eglin Air Force Base, Florida, a distance of 9,000 miles.

August 31
MARINES: In the Que Son Mountain region, the 11th Marines unleash one of their biggest bombardments of the war. For six hours commencing at midnight, 13,488 rounds rain down on 53 selected bases, followed by an additional two hours of air strikes. The 7th Marines then move in to conduct mop-up operations.

September 1
AVIATION: In Saigon, South Vietnam, General Lucius D. Clay, Jr., is appointed head of the Seventh Air Force.

September 5–October 8
MILITARY: In Thua Thien Province, South Vietnam, Operation Jefferson Glen is launched by the 101st Airborne Division. It is designed to protect the government's programs in the countryside and accounts for 2,026 Communist dead over the next 399 days.

September 6
TERRORISM: After radical Palestinians hijack three airliners and force them to fly to the Middle East, C-130s and F-4Cs are deployed at Incirlik Air Base, Turkey, to mount a possible rescue attempt; the operation is called off once all passengers are released.

September 10
MARINES: At Camp Pendleton, California, the Marine Corps Tactical System Support Activity commences to evaluate all tactical systems and related equipment within the Marine Corps.

September 11
NAVAL: In the eastern Mediterranean, the Sixth Fleet goes on alert for a potential evacuation of passengers from an airliner that was hijacked to Jordan.

September 13
MILITARY: In Washington, D.C., President Richard M. Nixon orders 800 military personnel from all four branches to provide security for international passenger flights originating in the United States. The code name is Operation Grid Square.

September 15
MARINES: A recruiting station in the Bronx, New York, is damaged by a bomb allegedly set off by the radical Weather Underground group.

September 17
NAVAL: In the latest cost-cutting measure, the navy declares that an additional 38 vessels are slated for deactivation, including the carrier *Shangri-La*. Since January 1969, 286 older vessels have been mothballed.

September 17–October 28
AVIATION: Operation Fig Hill commences as transports from the Military Airlift Command (MAC) and the U.S. Air Force Europe (USAFE) begin flying in relief supplies and heavy equipment to Jordan in the wake of escalating violence with Palestinian refugees.

September 18–21
AVIATION: A force of 76 marine helicopters transport 14 artillery pieces belonging to the 11th Marines to a remote mountain top outside Da Nang to create Fire Base Dagger. However, Operation Catawba Falls is intended as a ruse to convince Communist units that a ground assault is pending.
MARINES: At Da Nang, while Operation Catawba Falls unfolds, marine units redeploy without enemy interference. The enemy are apparently taken in by the ruse.

September 19
MARINES: In the eastern Mediterranean, once Jordanian forces begin removing armed Palestinians from their territory, the 8th Marine Amphibious Brigade is dispatched to the Sixth Fleet as reinforcements. There it joins the 2nd Battalion, 2nd Marines as a possible landing force, if needed.

September 21
MARINES: In the I Corps tactical zone, South Vietnam, the Marine Combined Action Force headquarters is deactivated. Only the 600 men of the 2nd Combined Action Group remain active in Quang Nam Province.

September 28–November 31
AVIATION: The Air Force commences Operation Fig Hill to assist the Kingdom of Jordan with casualties incurred during bloody battles with Palestinian radicals.

Over 200 army and air force medical personnel are flown in, who perform 1,200 medical procedures before returning to bases in western Europe. Air Force transports also deliver 186 tons of medicine, equipment, and other relief supplies.

October 1
MARINES: The number of marines serving in South Vietnam is only 29,600.

October 2
AVIATION: At Hurlburt Field, Florida, Bell deploys its twin-engine UH-1N Twin Huey helicopter for trial runs with the Special Operations Center. Ultimately, 79 of these rugged machines are acquired for air force use.

October 7
MILITARY: In Washington, D.C., a special House Armed Services Subcommittee is informed by the Department of the Navy that over 7,000 sailors and marines will be dishonorably discharged for drug violations this year.
MARINES: The fire base at Chu Lai, South Vietnam, is turned over to army units.

October 15
MARINES: The former marine base at Ah Hoa, South Vietnam, is turned over to ARVN units.

October 15–30
MARINES: In the Philippines, U.S. and Philippine marines execute a training exercise called Fortress Light.

October 21
AVIATION: At Edwards Air Force Base, California, the X-24A lifting body performs its first supersonic speed flight for the Flight Test Center.
• In the wake of Typhoon Joan, helicopters of HMM-64 arrive in the Philippines to conduct relief-and-rescue operations.

October 29
NAVAL: In Washington, D.C., Secretary of the Navy John H. Chaffee announces that, as of July 1971, the navy will consist of less than 700 vessels. At that time, no less than 234 will have been either deactivated or decommissioned, but he considers greater reductions as dangerous to national security.

October 30
MARINES: In a cost-cutting measure, the Marine Corps disbands the 4th Armored Artillery Company, the only remaining formation of its kind, which had been in service since 1952.

November 1
MEDICAL: At Wurtsmith Air Force Base, Michigan, air force physicians begin treating Chippewa tribesmen as part of the Domestic Action Program.
• A host of bare-base mobility equipment is tested at North Field, South Carolina, by the 336th Tactical Fighter Squadron. Among the items scrutinized are expendable shelters, hangars, control towers, and water systems.

November 13
MEDICAL: Air force medical technicians begin receiving specialized clinical training to allow them to perform many tasks, such as suturing wounds, and applying or removing casts, previously performed by doctors.

1970

November 17–December 16
AVIATION: At Dacca, East Pakistan, C-141 Starlifters from the Military Airlift Command (MAC) begin conveying supplies and equipment to help victims of recent tidal waves along the coast. The transports fly in 140 tons of relief supplies, sometimes from as far away as 10,000 miles.

November 18
AVIATION: Near Da Nang, South Vietnam, a CH-46 Skyknight helicopter slams into a mountainside, killing 15 marines.

November 19
MARINES: At Quantico, Virginia, the Marine Corps announces that it is resuming annual rifle squad competition commencing next fall. The practice was stopped in 1965 due to Vietnam War commitments.

November 20
AVIATION: On the 30th anniversary of the Air Force Southern Command, transports and personnel are dispatched to Colombia to assist the victims of heavy flooding.

November 21
AVIATION: U.S. Air Force brigadier general Leroy J. Manor leads several CH-53 helicopters in a daring commando raid on the Son Tay prison camp, 23 miles west of Hanoi, North Vietnam.
• During the commando raid at Son Tay prison camp, North Vietnam, F-105 Thunderchiefs drop bombs as a diversion for the attack while direct support is provided by five A-1 Skyraiders. The commandos are also escorted to and from the area by a Lockheed C-130E Combat Talon aircraft.
• Carrier aircraft from the *Hancock, Oriskany,* and *Ranger* assist air force jets in attacking missile and antiaircraft artillery sites below the 19th parallel. This move is undertaken in response to recent attacks upon American reconnaissance planes.
MILITARY: Helicopter-borne Special Forces under Colonel Arthur "Bull" Simons mount Operation Kingpin, a daring helicopter-borne raid against Son Tay prison camp, 23 miles west of Hanoi. The raiders kill 25 North Vietnamese without loss and storm the camp, only to find it abandoned. The commandos return home empty-handed. The assault was covered by a seven-hour bombing raid against Hanoi to remind the Communists of America's military presence.
MARINES: In the Mediterranean, the Seventh Fleet's Landing Force Alpha is renamed the 31st Marine Amphibious Unit (MAU). This designation now refers to any unit built up around a landing battalion and a helicopter squadron.

December 1
MILITARY: The Atomic Energy Commission reports that 24 underground nuclear tests have been conducted in the course of the year at Nevada test sites.

December 5
AVIATION: At Hill Air Force Base, Utah, the 945th Military Airlift Group, Air Force Reserve, supports the Domestic Action Program by delivering 40,000 pounds of food and clothing to Navajo Indians across four western states.

1970

December 15
NAVAL: The United States announces that it is constructing a $10 million naval facility on the island of Diego Garcia, Indian Ocean. This is presently a British possession and close enough to the Persian Gulf to allow a strategic presence there.

December 16
AVIATION: At Pease Air Force Base, New Hampshire, the first FB-111 strategic bombers are delivered to the 509th Bombardment Wing.

December 21
AVIATION: The new Grumman F-14 Tomcat air superiority fighter flies the first time; it becomes the standard navy interceptor over the next three decades.
MILITARY: The Nixon administration announces a speedy phase out of defoliation operations in Southeast Asia.

December 22
MILITARY: Congress places restrictions on the presence of U.S. forces or advisers in either Laos or Cambodia.

December 24
MARINES: In I Corps tactical zone, South Vietnam, Lieutenant General Donn J. Robertson is appointed the new commander of the III Marine Amphibious Force.

December 31
MARINES: Marine Corps personnel levels have dipped to 231,667 of which 25,394 are still in Vietnam. Losses for the year are 535 killed and 4,278 wounded.
• In the I Corps tactical zone, the 1st Marine Division conducts Operation Imperial Lake, which results in the death of 196 Communist troops at a cost of 22 dead and 158 wounded.

1971

January
MILITARY: Army manpower levels in South Vietnam continue to decrease to 250,700, although the force is further smitten by poor morale, drug use, and mounting insubordination. U.S. Army Chief of Staff general William C. Westmoreland also commissions the Board for Dynamic Training under Colonel Paul F. Gorman, to find ways of enhancing combat arms training.

January 1
MILITARY: Operation Keystone Robbin removes the 1st and 2nd Brigades of the 1st Cavalry Division from South Vietnam, along with the 11th Armored Cavalry Regiment, and the 2nd Brigade, 25th Infantry Division.

January 4
MARINES: In Washington, D.C., Commandant Chapman declares that the Marines Corps is going to adhere more closely than ever to traditions of strict discipline and good conduct. Nor will it relax its appearance standards.

January 6
AVIATION: The first group of AV-8A Harrier jump jets is delivered to Marine Corps units. This revolutionary British design is capable of vertical takeoffs and landings (VTOL) through use of adjustable nozzles on the wingtips and fuselage.
MILITARY: In Washington, D.C., Secretary of War Melvin Laird declares that the process of Vietnamization is advancing ahead of schedule and that all combat missions for U.S. troops will end by midsummer.

January 6–26
MARINES: The 31st Marine Amphibious Unit deploys in the Gulf of Thailand after Malaysia is battered by over 100 inches of rainfall and experiences severe flooding. They remain on station, if needed, over the next three weeks.

January 8
AVIATION: At Minot Air Force Base, North Dakota, the final deployment of Minuteman missiles renders the tactical squadron in charge of them operational. At this juncture, a squadron consists of 50 unmanned silo launchers connected to five manned launch-control centers.

January 11–March 29
MARINES: Around Da Nang, South Vietnam, the 1st Battalion, 1st Marines and various reconnaissance units scour the countryside looking for North Vietnamese rocket units who have been attacking the airfield lately. Little contact with the enemy results.

January 13
MARINES: In South Vietnam, the sixth round of troop removals includes 12,988 marines, including headquarter units of the 1st Marine Division and 1st Marine Aviation Wing (1st MAW), the 5th Marines, parts of the 11th Marines, and several squadrons.

January 14
MILITARY: In Washington, D.C., President Richard M. Nixon signs a congressional bill repealing the 1964 Tonkin Gulf Resolution.

January 19
MARINES: South of Hoi An, South Vietnam, Company G, 2nd Battalion, 5th Marines, repels an attack on its outpost, killing 12 enemy soldiers.

January 20
NAVAL: The Navy Department announces that the number of new helicopter assault ships (LHA) is being reduced from nine to five.

January 20–21
AVIATION: The Department of Defense candidly admits that marine helicopters on the *Iwo Jima* and *Cleveland* have been supporting South Vietnamese forces in Cambodia.
MARINES: During Operation Upsher Stream, Company B, 1st Battalion, 1st Marines suffers 11 casualties to booby traps. Subsequently, a CH-46 Skyknight helicopter attempting to medivac the wounded is shot down and crashes, killing four marines and wounding 16.

January 22–February 8
AVIATION: Commander Donald H. Lilienthal pilots a Lockheed P-3 Orion a record 15,963 miles from Naval Air Station Atsugi, Japan, to Naval Air Station Patuxent River, Maryland.

January 28
AVIATION: In South Vietnam, UC-123B sprayer aircraft conduct their final Operation Ranch Hand defoliation mission.
MILITARY: In Washington, D.C., President Richard M. Nixon seeks a two-year extension of the draft while also pushing a 50 percent pay raise for new recruits. He aspires to have an all-volunteer force in place by the middle of the decade.

January 30–February 7
MILITARY: In the I Corps, Operation Lam Son 719/Dewey Canyon II unfolds as the 1st Brigade, 5th infantry Division moves west along Route 9 toward the old Marine Corps base at Khe Sanh, while the 101st Airborne Division prepares to move back into the A Shau Valley. Both moves are actually a strategic distraction from the impending South Vietnamese thrust into Laos.

January 31–February 9
AVIATION: Captain Alan B. Shepard is the seventh man to walk on the moon's surface, a decade after his initial suborbital flight in a Mercury space capsule. He is also the first astronaut to hit a golf ball 400 yards while using an improvised club.

February 2
NAVAL: The Sixth Fleet departs Izmir, Turkey, after a round of anti-American demonstrations erupt.

February 3
MARINES: In light of upcoming budget cuts, the Marine Corps convenes a board to select those lieutenant colonels, majors, and captains to be released from active duty.

February 8–March 6
AVIATION: Operation Lam Son 719 in Laos receives active support from marine helicopters of HMH-463 and HML-367, along with several marine aviation air strikes. A CH-53 helicopter is shot down during 2,992 sorties.
MILITARY: Operation Lam Son 719 continues as a force of 16,000 South Vietnamese troops, backed by heavy American air power, moves along Route 9 and attacks Communist sanctuaries in neighboring Laos. Lieutenant General James W. Sutherland directs the movements of XXIV Corps, which operates 700 helicopters supporting ARVN units. However, the thrust eventually bogs down as the North Vietnamese rush additional troops into the region.

February 11
DIPLOMACY: The United States and the Soviet Union conclude a treaty prohibiting the deployment of nuclear weapons on the ocean floor.
NAVAL: In Washington, D.C., Chief of National Operations admiral Elmo Zumwalt ends the traditional practice of hiring Filipinos to serve as mess stewards.

February 12–March 6
MARINES: Off North Vietnam, the 31st Marine Amphibious Unit is stationed 50 miles east of the coast to provide a diversion while Operation Lam Son 719 unfolds in Laos.

February 16
MARINES: At Quantico, Virginia, the Staff NCO Academy officially opens.

February 18
AVIATION: Northeast of Phu Bai, a CH-53D Sea Stallion explodes in flight, killing all seven marines onboard.
• Marine Corps MHL-367 receives its first four Bell AH-1J Sea Cobras for testing under combat conditions.

February 21–25
AVIATION: After six states in the Midwest are hit by snowstorms and tornadoes, aircraft of the Air National Guard provide disaster relief missions to the afflicted areas.

February 27
AVIATION: Air force transports begin Operation Haylift to assist farmers in snow-bound Kansas in feeding their stranded cattle. They air drop 35,000 bales of hay to feed a quarter of a million head of cattle.
• In Laos, three A-4 Skyhawks of VMF-311 knock out three Soviet-made PT-76 tanks that were attacking a South Vietnamese outpost.

March
AVIATION: Marine Corps aircraft and helicopters fly 20,435 sorties this month, including 160 over North Vietnam.

March 1
MILITARY: The 5th Special Forces Group departs South Vietnam, although some personnel remain behind as instructors with the Special Advisory Group.

March 2
AVIATION: The air force begins a policy of allowing female personnel who become pregnant the option of remaining on duty or being temporarily discharged for 12 months, then resuming active service.

March 4–April 6
MILITARY: In Laos, South Vietnamese forces capture an enemy command center at Tchepone, then declare victory and commence a hurried withdrawal. North Vietnamese units harry them every step of the way and many have to be evacuated by air. By the time the incursion ends, 108 helicopters have been downed with a further 618 damaged. The Americans lose 215 dead from a total casualty list of 1,402 casualties.

March 5
MILITARY: In light of recent tensions, Secretary of Defense Melvin Laird announces that all recruits entering military service receive classes in race relations.
NAVAL: In Washington, D.C., Chief of Naval Operations admiral Elmo R. Zumwalt champions creation of new offices for the deputy chief of naval operations for air warfare, surface, and submarines.

March 10
AVIATION: Southwest of Kadena Air Base, Okinawa, air force helicopters rescue 10 Japanese fishermen who have been shipwrecked on a coral reef.

March 15
MILITARY: At Bien Hoa, South Vietnam, two lieutenants are killed after an African-American soldier rolls a grenade into an officers' barracks. Racial altercations and attacks against officers ("fraggings") are on the rise, which results in 86 deaths and 788 injuries during the war.

March 16
AVIATION: The Kaman SH-2D Seasprite Light Airborne Multipurpose System helicopter flies for the first time. This craft, fitted with advanced sensors and processors that are linked by computer to surface vessels, greatly extends the range through which surfaced or submerged targets can be detected and destroyed.

March 17
AVIATION: At Auburn University, Alabama, Jane Leslie Holley becomes the first woman tended a second lieutenant's commission through the U.S. Air Force ROTC program.

March 18
AVIATION: Captain Marcelite C. Jordon is the first female officer to successfully graduate from the Aircraft Maintenance Officer School.
NAVAL: In Washington, D.C., Secretary of the Navy John H. Chaffee testifies before a Senate committee and candidly admits that there exists a pervasive drug problem along with growing racial tensions in the U.S. Navy and Marine Corps.

March 28
MILITARY: In Quang Tin Province, South Vietnam, Firebase Mary Ann is attacked by Viet Cong sappers in the early morning hours. The 231 defenders from Company C, 1st Battalion, 46th Infantry, backed by some artillery, are caught off guard and their defense is poorly mounted. By the time the Communists withdraw, 30 Americans are killed and 82 injured. Consequently, American Division commander Major General James L. Baldwin and 196th Brigade commander Colonel William S. Hathaway are relieved of duty.

March 29
MILITARY: At Fort Benning, Georgia, a military court finds Lieutenant William Calley guilty of murdering 22 Vietnamese at My Lai; he is sentenced to life imprisonment at hard labor, but the term is reduced to 10 years before he is pardoned in November 1974 by Secretary of the Army Howard Callaway.

March 30
MARINES: Having raised $4.7 million to assist the South Vietnamese people, the Marine Corps Reserve Civic Action Fund closes.

March 31
NAVAL: At Charleston, South Carolina, the fleet ballistic missile submarine *James Madison* departs on its first deterrence patrol armed with Poseidon C-3 missiles. Moreover, the navy establishes an office to develop the newer, more capable Undersea Long-Range Missile System, or Trident.

April 1
AVIATION: At Naval Air Station Norfolk, Virginia, the Helicopter Mine Counter-measures Squadron 12 (HM-12) is established, being the first units of its kind in naval aviation.

April 7
AVIATION: At Kelly Air Force Base, Texas, Lieutenant Susanne M. Ocobock is the first female air force civil engineer.
• The marines receive their first twin-engine UH-1N Huey helicopter for evaluation.
MILITARY: In Washington, D.C., President Richard M. Nixon declares that a further 100,000 troops will be withdrawn from Southeast Asia over the course of the year.

April 8
MILITARY: Operation Lam Son 719 is formally concluded. The performance of South Vietnamese troops in Laos was adequate at first, but discipline fell apart during the chaotic withdrawal and much valuable equipment was abandoned.

April 11
AVIATION: In Washington, D.C., *Apollo II* astronaut Michael Collins is appointed the first director of the National Air and Space Museum, Smithsonian Institution.

April 12
NAVAL: Off the southernmost coast of South Vietnam, U.S. Navy and South Vietnamese gunboats intercept and sink a 160-foot North Vietnamese trawler attempting to pass through their surveillance line.

April 13
MILITARY: In Washington, D.C., Secretary of Defense Melvin Laird reiterates that combat roles for the U.S. Army and Marine Corps will end by summer, but that navy and air force units would remain on station until further notice.

The SR-71 Blackbird aircraft (*National Archives*)

April 14
Marines: At Camp Pendleton, California, the 5th Marine Amphibious Brigade disbands while the 1st Marine Division assumes control of all ground forces stationed there.
• The 3rd Marine Amphibious Brigade is activated at Da Nang, South Vietnam, once III Marine Amphibious Force is relocated to Okinawa. Its purpose is to service marines still operating in South Vietnam and consists of the 1st Marines, the 1st Battalion, 11th Marines, and Marine Air Groups 11 and 16.

April 16
Aviation: At Beaufort, South Carolina, the first three AV-8A Harrier jump jets are assigned to VMA-513, which becomes the first Harrier squadron in the service.

April 23
Marines: A large detachment heads to sea from Camp Lejeune, North Carolina, in a show of force to squelch any Cuban ambitions on the island of Haiti following the death of dictator François Duvalier.

April 26
Aviation: An SR-71 Blackbird piloted by Lieutenant Colonel Thomas B. Estes and Lieutenant Colonel Dewain C. Vick, 9th Strategic Reconnaissance Wing, completes a world speed record by traveling 15,000 miles in 10 hours and 30 minutes nonstop. They receive the Mackay Trophy for their achievement.

April 28
Naval: Captain Samuel L. Gravely, Jr., becomes the first African-American rear admiral in navy history thanks to Chief of Naval Operations Elmo R. Zumwalt. Gravely is one of 49 officers elevated to that rank this year.

April 30
Military: As most American combat units have been withdrawn, I and II Field Forces are replaced by the Second and Third Regional Assistance Commands (SRAC, TRAC) while the Mekong Delta receives the new Delta Regional Assistance Command (DRAC). All are staffed by U.S. advisers.

May 1
Medical: The hospital ship *Sanctuary* leaves South Vietnam after four years of continuous service.

May 1–7
Marines: Detachments from Quantico, Virginia, Marine Barracks 8th and I, and Camp Lejeune, North Carolina, are deployed near Washington, D.C., to counter any violence arising from antiwar demonstrations.

May 1–November 30
Military: Keystone Oriole unfolds with the Americal Division, the 173rd Airborne Brigade, and other units totaling 71,000 men departing South Vietnam.

May 7
Marines: In South Vietnam, the 3rd Marine Amphibious Brigade ceases all ground and fixed wing combat operations prior to shipping back to the United States.

May 11

MARINES: In South Vietnam, the 2nd Combined Action group disbands, bringing an end to the CAP program.

June 14

AVIATION: The super secret KH-9 Big Bird spy satellite is launched into orbit.

June 16

AVIATION: The onset of civil war in East Pakistan (now Bangladesh), results in Operation Bonny Jack to airlift 23,000 refugees from Tripura to Gauhjati, India. Other transports bring in 2,000 tons of food and medicine to assist the refugees, along with over 1 million doses of anticholera vaccine.

June 26

AVIATION: At Phan Rang Air Base, South Vietnam, the 35th Tactical Fighter Wing phases out its F-100 Super Sabres from front-line operational duties.

June 27

MARINES: In South Vietnam, the 3rd Marine Amphibious Brigade is deactivated and shipped back to the United States. Only 547 marines remain behind in advisory capacities.

June 30

MARINES: At this stage of the war, Marine Corps personnel levels stand at 21,765 officers and 190,604 enlisted men.

July 1

AVIATION: Historic Selfridge Air Force Base, Michigan, is the first such facility turned over to the Air National Guard by the Aerospace Defense Command.
MILITARY: In Washington, D.C., Robert F. Froehlke becomes the tenth secretary of the army; during his tenure he oversees the final departure of American troops from Vietnam and implements the new all-volunteer army plan.

July 9

NAVAL: In Washington, D.C., Secretary of the Navy John H. Chaffee exempts sailors and marines who voluntarily disclose illegal drug use from disciplinary action and dishonorable discharge.

July 9–10

MARINES: In Arizona, the Navaho Code Talkers of World War II fame hold their first reunion.

July 11–22

AVIATION: Over southeastern Texas, seven UC-123K Providers and eight C-47 Skyrains commence Operation Combat Vee by spraying insecticide over mosquito breeding grounds to halt an onset of Equine Encephalomyelitis. This actions proceeds under the direction of the Department of Agriculture and 2.5 million acres are covered.

July 12

AVIATION: In Washington, D.C., President Richard M. Nixon appoints former air force general Benjamin O. Davis to serve as assistant secretary of transportation. Davis is also the first African American who is an air force major general.

1971

July 16
AVIATION: In Washington, D.C., Colonel Jeanne M. Holm, director of Women of the Air Force (WAF), becomes the first female general officer in the air force by being promoted to brigadier general.

July 20
MARINES: A report in the newspaper *Cleveland Plain Dealer* claims that the Marine Corps has the highest rates of desertion in the U.S. military, 59.6 men per 1,000.

July 23
AVIATION: The Department of Defense signs a $70 million contract with the Hughes Aircraft Company to construct 2,000 AGM-65A Maverick, television-guided air-to-surface missiles. These weapons are destined for use on F-4E Phantom II and A-7 Corsair II aircraft.

July 26–August 7
AVIATION: At Cape Kennedy, Florida, the *Apollo 15* mission is launched into lunar orbit with an all-air force flight crew. They carry the unique Lunar Roving Vehicle (LRV) to enhance exploration of the moon's surface. Their lunar jaunts in this vehicle are televised in color for millions of viewers back on Earth.

July 29
AVIATION: The National Aeronautics and Space Administration (NASA) terminates the X-24A lifting body program after it has yielded tremendous amounts of data, which will be applied to the forthcoming space shuttle program.

August 1
AVIATION: In Saigon, South Vietnam, General John D. Lavelle assumes command of the Seventh Air Force.

August 6
MARINES: To help ease racial tensions in the Marine Corps, the Advisory Committee for Minority Affairs holds its first meeting.

August 7
MILITARY: In Quang Tri Province, a small reconnaissance team led by Lieutenant Loren D. Hagen is pinned down by North Vietnamese forces. The Americans fight back fiercely, but, when several are wounded, Hagan crawls on the ground to rescue them. He is killed during the process, winning the final Medal of Honor from this war.

August 7–12
MARINES: At the Interservice Rifle Team Match, marines win 12 of 13 contests as well as the 1,000-yard team match at the 10th Annual Interservice Rifle Championships.

August 11
MARINES: In Washington, D.C., Secretary of the Navy John H. Chaffee instructs base commanders to inform local government leaders that any violations of fair housing practices would factor largely in future base closings.

1971

August 13
AVIATION: The Marine Corps Night Observation Gunship System, consisting of a pair of specially rigged OV-10 Broncos, finishes the last of 207 missions to test a 20mm cannon with an infrared target acquisition system.

August 19
NAVAL: Off South Vietnam, ships of the Seventh Fleet shell Communist rocket and mortar positions below the Demilitarized Zone (DMZ).

August 26
NAVY: Alan B. Shepard, a naval officer and America's first man into suborbital space, is promoted to rear admiral.
MARINES: The first LVTP-7 assault amphibian vehicle is delivered; it is capable of hauling 25 fully armed troops ashore and is partly propelled by a water-jet drive pushing it through the surf at 8.4 miles per hour.

August 28
MARINES: In San Diego, the Marine Recruiting Depot and the Naval Training Center declare that all new recruits will be subject to testing for drug use.

September 10
AVIATION: At Tan Son Nhut Air Base, South Vietnam, the 17th Special Operations Squadron flies its last mission before turning the last of its AC-117G Shadow gunships over to the South Vietnamese air force.

September 12–16
AVIATION: In the wake of Hurricane Edith, air force transports convey humanitarian and relief supplies to thousands of victims in Nicaragua. A radio jeep also arrives to coordinate the activities of rescue helicopters that arrive subsequently.

September 14
AVIATION: At McClellan Air Force Base, California, a flight of 15 C-7 Caribou aircraft arrive after completing an 8,000-mile return flight from Cam Rahn Bay, South Vietnam. This Canadian-built aircraft proved invaluable by flying food, ammunition, and other supplies to troops from primitive airstrips.

September 19
MARINES: At Parris Island, South Carolina, two recruits die during unrelated training exercises.

September 21
AVIATION: Over Dong Hoi, North Vietnam, a strike force of 200 tactical fighters employing Loran (long-range aid to navigation), conducts the first all-instrument air strike of the war by hitting and destroying oil and fuel storage areas. An estimated 350,000 gallons of fuel are destroyed.

September 22
MARINES: To smooth out interpersonal relations among members, the Marine Corps Human Relations Instructors School is created. Hereafter, all marines will receive human relations training.

1971

September 25–29
AVIATION: On Okinawa, aircraft of the 1st Marine Aviation Wing (1st MAW) rush medicine and supplies to the southern Ryukyu Islands in the wake of Typhoon Bess.

October 1
AVIATION: Richard D. Kisling is appointed the new chief master sergeant of the air force.
NAVAL: At San Diego, California, the carrier *Constellation* departs to begin a sixth tour on Yankee Station in the Gulf of Tonkin.

October 9–22
MARINES: In Turkey, NATO Exercise Deep Furrow commences as marines from the United States join forces from Great Britain and Italy in a series of amphibious landings.

October 11
MARINES: At Hampton, Virginia, Lieutenant General Lewis B. "Chesty" Puller dies, still very much a Marine Corps icon.

October 28
AVIATION: In Washington, D.C., Michael Collins, director of the National Air and Space Museum, announces that spending for the new museum has been slashed from $70 million to $40 million owing to Vietnam War expenditures.

November 3
AVIATION: Jets of VMA-214 qualify on the carrier *Hancock*; this is the first time that a marine squadron has operated on a flattop since the start of the Vietnam War.

November 7–8
AVIATION: The MiG airfields at Dong Hoi, Vinh, and Quan Lang, North Vietnam, are struck by air force fighter bombers.

November 12
MILITARY: In Washington, D.C., President Richard M. Nixon declares that another 45,000 combat troops will be withdrawn from Vietnam by February 1, 1972, continuing his policy of Vietnamization. Accordingly, combat-related deaths for the year total 1,302 as opposed to 14,592 for the same period in 1968.

December 1
MILITARY: Operation Keystone Mallard unfolds as the 101st Airborne Division, the famed "Screaming Eagles," withdraws from Vietnam and redeploys back to Fort Campbell, Kentucky. They spent a total of 1,573 days in the field.

December 10
NAVY: The onset of war between Pakistan and India results in a task force formed around the carrier *Enterprise* being dispatched to the Bay of Bengal to evacuate citizens and foreigners, if necessary.
MARINES: Units of the Seventh Fleet, including the 31st Marine Amphibious Unit, are dispatched from Vietnam to the Indian Ocean in response to a war between India and Pakistan. They remain in the area through July 1972 in the event American civilians will have to be evacuated.

Howard, Robert L.   (1939–2009)
Army officer

Robert L. Howard was born in Opelika, Alabama, on July 11, 1939, and he enlisted in the U.S. Army in July 1956. An excellent soldier, Howard served as a paratrooper, rose steadily to sergeant, and he also received an associate's degree in business from the University of Maryland in 1962. By this time that the United States was becoming increasingly embroiled in the Vietnam conflict and Howard transferred from the 82nd Airborne Division to the 3rd Special Force Group, the elite Green Berets. Howard performed five tours of duty with the top-secret Military Assistance Command Vietnam Studies and Observations Group (MAC-SOG), which was heavily engaged in clandestine reconnaissance missions in North Vietnam, Laos, and Cambodia. He formed part of an understrength, 60-man reconnaissance company based at Kontum, which, with five Medal of Honor recipients, was the army's most highly decorated unit of the Vietnam War. For his part, Howard was wounded 14 times over a 54-month period, and he received eight Purple Hearts. He was also nominated three times for the Medal of Honor in three separate actions over a 13-month period. The first two nominations were downgraded to two Distinguished Service Crosses owing to the classified nature of his missions. It was after the third time, while serving on a top-secret mission to rescue a fellow soldier in Cambodia, that he finally received the coveted award.

On December 30, 1968, Howard's platoon was helicoptered in deep behind enemy lines and was almost immediately attacked by two companies of North Vietnamese. He was wounded in the first attack, yet he rushed forward under heavy fire to rescue his superior officer. Howard then rallied the survivors into a coherent defensive perimeter and withstood repeated enemy attacks for three-and-a-half hours until helicopters could be called in. Ignoring his own grievous wounds, Howard was literally the last man to be evacuated and spent several months in the hospital recuperating. In addition to the Medal of Honor, which was presented to him in 1971 by President Richard Nixon, he was also commissioned from master sergeant to first lieutenant. He also received the Distinguished Service Cross, the nation's second highest honor, and a Silver Star, the nation's third highest award. After the war, Howard returned to Fort Benning, Georgia, to serve as an airborne instructor at the Infantry School and he also served several years as a company commander in the 2nd Battalion, 75th Rangers. On September 29, 1992, he retired from active duty as a colonel, concluding a distinguished 36 years of service, of which 33 were spent on airborne status. Howard died on December 23, 2009, in Waco, Texas, the most heavily decorated soldier of the Vietnam War whose medal count exceeds that of World War II's famous soldier, Audie Murphy. Unlike Murphy, Howard was never touted as a national hero and his deeds are little known outside military circles.

December 14
AVIATION: Jets of Marine Corps VMA(AW)-224 deploy on the carrier *Coral Sea* for possible action over North Vietnam.

December 20
AVIATION: A helicopter launched from the assault ship *Tripoli* crashes into the Bay of Bengal off Libya; four marines are killed.

December 21
MARINES: The Civilian Pilot Training Program begins to attract more qualified candidates into marine aviation units for the Platoon Leader Class commissioning program.

December 26–30
AVIATION: American warplanes engage in their heaviest-ever bombardment of North Vietnam once air offensives resume.
DIPLOMACY: To push North Vietnam back to the negotiating table in Paris, France, President Richard M. Nixon orders a resumption of full-scale bombing in North Vietnam below the 20th parallel. These are the largest aerial attacks mounted since 1968, totaling more than 1,000 sorties.
MILITARY: As of this date, there are 156,800 Americans in South Vietnam.

December 31
NAVAL: Another bit of navy tradition falls by the wayside after the rope works at the Boston Naval Shipyard, Massachusetts, closes. This unit has provided the navy with all its rope since the administration of President Andrew Jackson. Henceforth, rope supplies will be handled by private companies.
MARINES: In Washington, D.C., General Robert E. Cushman gains appointment as the 25th commandant of the Marine Corps to replace General Chapman, who is recently deceased.
• In South Vietnam, marine casualties for the year total 41 dead and 476 wounded. There are presently only 175,000 American servicemen in all of Southeast Asia.

1972

January
MILITARY: Army troop strength is down to 109,000 men, all volunteer advisers. Despite the continuing drawdown, General Creighton W. Abrams sees mounting evidence of a massive Communist offensive in the offing.

January 1
MARINES: Headquarters Marine Corps raises reenlistment standards to include a high school diploma or equivalent.

January 5
AVIATION: In Washington, D.C., President Richard M. Nixon declares that $5.5 billion will be appropriated for the new space shuttle program.

January 5–February 28
AVIATION: Near Tucson, Arizona, Marine Air Control Unit 7 is directed to operate a radar site to support the Bureau of Customs' Operation Grasscatcher, a concerted attempt to curtail illegal air traffic crossings from Mexico.

January 12
AVIATION: At Beaufort, South Carolina, VMA-542 is reactivated and fully equipped with AV-8A Harrier jump jets.

January 13
MILITARY: In Washington, D.C., President Richard M. Nixon announces the withdrawal of an additional 70,000 American combat troops by the end of the year, which will reduce overall remaining troop strength to 69,000.

January 14
MARINES: In Washington, D.C., the Department of Defense releases manpower cuts that will drop overall military manpower to its lowest levels since 1951. For the marines, this entails a decline to 193,000 men and women.

January 17–27
MARINES: At Reid State Park, Maine, Operation Snowy Beach unfolds as elements of the 2nd Marine Division and the 2nd Marine Air Wing (2nd MAW) stage cold-weather landings in conjunction with the Atlantic Fleet.

January 19
AVIATION: Over North Vietnam, an F-4 from the carrier *Constellation* shoots down a MIG-21 in the navy's first aerial victory since March 1970.

January 21
AVIATION: The prototype of the Lockheed S-3 Viking, the navy's first jet-propelled antisubmarine aircraft, makes it maiden flight.

January 31
AVIATION: At Palmdale, California, the last production T-38 Talon jet trainer is accepted by the Air Training Command.

February 8
AVIATION: In Washington, D.C., the Joint Chiefs of Staff (JCS) authorizes up to 1,200 B-52 sorties per month over Southeast Asia.
•   AV-8A Harriers of VMA-513 undergo operational evaluation onboard the helicopter assault ship *Guam*.

February 17
AVIATION: At Andrews Air Force Base, Maryland, President Richard M. Nixon boards a Boeing VC-137 (a highly modified 707) belonging to the 89th Military Airlift Wing, and departs for Beijing, China. Nixon is about to make history as the first chief executive to visit China, where he negotiates with Mao Zedong and Chou En-lai. This is the first official contact between national leaders since 1949.

February 20
AVIATION: An air force HC-130H, flying nonstop from Taiwan to Illinois, sets a new world record for unrefueled turboprop flight.

March 10
MILITARY: Final elements of the 101st Airborne Division are the last remaining army combat troops to leave South Vietnam.

1972

March 19

MILITARY: In South Vietnam, responsibility for the five northernmost provinces falls to Major General Frederick J. Kroesen, Jr., head of the newly created First Regional Assistance Command (FRAC).

March 23

DIPLOMACY: In Paris, France, the United States suspends peace talks in the face of Communist intransigence.

March 28

AVIATION: Over North Vietnam, two F-4 Phantom IIs from the carrier *Coral Sea* share credit for downing a MiG-17.

March 30

AVIATION: After North Vietnamese troops attack across the Demilitarized Zone (DMZ) and penetrate deeply into South Vietnam, President Richard M. Nixon orders a full-scale resumption of bombing in North Vietnam. Consequently, the Joint Chiefs of Staff authorizes up to 1,800 B-52 sorties per month throughout Southeast Asia.

MILITARY: The North Vietnamese Army launches its "Easter Offensive," the largest conventional attack of the war by attacking Quang Tri near the Demilitarized Zone (DMZ), Kontum in the Central Highlands, and An Loc north of Saigon. They employ the services of no less than 14 divisions and 26 separate regiments totaling 140,000 men, backed by ample heavy artillery and 1,200 tanks and armored vehicles. The only U.S. troops involved are advisers posted with combat units and air cavalry gunships.

March 30–May 1

MILITARY: North Vietnamese forces pour across the Demilitarized Zone (DMZ) into Quang Tri Province and besiege the capital at Quang Tri. The South Vietnamese 3rd Division is all but destroyed and Team 155 under Colonel Donald J. Metcalf, the largest advisory team of the war, is evacuated by helicopter. This becomes the first provincial capital to fall to the Communists since Hue in 1968.

April 1

AVIATION: In light of the Communist Easter Offensive, the Military Air Command (MAC) commences Operation Constant Guard, which transports the entire 49th Tactical Fighter wing–3,195 airmen and 1,600 tons of cargo–from Holloman Air Force Base, New Mexico, to Takhil, Thailand, in only nine days.

• The navy withdraws Attack Squadron Light 4 (VAL-4) from operations in-country, a day after the North Vietnamese commence their Easter Offensive.

• At Randolph Air Force Base, Texas, the Air Training Command establishes the Community College of the Air Force.

MARINES: Off South Vietnam, the 31st Marine Amphibious Group and the 1st Battalion, 9th Marines are positioned to evacuate American military advisers and civilians if the need arises.

April 2

MARINES: Outside Dong Ha, South Vietnam, a North Vietnamese tank thrust down Route 1 stalls after Captain John W. Ripley, a Marine adviser, blows up a bridge over the Cua Viet River.

April 5–May 12

MILITARY: In Binh Long Province, South Vietnam, the city of An Loc is mobbed by thousands of North Vietnamese regulars, backed by Soviet-made PT-76 and T-45 tanks. To rescue the single South Vietnamese division present, Major General James F. Hollingsworth orders in major air strikes and sweeps by AH-1G Cobra helicopter gunships. The Communists are decimated by American air power and forced back into the jungle.

April 6

AVIATION: Over North Vietnam, aerial bombing north of the Demilitarized Zone (DMZ) resumes for the first time since October 1968. For navy carriers, this entails launching an average of 191 combat sorties per day over the ensuing week.

• At Da Nang, South Vietnam, reinforcements arrive in the form of Marine Air Group 15 (MAG-15) and F-4 Phantom IIs of VMFA-115 and 232. They are there to provide close air support to hard-pressed ARVN units.

NAVAL: In light of the Communist Easter Offensive, navy surface vessels loose 117,000 artillery rounds along coastal targets in both North and South Vietnam.

April 7

AVIATION: In Saigon, South Vietnam, General John W. Vogt, Jr., takes charge of the Seventh Air Force.

April 7–May 13

AVIATION: The air force commences Operation Constant Guard by shuttling 200 aircraft from the United States to South Vietnam to help blunt the Communist Easter Offensive there.

April 8

MARINES: In the Gulf of Tonkin off Vietnam, the headquarters of the 9th Marine Amphibious Brigade deploys to take command of all marine amphibious forces still in theater.

April 10

AVIATION: Over North Vietnam, B-52 bombers resume air raids for the first time since October 1968.

April 10–13

NAVAL: Over a four-day period, SEAL Lieutenant Thomas R. Norris, assisted by a few South Vietnamese, drops behind enemy lines to rescue two downed American airmen. He wins a Medal of Honor.

April 11

MARINES: Off Vietnam, the 33rd Marine Amphibious Unit joins the 31st MAU to form one of the largest amphibious forces deployed since the Korean War.

April 14
AVIATION: At Da Nang, South Vietnam, a dozen F-4 Phantom II jets of VMFA-212 arrive from Kaneohe, Hawaii.

April 16–27
AVIATION: The *Apollo 16* space capsule piloted by Captain John W. Young, Lieutenant Commander Thomas K. Mattingly, and Lieutenant Commander Charles F. Duke, land on the moon for an extended walk of 71 hours, then return to Earth safely.
DIPLOMACY: In Paris, France, peace talks between the United States, South Vietnam, and North Vietnam resume but no progress is made before they are broken off again on May 4.

April 17
AVIATION: Operation Linebacker I commences as B-52 bombers begin pounding targets in North Vietnam above the 20th parallel for the first time since March 1968.

April 21
AVIATION: In response to the use of Soviet tanks by North Vietnamese forces, the army rushes in supplies of tube-launched, optically tracked antimissiles (TOWs) for use on helicopter gunships of the 1st Aviation Brigade at Tan Son Nhut Air Base.

April 25
NAVAL: In Washington, D.C., John W. Warner gains appointment as the 61st secretary of the navy.

April 27
AVIATION: In North Vietnam, air force fighter bombers using 2,000-pound Paveway I laser-guided bombs drop several spans of the Thanh Hoa Bridge, something that had not been accomplished in 871 previous sorties. This is also the combat debut of precision-guided munitions.
NAVAL: Captain Alene B. Duerck, Nurse Corps, become the first female rear admiral in navy history.

April 30
MILITARY: In South Vietnam, the Studies and Observations Group (SOG) responsible for clandestine operations in Cambodia, Laos, and North Vietnam, is disbanded and replaced by Advisory Group 158 to support South Vietnamese SOF efforts.

May
AVIATION: This month the last remaining Martin B-57 Canberras are phased out from active duty and return to the United States for internment.
• Navy pilots enjoy their best month over North Vietnam by bagging a total of 16 MiGs. The cruiser *Chicago* also shoots down an unidentified aircraft at extreme range with a Talos missile.

May 1
MILITARY: In the northernmost province of South Vietnam, Quang Tri City falls to the North Vietnamese onslaught.

May 1–June 30
MILITARY: Increment XII (Operation Pheasant) results in the removal of the final major combat units from South Vietnam: the 3rd Brigade, 1st Cavalry Division, and the 19th Infantry Brigade.

May 5
TECHNOLOGY: The Pave Phased Array Warning System (PAWS) to detect sea-launched ballistic missiles is declared operationally ready.

May 6
AVIATION: Over North Vietnam, F-4 Phantom II jet fighters from VF-111 and VF 57 (*Coral Sea*) and VF-114 (*Kitty Hawk*) shoot down two MiG-17s and two MiG-21s.

May 8
AVIATION: Over Haiphong, North Vietnam, Operation Pocket Money commences as A-7 Corsair II and Marine Corps A-6 Intruders begin dropping 36 Mk-52-2 magnetic/acoustic sea mines in the harbor. The ports of Hong Gai, Cam Pha, Than Hoa, Vinh Quang Ki, and Dong Hoi are similarly treated. Over the next eight months over 11,000 mines are sown in Communist waters.
• Over North Vietnam, an F-4 Phantom II flown by Lieutenants Randall J. Cunningham and William Driscoll shoot down their second MiG-17 with a Sidewinder missile.

An A-4F *Skyhawk* aircraft preparing to launch from the flight deck of the attack aircraft carrier USS *Hancock* (U.S. Navy)

1972

NAVY: Rear Admiral Rembrandt C. Robinson, commanding Destroyer Flotilla 11, dies when his helicopter crashes in the Gulf of Tonkin. He is the first flag officer to die in the war.

May 10
AVIATION: The Fairchild YA-10 prototype performs its maiden flight. This is a ground-attack aircraft designed to withstand intense antiaircraft fire.
• Navy fighters enjoy a banner day over North Vietnam when they down 10 Soviet built MiGs; five are claimed by two F-4 Phantom II crews from VF-96 (*Constellation*). Three of these fall to Lieutenants Randall Cunningham and William P. Driscoll, making a total of five kills for the duo; they are the navy's only aces of the Vietnam War and receive the Navy Cross.

May 10–October 23
AVIATION: Air force fighter bombers commence Operation Linebacker I, the latest round of sustained aerial bombing against North Vietnam. F-4 Phantom IIs of the 8th Tactical Fighter Wing severely damage the Paul Doumer Bridge, Hanoi, with new laser-guided munitions.

May 12
AVIATION: A C-130 from U.S. Air Force Europe (USAFE) delivers 5,000 pounds of medical equipment from Stuttgart, Germany, to a new medical facility in Sile, Turkey.
• Near Hue City, South Vietnam, helicopters of HMM-164 transport Vietnamese marines into combat during a raid behind Communist lines.

May 13
AVIATION: Over North Vietnam, air force F-4 Phantom IIs perform a follow-up raid against the Paul Doumer Bridge, Hanoi, finally dropping one of its bridge spans through a combination of laser-guided and conventional bombs. It remains out of commission for the remainder of the year.

May 14
MILITARY: In Kontum, Central Highlands, Vietnam, North Vietnamese units make a third determined thrust at the provincial capital, which is defended by the South Vietnamese 23rd Division. The garrison, amply assisted by American air power and a group of seasoned advisers under John Paul Vann, a former officer turned civilian operative, drives them back.

May 15
DIPLOMACY: Civilian administration of the Ryukyu Islands, including Okinawa, reverts back to Japan after a 27-year period of American control.

May 16–25
MARINES: Along the Carolina coasts, Operation Exotic Dancer V commences among 50,000 personnel of the II Marine Amphibious Force, the 2nd Marine Division, and the 2nd Marine Air Wing (2nd MAW).

May 17
AVIATION: A large force of marine aircraft, including 32 A-4 Skyhawks from VMA-211 and 311, deploy at Bien Hoa Air Base, Saigon, South Vietnam, from Iwakuni, Japan.

May 23

AVIATION: Over North Vietnam, an F-4 Phantom II jet piloted by Lieutenant Commander Ronald E. McKeown and Lieutenant John C. Ensch of VF-161 (*Midway*), shoot down two MiG-17s. This concludes a winning streak of 17 kills for the month.

May 25

DIPLOMACY: In Moscow, Soviet Union, Secretary of the Navy John W. Warner and Soviet admiral of the fleet Sergei G. Gorshkov sign the Incidents at Sea Agreement to reduce the chances of hostile incidents on the high seas.

May 26

DIPLOMACY: In Vienna, Austria, President Richard M. Nixon and General Secretary Leonid I. Brezhnev conclude the Strategic Arms Limitation Treaty (SALT) to limit the construction of antiballistic missile (ABMs) systems, as well as land-based and submarine-launched nuclear missiles. These limitations are imposed for five years only.

June

MARINES: In the Wyoming Valley, Pennsylvania, marine reserve unit render humanitarian assistance for survivors of flooding occasioned by Hurricane Agnes.

June 1

MILITARY: In Washington, D.C., Secretary of Defense Melvin Laird announces that recruits joining a U.S. Army or Marine Corps combat arm would receive a $1,500 bonus and a four-year enlistment. This is a temporary expedient to test the appeal of an all-volunteer force.

June 9

MILITARY: Senior military adviser John Paul Vann dies when his helicopter crashes while surveying the battle scene at Kontum, Central Highlands, South Vietnam. A civilian with the equivalent rank of major general, he is the highest-ranking American fatality of the Vietnam War.

June 11

AVIATION: Over Hanoi, North Vietnam, B-52 bombers destroy a hydroelectric power plant using laser-guided bombs.

June 16

AVIATION: At Nam Phong, Thailand, a force of marine F-4 Phantom IIs belonging to VMFA-115 deploys for the first time. Combat sorties begin immediately.

NAVAL: At Annapolis, Maryland, Vice Admiral William P. Mack gains appointment as the 47th superintendent of the U.S. Naval Academy.

June 20

AVIATION: At Nam Phong, Thailand, marine A-6 Intruders of VMA-533 arrive from Iwakuni, Japan.

June 22

AVIATION: At Kontum, Central Highlands, South Vietnam, TOW-armed helicopter gunships of the 1st Aviation Brigade have accounted for two dozen tanks, four armored personnel carriers, seven trucks, and two artillery pieces.

1972

- Marine HMA-369 arrives of South Vietnam with the first seven Bell AH-1J Sea Cobras. They are to perform reconnaissance and interdiction missions along the North Vietnamese coast.

June 25
MILITARY: In the III Corps tactical zone, South Vietnamese troops break the siege of An Loc without the help of American ground forces. Victory here signals the end of the Communist Easter Offensive.

June 27
AVIATION: The air force begins transferring all its Fairchild C-123 Provider aircraft to the South Vietnamese air force.
MARINES: North of the Cua Viet River, South Vietnam, the 31st and 33rd Marine Amphibious Units make several feints along the coast to distract North Vietnamese forces from attacking south.

June 28
MILITARY: In the former I Corps tactical zone, South Vietnamese forces begin a concerted counterattack to drive North Vietnamese units out of the region.

June 29
AVIATION: Helicopters of the 9th Military Amphibious Brigade convey two Vietnamese battalions behind enemy lines south of Quang Tri City, South Vietnam.
- Over Quang Tri Province, an OV-10A Bronco flown by Captain Steven L. Bennett, 20th Tactical Air Support Squadron, makes an impromptu strafing attack on Communist forces about to attack an allied unit. His plane is hit by antiaircraft fire that cripples his aircraft and destroys his observer's parachute. Refusing to abandon his crewman, Bennet elects to ditch in the Gulf of Tonkin and drowns. Bennett wins a posthumous Medal of Honor for saving his observer's life.
MILITARY: In Saigon, South Vietnam, MACV commander General Creighton W. Abrams is replaced by General Frederick C. Weyand.
- The 196th Infantry Brigade, the final army combat unit in South Vietnam, departs.

June 30
MILITARY: In Washington, D.C., General Bruce Palmer, Jr., replaces General William C. Westmoreland as the new army chief of staff.
NAVAL: The Senate approves the nomination of Admiral Thomas Moorer ro serve a second two-year term as chairman of the Joint Chiefs of Staff (JCS).
MARINES: At this juncture, Marine Corps personnel levels are 19,842 officers and 178,395 enlisted men.

July 8
MARINES: In Florida, the 2nd Battalion, 6th Marines deploys at Homestead Air Force Base in the event they are needed to restore order at the Democratic National Convention.

July 9
MILITARY: At An Loc, South Vietnam, Brigadier General Richard Tallman is killed by enemy mortar fire as he surveys the battle scene.

1972

July 11
AVIATION: As part of the National Aeronautics and Space Administration's Viking Project to land a space probe safely on Mars, the air force test launches a 962-foot-tall balloon system.

July 14
AVIATION: The carrier *America* arrives off South Vietnam, and VMFA-333 is one of a few marine squadrons to conduct bombing missions from a carrier deck.

July 21–August 15
AVIATION: Operation Saklolo unfolds as transports of the Pacific Air Forces (PACAF) convey 2,000 tons of medicine, relief supplies, and disaster relief teams to Luzon, Philippines, in the wake of heavy flooding.

July 22
MARINES: In the Philippines, units from the 9th Marine Amphibious Brigade perform humanitarian operations for flood survivors.

July 24
MARINES: At Norfolk, Virginia, the headquarters, 4th Marine Amphibious brigade is activated as a command element for any contingency force raised between an MAU and a Marine Amphibian Force (MAF) in size.

July 26
AVIATION: The National Aeronautics and Space Administration (NASA) announces that Rockwell International has been selected as the prime manufacturer of the new space shuttle.
• Transports of the Pacific Air Forces (PACAF) begin delivering 4 million pounds of food and medical supplies to victims of recent flooding in the Philippines.
NAVAL: In Washington, D.C., Congress votes to fund a fourth nuclear-powered carrier.

July 27
AVIATION: At Edwards Air Force Base, California, the McDonnell-Douglas YF-15A Eagle air superiority fighter prototype successfully completes its maiden flight.

July 31
MARINES: In Washington, D.C., Commandant Cushman ends the practice of "voluntary segregation" in Marine Corps living quarters, be they on land or at sea.

August 10
AVIATION: In Washington, D.C., the Army announces that it is cancelling its new and expensive Cheyenne attack helicopter because of cost concerns. However, it is moving ahead with its new Advanced Attack Helicopter concept for the near distant future.

August 11
AVIATION: At Edwards Air Force Base, Aviation, the prototype Northrop F-5E Tiger II lightweight fighter performs its maiden flight; it is designed for the export market.

NAVAL: Ensign Rosemary E. Nelson and Lieutenant Ann Kerr are the first women assigned to go to sea onboard the hospital ship *Sanctuary,* who are not part of the Nurse Corps. They serve as the supply officer and personnel officer, respectively.

August 11–26

MILITARY: Task Force Gimlet under Lieutenant Colonel Rocco Negris, consisting of the 3rd Battalion, 21st Infantry and assorted units, becomes the last combat unit withdrawn from South Vietnam. Those military personnel still present are advisers attached to South Vietnamese combat units.

August 12

AVIATION: Northeast of Hanoi, North Vietnam, marine captain Larry G. Richard, an exchange pilot flying with the Air Force 58th Tactical Fighter Squadron, shoots down a Communist MiG-21. He is the second marine aviator to score a kill in this war.

MILITARY: True to his pledge, President Richard M. Nixon announces that the last American ground forces have been withdrawn from South Vietnam.

August 19

MARINES: The 2nd Battalion, 6th Marines, is mobilized to prevent civil disturbances during the Republican National Convention.

August 19–20

AVIATION: Flood conditions along the Han River, South Korea, prompt air force HH-3 Jolly Green Giant and HH-43 Huskie helicopters to rescue 763 civilians from danger.

August 22

MARINES: At Da Nang, South Vietnam, Communist forces resort to ground assaults and mortar barrages in an attempt to disrupt the airfield, but they all are driven off before serious damage ensues.

August 26

AVIATION: Southwest of Hanoi, North Vietnam, an F-4J Phantom II belonging to VMFA-232 is shot down by a Communist MiG fighter.

August 27

NAVAL: Admiral James L. Holloway III directs four vessels of the Seventh Fleet on a nighttime bombardment of Haiphong, North Vietnam. Two Communist torpedo boats that sortie are sunk without loss to the Americans.

August 28

AVIATION: Over North Vietnam, Captain Richard S. Ritchie and his weapons officer, Captain Charles B. DeBellevue, shoot down their fifth MiG-21 to become the first ace of the war.

MILITARY: In Washington, D.C., President Richard M. Nixon declares that all draft calls will cease after June 30, 1972.

September 9

AVIATION: Over North Vietnam and flying in a different F-4 Phantom II, weapons officer Captain Charles B. DeBellevue shoots down his sixth MiG-21, becoming the top scorer of the Vietnam War.

1972

September 11
AVIATION: Air force fighter bombers armed with laser-guided bombs destroy the Long Bien Bridge in downtown Hanoi, North Vietnam.
• Over North Vietnam, a Marine Corps F-4 Phantom II flown by Major Lee Lasseter and Captain John Cummings shoots down a Communist MiG-21 and damages another. They are the third marine team to score an aerial kill.

September 11–30
MARINES: In Norway, marine reservists are present during the NATO exercise Strong Express, during which the new LVTP-7 amphibian assault vehicle debuts.

September 15
AVIATION: At Loring Air Force Base, Maine, B-52s of the 42nd Bombardment Wing are the first aircraft equipped with short-range attack missiles.

September 16
AVIATION: A Department of Defense report notes that naval and marine aviators have recorded their lowest accident rates in history this year.
MILITARY: In South Vietnam, Vietnamese marines recapture Quang Tri City from Communist forces after they had occupied it for 138 days.

September 22
AVIATION: In the Gulf of Tonkin, Commander Dennis R. Weichmann sets a naval aviation record after returning from his 501st combat sortie over North Vietnam.

October 2
AVIATION: At Vandenberg, California, an Atlas-Burner two-stage rocket launcher hurls two satellites into Earth orbit. The *Space Test Program 72-1* will measure radiation effects on spacecraft while *Radcat* serves as a passive radar and optical calibration target.

October 11
NAVAL: Off the Vietnam coast, a turret explosion onboard the cruiser *Newport News* kills 19 men and injures nine more.

October 12
MILITARY: In Washington, D.C., General Creighton Abrams becomes the 27th chief of staff of the army. He faces a huge task of rebuilding a demoralized force suffering from poor discipline and drug use, along with lower defense appropriations and antimilitary sentiment.
NAVAL: Off the coast of North Vietnam, a racial brawl develops on the carrier *Kitty Hawk* between black and white sailors; 60 men are injured before order is restored.

October 13
AVIATION: Over North Vietnam, weapons officer Captain Jeffrey S. Feinstein, flying in an F-4 Phantom II, becomes the sixth and final air force ace by downing his fifth Communist MiG-21.
• The three air force aces of the war, Captains Richard S. Ritchie, Charles B. DeBellevue, and Jeffrey S. Feinstein receive the Mackay Trophy for outstanding airmanship.

October 16
NAVAL: At Subic Bay, Philippines, 12 African-American sailors refuse to sail with their vessel, the fleet oiler *Hassayampa.* A brawl later breaks out between white and black sailors, and marines are sent onboard to restore order.

October 17
AVIATION: The versatile Harpoon antiship missile is test-fired for the first time. This weapon possesses a range of over 60 miles and can be launched from ships, submarines, or airplanes.

October 23
DIPLOMACY: In Washington, D.C., President Richard M. Nixon orders a halt to bombing North Vietnam above the 20th parallel to encourage progress at the Paris peace talks.

October 26
DIPLOMACY: In Paris, France, Secretary of State Henry Kissinger declares that "peace is at hand" with North Vietnamese negotiators. He announces that any remaining differences between the United States and North Vietnam can be resolved in a few more negotiating sessions.

October 31
AVIATION: At Langley Air Force Base, Virginia, the 22nd Air Defense Missile Squadron, is inactivated. It is the last unit armed with Bomarc surface-to-air missiles.
NAVAL: In North Vietnam, a SEAL team comes under fire and its lieutenant is injured. Engineman Second Class Michael E. Thornton dashes forward, kills several enemy soldiers, rescues his unconscious leader, pulls him through water for two hours until picked up, and brings him to safety. Thornton wins a Medal of Honor.

November 10
NAVAL: Admiral Elmo R. Zumwalt, chief of naval operations, reprimands 90 naval officers for recent racial unrest on the carriers *Kitty Hawk* and *Constellation* and outlaws all racist behavior in the service.

November 22
AVIATION: Over North Vietnam, an air force B-52 is struck by an SA-2 Guideline missile and severely damaged. The crippled bomber hobbles its way back as far as Thailand, where it crashes, and the crew safely ejects. This is the first Stratofortress lost in combat.

December 1
AVIATION: Forty-two-year-old Colonel Thomas P. Stafford, a veteran of *Gemini 6, Gemini 9,* and *Apollo 10,* becomes the youngest brigadier general in the air force.
MILITARY: For the first time since January 1965, MACV is able to announce that no American servicemen have died in Vietnam during the week.

December 7–19
AVIATION: *Apollo 17,* piloted by Captain Eugene A. Cernan, Commander Ronald E. Evans, and geologist Harrison H. Schmidt, circles the moon, makes a final

touch down on the lunar surface for the last time, and returns safely to Earth. This flight concludes the successful Apollo moon program; of seven missions, six were commanded by former naval aviators.

December 18
DIPLOMACY: In Paris, France, North Vietnamese negotiators inexplicably walk out of peace talks, prompting President Richard Nixon to take swift and decisive action to force them back.

December 18–29
AVIATION: President Richard M. Nixon orders Operation Linebacker II, a maximum effort against North Vietnam. Massed B-52 bombers strike the cities of Hanoi and Haiphong for the first time. Nixon's goal is to convince the Communists to return to peace talks in Paris or face annihilation from the air. To this end B-52 bombers fly 741 sorties while 769 defense suppression, combat air patrol, and chaff sorties are also executed. Air force and navy losses during this period amount to 15 B-52s, two F-111s, three F-4s, two A-7s, two A-6s, one EB-66, one HH-53, and one RA-5C.
• On December 18, Staff Sergeant Samuel O. Turner becomes the first B-52 tail gunner to shoot down a MiG-21 with a 20mm Vulcan tail gun.
• Throughout Operation Linebacker II, more than 1,300 refueling sorties are successfully performed by KC-135 Startotankers.

December 20
AVIATION: Over North Vietnam, Communist surface-to-air missiles shoot down six B-52 bombers in one day. Air force authorities blame the loss on repetitive routing to targets coupled with the lack of SAM-jammers on half of the B-52Gs. Consequently, the rest of Operation Linebacker II is performed with adequately equipped B-52Ds, and losses drop to acceptable levels.

December 24
AVIATION: Over North Vietnam, Airman First Class Albert E. Moore, a B-52 tail gunner, becomes the second and final person to shoot down a MiG-21 in this manner.
MILITARY: In Saigon, South Vietnam, legendary comedian Bob Hope gives his ninth and final Christmas show for the remaining American personnel there.

December 25
MILITARY: Army strength in South Vietnam shrinks by 700 officers and men to 16,100, its lowest level since 1965. This year there were 172 combat-related fatalities.

December 27
MARINES: In Washington, D.C., the Commandant's House and the Marine Barracks at 8th and I are listed with the National Register of Historic Places.

December 30
DIPLOMACY: In light of the fact that Communist negotiators agrees to resume the Paris Peace talks on January 8, 1973, President Richard M. Nixon halts all bombing north of the 20th parallel.

December 31
MILITARY: American troop strength in South Vietnam stands at 24,200 officers and enlisted men.

1973

January
MILITARY: As part of an overall rehabilitation effort, the army opens its Sergeant Major Academy to the first class. Hereafter, increasing emphasis is placed on better education and schools for junior NCOs.
• In South Vietnam, Operation Enhance unfolds as the army turns over 70,767 guns, 383 artillery pieces, 622 tracked vehicles, and 2,035 wheeled vehicles to its ARVN allies. A handful of American military advisers also remain in Phnom Penh, Cambodia, to oversea the transfer of arms there.

January 3
DIPLOMACY: In Paris, France, the North Vietnamese delegation signals its readiness to resume diplomatic negotiations.

January 4
MILITARY: In Washington, D.C., Secretary of Defense Melvin Laird, giving heed to a recent Supreme Court decision, ends all compulsory religious attendance in all military academies and armed services.

January 5
DIPLOMACY: In Washington, D.C., President Richard M. Nixon writes President Thieu of South Vietnam and pledges that the United States will retaliate swiftly and severely should the Communists violate terms of the peace accord.

January 8
AVIATION: Over North Vietnam, an F-4D Phantom II flown by Captain Paul D. Howman and Lieutenant Lawrence W. Kullman shoot down a Communist MiG with a radar-guided AIM-7 Sparrow missile. This is the last air force victory of the war.

January 12
NAVAL: Over the Tonkin Gulf, North Vietnam, an F-4 Phantom II piloted by Lieutenants Walter Kovalseki and James Wise of VF-161 (*Midway*) shoots down a Communist MiG-17 fighter with Sidewinder missiles. This is also the last of 59 enemy planes downed by naval aviators in this war.

January 15
MARINES: In Washington, D.C., President Richard M. Nixon, generally pleased by the resumption of peace talks in Paris, ends all bombing, mining, and shelling of targets in North Vietnam.

January 18
AVIATION: The Fairchild Republic Company contracts with the Department of Defense to manufacture the new A-X ground support aircraft for the air force. It enters service as the A-10 Thunderbolt II.

January 19
MARINES: At Naval Air Station Anacostia, D.C., a battalion of marines from Camp Lejeune, North Carolina, deploys as a precaution against political unrest during presidential inaugural ceremonies.

January 23

DIPLOMACY: In Washington, D.C., President Richard M. Nixon announces that a peace agreement has been reached with North Vietnam to end the war "and bring peace with honor to Vietnam."

January 23–February 3

MILITARY: North Vietnamese troops attack selected targets in an attempt to enlarge their holdings while South Vietnamese forces hold onto what they can before the cease-fire occurs.

January 27

AVIATION: Over South Vietnam, an F-4D Phantom II piloted by Commander Harley H. Hall of VF-143 (*Enterprise*) is shot down; his radar officer is rescued but Hall is declared missing in action and eventually declared dead. He is the final naval aviator lost in this war.

DIPLOMACY: Secretary of State Henry Kissinger signs a peace treaty in Paris along with representatives of North Vietnam, the Viet Cong, and South Vietnam, which puts in place an immediate cease-fire and the release of all American captives, coupled with the removal of all remaining U.S. forces from South Vietnam within 60 days.

MILITARY: In Washington, D.C., Secretary of Defense Melvin Laird declares the military draft over and a new volunteer force begins at once. Lieutenant Colonel William B. Nolde, an army adviser, becomes the final American soldier killed in South Vietnam when he is struck by fragments from an artillery round. His death comes only 11 hours before the cease-fire.

January 28

AVIATION: Carrier aircraft from the *Ranger* and *Enterprise* conduct air raids against Communist positions in Laos, despite the recent cease-fire. B-52s perform their final Arc Light mission of the war by dumping hundreds of tons of bombs on suspected Communist positions in South Vietnam. Arc Lights have been continuously employed since 1965.

MILITARY: To oversee the closing down of remaining American facilities in South Vietnam, the Defense Attaché Office (DAO) is created under Major General John E. Murray. It currently employs 50 soldiers and 1,200 civilian operatives.

MARINES: The recent Easter Offensive in South Vietnam has claimed the lives of 18 marines, while 68 were wounded and 21 are missing.

January 30

AVIATION: Marine Air Group 12 (MAG-12) flies from Bien Hoa, South Vietnam, and redeploys at Iwakuni, Japan.

MILITARY: In Washington, D.C., Elliot L. Richardson gains appointment as the 11th secretary of defense.

January 31

MARINES: Sergeant Major Clinton A. Puckett is appointed the sixth sergeant major of the Marine Corps.

February 1

AVIATION: The program to employ naval aviators in Marine Corps aviation, which stretches back to 1923, concludes with the retirement of the last four navy pilots.

1973

American prisoners of war, most of them downed pilots, were released from North Vietnam prison camps beginning on February 12, 1973, two weeks after the signing of a cease-fire agreement. *(United States Army)*

MILITARY: In Washington, D.C., the Department of Defense announces that it is tightening military disability standards to cut back on the number of officers retiring from active duty with disabilities.

February 9
MARINES: The 9th Marine Amphibious Brigade is deactivated with the exception of its headquarters. This is maintained to serve as a viable command element within III Marine Amphibious Force.

February 12
AVIATION: Operation Homecoming begins at Clark Air Force Base, the Philippines, as the North Vietnamese begin releasing the first of their acknowledged 591 prisoners of war. They are flown in air force C-141 Starlifters of the Military Airlift Command (MAC). Army captives released total 117 out of 164 known captured. Four marines are also released of the 26 thought to be held. For its efforts, MAC aircrews receive the Mackay Trophy.

February 16
MARINES: In Quang Tri City, the marines stop advising their Vietnamese counterparts and the last two advisers depart.

1973

February 22
DIPLOMACY: Once Laos arranges a cease-fire between Communist and noncommunist factions, the United States declares its intention to cease all military activities, clandestine or otherwise in that nation. However, Communist violation results in a resumption of B-52 strikes, which continue over the next two months.

February 24–July 18
AVIATION: In the Gulf of Tonkin, 31 CH-53 Sea Stallion helicopters begin minesweeping operations as part of Operation End Sweep.
NAVAL: In waters off Haiphong, North Vietnam, Operation End Sweep commences as the Seventh Fleet's Mine Countermeasure Force (Task Force 78) mine sweeper begins removing thousands of mines laid during the war years. Once finished, Task Force 78 is the last American unit to leave North Vietnamese territorial waters.

February 25
AVIATION: In Cambodia, jets of Marine Air Group 15 (MAG-15) continue flying tactical sorties against Khmer Rouge Communists.

March 4
MILITARY: In accordance with the Paris peace accords, Hanoi releases a second group of American prisoners of war.

March 14
MARINES: Sub Unit One, which has been providing support to South Vietnamese forces, becomes the last marine detachment to vacate the country.

March 16
MILITARY: Army Captain Floyd J. Thompson, who has been a captive of the Viet Cong for nine years, is released. He is the longest-held American captive of the war.

March 18
AVIATION: In Haiphong Harbor, North Vietnam, a CH-53D of HMH-463 crashes into the bay during minesweeping operations; all the crew are rescued.

March 20
AVIATION: American aircraft cover a supply convoy of eight vessels that ventures up the Mekong River to the Cambodian capital of Phnom Penh.

March 21
AVIATION: Over the Mediterranean, two C-130 Hercules transports, reportedly flying a reconnaissance mission, are attacked by two Libyan Mirage jet fighters. The aircraft evade their attackers and land safely in Greece.

March 28
AVIATION: As the final air force warplanes depart South Vietnam, many are redeployed to nearby Nakhon Phanom Air Base, Thailand, with the U.S. Support Activities Group.
• The highly effective 1st Aviation Brigade, U.S. Army, which helped pioneer the concept of helicopter gunships in combat, is deactivated and departs South Vietnam.

1973

March 29
MILITARY: In Saigon, MACV finally closes down after a decade in operation. However, General Frederic C. Weyand warns Congress that the survival of South Vietnam depends on the continuance of American economic and military aid. The Defense Attaché Office handles the few remaining military functions extant. North Vietnam also releases the final group of American prisoners of war.
• In Long Binh, the 18th Military Police Brigade is withdrawn from Vietnam, the last sizable army unit to depart. At the war's height no less than 30,000 military police were deployed throughout the country.

March 29–31
AVIATION: In Tunis, Tunisia, helicopters of HMH-362 perform disaster relief operations.

April
MARINES: In Managua, Nicaragua, the U.S. embassy is destroyed by a severe earthquake and six marine guards on station aid in rescue efforts.

April 5
MARINES: In Rome, Italy, a bomb demolishes the living quarters of marines guarding the U.S. embassy; there are no casualties.

April 10
AVIATION: The Boeing T-43A navigation trainer, a highly modified 737 airliner, performs its maiden flight.
• American aircraft begin airlifting gasoline and oil into the besieged capital of Phnom Penh, Cambodia.

April 13
AVIATION: Responsibility for training the shah of Iran's pilots in F-4 Phantom II operations is delegated to the U.S. Air Force Europe (USAFE).

April 16–17
AVIATION: Guam-based B-52s perform their final bombing missions in Southeast Asia by striking Communist targets in Laos after the latter violated cease-fire terms by overrunning villages in the Plaine des Jarres.

April 26
MILITARY: In Washington, D.C., the Department of Defense raises the combat arms enlistment bonus from $1,500 to $2,500. It applies only to the U.S. Army and Marine Corps.

May 14
AVIATION: At Cape Kennedy, the unmanned *Skylab 1* orbiting space station is launched, although it loses a meteoroid shield and one of two solar panels. New procedures will be developed for manning and operating the crippled station with a crew onboard.
MILITARY: In Washington, D.C., Howard H. Callaway gains appointment as the 11th secretary of the army. He completes the phase out of the military draft and also takes measures to reform the army command and staff structure.

• A Supreme Court decision rules that female members of the armed services are entitled to the same dependency benefits for their husbands as male servicemen have traditionally enjoyed for their spouses.

May 15
AVIATION: Operation Authentic Assistance unfolds as 19 C-130 transports begin delivering 9,250 tons of food and supplies to drought victims in Chad, Mali, and Mauritania, Africa.

May 18
AVIATION: The 81st and final C-5A Galaxy is delivered to the U.S. Air Force.

May 25–June 22
AVIATION: In Earth orbit, an astronaut crew comprised of Captain Charles C. Conrad, Commander Joseph P. Kerwin, and Commander Paul J. Weitz occupy the new *Skylab 2* and conduct experiments in space over the next 28 days. They also perform ongoing repairs to the damaged solar shield.

May 29
MARINES: When five soldiers and four marines are charged with misconduct while they were prisoners of war, the secretary of the navy dismisses all charges against them.

June 1
AVIATION: In Washington, D.C., Jeanne M. Holm, who was the first female brigadier general in the air force, receives her second star to major general.

June 13
AVIATION: The Boeing E-4A advanced airborne command post performs its maiden flight.

June 19
MILITARY: In Washington, D.C., Congress passes the Case-Church Amendment, which outlaws any military appropriations for Southeast Asia without congressional approval. Many critics have argued this signaled to the North Vietnamese that they could attack the South without fear of American intervention.

June 25
NAVAL: Former prisoner Rear Admiral James Stockdale files charges against a navy captain and a Marine Corps lieutenant colonel who were also captives. The secretary of the navy dismisses the charges, but issues letters of reprimand and forces them into retirement.

June 26
MARINES: The United States, having opened a liaison office in Beijing, China, marines are on hand to raise the American flag over the premises.

June 27
AVIATION: President Richard M. Nixon vetoes a congressional bill that would have stopped funding for aerial bombardment of Communist Khmer Rouge forces Cambodia. He later agrees to a cut-off date of August 15 for all such operations.
MILITARY: The cease-fire signed in Paris takes effect; the South Vietnamese army controls 75 percent of its territory and 85 percent of its population. Moreover,

the force is well-equipped with modern weaponry and the Americans promise additional aid if needed.

June 29
POLITICS: In Washington, D.C., the Democratic-controlled Congress passes a resolution halting all American air power in Cambodia after August 15. This makes possible a victory by the bloody Khmer Rouge Communists.

June 30
MARINES: Manpower levels in the Marine Corps stand at 19,282 officers and 176,816 enlisted men.

July 1
MILITARY: Conscription (draft) in the United States ends but the Selective Service still registers young men of military age.

July 3
MILITARY: In Washington, D.C., James R. Schlesinger gains appointment as the 12th secretary of defense.

July 15
AVIATION: Over South Vietnam, an A-7D Corsair II of the 354th Tactical Reconnaissance Wing completes the final combat mission of the Vietnam conflict. Since 1964 the air force has flown 5.25 million sorties over Southeast Asia at a cost of 1,737 aircraft lost in combat and a further 514 through accidents.

July 16
POLITICS: The Senate Armed Services Committee begins hearings on secret bombing raids made by the U.S. Air Force against Cambodian Communists in 1969 and 1970. Secretary of Defense James L. Schlesinger subsequently testifies that such actions were necessary for the protection of U.S. ground forces then in South Vietnam.

July 28–September 25
AVIATION: At Cape Kennedy, Florida, a crew of astronauts composed of Captain Alan Bean, Major Jack Lousma, and Dr. Owen Garriott lifts off into orbit to man the *Skylab* 3 orbiting space station; they remain for a record 59 days.

July 31
AVIATION: At Naval Air Station Imperial Beach, California, Light Helicopter Antisubmarine Squadron 33 (HSL-33) is established. This is also the first Light Airborne Multi-Purpose squadron.
• At Cherry Point, North Carolina, VMA-231 is reactivated and equipped with AV-8A Harrier jump jets.
MARINES: At Guantánamo Bay, Cuba, the 2nd Battalion, 8th Marines is relieved by a company-sized formation. This constitutes the first reduction in garrison forces since the 1960s.

August
MILITARY: In South Korea, Lieutenant Colonel Colin Powell takes charge of a battalion within the 2nd Infantry Division. His commander, Major General Henry Emerson, has instituted a rigorous regimen for increasing morale and discipline in his division.

1973

August 15
AVIATION: In accordance with congressional action, the air force halts bombing operations against the Communist Khmer Rouge forces in Cambodia, the final act of American involvement in Southeast Asia. Marine air operations originating from Nam Phong, Thailand, are also suspended. This concludes eight years of continuous raids by B-52 bombers and nine years by fighter bombers.
• From a base at Korat, Thailand, a Lockheed EC-121 performs the final aerial mission of the Vietnam War. Since February 1962, over 5.25 million missions have been flown over Southeast Asia, with more than 1,700 aircraft shot down.

August 20
AVIATION: Recent flooding victims in Pakistan are the object of transports from the Military Airlift Command (MAC), Tactical Air Command (TAC), and the Air Force Reserve (USAFR), which deliver over 2,400 tons of food, medicine, and supplies.

September
MARINES: The Marine Corps Enlisted Commissioning Education Program enrolls its first selectees. Male candidates study at The Citadel, Charleston, South Carolina, while female candidates study at the University of Seattle, Washington.

September 5
AVIATION: On *Skylab* 3, in Earth orbit, Captain Alan L. Bean sets a new record by remaining over 49 days in space. This breaks a previous record held by Captain Charles P. Conrad.

September 6
AVIATION: At Korat Royal Thai Air Base, Thailand, F-105 Thunderchiefs of the 561st Tactical Fighter Squadron depart for George Air Force Base, California.

September 10–21
MARINES: In the Hawaiian Islands, Marines join forces from Australia, Canada, and New Zealand in RimPac-73, a large combined naval exercise.

September 25
AVIATION: In Earth orbit, Marine lieutenant colonel Jack R. Lousma sets a record 59 days in space while working on the *Skylab* 3 space station.

October
AVIATION: At Elmendorf Air Force Base, Alaska, the Air Weather Service employs a ground-based liquid propane system for dispersing fog. In this manner, more air traffic is possible during bouts of inclement weather.

October 1
AVIATION: Thomas N. Barnes is appointed the new chief master sergeant of the air force.

October 5
NAVAL: The aircraft carrier *Midway* is the first such vessel homeported at Yokosuka, Japan. At least one, forward-based carrier operates from this port today.

October 6
NAVAL: In the Sinai Peninsula, the Egyptian attack upon Israeli defenses signals the start of the brief but bloody Yom Kippur War. The Sixth Fleet is placed on alert in the event of Soviet intervention.

October 12–April 6

AVIATION: As the Yom Kippur War continues, SR-71 Blackbirds fly a total of nine reconnaissance missions during Operation Giant Reach. As the name implies, all the aircraft involved are dispatched from bases in the United States.

October 14–November 14

AVIATION: The United States announces that it is beginning a major airlift of military supplies and equipment to Israel to counter recent Soviet support of Egypt and Syria in the Yom Kippur War. Operation Nickle Grass involves air force C-5A Galaxy and C-141 Starlifter aircraft, which ultimately deliver 22,000 tons of equipment. This breaks down into 145 C-5A sorties with 10,000 tons and 421 C-141 sorties with 11,600 tons. This influx of military hardware enables the Israelis to rebuff Arab attacks and strengthen their overall position.

October 17

DIPLOMACY: Several Arab nations announce an oil embargo against any nation supporting Israel during the recent conflict; this is directed mainly against the United States.

October 24

MILITARY: According to U.S. military intelligence, North Vietnam has used the cease-fire to enlarge its troop strength in South Vietnam by 70,000 men, 400 tanks, and 200 artillery pieces. A number of airfields and all-weather roads have been constructed from Quong Tri Province in the north to the Mekong Delta in the south.

October 25

MARINES: In light of Arab-Israeli violence, the 4th Marine Amphibious Unit and helicopters of HMM-201 are placed on alert in the eastern Mediterranean.

October 28

AVIATION: At Mather Air Force Base, California, the first production T-43 trainer aircraft is delivered.

November 7

MILITARY: In Washington, D.C., Congress passes the War Powers Act to curtail future military adventurism. It stipulates that the president must notify Congress within 48 hours of committing American forces into combat. Moreover, such forces must be withdrawn within 60 days unless Congress authorizes an extension.

November 9

MILITARY: In Washington, D.C., the Department of Defense announces severe fuel economy measures due to shortages arising from the Arab oil embargo.

November 14

TECHNOLOGY: The M203 40mm grenade launcher is adopted by the Marine Corps as a standard infantry weapon. It affixes directly onto the barrel of an M16 rifle, greatly enhancing unit firepower.

November 16–February

AVIATION: At Cape Canaveral, Florida, a Saturn 1B rocket carries the new *Sky-Lab 4* team aloft. The team is commanded by Marine Corps lieutenant colonel

1973

Gerald P. Carr over the next 84 days. A major activity onboard *Skylab* at this time is photographing the oncoming comet Kohoutek.

November 19
NAVAL: Vice Admiral Hyman G. Rickover (Retired), the father of the American nuclear navy, is promoted to full (four-star) admiral.

December 1
NAVAL: The navy launches the *Tarawa,* the first in a new series of general purpose amphibious assault ships. It can disembark marine detachments by landing craft, amphibious tracked vehicles, or helicopters.

December 5
MARINE: Another gender barrier falls after the marines adopt regulations allowing women to command units primarily made up of men.

December 13
AVIATION: At Fort Worth, Texas, General Dynamics rolls out its prototype YF-16 lightweight fighter. This is the first fighter craft to feature advanced "Fly-by-wire" computer technology to enhance pilot performance at high speed. It enters service as the F-16 Fighting Falcon, which still serves today.

December 19
AVIATION: The air force approves the purchase of 51 Fairchild/Republic A-10 Thunderbolt II ground attack aircraft, armed with a 30mm GAU-8A gatling gun.

December 20
MEDICAL: Lieutenants Jane O. McWilliams and Victoria M. Voge are the first women to become naval flight surgeons.

1974

January
MILITARY: As part of its rebuilding program, the army activates the 75th Infantry Regiment (Ranger) of three battalions. In Vietnam, the only remaining military personnel serve in the Defense Attaché Organization under Major General John E. Murray, who has little to do but watch South Vietnam crumble under hammer blows delivered by Communist forces.

January 16–19
AVIATION: Near Pinehurst, Idaho, the 48th Air Rescue and Recovery Squadron evacuates 93 people from flooded areas.

February 2
AVIATION: At Edwards Air Force Base, California, the General Dynamics F-16 Fighting Falcon lightweight fighter completes its initial flight; this is the first fighter craft to employ fly-by-wire (computer-assisted) technology.

February 11
MARINES: In Washington, D.C., Commandant Cushman declares that the Marines Corps will allow reservists to keep long hair, provided they wear a short-hair wig while drilling on weekends. As unsavory as it sounded, he was keeping military policy in line with recent Supreme Court decisions.

February 14
MARINES: At Quantico, Virginia, and Camp Butler, Okinawa, marines begin training on the Small Arms Remote Target System (SMARTS), an innovative rifle range system.

February 22
AVIATION: Lieutenant Barbara Ann Allen is the first woman to complete navy flight training and earn her golden wings as a naval aviator.

March 1
AVIATION: The Sikorsky CH-53E Sea Stallion heavy lift helicopter makes its initial flight. Designed expressly for the Marine Corps, this three-engined behemoth has twice the lifting capacity of the CH-53D.
MARINES: Female marines are now allowed to have billets on previously all-male bases, and rear-echelon billets with the Fleet Marine Force. The first 13 candidates are lodged with the 2nd Marine Air Wing (2nd MAW), Cherry Point, North Carolina, and the 1st Marine Division, Camp Pendleton, California.

March 7
NAVAL: A team of underwater archaeologists reports finding the wreckage of the famous Union warship *Monitor*, which sank off Hatteras, North Carolina, in 1862.

March 26
AVIATION: The Department of Defense announces that, owing to spare parts shortages and overdue maintenance, nearly 5,000 air force, navy, and marine aircraft are not operationally ready.

April 10
AVIATION: Minesweeping operations in the Suez Canal are begun by ships and aircraft of the United States, Great Britain, and France as per provisions of the Camp David Peace Accords. Air force C-130s are called in to support communications efforts as part of Operation Nimbus Star.

April 22–June 3
AVIATION: In the Suez Canal, Egypt, marine RH-53 Sea Stallion helicopters of HM-12 arrive and participate in Operation Nimbus Star by sweeping that waterway free of mines planted there in the 1973 Yom Kippur War.

May
AVIATION: At Myrtle Beach, South Carolina, the 354th Tactical Fighter Wing finishes it redeployment from distant Korat, Thailand.

June 4
AVIATION: At Fort Rucker, Alabama, Lieutenant Sally W. Murphy graduates from army flight school and becomes its first female helicopter pilot.

June 9
AVIATION: At Edwards Air Force Base, California, the Northrop YF-17 prototype performs its maiden flight. Although it lost the air force fighter competition to the General Dynamics YF-16, it is eventually acquired by the navy as the F/A-18 Hornet.

June 20
NAVAL: In Washington, D.C., J. William Middendorf gains appointment as the 62nd secretary of the navy.

1974

June 30
MARINES: Because the Naval Disciplinary Command, Portsmouth, New Hampshire, is being disbanded, Marine Corps prisoners serving exceptionally long sentences are transferred to army detention facilities at Fort Leavenworth, Kansas.
• In Saigon, South Vietnam, the Marine Security Guard at the U.S. embassy is lowered from 174 to 157 men.

July
MARINES: In Australia, the 33rd Marine Amphibious Unit begins the largest-ever peacetime training exercises held with Australian forces. The exercise includes troops from the United States, Australia, New Zealand, and Great Britain.

July 1
AVIATION: In Washington, D.C., General David C. Jones gains appointment as U.S. air force chief of staff.
NAVAL: In Washington, D.C., Admiral James L. Holloway becomes the 20th chief of naval operations.
• The Boston Navy Yard, Massachusetts, closes its gates as a cost-cutting measure, ending a rich and varied 174-year history. Many historic vessels were constructed here since the 1790s, including the famous frigate *Constitution*.
MILITARY: In Washington, D.C., U.S. Air Force general George S. Brown gains appointment as chairman of the Joint Chiefs of Staff (JCS).
MARINES: A new aptitude test, the Armed Services Vocational Aptitude Battery, is adopted by the Marine Corps for all recruits.

July 5
AVIATION: At Luke Air Force Base, Arizona, personnel of the 555th Tactical Fighter Squadron arrive from Udorn Royal Thai Air Base, Thailand, to become the first squadron equipped with F-15 Eagles.

July 22
AVIATION: On the disputed island of Cyprus in the eastern Mediterranean, helicopters of HMM-262 evacuate American citizens and foreign nationals during an invasion by Turkish forces. They depart the British base at Dhekelia for the helicopter assault ship *Coronado* offshore, which takes them, in turn, to Beirut, Lebanon, for safekeeping.

July 25
AVIATION: In the wake of a Turkish invasion of the island of Cyprus, C-130 transports are dispatched from western Europe to deliver 10,000 blankets, 7,500 cots, 600 tents, and two water trailers for use by refugees.
NAVAL: The Department of Defense contracts with the General Dynamics Corporation to design and construct the new generation of Trident fleet ballistic missile submarines.

July 27
AVIATION: During an airshow at Milwaukee, Wisconsin, a marine AV-8A Harrier jump jet crashes and burns during its demonstration; the pilot ejects and is unharmed.

LGM-30G Minuteman III missile being inspected inside a silo near Grand Forks Air Force Base, North Dakota *(Department of Defense)*

July 29
AVIATION: In Washington, D.C., Secretary of Defense James R. Schlesinger authorizes the U.S. Air Force to consolidate all military airlift aircraft under itself as a single manager.

August 9
MILITARY: In light of the resignation of Richard M. Nixon from the presidency, Gerald R. Ford succeeds him as the new chief executive and commander in chief.

August 13
AVIATION: At Iwakuni, Japan, VMA-513 deploys as the first Harrier-equipped jet attack squadron in the western Pacific.

August 17
AVIATION: Operation Compass Cope unfolds as the U.S. Air Force begins testing of its Teledyne remote piloted vehicle (RPV).

August 19
MARINES: On Cyprus, American ambassador Roger P. Davies dies in a riot despite the presence of a 15-man Marine Security Guard.

August 21–28
AVIATION: In the Philippines, helicopters from the 31st Marine Amphibious Unit assist survivors of recent heavy rains and flooding.

August 30
AVIATION: At Clark Air Base, Philippines, a C-5A Galaxy completes its first trans-pacific flight with refueling by landing after a flight of 21 hours, 30 minutes. The 10,600-mile mission originated at Dover Air Force Base, Delaware.
• At Kwangju, South Korea, helicopters of the 41st Air Rescue and Recovery Wing save 36 civilians from rising floodwaters.

September 1
AVIATION: In a record-breaking flight, an SR-71 piloted by Majors James V. Sullivan and Noel Widdifield fly from New York to London, England, in 1 hour and 54 minutes, averaging 1,800 miles per hour.

September 3
AVIATION: At Warren Air Force Base, Wyoming, the last operational Minuteman I intercontinental ballistic missile (ICBM) of the 90th Strategic Missile Wing is replaced by a new Minuteman III.

September 13
AVIATION: In another world record flight, Captains Buck Adams and William Machorek fly their SR-71 Blackbird from London, England, to Los Angeles, Cali-

fornia, in three hours, 47 minutes, and 39 seconds; they averaged 1,436 mile per hour.

September 16
AVIATION: The 8th Tactical Fighter Wing finishes its redeployment from Ubon Airfield, Thailand, to Kunsan Air Base, South Korea.
MILITARY: In another gesture at national healing, President Gerald R. Ford declares a limited amnesty for Vietnam War draft dodgers. The process involves taking a loyalty oath and two years of community service, but veterans groups are quick to criticize the measure.

October 3
MILITARY: In Washington, D.C., General Frederic C. Weyand succeeds the late general Creighton W. Abrams as the 28th chief of staff of the army. He will address problems associated with enlarging the volunteer force as well as enhancing troop readiness.

October 24
AVIATION: A C-5A Galaxy hoists a Minuteman I missile to 19,500 feet, whereupon it is released by parachute above the Pacific Ocean, then ignites and successfully launches.

November 24
DIPLOMACY: President Gerald R. Ford and Soviet general secretary Leonid Brezhnev conclude the Vladivostok Strategic Arms Limitation Treaty to limit development of strategic delivery vehicles and multiple, independently targeted reentry vehicles (MIRVs).
NAVAL: The carrier *Constellation* enters the Persian Gulf, the first time an American warship has deployed there since 1948. This remains a region of increasing strategic and economic concern over the next three decades and sees increasing American military involvement.

December
AVIATION: At Cudjoe, Florida, the air force begins operating a balloon-borne radar called Seek Skyhook to monitor the Florida Strait separating Cuba and the United States.

December 1
AVIATION: All transport assets in the Tactical Air Command (TAC) are now transferred to the Military Airlift Command (MAC).

December 2
AVIATION: In Washington, D.C., the Department of Defense approves the joint air force–navy NAVSTAR global positioning satellite system intended to revolutionize global navigation and weapons delivery.

December 23
AVIATION: The Rockwell B-1A variable-geometry bomber performs its maiden flight by relocating from the factory at Palmdale, California, to Edwards Air Force Base.

1975

AVIATION: This year the army conducts intense testing of prototypes for its new advanced attack helicopter, a choice that ultimately falls upon Hughes Aircraft AH-64 Apache.

January
MILITARY: As Communist forces continue to violate the Paris peace accords and attack South Vietnam, there is very little that the handful of advisers still extant can do except watch the country die.

January 11
AVIATION: As Phnom Penh, Cambodia, is surrounded and cut off by Communist Khmer Rouge forces, air force transports begin an emergency airlift to bring in needed supplies and ammunition to the defenders.

January 13
AVIATION: In Washington, D.C., Secretary of the Air Force Dr. John L. Lucas agrees to purchase a fleet of new, lightweight, and highly sophisticated General Dynamics F-16 jet fighters.

January 16–February 1
AVIATION: The F-15 Streak Eagle, a stripped-down pre-production aircraft flown by three different test pilots, sets eight world time-to-climb records, including 98,425 feet in only three minutes and 28 seconds. Consequently, Majors Roger J. Smith, David W. Peterson, and Willard R. MacFarlane all win the Mackay Trophy.

January 15
MARINES: In Washington, D.C., the Supreme Court overturns the ruling of a lower court and upholds a law mandating retirement of all male officers who have been twice passed over for promotion.

January 27
MILITARY: In Cambodia, the Communist Khmer Rouge forces of Pol Pot are poised to storm the capital of Phnom Penh as government defenses wilt.
NAVAL: In Corfu, Greece, anti-American agitation and mob attacks against two officers require the destroyer *Richard E. Byrd* to hoist anchor and depart.

February 1
AVIATION: A McDonnell Douglas F-15 fighter jet dubbed *Streak Eagle* sets several world speed records in the time-to-climb category.
MARINES: In an attempt to raise enlistment standards, the Marine Corps begins emphasizing the general-technical score of the new Armed Services Vocational Aptitude Battery.
• At Marine Air Station Corps, Cherry Point, North Carolina, Sergeant Major Eleanor L. Judge is appointed the first woman to hold the top enlisted slot in the Headquarters Squadron.

February 7
AVIATION: An LTV Corsair II fitted with the DIGITAC (digital flight control system) begins flight testing. This computerized fly-by-wire system is intended

Weyand, Frederick C. (1916–)
Army general

Frederick Carleton Weyand was born in Arbuckle, California, on September 15, 1916, and, after graduating from the University of California, Berkeley, in 1939, he joined the Coast Artillery Reserve as a lieutenant. During World War II he served as an intelligence officer in Burma under General Joseph W. Stilwell, and remained in the Pacific for several years until 1949, when he enrolled in the Infantry School at Fort Benning, Georgia. Weyand proved himself a competent officer and he also passed through the Armed Forces Staff College in 1957 and the National War College in 1958. After serving with the Berlin garrison as a temporary brigadier general in 1960, he became a major general in November 1962 and assumed command of the 25th Infantry Division in Hawaii (1964–66). Weyand arrived in South Vietnam with his division in March 1966 and was posted with the III Corps tactical zone, whose troops were responsible for the security of Saigon. He fought in Operations Cedar Falls and Junction City with distinction. The following year he was appointed commander of the II Field Force, a corps-size formation. In January 1968 he performed exceptionally well during the infamous Tet Offensive. Weyand grew suspicious of the volume of Communist radio traffic he was receiving and convinced General William C. Westmoreland to transfer the bulk of his battalions from the Cambodian border to the Saigon region. The Americans, thus strengthened, were able to quickly recapture the city of Hue and severely punish the Viet Cong when they emerged.

Weyand departed South Vietnam in August 1968 and proceeded to Paris, France, to serve as the American military adviser during peace talks there. He returned in September 1970 as deputy commander of the Military Assistance Command, Vietnam (MACV), and, in June 1972, he succeeded General Creighton Abrams as commander. Weyand was preoccupied with the dangerous task of winding down the American military presence in Southeast Asia while providing military supplies to the South Vietnamese army. On March 29, 1973, he departed Vietnam to serve as commander in chief, U.S. Army, Pacific, and army chief of staff in October 1974, becoming the first non–West Point graduate to hold that office. In March 1975 President Gerald Ford dispatched him back to Vietnam to assess the mounting crisis, and Weyand advised him that the government there needed drastic American aid if it were to survive the ongoing Communist onslaught. He also personally informed President Nguyen Van Thieu that the United States would not intervene militarily on his behalf. When such aid was not forthcoming from Congress, South Vietnam fell a month later. Weyand concluded his 36-year military career by retiring from active duty in October 1976 as a full general. For the six years he served in South Vietnam, he was regarded as one of America's most capable and experienced combat commanders.

to allow inherently unstable aircraft designs such as the F-117 Nighthawk to fly stable.

February 16

AVIATION: At Fairchild Air Force Base, Washington, Brigadier General Eugene D. Scott becomes the first navigator (nonpilot) to command an aerial unit when he takes charge of the 47th Air Division.

February 23

MARINES: In Washington, D.C., the Department of Defense announces the end of two-year enlistments by the end of the current fiscal year. Afterward, the shortest enlistment term is a three-year hitch.

February 28

MARINES: In the Gulf of Thailand, recent gains by the Communist Khmer Rouge results in the 31st Marine Amphibious Unit (2nd Battalion, 4th Marines and helicopters of HMH-462) being deployed for possible evacuation services.

March

MARINES: In an attempt to identify and possibly rehabilitate drug abusers in the ranks, the Marine Corps resumes urinalysis testing as per a new Department of Defense policy.

March 3

NAVAL: The Navy Department reveals that its strength will slip to 490 ships as of June 30, 1976.

March 5

AVIATION: At March Air Force Base, California, the last T-29 navigation training sortie is performed by students.

MILITARY: Throughout South Vietnam, reconstituted North Vietnamese Army (NVA) units begin an all-out spring offensive in the Central Highlands region.

MARINES: A recent spate of rocket attacks on the national airport in Phnom Penh, Cambodia, forces navy and marine helicopters to begin evacuating American civilians to a helicopter carrier offshore.

March 17

MILITARY: In South Vietnam, ARVN forces abandon the central provinces of Kontum, Pleiku, and Darlac to advancing Communists.

March 18

NAVAL: Word is leaked of a 1974 CIA attempt to raise a sunken Soviet missile submarine with the salvage vessel *Glomar Explorer.* Over $250 million is spent but only the front third of the Russian vessel is recovered.

March 21

AVIATION: A C-141 Starlifter crashes into the Olympic Mountains, Washington, with no survivors. Given the remoteness of the location, Air Rescue and Recovery Service personnel spend the next four months retrieving bodies and equipment.

March 22
AVIATION: At Kaneohe, Hawaii, helicopters of HMH-463 are ordered on to the carrier *Hancock* for immediate departure for Southeast Asia.

March 25
AVIATION: With Communist forces closing in on Da Nang, South Vietnam, the Military Airlift Command (MAC) becomes the single coordinating body for a massive aerial evacuation of civilians. They evacuate 10,000 people a day for several days.
MILITARY: The ancient capital of Hue, South Vietnam, falls a second and final time to Communist forces.
• U.S. Army Chief of Staff general Frederick C. Weyand arrives in South Vietnam to evaluate the developing military crisis there.

March 27
MILITARY: U.S. Army Chief of Staff general Frederick C. Weyand ventures to Saigon, South Vietnam, for a high-level conference with government officials. He is convinced that the country cannot survive without continuing military assistance from the United States, especially air power.
MARINES: In light of South Vietnam's impending collapse, the Amphibious Evacuation Support Group (1st Battalion, 4th Marines, and helicopters of HMM-165) are ordered to sail from Okinawa to Southeast Asia.

March 29
AVIATION: Air force transports begin emergency airlifts of military supplies and other vital equipment directly into Saigon, South Vietnam.
MARINES: At Da Nang, South Vietnam, the Marine Security Guard begins the seaborne evacuation of American nationals and foreign nationals before the city falls to Communist forces.

March 31
AVIATION: The transport assets of the Pacific Air Forces (PACAF), Alaskan Air Command, and U.S. Air Forces in Europe are all transferred to the Military Airlift Command (MAC). This consolidates all military airlift equipment into a single, unified command.
MILITARY: The conditional amnesty program for draft dodgers initiated by President Gerald R. Ford ends today after only 22,500 men come forth to accept it out of 124,400 eligible.

April 1
DIPLOMACY: One step ahead of the Communist triumph, General Lon Nol departs Phnom Penh, Cambodia, for a new home in Indonesia.
MARINES: At Nha Trang, South Vietnam, the Marine Security Guard is helicoptered to Saigon ahead of Communist forces.

April 2
MARINES: The Military Sealift Command has chartered four civilian merchant ships to evacuate 4,000 South Vietnamese refugees, one vessel is crammed with 16,000 people. Marine security forces are onboard to maintain order.

April 4

AVIATION: A Lockheed C-5A Galaxy transport crashes after takeoff from Saigon, South Vietnam, killing 176 civilian refugees, mostly orphaned children. This accident concludes Operation Baby Lift.

• The air force details several C-130 transports to begin the evacuation of refugees from Phnom Penh before the city falls to Khmer Rouge Communists.

MARINES: In Cam Ranh Bay, South Vietnam, the Amphibious Evacuation Support Group assists thousands of refugees fleeing the Communist onslaught.

April 5

MILITARY: In Cambodia, as Communist Khmer Rouge forces close in on the capital of Phnom Penh, Operation Eagle Pull prepares to evacuate all remaining army personnel and advisers under Brigadier General William Palmer. They will be airlifted out by helicopter.

April 7

MARINES: In the Philippines, the 33rd Marine Amphibious Unit (1st Battalion, 9th Marine and helicopters of HMM-165) are activated for possible deployment in Vietnam.

April 8

MILITARY: In Washington, D.C., U.S. Army Chief of Staff general Frederick C. Weyand informs Congress that the fall of South Vietnam is imminent without major American military assistance. No such assistance is forthcoming.

April 9

MILITARY: Communist forces penetrate the outer defenses of Saigon, South Vietnam, placing them only 37 miles away from the city.

April 10

AVIATION: The B-1A Lancer achieves supersonic flight for the first time.

April 11

NAVAL: The carrier *Hancock* and helicopters of HMH-463 deploy off the Cambodian coast.

April 12

AVIATION: Marine CH-53 Sea Stallion helicopters of HMH-462 and 463 continue Operation Eagle Pull by evacuating a further 287 people from Phnom Penh, Cambodia.

NAVAL: In light of surging Communist Khmer Rouge forces in Cambodia, Operation Eagle Pull continues in the Gulf of Siam to safely evacuate Americans and other nationals from the capital of Phnom Penh. The amphibious assault ship *Okinawa* and the carrier *Hancock* deploy helicopters to remove 276 people, including Ambassador John G. Dean and Cambodian president Saukhm Khoy. A horrid fate awaits those who cannot escape vengeful Khmer Rouge soldiers under the fanatical Pol Pot.

MARINES: As helicopters evacuate Americans and foreign nationals at Phnom Penh, Cambodia, the 2nd Battalion, 4th Marines deploys around the airport under heavy fire to provide security.

April 17
MILITARY: Phnom Penh, capital of Cambodia, falls to communist Khmer Rouge forces under Pol Pot. What follows is a holocaust when one-half of the country's population is slaughtered in what becomes known as the "Killing Fields."

April 18
AVIATION: All Strategic Air Command (SAC) air refueling wings are transferred to the Air Force Reserve and Air National Guard, which are now required to support SAC alert operations.

April 19
AVIATION: Marine Air Group 39 (MAG-39) is activated onboard the command vessel *Blue Ridge* to direct evacuation activities of HMH-462 and 463, HMM-165, HML-367, and HMA-369.
MARINES: The 31st, 33rd, and 35th Marine Amphibious Units are consolidated into the 9th Marine Amphibious Brigade for the purpose of evacuating refugees from South Vietnam.

April 20
NAVAL: The carrier *Hancock* deploys off South Vietnam with helicopters of HMH-463 onboard.

April 21
AVIATION: The B-1A Lancer completes its first successful aerial refueling.
DIPLOMACY: In Saigon, President Thieu makes an emotional televised address in which he resigns from office and also denounces the United States for abandoning the nation.
MARINES: On Guam, the Marine Barracks begins setting up camp facilities for an influx of South Vietnamese refugees.

April 28–October 31
MARINES: At Camp Pendleton, California, Marine Air Group 13 (MAG-13) is tasked with constructing holding facilities for the first wave of an expected 130,000 South Vietnamese refugees.

April 29–30
AVIATION: In Saigon, South Vietnam, as North Vietnamese forces close in upon the capital, Operation Frequent Wind commences as 68 marine and 10 air force helicopters evacuate 6,978 Americans and foreign nationals to the carrier *Midway* offshore. This is the largest such aerial operation in history and lasts 17 hours. Two Marines die when their CH-46 Skyknight and AH-1J Sea Cobra helicopters crash. This is also the combat debut of the F-14A Tomcat jet fighter, which flies top cover throughout the evacuation.
•   In Saigon, South Vietnam, Operation New Life commences as C-130s and C-141s of the Military Airlift Command (MAC) pull another 45,000 people from danger, including 5,600 American citizens.
•   Aircraft of the South Vietnamese air force, including C-130s, F-5s, and AT-37s are evacuated to bases in Thailand to prevent their capture.
NAVAL: In the South China Sea, the Seventh Fleet's Task Force 76 commences Operation Frequent Wind to evacuate all American military and civilian person-

nel from impending capture by advancing Communist forces, including Ambassador Graham Martin. Vessels of the Military Sealift Command also take on several thousand refugees fleeing the country by sea.

• The conflict in Southeast Asia reaches its ignominious conclusion in a decisive Communist victory. The United States has lost 6,598 officers, 1,276 warrant officers, and 50,274 enlisted men attempting to stem the tide; a total of 58,148.

MARINES: In South Vietnam, Communist forces rocket Tan Son Nhut Airfield in Saigon, killing two marines and destroying a C-130 transport. Meanwhile, the 9th Marine Amphibious Brigade commences Operation Frequent Wind to assist the removal of several thousand refugees to safety.

• The U.S. presence in South Vietnam ends as the last 10 marine security guards depart the American embassy at 8:35 A.M.

April 29–September 16

AVIATION: Operation New Arrivals unfolds as C-130s, C-141s, and commercial airliners transport 121,562 Indochinese refugees to new lives in the United States from staging areas throughout the Pacific.

April 30

MILITARY: Saigon, South Vietnam, falls to Communist forces, completing the conquest and reunification of that nation by force. General Duong Van Minh, who succeeded President Thieu, declares the country's unconditional surrender.

May 2

AVIATION: The Northrop YF-17 prototype is selected by the navy as its new fighter/bomber and it enters service as the F/A-18 Hornet. This remains the tactical mainstay of naval aviation to present times.

May 3

NAVAL: The navy commissions the 81,600-ton *Nimitz*, the nation's second nuclear-powered aircraft carrier. This vessel carries 100 aircraft and has a top speed of 30 knots.

May 7

NAVAL: In a period of cold war thaw, the frigate *Leahy* and destroyer *Tatnall* make a goodwill visit to the Soviet port city of Leningrad (St. Petersburg) while Soviet destroyers *Boykiy* and *Zhguchiy* visit Boston, Massachusetts.

May 12

AVIATION: In response to the Khmer Rouge seizure of the SS *Mayaguez*, transports of the Military Airlift Command (MAC) carry Marines and their equipment from the Philippines and Okinawa to Thailand.

NAVAL: In the Gulf of Thailand, Communist Khmer Rouge forces capture the U.S. merchant vessel SS *Mayaguez*. President Gerald R. Ford warns them to release the vessel and its 40-man crew immediately or face the consequences.

May 14–15

AVIATION: Eight helicopters of the 3rd Aerospace Rescue and Recovery Group and the 21st Special Operations Squadron transport 230 Marines to Kho Tang Island to look for the SS *Mayaguez* crew. Instead, they encounter strong resistance from dug-in Khmer Rouge forces, who shoot down three helicopters and damage two more. The marines are pinned by heavy fire until assisted by air force A-7s, F-4s, OV-10s, and AC-130s, then they are successfully extracted. Several Air Force Crosses are awarded for heroism and Major Robert W. Undorf also win a Mackay Trophy.

NAVAL: President Gerald R. Ford orders air, sea, and land elements into action to rescue the American cargo vessel SS *Mayaguez* after it is captured by Khmer Rouge guerrillas off Cambodia. Military operations are supported by carrier aircraft launched from the *Coral Sea* and the vessel itself is towed to freedom by the destroyer *Harold E. Holt.* Congress and the American people laud the action as a blow against international piracy.

MARINES: Company D, 1st Battalion, 4th Marines, swings into action and boards the SS *Mayaguez,* since abandoned by Khmer Rouge forces, and it is quickly secured. Meanwhile, air force helicopters drop elements of the 2nd Battalion, 9th Marines on nearby Koh Tang Island to look for the crew and a stiff firefight ensues. The captives are not on the island, but they are subsequently released and rejoin the *Mayaguez* by fishing boat. American losses are three helicopters downed, 15 men killed, 50 wounded, and three missing.

May 29

MARINES: Sergeant Major Henry H. Black becomes the seventh sergeant major of the Marine Corps.

June 5

NAVAL: At Suez, Egypt, the guided cruiser *Little Rock* is the first foreign vessel to transit through the Suez Canal once that waterway has been cleared of mines and other obstructions.

The Vietnam War saw the introduction of the gunship, modified C-47s and C-130s, capable of pouring concentrated fire onto ground positions. Pictured is an AC-130. (*U.S. Air Force*)

June 6
AVIATION: At U-Tapao, Thailand, the final 16 B-52 Stratofortresses begin redeploying back to the United States.

June 15
AVIATION: In Thailand, the final F-111 departs for a new billet back in the United States.

June 17
AVIATION: In Montana, helicopters from the 37th Air and Rescue Squadron save 131 victims of heavy flooding throughout that state.

June 30
MARINES: In Washington, D.C., General Louis H. Wilson, Jr., who won a Medal of Honor on Guam in 1944, gains appointment as the 26th commandant of the Marine Corps.

July 1
AVIATION: Air National Guard KC-135s begin supporting Strategic Air Command (SAC) operations for the first time. The ANG and Air Force Reserve continue transitioning to jet tankers over the next four years.

July 15–24
AVIATION: Three American astronauts rendezvous with two Soviet cosmonauts and link up with their *Soyuz* spacecraft. The combined crews carry out a number of scientific experiments before returning safely to Earth.

July 31
AVIATION: After 18 years of useful service, the Air National Guard (ANG) retires its last F-104 Starfighters.

August 1
NAVAL: At Annapolis, Maryland, Rear Admiral Kinnaird R. McKee is appointed the 48th superintendent of the U.S. Naval Academy.

August 5
MILITARY: In Washington, D.C., Martin R. Hoffman becomes the 12th secretary of the army. His main preoccupation will be rebuilding the military in the wake of Vietnam.

August 7
AVIATION: At Ramstein Air Base, West Germany, two C-141 Starlifters depart for Bucharest, Romania, to assist victims of extensive flooding along the Danube River.

August 8–15
AVIATION: In California, C-130 transports of the Air Force Reserve and Air National Guard drop 1,400 tons of retardant on several forest fires.

August 23
MILITARY: The Communist Pathet Lao completes the conquest of Laos; all the states of Indochina are now ruled by Communist dictatorships.

1975

August 27
MILITARY: Governor James Rhodes of Ohio and 27 National Guardsmen are cleared of all charges stemming from the shooting of 13 students at Kent State University in May 1970.

September 1
AVIATION: Major General Daniel "Chappie" James is promoted to full general, becoming the first African-American officer to wear four stars.

September 20
NAVAL: At Pascagoula, Mississippi, the new 7,50-ton destroyer *Spruance* is commissioned, being the navy's first class of warships powered by a gas turbine; no less than 30 ships are built.

October
MARINES: Marine detachments conduct amphibious operations along the coast of northern Germany as part of the NATO Exercise Autumn Forge. This is the first time marines have trained in Germany since 1918.

October 7
MILITARY: In Washington, D.C., President Gerald R. Ford signs legislation that allows women to enroll at all four service academies and receive regular commissions.

October 8
MILITARY: The army declares that, commencing next year, the U.S. Military Academy will accept applications from women.

October 22
MILITARY: Sergeant Leonard Matlovich is discharged from the military after revealing his homosexuality. His discharge is subsequently upgraded to honorable, owing to his status as a decorated Vietnam veteran.

October 29
AVIATION: At Nellis Air Force Base, Nevada, the air force accepts delivery of the first Northrop F-5E Tiger II jet fighter. It is destined to play a central role in future "Red Flag" pilot training maneuvers.

October 31
AVIATION: The revolutionary Boeing E-3A Sentry, an advanced aerial command and control center, performs its maiden flight.

November
AVIATION: The air force reveals the existence of its Have Blue Project, which is developing the first radar-resistant, or stealth, warplane.

November 10
MARINES: The Marine Corps celebrates the 200th anniversary of the founding of the Continental Marines in 1775.

November 20
MILITARY: In Washington, D.C., Donald H. Rumsfeld is appointed the 13th secretary of defense.

November 22
NAVAL: During night maneuvers in the Mediterranean, the guided missile frigate *Belknap* collides with the carrier *John F. Kennedy*; the frigate loses seven killed and 47 injured while the carrier has one sailor missing.

November 29
AVIATION: Stung by the mediocre results of air force crewmen during Vietnam era dogfights, the first new Red Flag training program is unveiled at Nellis Air Force Base, Nevada. Its purpose is to provide realistic air-to-air combat training for prospective fighter pilots. They are pitted against crack instructor crews whose F-5E Tiger IIs closely mimic Soviet-style tactics and aircraft. The program runs annually today and has trained over 500,000 pilots from all four services and 23 allied nations.

December 6
AVIATION: In light of tactical lessons learn in Vietnam, the new F-4G Wild Weasel aircraft performs its maiden flight. The air force acquires 116 such aircraft for the express purpose of surface-to-air missile (SAM) suppression.

James, Daniel   (1920–1978)
Air Force general

Daniel James was born in Pensacola, Florida, on February 11, 1920, the youngest of 17 children. His mother, a schoolteacher, imbued in him an abiding sense that excellence could surmount any obstacle, including racial hostility. James was fascinated by airplanes at Pensacola Naval Air Station but, because the navy did not allow African Americans to serve as pilots, he attended the Tuskegee Institute from 1937 to 1942, then earned his wings through the Civilian Pilot Training Program. During World War II James flew P-40s and P-51s with the famed Tuskegee Airmen under Colonel Benjamin O. Davis. In April 1945 he was arrested by participating in one of the first civil rights sit-ins at Freeman Field, Indiana, where he met and befriended the great civil rights attorney Thurgood Marshall, a future Supreme Court justice. The armed forces were ordered integrated by President Harry S. Truman in 1947, and James continued advancing due to his determination and skill as a leader. During the Korean War he flew over 100 missions as head of the 12th Fighter Bomber Squadron, then reported to Otis Air Force Base, Massachusetts, to command the 58th Fighter Interceptor Squadron. Dynamic and gregarious, James's outsized personality and community activism led to an award as Outstanding Man of the Year by the Massachusetts Junior Chamber of Commerce. During the Vietnam War James commanded the Eighth Tactical Fighter Wing, operating out of Udon, Thailand, and he flew an additional 78 combat missions in F-4 Phantom II jet fighters. On January 2, 1967, he led the "Bolo MiG-Sweep" over North Vietnam, which accounted for seven MiG-21s, the highest total of enemy aircraft claimed in a single day.

1976

JANUARY: Army personnel stands at 779,412 officers and men arrayed in 16 active divisions. The service still grapples with problems arising from apathy, drug use, and lingering racism.

January 9
AVIATION: At Langley Air Force Base, Virginia, the first McDonnell Douglas F-15 Eagle air superiority fighter arrives to join the 1st Tactical Fighter Wing. This is the first jet fighter in history to possess greater thrust than its overall weight, allowing it to literally climb straight up.

January 19
AVIATION: At Nellis Air Force Base, Nevada, the 180th Tactical Fighter Group is the first Air National Guard unit to cycle through the Red Flag program.

January 31
AVIATION: At Udorn Air Base, Thailand, the air force prepares to turn all its facilities over to the Royal Thai Air Force as the Americans continue pulling out of Southeast Asia. The Americans have run the facility since October 1964.

James returned home in 1967 and used his oratorical skills and commanding persona to rigorously defend the Vietnam War against political opponents. In 1969 he took command of Wheelus Air Force Base, Libya, and he handled the withdrawal of American forces there with diplomacy and tact. He then served at the Pentagon and Military Airlift Command (MAC), rising successively to brigadier general in 1970, major general in 1972, and lieutenant general in 1973. On September 1, 1975, James made history by becoming the first African American of any service branch to reach four-star rank. He assumed command of the North American Air Defense Command (NORAD), which was responsible for defending the United States against a surprise nuclear attack from the Soviet Union. As such, he was the only other person, besides the president of the United States, who could authorize a nuclear strike. "Chappie" James concluded 35 years of distinguished service by retiring in Febru-

Daniel James meets with two government officials in the Pentagon. *(U.S. Army)*

ary 1978. Unfortunately, he died of a heart attack in Colorado Springs, Colorado, on February 25, 1978, prior to delivering one of his trademark speeches about individualism and personal doggedness. The F4C Phantom II he flew in Vietnam presently stands guard outside Tuskegee University, Alabama.

February 5–March 3
AVIATION: A devastating earthquake in Guatemala leads to Project Earthquake, during which Military Airlift Command (MAC) transports deliver 1,000 tons of food and medical supplies, along with 700 personnel, to the region.

February 12
NAVAL: Captain Fran McKee is the first female naval officer selected for promotion to rear admiral.

March 1
AVIATION: On Taiwan, the U.S. Air Force ceases all operations at Taipei Air Station, concluding a two-decade presence there.

March 5
AVIATION: The United States tests its new long-range Air Launch Cruise Missile (ALCM), which gives added punch and penetration power to its aging fleet of jet bombers.

March 13
MARINES: After a mentally deficient recruit dies of injuries received in a late 1975 pugil stick bout, Congress opens an investigation into marine recruit training.

March 15
AVIATION: A Titan IIIC rocket launcher hurls *Les-8* and *Les-9*, two nuclear-powered communications satellites, into Earth orbit.

March 22
AVIATION: The Fairchild/Republic A-10 begins its operational and test evaluations at Davis Monthan Air Force Base, Arizona. Though straight-winged, this aircraft is both heavily armed and armored for a close support role, and it sports a tank-killing 30mm GAU gatling gun in the nose firing heavy, depleted uranium rounds.
• The Strategic Air Command (SAC) ends its presence in Southeast Asia by withdrawing the final U-2 aircraft from U-Tapao Air Field, Thailand.

March 22–June 9
AVIATION: After destructive typhoons ravage Guam and the Philippines, C-130s, C-141s, and C-5As of the Military Airlift Command (MAC) arrive to provide relief and rescue over 700 survivors.

March 26
AVIATION: At Edwards Air Force Base, California, the NASA Flight Research Center is renamed after the agency's former deputy administrator, Hugh L. Dryden.

March 28
AVIATION: Off the California coast, an A-6 Intruder fires the first Tomahawk cruise missile. This is a second-generation guided missile with an extremely accurate terrain-following radar.

April 1
AVIATION: At RAF Alconbury, England, the 527th Tactical Fighter Aggressor Squadron is activated by U.S. Air Force in Europe (USAFE) to provide fighter and reconnaissance pilots with advanced training.

1976

April 2

AVIATION: The last Douglas C-118A Liftmaster is flown to the "bone yard" at Davis Monthan Air Force Base for storage and ultimate disposal.

April 28–May 15

AVIATION: At Twenthe Air Base, the Netherlands, air crews from the U.S. Air Force in Europe (USAFE) participate in the first Allied Air Forces Central Europe Tactical Weapons meet.

May 6–June 5

AVIATION: At Aviano Air Base, Italy, air force personnel are called upon to assist the victims of destructive earthquakes that struck the Friuli region to the northeast.

May 7

MILITARY: At South Dakota State University, Martha Hahn becomes the first female lieutenant commissioned through ROTC. The ceremony is conducted by General William E. DuPuy, head of U.S. Army Training and Doctrine Command (TRADOC), who is also an alumnus of South Dakota State, class of 1941.

May 13–June 9

AVIATION: In the wake of Typhoons Olga and Pamela, which ravaged portions of Guam and the Philippine Islands, Air Rescue and Recovery helicopters are called into save 734 survivors. Military Airlift Command (MAC) transports also fly in 2,652 tons of relief and medical supplies.

May 21

AVIATION: The new Surface-to-Air Missile D, which has been in development since the 1960s, enters the service as the Patriot.

May 29

NAVAL: The navy commissions the *Tarawa*, the first multipurpose helicopter assault ship with a flight deck for handling helicopters and new AV-8A Harrier jump jets. It can also carry 1,900 fully equipped marines.

June 5

AVIATION: Over the White Sands Missile Range, New Mexico, an A-6 Intruder successfully launches a fully guided Tomahawk cruise missile for the first time. This remains a standard offensive weapon in navy arsenals today.

June 7–24

AVIATION: In South Korea, Operation Team Spirit unfolds over the next three weeks in a major test of that nation's tactical air control system. Several bases are involved in what becomes one of the largest such tactical exercises in the world.

June 20

NAVAL: In Beirut, Lebanon, elements of the Sixth Fleet evacuate civilians and foreign nationals in the wake of factional violence.

June 27

AVIATION: At Vandenberg Air Force Base, California, a Titan II intercontinental ballistic missile (ICBM) is launched for the first time with a universal space guidance system in place.

1976

June 28
AVIATION: In Colorado Springs, Colorado, the first woman cadet, Joan Olsen, is admitted to the U.S. Air Force Academy.

July 1
MILITARY: In Washington, D.C., the National Air and Space Museum, Smithsonian Institution, is opened to the public. It hosts over 20 million visitors in only two years, a benchmark making it the most visited museum in the world.

• At Fort Monroe, Virginia, the new Field Manual FM-100-5 is issued at the behest of General William E. DuPuy, the head of TRADOC. Unlike earlier editions, the new version emphasizes aggressive, small unit tactics coupled with rigorous training and heavy fire power. The new tactics are specifically designed to wear down numerically superior Warsaw Pact units in a European conflict. This is also the conceptual beginning of the "AirLand Battle," which closely integrates air power and ground forces to overpower an enemy.

July 7
MILITARY: At the U.S. Military Academy, West Point, New York, the first female cadets are enrolled in the class of 1980. Ultimately, 119 are accepted.

July 12
MILITARY: In Washington, D.C., Secretary of the Army Martin R. Hoffman overturns an earlier decision to eliminate the Chemical Corps after learning that the Soviet Union is placing renewed emphasis on chemical and biological warfare.

July 15
AVIATION: At Mather Air Force Base, California, U.S. Navy and Marine Corps navigators report for training alongside their U.S. Air Force counterparts. This is the first time such instruction has been consolidated for all three services.

July 20
AVIATION: The *Viking 1* probe makes a soft landing on Mars and beams back the first televised images from the Red Planet. This is also the seventh anniversary of man's first walk on the moon.

July 27
NAVAL: Off Beirut, Lebanon, the amphibious transport dock *Coronado* evacuates 160 Americans and 148 foreign nationals during a period of civil war. The operation is covered by jets from the carriers *America* and *Nimitz*.
MARINES: Civil war in Beirut, Lebanon, prompts the 32nd Marine Amphibious Unit to go ashore to rescue American citizens.

July 27–28
AVIATION: Over Edwards Air Force Base, California, an SR-71 Blackbird flown by Majors Adolphus Bledsoe and John T. Fuller establishes three world records: an absolute speed record of 2,092 miles per hour with a 2,200 pound payload, an absolute jet speed record of 2,193 miles per hour over a 15–25 kilometer course, and an absolute sustained altitude in level flight of 85,069 feet.

July 28
AVIATION: A Lockheed SR-71 Blackbird flown by Captain Eldon W. Joersz and Major George T. Morgan sets new speed and altitude records of 2,193 miles per

hour at 85,069 feet over a 15–25 kilometer straight course. Another Blackbird flown by Captain Robert C. Helt and Major Lang A. Elliot reaches an altitude of 85,069 feet, both absolute and jet records for altitude in horizontal flight.

August 1–2
AVIATION: In Big Thompson Canyon, Colorado, two air force UH-1 helicopters are dispatched to save 81 people stranded by flash floods.

August 18
MILITARY: At Panmunjom, Korea, Captain Arthur Bonifas and Lieutenant Mark Barrett are attacked and killed by North Koreans as they prune a tree obstructing surveillance of the Demilitarized Zone (DMZ) between North and South Korea. Four other soldiers are injured in the fracas and American forces are placed on full alert in consequence.

August 20
AVIATION: Following the murder of two American officers by North Koreans, C-5A Galaxy and C-141 Starlifter transports convey air and ground crewmen to various air bases throughout South Korea.

August 21
MILITARY: Operation Paul Bunyon, a show of force that includes fully armed soldiers, helicopter gunships, and B-52 bombers, unfolds as American soldiers return to the Demilitarized Zone (DMZ) in South Korea, and prune several trees under North Korean noses. The late Arthur Bonifas is also posthumously promoted to major and the UN compound at Panmunjom is renamed Camp Bonifas.

August 23
MILITARY: In Washington, D.C., Secretary of the Army Martin R. Hoffman announces that the 149 West Point cadets implicated in a cheating scandal can regain admittance following a one-year probationary period for "reflection." The decision is criticized by several ranking officers, including Brigadier General Walter R. Ulmer, the academy commandant.

August 28
NAVAL: In the Ionian Sea, the frigate *Voge* collides with a Soviet Echo II guided-missile submarine, with both vessels suffering damage.

September 1
MARINES: The old sateen (green) uniform gives way to a new, camouflage utility design.

September 6
AVIATION: On Hokkaido, Japan, Soviet pilot Lieutenant Vicktor Belenko defects with his top-secret MiG-25 Foxbat fighter; the craft is closely examined by air force authorities before being returned to the Russians on November 15. The craft provides valuable insights into Soviet aircraft construction and electronics, which prove to be a deft combination of brilliant and primitive.

September 9
AVIATION: At the White Sands Missile Range, New Mexico, testing of the new air-launched cruise missile (ALCM) begins as it guides itself along preset coordinates.

September 14
NAVAL: In the Atlantic Ocean north of Scotland, the carrier *John F. Kennedy* and the destroyer *Bordelon* collide; the latter loses six killed and is damaged beyond repair. This is the *Kennedy*'s second major accident in only 10 months.

September 16
DIPLOMACY: Eniwetok Atoll, site of the first American hydrogen bomb detonation, is returned to the original inhabitants after several decades of cleaning up residue radioactivity.

September 29
AVIATION: Another gender barrier falls at Williams Air Force Base, Arizona, when 10 women enter undergraduate pilot training for the first time since World War II.

September 30
NAVAL: The navy decommissions the *Oriskany,* the last-surviving *Essex*-class carrier and a veteran of the Korean War and the Vietnam War.

October 1
MILITARY: In Washington, D.C., General Bernard W. Rogers gains appointment as the 28th army chief of staff. He is also the last World War II veteran to hold this position.

October 7
NAVAL: In a new organization scheme, the 12 Navy Commands in the continental United States are consolidated into only four, with headquarters at Seattle, Washington; Great Lakes, Illinois; Philadelphia, Pennsylvania; and Washington, D.C.

November 13
NAVAL: The navy commissions the *Los Angeles,* the first in an entirely new generation of nuclear attack submarines. With a length of 360 feet and a submerged speed of 30 knots, these are the largest vessels of their class ever built. Moreover, they are armed with Tomahawk, Sub-Harpoon, and SUBROC missiles.

November 23
MILITARY: At Fort Rucker, Alabama, the Silver Eagles precision-flying helicopter team is disbanded for budgetary reasons. In their four-year existence, they operated OH-6A Cayuse and OH-58A Kiowa helicopters.

November 29
AVIATION: After an earthquake devastates parts of Turkey, C-141 Starlifters of the Military Airlift Command (MAC) begin flying in medical and relief supplies to Incirlik Air Base, Turkey.

December 8
AVIATION: At Fort Worth, Texas, the first production General Dynamics F-16 Fighting Falcon successfully performs its maiden flight.

December 15
MILITARY: The Borman Commission, headed by former astronaut Frank Borman, releases its final report relative to the West Point cheating scandal. Its several recommendations include allowing accused students to be readmitted, halting

1976

further investigations, and placing greater emphasis on the Cadet Honor Code. The army accepts most of these recommendations.

December 19
AVIATION: The new KH-11 Kennan reconnaissance satellite is launched, being the first capable of relaying real-time, digitally enhanced images back to Earth.

1977

January 1
AVIATION: At Holloman Air Force Base, New Mexico, the 479th Tactical Training Wing is formed with three squadrons of Northrop T-38 Talon aircraft. These have been modified to carry gunsights and practice bomb dispensers. The 479th also constitutes the backbone of the Fighter Lead-in School for future combat pilots.
MILITARY: At Arlington Hall, Virginia, army intelligence activities are consolidated through creation of the new U.S. Army Intelligence and Security Command (INSCOM) under Brigadier General William I. Rolya.

January 8
AVIATION: At Marietta, Georgia, Lockheed unveils the first stretched YC-141B Starlifter, which is 23 feet longer than the original model and, being equipped with an aerial fueling receptacle, has both increased cargo capacity and unlimited range.

January 10
AVIATION: In Washington, D.C., Chief of Naval Operations admiral Arleigh Burke receives the Medal of Freedom, the nation's highest civilian decoration.

January 16
NAVAL: In Barcelona, Spain, the amphibious transport dock *Trenton* collides with the Spanish merchant vessel *Urlea,* killing 49 sailors and marines.

January 18
AVIATION: Off Cape Canaveral, Florida, the new C-4 Trident ballistic missile is successfully test-launched for the first time. These large weapons, possessing a range of 4,350 miles, are designed for the new *Ohio*-class ballistic submarines, which are due to arrive soon.

January 20
MILITARY: In Washington, D.C. Jimmy Carter is sworn in as the 39th president and commander in chief.

January 21
MILITARY: President Jimmy Carter grants unconditional amnesty to all remaining draft dodgers from the Vietnam War. An estimated 13,000 are still residing in Canada.

January 31–February 11
AVIATION: In the wake of a massive winter storm that blankets and paralyzes much of western New York and Pennsylvania, transports of the Military Airlift Command (MAC) deliver 1,160 tons of snow removal equipment and 495 operating personnel to Buffalo and Pittsburgh.

February 14
MILITARY: In Washington, D.C., Clifford Irving becomes the first African American appointed as the 13th secretary of the army.
NAVAL: W. Graham Clayton, Jr., gains appointment as the 63rd secretary of the navy.

February 18
AVIATION: The space shuttle *Enterprise* makes its first captive flight atop a specially modified Boeing 747.

March 1
AVIATION: At RAF Lakenheath, England, the 48th Tactical Fighter Wing receives its first F-111F strike fighters.

March 9
MILITARY: President Jimmy Carter declares that all U.S. military personnel will be withdrawn from South Korea within five years.

March 10
AVIATION: Another gender barrier falls when the first women navigator candidates arrive at Mather Air Force Base, California, for undergraduate navigation instruction.

March 17
MARINES: In Barcelona Harbor, Spain, a merchant vessel strikes a landing craft carrying a liberty party from the 34th Marine Amphibious Unit; 24 marines and 25 sailors are drowned.

March 23
AVIATION: At Tinker Air Force Base, Oklahoma, the first Boeing E-3A Sentinel is deployed with the Tactical Air Command (TAC). This highly sophisticated aircraft is instantly recognizable due to the large rotating antenna disc on the top of its fuselage. Thus, the U.S. Air Force initiates a revolution in command and combat functions by air fielding the first fleet of Airborne Warning and Control System (AWACS), which can monitor and direct several warplanes in combat simultaneously.

March 24
AVIATION: The stretched YC-141B Starlifter performs its maiden flight for the first time.

March 26–April 11
AVIATION: In South Korea, Exercise Team Spirit '77 involves 548 air force, navy, and Marine Corps aircraft, which fly a total of 6,400 sorties.

March 27–30
AVIATION: The worst aviation disaster in aviation history occurs when two Boeing 747 Jumbojets from Pan Am and KLM collide on Tenerife, Canary Islands, killing 500 people. Air force C-130s are immediately dispatched to the scene with medical personnel and equipment and fly crash victims to nearby Las Palmas, where C-141 Starlifters take them to the United States for treatment.

1977

March 31
MARINES: Sergeant Major John R. Massaro becomes the eighth Sergeant Major of the Marine Corps.

April 14
AVIATION: A pair of Soviet Tu-95 Bear maritime reconnaissance aircraft suddenly appear on the radar scopes off Charleston, South Carolina, then slip below radar coverage and reappear off Jacksonville, Florida. No serious harm results other than a major embarrassment to air force air defenses.

April 28
MILITARY: Christopher J. Boyce and Andrew Lee are convicted of selling the Soviets top-secret American satellite information; Boyce is sentenced to 40 years in jail, Lee to life.

May
AVIATION: In Colorado, the U.S. Air Force Academy selects the DeHaviland DHC-6 Twin Otter for its parachute jump program. It receives the new designation UV-18B and operates from nearby Peterson Air Force Base.

May 2
AVIATION: A major gender barrier falls as Lieutenant Christine E. Schott becomes the first female undergraduate pilot to solo in a T-38 Talon jet training aircraft.

May 17
MARINES: In the Washington Navy Yard, D.C., the Marine Corps Historical Center opens for research.

May 19
AVIATION: A B-52 bomber flown by instructor pilot Captain James A. Yule experiences a severe inflight emergency, but Yule manages to keep his craft flying and lands safely. He wins a Mackay Trophy for his achievement.

May 26
MARINES: Males and females graduate from the Marine Corps Basic School for the first time.

June 10
MILITARY: In Washington, D.C., Secretary of the Army Clifford Alexander restores to Dr. Mary Walker her Medal of Honor, which she received for distinguished service during the Civil War. It was rescinded in 1917 in an attempt to correct errors in the issuance of medals. Walker remains the only female recipient.

June 19
AVIATION: A C-5A Galaxy flown by Captain David M. Sprinkel of the 436th Military Airlift Wing lands at Sheremetyevo Airport in Moscow, Soviet Union, bringing a huge, superconducting electromagnet and supporting equipment in a scientific energy research exchange. The 5,124-mile flight originated in Chicago, Illinois, and required two in-flight refuelings to complete. Sprinkel's crew wins a Mackay Trophy for their efforts.

June 30

AVIATION: Fulfilling a campaign promise, President Jimmy Carter cancels production of the new Rockwell B-1A strategic jet bomber, although he allows four prototypes to continue flying for testing purposes.

MARINES: Headquarters Marine Corps abolishes the director of women marines as female marines no longer exist as a separate category.

• At this point in the cold war, marine manpower levels are 18,650 officers and 176,057 enlisted men.

July 12

MILITARY: In Washington, D.C., President Jimmy Carter requests funding to build enhanced radiation weapons, the so-called neutron bomb, which features a lower yield and smaller blast results. The weapon is slated for deployment with Lance missiles and 155mm howitzer units, but it goes no further than the developmental stage.

July 14

AVIATION: Along the Demilitarized Zone (DMZ), South Korea, an army CH-47 Chinook transport helicopter strays into North Korean airspace and is shot down. Three Americans are killed and one wounded; all are returned to Panmunjom within days.

August 3

AVIATION: At Colorado Springs, Colorado, Cadet Colonel Edward A. Rice becomes the first African American to serve as cadet wing commander, the highest cadet leadership position on campus.

August 4

AVIATION: At Davis Monthan Air Force Base, the last operational Lockheed T-33 jet trainer, the beloved "T-Bird," flies in for a rendezvous with the Bone Yard.

August 12

AVIATION: At Edwards Air Force Base, California, the Space Shuttle *Enterprise* is released from a specially modified Boeing 747 and successfully performs its first unpowered glide flight from 22,800 feet. It is flown by two air force veterans, Fred Haise and C. Gordon Fullerton, whose landing is observed by a crowd estimated at 80,000 people.

August 15

AVIATION: Over California, two C-130B Hercules aircraft make a total of 38 fire-retardant drops on several major forest fires.

September 1

AVIATION: At Kaneohe, Hawaii, HMM-265 is reactivated after seven years in hiatus.

September 2

AVIATION: Another gender barrier falls when the first female air force pilots receive their wings at Williams Air Force Base.

September 3

AVIATION: The air force incinerates its last remaining stocks of the defoliant Agent Orange at sea, west of Johnson Island in the Pacific. This substance has been implicated in outbreaks of cancer associated among those working with it.

1977

September 7
DIPLOMACY: In Washington, D.C., President Jimmy Carter and Panamanian strongman Omar Torrijos conclude a treaty that will turn over the Panama Canal zone to Panama by 2000. A second agreement insures the neutrality of the canal zone in the event of war.

September 28
MILITARY: At Fort McClellan, Alabama, the Women's Army Corps graduates its last class of 129 attendees of the Officers Orientation Course.

September 30
AVIATION: At Charleston, South Carolina, a C-141 Starlifter takes off without navigation equipment and flies directly to the Rota Naval Air Station, Spain, using a Delco internal navigation system.

October 1
AVIATION: At Howard Air Force Base, Panama Canal Zone, Operation Volant Oak commences as Air Force Reserve and Air National Guard C-130 aircraft and crews begin quarterly deployments.

October 12
AVIATION: At Mather Air Force Base, the first five women graduates from undergraduate navigator training (UNT); three of the women end up with the Military Airlift Command (MAC).

October 21
AVIATION: Over Mindoro Island, the Philippines, a marine CH-53D helicopter crashes, killing 23 marines and injuring 13.

November 17
MARINES: At Camp Pendleton, California, the 1st Battalion, 4th Marines arrives as part of a new unit deployment plan (UDP) that rotates units to the Far East for six months to maintain unit cohesion and hone combat skills.

November 18
MILITARY: At the White Sands Missile Range, New Mexico, the first flight tests of the new Pershing II ballistic missile are successfully conducted. This new battlefield nuclear weapon is designed to counter a threat posed by the Soviet SS-20 missile.

November 21
MILITARY: At Fort Bragg, North Carolina, the 1st Special Forces Operational Detachment-Delta (1st SFOD-D) is created under Colonel Charles "Chargin' Charlie" Beckwith. In contrasts to existing Special Forces, which are largely instructional and reconnaissance units, Delta Force is a counterterrorist unit specializing in hostage rescues. Its field operations remain highly classified and the army continues to disavow its existence.

November 30
AVIATION: In Japan, the air force returns control of Tachikawa Air Base to the government for the first time since 1945.

December 6
AVIATION: At Hahn Air Base, West Germany, the first contingency launch and recovery airfields are constructed as part of the overall survivability program instituted by the U.S. Air Force in Europe (USAFE).

1977

December 17
NAVAL: The navy commissions the frigate *Oliver Hazard Perry*, the first of 51 vessels comprising this class.

December 20
MILITARY: In Washington, D.C., Secretary of the Army Clifford Alexander announces that while many positions within the army are open to women, they remain excluded from combat arms, including infantry, armor, engineers, and air-defense units.

1978

January
AVIATION: A C-141 Starlifter is dispatched by the Military Airlift Command (MAC) to Alberta, Canada, with Department of Energy personnel and equipment after a nuclear-powered Soviet satellite breaks up over the Canadian wilderness.
MILITARY: After the Midwest and Northeast are struck by a massive blizzard that dumps 30 inches of snow, thousands of National Guard, reservists, and regular army troops are mobilized to assist stranded civilians.

January 24
AVIATION: In their first operational deployment to the Western Pacific, eight F-15 Eagles fly from Langley Air Force Base, Virginia, to Osan Air Base, South Korea.
MILITARY: The 761st Tank Battalion, comprised mostly of African Americans, receives a Presidential Unit Citation, 33 years after World War II. It fought exceptionally well during the dash across northern France in 1944.

February 1
AVIATION: Off the California coast, a Tomahawk missile is successfully fired underwater for the first time by the submarine *Barb*.

February 8–17
AVIATION: Operation Snow Blow II unfolds as air force C-5As, C-130s, and C-141s convey over 2,300 tons of snow-removal equipment and over 1,000 passengers to heavily hit parts of southern New England.

February 9
AVIATION: The navy initiates the revolutionary Fleet Satellite Communications System, which provides improved command and control functions for the fleet, anywhere in the world.
MILITARY: The army adopts a new kelvar helmet, strongly reminiscent of the German helmets of World Wars I and II, to replace the old M1 "steelpot." New and more effective kelvar body armor is also taken into service.

February 22
AVIATION: An Atlas F booster rocket hurls *NAVSTAR 1* (Navigation System with Timing and Range), the first Global Positioning System (GPS), into Earth orbit. This is the first of 24 such devices intended to revolutionize both navigation and weapons accuracy. The final element does not reach space until 1994.

February 25–26
AVIATION: A C-141 Starlifter is dispatched by the Military Airlift Command to convey 12 burn specialists from Newark, New Jersey, to Waverly, Tennessee, following a propane-filled railway tank car explosion.

March 11
NAVAL: A navy milestone is reached when the fleet ballistic submarine *Abraham Lincoln* becomes the first vessel of its class to complete 50 operational patrols. This translates into 8½ years submerged and a distance of 420,000 miles.

March 19
AVIATION: The U.S. Air Force in Europe (USAFE) arranges for air force F-15 Eagles and navy F-14 Tomcats to begin joint training operations against each other.

March 23
AVIATION: Captain Sandra M. Scott becomes the first female tanker aircraft commander to conduct KC-135 refueling operations for the Strategic Air Command (SAC).

April 7
MILITARY: President Jimmy Carter decides to postpone development of the so-called neutron bomb, which utilizes high radiation bursts to kill people while inflicting relatively little damage on property or surroundings.

April 9–11
MARINES: At Twenty-Nine Palms, California, the 5th Marine Amphibious Brigade wages Palm Tree 5-78, a live-fire exercise involving 6,000 troops. This is the largest maneuver of its kind held at Twenty-Nine Palms.

May 6
MARINES: At Quantico, Virginia, the Marine Corps Aviation Museum is opened at Brown Field.

May 11
MARINES: Colonel Margaret A. Brewer becomes the first female marine to reach the grade of brigadier general.

May 20–23
AVIATION: Two C-5A Galaxies piloted by Captains Robert F. Schultz and Todd H. Hohberger endure crew fatigue and other hardships while conveying French and Belgian troops to Africa during Operation Zaire I. Once there they help evacuate European citizens threatened by a revolt by Katanga rebels. For their actions, Schultz and Hohberger win the Mackay Trophy.

May 31–June 16
AVIATION: Continuing strife in Zaire results in Operation Zaire II, during which Air Force transports convey 1,600 tons of supplies and 1,225 peacekeeping troops in 72 sorties.

July 1
NAVAL: In Washington, D.C., Admiral Thomas B. Hayward gains appointment as the 21st chief of naval operations.

July 6
MARINES: At Camp Lejeune, North Carolina, Force Troops are renamed the 2nd Force Service Support Group; Force Troops at Camp Pendleton, California, and on Okinawa are also redesignated.

July 12
AVIATION: The last Boeing KC-97L Stratofreighter is dropped from the air force inventory following a quarter century of distinguished service.

July 27
AVIATION: At Bentwaters/Woodbridge RAF air bases, England, the 81st Tactical Fighter Wing deploys, bringing with them the first operational Fairchild/Republic A-10 Thunderbolt IIs. This aircraft is covered by so many protuberances that it acquires the affectionate name "Warthog."

August 14–16
AVIATION: In Khartoum, Sudan, air force C-141s arrive with 26 tons of food and medical supplies for victims of recent flooding.

August 17
AVIATION: At Fort Worth, Texas, the first production model General Dynamics F-16 Fighting Falcon is delivered to air force authorities.
NAVAL: After President Jimmy Carter vetoes a defense appropriations bill that included funding for a new carrier that he felt was unnecessary, Admiral James L. Holloway III testifies before Congress and convinces them to override Carter's veto.

August 18
AVIATION: At McConnell Air Force Base, Kansas, Airman First Class Tina M. Ponzer becomes the first female to perform missile maintenance with the 381st Strategic Missile Wing.

August 21
MARINES: At Twenty-Nine Palms, California, 2,000 reserve marines join the first Combined Arms Exercise (CAX), a challenging, air-ground live-fire operation that becomes a fixture of modern Marine Corps training.

August 24
AVIATION: Tragedy strikes the 381st Strategic Missile Wing at McConnell Air Force Base, Kansas, when escaping oxidizer from a Titan II launch complex kills two people and damages a silo.
• At RAF Bentwaters/Woodbridge, the first three A-10 Thunderbolt IIs deploy with the 81st Tactical Fighter Wing. These are also the first aircraft of their kind assigned to the U.S. Air Force in Europe, where they are expected to play a significant role in breaking up any Soviet armored attacks.

August 26
AVIATION: In a breakthrough gesture, the Communist government of Laos returns the remains of four U.S. servicemen killed in the Vietnam conflict.

August 28
NAVAL: At Annapolis, Maryland, Rear Admiral William P. Lawrence gains appointment as the 49th superintendent of the U.S. Naval Academy.

1978

September 16
AVIATION: At McConnell Air Force Base, Kansas, Lieutenant Patricia M. Fornes of the 381st Strategic Missile Wing is the first female officer to stand Titan II alert.

September 25
MILITARY: At the Redstone Arsenal, Alabama, the Hellfire AGM-114 laser-guided missile is successfully tested against ground targets. This particularly lethal device is intended for use in helicopter gunships.

October 17
MILITARY: Near the Demilitarized Zone (DMZ), South Korea, American and Korean troops uncover a North Korean tunnel dug four miles from Panmunjom. The tunnel runs along the traditional invasion route to Seoul and can accommodate several thousand heavily armed troops.

October 20
MILITARY: In Washington, D.C., President Jimmy Carter abolishes the Women's Army Corps (WAC) as a separate entity within the U.S. Army. Henceforth, all female personnel will be directly integrated into standing, noncombat army formations.
• At Fort McClellan, Alabama, Brigadier General Mary E. Clarke of the Army Military Police and Chemical Schools becomes the first female major general in army history. Previously, she was the last WAC director.
NAVAL: In Chesapeake Bay, the Coast Guard training cutter *Cuyahoga* accidentally collides with the Argentine freighter *Santa Cruz II* and sinks with a loss of 11 men.
MARINES: President Jimmy Carter signs legislation elevating the commandant of the Marine Corps to a full-fledged member of the Joint Chiefs of Staff (JCS).

October 23
AVIATION: The 24th Composite Wing dispatches two UH-1N Iroquois helicopters and one O-2A aircraft to Costa Rica to fly flood-assistance missions.

November
AVIATION: The air force orders its first stealth aircraft, the Lockheed F-117 Night Hawk, into production. It possesses the world's first radar-absorbing design.

November 1
MILITARY: At Fort McClellan, Alabama; Fort Jackson, South Carolina; Fort Dix, New Jersey; and Fort Leonard Wood, Missouri; male and female recruits are integrated into the same basic training units.
NAVAL: Nine female ensigns, recently graduated from the U.S. Naval Academy, are the first women assigned to serve in ships other than hospital vessels and transports.

November 18
AVIATION: The revamped Northrop F-18 prototype makes its maiden flight and enters service as the Hornet.

November 22–29
AVIATION: HH-53 Jolly Green Giant helicopters of the 55th Aerospace Rescue and Recovery Squadron (ARRS) help transport 900 bodies from Jonestown, Guyana,

to makeshift morgues in nearby Georgetown. They are fueled between stations by HC-130 aircraft. These people died in a bizarre mass suicide.
• At Boston, Massachusetts, the air force dispatches a C-141 Starlifter with six medical specialists and their equipment to Algiers, Algeria, to attend the critically ill president.

November 28
AVIATION: A C-141 Starlifter conveys 911 bodies of a mass suicide at Jonestown, Guyana, to Dover Air Force Base for identification and burial.

November 30
AVIATION: At Hill Air Force Base, Utah, the final Boeing Minuteman II intercontinental ballistic missile (ICBM) is delivered.

December 8–9
AVIATION: In Tehran, Iran, air force C-5A Galaxies and C-141 Starlifters hastily evacuate 900 citizens as the shah's regime begins collapsing.

December 16
MARINES: The announcement of normalized relations between the United States and the People's Republic of China leads to anti-American riots in Taipei, Taiwan. Marine security guards are forced to drive off protestors with tear gas and nightsticks.

December 27
NAVAL: Responding to a rising tide of internal strife in Iran, the carrier *Constellation* positions itself off Singapore in the event it is needed in the Persian Gulf region.

1979

January
MILITARY: Army manpower levels drop to 758,852, their lowest level since 1950.

January 1
MILITARY: In light of increasing use of unauthorized headgear worn by soldiers, U.S. Army Chief of Staff Bernard W. Rogers issues a directive allowing berets to be worn by Rangers (black) and Green Berets (green).

January 6
AVIATION: At Hill Air Force Base, Utah, the 388th Tactical Fighter Wing receives the first operational F-16 Falcon. This multirole aircraft is capable of performing air superiority and close support missions.

January 16
DIPLOMACY: A rising tide of Islamic extremism forces the shah of Iran to abdicate and flee the country, and threatens to roil the entire Persian Gulf region with anti-Western unrest.

January 26
AVIATION: The first F-16 Fighting Falcons are turned over to the Belgian air force.

January 29
AVIATION: All E-3A Sentry AWACS aircraft accept responsibilities as part of the continental air defense mission.

February 6
NAVAL: At the ports of Bandar Abbas and Char Bahar, Iran, 200 Americans and 240 foreign nationals are evacuated by the command ship *La Salle*, the destroyers *Blandy, Decatur, Hoel,* and *Kincaid,* and the frigate *Talbot*.

February 14
MARINES: In Tehran, Iran, Muslim fanatics attack the U.S. embassy, taking several marine guards prisoner for a week.

February 27
AVIATION: At St. Louis, Missouri, the improved F-15C Eagle performs its maiden flight.

March 9
AVIATION: Operation Flying Star unfolds as two E-3A AWACS aircraft are dispatched to Saudi Arabia following perceived threats from revolutionary Iran.

March 31
AVIATION: Over the Yellow Sea, an H-3 helicopter flown by Major James E. McArdle, Jr., rescues 28 Taiwanese seamen whose ship had run aground. For his efforts he wins the Mackay Trophy.
• The nuclear accident at Three Mile Island, Pennsylvania, results in C-5 Galaxy, C-141 Starlifter, and C-130 Hercules transports flying in lead-shielding and testing equipment to the afflicted area.

April
AVIATION: At Fort Rucker, Alabama, the army receives its first Sikorsky UH-60 Black Hawk transport helicopters that will replace the aging Bell UH-1 Hueys. This new vehicle is faster, carries more troops, and is more crash-survivable than older machines.

April 3–5
AVIATION: At Nandi International Airport, Fiji, two C-141s deliver 20 tons of food and supplies in the wake of Typhoon Meli.

April 10
AVIATION: Off Cape Canaveral, Florida, the first submerged launching of a C-4 Trident ballistic missile is made by the submarine *Francis Scott Key*; within a month, this vessel makes the first deterrence cruise entirely armed with Trident missiles.

April 13
AVIATION: The Military Airlift Command (MAC) dispatches a C-141 Starlifter with 20 tons of vegetable seed to assist famished inhabitants of Kamina, Zaire.

April 19–20
AVIATION: After earthquakes ravage Adriatic coastal regions, transports of the Military Airlift Command (MAC) deliver 139 tons of humanitarian supplies to Titograd International Airport, Yugoslavia.

May

Aviation: At Sembach Air Base, West Germany, the first forward operating Base (FOB) for A-10 Thunderbolt IIs is activated. This is a new phase in tactical planning that will allow air force jets to operate closer to the front in the event of a Soviet invasion.

May 2–3

Aviation: In Central Europe, two E-3A Sentry AWACS aircraft begin their first overseas training mission.

June–July

Marines: At Managua, Nicaragua, the marine guard helps evacuate 1,423 U.S. citizens and foreign nationals while Communist Sandinista forces overthrow the Somoza regime.

June 1

Aviation: At Lackland Air Force Base, Texas, the Air Force Community College departs for a new home as part of the Air University, Maxwell Air Force Base, Alabama.

• RAF Fairford, England, is activated as a base to support ongoing Strategic Air Command (SAC) tanker operations.

June 5

Aviation: In Washington, D.C., President Jimmy Carter authorizes development of the new MX intercontinental ballistic missile (ICBM).

June 20

Aviation: Lieutenant Donna A. Spruill becomes the first woman to qualify in a fixed wing airplane; to do so she was required to make several landings in a Grumman C-1 Trader onboard the carrier *Independence*.

June 22

Military: In Washington, D.C., General Edward C. Meyer is appointed the 29th secretary of the army. His tenure is spent in determining ways to make the army more easily and quickly deployable overseas.

June 25

Terrorism: In Belgium, General Alexander Haig, supreme allied NATO commander, narrowly escapes an assassination attempt when a bomb explodes near his motorcade. The device has apparently been placed by the Red Army Faction, an ultra-Left terrorist group.

July 1

Marines: In Washington, D.C., General Robert H. Barrows becomes the 27th commandant of the Marine Corps.

July 8–16

Aviation: To test the Single Integrated Operational Plan (SIOP), Operation Global Shield '79, which involves 100,000 members of the Strategic Air Command (SAC), commences. This intricate nuclear war plan exercise also involves hundreds of bombers, tankers, and missiles being placed on alert or dispersed to various locations. Hereafter, Global Shield remains an annual SAC exercise for the remaining cold war years.

1979

July 9
AVIATION: The *Voyager 2* space probe reaches the giant planet Jupiter and begins sending back incredible televised images of various Jovian moons and the planet's storm-swept surface.

July 19
NAVAL: As thousands of Vietnamese "boat people" flee Communist oppression and tyranny at home, President Jimmy Carter instructs the Seventh Fleet to begin rescuing them. A total of 1,800 are taken aboard this year, but many more perish at sea.

July 26
AVIATION: At Vandenberg Air Force Base, California, the air force test-launches its 400th Minuteman missile.

August 15
MARINES: Sergeant Major Leland D. Crawford becomes the ninth sergeant major of the Marine Corps.

August 31–November 21
AVIATION: Throughout the Caribbean, Military Airlift Command (MAC) cargo planes begin delivering 2,900 tons of relief supplies to islands devastated by Hurricanes David and Frederic.

September 1
MILITARY: Colonel Hazel W. Johnson, chief, U.S. Army Nurse Corps, becomes the first female African American promoted to brigadier general.

September 12
AVIATION: At RAF Fairford, England, the first two KC-135 Stratotankers deploy to assist Strategic Air Command (SAC) refueling operations.

September 15–22
AVIATION: Over Southern California, Air Force Reserve and Air National Guard C-130s fly 250 sorties, dropping 732,000 gallons of water and flame retardant in a massive firefighting operation.

October 1
AVIATION: The air force begins phasing out the Air Defense command by parceling out its responsibilities to the Strategic Air Command (SAC) and the Tactical Air Command (TAC).
MILITARY: In Washington, D.C., Secretary of the Army Clifford Alexander orders that enlistment qualifications between men and women be made identical.

October 17
MARINES: Responding to news that the Soviets have deployed a combat brigade for training purposes in Cuba, President Jimmy Carter orders the amphibious assault ship *Nassau* to land 1,800 marines at Guantánamo Bay.

October 19
AVIATION: At Yokota Air Base Japan, specially equipped C-141 Starlifters transport 38 severely burned marines back to Kelly Air Force Base, Texas, for treatment.

MARINES: At Camp Fuji, Japan, 13 marines of the 2nd Battalion, 4th Marines, are killed when Typhoon Tip punctures a 5,000-gallon fuel bladder and the gasoline ignites a barracks.

October 25
NAVAL: In Washington, D.C., Edward Hidalgo gains appointment as the 64th secretary of the navy; he is also the first Hispanic to hold that office.

October 26
AVIATION: At St. Louis, Missouri, McDonnell Douglas terminates production of its legendary F-4 Phantom II after a run of 5,000 machines.

October 30
MARINES: In San Salvador, El Salvador, the marine security detachment beats back an assault by 200 armed leftists until local authorities can restore order; two marines are injured.

November
MILITARY: The army adopts the camouflage Battle Dress Uniform (BDU), presently worn by paratroopers, rangers, and Special Forces as its standard field uniform. This replaces the standard green fatigues.

November 4
TERRORISM: In Tehran, Iran, militants students storm the U.S. embassy, seizing 52 hostages. Among them are Colonel Charles W. Scott and Master Sergeant Regis Ragan of the U.S. Military Assistance Advisory Group, who are held for the next 444 days. The marine security detachment, numbering 13 men, is also taken and held. President Jimmy Carter, however, seeks a peaceful, diplomatic end to the crisis.

November 20
TERRORISM: The U.S. embassy in Islamabad, Pakistan, is besieged by a hostile mob while seven marine security guards hold them off; one marine is killed.

November 21
MARINES: In Karachi, Pakistan, a hostile mob surrounds the U.S. consulate and they are restrained by marine security guards. However, because this detachment had two women present, the pilot program to integrate female personnel into embassy detachments is ended.

December
MARINES: In Washington, D.C., the secretary of defense announces a new doctrine, which requires the Marine Corps to establish a Maritime Prepositioning Force (MPF) of three squadrons, each consisting of five cargo ships with sufficient equipment and supplies to supply a Marine Amphibious brigade for 30 days.

December 2–21
AVIATION: After Typhoon Abby ravages the Majuro Atoll, Marshall Islands, Military Airlift Command (MAC) transports begin delivering 650 tons of relief supplies and 250 medical personnel to assist survivors.

December 3
TERRORISM: Near San Juan, Puerto Rico, terrorists fire upon a bus carrying naval personnel to Sabana Seca Naval Communications Center; two sailors are killed and 10 are wounded.

1979

December 7

MILITARY: Near the Demilitarized Zone (DMZ), South Korea, a patrol from the 2nd Division wanders into a North Korean minefield, killing one soldier and wounding two others.

December 12

AVIATION: The prototype SH-60 Seahawk, a navalized version of the army's UH-60 Blackhawk, flies for the first time; it remains a standard helicopter design with the fleet today.

December 14

MILITARY: In light of increasing Soviet strides in chemical and biological warfare, the U.S. Army chemical School reopens its doors at Fort McClellan, Alabama.

December 20

AVIATION: An Advanced Maneuvering Reentry Vehicle (AMARV) is launched onboard a Minuteman I Missile for the first time. This device employs a fully autonomous navigation system to avoid enemy antimissile weapons launched at it.

December 27

MILITARY: In Kabul, Afghanistan, Soviet special forces help spark a coup that brings down the current regime and installs a Communist puppet state. The Red Air Force begins airlifting thousands of troops into the country.

1980

January

MILITARY: The Soviet invasion of Afghanistan and the Iranian hostage situation leads to upswings in army recruitment, which boosts overall strength to 777,036 officers and men.

January 2–4

AVIATION: During a rather busy period, Military Airlift Command (MAC) transports deliver relief supplies to earthquake victims on Terceira Island, Azores. Two C-141s from the 437th Military Airlift Wing deliver 700 tents and 1,000 blankets. A C-141 from the 86th Military Airlift Squadron conveys 17 tons of humanitarian relief supplies for victims of Cyclone Claudette on the Indian Ocean island of Mauritius.

January 8

AVIATION: The government reveals that 300 air force personnel had taken part in military exercises in Egypt December last, a sign of growing rapprochement with that Arab nation.

January 10

NAVAL: Ensign Roberta McIntyre, serving onboard the submarine tender *Dixon*, becomes the first female naval officer to qualify in surface warfare.

January 14

NAVAL: In light of tensions with Iran, the carriers *Nimitz* and *Kitty Hawk* are ordered to join the *Midway* in the Persian Gulf with their respective battlegroups.

Grumman F-14A *Tomcat* flying alongside a Soviet TU-95RT *Bear D* maritime patrol aircraft. *(U.S. Navy)*

January 28
NAVAL: The Coast Guard buoy tender *Blackthorn* accidentally strikes the oil tanker *Capricorn* near the Skyway Bridge in Tampa Bay, Florida, killing 23 sailors.

February 5
NAVAL: In Washington, D.C., John F. Lehman, Jr., is appointed the 65th secretary of the navy. The centerpiece of his tenure is acquiring a 600-ship navy to ensure American national security.

February 25–28
AVIATION: Over the Philippines, F-15 Eagles launched from Clark Air Base intercept four Soviet Tu-95 Bear reconnaissance aircraft attempting to penetrate the local air defense zone.

February 28
MILITARY: The army deploys its first turbine-powered M1 Abrams tanks, which are still among the world's greatest fighting vehicles. These replace the older M60

1980

Patton tanks, even though both are armed with the same 105mm main gun. The M1A1, which arrives in 1985, boasts a more powerful, German-designed 120mm cannon.

March 1
MILITARY: President Jimmy Carter authorizes deployment of the new Rapid Deployment Joint Task Force (RDF), consisting mostly of members of the 82nd Airborne Division with Special Forces and Rangers units attached as needed.
NAVAL: The repair ship *Vulcan* completes the first six-month deployment of a U.S. Navy vessel with 57 women as part of its crew.
MARINES: The Rapid Deployment Joint Task Force (RDJTF) is established at Tampa, Florida, under Lieutenant General Paul X. Kelley. This is a headquarters unit intended to quickly assert control of amphibious and airborne quick-response units in times of crisis. Its initial focus is the Middle East.

March 12–14
AVIATION: Two B-52 bombers from the 644th Bombardment Squadron are ordered to fly around the world in order to locate Soviet warships in the Arabian Sea. The planes cover 22,000 miles in 43 hours at an average speed of 488 miles per hour. This is the third time since 1949 and 1957 that Strategic Air Command (SAC) bombers have circumnavigated the globe nonstop; the crews involved win a Mackay Trophy.

March 31
AVIATION: The air force turns over control of Naha Air Base, Okinawa, to the government of Japan for the first time since 1945.

April 2
MILITARY: In Washington, D.C., Secretary of Defense Harold Brown announces that members of the Women's Army Auxiliary Corps (WAAC) of World War II are to be considered military personnel for laws pertaining to the Veterans Administration.

April 6
AVIATION: At Beale Air Force Base, California, the C-141B Stratolifter performs its first operational mission by flying to RAF Mildenhall, England, which it completes in 11 hours and 12 minutes. One inflight refueling is also necessary.

April 7
AVIATION: In light of rising tensions between the United States and Iran, all Iranian military personnel currently attending military schools are ordered out of the country within four days. Several are forced to depart the Air Training Command.
DIPLOMACY: Five months into the hostage crisis, President Jimmy Carter orders diplomatic relations with Iran severed.

April 18
AVIATION: At Vandenberg Air Force Base, California, a $3 million Data Transfer System is constructed to assist space shuttle, missile testing, and global positioning system (GPS) satellite network.

April 22
AVIATION: Elements of the 33rd Aerospace Rescue and Recovery Squadron attempt to rescue 900 passengers from a ferry that sank 150 miles southeast of Manila, Philippines.

April 24
TERRORISM: After several months of failed negotiations to secure American hostages held in Tehran, Iran, by military students, President Jimmy Carter authorizes Operation Eagle Claw, a helicopter-borne commando mission to rescue them by force. This consists of a rescue team comprised of Delta Force operatives, Rangers, and Special Forces under Colonel Charles Beckwith. They are conveyed inland in eight RH-53 helicopters launched from the carrier *Nimitz*. At least three of the helicopters suffer from mechanical malfunctions as a result of encountering a dust storm and abort, at which point Beckwith cancels the attempt. However, the mission comes to grief at a landing zone christened Desert One, when an EC-130 transport and a helicopter collide in a sand storm, killing eight Americans and wounding five. Failure here occasions the rise of the U.S. Central Command (CENTCOM) to better orchestrate military operations in this theater.

May
AVIATION: Lieutenant Mary L. Wittick becomes the first female to attend air force helicopter flight training.

May 18–June 5
AVIATION: The powerful eruption of Mount St. Helens results in aircraft from the Aerospace Rescue Service (ARRS), Military Airlift Command (MAC), and the 9th Strategic Reconnaissance Wing to fly humanitarian and rescue missions to afflicted persons throughout the region. SR-71 Blackbirds also fly photographic sorties to assist ground rescue teams.

May 25
AVIATION: Radar-equipped OV-1 Mohawk reconnaissance aircraft operated by the Oregon National Guard are called in to survey the condition of Mount St. Helens following its violent eruption.
MILITARY: In the wake of the destructive Mount St. Helens eruption, National Guard troops are mobilized to search for survivors.

May 28
MILITARY: The service academies graduate their first women officers, with 61 from West Point, 55 from Annapolis, and 97 from the Air Force Academy.

June
MILITARY: Army chow, never exactly gourmet fare, takes a decided turn for the better when the new Meals-Ready-to-Eat (MREs) are adopted as standard field rations. The lowly C-rations have been replaced by dehydrated foods in airtight pouches, packing much higher nutritional content.

June 27
MILITARY: In another belated response to the Soviet invasion of Afghanistan, President Jimmy Carter signs legislation reactivating draft registration for 19- and 20-year-old men.

1980

June 30
MARINES: Presently, Marine Corps manpower levels stand at 18,198 officers and 170,271 enlisted men and women.

July
MARINES: At Twenty-Nine Palms, California, the 7th Marine Amphibious Brigade headquarters is activated as the first Marine Prepositioning Force (MPF). Once fully organized, it is ready to deploy by air to any port where an MPF squadron is located.

July 8
AVIATION: The McDonnell Douglas FSD F-15B (F-15E Strike Eagle) performs its maiden flight. This is a two-seat version with a Weapons Systems Officer (WSO) and is modified for ground strike roles.
NAVAL: Off Cuba, a force of 11 navy vessels and some P-3 maritime patrol craft assist 115,000 refugees fleeing from the Communist dictatorship of Fidel Castro. This goes down in history as the Mariel Boat Lift.

July 10–October 3
AVIATION: At Moody Air Force Base, Georgia, 12 F-4E Phantom IIs deploy to Egypt during Operation Proud Phantom, This is a training exercise to help the Egyptian air force, which recently acquired Phantom IIs of their own, to properly operate their aircraft.

July 28–30
AVIATION: At Clark Air Force Base, Philippines, the 3rd Tactical Fighter Wing dispatches four F-4E Phantom IIs to Tengah Air Base, Singapore. This is the first goodwill mission mounted by the air force since Singapore gained its independence in 1965.

July 30–August 1
AVIATION: Three C-130s dispatched from the 146th and 433rd Tactical Airlift Wings drop 10,500 gallons of fire retardant on raging forest fires in the San Bernardino National Forest, California.

August 7–16
AVIATION: After Hurricane Allen ravages Haiti and St. Lucia in the Caribbean, the Air Force Southern Command deploys transports to deliver 61 tons of relief supplies and a 107-person cleanup crew.

August 14
AVIATION: At Dobbins Air Force Base, Georgia, the first C-5A with modified wings makes its maiden flight. All 77 of these aircraft in service will be similarly modified to extend their service life into the 21st century.

August 22
NAVAL: At Annapolis, Maryland, Vice Admiral Edwin C. Waller III gains appointment as the 50th superintendent of the U.S. Naval Academy.

September 2
AVIATION: The air force provides an Air Weather Service detachment to assist NASA operations at the Johnson Space Center, Houston, Texas.

1980

September 10
AVIATION: In the wake of Typhoon Orchid, an HH-3E Jolly Green Giant helicopter is dispatched from Osan Air Base, South Korea, to rescue 229 people struggling in the Sea of Japan.
MILITARY: At Fort Lewis, Washington, the 9th Infantry Division begins experimenting with a smaller, lighter formation of 17,773, with the approval of U.S. Army Chief of Staff general Edward C. Meyer. Two years later the focus of divisional activities shifts to that of a more "motorized" organization.

September 16
AVIATION: Off Libya, a Libyan MiG-23 fighter attacks an air force RC-135 electronic surveillance aircraft, which employs drastic maneuvering to avoid being hit. Recently, the United States has stepped up electronic intelligence missions along Libya's coast.

September 18
MILITARY: At Little Rock Air Force Base, Arkansas, a Titan II missile of the 308th Strategic Missile Wing explodes in its silo, killing one airman and injuring 21.

September 20
AVIATION: The Pacific Air Forces (PACAF) dispatches two F-15s and an E-3A on goodwill trips to New Zealand, Malaysia, Singapore, and Thailand.

September 30
NAVAL: The Service Life Extension Program commences with the carrier *Saratoga*. It is designed to increase the longevity of warships in active service.

October 1
AVIATION: As the bloody Iran-Iraq War continues, Operation Elf One places E-3A AWACS aircraft and KC-135 tankers in Saudi Arabia to closely monitor military communications. They remain in place over the next eight years.
NAVAL: In Washington, D.C., the Office of Naval Warfare replaces the earlier designation of Office of Antisubmarine Warfare and Ocean Surveillance.

October 3
AVIATION: Over the Pacific Ocean, an HH-3 Jolly Green Giant helicopter piloted by Captain John J. Walters rescues 61 passengers from the Dutch cruise ship *Prinsendam* after it catches fire 120 mile south of Yakutat, Alaska. Captain Walters receives a Mackay Trophy for his efforts.

October 11
NAVAL: In light of continuing tensions with Iran and concerns over Saudi Arabian security, the guided-missile cruiser *Leahy* is ordered to the Persian Gulf to assist air force E-3 Airborne Warning and Control Systems (AWACS) aircraft already there.

October 12–23
AVIATION: Transports of the Military Airlift Command (MAC) begin transporting 400 tons of relief supplies and medical personnel to El Asnam, Algeria, following a destructive earthquake that kills 6,000 people.

October 16
MILITARY: At Fort Irwin, California, the new National Training Center (NTC) opens for service. This unique facility covers 1,000-square miles of the Mojave Desert, is highly automated with computers and laser equipment, and becomes the army's premier testing and training grounds for large-scale maneuvers.

October 17
AVIATION: In Washington, D.C., the secretary of defense orders the army to take control of Wheeler Air Force Base. That branch has been the principal user of the base since it was reactivated in 1952.

October 18
NAVAL: The guided missile cruiser *Arkansas* is commissioned, being the last nuclear-powered vessel acquired by the U.S. Navy; a total of eight are now in service.

October 20–23
AVIATION: The Southern Air Division routes transport aircraft to Nicaragua and conveys 40 tons of food and relief supplies in the aftermath of recent flooding there.

November 5
MILITARY: In light of budgetary restrictions, a new freeze in army civilian employee hiring requires soldiers to undertake tasks usually performed by civilians.

November 12–14
AVIATION: At Hahn Air Base, West Germany, the 50th Tactical Fighter Wing is ordered by U.S. Air Force in Europe (USAFE) to carry out its wartime mission in a simulated chemical warfare environment.

November 12–25
AVIATION: In Egypt, Rapid Deployment Force elements of the U.S. Air Force in Europe (USAFE) participate in Operation Bright Star, the first joint exercise held with Egyptian forces.

November 13
NAVAL: The Navy Department announces that 81-year-old Admiral Hyman Rickover will be retiring after his current extension expires on January 31, 1982. He has been in the forefront of the American nuclear navy for over three decades.

November 20
AVIATION: At RAF Lakenheath, the 48th Tactical Fighter Wing receives the first operational Pave Tack F-111. The Pave Tack system allows bombing missions under 24-hour, high- and low-altitude bomb runs.

November 21
AVIATION: Over Las Vegas, Nevada, helicopters from Nellis Air Force Base swoop in to rescue 310 guests from the burning 26-story MGM Grand Hotel.

November 23–December 2
AVIATION: Severe earthquakes around Naples, Italy, prompt the U.S. Air Force in Europe (USAFE) to dispatch transports with 300 tons of blankets, tents, and medical supplies for the survivors.

November 25
AVIATION: In England, the 26h Tactical Fighter Training Aggressor Squadron flies T-38 Talons for the last time. These aircraft are returned to the Air Training Command and replaced by F-5E Tiger II jets.

November 25–29
AVIATION: East of Los Angeles, California, transports of the Military Airlift Command (MAC) and the Air Force Airlift Readiness Center drop five tons of retardant on 11 fires raging in four different counties.

December 10
AVIATION: As the Iran-Iraq War rages in full fury, four additional Boeing E-3A AWACS aircraft are deployed to Ramstein Air Base, West Germany, to help monitor military events throughout the Middle East. An additional four E-3As are deployed to Europe to keep tabs on the ongoing crisis in Poland.

December 12
AVIATION: At Maxwell Air Force Base, Alabama, the Community College of the Air Force is accredited by the Commission on Colleges of the Southern Association. The degree program in question is an associate in applied science.

December 22
NAVAL: At Norfolk, Virginia, the carrier battle group consisting of the carrier *Dwight D. Eisenhower* and cruisers *South Carolina* and *Virginia* return to home port after 251 days at sea; this is the longest deployment of naval vessels since the end of World War II.

1981

January
MILITARY: In an attempt to boost recruiting, the U.S. Army Recruiting Command unveils its "Be all that you can be" campaign. This proves to be one of the most successful advertising efforts of the 20th century and brings in numerous high-quality recruits.

MARINES: The United States concludes an agreement with Norway to allow prepositioning supplies to be stored in special caves for possible use by Marine Corps forces in the event of a Soviet attack.

January–June
AVIATION: Military Airlift Command (MAC) transports based at Corpus Christi, Texas, and Little Rock, Arkansas, deliver 500 tons of military supplies to the government of El Salvador to help stave off a Communist insurgency supported by neighboring Nicaragua.

January 10–11
AVIATION: At Griffiss Air Force Base, New York, the first two Boeing air-launched cruise missiles (ALCMs) are delivered to the 416th Bombardment Wing for testing and maintenance training purposes. These revolutionary weapons possess a 1,500-mile range, carry nuclear or conventional warheads, and navigate through a precise terrain-contour matching system that allows high-speed ingress at low altitude.

January 12
TERRORISM: In Puerto Rico, nine A-7D Corsair II aircraft belonging to the 156th Tactical Fighter Group, Air National Guard, are destroyed by terrorists.

January 20
MILITARY: In Washington, D.C., Caspar Weinberger is appointed the 15th secretary of defense.
• In Washington, D.C., Ronald W. Reagan is sworn in as the 40th president of the United States and commander in chief.
TERRORISM: As if on cue, the Iran Islamic regime releases all American hostages following 444 days of captivity; apparently they decline seeking confrontation with a new, more assertive American government. The hostages are flown to Rhein-Mein Air Base, West Germany, on two Military Airlift Command (MAC) C-9 Nightingales.

January 22
MILITARY: In Washington, D.C., former U.S. Army general Alexander M. Haig is appointed the new secretary of state. He is only the second soldier to hold that position after George C. Marshall.

January 23
AVIATION: The 6594th Test Group dispatches two helicopters, which perform a hoist pickup of an injured seaman from a merchant vessel 240 miles west of Honolulu, Hawaii.

January 25
AVIATION: An air force VC-137 transport flies 52 former American hostages from Wiesbaden, West Germany, to the United States and freedom.

January 29
MILITARY: In Washington, D.C., John O. Marsh, Jr., gains appointment as the 14th secretary of the army. In time he becomes the longest serving secretary.

February 5
NAVAL: In Washington, D.C., John F. Lehman, Jr., a former staffer on the National Security Council, gains appointment as the 65th secretary of the navy. His quest to obtain a 600-ship navy becomes a centerpiece of the Reagan administration's defense buildup.

February 10
AVIATION: In Las Vegas, Nevada, three U-1 helicopters dispatched by the 57th Fighter Weapons Wing rescue nine guests trapped on the roof of the 30-story Las Vegas Hilton. The flames are partially extinguished by firefighters from Nellis Air Force base.

February 24
MILITARY: In Washington, D.C., President Ronald W. Reagan awards Special Forces Master Sergeant Ray Benavidez a Medal of Honor 13 years after his display of heroism on the battlefield in Vietnam. Originally, he received a Distinguished Service Cross for rescuing several Special Forces members under fire.

February 26–March 6
AVIATION: In the wake of severe earthquakes in central Greece, the 7206th Air Base Group, Hellenikon Air Base, assist relief efforts with supplies and equipment.

February 27
MILITARY: The army begins deploying its new Stinger, second-generation, shoulder-launched, surface-to arm missile to infantry units in Europe. It replaces the earlier and less capable Redeye missile system.

March 1
AVIATION: Marine HMH-464 is equipped with Sikorsky CH-53E Super Stallion helicopters, capable of inflight refueling and carrying twice the payload of earlier versions.

March 4
NAVAL: In Washington, D.C., Secretary of Defense Caspar Weinberger states that the battleships *Iowa* and *New Jersey,* and the carrier *Oriskany,* are slated for reactivation.

March 12
AVIATION: Peterson Air Force Base, Colorado, is chosen by the Aerospace Defense Command as the backup facility for the North American Aerospace Defense Command (NORAD) in the event of a peacetime technical failure.

March 17
AVIATION: The Strategic Air Command (SAC) takes delivery of its first McDonnell Douglas KC-10 Extender, which carries more fuel and cargo than the current KC-135 aircraft it will replace.

March 18
AVIATION: The 18th Tactical Fighter Wing accepts delivery of 80 F-15 Eagles and transfers its 79 F-4 Phantoms to other commands. This completes the conversion of the Pacific Air Forces to F-15 standards.

April 1
AVIATION: Ever concerned with honing the skills of its fighter pilots, the air force deploys the 527th Tactical Fighter Training Aggressor Squadron to RAF Alconbury, England. It is equipped with Northrop F-5E Tiger IIs, which simulate Soviet fighters during air-to-air combat drills.

April 3
MILITARY: Colonel Harry G. Summers publishes his seminal text *On Strategy: The Vietnam War in Context.* In it, the author maintains that the United States should have waged a conventional war against the Viet Cong and North Vietnamese, instead of gradually escalating guerrilla conflict that allowed the enemy time to adapt. This document is a product of the Strategic Studies Institute of the Army War College.

April 8
MILITARY: In New York City, General Omar N. Bradley dies; at the time he is the army's senior officer and last five-star general.

1981

Haig, Alexander M.   (1924–2010)

Army general, secretary of state

Alexander Meigs Haig was born in Philadelphia, Pennsylvania, on December 2, 1924, and he gained admittance to the U.S. Military Academy in 1944. He was commissioned a second lieutenant four years later and served with distinction with the X Corps in Korea under General Edward M. Almond. Haig rose to captain in 1950 and held routine assignments over the next 15 years and also obtained a master's degree in international relations at Georgetown University in 1961. He subsequently served as assistant to Secretary of the Army Cyrus Vance before returning to active duty in Vietnam. In 1966 Haig helped to win the Battle of Ap Gu while leading the 26th Infantry Regiment, and he returned to the United States as a colonel and part of President Richard M. Nixon's inner circle. He helped to craft Nixon's successful visit to China in 1972, and, that September, Nixon promoted him two grades to full general over the heads of 240 officers with more seniority. Haig served the next president, Gerald Ford, with an appointment as NATO supreme allied commander, and was largely responsible for upgrading nuclear forces, training, and strategy. However, he disagreed with President Jimmy Carter's vacillating policy toward the Soviet Union and resigned his commission in July 1979.

In 1980 Haig's outspoken criticism of Carter came to the attention of President Ronald W. Reagan, who appointed him the new secretary of state. Haig crafted a deliberately confrontational strategy toward the Soviet Union and its Commu-

nist allies, which included sending military aid to Afghan freedom fighters and arming the Nicaraguan contra rebels in their struggle against the Communist Sandinistas. He also persuaded the administration to deploy new Pershing II and cruise missiles in Western Europe to counter the Soviet buildup of nuclear SS-20 missiles in the East. However, he clashed strongly with Vice President George H. W. Bush and Secretary of Defense Caspar Weinburger, who felt that clandestinely arming the contras against the congressional will was illegal. Haig was also embarrassed and frustrated by his inability to prevent two nominal allies, Great Britain and Argentina, from going to war over the Falkland Islands in 1982. Afterwards, he sided with the British and provided them logistical support, which won him few friends in Latin America. He also made a major misstep following the attempted assassination of President Reagan in March 1981 by declaring himself "in charge of the White House." Feeling that his presence in the administration was counterproductive to President Reagan, Haig tended his resignation in June 1982. He resided in Washington, D.C., and made an unsuccessful bid for the Republican Party presidential nomination in 1988. He continued to serve as a political commentator on television until his death on February 20, 2010. Haig's legacy as one of the most effective secretaries of state, whose policies helped defeat communist regimes in Russia, Afghanistan, and Nicaragua, is secure.

April 9

NAVAL: South of Sasebo, Japan, the fleet ballistic missile submarine *George Washington* collides with the Japanese merchantman *Nissho Maru* while surfacing, killing two crewmen from the latter. The submarine captain is relieved of duty and receives a letter of official reprimand.

April 12–14

AVIATION: At Cape Canaveral, Florida, the space shuttle *Columbia* is launched for the first time with an all-navy crew consisting of Captain John W. Young and Captain Robert L. Crippen. This milestone flight involves taking off like a rocket and then returning to Earth as a conventional airplane. Communication with the shuttle in space is also facilitated by the Aerospace Defense Command and the Air Force Communications Command.

April 13

AVIATION: Two Marine Corps Harrier jump jet squadrons are deployed on an assault vessel to test how well they augment fixed-wing elements in the fleet during a contingency.

April 21

DIPLOMACY: The United States agrees to sell Saudi Arabia $1 billion worth of advanced military equipment, including five sophisticated AWACS electronic aircraft, despite protests from Israel.

April 24

MILITARY: The government announces that a new military command will be created for protecting American interests in the Persian Gulf region.

May 2

AVIATION: At White Sands Missile Range, New Mexico, an aerial target drone is successfully shot down by the Airborne Laser Laboratory (ALL) aircraft. This is a modified KC-135 carrying a carbon dioxide laser.

May 28

AVIATION: Off the Florida coast, a Marine EA-6B Prowler crashes on the carrier *Nimitz* during a night landing; all four marines onboard are killed, along with 10 sailors. A further 48 men are injured and 20 aircraft are damaged or destroyed.

June 14

AVIATION: The 32nd and 36th Tactical Fighter Wings, U.S. Air Force in Europe (USAFE) contribute a total of seven F-15s to the Tactical Air Command's Red Flag exercise.

June 17

NAVAL: At Charleston, South Carolina, the fleet ballistic missile submarine *James K. Polk* returns to port, concluding the 2,000th cold war deterrent patrol made by navy vessels.

June 18

AVIATION: At Tonopah Test Range, Nevada, the revolutionary Lockheed F-117 Night Hawk stealth aircraft makes its first successful flight at night. Extreme secrecy surrounds the test program until 1988.

1981

June 25
MILITARY: The U.S. Supreme Court rules that draft registration can exclude women without violating the U.S. Constitution.

June 27
NAVAL: The fleet ballistic submarine *James K. Polk* completes the navy's 2,000th deterrence patrol.

July
AVIATION: South of Osan Air Base, South Korea, helicopters of the 33rd Aerospace Rescue and Recovery Squadron (ARRS) assist 118 people from rising floodwaters.

July 1
NAVAL: In Washington, D.C., Admiral James D. Watkins gains appointment as the 22nd chief of naval operations.

July 27
NAVAL: The destroyer *Kidd* is commissioned by the navy; this vessel was originally intended for service with the Iranian navy but has since been retained in American service. It differs from other *Spruance*-class destroyers in being armed with missiles.

August 3
AVIATION: Once civilian air traffic controllers stage an illegal strike, air force controllers are called in to fill in the gaps and allow commercial air travel to continue safely.

August 10
MILITARY: President Ronald W. Reagan, determined to increase pressure on the Soviet Union, authorizes production of the new neutron warhead for missiles and artillery.

August 15
AVIATION: At Griffiss Air Force Base, New York, the first B-52G bomber outfitted to carry air-launched cruise missiles (ACLMs) is deployed. This adds new and potentially lethal capabilities to the aging aircraft.

August 19
AVIATION: VF-41 F-14 Tomcats from the carrier *Nimitz* down two Libyan Su-22 jets over the Gulf of Sidra, 60 miles from the Libyan coast, after they fired on the Americans in international airspace. Previously, Libyan dictator Moammar Qaddafi had proclaimed a "line of death" that any American vessel would face should it cross.

August 22
NAVAL: In Annapolis, Maryland, Vice Admiral Edwin C. Waller III gains appointment as superintendent of the U.S. Naval Academy.

September 14
AVIATION: At Kunsan Air Base, South Korea, the first operational F-16 Falcons from the Pacific Air Forces (PACAF) are deployed.

September 15
AVIATION: The Strategic Air Command (SAC) accepts delivery of its first Lockheed TR-1A strategic reconnaissance aircraft; this is the latest version of the venerable U-2 spyplane and can perform all-weather operations from altitudes of 70,000 feet.

• At RAF Lakenheath, the 494th Tactical Fighter Squadron deploys; this is the first unit equipped with Pave Tack laser-guided weapons systems mounted on their F-111s.

TERRORISM: In West Germany, a car driven by General Frederick J. Koersen is attacked by terrorists firing a rocket-propelled grenade (RPG) launcher. However, he and his wife emerge unscathed. This is the latest attack by the Red Army Faction terror outfit.

September 21
AVIATION: At Clark Air Force Base, Philippines, helicopters of the Aerospace Rescue and Recovery Squadrons (ARRS) rescue members of the grounded Philippine destroyer *Datu Kalantiaw*; in the past 35 years, the ARRS has rescued 20,000 people.

October
AVIATION: At Sheppard Air Force Base, the Euro-NATO Joint Jet Pilot Training Program commences.

October 1
AVIATION: At Mather Air Force Base, California, the Air Training Command initiates a program to train German weapons systems officers for service in the European Tornado fighter-bomber.

NAVAL: The fleet ballistic missile submarine *Robert E. Lee* completes the final cold war deterrent cruise while armed with aging Polaris A-3 missiles.

October 2
MILITARY: In Washington, D.C., President Ronald Reagan rises to the challenge of an aggressive Soviet Union by articulating a five-point buildup of American military strength. This includes production of 100 Rockwell B-1B Lancer strategic bombers, deployment of 100 new MX Peacekeeper missiles in existing super-hardened silos, and resumed development of the neutron bomb intended to wipe out Soviet tank columns without destroying Western Europe.

• Secretary of Defense Frank P. Carlucci orders the Titan II intercontinental ballistic missiles in service with the Strategic Air Command (SAC) inactivated. These obsolete, liquid-fueled weapon are to be replaced by the solid-fuel MX.

October 14
AVIATION: Following the assassination of Egyptian president Anwar Sadat, the Tactical Air Command (TAC) deploys two E-3A Sentry aircraft to monitor regional events in the Middle East.

October 20
MILITARY: At Fort Myer, Virginia, the army officially christens its new armored personnel carrier the M2/3 Bradley.

1981

October 21
AVIATION: At Sheppard Air Force Base, Texas, the Euro-North Atlantic Treaty Organization Joint Jet Pilot Training Program begins training candidates from NATO members. It is run along lines conducted by the German air force since 1966.

October 28
DIPLOMACY: President Ronald Reagan, determined to cement the strategic country of Saudi Arabia as an ally in the struggle with global communism and Islamic militarists in Iran, convinces Congress to sell the Savdis advanced F-15 Eagle fighter jets and sophisticated Airborne Warning and Control Systems (AWACS).

November 5
AVIATION: At Mountain Home, Idaho, the 388th Electronic Combat Squadron (ECS) deploys the first EF-111A Raven. Popularly known as the "Spark Vark," it is intended to replace all EB-66 and EB-57 aircraft in electronic warfare and defense suppression.

November 11
NAVAL: At Groton, Connecticut, the 18,700-ton fleet ballistic missile submarine *Ohio* is commissioned, being especially designed to carry 24 Trident missiles; 18 vessels are constructed in this class.

November 13
NAVAL: In Washington, D.C., 81-year-old Admiral Hyman Rickover is eased from active duty when his service extension is not renewed. As a sop, he gains appointment as a presidential adviser on nuclear science.

November 18
MEDIA: President Ronald W. Reagan give a televised address, broadcast live throughout Europe, outlining his decision to deploy medium-range Pershing II and cruise missiles if the Soviet Union does not dismantle all of its offensive weaponry in Eastern Europe.

November 23
AVIATION: Operation Bright Star '82 unfolds as eight B-52 bombers fly 15,000 miles from North Dakota to Egypt to drop training bombs on a practice airfield target. This is the longest B-52 bombing mission to date and concludes in 31 hours and three air refuelings.

December
MARINES: This month the 10th Marines, an artillery unit, is equipped with new M198 155mm howitzers.

December 1
MARINES: In Washington, D.C., Commandant Barrow institutes a stepped-up war against drug use in the Marine Corps through increased urinalysis.

December 17
TERRORISM: In Verona, Italy, the Italian terrorist Red Brigade kidnaps General James L. Dozier from his apartment.

December 31
AVIATION: At Hahn Air Base, West Germany, the first operational F-16s assigned to the U.S. Air Force in Europe (USAFE) are deployed with the 50th Tactical Fighter Wing.

1982

January
MILITARY: The 82nd Airborne Division is assigned the duty as UN Multinational Force and Observers (MFO) in the Sinai Peninsula between Egypt and Israel. It remains the army's longest-running peacekeeping mission.

January 13
AVIATION: In Washington, D.C., Air Florida Flight 90 crashes into the icy Potomac River after takeoff, prompting soldiers of the Military District of Washington to assist in the recovery of victims and wreckage.

January 17
AVIATION: Off Cape Kennedy, Florida, the fleet ballistic missile submarine *Ohio* fires a submerged Trident missile for the first time. Each Trident carries 14 independently targeted reentry warheads and has a range of 4,000 miles.

January 18
AVIATION: At Indian Springs, Nevada, four T-38 Talons belonging to the Thunderbirds demonstration team crash into the desert floor, killing four pilots. Accidents in the previous May and September also took the lives of two pilots.
TERRORISM: In Paris, France, Lieutenant Colonel Charles R. Ray, a military attaché at the American embassy, is assassinated by an unknown gunman.

January 26
AVIATION: At Edwards Air Force Base, California, major general and former astronaut Michael Collins flies his final flight in an F-16, then retires from active duty.

January 28
AVIATION: The first C-5A Galaxy transport to receive new wings is delivered to the Lockheed-Georgia plant. The cost of modifying 76 transports will set the taxpayers back $1.4 billion over the next few years.
TERRORISM: In Italy, Italian antiterrorist police, assisted by Delta Force commandos, rescue General James L. Dozier from captivity.

February 5
AVIATION: The Tacit Blue stealth technology demonstrator makes its first secret flight. The so-called Whale, built by Northrop, makes a total of 135 clandestine flights to evaluate radar cross-reduction techniques.

February 13
AVIATION: F-14 Tomcats of VF-84, flying from the carrier *Nimitz*, complete the first missions to employ the new Tactical Air Reconnaissance Photographic System (TARPS) to provide low-to-medium altitude photographic capabilities for the fleet.

February 24
AVIATION: At Geilenkirchen Air Base, West Germany, the first of 18 Boeing E-3A Sentry AWACS aircraft assigned to NATO arrives.

March 1
NAVAL: An era in submarine warfare ends when the *Robert E. Lee,* the navy's last Polaris ballistic missile submarine in service, is redesignated an attack submarine. The Polaris submarines served with distinction for 21 years.

March 3
AVIATION: At Suwon Air Base, South Korea, the first six A-10 Thunderbolt IIs arrive to participate in Project Commando.

March 13
NAVAL: The supercarrier *Carl Vinson* is commissioned, bringing the total number of carriers in service to 14.

March 16
NAVAL: In Washington, D.C., Vice President George H. W. Bush announces that the navy will join the campaign to curb the influx of illegal drugs from outside the country. To that end, several Grumman E-2 Hawkeye airborne early warning aircraft, along with several Coast Guard vessels, will be earmarked for that vital mission.

March 24
AVIATION: The U.S. Air Force in Europe (USAFE) assigns Comiso Air Base, Sicily, as a storage/launching site for new cruise missiles.

May 3
MILITARY: After a three-year experiment, the army abandons same-sex basic training units and reverts back to segregating them by gender.

May 4–8
AVIATION: The air force deploys an E-3A Sentry AWACS plane to Turkey for the first time.

May 16
TERRORISM: At San Juan, Puerto Rico, one sailor is killed and three wounded in a terrorist attack; the victims are from the amphibious vessel *Pensacola.*

May 30
DIPLOMACY: Spain, which has long-hosted American military bases, formally joins NATO.

June 10
AVIATION: At Castle Air Force Base, California, a KC-135 aircraft belonging to the 924th Air Refueling Squadron, Strategic Air Command (SAC), flies for the first time with an all-female crew. Their five-hour training mission includes a midair refueling with a B-52 bomber.

June 14
AVIATION: At Hahn Air Force Base, West Germany, the 313th Tactical Fighter Squadron becomes the first operational F-16 Falcon unit in the U.S. Air Force in Europe (USAFE).

June 18
MILITARY: In Washington, D.C., General John W. Vessey, the army vice chief of staff, gains appointment as the 10th chairman of the Joint Chiefs of Staff. He is also the fifth army general to serve as chairman.

June 20
NAVAL: In the South China Sea, an unidentified vessel fires a machine gun at the guided-missile cruiser *Sterett,* and destroyers *Lynde McCormick* and *Turner Joy;* warning shots are fired at the intruder, whose identity is never learned.

June 21
AVIATION: Over Antarctica, a Strategic Air Command (SAC) KC-10 Extender delivers 67,400 pounds of aviation fuel in support of Military Airlift Command (MAC) resupply operations. This occurs only 750 miles from the South Pole, making it the southernmost inflight refueling by an American aircraft.

June 24–25
NAVAL: At Juniyah, Lebanon, the amphibious ships *Nashville* and *Heritage* evacuate 600 Americans and foreign nationals seeking to escape from fighting that results from Israel's invasion of that battered nation.
MARINES: The 32nd Marine Amphibious Unit goes ashore at Juniyah, Lebanon, to help evacuate American citizens trapped there in the wake of the Israeli invasion.

June 26
MARINES: In Washington, D.C., General Paul X. Kelley gains appointment as the 28th commandant of the Marine Corps.

June 30
MARINES: At present, Marine Corps manpower levels are 18,975 men and 173,405 enlisted men and women.

July 1
AVIATION: At RAF Greenham Common, England, the 501st Tactical Missile Wing deploys as the first ground-launched cruise missile (GLCM) wing in Europe. A total of six Gryphon-equipped missile wings will be deployed there.
NAVAL: In Washington, D.C., Admiral James D. Watkins gains appointment as the 22nd chief of naval operations and the third successive submariner to do so.

July 2
AVIATION: At Davis Monthan Air Force Base, the 570th Strategic Missile Squadron deactivates its final Titan II intercontinental ballistic missile (ICBM).

July 6
DIPLOMACY: In Washington, D.C., President Ronald W. Reagan announces that marines currently deployed in Lebanon will become part of a Multinational Peacekeeping Force. Moreover, they will safeguard the evacuation of Palestinian Liberation Organization (PLO) members once a cease-fire has been achieved.

July 6–13
AVIATION: To assist refugees from the civil war in Chad, Africa, a C-130 Hercules transport conveys 113 tons of food supplies.

July 15
AVIATION: At Vandenberg Air Force Base, California, the 1,500th missile test is launched by the Strategic Air Command (SAC).

August 4
AVIATION: To extend the life and performance of the venerable KC-135 tanker aircraft, the first one retrofitted with CFM-56 turbofan engines performs its maiden flight. These new power plants will extend the life of the KC-135 well into the 21st century.

August 5
POLITICS: In a major victory for President Ronald W. Reagan, the Democratic-controlled House of Representatives rejects a bill that would freeze American and Soviet nuclear arsenals at current levels.

August 25–September 10
NAVAL: Vessels of the Sixth Fleet land the 32nd Marine Amphibious Unit at Beirut, Lebanon, as part of an international peacekeeping force. They also supervise the evacuation of 12,000 Palestinians onto merchant vessels during a major relocation of refugees. They depart when the last refugees are removed.
MARINES: At the request of the Lebanese government, the 32nd Marine Amphibious Units go ashore and occupy Beirut to help restore order as part of a multinational force. Once the evacuation of Palestinians is complete, the mission terminates.

August 30
AVIATION: At Edwards Air Force Base, California, the Northrop F-20 Tigershark, a lightweight air superiority fighter, performs its maiden flight.
MILITARY: In Japan, Lieutenant General Roscoe Robinson, Jr., becomes the first African American promoted to full (four-star) general.

August 31
NAVAL: At Annapolis, Maryland, Rear Admiral Charles R. Larson is appointed the 51st superintendent of the U.S. Naval Academy.

September 1
AVIATION: At Peterson Air Force Base, Colorado, the Air Force Space Command is activated.

September 2
AVIATION: At Farnborough, England, B-1B prototype no. 4 lands following an 14-hour nonstop flight from Edwards Air Force Base, California. This is also the first overseas deployment of any B-1B.

September 16
AVIATION: A B-52 flown by Captain Ronald L. Cavendish survives a crippling inflight emergency and manages to land safely through superior airmanship. Cavendish and his crew receive the Mackay Trophy for their efforts.

September 21
AVIATION: At Griffiss Air Force Base, New York, a B-52G from the 416th Bombardment Wing fires a cruise missile in its first operational test. An ongoing

program is modifying 16 B-52s at this base to carry six cruise missiles (ALCMs) under each wing.

September 29
NAVAL: Vessels of the Sixth Fleet embark the 1,200 men of the 32nd Marine Amphibious Unit at Beirut, Lebanon, and join French, British, Italian, and Australian troops as part of an international peacekeeping force. The marines are positioned at Beirut International Airport.

September 30
MILITARY: One marine is killed and three others wounded while trying to diffuse a bomb in Beirut, Lebanon.

October 1
NAVAL: At Bangor, Washington, the fleet ballistic submarine *Ohio* embarks on its first cold war deterrence cruise, armed with Trident missiles.

October 18
MARINES: Plans are announced to accept deliveries of the new High Mobility Multipurpose Wheeled Vehicle (HMMWV—or Hummer) to replace the beloved jeep.

October 22
MARINES: As soon as stocks of old C rations are depleted, marines will be victualed by the new meals-ready-to-eat (MRE) rations.

October 30
MARINES: In Beirut, Lebanon, the 24th Marine Amphibious Unit lands to relieve the 32nd MAU.

November 9
MARINES: In Washington, D.C., the commandant announces deliveries of the new M16A2 rifle, which will replace the older M16 variant.
• At Wahibah, Oman, the 31st Marine Amphibious Unit conducts Jade Tiger 83, a four-day exercise, in concert with Omani forces.

November 13
MILITARY: In a move of iconic importance, the Vietnam Veterans Memorial is dedicated in Washington, D.C. The names of all 59,800 servicemen and women killed in that conflict are etched in the memorial walls. Jan Scruggs, formerly of the 199th Light Infantry brigade, led the effort to raise funding for the shrine.

November 14–19
AVIATION: At Eskisehir Air Base, Turkey, the 527th Tactical Fighter Training Aggressor Squadron deploys three F-5E Tigers to help train the Turkish air force with Soviet-style tactics.

November 16
AVIATION: At Edwards Air Force Base, California, the space Shuttle *Columbia* lands safely; this is the first occasion on which a space vehicle orbits Earth with four crewmen.

November 22
MILITARY: President Ronald Reagan proposes constructing 100 MX Peacekeeper missiles with multiple warheads and deploying them in dense-pack silos, which are held easier to defend. Total costs are projected at $26 billion.

November 23
NAVAL: The guided-missile cruiser *Mississippi,* assisted by a Coast Guard boarding party, is the first U.S. Navy vessel to help seize a drug-smuggling vessel at sea.

December 7
MARINES: In Washington, D.C., President Ronald Reagan replaces the Rapid Deployment Joint Task Force (RDJTF) with the Central Command, a unified, all-service headquarters whose primary responsibility is the Middle East, Southwest Asia, and the Indian Ocean.

December 16
AVIATION: At Griffiss Air Force Base, New York, the 416th Bombardment places its first air-launched cruise missile (ACLM) on alert.

December 24–30
AVIATION: A severe earthquake in the Yemen Arab Republic prompts the Military Airlift Command (MAC) to convey 87 tons of supplies and equipment to assist survivors.

December 28
NAVAL: The World War II–vintage battleship *New Jersey* is pressed into service a third time as part of President Ronald W. Reagan's efforts to strengthen and enlarge the U.S. Navy. The vessel is now outfitted with 16 Harpoon antiship missiles and 32 Tomahawk cruise missiles.

1983

January 1
MILITARY: The Rapid Deployment Joint Task Force (RDF) is redesignated the U.S. Central Command (CENTCOM) at MacDill Air Force Base, Florida. This unified command coordinates military operations in over 25 countries, worldwide, and is initially headed by Lieutenant General Robert C. Kingston.

January 7
AVIATION: The new McDonnell Douglas F/A-18 Hornet, which is intended to replace the venerable A-4 Skyhawks and F-4H Phantom IIs, debuts with marine squadron VMFA-3124.

January 22
NAVAL: The new guided-missile cruiser *Ticonderoga* is commissioned, being the first vessel equipped with a highly automated Aegis weapon system; it is also the lead ship in a class that ultimately contains 27 vessels.

February
AVIATION: At Lagos, Nigeria, a C-141 Starlifter conveys 15 tons of communications equipment to replace a telecommunication center that has burned down.
MARINES: Following the U.S. Army's lead, the Marine Corps adopts the new Kevlar helmet to replace the old M1 steel "pot."

February 1
AVIATION: In a show of solidarity against regional Communist-inspired insurgencies, air force units visit Honduras to participate in Operation Ahus Tara

I with forces from Central American countries. Specifically, it is aimed at the Communist dictatorship in Nicaragua, which has been fomenting guerrilla wars throughout the region.
• At Davis Monthan Air Force Base, Arizona, the 868th Tactical Missile Training Squadron begins training with ground-launched cruise missiles (GLCMs) intended to be deployed in Europe.

February 2
AVIATION: At Luke Air Force Base, Arizona, the air force begins training pilots to fly the new F-16 Fighting Falcons.
MARINES: In Lebanon, a squad of Israeli tanks, attempting to pass through a U.S. checkpoint, is halted by Captain Charles B. Johnson when he steps in front of them, armed only with a .45-caliber pistol.

February 3
AVIATION: The entire force of Minuteman III intercontinental ballistic missiles is retrofitted with new reentry systems designed to enhance their retaliatory capabilities.

February 15
MARINES: In Beirut, Lebanon, the 24th Marine Amphibious Unit is relieved by the 22nd MAU.

March
AVIATION: At Langley Air Force Base, Virginia, the Air Force Thunderbirds demonstration team flies for the first time in their new F-16 fighters.

March 1
AVIATION: At Scott Air Force Base, Illinois, the Twenty-Third Air Force is organized as a diverse command capable of executing missions involving combat rescue, weather reconnaissance, missile site security, and aircrew special operations training.
• Once the 1st Special Operations Wing transfers to Hurlburt Field, Florida, that facility is reassigned from the Tactical Air Command (TAC) to the Military Airlift Command (MAC).

March 7
AVIATION: In South Korea, Team Spirit '83 commences as three wings of B-52Gs simulate minelaying operations off the coast.

March 15–28
AVIATION: At the Pacific Missile Test Range, Kwajalein, a B-52 successfully fires three navy AGM-Harpoon antiship missiles as the Strategic Air Command (SAC) seeks ways of performing sea interdiction missions.

March 22
MILITARY: After a seven-year period of intense testing, the U.S. Army Tank-Automotive and Armaments Command awards a contract to obtain 55,000 High-Mobility Multipurpose Wheeled Vehicles (HMMWV, or Hum-Vees) to replace the standard M551 utility "Jeep." Several versions are planned, including those armed with TOW antitank missiles.

March 31
MILITARY: At Fort Riley, Kansas, the first battery of M270 Multiple Launch Rocket Systems (MLRS) deploys with the 1st Infantry Division. Each battery can fire 12 M26 rockets, laden with smaller submunitions, over a distance of 19 miles. It is also the first multiple-rocket system acquired by the army since the Korean War.

April
MILITARY: The army assigns its first Bradley armored fighting vehicles (AFVs) to various cavalry and mechanized infantry units. These are heavily armed and armored, and capable of firing TOW antitank weapons, along with a 25mm chain gun (cannon) and several machine guns. Moreover, each Bradley can carry a squad of infantry in comparative safety throughout a modern combat environment.

April 1
AVIATION: The Strategic Air Command (SAC) yields four installations and 31 operational units to Space Command, as the majority of these are concerned with missile warning and space surveillance missions.

April 1–8
AVIATION: Flooding in Panama and earthquakes in Colombia prompt a C-130 Hercules aircraft to transport 34 tons of shelters, medical supplies, and electric generators to assist the survivors.

April 5–10
AVIATION: With southeastern Louisiana severely flooded by torrential rains, air force C-141 Starlifters convey 83 tons of food and medicine to victims.

April 11
MILITARY: A presidential panel recommends that the United States acquire 100 new MX Peacekeeper missiles and install them inside existing silos in Wyoming and Nevada.

April 12
AVIATION: For the first time since World War II, the army establishes a separate aviation branch to facilitate the deployment and development of helicopters and light aircraft.

April 18
TERRORISM: In Beirut, Lebanon, the U.S. embassy is destroyed by a bomb blast that kills 61 people, including 17 Americans (of whom three are soldiers and one a marine).

April 26
AVIATION: At Davis Monthan Air Force Base, the first ground-launched cruise missile (GLCMs) training crews are graduated and assigned to a tactical missile wing in Europe.

May 1
AVIATION: In the Caribbean, air force aircraft commence surveillance missions over the Bahamas to assist law-enforcement agencies in suppressing drug smuggling from offshore.

May 24
MILITARY: Congress authorizes $625 million for the first batch of MX (Peacekeeper) missiles after President Ronald W. Reagan promises the Democrats to be more flexible in dealing with the Soviet Union during scheduled arms control talks.

May 30
MARINES: At Beirut, Lebanon, the 24th Marine Amphibious Brigade arrives to replace the 22nd MAU.

June
MILITARY: At Fort Leavenworth, Kansas, the School of Advanced Military Studies (SAMS) opens, which teaches its pupils military theory, history, and execution-based practical exercises.

June 4
AVIATION: At Hill Air Force Base, Utah, the few remaining F-105s in the Air Force Reserve stage a final flyby before being retired from active service.

June 10
AVIATION: At the U.S. Naval Test Pilot School, Patuxent River, Maryland, Colleen Norris becomes the first female naval aviator to graduate.

June 17
AVIATION: At Vandenberg Air Force Base, California, an MX (Peacekeeper) missile is launched for the first time with multiple dummy warheads that splash down in the Kwajalein test range.

June 18
AVIATION: At Cape Canaveral, Florida, scientist Sally J. Ride is the first American woman in space when she accompanies the *Challenger* space shuttle into orbit.

June 23
MILITARY: In Washington, D.C., General John A. Wickham is appointed the army's 30th chief of staff. He continues the policies of his predecessor in rendering the army more easily transported to trouble spots around the world.

June 26
AVIATION: The Military Airlift Command dispatches three C-130 Hercules aircraft to northwestern Peru to provide relief supplies to victims of flooding.

June 28
MARINES: Sergeant Major Robert E. Cleary is appointed the 10th sergeant major of the Marine Corps.

June 30
MARINES: At this date, Marine Corps personnel stands at 19,983 officers and 174,106 enlisted men and women.

July 1
AVIATION: In light of the ongoing Iran-Iraq War, the air force deploys a provisional support squadron at Riyadh Air Base, Saudi Arabia. The oil-rich region of the Persian Gulf remains an area of vital strategic interest to the United States and the West.

1983

July 7
AVIATION: At McEntire Air National Guard Base, South Carolina, the first F-16As delivered to a National Guard unit arrive at the home of the 169th Tactical Fighter Group.
• General Dynamics completes its 1,000th F-16 Falcon of the 2,165 ordered by the air force.

July 24–August 6
AVIATION: The air force dispatches two UH-1 helicopters to deliver medical supplies and personnel to flood victims in western Ecuador.

July 26
MARINES: At Camp Lejeune, North Carolina, the 6th Amphibious Marine Brigade activates as the latest headquarters dedicated to the Marine Prepositioning Force (MPF) mission.

July 26–September 12
NAVAL: At various times the carriers *Ranger* and *Coral Sea,* and the battleship *New Jersey,* deploy off the coasts of Central and South America in a show of force against a number of Communist insurgencies there.

August
AVIATION: The 907th Tactical Airlift Group dispatches three C-123 Providers to spray insecticide over 11 Minnesota counties to fight an encephalitis epidemic.

August 1
AVIATION: At Andrews Air Force Base, Maryland, a microburst packing 120 mile-per-hour winds inflicts $465,000 in damages.

August 7
TERRORISM: At Hahn Air Base, Germany, a bomb, presumably planted by anti-nuclear activists, explodes at the officer's club.

August 10
AVIATION: In Washington, D.C., Secretary of Defense Caspar W. Weinberger announces that the air force will deploy 100 MX (Peacekeeper) missiles in existing Minuteman silos.

August 15–September 15
AVIATION: In support of an ongoing security assistance program, the air force dispatches 12 Starlifters to convey 185 tons of cargo to the African nation of Chad.

August 28
MARINES: An outpost comes under fire from one of many hostile factions in Beirut, Lebanon, and marines receive permission to fire back in self defense.

August 29
MARINES: At Beirut Airport, Lebanon, marine positions are heavily shelled by militant factions; two marines are killed and 14 wounded. Thereafter, marine artillery is ordered to provide counterbattery fire wherever possible and repeated exchanges grow more common.

1983

August 30
AVIATION: On the space shuttle *Challenger*, Lieutenant Colonel Guion S. Bluford becomes the first African American to ride in space.

August 31
NAVAL: In Annapolis, Maryland, Rear Admiral Charles R. Larson gains appointment as the 51st superintendent of the U.S. Naval Academy.

September 1
AVIATION: A Korean Airlines 747 is shot down by Soviet fighters after it strays over Sakhalin Island and air force HC130 transports of the 33rd Aerospace Rescue and Recovery Squadron are deployed from Kadena Air Base, Okinawa, to comb the waters for survivors; all 269 passengers perish.
MILITARY: The first MLRS rocket battery deploys to Germany as part of the 8th Infantry Division.
NAVAL: Off the Kamchatka Peninsula, Soviet Union, U.S. Navy vessels assist the search for wreckage and survivors from Korean Air Lines Flight 007, which was shot down by the Soviets after it strayed into their airspace.
MARINES: A force of 2,000 marines is dispatched to war-torn Lebanon as part of an international peacekeeping force.

September 3–25
AVIATION: To support American marines in Lebanon, the Military Airlift Command (MAC) commences Operation Rubber Wall, and delivers 4,000 tons of supplies in 100 heavy-lift missions. The effort involves 85 C-141 Starlifters, 24 C-5 Galaxies, and four C-130 Hercules sorties.

September 5
AVIATION: A Strategic Air Command (SAC) KC-135 piloted by Captain Robert J. Goodman refuels an F-4E Phantom II jet four times over water and even tows it along with the refueling boom until it lands safely. Goodman and his crew receive the Mackay Trophy for their efforts.

September 8
NAVAL: In Beirut, Lebanon, the frigate *Bowen* supplies close support fire to assist marines deployed there as an international peacekeeping force. Her 5-inch guns are trained on Druze militiamen who had been firing on the Marines with small arms and mortars.

September 12
MARINES: At Beirut, Lebanon, the 31st Marine Amphibious Brigade arrives off the coast from the Indian Ocean and remains there until October 1.

September 13
MILITARY: In light of attacks by Muslim extremists, President Ronald W. Reagan authorizes U.S. Marine contingents deployed in Lebanon to call for naval support fire and air strikes to protect themselves.

September 15
MILITARY: Reversing itself after the Soviet downing of Flight 007, the Democratic-controlled House of Representatives votes to approve a $187.5 billion defense

bill that includes funding for both the MX Peacekeeper missile and B-1B Lancer bomber, along with a new generation of chemical weapons.

September 19
NAVAL: Off the Lebanese coast, the guided-missile cruiser *Virginia* and the destroyer *John Rodgers* unleash 338 5-inch rounds near the approaches of Sug el-Gharb village to support the Lebanese army there. This marks a shift in American policy; heretofore warships fired only in defense of marine positions.

September 25
NAVAL: In a sign of the seriousness of American involvement in Lebanese affairs, the battleship *New Jersey* arrives off the coast of that wartorn nation.

September 26
MARINES: At Beirut, Lebanon, a cease-fire is called between the marines and several militant factions, but sniping persists on both sides.

September 28
AVIATION: The EF-111A Raven electronic warfare aircraft become operational after extensive resting. Pilots dub it the "Spark Vark" because of its extensive electronic suite.

September 30
AVIATION: The first production batch of Hughes AH-64A Apache attack helicopters roll out of the factory.

October 1
AVIATION: At Davis Monthan Air Force Base, Arizona, the last operational B-52D is retired to the "bone yard."
MILITARY: At Fort Gillem, Georgia, the 2nd U.S. Army is activated to oversee Reserve units in Kentucky, Tennessee, North Carolina, South Carolina, Mississippi, Alabama, and Georgia.
NAVAL: The Naval Space Command is organized under Captain Richard Truly, a former astronaut. This consolidates several space services into one centrally administered unit.

October 4–5
AVIATION: The 30th Special Operations Squadron sends four CH-3 helicopters to Maricopa, Arizona, to rescue 57 civilians trapped by floodwaters.

October 6
AVIATION: The Strategic Air Command (SAC) modifies three of its B-52Gs to carry and fire the AGM-Harpoon antiship missile. These aircraft are intended to perform maritime interdiction missions.

October 13
AVIATION: In Washington, D.C., the National Air and Space Museum, Smithsonian Institution, announces that it is building a large annex at Dulles International Airport to house the Concorde, the space shuttle *Enterprise*, and the B-29 *Enola Gay*.

October 19
MARINES: The 22nd Marine Amphibious Brigade is en route to Beirut, Lebanon, when a Communist coup on the island of Grenada forces it to change course for

the Caribbean. Apparently, 1,000 American citizens, mostly students at the St. George Medical School, stand to be held hostage.

October 22
DIPLOMACY: The Organization of Eastern Caribbean States, fearful that Grenada will become a Soviet outpost for exporting revolutionary activities, asks the United States to intervene on that island.

October 23
AVIATION: Transports of the Military Airlift Command (MAC) convey 239 dead and 95 wounded marines from Beirut, Lebanon, to European and American hospitals for treatment or burial.

TERRORISM: An explosive-laden truck driven by suicide jihadists explodes in the 24th Marine Amphibious Unit compound at Beirut, Lebanon, killing 241 and wounding 71 men of the 1st Battalion, 8th Marines. This is the highest one-day death toll of marines since World War II. Minutes later, a second truck bomb also kills 58 French soldiers of a peacekeeping force. This murderous act prompts President Ronald Reagan to reevaluate the marines' role in the peacekeeping mission there.

October 25–30
AVIATION: Transports of the Military Airlift Command (MAC) and the Air Force Reserve fly 11,389 passengers and 7,709 tons of cargo during Operation Urgent Fury in Grenada. A total of 496 sorties are flown by C-141 Starlifters, C-5 Galaxies, and C-130 Hercules aircraft.

A Sikorsky CH-53D *Sea Stallion* helicopter hovers above the ground during Operation Urgent Fury in Grenada. *(Department of Defense)*

• Over Grenada, a flight of MC-130s drops paratroopers on Point Salines, Grenada, and Lieutenant Colonel James J. Hobson, Jr., manages to keep his aircraft under control despite intense antiaircraft fire, guiding the mission to success. For this he wins a Mackay Trophy.

MILITARY: In response to the takeover of the Caribbean island nation of Grenada by Marxist revolutionaries, who killed prime minister Maurice Bishop and took over 1,100 American medical students hostage, President Ronald W. Reagan unleashes Operation Urgent Fury to rescue them. U.S. Air Force, Marine Corps, Army Rangers, the 82nd Airborne Division, and U.S. Navy SEALS all come ashore and crush an armed force bolstered by Cuban soldiers, taking the whole captive. The attack begins at dawn with a low-altitude parachute assault by the 2nd Ranger Battalion, 75th Infantry, against the unfinished Soviet airstrip at Port Salines. They overcome stiff resistance by Cuban and Grenadian forces and secure their objective by 8:50 A.M.

NAVAL: Overall command of Operation Urgent Fury is entrusted to Vice Admiral Joseph Metcalf III. It commences before dawn when a U.S. Navy SEAL team infiltrates the capital of St. George's and captures Government House. Governor General Sir Paul Scoon is released from captivity, although Communist forces besiege the liberators.

MARINES: A force of 400 men from the 22nd Marine Amphibious Brigade are helicoptered from the assault ship *Guam* to Pearls Airport, the island's only operational airfield. The balance of the brigade lands subsequently at Grand Mal Bay; three marine aviators are killed in action.

October 26
AVIATION: At the Tonopah Test Range, the initial batch of five F-117 Nighthawks reaches initial operational capability. Meanwhile, the activity of 18 A-7 Corsair IIs provide a convenient cover for ongoing operations.

• On Grenada, Governor General Sir Paul Scoon is helicoptered to the assault ship *Guam* for his own safety, while hundreds of American students are airlifted from the Point Salines airstrip.

MARINES: The first deliveries of the LAV-25, the first wheeled light-armored vehicle in Marine Corps history, are completed.

• Men of the 22nd Marine Amphibious Unit (SOC) relieve U.S. Navy SEALs besieged at Government House, Grenada.

October 27
AVIATION: In Spain, B-52 Stratofortresses deploy at air bases for the first time.

MILITARY: American forces on Grenada round up 638 Cuban prisoners, who have suffered 24 killed and 59 wounded. An additional 45 Grenadian soldiers are slain in combat. American losses are 18 dead and 166 wounded, mostly through friendly fire. The Soviet diplomatic delegation on the island is also placed on an American transport plane and removed to Cuba at once.

November 1
NAVAL: In Washington, D.C., retired admiral Hyman G. Rickover is awarded a second congressional gold medal, a distinction he shares only with general and president Zachary Taylor.

- In the Arabian Sea, a fire breaks out in the engine room of the carrier *Ranger*, which kills six sailors and injures 35.

November 1–5
AVIATION: A severe earthquake rattles northern Turkey, so the Military Airlift Command (MAC) dispatches four C-141 Starlifters and six C-130s Hercules transports to convey 234 tons of relief supplies to the survivors.

November 8
NAVAL: In Washington, D.C., 76-year-old Captain Grace M. Hopper, who was partly responsible for inventing computer-programming languages, is promoted to commodore.

November 11
MILITARY: The United States deploys the first of 160 cruise missiles in Great Britain, much to the consternation of the Soviet Union and the European peace movement. All told, the Americans deploy 571 medium-range missiles to counter similar Soviet weapons.

November 17
NAVAL: In the Arabian Sea, the destroyer *Fife* collides with the Soviet missile frigate *Razyashchiy* as it attempts to approach close to the carrier *Ranger*; the collision results in minor damage and no casualties.

November 19
MARINES: In Beirut, Lebanon, the 22nd Marine Amphibious Unit comes ashore to relieve the 24th MAU.

November 23
AVIATION: In Bonn, West Germany, the parliament ignore the protests of the Greens and pro-Communist radicals and approves deployment of air force ground-launched cruise missiles (GLCMs) and U.S. Army Pershing II ballistic missiles.

December
MILITARY: The bulk of American forces involved in Operation Urgent Fury are gradually withdrawn from the Caribbean island of Grenada. This small but successful action witnessed the combat debut of UH-60 Black Hawk helicopters and over 100 female military personnel.

December 3
AVIATION: The Strategic Air Command (SAC) begins disbanding its Titan II intercontinental ballistic missiles (ICBMs) by inactivating the 571st Strategic Missile Squadron.

December 4
AVIATION: A force of 28 navy warplanes from the carriers *Independence* and *John F. Kennedy* attack Syrian antiaircraft and missile batteries near Beirut, Lebanon. Good results are achieved but an A-6 flown by Lieutenant Mark A. Lange is shot down; Lange is killed and his navigator, Robert O. Goodman, is captured. An A-7 flown by Commander Edward K. Andrews is also lost, although the pilot is rescued.

1983

MARINES: A heavy bombardment of marine positions near Beirut, Lebanon, results in eight dead and two wounded. Prolonged exchanges of firepower with Druze militiamen resume.

December 6

AVIATION: At Langley Air Force Base, Virginia, the new National Transonic Wind Tunnel is dedicated; this new device is expressly intended for research on the faster jets being designed or under construction.

December 14

NAVAL: East of Beirut, Lebanon, the battleship *New Jersey* unleashes its 16-inch guns against militant Druze extremists for the first time.

TERRORISM: The U.S. embassy in Kuwait is struck by a truck bomb, killing dozens of innocent bystanders. Marine security guards protect the smoldering remnants.

December 15

AVIATION: Despite the pleas of antinuclear protestors, the 56th Field Artillery Brigade is the first NATO unit to deploy new Pershing II tactical nuclear missiles. This weapon has a range of over 1,000 miles, enhanced accuracy, and carries a warhead ranging from five to 50 kilotons in yield.

December 23

AVIATION: The 390th Electronic Combat Squadron becomes the first operational unit with General Dynamics EF-11A Ravens.

1984

January

MILITARY: Although army manpower levels are basically stabilized, the force is increasingly capable owing to the mass deployment of several new and advanced weapons systems. Plans are also being drawn up to convert the 7th Infantry Division into a highly mobile "light" formation.

January 1

AVIATION: The new Global Positioning System (GPS) is taken over by the Space Command.

January 3

DIPLOMACY: After the Reverend Jesse Jackson meets Syrian president Hafez al-Assad in Damascus, Syria, Lieutenant Robert O. Jackson, who was shot down on December 4, 1983, is released.

January 12

AVIATION: At Cherry Point, North Carolina, the 2nd Marine Air Wing (2nd MAW) accepts its first deliveries of improved AV-8B Harrier jump jets.

January 21

MILITARY: The American antisatellite missile system completes its first test in being launched by an F-15 fighter and positing a dummy miniature-vehicle emulator.

January 26

AVIATION: At the Army Aviation Center, Fort Rucker, Alabama, the first Hughes Aircraft AH-64 Apache attack helicopters are deployed. This aircraft is destined to replace the 20-year-old Bell AH-1 Cobra and is equipped with a powerful 30mm chain gun and highly accurate Hellfire laser-guided missiles.

January 28
AVIATION: At Hill Air Force Base, Utah, the 419th Tactical Fighter Wing trades its aging F-105 Thunderchiefs for new F-16 Falcons. They are also the first Air Force Reserve unit so equipped.

January 31
AVIATION: The new AGM-81A Firebolt target vehicle hits Mach 1.4 at 104,000 feet, breaking world records for speed and altitude.

February 1
MARINES: Rather than lose more men to internecine civil strife, President Ronald W. Reagan orders marine detachments stationed at Beirut, Lebanon, withdrawn.

February 3
AVIATION: At RAF Upper Heyford, England, the 20th Tactical Fighter Wing becomes the first EF-111A Raven unit deployed with the U.S. Air Force in Europe (USAFE).

February 3–11
AVIATION: Lieutenant Colonel Robert L. Stewart becomes the first soldier astronaut to accompany a space shuttle into orbit when he rides the *Challenger* into orbit.

February 4
AVIATION: The HH-60 Night Hawk, a combat rescue version of the Black Hawk helicopter, performs its maiden flight. However, funding for construction is not forthcoming and the project is cancelled.

February 7
AVIATION: In Earth orbit, Captain Bruce McCandless makes the first untethered space walk from the space shuttle *Challenger* while operating a manned maneuvering unit.

DIPLOMACY: In Washington, D.C., President Ronald W. Reagan announces his decision to withdraw marines from the multinational peacekeeping force in Beirut, Lebanon.

February 8
NAVAL: In light of continuing tensions in Lebanon, the battleship *New Jersey* fires 288 16-inch shells upon Syrian and Druze positions in the Bekaa Valley, wiping out eight artillery batteries and killing the Syrian general in charge of Lebanon.

February 9
NAVAL: Off Lebanon, destroyers *Caron* and *Moosbrugger* fire 400 5-inch rounds against hostile positions along the shore. This is also the heaviest American bombardment of the Lebanese civil war.

February 10–11
AVIATION: With the situation in Lebanon spiraling out of control, navy and marine helicopters evacuate several hundred American citizens and foreign nationals from Beirut.

February 14
NAVAL: The guided-missile destroyer *Claude V. Ricketts* shells Syrian-held positions east of Beirut.

February 21–26
MARINES: The 22nd Marine Amphibious Brigade withdraws from Beirut, Lebanon, and redeploys on vessels of the Sixth Fleet offshore. The only marines remaining are those posted as embassy guards.

February 23
AVIATION: The F-15C Eagle officially replaces the aging F-4 Phantom II in the Tactical Air Command (TAC) as its standard air-superiority fighter.

February 24
AVIATION: The air force chooses the McDonnell Douglas F-15E Strike Eagle over the delta-wing General Dynamics F-16XL as its next dual role fighter bomber; almost 400 are acquired and are still in service today.
• Two C-141 Starlifters land at Cherry Point, North Carolina, in support of withdrawing U.S. Marines from Larnaca, Cyprus, and Lebanon.

March 6
AVIATION: Over Canada's Northern Test Range, a B-52G from the 319th Bombardment Wing test launches an air-launched cruise missile (ALCM) for the first time.

March 19–April 9
AVIATION: Recent threats against Egypt and Sudan by Libya result in an E-3A Sentry aircraft being dispatched to the region. This is joined by 17 C-141 Starlifter and 28 C-5 Galaxy missions to convey military supplies to the Egyptians.

March 21
NAVAL: In the Sea of Japan, the carrier *Kitty Hawk* collides with a Soviet Victor I-class nuclear attack submarine that surfaces in its path; the latter is so heavily damaged that it has to be towed to a Soviet naval base at Vladivostok.

March 24
AVIATION: In South Korea, a CH-53 crashes during Ream Spirit 84 exercises, killing 18 U.S. Marines and 11 Republic of Korea (ROK) Marines.

April 2
NAVAL: In the South China Sea, the frigate *Harold E. Holt* is struck by three signal flares fired at it by the Soviet aircraft carrier *Minsk* as it passed to within 300 yards, but no damage results.

April 4
MARINES: At Camp Lejeune, North Carolina, the LAV-25 equipped 2nd Light Armored Vehicle Battalion is organized.

April 6
AVIATION: Astronauts from the space shuttle *Challenger* conduct the first satellite repair program by using the Canadian-built "arm" to grasp an ailing satellite, repair it, and then restore it to orbit.

USS *Iowa* fires a full broadside during a target exercise near Vieques Island, Puerto Rico. *(Department of Defense)*

• The 375th Aeromedical Airlift Wing acquires the first of 80 Learjet C-21A aircraft, which gradually replace its older Cessna CT-39 Sabreliners.

April 11
AVIATION: The 375th Aeromedical Airlift Wing receives its first Beech C-12F operational support aircraft; a total of 40 are purchased.

April 15
TERRORISM: At Oshakati, Namibia, a land mine planted by Marxist guerrillas kills an American diplomat and the army attaché.

April 19
AVIATION: At Robins Air Force Base, Georgia, construction begins on the phased array, sea-launched ballistic missile warning system.

April 28
NAVAL: The World War II–vintage battleship *Iowa* is recommissioned into active service.

May 2
NAVAL: In New Orleans, Louisiana, the new Bell Aerospace Textron landing craft air-cushion (LCAC) debuts. It is hoped this new hovercraft design will bring better speed and range to amphibious operations.

1984

May 16

AVIATION: Afghan refugees at Peshawar, Pakistan, receive 22 tons of medical supplies from C-141 Starlifters dispatched by the Military Airlift Command (MAC).

May 25

AVIATION: The Vietnam War's unknown soldier returns home aboard a C-141 Starlifter for internment at Arlington National Cemetery. He is subsequently identified as U.S. Air Force lieutenant Michael J. Blassie and reburied in his home town of St. Louis, Missouri.

May 28

MILITARY: This Memorial Day, President Ronald Reagan offers a tribute to the only unidentified serviceman killed in Vietnam.

June

AVIATION: A Schweizer TG-7A motor glider is delivered to the U.S. Air Force Academy for airmanship programs and is relegated to the 94th Air Training Squadron.

June 10

MILITARY: The army experimental antiballistic missile system fired from Vandenberg Air Force Base, California, scores a direct hit on a target missile launched from Kwajalein Atoll in the Pacific. This is the equivalent of hitting a bullet with a bullet.

June 15

AVIATION: At Dyess Air Force Base, Texas, a C-130 Hercules from the Military Airlift Command (MAC) flies to Kansas City, Missouri, with 4.5 tons of pumping equipment to assist efforts to fight floods in that part of the state.
• At Vandenberg Air Force Base, California, an MX (Peacekeeper) missile is flight-tested with a Mark-21 test reentry vehicle for the first time.

June 16

AVIATION: At Fort Forth, Texas, the improved F-16C Falcon performs its maiden flight. This new design is equipped with improved Heads up Display (HUD) instrumentation and improved multimode radar.

June 20

AVIATION: The 384th Air Refueling Wing, Strategic Air Command (SAC), receives its first KC-135R Stratotanker aircraft. This version is equipped with new CFM-56 fan jet engines, which possess higher thrust and lower fuel consumption.

June 21

AVIATION: A Military Airlift Command (MAC) C-141 Starlifter loaded with supplies for U.S. Antarctic bases at McMurdo Sound is refueled en route by a KC-10 Extender from the 22nd Air Refueling Wing flying out of Christchurch International Airport, New Zealand.

June 25–26

AVIATION: In the Gulf of Sidra off Libya, F-14 Tomcats launched from the carrier *Saratoga* fly to demonstrate American rejection of that nation's claim to international waters.

June 30
AVIATION: The air force closes Hancock Field, New York, after 32 years of operations.
MARINES: At this time, Marine Corps manpower levels stand at 20,366 officers and 175,848 enlisted men and women.

July
AVIATION: At Loring Air Force Base, Maine, the first deliveries of AGM-84 Harpoon antiship missiles are accepted by the 69th Bombardment Squadron. These are to be carried on B-52 bombers for shipping interdiction at sea.

July 14
NAVAL: In Maryland, the *Corporal Louis J. Hauge, Jr.,* the first vessel expressly designed for the Marine Prepositioning Force, is launched.

July 31
AVIATION: At Davis Monthan Air Force Base, Arizona, the 390th Strategic Missile Wing is the first Titan II unit to be deactivated.

August
MILITARY: The army continues with plans to lighten several existing formations to make them more mobile, including the 6th and 25th Infantry Divisions, and the famous 10th Mountain Division.

August 7–October 2
AVIATION: Operation Intense Look unfolds as the United States begins minesweeping efforts in the Red Sea at the request of Egypt and Saudi Arabia after several commercial vessels mysteriously exploded and sank. In support of this effort, air force transports convey 1,300 tons of cargo and 1,000 military personnel to the region.

August 8
AVIATION: In Europe, the first C-23 Sherpa begins operating as a small cargo/liaison aircraft that flies between airfields and depot centers.

August 17
AVIATION: In the Gulf of Suez, Helicopter Mine Countermeasure Squadron 14 (HM-14), operating from the amphibious transport dock *Shreveport*, begins a 22-day operation clearing mines from that strategic waterway.

August 19–20
AVIATION: The 22nd Air Force dispatches two C-141 Starlifters to evacuate 382 American military and civilian personnel from Johnson Island, 715 miles from Hawaii, as Typhoon Kell approaches.

August 28
AVIATION: In a significant political and military development, a C-5 Galaxy touches down at Florennes Air Base, Belgium, with the first supply of ground-launched cruise missiles (GLCMs). The noisy and KGB-orchestrated antimissile movement throughout Europe, sensing the futility of their efforts, begins disbanding.

1984

August 29
AVIATION: At Sembach Air Base, Germany, the last OV-10 Broncos depart after performing for a decade with the U.S. Air Force Europe (USAFE).

September 2–3
AVIATION: In South Korea, helicopters of the 38th Aerospace Rescue and Recovery Squadron (Arrs) save 148 stranded civilians in a recent flood.

September 4
AVIATION: At Palmdale, California, the first production B-1B Lancer intercontinental strategic bomber is rolled out of the factory for flight testing.

September 10
MILITARY: The School of the Americas is relocated from Fort Gulick, Panama Canal Zone, to Fort Benning, Georgia, in accordance with provisions of the 1977 Panama Canal Treaty. The school serves as a training agency to foster close cooperation between the U.S. Army and those of Latin American nations.

September 14–18
AVIATION: Retired air force colonel and aeronaut Joe Kittinger, Jr., flies a balloon nonstop from Caribou, Maine, to Savona, Italy, a 3,550-mile journey covered in 84 hours. He also establishes a new balloon distance record.

September 20
TERRORISM: In Beirut, Lebanon, the U.S. embassy annex is bombed and 23 people are killed. The dead include Petty Officer Michael R. Wagner, while two sailors and four marine guards are wounded. U.S. ambassador Reginald Bartholomew is also killed.

September 28
AVIATION: After a hiatus of 13 years, marine helicopter squadron HMM-364 is resurrected at Kaneohe Bay, Hawaii.

October 1
MILITARY: At Fort Sheridan, Illinois, the 4th U.S. Army is activated to oversee Army Reserve units in Ohio, Michigan, Illinois, Indiana, Iowa, Minnesota, and Wisconsin.

October 11–14
AVIATION: In San Juan, Puerto Rico, transports of the Military Airlift Command (MAC) convey Secret Service vehicles for use by Pope John Paul II during his visit to the island.

October 18
AVIATION: At Palmdale, California, the first operational B-1B, christened *Star of Abilene*, performs its maiden flight ahead of schedule.

October 18–20
AVIATION: After Colorado and New Mexico are struck by heavy snowstorms, the Air Force Rescue Coordination Center directs search-and-rescue operations that save 47 lives.

1984

October 23–24

AVIATION: During a sentimental tour of the Philippines by General Douglas MacArthur's veterans, a fire breaks out at the Pines Hotel in Baguio. An H-3 helicopter from the 31st Aerospace Rescue and Recovery Squadron (ARRS) lifts nine people trapped on the roof to safety. A C-130 Hercules transport also carries 48 injured people to Clark Air Base for treatment.

October 25

AVIATION: At Salto di Quirra, Sardinia, F-4Es of the 86th Tactical Fighter Wings participate in live missile fire exercises with U.S. Navy units.

November 2

AVIATION: At McConnell Air Force Base, Kansas, a fire erupts as a Titan II missile is being drained of liquid fuel; the incident threatens to delay deactivation of this system.

November 19

AVIATION: At Bogotá, Colombia, two C-141 Starlifters from the Military Airlift Command deliver vehicles, small arms, and ammunition to the U.S. embassy after it is threatened by drug lords.

November 20

AVIATION: In Washington, D.C., President Ronald W. Reagan approves creation of a new, unified United States Space Command.

November 23

MILITARY: Along the Demilitarized Zone (DMZ), South Korea, a Communist defector suddenly breaks for American lines, triggering a huge fire fight near the Panmunjom Truce Compound; one American is injured.

November 30

NAVAL: After the Cuban government refuses an American request to allow a Coast Guard vessel to rescue a disabled American ship that had drifted into Cuban waters, the *Nimitz* battle group deploys offshore and the Cuban government allows the vessel to be towed.

December 1

AVIATION: At Kelly Air Force Base, Texas, the first C-5A Galaxy is delivered to the Air Force Reserve.

December 2–4

AVIATION: When the *Carl Vinson* and *Midway* carrier battle groups sail to within 50 miles of Vladivostok, Russia, the Soviets respond by dispatching over 100 aircraft and vessels in their direction.

December 11–12

AVIATION: Survivors and two wounded victims of a hijacked Kuwaiti airliner are flown by C-141 Starlifters to Rhein-Main Air Base, West Germany, and thence to the United States.

December 20

AVIATION: In the aftermath of a collapsed tunnel in Huntington, Utah, two C-130 Hercules aircraft convey 23.8 tons of emergency equipment to help rescue the 27 coal miners trapped there. Although the equipment allows rescue parties to reach the miners, all had died from smoke inhalation beforehand.

December 22
MILITARY: At Pontiac, Michigan, the U.S. Military Academy wins its first post-season football bowl game by defeating the University of Michigan at the Cherry Bowl.

December 22–March 1985
AVIATION: Ongoing famine in the Sahel region of Africa results in eight Military Airlift Command (MAC) C-141 Starlifters being dispatched with 200 tons of food and medical supplies to Kassala, Sudan.

1985

January
AVIATION: Headquarters, Strategic Air Command (SAC) determines that the recent leak of a Titan II ICBM at McConnell Air Force Base could have been prevented with better procedures. The continuing deactivation of Titan IIs continues ahead as scheduled.

January 1
AVIATION: Having spent 13 hours of flight time attempting to lower the nose gear, Colonel David E. Faught, 97th Bombardment Wing, makes a successful nose gear-up landing without serious damage to the aircraft, a KC-135. He wins a Mackay Trophy for his efforts.

January 4
AVIATION: Major Patricia M. Young is appointed commander of Detachment 1, 20th Missile Warning Squadron. She is the first female to lead an Air Force Space Command unit.

January 5
AVIATION: After an Eastern Airlines Boeing 727 crashes in the Andes Mountains, the Military Airlift Command (MAC) dispatches a C-141 Starlifter carrying a Sikorsky S-70 helicopter to look for the wreckage and any possible survivors.

January 18–23
AVIATION: The Military Airlift Command (MAC) orders C-141 Starlifter flights to the Sudan to assist ongoing relief efforts there; 62 tons of food are delivered.

January 19–21
AVIATION: After Typhoon Eric devastates Viti Levu, Fiji, the 75th and 312th Military Airlift Squadrons send two C-5 Galaxies and one C-141 Starlifter with 186 tons of relief supplies to assist the survivors.

January 24–27
AVIATION: At Cape Canaveral, Florida, the space shuttle *Discovery* blasts off under Colonel Loren J. Shriver on its first all-military mission. This is also one of the shortest shuttle missions, lasting only 73 hours, 33 minutes.

January 28
AVIATION: At Kunsan Air Base, South Korea, two H-3 Jolly Green Giant helicopters return after rescuing 10 shipwrecked Korean fishermen.

January 31
MILITARY: Another military icon falls to the wayside as the army decides to replace its famous M1911A1 .45 caliber automatic pistol, in service since 1911, with the smaller Beretta M9 9mm pistol.

February 2
DIPLOMACY: At the conclusion of ANZUS Exercise Sea Eagle, the government of New Zealand denies permission for the destroyer *Buchanan* to dock there, citing its undesirability as a nuclear-armed or nuclear-powered vessel. However, both the United States and Great Britain conform to their policy of neither admitting nor denying the presence of nuclear weapons onboard their warships.

February 3
AVIATION: At Howard Air Force Base, Panama, C-141 Starlifters of the Military Airlift Command (MAC) are sent to Argentina after a devastating earthquake to aid 12,000 refugees.

February 4
AVIATION: The Strategic Air Command (SAC) institutes the practice of gender-specific missile launch crews (either male of female) for Minuteman and Peacekeeper facilities. Previously, women were restricted to Titan II launch sites.

February 18
GENERAL: Former general and Vietnam commander William Westmoreland and CBS network reach an out-of-court settlement in the former's $120 million libel suit against the network. The general asserts that CBS falsely accused him of misrepresenting Communist manpower and strength.

March
MILITARY: Due to budgetary constraints, the army ceases its support for athletes training for the modern Olympic pentathlon, which includes running, swimming, fencing, shooting, and horseback riding.

March 5–9
AVIATION: Air force transports complete four famine-relief missions by flying in 123 tons of food to victims in Sudan, Niger, and Mali.

March 8
AVIATION: In the Bahamas, police and U.S. Drug Enforcement Agency officials bust a $320 million cocaine smuggling effort with the help of helicopters provided by the Military Airlift Command. Joint drug interception campaigns continue the following month.

March 15
AVIATION: In Chile, a Military Airlift Command C-5 Galaxy arrives with 1,000 rolls of plastic sheeting to shelter victims of a devastating earthquake that struck in February.

March 24
MILITARY: In Ludwigslust, East Germany, a Soviet sentry shoots and kills Major Arthur D. Nicholson of the U.S. Military Liaison Mission. He is considered the last American killed in the cold war and receives a posthumous Purple Heart and the Legion of Merit.

March 25
AVIATION: The air force relaxes its prohibitions against allowing women to serve in combat conditions by allowing them to serve as forward air controllers (FAC) and as crew members on C-130 transports and gunships.

April 4
AVIATION: Retired air force leader James H. Doolittle is elevated to full general, four-star rank. He is the first Air Force Reserve officer so honored.

April 5
AVIATION: When a large fire devastates 7,000 acres across six counties in drought-stricken western North Carolina, two C-141 Starlifters and a C-130 Hercules arrive with 10 tons of fire-fighting equipment, 21,000 gallons of fire retardant, and 190 firefighters to assist.

April 20
AVIATION: By this date, the first B-52 crews completely trained in Harpoon anti-ship missile operations are graduated.

April 29–May 17
AVIATION: At Spangdahlem Air Base, West Germany, U.S. Air Force in Europe sponsors Salty Demo, a basewide exercise to gauge that facility's ability to defend itself against an attack and presumed combat operations.

April 30
GENERAL: On the 10th anniversary of the fall of Saigon to Communist North Vietnamese forces, hundreds of people attend ceremonies at the Vietnam War Memorial in Washington, D.C. This long, black wall lists the names of all 58,022 men and women who perished in that conflict, now viewed by a majority of Americans to have been a mistake.

May 6
AVIATION: Over the Sea of Japan, a CH-53D crashes into the ocean, killing 17 marines.

May 20
NAVAL: U.S. Navy chief warrant officer John A. Walker, Jr., is arrested by the FBI for espionage and charged with providing top-secret information to the Soviet Union since 1967, including information on American surface and submarine operations and keys to deciphering encrypted radio transmissions; the damage Walker inflicted on the navy is regarded as incalculable.

May 24
MARINES: According to revised Marine Corps orders, female marines are subject to increased amounts of combat-related training, especially in the fields of marksmanship and defensive tactics.

May 31
MARINES: At Camp Pendleton, California, the 1st Light Armored Vehicle Battalion is organized.

June 14
MARINES: In Washington, D.C., Commandant Kelley institutes a pilot program to familiarize Marine Amphibious Units with certain special operations.

June 14–30
TERRORISM: Shiite extremists seize Trans World Airlines Flight 847 midway on a flight between Athens and Rome, and force it to land at Beirut, Lebanon. U.S. Navy steelworker second class Robert D. Walker is murdered by the hijackers, but subsequent negotiations free the 39 hostages on June 30.

June 19
TERRORISM: In El Salvador, Communists open fire at an outdoor café, killing 13 people; four off-duty marine embassy guards are among those slain.

June 21–July 25
AVIATION: In southern Idaho, a severe locust infestation prompts the dispatch of three C-123K Providers for aerial spraying purposes. They cover 795,000 acres in 73 sorties.

June 29
AVIATION: The air force accepts delivery of its first Rockwell B-1B Lancer strategic bomber; only 100 are scheduled for acquisition owing to their considerable expense.
• At Andersen Air Force Base, the 60th Bombardment Squadron becomes the second B-52G unit equipped and trained to fire Harpoon antiship missiles.
• At Naval Air Station New Orleans, Louisiana, the 159th Tactical Fighter Group is the first Air National Guard unit equipped with F-15 Eagles.

June 30
AVIATION: At Vandenberg Air Force Base, California, the final MX (Peacekeeper) test is conducted by the Air Force Space Command.

July 1
AVIATION: At Carswell Air Force Base, Texas, the 7th Bombardment Wing is the first B-52H unit equipped to operate air-launched cruise missiles (ACLMs).
• A C-141 Starlifter from the 438th Military Airlift Wing transports 39 passengers from TWA Flight 847, which had been hijacked and flown to Lebanon, to Rhein-Main Air Base, West Germany. They are greeted upon arrival by Vice President George H. W. Bush.

July 2–10
AVIATION: A series of huge forest fires in California and Idaho results in C-141 Starlifters flying 285 firefighters to staging areas, while C-130s complete 200 sorties spreading 450 tons of flame retardant across 1.5 million acres.

July 7
AVIATION: At Dyess Air Force Base, Texas, the 96th Bombardment Wing, Strategic Air Command (SAC) receives the first operational B-1B Lancer.

1985

July 10
NAVAL: In Washington, D.C., Admiral William J. Crowe is nominated to serve as the 11th chairman of the Joint Chiefs of Staff.

July 15
AVIATION: During the United States Atlantic Command exercise Readex '85-2, two B-52Gs from the 42nd Bombardment Wing simulate Harpoon missile launches for test and evaluation purposes.

July 30
AVIATION: The Bomarc aerial target drone (CQM-10B) program is officially terminated.

August 12–15
AVIATION: A C-5 Galaxy of the 436th Military Airlift Wing responds to a request from the State Department by delivering 35 tons of food and equipment to famine victims in western Sudan.

August 23
AVIATION: At Vandenberg Air Force Base, California, a Minuteman missile is "cold launched" out of its silo using compressed air. The missile ignites once it is airborne, resulting in less damage to the silo and a quicker reload time.

August 27
MILITARY: In Washington, D.C., Secretary of Defense Casper Weinberger halts production and development of the controversial M988 Sergeant York antiaircraft system, following a trouble-plagued past. Total cost to the taxpayers: $1.8 billion.

September 10
AVIATION: The Lockheed C-5B Galaxy performs its maiden flight; the air force acquires 50 of these giant transports by April 1989.

September 13
AVIATION: The orbiting satellite Defense Department P78-1 is destroyed by a Vought ASM-135 antisatellite missile fired by an F-15 Eagle while 290 miles above the Earth. This is also the first-ever successful satellite interception.

September 21–30
AVIATION: Air force transports deliver over 360 tons of food and medicine to survivors of a devastating earthquake in Mexico City, Mexico.

September 23
AVIATION: A transport from the 89th Military Airlift Wing conveys the first lady, Nancy Reagan, to Mexico City, Mexico, to express official U.S. condolences and present the government with a check for $1 million.

October 1
MILITARY: In Washington, D.C., Admiral William J. Crowe is appointed chairman of the Joint Chiefs of Staff (JCS).
•   The ranks of Specialist Five and Specialist Six, in service since 1958, are eliminated by the army because they have performed work more in line with noncommissioned officers.

October 7–10
TERRORISM: In the Mediterranean Sea, Palestinian terrorists hijack the Italian ocean liner *Achille Lauro,* killing Leon Klinghoffer, an elderly American tourist. Subsequent negotiations allow the terrorists to depart, and they leave on an Egyptian Air Boeing 737.

October 11
AVIATION: An Egyptian airliner carrying terrorists responsible for the hijacking of the Italian cruise ship *Achille Lauro* is intercepted by navy F-14 Tomcat fighters from the carrier *Saratoga* and forced to fly to Italy for internment. President Ronald W. Reagan exclaims to terrorists everywhere that, "You can run but you can't hide." However, the Italians release the terrorists.
• A C-141 Starlifter from the 438th Military Airlift Wing transports 11 American hostages from the *Achille Lauro* from Egypt to Newark, New Jersey.

October 12
MILITARY: At Fort Drum, New York, the 10th Mountain Division is activated while the National Guard 29th Division (Maryland and Virginia) is reorganized as a light infantry division capable of deploying in terrain deemed impractical for armor and mechanized forces.

October 15
AVIATION: Off Camp Lejeune, North Carolina, a CH-46 Skyknight crashes into the ocean, killing 14 marines and a navy chaplain.
• At Edwards Air Force Base the first flight of the T-46A next generation trainer occurs.

October 16
AVIATION: The crew of the shipwrecked Philippine vessel *Marcos Faberes* is rescued by two air force H-3 Jolly Green Giant helicopters.

October 18
AVIATION: A General Dynamics F-111A, fitted with a mission adaptive wing (MAW), performs its maiden flight.

November 1
AVIATION: Ignoring protests from antinuclear groups and KGB-orchestrated peace movements, the Dutch government approves the deployment of air force ground-launched cruise missiles at Woensdrecht, the Netherlands.

November 4
AVIATION: In the Shenandoah Valley, Virginia, helicopter missions orchestrated by the Air Force Rescue Coordination Center save 47 lives from rapid floodwaters.

November 8
MILITARY: In Washington, D.C., the new Defense Authorization Act creates the new Prisoner of War Medal for all U.S. service members. All former POWs taken from April 5, 1917, to the present are eligible, although none of the armed forces request it.
NAVAL: The rank of commodore is changed to rear admiral.

1985

November 15–18
AVIATION: Air force transports lift 50 tons of food and supplies to Colombia in the wake of a severe volcanic eruption.

November 21
NAVAL: Jonathan Jay Pollard, a U.S. naval intelligence analyst, is arrested and charged with spying for Israel, along with his wife. Tried and convicted, he is currently serving a life sentence in a military prison.

November 27
MARINES: At Tampa, Florida, General George B. Crist assumes control of the Central Command; he is the first marine officer to head a unified command.

December
MARINES: Following a period of intense training, the 26th Marine Amphibious Brigade is declared special operations capable (SOC).

December 6
AVIATION: At Barksdale Air Force Base, Louisiana, the arrival of the 19th KC-10 Extender aircraft completes the first fully operational tanker squadron employing that aircraft.

December 12
AVIATION: A chartered Arrow Air airliner crashes near Gander, Newfoundland, Canada, killing 248 members of the 3rd Battalion, 502nd Infantry, 101st Airborne Division as they are returning from peacekeeping activities in the Sinai Peninsula. Eight civilians onboard also perish. Air force C-141s and C-130s are required to airlift all the bodies back to the United States, along with 125 tons of cargo necessary for the cleanup. This remains the worst-ever military aviation disaster.

December 18
AVIATION: Off Lubang, Philippines, 78 passengers from the sinking ship *Asuncion Cinco* are rescued by helicopters dispatched by the Western Pacific Rescue Coordination Center.

December 31
AVIATION: The air force awards a contract to McDonnell Douglas to build the new C-17A long-range, heavy-lift cargo transport. This aircraft will possess the lifting capability of the C-5A Galaxy with the short field landing abilities of the C-130 Hercules.

1986

January 8
AVIATION: At Altus Air Force Base, Oklahoma, the first improved C-5B Galaxy transport aircraft is delivered to the Military Airlift Command (MAC).
• At Eielson Air Force Base, Alaska, the air force installs the first overseas meteorological data system circuit to replace obsolete weather teletype systems in place.

January 28
AVIATION: At Cape Canaveral, Florida, tragedy strikes when the space shuttle *Challenger* explodes shortly after liftoff. U.S. Navy commander Michael Smith

Crowe, William J.   (1925–2007)
Admiral

William James Crowe was born in La Grange, Kentucky, on January 2, 1925, and raised in Oklahoma City. He entered the U.S. Naval Academy in 1946 under a war-accelerated course of study, graduated in 1947, and qualified for submarine service in 1950. Crowe handled his affairs competently, rose steadily through the ranks and, while serving in Washington, D.C., as assistant to the naval aide of President Dwight D. Eisenhower, he enrolled in night classes at the Washington University Law School. Crowe continued honing his scholarly bent by obtaining a master's degree in personnel administration from Stanford University in 1956 and a doctorate in political science from Princeton University in 1965. To obtain the latter, he reputedly turned down Admiral Hyman G. Rickover's invitation to serve in the nuclear-powered submarine force. Two more years of work commanding Submarine Division 31 at San Diego, California, followed, and, after a lengthy stint with the Plans and Policy Deputy's Office in Washington, D.C., Crowe volunteered for service in Vietnam as a naval adviser to the Vietnamese Riverine Force. He became a rear admiral in 1973, served several tours in the Pentagon, and obtained his fourth star to rear admiral in 1980. It was while serving as commander in chief of the Pacific Command that he met President Ronald W. Reagan, who was so impressed with Crowe's command of global affairs that he appointed him the new chairman of the Joint Chiefs of Staff. Crowe was also the first chairman to benefit from the Goldwater-Nichols Act of 1986, under which he served as the senior military adviser to the chief executive and the senior military commander of all military branches.

As chairman, Crowe confronted a world engaged in rising terrorism. In 1986 he advocated several sharp actions against Libyan strongman Muammar Qaddafi, which induced a lessening of Libyan terrorist activ-

is among those killed, along with air force pilots Francis R. Scobee, Gregory B. Jarvis, Ellison S. Onizuka, civilians Judith A. Resnick and Michael J. Smith, and schoolteacher Christa McAuliffe. Modifications are subsequently made to the "O-rings" on each booster rocket, but regular shuttle missions do not resume until September 1988.

NAVAL: The nuclear-powered submersible *NR-1* proves instrumental in retrieving many pieces of the wrecked *Challenger* shuttle from the ocean floor.

February 3
MILITARY: At Fort Benning, Georgia, the 75th Ranger Regiment is organized from the 75th Infantry Regiment. It consists of three battalions under the command of Colonel Wayne A. Downing and is assigned to the 1st Special Operations Command.

February 18–22
AVIATION: Along the Russian and Yuba Rivers, northern California, air force H-3s, HH-53s, and C-130s of the 49th and 129th Aerospace Rescue and Recovery

☆ ☆ ☆ ☆ ☆ ☆ ☆ ☆ ☆ ☆ ☆ ☆ ☆ ☆ ☆

ities. He also supported reflagging neutral tankers in the Persian Gulf, which led to several harsh blows dealt to Iranian naval forces. But Crowe, a consummate diplomat, also engaged his Soviet opposites cordially by inviting Marshal Sergei Akhromeyev to the Pentagon to sign the Intermediate Nuclear Forces (INF) Treaty. In June 1989, he and Soviet general Mikhail Moiseyev concluded the Agreement on the Prevention of Dangerous Military Activities to lower tensions in the last years of the cold war. Crowe resigned from active duty in September 1989 and was replaced by General Colin Powell. He published his memoirs, *The Line of Fire*, in 1993 and, the following year, President Bill Clinton appointed him U.S. ambassador to Great Britain. He served in this office until 1997, and then returned to hold corporate positions while teaching international security at the Naval Academy, Princeton University, and George Washington University. Crowe died on October 18, 2007, in Bethesda, Maryland, one of the most astute sailor-diplomats of his generation.

Admiral William Crowe, former chairman of the Joint Chiefs of Staff (*Department of Defense*)

Groups help evacuate over 500 civilians stranded by severe flooding. A total of 3,000 sandbags are also delivered to army troops on the ground.

February 25–26
AVIATION: In the wake of a disputed election in the Philippines, five H-3 Jolly Green Giant helicopters from the 31st Aerospace Rescue and Recovery Squadron (ARRS) convey President Ferdinand Marcos and 51 people in his entourage to Clark Air Base for ultimate removal to Hawaii.

March 3
AVIATION: At Shaw Air Force Base, South Carolina, the reconnaissance OT-38 Talon replaces the Cessna O-2 aircraft.

March 4
AVIATION: Exercise Bright Star unfolds as aircraft from the United States and Egypt conduct their first joint exercise. This is also the first time that foreign aircraft have been refueled in midair by air force tankers.

March 5
AVIATION: An emergency situation during Operation Coronet East requires a KC-10 Extender to be launched in zero visibility weather. Once over the Atlantic, this aircraft, piloted by Captain Marc C. Felman, refuels a KC-10 and three navy A-4 Skyhawks that were nearly out of fuel. Felman and his crew win a Mackay Trophy for their efforts.
• In accordance with the 1986 McCollum Amendment, the air force begins transporting Afghan refugees and patients from the Soviet invasion from Pakistan to the United States.

March 22
NAVAL: Off Midway Atoll, the ballistic submarine *Georgia* collides with the ocean-going tug *Secota* during a routine crew transfer, resulting in two deaths.

March 23–24
AVIATION: In the Gulf of Sidra, Libyan antiaircraft batteries fire missiles at navy warplanes belonging to the *Coral Sea* and miss. On the following day, Operation Prairie Fire unfolds as six A-6 aircraft from the carrier *America* attack and sink two Libyan patrol boats and a guided missile corvette with Harpoon antiship missiles. Freedom of navigation in the gulf has been deftly underscored.

March 25
AVIATION: At Whiteman Air Force Base, Missouri, the 351st Strategic Missile Wing activates the first all-women Minuteman missile crew on alert.

March 27
AVIATION: The first Bell Textron AH-1W Super Cobra is delivered to the Marine Corps.

March 29
AVIATION: Lieutenant Commander Donnie L. Cochran is the first African-American pilot chosen to fly with the navy's Blue Angels precision flying team.

April 1
AVIATION: The Marine Corps begins reorganizing three attack helicopter and three light helicopter squadrons into six light attack squadrons (HLMA), equipped with UH-1 Hueys and AH-1 Cobras.

April 5
TERRORISM: An American sergeant is killed and 60 others wounded when a bomb explodes at a discotheque in West Germany. The American government suspects Libyan agents are behind the blast and prepares to act accordingly.

April 5–6
AVIATION: At Osan Air Base, South Korea, four C-141 Starlifters and one H-3 Jolly Green Giant helicopter from the 63rd Airlift Wing convey fire-suppressant foam to extinguish a large jet fuel tank fire. Burn victims are also conveyed to medical facilities in Seoul for treatment.

April 14–15
AVIATION: Operation El Dorado Canyon unfolds as a strike force of 24F-111F bombers from the Statue of Liberty Squadron, 48th Tactical Fighter Wing,

launches from Great Britain and performs a retaliatory strike against Tripoli, Libya. To get there, these aircraft, lacking overflight permission from Spain and France, fly a 5,500-mile round trip around continental Europe. Nonetheless, the attackers inflict heavy damage on the Jumahiriya Military Barracks and Benina Military Airfield. The attack is joined by carrier strike craft launched from the *America* and *Saratoga,* including jets from VMFA-314 and 323. One F-111 is lost in action, presumably to a surface-to-air missile.

• No less than 28 KC-10 Extenders and KC-135 Stratotankers are employed during Operation El Dorado Canyon, and they refuel the F-111 strike force six times in complete radio silence.

MILITARY: At Fort Monroe, Virginia, Major General Robert E. Wagner is appointed to head the new U.S. Army ROTC Cadet Command. It is assigned as part of the Training and Doctrine Command (TRADOC) and oversees ROTC programs at more than 400 colleges and universities and also 800 high schools with Junior ROTC programs. The army currently obtains more than 70 percent of its commissioned officers from ROTC.

April 15
TERRORISM: At Yokota Air Base, Japan, a rocket bomb lands inside the perimeter fence causing minor damage.

April 18
AVIATION: At Vandenberg Air Force Base, California, a Titan 3D rocket booster explodes on liftoff; Space Launch Complex Four sustains damage and does not become operative again until August 15.

April 28–May 7
AVIATION: In the wake of a nuclear reactor accident at Chernobyl, Soviet Union, the Air Weather Service launches several WC-130s to track and analyze the radioactive fallout with air samples.

May 6
NAVAL: In an impressive show of force, the nuclear-powered submarines *Archerfish, Hawkbill,* and *Ray* all surface at the North Pole for the first time.

May 10
NAVAL: The historic battleship *Missouri,* upon which the ceremonies ending World War II took place, is recommissioned into active service.

June 17
AVIATION: The air force retires its final UC-133K Provider from spraying activities.

July
AVIATION: The first C-141 Starlifters are delivered to units of the Air Force Reserve and Air National Guard.

July 1
NAVAL: In Washington, D.C., Admiral Carlisle A. H. Trost gains appointment as the 23rd chief of naval operations.

July 19
AVIATION: In Europe, Rapier surface-to-air missile units are declared operational by the U.S. Air Force in Europe (USAFE).

July 19–28
AVIATION: Severe drought conditions across the southwestern United States result in Operation Southern Haylift as 24 C-141s and eight C-130s carrying 19,000 bales (536 tons) of hay to livestock farmers living in the afflicted areas.

July 27
AVIATION: In Damascus, Syria, an air force C-9 Nightingale transports Father Lawrence Jenco, recently released by Muslim extremists, to medical facilities at Rhein-Main Air Base, West Germany.

August 27–29
AVIATION: In Cameroon, West Africa, a C-130 Hercules of the 50th Tactical Airlift Squadron delivers 250 tents to villagers fleeing toxic volcanic fumes escaping from Lake Nyos.

August 29
AVIATION: In Norway, a CH-46 Skyknight helicopter crashes, killing eight marines and injuring 13 more.

September 1
AVIATION: At Davis Monthan Air Force Base, Arizona, the last operational Cessna O-2 Bird Dog is retired and sent to the "bone yard."

September 5
AVIATION: At Karachi Airport, Pakistan, a C-141 Starlifter transports Americans injured during a hijacking attempt to medical facilities in Frankfurt, West Germany.

September 11
MARINES: At Twenty-Nine Palms, California, the 3rd Light Armored Vehicle Battalion is organized.

September 18–20
AVIATION: At Luzon, Philippines, two C-5 Galaxies of the 436th Military Airlift Wing convey 93 tons of food and medical supplies under terms of the Foreign Assistance Act of 1985.

September 20
NAVAL: In a nod to tradition, Secretary of the Navy John F. Lehman orders brown shoes reinstituted as part of the uniforms of naval officers and chief petty officers assigned to aviation units.

September 22
MARINES: A new directive from the commandant of the Marine Corps mandates that senior NCOs replace all officers at the SNCO Academies at Quantico, Virginia; Camp Lejeune, North Carolina; and El Toro, California.

October 1
MILITARY: In Washington, D.C., the Goldwater-Nichols Act is signed into law by President Ronald W. Reagan. A significant reform, it centralizes all operational authority through the chairman of the Joint Chiefs of Staff, who now serves as the president's senior military adviser. The act streamlines the chain

of command from the president to the secretary of defense to respective theater commanders. The position of vice chairman of the Joint Chiefs of Staff is also created.

October 10

AVIATION: The LGM-118A, or Peacekeeper, intercontinental ballistic missile is placed on operational alert for the first time. It is capable of attacking up to 10 different targets with a multiple independent reentry vehicle (MIRV) warhead.

October 11–16

AVIATION: San Salvador, capital of El Salvador, is destroyed by an earthquake, prompting air force transports to begin delivering food and relief supplies to survivors.

November 5

NAVAL: In China, the cruiser *Reeves*, the destroyer *Oldendorf*, and the frigate *Rentz* become the first U.S. Navy warships to make a friendly port call in 37 years.

December 4

MILITARY: In the Panama Canal Zone, U.S. Army South is activated to coordinate the multiservice U.S. Southern Command through a single army headquarters. Major General James R. Taylor is the first commander from his headquarters at Fort Clayton in the Panama Canal Zone.

The controversial MX or Peacekeeper missile (*U.S. Air Force*)

December 7

AVIATION: In the wake of Typhoon Kim, a WC-130 Hercules of the 54th Weather Reconnaissance Squadron lands on Saipan, Mariana Islands, to deliver seven tons of relief supplies, food, and Christmas toys for the children.

December 10

AVIATION: Several miles off Destin, Florida, air force helicopters rescue 19 members of the Norwegian research ship *Geco Alpha* after it caught fire. Casualties are flown to Eglin Air Force base for treatment.

December 14–23

AVIATION: At Edwards Air Force Base, California, the experimental *Voyager* aircraft, piloted by Richard G. Rutan and Jeana L. Yeager, lifts off and flies 25,000 miles, nonstop and unrefueled, around the world. Rutan wins a Collier Trophy for his record, nine-day flight.

December 18

AVIATION: In the South China Sea, two H-3 Jolly Green Giant helicopters of the 31st Aerospace Rescue and Recovery Squadron (ARRS) hoist up 13 survivors from a sinking Filipino vessel. Casualties are delivered to medical facilities at Cubi Air Station, Philippines, for treatment.

1986

December 22
AVIATION: At F. E. Warren Air Base, the deployment of a 10th Peacekeeper intercontinental ballistic missile (ICBM) leads to all weapons being placed on operational status.

December 31
AVIATION: In San Juan, Puerto Rico, H-3 Sea King helicopters of Composite Squadron 8 (VC-8) rescue 75 people stranded on the roof of the Dupont Plaza Hotel during a fire.

1987

January
MILITARY: Although the number of army personnel is stable, the number of active divisions has risen to 18, the largest number in service at the height of the Vietnam War in 1968.

January 10
MARINES: Sergeant Clayton J. Lonetree is arrested and charged with trading national secrets in exchange for sex while he served in the U.S. embassy guard detail in Moscow, Soviet Union. He is the first member of the Marine Corps ever charged with disloyalty and receives a 30-year sentence and a $5,000 fine.

January 16
AVIATION: At the Tonopoh Test Range, Nevada, a B-1B Lancer fires a short-range attack missile (SRAM) for the first time.

February 3
AVIATION: At Eglin Air Force Base, Florida, the 55th Aerospace Rescue and Recovery Squadron receives the first Sikorsky UH-60A Black Hawk helicopters. These machines are to be retrofitted with Pace Low III infrared systems to facilitate long-range search-and-rescue missions.

February 13–15
AVIATION: On Vanuatu, New Hebrides, two C-141 Starlifters and two C-130 Hercules transport 64 tons of tents and plastic sheeting to survivors of Typhoon Uma.

February 16
AVIATION: In San Antonio, Texas, the Joint Military Medical Command is activated; it is staffed by both army and air force personnel.

March 7
NAVAL: The so-called tanker war begins in the Persian Gulf as Iran and Iraq begin attacking oil tankers sailing with each other's oil. President Ronald W. Reagan, anxious to keep the flow of petroleum to the West unimpeded, announces that 11 Kuwaiti tankers will be reflagged with American colors to protect them from Iranian attack.

March 31
MILITARY: In El Paraiso, El Salvador, Special Forces Sergeant Gregory Frontius is killed in a shoot-out with FMLN Marxist guerrillas, currently receiving military aid from Communists in Nicaragua.

April 9
MILITARY: In light of prevailing world realities, the Special Forces Branch is established as a basic branch of the U.S. Army. The military is placing renewed emphasis on special operations around the world in the fight against communism and terrorism.

April 10
NAVAL: In Washington, D.C., James H. Webb gains appointment as the 66th secretary of the navy.

April 14
AVIATION: A B-1B Lancer flying out of Dyess Air Force Base, Texas, flies 9,400 miles in 21 hours and 40 minutes while utilizing five inflight refuelings. This is also the type's longest flight to date.

April 15
MILITARY: The navy initiates the Special Operations Command (SOCOM), which brings the special forces of all four branches of the armed services under a unified command.

April 16
MARINES: At Norfolk, Virginia, the Marine Corps Security Force Battalion, Atlantic is organized while restructuring various detachments at sea and the Marine Barracks.

April 21
NAVAL: Off the Virginia coast, the frigate *Richard L. Page* collides with the fishing boat *Chickadee* in foggy weather, sinking it.

May 5
AVIATION: At Little Rock Air Force Base, Arkansas, the last liquid-fueled Titan II intercontinental ballistic missile (ICBM) is retired from active service. This was the largest ballistic missile ever fielded by the United States during the cold war years.
POLITICS: Lieutenant Colonel Oliver L. North and Rear Admiral John M. Poindexter are charged with misbehavior during the so-called Iran-Contra scandal. In televised congressional hearings, North gains national notoriety as "the marine who took the hill" during a spirited defense of his actions.

May 6
AVIATION: At Sembach Air Base, West Germany, the first EC-130H Compass Call aircraft is delivered to the 43rd Electronics Combat Squadron.

May 14
AVIATION: In the Persian Gulf, the destroyer *Coontz* prepares to engage an Iraqi Mirage F-1 fighter that approaches to within 10 miles of it, then turns around.

May 17
AVIATION: In the Persian Gulf, the frigate *Stark* is struck by a pair of French-made Exocet missiles fired by an Iraqi F-1 Mirage; 37 sailors are killed and the vessel is badly damaged. The vessel's defensive measures were not operational at the time of the attack, despite the element of danger present, so the captain and the tactical action officer receive letters of reprimand and resign.

May 19
DIPLOMACY: The Iraqi government of Saddam Hussein acknowledges responsibility in launching the missile that struck the *Stark* but declares the incident will not alter relations between the two countries; President Ronald W. Reagan announces his decision to fly the American flag on Kuwaiti oil tankers in the Persian Gulf to protect them as the Iraq-Iran War rages.

June 1
AVIATION: The air force establishes its Special Operations Command.

June 10
AVIATION: At the Paris Air Show, France, the B1-B Lancer makes its European debut.

June 23
MILITARY: In Washington, D.C., Major General Carl E. Vuono gains appointment as the 31st army chief of staff.

June 26
MARINES: Sergeant Major David W. Somers is appointed the 11th sergeant major of the Marine Corps.

June 30
MARINES: Manpower levels of the Marine Corps peak at 20,047 officers and 179,478 enlisted men and women. This is the highest level since the end of the Vietnam War.

July 1
MARINES: In Washington, D.C., General Alfred M. Gray gains appointments as the 39th commandant of the Marine Corps.

July 4–September 17
AVIATION: A Rockwell B-1B Lancer flown by Lieutenant Robert Chamberlain establishes 12 new world records for speed and payload combinations. Another B-1B flown by Major Brent A. Hedgpeth sets another nine speed records. Consequently, the B-1B System Program Office, Air Force Systems Command, wins a Mackay Trophy.

July 15–22
POLITICS: Admiral John Poindexter testifies before the House Foreign Affairs Committee to determine responsibility in the Iran/contra arms for hostages swap.

July 17
AVIATION: At Hurlburt Field, Florida, the first Sikorsky MH-53J Pave Low helicopter is delivered by the Air Force Logistics Command and begins operational service within a year. This machine is equipped for poor weather/ nighttime operations and becomes closely associated with Special Forces.

July 22–December 21
AVIATION: With the Iran-Iraq War now spilling over into the Persian Gulf, Operation Earnest Will unfolds as air force E-3A Sentry aircraft begin routine patrols. C-5A Galaxy and C-141 Starlifter transports also convey minesweeping equip-

ment into the region while air force tankers support navy aircraft patrolling the gulf waters.

July 24

AVIATION: After the tanker *Bridgeton* strikes a mine in the Persian Gulf, eight RH-53D helicopters begin minesweeping operations to secure the safe passage of neutral shipping.

NAVAL: The United States commences Operation Earnest Will by providing protection to reflagged Kuwaiti oil tankers in the Persian Gulf.

MARINES: The 24th Marine Amphibious Unit deploys to the Persian Gulf once the *Bridgeton,* an American-flagged tanker, strikes a mine laid by the Iranians. They are there to assist the navy in keeping that valuable waterway open to commercial traffic.

July 27

AVIATION: Helicopter mine countermeasure squadron HM-14 arrives in the Persian Gulf after an Iranian mine damages the reflagged tanker *Bridgeton* on July 24.

August 4

NAVAL: At Pascagoula, Mississippi, the amphibious assault ship *Wasp* is launched; this vessel is intended to replace the earlier *Iwo Jima* class of helicopter carriers.

August 8

AVIATION: To counter Iranian mine-laying operations in the strategic Persian Gulf, Special Force MH-6 Little Bird helicopters begin patrolling the waters at night. They are under orders to stop any Iranian vessels threatening the free transit of any merchant ships and tankers through the gulf.

August 24

NAVAL: In a sign of rising tension throughout the Persian Gulf, when the destroyer *Kidd* is approached by two Iranian dhows, warning shots are fired to force them back. The frigate *Jarrett* also interposes his vessel between a convoy he is escorting and an Iranian warship.

MARINES: A military court convicts Sergeant Clayton J. Lonetree of espionage on behalf of the Soviet embassy while serving as a marine security guard at the U.S. embassies in Vienna and Moscow.

August 31–September 9

AVIATION: Across the coastal regions of Oregon and northern California, C-130 and C-141 aircraft deliver 2,511 tons of fire retardant and a crew of firefighters to combat a fire blazing across 970 square miles.

September 10

NAVAL: The battleship *Iowa* is assigned VC-6, Detachment One, which is the first squadron of Pioneer remotely controlled vehicles.

September 17

AVIATION: A Rockwell B-1B Lancer flown by Major Brent A. Hedgpeth establishes nine new world records in a single five-hour sortie by carrying 66,140 pounds for 3,107 miles and at a speed of 655 miles per hour.

September 21
NAVAL: An army MH-6 Little Bird helicopter launched from the frigate *Jarrett* attacks and damages the Iranian landing craft *Iran Air* after it is caught deploying mines in the Persian Gulf. The vessel is then stormed by SEALs and taken under tow. The crew of 26 Iranians is released shortly afterward.

September 24
AVIATION: Over Beijing, China, the Air Force Thunderbirds demonstration squadron performs before a crowd of 20,000 spectators.

September 28
AVIATION: The first B-1B crashes during a training mission after a severe bird strike.

October 1
AVIATION: The Space Command assumes control over Onizuka Air Force Station, California, and the Air Force Satellite Control Network, a set of worldwide remote-tracking stations.
• At Hickham Air Force Base, Hawaii, and Clark Air Base, Philippines, the Pacific Air Forces retire all their venerable T-33 jet trainers after 32 years.

October 8
AVIATION: In the Persian Gulf, An army MH-6 Little Bird helicopter attacks a group of four Iranian speedboats after one of their number shot at them. One boat is sunk, two are captured; two Iranians die of their wounds.
MARINES: The Marine Amphibious Group Task Force (MAGTF) 1-88 sails onboard the *Okinawa* in order to relieve the 24th Marine Amphibious Unit then on duty in the Persian Gulf.

October 9
MARINES: At Portsmouth, New Hampshire, the Marine Barracks closes in a cost-cutting measure. This is the second-oldest marine post in the nation, dating to 1813.

October 16
NAVAL: In the Persian Gulf, an Iranian battery on the Fao Peninsula fires a Chinese-built Silkworm missile at the reflagged Kuwaiti tanker *Sea Isle City,* damaging it.

October 19
NAVAL: In the Persian Gulf, the guided-missile destroyers *Hoel* and *Kidd,* and the destroyers *John Young* and *Leftwich,* shoot up two older Iranian oil platforms in retaliation for missile attacks against neutral shipping. No casualties are reported. The platforms had been used for military purposes and were singled-out for destruction.

November 1
MILITARY: At Fort Benning, Georgia, the army establishes the Ranger Training Brigade along with four Ranger Training Battalions. This is to impart meaningful training on Ranger and Long-Range Surveillance officers.

November 19
AVIATION: The Northrop Corporation contracts with the air force to design and construct the B-2, the next generation of stealth aircraft.

November 24
AVIATION: A B-1B Lancer successfully deploys an air-launched cruise missile (ACLM) for the first time.
MILITARY: In Washington, D.C., Frank C. Carlucci gains appointment as the 16th secretary of defense.

December 5
AVIATION: Luzon, Philippines, still reeling from the effects of Typhoon Nina, is assisted by six C1-30 Hercules transports from the 374th Tactical Airlift Squadron, which bring in 34 tons of supplies, clothing, and rice to assist the victims.

December 6
MARINES: In San Diego, California, a restructuring of marine security forces leads to the closing of the Sea School, which has operated there since 1923.

December 8
AVIATION: The recently signed Intermediate-Range Nuclear Forces Treaty (INF) between the United States and the Soviet Union calls for the removal of all Pershing II, ground-launched cruise missiles, and SS-20 missiles from Europe by 1991. Presidents Ronald W. Reagan and Mikhail S. Gorbachev are the signatories. This results in the deactivation and removal of six air force tactical missile wings (TMW) throughout Europe.

December 12
NAVAL: In the Persian Gulf, the destroyer *Chandler* deploys its helicopters to evacuate 11 crewmen from the sinking Cypriot tanker *Pivot* after it is attacked by Iranian speedboats.

December 25
NAVAL: In the Persian Gulf, the frigates *Elrod* and HMS *Scylla* use helicopters to rescue 20 crewmen from the South Korean–flagged tanker *Hyundai* after it was attacked by an Iranian frigate.

December 27
TERRORISM: In Barcelona, Spain, a terrorist attack upon a United Services Organization club kills one sailor and injures five others.

1988

January
MARINES: In Washington, D.C., Secretary James Webb, a former marine, orders that Naval Academy midshipmen seeking a Marine Corps commission will have to pass through the Officer Candidate School at Quantico, Virginia, first.

January 1
AVIATION: The Strategic Air Command (SAC) allows mixed male/female teams to serve as Minuteman and Peacekeeper strategic missile crews for the first time.

January 20
AVIATION: At Palmdale, California, the 100th and final Rockwell B-1B Lancer strategic bomber rolls off the assembly line.

January 25–28
AVIATION: Two C-5 Galaxy transports from the 60th Military Airlift Wing arrive in Manila, Philippines, bringing 102 tons of medical supplies to refresh the stocks of Americares, a private relief organization.

February 5
MARINES: As of this date the name of all marine amphibious groupings will add the title "expeditionary" to their titles, a reflection of the wider capabilities they project.

February 12
NAVAL: In the Black Sea, the guided-missile cruiser *Yorktown* and the destroyer *Caron* are challenged by two Soviet patrol frigates who bump into them. Other than a flurry of diplomatic protests, no action results.

February 17
TERRORISM: Along the Israel-Lebanon border, marine lieutenant colonel William R. Higgins, on station as a UN observer, is kidnaped and subsequently killed by militants.

February 19–22
AVIATION: After Typhoon Roy batters the Marshall Islands, a C-141 of the 86th Military Airlift Wing conveys 50 tons of construction materials to repair housing.

February 22
NAVAL: In Washington, D.C., Secretary of the Navy James H. Webb vocally resigns from office after accusing Secretary of Defense Frank Carlucci of failing to support a 600-ship navy.

March 16
CRIME: Admiral John Poindexter, Lieutenant Colonel Oliver North, and two other individuals are indicted by a federal grand jury for their roles in the illegal Iran-contra scandal.

March 16–28
AVIATION: In Honduras, air force transports convey 3,200 army troops during Operation Golden Pheasant to counter Sandinista threats to the region.
MILITARY: In response to Nicaraguan Sandinista (Communist) incursions into Honduras, President Ronald W. Reagan announces the temporary deployment of 3,200 army troops under the title of Operation Golden Pheasant. The units involved are the 1st and 2nd Battalions, 504th Infantry, 82nd Airborne Division, and 7th Infantry Division (Light). Their presence is sufficient to deter Nicaraguan activities and they are eventually withdrawn without incident.

March 24
NAVAL: In Washington, D.C., William L. Ball gains appointment as the 68th secretary of the navy.

April
AVIATION: When political instability threatens the safety of Americans living in Panama, eight C-5 Galaxies and 22 C-141 Starlifters from the Military Airlift Command (MAC) covey 1,300 security specialists there as a precaution.

1988

April 14
DIPLOMACY: The Soviet Union, having invaded Afghanistan in December 1979 and having been thwarted by Afghani freedom fighters bolstered by U.S. military aid, signs an agreement with the United States, Pakistan, and Afghanistan to remove all its troops from the region. This is a major victory for the United States and its allies, although it portends ill for subsequent events there.
NAVAL: In the Persian Gulf, the frigate *Samuel B. Roberts* strikes an Iranian mine, causing a 21-foot-long hole in its hull and extensive damage. Ten sailors are injured.

April 17–July 23
AVIATION: A C-5A Galaxy piloted by Captain Michael Eastman of the 436th Military Airlift Wing delivers nuclear-test monitoring equipment to the Soviet Republic of Kazakhstan to support joint verification experiments. They land near the site where the first Soviet atomic weapon was detonated in 1949; Eastman and his crew win the Mackay Trophy for the efforts.

April 18
AVIATION: Air force tankers are actively engaged refueling navy aircraft in a confrontation with Iranian forces.
• During Operation Preying Mantis, a Marine Sea Cobra helicopter is downed, possibly by an Iranian missile; its crew of two is killed.
NAVAL: In the Persian Gulf, Operation Preying Mantis unfolds as U.S. Navy warships and jet bombers conduct a retaliatory action for the recent mine strike on the frigate *Samuel B. Roberts*. Initially, the destroyer *Merrill* shells and destroys an oil platform employed as command-and-control center for attacks on neutral shipping. A second platform is eliminated by the guided-missile cruiser *Wainwright,* and frigates *Simpson* and *Bagley.* Meanwhile, A-6 Intruders launched from the carrier *Enterprise* fire Harpoon missiles that sink the fast patrol boat *Joshan* and the frigate *Sahand.* Finally, the destroyer *Joseph Strauss* joins A-6 and A-7 aircraft in pummeling the Iranian frigate *Sabalan,* which is allowed to return to port in severely damaged condition upon the orders of the president.
MARINES: In the Persian Gulf, Contingency MAGTF 2-88 swings into action in storming the Iranian oil platform *Sassan,* which had been used for gathering military intelligence.

April 24
NAVAL: Off Cape Kennedy, Florida, the elderly diesel-electric submarine *Bonefish* has a battery explosion that kills three of its crew. The vessel is towed to Charleston, South Carolina, and decommissioned.

April 26
AVIATION: At the White Sands Missile Range, New Mexico, the army successfully fires its first Army Tactical Missile System (ATACMS). This weapon is designed for penetrating hardened targets and some variants eventually boast a range of over 100 miles.

April 29
NAVAL: In Washington, D.C., Secretary of Defense Frank Carlucci announces that the navy will protect all friendly, neutral shipping in the Persian Gulf.

April 30

AVIATION: At McConnell Air Force Base, Kansas, the 100th and final Rockwell B-1B Lancer is delivered to the 384th Bombardment Squadron.

May

AVIATION: This month C-5 Galaxy transports convey 73 tons of relief supplies from Kadena Air Base, Okinawa, to Islamabad, Pakistan, for refugees fleeing the onset of civil war in neighboring Afghanistan.

MARINES: Female marines are allowed to serve as embassy security personnel for the first time since the 1970s.

May 23

AVIATION: At Arlington, Texas, the Bell Textron V-22 Osprey, an airplane/helicopter hybrid machine, debuts for the first time. This revolutionary craft will eventually replace aging CH-46 Skyknight helicopters in the Marine Corps.

June 1

MILITARY: The Army Engineering School at Fort Belvoir, Virginia, is relocated to Fort Leonard Wood, Missouri, after 68 years at the former locale. It is soon joined by the Chemical School and the Military Police School.

June 2–August 11

AVIATION: The outbreak of sectarian warfare in southern Sudan results in thousands of refugees and prompts transports of the 60th and 436th Military Airlift Wings to convey 70 tons of plastic sheeting for shelters, along with food and medical supplies.

June 28

TERRORISM: In Athens, Greece, naval attaché Captain William E. Nordeen is killed by a car bomb planted in his automobile.

July 2

NAVAL: In the Persian Gulf, an Iranian speedboat fires on a Danish supertanker and is driven off by warning shots from the frigate *Elmer B. Montgomery.*

July 3

AVIATION: In the Persian Gulf, Iranian speedboats have fired on American helicopters working in that region. Hours later, the guided-missile cruiser *Vincennes* picks up a radar contact with a large aircraft approaching them. This turns out to be an Iranian A-300 Airbus, and it is mistaken at long range for an Iranian F-14 fighter. The craft is shot down over the Strait of Hormuz by the *Vincennes,* killing all 290 passengers and crew. In fairness to the commander, the aircraft had been warned repeatedly as it approached, but it refused to respond. Rather than risk a potential suicide attack on his vessel, the captain ordered the aircraft downed. Regardless, President Ronald W. Reagan issues a formal apology to the Iranian people and offers compensation to families of the deceased. A navy investigation concludes that Captain Will C. Rodgers acted responsibly, given the information he had at his disposal.

July 7

AVIATION: After three decades of distinguished service, the last F-106 Delta Darts are ordered dropped from the air force inventory.

1988

August 1
AVIATION: The last three F-106 Delta Darts are retired from active service by the 177th Fighter Group. Many surviving aircraft end up as remote-controlled target drones.

August 15–28
AVIATION: Air force C-5 Galaxies from the Military Airlift Command (MAC) fly in 500 UN peacekeepers to maintain and monitor a cease-fire between Turkey and Iraq.

August 18
NAVAL: At Annapolis, Maryland, Rear Admiral Virgil L. Hill, Jr., gains appointment as the 53rd superintendent of the U.S. Naval Academy.

August 22–October 6
AVIATION: As forest fires devastate Yellowstone National Park, the Military Airlift Command (MAC) flies in 4,000 firefighters and 2,500 tons of equipment directly into the disaster zone. Other transports are fitted with spraying equipment and apply flame retardant over thousands of acres.

August 25–31
AVIATION: Once the onset of civil war creates an acute refugee problem in Somalia, a C-141 Starlifter belonging to the 41st Military Airlift Squadron delivers a 200-bed emergency hospital weighing 200 tons.

August 28
AVIATION: A C-141 Starlifter from the 20th Military Airlift Squadron delivers 29 tons of medical supplies and hospital equipment to medical facilities on the island of São Tomé off the west coast of Africa.

September
AVIATION: To deter any North Korean aggression during the Olympics held in Seoul, South Korea, an Air Force E-3A Sentry aircraft, escorted by fighters, patrols the airspace above the peninsula.

September 9
AVIATION: At Karnack, Texas, and in accordance with the recent INF Treaty, the army begins destroying the first of its Pershing II missiles. The devices are static fired and then crushed flat by hydraulic presses. Half a world away, Soviet SS-20 missiles are slated for the same fate.

September 10–15
AVIATION: Catastrophic flooding in Bangladesh leaves 28 million people homeless so no less than four Airlift Wings–the 60th, 62nd, 63rd, and 436th–are employed bringing 100 million tons of humanitarian supplies to the victims.

September 28
NAVAL: The newly passed 1989 Defense Authorization Act brings the Department of Defense into the War on Drugs as a detection and monitoring agency. Apprehension of violators, however, will remain with the Coast Guard.

1988

The Boeing B-2 Spirit is the USAF's only strategic stealth bomber. *(U.S. Air Force)*

September 29
AVIATION: Two and a half years after the *Challenger* space shuttle disaster, the stand down ends when *Discovery* is launched into orbit under U.S. Air Force colonel Richard O. Covey.

October 22
NAVAL: The World War II–era battleship *Wisconsin* is recommissioned, marking the first time that all four *Iowa*-class battleships are in service again.

October 25
AVIATION: Severe flooding at Marikina, Philippines, results in two HH-3 Jolly Green Giant helicopters from the 31st Aerospace Rescue and Recovery Squadron (ASSR) assisting 27 stranded residents over an eight-hour period.

November 9
AVIATION: The 709th Military Airlift Squadron dispatches a C-5 Galaxy with a mobile dental clinic and two ambulances to Niamey, Niger, at the behest of the U.S. State Department.

November 10
AVIATION: The air force reveals the existence of the Lockheed F-117A Nighthawk to the public. A stealthy light bomber, it employs the smallest radar cross-section of any aircraft at the time and is virtually invisible to radar. The air force acquires 59 F-117s at a cost of $42.6 million apiece.

November 16–30
AVIATION: At Dakar, Senegal, aircraft of the 60th, 63rd, 437th, and 438th Military Airlift Wings deliver tons of insecticide to help thwart a major locust infestation.

November 22
AVIATION: At Palmdale, California, the new Northrop B-2 Spirit bomber is publicly revealed for the first time; it is reputedly invisible to radar and also costs a whopping $1 billion per aircraft. The air force aspires to order 132 such aircraft as its new front-line bomber.

November 29
AVIATION: The air force accepts delivery of its 60th and final KC-10 Extender. This particular model employs wing-mounted refueling pods to complement its centerline boom.

December
NAVAL: With the end of the Iran-Iraq War, tensions in the Persian Gulf decline to the point where the role of the navy is reduced to monitoring U.S. flag vessels.

December 9
AVIATION: A destructive earthquake ravages Yerevan, Armenia–then part of the Soviet Union–and Party Secretary Mikhail Gorbachev permits Military Airlift

1988

Command (MAC) transports to enter Russian airspace unimpeded and deliver 300 tons of relief aid.

December 12

AVIATION: In the Pacific Ocean between the Philippines and Japan, a helicopter from the 33rd Aerospace Rescue and Recovery Squadron (ARRS) saves 11 passengers on a life raft once their vessel, *Selina,* sinks. They are taken to Clark Air Base for treatment, then released.

December 22

AVIATION: The Grumman Company begins modifying the second E-8A JSTARS command-and-control aircraft; the two E-8As will be deployed during Operation Desert Storm while still in their developmental stage.

1989

January 4

AVIATION: Several navy F-14 Tomcats of VF-32 from the carrier *John F. Kennedy* shoot down two Libyan MiG-23 jets over the Gulf of Sidra after a tense standoff. They had apparently approached the American jets in a hostile manner before the incident.

January 7

AVIATION: At Camp Pendleton, California, helicopter squadron HMA-775 is activated as part of the 4th Marine Air Wing (4th MAW).

January 7–20

AVIATION: To support Medfly '89, a joint-service humanitarian effort, two C-130 Hercules from the 167th Tactical Airlift Group arrive at Monrovia, Liberia, to deliver medical supplies and personnel.

January 10

AVIATION: A B-52 bomber test launches the AGM-136 Tacit Rainbow missile for the first time. This advanced weapon is designed to fly to specific coordinates and then loiter in the area until radar energy is detected and identified, whereupon the missile hones in and destroys the target.

January 20

MILITARY: In Washington, D.C., George H. W. Bush is sworn in as the 41st president of the United States and commander in chief.

February

AVIATION: The 63rd Military Airlift Wing dispatches two C-141 Starlifters to Dakar, Senegal, with 20 tons of insecticide to control swarming locusts.

February 16

AVIATION: The T-38 Talon production line is closed by Northrop after manufacturing its 3,806th supersonic jet trainer.

March

MARINES: The Fleet Marine Manual 1, *Warfighting,* is issued at the behest of its staunchest advocate, General Al Gray. It advocates battle based on maneuver instead of traditional attrition, and it becomes required reading for all officers and staff NCOs.

March 3
Marines: Force restructuring results in the 2nd Battalion, 6th Marines and 3rd Battalion, 1st Marines being accorded cadre status. However, all 24 remaining active-duty battalions are enlarged with the addition of a fourth rifle company.

March 20
Aviation: In South Korea, the crashes of a CH-46 and a CH-53D helicopter during the Team Spirit '89 exercise kill 17 marines and one navy corpsman.

March 21
Military: In Washington, D.C., Richard B. Cheney is appointed the 17th secretary of defense.
Naval: Off Cape Kennedy, Florida, the fleet ballistic submarine *Tennessee* launches the Trident II D-5 missile underwater for the first time. The result is a spectacular failure that cartwheels through the sky and has to be destroyed in midflight.

March 27
Aviation: In Alaska, Military Airlift Command (MAC) transports convey over 1,000 tons of cleanup equipment after the *Exxon Valdez* tanker spills 10 million gallons of oil along the coastline.

April
Aviation: The 436th Military Airlift Wing delivers 32 pallets of relief supplies to undernourished inhabitants of Gambia, Equatorial Guinea, and Chad.

April 17
Aviation: Over Saudi Arabia, the Boeing E-3A Sentry aircraft christened Elf One returns to Tinker Air Force Base, Oklahoma, after serving eight years on station.
•   The 50th and final Lockheed C-5B Galaxy transport is delivered to the U.S. Air Force.

April 19
Naval: While conducting a firing test of its main battery off Puerto Rico, the battleship *Iowa* suffers from a catastrophic turret explosion that kills 47 sailors. Quick flooding of the powder magazine below the turret prevents a catastrophic explosion. Several official investigations of the mishap are undertaken.

April 21
Military: In Quezon City, the Philippines, Marxist guerrillas assassinate Colonel James N. Rowe of the Joint United States Military Advisory Group (JUSMAG). The Americans are presently providing advanced counterinsurgency training to Filipino units.

May 11
Diplomacy: The refusal of Panamanian dictator Manuel Noriega to allow free elections results in increased tension with the United States. Consequently, additional military forces are dispatched to the Panama Canal Zone.

May 13–18
Aviation: Operation Nimrod Dancer unfolds as air force transports fly in 2,600 marines into Panama, along with 3,000 tons of equipment, in response to recent threats to U.S. military personnel.

May 15
NAVAL: In Washington, D.C., H. Lawrence Garrett III, gains appointment as the 68th secretary of the navy.

May 16–June 29
AVIATION: Continuing political unrest in Panama results in Operation Blade Jewel, during which air force transports evacuate 6,000 nonessential personnel from the region.

May 30
AVIATION: A CH-46 Skyknight helicopter belonging to the amphibious transport *Denver* crashes at sea, killing 13 marines and a navy corpsman.

June 9–11
AVIATION: The Military Airlift Command (MAC) sends several transports to the Soviet Union with humanitarian supplies for victims of a terrible train wreck near Ufa of the Trans-Siberian Railroad, resulting in 850 casualties.

June 10
AVIATION: At Edwards Air Force Base, California, Captain Jacquelyn S. Parker is the first woman to graduate from the Air Force Test Pilot School.

June 14
AVIATION: At Cape Canaveral, Florida, the new Titan IV heavy-lift rocket booster, almost 20 stories tall, is launched for the first time and carries a Department of Defense satellite into orbit.
NAVAL: Off the California coast, the nuclear submarine *Houston* snares a tow bale dangling from the commercial tugboat *Barcelona,* and drags the vessel underwater. One civilian dies in consequence.

July 6
AVIATION: In Washington, D.C., President George H. W. Bush awards noted aviator James H. Doolittle the Presidential Medal of Freedom. Significantly, Doolittle is the only American to receive this medal and a Medal of Honor, the nation's two highest awards.
•   The final Pershing II ballistic missile is destroyed in accordance with the Intermediate Range Nuclear Force Treaty.

July 11
MARINES: In Washington, D.C., the commandant, always seeking to upgrade the professional horizons of the corps, establishes the Marine Corps Professional Reading Program for all NCOs, SNCOs, and officers.

July 17
AVIATION: At Edwards Air Force Base, California, the new Northrop-Grumman B-2 Spirit stealth bomber completes its first flight; with a price tag of nearly $1 billion apiece these are the most expensive aircraft ever constructed and flown.

July 21–August 8
NAVAL: A thaw in the cold war occurs when the Soviet missile cruiser *Marshal Ustinov,* the missile destroyer *Otlichny,* and the oiler *Genrikh Gasanov* pay a friendly visit to Norfolk, Virginia. Concurrently, the guided-missile cruiser *Thomas*

Gates and the guided-missile frigate *Kauffman* make a port visit to Sevastopol in the Crimea.

August 1
MARINES: To further enhance the educational prospects of marines, the Marine Corps University is established to oversee various programs. This institution includes the Basic and Amphibious Warfare Schools, the Command and General Staff, and 17 noncommissioned officer schools.

August 14
MILITARY: In Washington, D.C., Michael P. Stone gains appointment as the 15th secretary of the army. He is also the first foreign-born secretary, having served in the Royal Navy during World War II.

August 16
AVIATION: The Pacific Air Forces hosts the first Pacific Air Chiefs Conference, which is attended by ranking airmen from Australia, Japan, the Philippines, Singapore, Malaysia, and Brunei. The top issues discussed are promoting regional cooperation and security through air power.

September 7
NAVAL: An accident investigation concludes that the turret accident onboard the battleship *Iowa* was the result of a suicidal act of sabotage by a sailor, Gunner's Mate Second Class Clayton Hartwigg.

September 19–21
AVIATION: After Hurricane Hugo ravages the coast of South Carolina, Military Airlift Command (MAC) transports convey 4,300 tons of humanitarian supplies while RF-4C Phantom II reconnaissance aircraft, operating from nearby Shaw Air Force Base, provide photo coverage of the storm's path to National Guard troops conducting rescue operations.

October 1
AVIATION: General Hansford T. Johnson becomes the first U.S. Air Force Academy graduate to wear four stars.
MILITARY: General Colin Powell is selected by President George H. W. Bush as the sixth chairman of the Joint Chiefs of Staff; he is the first African American so honored and, aged 52 years, also the youngest.

October 3
AVIATION: Lockheed delivers its last production U-2R spyplane to the air force, which now operates a fleet of nine U-2Rs, 26 TR-1As, and two TR-1Bs.

October 4
AVIATION: Captain Jeffrey K. Beene, flying a B-1B Lancer, of the 96th Bombardment Wing manages to make a nose-wheel-up landing without seriously damaging the aircraft; he and his crew win the Mackay Trophy.
• Ar McMurdo Station, Antarctica, a C-5 Galaxy from the 60th Military Airlift Wing lands for the first time without skies and unloads two UH-1N Huey helicopters, 84 tons of supplies, and 72 passengers.

★ ★ ★ ★ ★ ★ ★ ★ ★ ★ ★ ★ ★ ★ ★

Powell, Colin L.   (1937–   )
Army general, secretary of state

Colin Luther Powell was born in the Harlem district, New York City, on April 5, 1937, a son of Jamaican immigrants. He enrolled in the local ROTC program while attending the City College of New York and was commissioned a second lieutenant in the U.S. Army in 1958. Powell served actively over the next four decades, including two tours in Vietnam in which he was wounded and highly decorated. Back home, he accepted a number of high-profile political positions within the Office of Management and Budget and the Department of Energy. He rose to brigadier general in 1979, served as a National Security Advisor under President Ronald Reagan, and, in 1989, made history when President George H. W. Bush appointed him the nation's first African-American chairman of the Joint Chiefs of Staff, the nation's highest military post. In this office he was responsible for helping to orchestrate Operation Desert Shield and Desert Storm in response to the 1991 Iraqi invasion of Kuwait. He worked closely with General H. Norman Schwarzkopf during the run-up to the ensuing Gulf War, and he became a familiar national figure by appearing nightly on national television. His reassuring presence, smooth persona, and high popularity ratings gave rise to speculation about a potential run for the presidency. Powell was reappointed to the JCS in 1991 after President Bush awarded him a Presidential Medal of Freedom for his services. However, he disagreed strongly with cuts in military spending proposed by President Bill Clinton and resigned from office in September 1993. The following year he served with

General Colin L. Powell *(Library of Congress)*

an American delegation to Haiti, which convinced the ruling junta to restore the country to democracy without bloodshed.

Powell continued as a private citizen for several years and, in 1995, he published his best-selling memoir, *My American Journey*. He briefly considered running for president as a Republican but, as an exponent of affirmative action for minorities, felt his

(continues)

1989

(continued)

chances were unrealistic and he withdrew from consideration in December 1995. However, in 2001 President George W. Bush appointed him the nation's first African-American secretary of state, responsible for the nation's diplomacy. His task grew increasingly complex in the wake of the September 11, 2001, attacks upon the World Trade Center in New York and the Pentagon in Washington, D.C., followed by Bush's policy to invade Iraq and rid that country of dictator Saddam Hussein. It was Powell's task to lay out the American position to a skeptical United Nations, which he did with verve and style, although the American claim of Iraqi weapons of mass destruction (WMD) has since been discounted. Powell was stung by criticism that he failed to garner sufficient international backing for Operation Iraqi Freedom, and he concluded half a century of service to the nation by retiring in January 2005. He was replaced by another African American, Condoleezza Rice.

October 11
NAVAL: On the amphibious assault ship *Iwo Jima*, an officer and a seaman are killed when struck accidentally by rounds fired from a Phalanx onboard the cargo ship *El Paso*.

October 17
AVIATION: San Francisco, California, is heavily damaged by an earthquake, and transports from the Military Airlift Command (MAC) fly in 250 tons of supplies.

October 29
AVIATION: In the Gulf of Mexico, a T-2 Buckeye training craft crashes onto the flight deck of the training carrier *Lexington*, killing the pilot and four deck crewmen.

October 30
AVIATION: During a bombing exercise in the Indian Ocean, an F/A-18 Hornet accidentally drops a 500-pound bomb of the guided-missile cruiser *Reeves*, injuring five sailors.

November 9
POLITICS: In an act of historic significance, citizens of East and West Berlin begin tearing down the Berlin Wall, the very symbol of Communist oppression, while bemused East German security forces look on passively. The cold war has ended in a decisive victory for the United States and its Western allies.

November 14
NAVAL: In light of the recent spate of accidents on naval vessels, U.S. Chief of Naval Operations admiral Carlisle Trost orders the fleet to stand down for a review of basic safety procedures. Two days later, he testifies before Congress that 67 major mishaps have cost $1 million, although he finds the rate still too high.

December 2

NAVAL: The guided-missile cruiser *Belknap* arrives off Malta to serve as a meeting place for talks between Presidents George H. W. Bush and Mikhail S. Gorbachev, but stormy weather prevents their meeting onboard.

December 7

NAVAL: In the Persian Gulf, the battleship *New Jersey* arrives on a five-day good-will cruise to Bahrain and the United Arab Emirates. This is also the first battle-ship to visit these waters.

December 11

EXPLORATION: A report issued by the National Geographic Society claims that Admiral Robert E. Peary did not reach the North Pole on April 6, 1909, and he based his claim on either falsified data or simple human error.

December 14

AVIATION: Women make their entry as combat crew members by serving in C-130 and C-141 airdrop missions for the first time.

December 16

MILITARY: As tensions increase between Panama and the United States, U.S. Marine Corps lieutenant Robert Paz is killed by Panamanian guards at a roadblock.

NAVAL: In Panama City, Panama, a navy officer and his wife are taken into cus-tody and physically abused by Panamanian guards after witnessing an incident in which armed guards fired on a car driven by four American officers.

Marines of Company D, 2nd Light Armored Infantry Battalion, with their LAV-25 light armored vehicles during Operation Just Cause in Panama, 1989. *(Department of Defense)*

December 20–24

AVIATION: Six F-117s of the 37th Tactical Fighter Wing and special operations AC-130H aircraft from Air Force Special Operations Command participate in the opening phases of Operation Just Cause, Panama. Military Airlift Command (MAC) transports also fly in 9,500 troops from Pope Air Force Base, North Carolina, and help execute the biggest nighttime combat airdrop since World War II. Air Force Reserve aircraft fly in 6,000 passengers and 3,700 tons of supplies into the region as hostilities unfold.

• The AC-130H named *Air Papa 06* from the 16th Special Operations Squadron distinguishes itself in combat during Operation Just Cause by destroying numerous barracks and antiaircraft gun emplacements at La Comandancia (Panamanian Defense Force headquarters) without inflicting collateral damage to civilian buildings nearby. They win a Mackay Trophy for their mission.

MILITARY: President George H. W. Bush responds to Panamanian aggression by unleashing Operation Just Cause, a concerted invasion by U.S. armed forces under General Maxwell R. Thurman, which quickly overrun General Manuel Noriega's self-defense forces. The units involved include the XVIII Airborne Corps, 7th Infantry Division (Light), 193rd Infantry Brigade, 75th Ranger Regiment, Special Forces, and part of the 82nd Airborne Division. Significantly, Captain Linda Bray, leading the 988th Military Police Company, is the first woman to direct American troops into action.

NAVAL: In Panama, several SEAL teams participate in Operation Just Cause by disabling a boat and a car used by dictator Manuel Noriega, preventing his escape. SEALS are also engaged in a heavy fire fight with Panamanian security forces at Paitilla Airport; four navy personnel are killed and nine wounded in various actions.

MARINES: During Operation Just Cause, a platoon of marines from the Fleet Antiterrorism Security Team (FAST), the Marine Corps Security Force Company, and units from the infantry and armored infantry engage Panamanian defense forces; one marine is killed.

December 29–31

AVIATION: In the wake of a bloody anticommunist uprising in Bucharest, Romania, two C-130 Hercules from the Military Airlift Command (MAC) fly in 30 tons of medical supplies to treat the victims.

1990

January 3

AVIATION: In Panama, dictator Manuel Noriega takes refuge in the Vatican diplomatic mission until he is coaxed into surrendering. The former dictator is then packed onto an air force C-30 and extradited back to the United States to face drug trafficking charges in Miami, Florida.

• American losses in Operation Just Cause are 23 killed and 322 wounded, mostly by friendly fire, while Panamanian casualties total 314 dead and 124 wounded. The AH-64 Apache attack helicopter successfully debuts in this action, as does the lethal Hellfire laser-guided missile.

January 25
NAVAL: As a cost-cutting expedient, Secretary of Defense Dick Cheney announces the retirement of 54 warships, including two battleships and five nuclear attack submarines.

January 31
AVIATION: The decade-old Operation Coronet Cove, which rotated Air National Guard units into the Panama Canal Zone, is terminated after 13,000 sorties.

February
AVIATION: Aircraft from the 436th Military Airlift Wing and the 463rd Tactical Airlift Wing fly to Monrovia, Liberia, with 30 tons of relief supplies for refugees fleeing an ongoing civil war.

February–March
AVIATION: Transports belonging to the 60th and 63rd Military Airlift Wing deliver 410 tons of relief supplies to Western and American Samoa in the wake of Typhoon Ofa.

February 21
MILITARY: In Colón Province, Panama, a crash between two helicopters in a driving rainstorm kills 11 soldiers of the 7th Infantry Division.

February 23
AVIATION: Aircraft of the 435th Tactical Airlift Wing convey 11 tons of food, medical supplies, and 60 medics to combat an ongoing epidemic in Senegal.

February 26
AVIATION: The legendary Lockheed SR-71 Blackbird is retired from active service owing to extreme operating costs and improvements in satellite photography.

February 27
NAVAL: In Washington, D.C., Admiral David E. Jeremiah gains appointment as the second vice chairman of the Joint Chiefs of Staff.

March 1
MILITARY: In the Fulda Gap between East and West Germany, the 11th Armored Cavalry performs the last border patrol of the cold war.

March 6
AVIATION: A Lockheed SR-71 Blackbird sets four transcontinental air speed records by flying 2,124 miles per hour on a transcontinental crossing. Once parked at Dulles International Airport, Washington, D.C., it is handed over to the National Air and Space Museum, Smithsonian Institution, to be put on permanent display.

March 9
NAVAL: The Department of Defense reports that it will be spending $877 million on the war on drugs in fiscal year 1990 and $1.2 billion for FY 1991. These activities include increased surveillance activities and completion of the aerostat radar screen across the southern border.

March 29–April 23
NAVAL: The fleet ballistic submarine *Tennessee* is the first submersible to make a deterrent patrol carrying the new Trident D-5 missiles.

April 4
AVIATION: The 60th and final KC-10 Extender tanker/cargo aircraft is delivered to the air force.

April 11
AVIATION: In Europe, a C-5 Galaxy is loaded with the first Pershing II missiles destined to be destroyed under provisions of the recent INF Treaty between the United States and the Soviet Union.

April 21
AVIATION: At Nellis Air Force Base, Nevada, the Lockheed F-117 Nighthawk is put on public display for the first time and is viewed by an estimated 100,000 visitors.

April 24
AVIATION: At Cape Canaveral, Florida, the seminal Hubble Space Telescope is placed into orbit by the space shuttle *Discovery.* In time, this device provides the most detailed photographic images of the universe collected to date.

April 30
NAVAL: At Norfolk, Virginia, the aircraft carrier *Coral Sea* is decommissioned after 42 years of service. This lowers to 14 the number of carrier battle groups in service.

May 4
AVIATION: The air force approves the use of the AIM-120A advanced medium-range air-to-air missile (AMRAAM) on fighter craft.

May 8
NAVAL: Off Norfolk, Virginia, the guided-missile destroyer *Conyngham* experiences a fire in its boiler room, killing one sailor and injuring 18; this vessel is decommissioned later this year.

May 22
AVIATION: The Special Operations Command (SOC) is created from the Twenty-Third Air Force.

June 15
AVIATION: In Washington, D.C., Secretary of the Air Force Donald B. Rice releases the post–cold war study *Global Reach–Global Power,* which provides a transitional strategic blueprint for the post–cold war air force.

June 20
NAVAL: Off Japan, the carrier *Midway* has a fire in a storeroom, which kills two sailors and injures 16.

June 27–29
NAVAL: The guided-missile carrier *Yarnell* and the guided-missile frigate *Kaufman* drop anchor at Gdańsk, Poland, on a goodwill tour; they are the first American warships to visit that port in 45 years.

1990

June 29
NAVAL: In Washington, D.C., Admiral Frank B. Kelso is appointed the 24th chief of naval operations.

June 30
MARINES: Presently, Marine Corps personnel levels stand at 19,958 officers and 176,694 enlisted men and women.

July 1
AVIATION: In Washington, D.C., General Michael J. Dugan gains appointment as U.S. Air Force chief of staff.

July 12
AVIATION: Lockheed delivers the final production F-117 Nighthawk to the air force; 59 have been acquired in all.
NAVAL: Commander Rosemary B. Mariner becomes the first woman to head an operational aircraft squadron when she officially takes control of Tactical Electronics Warfare Squadron 34 (VAQ-34).

July 17
AVIATION: The city of Baguio, Philippines, is destroyed by a severe earthquake and the air force beings flying in 600 tons of relief equipment to look for survivors. An additional 2,475 passengers are also flown to medical facilities for treatment. Personnel from nearby Clark Air Base are also on hand to assist refugees.
DIPLOMACY: In an ominous televised speech, Saddam Hussein of Iraq demands that Kuwait reduce its oil production from Rumalia Field, which extends under Iraqi territory, and settle ongoing border disputes. Failing this, he intends to invade, a threat that few take seriously at the time.

July 24
AVIATION: An important benchmark occurs when the EC-135 Looking Glass aircraft, intended to control and coordinate nuclear command posts in the event of a nuclear war, stands down. In three decades of service and hundreds of thousands of flying hours, the aircraft never experienced a single accident.

July 30
DIPLOMACY: In Jeddah, Saudi Arabia, representatives from that nation, Kuwait and Iraq meet to arrange reconciliation, but no progress is made.
MILITARY: The Central Intelligence Agency deduces that at least 100,000 Iraqi troops are poised on the borders of Kuwait as an invasion looms.

August–September
AVIATION: The first space system infrastructure capable of directly supporting a military conflict is initiated by the Air Force Space Command (AFSPACECOM). Its many functions include relaying communications, navigation, and meteorological information, along with detecting short-range ballistic missile launches.

August 2
DIPLOMACY: Resolution 660 is quickly passed by the UN Security Council, which calls for the immediate withdrawal of Iraqi forces from Kuwait. Hussein defiantly refuses to relinquish the country, which he is reclaiming as an oil-rich province.

MILITARY: In one of the gravest military miscalculations of the 20th century, Iraqi dictator Saddam Hussein orders his forces to invade and occupy Kuwait, an American ally and major oil exporter. President George H. W. Bush issues several executive orders declaring a national emergency while the Joint Chiefs of Staff review CENTCOM Operations Plan 1002-90, a highly classified contingency plan for transferring major American forces into the region over a period of three to four months.

August 4
MILITARY: In New York City, General H. Norman Schwarzkopf briefs the National Security Council about the military options available for Kuwait. He maintains that it will take a minimum of 17 weeks to build up sufficient military forces in theater to drive the Iraqis out. The possibility that Saddam Hussein will use chemical weapons is also discussed. At Fort Benning, Georgia, the Army Central Command (ARCENT) under Lieutenant General John Yeosock begins preliminary planning for action in the Persian Gulf region. He is assisted by Major General William G. Pagonis, director of logistics, and other high-ranking staff officers.

August 5
NAVAL: Operation Sharp Edge unfolds off the coast of wartorn Liberia, as the amphibious assault ship *Saipan* helps evacuate 2,609 American and foreign nationals from the capital of Monrovia by the time the operation concludes on December 3.
MARINES: Off Monrovia, Liberia, units from the 22nd Marine Expeditionary Unit come ashore to assist in the evacuation of citizens and foreign nationals.

August 6–7
MILITARY: The U.S. Army kicks into high gear as several divisions receive their deployment orders to Saudi Arabia. They include the 82nd Airborne Division and the 24th Infantry Division. Within 24 hours the 1st Cavalry Division, the 1st Brigade, 2nd Armored Division, the 101st Airborne Division, and the 3rd Armored Cavalry Regiment are ordered to ship out under the operation entitled Desert Shield. General H. Norman Schwarzkopf, who has a particular expertise in this region, is chosen as commander. The Americans are under an extreme urgency to secure the Saudi oil fields from a potential Iraqi attack.

August 7
AVIATION: At Langley Air Force Base, Virginia, the 71st Tactical Fighter Squadron (TFS), 1st Tactical Fighter Wing, begins deploying 24 F-15C Eagles on an 8,000-mile flight to Dhahran, Saudi Arabia. The flight is made in 15 hours with the help of 12 inflight refuelings.
DIPLOMACY: In Washington, D.C., President George H. W. Bush insists that Iraqi aggression against Kuwait "will not stand" and formally orders a buildup of American military forces in the region to drive Saddam Hussein out of that strategic oil-producing country.
MILITARY: The U.S. Army begins gearing up for Operation Desert Shield to protect Saudi Arabia and its oil fields from a possible Iraqi attack.

Naval: The carrier *Dwight D. Eisenhower* passes through the Suez Canal and enters the Red Sea, where it joins the carrier *Independence* in the Gulf of Oman. Their combined air wings are presently the only coalition aircraft available for immediate use in the Persian Gulf region.

August 8

Aviation: At Dhahran, Saudi Arabia, the first Air Force Reserve C-141 Starlifter lands, becoming the first American aircraft to deploy in the theater. They are joined shortly afterward by F-15Cs from the 1st Tactical Fighter Wing as additional AWACS aircraft to assist Saudi AWACS already flying over the kingdom. In response to a request from General H. Norman Schwarzkopf, U.S. Air Force vice chief of staff Lieutenant General Mike Loh orders the Air Staff Planning Group (Checkmate) under Colonel John Warden to initiate plans for conducting a strategic air war against Iraqi forces.

Military: At Savannah, Georgia, the 2nd Brigade, 24th Infantry Division boards transports for a rapid transit to Saudi Arabia. The entire division is assembled there by September 12.

August 8–9

Military: In Dhahran, Saudi Arabia, the 2nd Brigade, 82nd Airborne Division, under Colonel Richard Rokosz is the first large American unit airlifted into the theater. Shortly after, they are joined by staff officers of the soon-to-arrive XVIII Airborne Corps.

August 9

Aviation: The new Eleventh Air Force is created from the old Alaskan Air Command and is assigned to the Pacific Air Forces (PACAF).

August 10

Aviation: At Central Command (CENTCOM), MacDill Air Force Base, Florida, Colonel John Warren of Air Staff presents a preliminary draft for air operations in the Persian Gulf to General H. Norman Schwarzkopf. General Charles Horner also begins drawing up contingency plans for air power in the event that Iraqi forces attack Saudi Arabia before the Americans can deploy there in force.

• Detachments of F-16s from Shaw Air Force Base, South Carolina, and C-130s from Pope Air Force Base, North Carolina, begin filtering into Saudi Arabia.

Marines: In accordance with Operation Desert Shield, the 7th Marine Expeditionary Brigade begins airlifting from the United States to Al Jubayl, Saudi Arabia. Once there it will join up with its assigned Marine Prepositioning Force (MPF) squadron.

August 11

Military: In Saudi Arabia, Colonel David Whately and the 7th Transportation Group arrive from Fort Eustis, Virginia. They are tasked with managing the huge influx of men and materiel en route to the theater.

August 12

Aviation: At Dhahran, Saudi Arabia, the first 32 KC-135 tanker aircraft begins deploying, the first of over 300 Kc-135s and KC-10s scheduled to arrive. These

Schwarzkopf, H. Norman   (1934–)
Army general

Herbert Norman Schwarzkopf was born in Trenton, New Jersey, on August 22, 1934, the son of an army officer. He traveled abroad with his father on a year-long visit to Iran in the 1940s and was indelibly impressed by this youthful encounter with Islamic religion and culture. Schwarzkopf subsequently attended the U.S. Military Academy, receiving his lieutenant's commission in 1956. After gaining his airborne wings, he served with the elite 101st Airborne Division before becoming a member of the army's elite Berlin brigade. In 1964 he left the military briefly to obtain a master's degree in missile engineering from the University of Southern California. Schwarzkopf then fulfilled several tours of duty in Vietnam, where he was decorated for bravery with his third Silver Star before rising to brigadier general in 1978 and major general in 1982. The following year he served as ground force commander during Operation Urgent Fury, the U.S.-sponsored liberation of Grenada from Marxist revolutionaries.

Afterwards, he wrote a scathing critique of operations that generated badly needed reforms. Schwarzkopf received his fourth Silver Star in 1988 and spent a year at the Pentagon as deputy chief of staff. He then transferred as head of the United States Central Command (CENTCOM), headquartered at Tampa, Florida, tasked with providing security for American interests throughout the Middle East. In the spring of 1990, mindful of the declining Soviet threat to the region, he conducted hypothetical war games that substituted Iraq's dictator Saddam Hussein as a potential aggressor. The following August Hussein actually invaded neighboring Kuwait and President George H. W. Bush authorized Schwarzkopf to initiate appropriate measures for his eviction.

Using his existing Iraq plan, Schwarzkopf spent the ensuing six months assembling a 27-nation coalition to oust the Iraqis from Kuwait. Many Arab nations proved willing to assist, and Schwarzkopf,

are shortly joined by MH-53J Pave Low helicopters from the 1st Special Operations Wing.

NAVAL: To enforce a United Nations embargo of Iraq, U.S. Navy vessels begin a naval quarantine of the Persian Gulf region.

August 12–14
MILITARY: In Saudi Arabia, Operations Dragon I and II unfold as the 82nd Airborne Division forms a defensive perimeter around the ports of al-Jubayl, Dhahran, and ad-Damman. They have on hand 4,575 soldiers, a company of M551 Sheridan light tanks, and a battalion of 105mm howitzers.

August 13
MILITARY: In light of the fact that the Iraqi army employs hundreds of Scud Soviet-made ballistic missiles, the army deploys its first PAC-2 Patriot surface-to-air missile unit, Battery B, 2nd Battalion, 7th Air Defense Artillery.

by dint of his training in Middle Eastern affairs, melded this awkward assemblage of Western and Middle Eastern armies into a formidable military force of 500,000 men. Operation Desert Shield, the buildup of forces in the Gulf region, succeeded without any serious problems. Thus, when Hussein refused a United Nations order to leave Kuwait, Schwarzkopf commenced Operation Desert Storm to drive them out in January 1991. He began the Gulf War with a month-long aerial bombardment of Iraqi defenses and antiaircraft sites, which left their ground forces vulnerable to assault. When this failed to induce Hussein to depart, he enacted a well-executed flanking movement that routed the Iraqis, inflicted 100,000 casualties in little over 100 hours of fighting, and effectively liberated Kuwait. Schwarzkopf retired from the military in 1991 and published his memoir entitled *It Doesn't Take a Hero* (1992). He was also made an honorary private first class in the French Foreign Legion, the only American so honored. Today Schwarzkopf lives in Florida, where he frequently serves as a TV military commentator and analyst.

General H. Norman Schwarzkopf, here receiving Kuwait's highest decoration. *(U.S. Air Force)*

August 14

AVIATION: In Washington, D.C., the Department of Defense announces the presence of E-3 AWACS, KC-10s, KC-135s, and RC-135s in the Persian Gulf theater.

DIPLOMACY: Ships from the Soviet Union join the naval quarantine against Iraq.

MILITARY: In Saudi Arabia, deployment of the XVIII Airborne Corps is assisted by photo intelligence provided by an army satellite.

August 15

AVIATION: Top-secret F-117 stealth aircraft belonging to the 37th Tactical Fighter Wing (TFW) deploy from Tonopah, Nevada, and they are soon joined by F-4G Wild Weasels flying in from George Air Force Base, California.

MILITARY: In Saudi Arabia, the 1st and 3rd Brigades, 82nd Airborne Division, deploy for battle.

August 16
AVIATION: At Myrtle Beach Air Force Base, California, the first wave of Fairchild A-10 Thunderbolt IIs departs for service in Saudi Arabia.

August 17
AVIATION: In Washington, D.C., President George H. W. Bush mobilizes the Civil Reserve Air Fleet for the first time since 1952. These aircraft are pressed into service as troop carriers to accelerate the buildup of forces in the Persian Gulf.

• Once General H. Norman Schwarzkopf approves the initial air campaign strategy, Colonel John Warden is dispatched to Saudi Arabia to personally brief General Charles Horner on it.

• The Defense Satellite Communications Systems (DSCS) is established by the Air Force Space Command to facilitate command links to Operation Desert Storm.

MILITARY: Iraqi forces occupying Kuwait are heavily reinforced and begin constructing defensive structures, or sand berms, along the Saudi border.

• The military buildup in Saudi Arabia continues as a brigade of the 101st Airborne Division deploys from Fort Campbell, Kentucky. The remaining two brigades are embarking on ships at Jacksonville, Florida, and all three will assemble with their equipment by September 22.

MARINES: In accordance with Operation Desert Shield, the 4th Marine Expeditionary Brigade begins embarking on vessels at Morehead City, North Carolina, for the Persian Gulf.

August 18
NAVAL: In the Persian Gulf, the guided-missile frigate *Reid* and frigate *Bradley* fire warning shots across the bows of two Iraqi tankers attempting to leave. The guided-missile cruiser *England* and the guided-missile destroyer *Scott* also divert freighters from docking in the Persian Gulf and northern Red Sea.

August 19
AVIATION: A force of 18 F-117s Nighthawks from the 415th Tactical Fighter Squadron arrives at Mushait Air Base, Saudi Arabia, for service during Operation Desert Shield.

MARINES: On Okinawa, the 1st Battalion, 6th Marines begins embarking for service in Operation Desert Shield.

August 20
AVIATION: In Saudi Arabia, General Charles Horner declares that there is sufficient American air power in Saudi Arabia to defend it against any Iraqi attack. At this time he is also briefed by Colonel John Warden as to the overarching campaign for waging a strategic air war.

MARINES: In Saudi Arabia, Lieutenant General Walter E. Boomer arrives to take charge of I Marine Expeditionary Force. He is ordered to command all marine units in Operation Desert Shield except those still afloat.

Horner, Charles A. (1936–)
Air Force general

Charles A. Horner was born in Davenport, Iowa, on October 19, 1936, and he attended the University of Iowa while pursuing a bachelor of arts degree. He was also commissioned a second lieutenant through the ROTC program on campus and reported for flight training at Laredo Air Force Base, Texas. Horner earned his wings as an F-100 pilot in 1960 and flew three years with the 492nd Tactical Fighter Squadron at RAF Lakenheath, England. In December 1963 he switched to flying F-105s with the 4th Tactical Fighter Wing at Seymour Johnson Air Force Base, North Carolina, and, two years later, he served in the Vietnam War at Korat Royal Thai Air Base in Thailand. At this post Horner completed 41 combat missions over North Vietnam as a fighter bomber. Between 1966 and 1967 he rotated back to Nellis Air Force Base, Nevada, to serve as an F-105 instructor, then returned to Thailand in May 1967 to fly an additional 70 combat missions as a Wild Weasel pilot, deliberately luring out Communist air defenses so that they could be identified and destroyed. In 1972 he also attended William and Mary College to obtain a master's in business administration. Horner handled his affairs capably and in July 1985 he became a major general and deputy chief of staff for Plans, Headquarters, Tactical Air Command, Langley Air Force Base, Virginia. In March 1987 he served as commander, 9th U.S. Air Force and U.S. Central Command Air Forces based at Shaw Air Force Base, South Carolina.

Horner's greatest test came in August 1991 after Saddam Hussein invaded Kuwait with a massive army. He was appointed commander in chief–Forward, U.S. Central Command and directed the opening phases of Operation Desert Shield while General H. Norman Schwarzkopf was still stateside. He oversaw the buildup of several hundred aircraft and supporting units from the U.S. Air Force and its coalition partners. When Operation Desert Storm commenced the following January, Horner had at his disposal 2,700 warplanes from 14 nations, and these planes flew over 100,000 missions prior to the ground phase of the campaign. Their accurate bombing gutted Iraqi air defenses and armored formations, allowing the main attack to conclude after only 100 hours of fighting with extremely light losses. For his part, Horner was promoted to full general on July 1, 1992, and appointed to head the North American Aerospace Defense Command and the U.S. Space Command. Horner was responsible for the utilization of space for national purposes through a large network of satellites in orbit and ground stations around the globe. This assignment was followed by a stint as commander of the Air Force Space Command at Peterson Air Force Base, Colorado, after which he retired from active service on September 30, 1994. He currently resides in Fort Walton Beach, Florida, and serves on the board of directors for the U.S. Institute of Peace. During his tenure in the Persian Gulf, military air power was never more effective and decisive in battle.

• Off Liberia, units belonging to the 26th Marine Expeditionary Unit arrive to replace the 22nd MEU as part of Operation Sharp Edge.

August 21
AVIATION: By this date, the U.S. Air Force has deployed A-10s, C-130s, E-3 AWACS, F-4Gs, F-15s, F-15Es, F-16s, F-117s, KC-135, KC-10,s and RC-135s in theater. This is the largest concentration of military aircraft outside the United States since the Vietnam War.
• When the air force requests the services of 6,000 reservists, no less than 15,000 volunteer to serve with Operation Desert Shield.

August 22
AVIATION: By this date, Air Force Reserve personnel have flown 8,000 soldiers and 7 million tons of military cargo into Saudi Arabia for service in Operation Desert Storm. Moreover, 20,000 reservists and 12,000 Air National Guardsmen will be called up for service in the Persian Gulf.
MILITARY: In Washington, D.C., Executive Order 12727 is signed by President George H. W. Bush to mobilize 200,000 army reservists for six months of active service. This is the largest activation of reservists since the Korean War.
• In Saudi Arabia, a brigade of the 82nd Airborne Division is redeployed to advance positions in the desert (Forward Operating Base Essex) to help blunt any possible Iraqi attacks. Operating temperatures at the time exceed 100 degrees Fahrenheit.
MARINES: President George H. W. Bush orders 31,000 marine Reservists mobilized for active duty in Operation Desert Shield.

August 23
AVIATION: At Andrews Air Force Base, Maryland, the first of two VC-25a (highly modified Boeing 747s) deploy with the 89th Military Airlift Wing. Once a president is onboard, the aircraft in question receives the call sign *Air Force One*.
• In Washington, D.C., Secretary of Defense Dick Cheney authorizes the air force to mobilize its Reserve components for service in the Persian Gulf; 20,000 are called to the colors to serve in the Persian Gulf crisis.

August 24
AVIATION: At Birmingham, Alabama, the 117th Tactical Reconnaissance Wing dispatches six of its RF-4C Phantom II aircraft to the Persian Gulf region, to be joined by similar aircraft sent by the 67th Tactical Reconnaissance Wing, Bergstrom Air Force Base, Texas.

August 25
MARINES: In Hawaii, men of the 1st Marine Expeditionary Brigade begin flying out to al-Jubayl, Saudi Arabia, where ships of its MPF await.

August 28
AVIATION: At Torrejon, Spain, F-16 fighters are sent in a new deployment to airfields in Qatar, another Persian Gulf ally.
DIPLOMACY: The Iraqi government declares that Kuwait is its 19th province.
POLITICS: In Washington, D.C., President George H. W. Bush meets with 170 congressional members and delineates U.S. objectives in Kuwait: the unconditional withdrawal of all Iraqi forces and restoration of the legitimate Kuwaiti government. Security for the Persian Gulf region and the protection of Americans abroad are also highlighted.

August 29
AVIATION: At Ramstein Air Base, West Germany, a C-5 Galaxy, laden with military supplies for the Persian Gulf, crashes on takeoff, killing 13 people. Staff Sergeant Lorenzo Galvin, Jr., wins the Airman's Medal for heroic efforts to assist crash victims.

August 31
MILITARY: Colonel Jesse Johnson leads the 5th Special Forces Group to Saudi Arabia to train various Arab coalition armies. In time, they are joined by the 3rd and 10th Special Forces Group and some Delta Force contingents.
NAVAL: In the Persian Gulf, the guided-missile cruiser *Biddle* stops and searches the Iraqi freighter *Al Karamah*; it is found to be empty and allowed to proceed to Jordan.

September 1
MILITARY: At Forward Operating Base Essex, Saudi Arabia, men of the 82nd Airborne Division are relieved by the 101st Airborne Division, who promptly rename the position Forward Operating Base Bastogne.

September 2
MARINES: Once in theater, the 7th Marine Expeditionary Brigade is disbanded and incorporated into the I Marine Expeditionary Force, which now consists of the 1st Marine Division and 1st Marine Air Wing (1st MAW).

September 3
MILITARY: In the Saudi Arabian desert, Operation Desert Dragon II unfolds as the 101st Airborne Division erects two addition Forward Operating Bases called FOB Normandy and FOB Carentan to the west of FOB Bastogne.

September 5
AVIATION: Five C-130 units from the Air National Guard (ANG) begin arriving in Saudi Arabia.
NAVAL: In San Diego, California, the fleet tender *Acadia* departs with a crew of 1,260, including 360 women. This is the first wartime test of a combined sex crew in wartime.

September 6
AVIATION: Lieutenant General Claire L. Chennault, who commanded the famous "Flying Tigers" of World War II, is commemorated when the U.S. Post Office issues a 40-cent stamp with his portrait.

September 7
MILITARY: In the Saudi Arabian desert, the 1st and 2nd Brigades of the 24th Infantry Division deploy, and they are soon joined by the 12th Aviation Brigade.
MARINES: The special operations capable 13th Marine Expeditionary Unit (SOC) deploys in the Persian Gulf, where it will remain under navy control.

September 8
AVIATION: Colonel Marcelite Jordan Harris becomes the first African-American woman to make brigadier general in the U.S. Air Force. In this post she becomes director of Air Training Command's technical training.
• The first wave of AC-130H gunships from the 16th Special Operations Squadron arrive in Saudi Arabia.

Boomer, Walter E. (1938–)
Marine Corps general

Walter E. Boomer was born in Rich Square, North Carolina, on September 22, 1938, and he received a second lieutenant's commission in the Marine Corps while pursuing his bachelor's degree from Duke University in 1960. He rose to captain in 1965 and saw service in Vietnam from 1966 to 1967 as a company officer, winning a Silver Star for valor. After passing through the Amphibious Warfare School at Quantico, Virginia, Boomer returned to Southeast Asia in 1971 as an adviser to South Vietnamese marines, and he was under fire throughout the Communist Easter Offensive the following year. After additional study at the American University, he taught management at the U.S. Naval Academy as the Management Department chairman, and rose to lieutenant colonel in 1976. Boomer served several years in various posts, rising to brigadier general in April 1986 and took command of the 4th Marine Division, Fleet Marine Force, New Orleans. Boomer rose to major general on March 14, 1989, and lieutenant general on August 8, 1990, around the same time that Iraqi dictator Saddam Hussein launched his invasion of Kuwait. On August 15, 1990, Boomer arrived in Saudi Arabia as commanding general, U.S. Marine Forces Central Command and I Marine Expeditionary Force. In time this consisted of the 1st and 2nd Marine Divisions, the 3rd Marine Air Wing, and the U.S. Army Tiger Brigade from the 2nd Armored Division. The unit gave marines the added punch of ultramodern army M1 Abrams tanks to supplement their older M60 Pattons.

As Operation Desert Shield gave way to Desert Storm, Boomer favored a direct amphibious assault on the port of Ash-Shu'yabah, 20 miles south of Kuwait City, to provide the I MEF with a supply base before pushing north. Such a move would also preempt any Iraqi counterattacks against the main overland thrust. How-

September 13
AVIATION: In Riyadh, Saudi Arabia, U.S. Air Force brigadier general Buster Glosson, deputy commander, Joint Task Force Middle East, briefs General H. Norman Schwarzkopf and Colin Powell on the completed operational air war plan that will follow Operation Desert Shield.

September 14
MILITARY: The 197th Infantry Brigade makes its appearance in the Saudi Arabian desert, having shipped in from Fort Benning, Georgia. It is attached to the 24th Infantry Division until that formation's 48th Infantry Brigade can deploy on November 30.
• Camps Red, Gold, and White are founded by the 82nd Airborne Division at Ab Qaiq, Saudia Arabia.

ever, he deferred to Coalition Commanding General H. Norman Schwarzkopf to
cancel any landings on the coast for fear
that they would prove too costly and would
delay the overland offensive. In return,
Schwarzkopf approved Boomer's request
to delay the attack from February 22, 1991,
to February 24, to allow the marines more
time to redeploy. Kuwait City was liberated
during the so-called 100 hours campaign
by marines, who had no trouble dealing
with dug-in Iraqi infantry. After the Gulf
War, Boomer arrived at Camp Pendleton, California, as commanding general, I
Expeditionary Force/commanding general,
Marine Corps Base, where he remained
until September 1991. He subsequently
served as the commanding general, Marine
Corps Combat Development Command,
rose to full general as of September 1,
1992, and performed his final duty as assistant commandant of the Marine Corps in
Washington, D.C. Boomer retired from the
marines on September 1, 1994, and presently serves as chairman and CEO of the
Rogers Corporation. Among his numer-

General Walter E. Boomer (U.S. Marine Corps)

ous awards are the Distinguished Service
Medal, two Silver Stars, two Bronze Stars,
and the Legion of Merit.

September 16

MILITARY: At Fort Hood, Texas, the 1st Cavalry Division begins shipping out men
and equipment under the aegis of Brigadier General John Tilleli. Once deployed,
it is joined by the 1st Brigade, 2nd Armor Division, until the 155th Armored Brigade is ready for service overseas.

NAVAL: In the Persian Gulf, the Bahamian-rigged tanker *Daimon* is intercepted by
the destroyer *O'Brien*, becoming the 1,000th vessel to be stopped and searched.

September 17

AVIATION: In Washington, D.C., Secretary of Defense Dick Cheney relieves U.S.
Air Force chief of staff Michael J. Dugan for unauthorized comments made to the
media relative to Operation Desert Shield.

MARINES: Final elements of the 4th Marine Expeditionary Brigade deploy in the
Persian Gulf and are retained under navy command.

September 18–28
AVIATION: Transports of the 436th and 438th Military Airlift Wings deliver tons of blankets, tents, cots, and other equipment for the 100,000 foreign workers fleeing Kuwait for Jordan.

September 20
DIPLOMACY: In Baghdad, Iraq, the Revolutionary Command Council announces that a withdrawal from Kuwait is impossible and that the "mother of all battles" is shaping up.

September 27
NAVAL: In the Gulf of Aqaba, Jordan, the Iraqi tanker *Tadmur* is intercepted by the frigate *Elmer B. Montgomery*, which places a crew onboard after firing shots across the bow.

September 29
AVIATION: The new Lockheed/General Dynamics YF-22A Raptor air superiority/stealth fighter prototype makes its initial flight on a ferry flight to Edwards Air Force Base, California.

October 1
AVIATION: The Air Force Space Command assumes control of Patrick Air Force Base, Florida, from the Air Force Systems Command.

October 1–4
NAVAL: The carrier *Independence* passes through the Straits of Hormuz and enters the Persian Gulf, marking the first time a vessel of this kind has operated in such cramped waters since 1974. The visit is deemed successful and the vessel departs three days later.

October 10
AVIATION: In the Persian Gulf, air force fighter and fighter bomber units begin training exercise to familiarize themselves with desert warfare. To underscore that point, F-15Cs are already performing combat air patrols (CAP).

October 30
AVIATION: In Washington, D.C., General Merrill A. McPeak gains appointment as the new air force chief of staff.
• To expedite the shipment of certain crucial items to the Persian Gulf, air force transports commence Operation Desert Express.
NAVAL: In the Persian Gulf, the amphibious assault ship *Iwo Jima* experiences a steam leak in its fire room, which kills 10 sailors.

November 3
AVIATION: Over Edwards Air Force Base, California, the prototype YF-22A Advanced Technology Fighter (ATF), which employs two General Electric YF120 turbofan engines, becomes the first jet aircraft to achieve supersonic speed with the use of afterburners through a process known as "supercruise" at 40,000 feet.

1990

November 6
MILITARY: The army begins replacing its M1 Abrams tanks with the newer, more powerfully armed M1A1s, which sport a German-made 120mm cannon.

November 8
MILITARY: Gearing up for an inevitable showdown with Iraqi dictator Saddam Hussein, President George H. W. Bush orders an increase in American and allied forces in the Persian Gulf to 430,000 men. Part of this entails shipping the VII Corps under Lieutenant General Frederick M. Franks from Germany to Saudi Arabia. A total of 200,000 men, 6,000 tracked vehicles, and 59,000 wheeled vehicles are relocated by mid-February 1991.
• At Fort Riley, Kansas, the 1st Infantry Division (Mechanized) under Major General Thomas G. Rhame is ordered to prepare for deployment overseas. Because only two brigades can be organized in time, the third brigade will be supplied by the 2nd Armored Division.
MARINES: As part of a general buildup in the Persian Gulf, the 2nd Marine Division, 5th Marine Expeditionary Brigade, and 2nd Marine Air Wing (2nd MAW) are ordered deployed with I Marine Expeditionary Force.

November 13–14
MILITARY: In Washington, D.C., President George H. W. Bush extends the service term for reservists in Operation Desert Shield by an additional 180 days. Within hours, Secretary of Defense Dick Cheney mobilizes an additional 80,000 reservists and National Guard troops.

November 17
AVIATION: To enhance Desert Shield communications, a DSCS II satellite is placed above the Indian Ocean by the Air Force Space Command.

November 21
AVIATION: A-10 Thunderbolt IIs from Davis Monthan Air Force Base deploy to Saudi Arabia.

November 27
MILITARY: At Fort Bragg, North Carolina, the 1st Special Operations Command is reorganized and redesignated the U.S. Army Special Operations Command (Airborne). The U.S. Army Reserve Special Operations Command is also retitled the U.S. Civil Affairs and Psychological Operations Command.

November 29
DIPLOMACY: Resolution 678, authorizing the use of force against Iraqi forces occupying Kuwait, passes the United Nations Security Council. It also grants Saddam Hussein a grace period, one last chance to pull out, but he ignores it.

December 1
MILITARY: In Washington, D.C., Secretary of Defense Dick Cheney enlarges the reservist call up to 115,000 men and women.
MARINES: In California, the 5th Marine Expeditionary Brigade and the special operations capable 11th Marine Expeditionary Unit (SOC) set sail for the Persian Gulf.

1990

December 1–2
AVIATION: At Osan Air Base, South Korea, two MH-60 Pave Hawk helicopters of the 38th Air Rescue Squadron save 22 shipwrecked sailors from a grounded Panamanian vessel six miles offshore.

December 5
AVIATION: The 152nd Tactical Reconnaissance Group dispatches its RF-4Cs to airfields in Saudi Arabia.

December 18
MARINES: The first M1A1 Abrams tanks accepted into the Marine Corps are delivered to the 2nd Tank Battalion.

December 22
MILITARY: In Saudi Arabia, the first unit of the VII Corps, the 2nd Armored Cavalry Regiment under Colonel Don Holder, arrives from Germany.

December 26
NAVAL: In the Arabian Sea, an international flotilla, including the destroyers *Fife* and *Oldendorf,* the guided-missile frigate *Trenton,* and the amphibious transport dock *Shreveport* intercept and board the so-called peace ship *Ibn Khaldoon.* Tense moments result after the crew on the latter attempt to grab weapons from the boarding crew, and warning shots are fired in the air. The vessel is found to be carrying contraband cargo and redirected into a port.

December 27
MILITARY: In Riyadh, Saudi Arabia, General Colin Powell and Secretary of Defense Dick Cheney are briefed by General H. Norman Schwarzkopf as to his forthcoming strategy. He intends to launch a vast flanking movement by the VII Corps and XVIII Airborne Corps from the western desert that will decisively turn the Iraqi right flank before they can react to it.

December 29
AVIATION: The 169th Tactical Fighter Group becomes the first Air National Guard (ANG) unit deployed in the Persian Gulf for active duty.

1991

January
MILITARY: At this critical juncture, the army consists of 710,821 officers and men in 18 divisions, with 200,000 deployed in the Arabian desert.

January 1
MILITARY: At Tactical Assembly Area (TAA) Thompson, northwest of King Khalid Military City, Saudi Arabia, elements of the 1st Armored Division, VII Corps, arrive and deploy under Major General Ronald H. Griffin. As the men settle into TAA Thompson, they begin an extensive set of drills and maneuvers with live gunnery.
MARINES: The 24th Marines are deployed to al-Jubayl, Saudi Arabia, where they will provide rear-area security throughout the I Marine Expeditionary Force area.

January 2
AVIATION: In Saudi Arabia, the 4th Tactical Fighter Wing (Provisional) is cobbled together from Air National Guard F-16s of the 174th Tactical Fighter Wing and the 169th Tactical Fighter Group.
MILITARY: On this day, the Central Command (CENTCOM) reveals U.S. military strength in the Persian Gulf to be 325,000 with more on the way.
MARINES: The outbreak of civil war in Mogadishu, Somalia, results in units of the 4th Marine Expeditionary Brigade being diverted from the Persian Gulf for service off the African coast. Their primary concern is the safety of U.S. embassy personnel trapped by the fighting.

January 2–5
AVIATION: Operation Eastern Exit commences off Somalia as helicopters from the amphibious assault ship *Guam* and the amphibious transport dock *Trenton* evacuate 65 American citizens caught up in civil strife there. Meanwhile, two CH-53Es, with a security force, are launched 466 miles from Mogadishu and conduct a long-range rescue mission under the noses of various armed militias. In two trips nearly 300 people are airlifted to safety, including the Soviet embassy staff.

January 3
DIPLOMACY: In Washington, D.C., President George H. W. Bush, seeking to avert the outbreak of hostilities, proposes that Secretary of State James Baker and Iraqi foreign minister Tariq Aziz meet in Geneva for a last chance at negotiated settlement.

January 4
NAVAL: A Spanish naval vessel halts the Soviet freighter *Dmitri Firmanov* in the Red Sea. The vessel is then boarded by Spanish and U.S. naval personnel, who uncover military equipment not listed on the cargo manifest. The vessel is detained in consequence.

January 5
AVIATION: Two CH-53E Sea Stallion helicopters depart from the amphibious landing dock *Trenton* and fly 460 miles to Mogadishu, Somalia, and land at the U.S. embassy compound there. En route they are refueled twice by KC-130 Hercules tankers.
NAVAL: Following the outbreak of civil war in Somalia, the amphibious assault ship *Guam* and the amphibious transport dock *Trenton* are detached from Operation Desert Shield and dispatched there.

January 6
AVIATION: Four waves of five CH-46 Skyknight helicopters are launched from the amphibious assault ship *Guam* and land in Mogadishu to assist in the evacuation of 200 citizens and foreign nationals.

January 7
AVIATION: The Defense Department announces cancellation of the McDonnell Douglas/General Dynamics A-12 Avenger stealth attack plane for the navy, already 16 months behind schedule and $2.7 billion over budget. With a projected total cost of $52 billion, this is the largest weapons program ever terminated.

MILITARY: According to the U.S. Central Command's (CENTCOM) intelligence section, Saddam Hussein has deployed 452,000 Iraqi troops (35 divisions), bolstered by 4,300 tanks and 3,100 artillery pieces.

January 8
MILITARY: At Riyadh, Saudi Arabia, Operation Quick Silver unfolds as the 3rd Brigade, 82nd Airborne Division deploys in response to a terrorist threat to the capital.
POLITICS: In Washington, D.C., President George H. W. Bush asks Congress for authorization to commit American forces to combat in the Persian Gulf if Iraq refuses to relinquish Kuwait.

January 9
DIPLOMACY: In Geneva, Switzerland, Secretary of State James Baker and Iraqi foreign minister Tariq Aziz discuss the Persian Gulf crisis for six and a half hours without resolution.

January 10
MILITARY: The 1st Brigade, 2nd Armored Division ("Tiger Brigade") under Colonel John B. Sylvester, is removed from the 1st Cavalry Division and reassigned to the 2nd Marine Division, I Marine Expeditionary Force, to provide them with enhanced firepower. At the time the marines are still saddled with M60A3 Patton tanks instead of more modern M1A1 Abrams tanks. Meanwhile, the British 7th Armoured Brigade rejoins the British 1st Armoured Division, then part of VII Corps.

January 11
AVIATION: At Riyadh, Saudi Arabia, the two pre-production E-8A JSTARS aircraft are deployed for eventual use against Iraq. This highly advanced reconnaissance platform is capable of real-time surveillance over a battlefield situation.

January 11–12
MARINES: The I Marine Expeditionary Force is reinforced by the II MEF and the 5th Marine Expeditionary Brigade. This assemblage constitutes one of the largest amphibious task forces since the Inchon operation of 1950.
POLITICS: In Washington, D.C., Congress hotly debates authority for U.S. military action against Iraq, although, as commander in chief, President George H. W. Bush does not need their permission to engage. Nonetheless, the House of Representatives votes 250–183 and the Senate votes 52–47 to implement UN Resolution 678.

January 12
DIPLOMACY: In Washington, D.C., Congress votes to authorize President George H. W. Bush to use force against Iraq.

January 14
MILITARY: The 1st Armored Division under Major General Ronald H. Griffin makes a reconnaissance of terrain west of the Saudi-Iraqi border, concluding it is passable for tanks and other tracked vehicles. This information, plus that subsequently obtained by U-2 overflights of enemy positions, allows the 1st and 3rd Armored Divisions to deploy farther west to avoid troop congestion on the ground.

January 15
AVIATION: Vandenberg Air Force Base, California, passes from the Strategic Air Command (SAC) to the Air Force Space Command.
DIPLOMACY: The deadline for Iraqi forces to evacuate Kuwait as per UN Resolution 678 expires.
MILITARY: In light of the threat of chemical warfare used against coalition forces by Saddam Hussein, men of the XVIII Airborne Corps begin taking antinerve agent pills as a precaution.

January 16
AVIATION: The first aerial mission of Operation Desert Storm commences as seven B-52Gs of the 2nd Bomb Wing launch from Barksdale Air Force Base, Louisiana, carrying the new AGM-86C conventional air-launched cruise missiles (ALCMs). With 35 hours of flight time ahead of them, round trip, this is also history's longest bombing mission.
MILITARY: On the eve of hostilities, Central Command (CENTCOM) declares that 425,000 U.S. troops are in the Persian Gulf region, along with forces of 19 nations and naval forces of 14 nations.
•   In Saudi Arabia, convoys begin transporting men and equipment of the VII Corps and XVIII Airborne Corps down the Tapline Road, gradually stretching in length to 120 miles. Operation Desert Shield is about to give way to Operation Desert Storm.

January 17
AVIATION: With the UN deadline for evacuating Kuwait having passed, American and coalition aircraft begin a concerted bombardment of Iraqi military targets, missile sites, communications facilities, and other targets deemed useful to Saddam Hussein's occupying forces. On the first day alone the air force and coalition warplanes mount 750 attack sorties while carrier aircraft contribute a further 228. The aerial campaign continues relentlessly for the next 38 days with devastating results and relatively light losses.
•   Among the first wave of aircraft to go in are AH-64A Apache helicopter gunships from the 1st Battalion, 101st Aviation Regiment, 101st Airborne Division under Lieutenant Colonel Richard A. Cody. Early shots fired by the laser-guided Hellfire missiles destroy two Iraqi early warning radar sites, paving the way for additional coalition aircraft to begin launching strikes. The army crews are guided in to their targets by air force MH-53 Special Operations helicopters.
•   Seven B-52Gs from Barksdale Air Force Base, Louisiana, unleash a salvo of 35 super accurate cruise missiles against communications and radar targets in Iraq.
•   F-117 light bombers steal past Iraqi radar defenses and begin bombing strategic targets throughout Baghdad while intense antiaircraft fire lights up the darkness. They account for 31 percent of all targets struck on the first day.
•   As General H. Norman Schwarzkopf begins his "Hail Mary maneuver," a massive outflanking movement, air force C-130 transports deliver 14,000 troops and 9,000 tons of cargo belonging to the army's XVIII Airborne Corps. This forward deployment suddenly places them on the Iraqi right flank.

• An F-16C flown by Captain Jon K. Kelk, 3rd Tactical Fighter Wing (TFW) gains the distinction of bagging the first Iraqi MiG-29 jet fighter.

DIPLOMACY: After some hesitation, the Turkish government votes to allow air force warplanes stationed at Incirlik Air Base to be used against targets in northern Iraq.

January 17

AVIATION: Aircraft from six carriers launch strikes against targets in Kuwait and Iraq as part of Operation Desert Storm. One F/A-18 Hornet flown by Lieutenant Commander Michael S. Speicher of VFA-81 (*Saratoga*) is shot down and the pilot is declared killed in action. This status is revised in time to missing/captured, although his body is not recovered until 2009.

MILITARY: The 2nd Battalion, 34th Armor (1st Division) begins rehearsing attacks on Iraqi earthen positions using plows and armored combat earthmovers.

NAVAL: Within hours of the decision to go to war, navy vessels in and around the Persian Gulf fire off 122 precision-guided Tomahawk cruise missiles. The honor of firing the first missile goes to the cruiser *San Jacinto* serving in the Red Sea.

January 17–February 28

AVIATION: The Air Force Reserve is extremely active during Operation Desert Storm. C-130 transports of the 1650th Tactical Airlift Wing complete 3,200 combat sorties while A-10 Thunderbolt IIs from the 706th Tactical Fighter Squadron fly 1,000 sorties against enemy targets. Despite this level of involvement, no Reserve aircraft are lost and no personnel are killed.

January 18

AVIATION: In a series of air battles over Iraq, coalition aircraft shoot down eight Iraqi MiG-29 and Mirage F-1 fighters, with the first two falling to a pair of F/A-18s piloted by Commander Mark I. Fox and Lieutenant Nick Mongillo of VFA-81 (*Saratoga*).

• Air force jets flying from Incirlik Air Base, Turkey, strike at military targets in northern Iraq to prevent forces there from concentrating against forces moving up from Saudi Arabia.

• Over Dhahran, Saudi Arabia, Patriot missiles fired by Battery A, 2nd Battalion, 7th Air Defense Artillery shoot down a Scud ballistic missile fired by Iraqi forces. Several other Scuds strike Tel Aviv, Israel, as the Patriot battalions there are not yet operational. When the government requests additional defenses against missiles, the army dispatches Task Force Patriot Defender, consisting of two battalions from the 10th Air Defense Brigade, from Germany.

• Battery A, 1st battalion, 27th Field Artillery, fires the first Army Tactical Missile System (ATACMS) rockets at Iraqi targets in occupied Kuwait, destroying an SA-1 missile battery. This event marks the debut of the multiple-launch rocket system (MLRS) in combat.

MILITARY: In Washington, D.C., President George H. W. Bush signs an executive order extending the tour of army reservists beyond 180 days. He also authorizes the call-up of 1 million reservists as needed.

NAVAL: In the Persian Gulf, the destroyer *Moosbrugger* dispatches a SEAL team that boards the Sudanese vessel *El Obeid*; this is the first vessel apprehended since the commencement of hostilities.

USS *John F. Kennedy* taking on fuel and ammunition from the USS *Joshua Humphreys* in the Red Sea during the Persian Gulf War (*U.S. Air Force*)

• In the Persian Gulf, the guide-missile frigate *Nicholas,* assisted by Helicopter Anti-submarine Squadron (Light) (HSL-44) and a Kuwaiti patrol boat, neutralize several Iraqi oil platforms with enemy troops firing shoulder-launched missiles at coalition aircraft. Five Iraqis are killed, eight are wounded, and 23 are taken captive.

January 19
AVIATION: Over Iraq, A-6 Intruder and A-7 Corsair II aircraft from the carriers *John F. Kennedy* and *Saratoga* fire new Standoff Land Attack Missiles against military targets for the first time.
• Iraqi surface-to-air missiles shoot down two F-16Cs belonging to the 614th Tactical Fighter Squadron and the pilots are captured. Along with six other coalition airmen, they are paraded before television.
• The Iraqis launch 10 Scud missiles into Israeli territory, injuring 10 civilians.
NAVAL: In the Red Sea, the submarine *Louisville* fires the first submerged Tomahawk cruise missile in history against targets in Iraq.

January 20
AVIATION: Over Dhahran, Saudi Arabia, several Iraqi Scud missiles are downed by Patriots fired by Batteries A and B, 2nd Battalion, 7th Air Defense Artillery.

MARINES: Artillery units attached to the I Marine Expeditionary Force commence bombarding Iraqi units on Kuwaiti soil.

January 21
AVIATION: An A-10 Thunderbolt II flown by Captain Paul T. Johnson braves intense antiaircraft fire to destroy an Iraqi vehicle threatening a downed navy F-14 pilot; he wins the Air Force Cross. Meanwhile, an MH-53J Pave Low helicopter piloted by Captain Thomas J. Trask, 20th Special Operations Squadron, flies in under fire to extract the pilot. Trask and his crew win the Mackay Trophy for their efforts.

January 22
AVIATION: Over Iraq, an F-15E flown by Colonel David W. Eberly and Lieutenant Colonel Tom Griffith are shot down in combat; Eberly and Griffith evade capture for the next three days but are finally taken near the Syrian border.
• Over the Persian Gulf, A-6 Intruder aircraft attack and disable an Iraqi T-43 class vessel, which have a mine laying capability.
MILITARY: Six Iraqi prisoners are taken in a sweep by the 3rd Armored Cavalry Regiment.

January 22–27
AVIATION: MiG aircraft sequestered in hardened aircraft shelters at Al Asad Air Base, Iraq, are hammered by F-111F "Aardvarks" using laser-guided "smart" bombs. Many grounded aircraft are destroyed in this fashion.

January 23
AVIATION: General Colin Powell, chairman of the Joint Chiefs of Staff, declares that air superiority has been achieved over Iraq. Enemy positions are being bombed with virtual impunity.
• In the Persian Gulf, A-6 Intruders attack an Iraqi *Al Qaddisiyah*-class tanker that was apparently collecting military intelligence, and disable it. An enemy hovercraft and patrol ship moored alongside are also sunk.
• A week of intense coalition aerial attacks leaves Iraq with only five air bases still functioning. Their surviving aircraft are reduced to 40 sorties per day.
MILITARY: Near Objective Falcon, Saudi Arabia, scouts of the 1st Battalion, 325th Infantry, 82nd Airborne Division begin nightly reconnaissance sorties to observe enemy positions.
• In Kuwait, Iraqi forces begin dumping millions of gallons of Kuwaiti oil into the Persian Gulf waters and torching hundreds of captured oil wells.

January 24
AVIATION: In the Persian Gulf, A-6 Intruder aircraft sink an Iraqi minelayer and minesweeper and 22 survivors are airlifted to safety by an SH-60 Seahawk helicopter from the guided-missile frigate *Curts*.
• Over the Persian Gulf a Saudi F-15C shoots down two Iraqi Mirage F-1 fighters armed with Exocet antishipping missiles.
• Today coalition air forces mount 2,570 sorties; over the past eight days the number is a staggering 14,750.
NAVAL: A SEAL team lands on a small island in the Persian Gulf and captures 51 Iraqi who had been shooting at coalition aircraft. All are evacuated by helicopters

from the destroyer *Leftwich* and the guided-missile frigate *Nicholas*. This is also the first portion of Kuwaiti territory to be liberated.

January 25
AVIATION: Air force fighter bombers begin employing new I-2000 bombs against hardened Iraqi aircraft shelters, destroying several MiG-29s sequestered inside.

January 26
AVIATION: With the Iraqi air force effectively neutralized, coalition forces begin concentrating their attacks on enemy ground forces in Kuwait.

January 27
AVIATION: Coalition forces acknowledge their air supremacy over Iraqi after 10 days of combat, freeing their aircraft to attack enemy targets at will. F-111s also hit oil pumping manifolds in Kuwait's main terminal at al-Ahmadi with guided GBU-15 bombs to halt the flow of crude oil into the Persian Gulf. This is the worst deliberately set oil spill ever.

January 28
MILITARY: Over Kwajalein Atoll in the Pacific, an army exoatmospheric reentry interceptor system (ERIS) successfully intercepts a dummy warhead launched at Vandenberg Air Force Base, California. The target is destroyed 160 miles above the ground after traveling 4,200 miles.

January 29
AVIATION: Over Al Khafji, Saudi Arabia, an AC-130H gunship is shot down with a loss of all 14 crew members but other air force planes pound the Iraqi forces and hold them in place for a counterattack.
• In the Persian Gulf, helicopters from the amphibious assault ship *Okinawa* attack Iraqi small craft around Umm al Maradum Island, sinking four.
MARINES: Detachments from the amphibious assault ship *Okinawa* seize Umm al Maradum Island in the Persian Gulf; this is the second small portion of Kuwaiti territory liberated by coalition forces.
• Inexplicably, Saddam Hussein orders three brigade-sized night attacks across the Kuwaiti border, one of which captures the Saudi town of Al Khafji. A total of 11 marines are killed by friendly fire.

January 31
MILITARY: In Iraq, two American soldiers from the 233rd Transportation Company, including Specialist Melissa A. Rathbun-Nealy, stray into Iraqi territory and are taken prisoner. Rathbun-Nealy is also the first female prisoner of the conflict.
• In order to prevent further Scud attacks upon Saudi Arabia and Israel, Major General Wayne A. Dowding of the Joint Special Operations Task Force (JSOTF) is ordered to hunt down Scud launchers and either destroy them or point them to coalition air forces. On hand are two squadrons from Delta Force, a company from the 1st Battalion, 75th Rangers, some Navy SEALS, and elements of the army 160th Special Operations Aviation Regiment (SOAR) or "Night Stalkers." The endeavor is moderately successful as Scud launchers are mobile and difficult to track down.

February 1
MILITARY: Along Phase Blue Line, Saudi Arabia, a 15-minute fire fight erupts between Iraqi forces and men from the 4th Battalion, 325th Infantry, 82nd Airborne Division. No losses are incurred by either side.

MARINES: In Saudi Arabia, Saudi and Qatari troops take the village of Al Khafji from Iraqi forces, backed by marine air, artillery, and observer support.

February 2
AVIATION: Over the Indian Ocean, a B-52 bomber based on Diego Garcia experiences electrical problems while returning for a bombing mission over Iraq and crashes. Three crew members are rescued but three are lost.

February 3
MILITARY: By this date, Operation Desert Shield is concluding as most allied ground units have completed their deployment to assigned assembly areas. Foremost among these are the VII Corps and the XVIII Airborne Corps in northwestern Saudi Arabia, which will figure prominently in Operation Desert Storm.

Fairchild A-10A Thunderbolt IIs, affectionately dubbed the "Warthog." This ground-support aircraft played a key role in Operation Desert Storm. (*San Diego Aerospace Museum*)

February 4

AVIATION: A remote-controlled Pioneer vehicle is used to spot artillery targets for the battleship *Missouri* for the first time.

NAVAL: In the Persian Gulf, the battleship *Missouri* fires its 16-inch guns in anger for the first time since World War II. Accurate shelling destroys several Iraqi command-and-control bunkers.

February 6

AVIATION: An A-10 Thunderbolt II flown by Captain Robert R. Swain, Jr., shoots down an Iraqi Gazelle helicopter with his 30mm cannon. This is the first aerial victory attributed to a "Warthog." Over Iraq, an F-14 Tomcat from VF-1 (*Ranger*) shoots down an Iraqi Mi-8 helicopter.

MILITARY: Final elements of the 3rd Armored Division under Major General Paul E. Funk arrive in Saudi Arabia and begin deploying. This is the final unit belonging to VII Corps.

MARINES: Marines of the Direct Support Command begin constructing a new forward logistics base dubbed Al Khanjar, which is fully operational within six days.

February 7

MILITARY: Along the Kuwaiti-Iraqi border, the first artillery raids of Desert Storm are conducted by the VII Corps and 1st Cavalry Division. These actions also mark the debut of the laser-guided Copperhead missile, which knocks out an enemy observation tower. These harassment attacks convince the Iraqi high command that coalition forces are planning a major push through the Wadi al-Batin, and they reinforce the area ahead of time.

February 9

AVIATION: Iraqi Scud missiles continue raining down on Israel, wounding 26 civilians.

• A-10 Thunderbolt IIs begin the process of "tank plinking" or destroying individual targets with precision-guided munitions, or "smart weapons." At this juncture, roughly 600 enemy tanks and armored vehicles have been destroyed, representing 15 percent of Saddam Hussein's overall military strength.

MILITARY: Coalition commander General H. Norman Schwarzkopf suggests that the opening phase of Operation Desert Storm commence between February 21 and 25, and President George H. W. Bush agrees.

February 11

AVIATION: This day coalition forces mount 2,900 strike sorties. A grand total of 61,862 have been completed for the 26-day period.

February 12

AVIATION: Over Baghdad, Iraq, air force fighter bombers use "smart bombs" to bring down the Martyr's Bridge, the Republic Bridge, and the July 14 Bridge.

February 13

AVIATION: Acting upon a tip from military intelligence, F-117s bomb the Al Firdos bunker in downtown Baghdad, Iraq, suspected of housing Saddam Hussein. The building, a civilian communications center, is flattened with the loss of several hundred dead, but the elusive dictator was not there. Thereafter, coalition air authorities more closely supervise combat strikes in the capital city.

MILITARY: Another large artillery raid commences as three MLRS missile batteries from the 42nd Field Artillery Brigade and the 1st Cavalry Division fire 216 rounds at Iraqi artillery positions. These, in turn, drop 140,000 "bomblets" upon exposed enemy positions.

February 14

AVIATION: An air force EF-111A "Spark Vark" crashes in Saudi Arabia after a bombing mission over Iraq; the two-man crew ejects but is apparently killed upon landing.

MILITARY: The 1st Armored Division, 9,000 vehicles strong, rumbles toward its Tactical Assembly Area (TAA) Garcia, just below the 2nd Armored Cavalry's position. Concurrently, the 3rd Armored Division positions itself to the west of this armored concentration.

February 15

DIPLOMACY: In Baghdad, Iraq, the five-man Revolutionary Council declares that they are willing to consider the UN resolution requiring Iraq to withdraw from Kuwait.

MILITARY: Coalition commander General H. Norman Schwarzkopf is briefed on the condition and morale of Iraqi prisoners. He learns that the Iraqi are tired of incessant warfare and would surrender readily except for minefields in their path, possible execution by the Republican Guard, and threats against family members. Many are of the opinion that the bulk of Iraqis will surrender the moment serious fighting starts.

February 16

AVIATION: This evening an AH-64A Apache helicopter gunship from the 1st Infantry Division accidentally fires Hellfire missiles at American personnel carriers as they worked their way through a sand berm along the Iraqi border. Two soldiers are killed and six others wounded in the first of several "friendly fire" episodes that follow.

February 17

AVIATION: By this time, coalition force aircraft have accounted for 1,300 of Saddam Hussein's 4,240 tanks and 1,100 of his 3,110 artillery pieces.

• A wave of AH-64A Apaches from the 2nd Battalion, 229th Aviation Regiment (101st Airborne Division) begin attacking and reducing Iraqi bunker complexes near the projected Main Supply Route New Market. They are joined by additional Apaches from Company C, 3rd Battalion, 502nd Infantry; around 40 Iraqis from the 45th Infantry Division surrender.

MILITARY: The VII Corps unleashes its largest bombardment to date with five battalions of artillery that smash various Iraqi air defenses. This allows AH-64A Apaches of the 2nd Squadron, 6th Cavalry (11th Aviation Brigade) to slip into enemy lines unopposed, and they destroy several communication facilities.

February 18
AVIATION: The XVIII Airborne Corps swings into action as helicopters from the 1st Battalion, 82nd Aviation Regiment (82nd Airborne Division) conduct a reconnaissance in force over Objective Rochambeau while other Apaches belonging to the 12th Aviation Brigade maul Iraqi troops at Objective White.
• An MH-60 Black Hawk from the 3rd Battalion, 160th Special Operations Battalion swoops in and rescues a downed F-16 pilot 40 miles north of the Iraqi border.
NAVAL: In the Persian Gulf, the amphibious assault ship *Tripoli* and the guided-missile cruiser *Princeton* strike mines and suffer damage. A total of seven crewmen are injured.

February 19
AVIATION: Baghdad, Iraq, is struck by a combination of F-4Gs and F-16s launched from Turkish air space. Today coalition forces mount a record 3,000 sorties for a total of 83,000 since the war began.
MILITARY: The 24th Infantry Division (Mechanized) rumbles forward to engage Iraqi troops while its attached aviation brigade provides support. An Iraqi border post is also eliminated by a direct hit from a Copperhead missile courtesy of Battery B, 4th Battalion, 41st Field Artillery.

February 20
AVIATION: Attack helicopters from the 82nd and 101st Airborne Division ravage nearby Iraqi positions near the Saudi border, inducing more than 400 of them to surrender. Meanwhile, the Iraqi 45th Infantry Division becomes an object of unwelcome attention by the 1st Battalion, 201st Field Artillery.
MILITARY: At Wadi al-Batin, Kuwait, the 1st Battalion, 5th Cavalry, 1st Cavalry Division forces its way through the Iraqi sand berm and begins fanning out into the desert, looking for enemy positions. They are subsequently attacked by Iraqi artillery and antitank guns before pulling back with three killed and nine injured.

February 21
AVIATION: At Freetown, Sierra Leone, a C-141 Starlifter from the 438th Military Airlift Wing arrives bearing 55 tons of food and medicine for victims of hardships there.

February 23
AVIATION: Air force B-52Gs continue pounding the Iraqi Republican Guard positions as other Iraqi troops continue setting Kuwaiti oil wells on fire.
MILITARY: In Washington, D.C., President George H. W. Bush declares to the world that the liberation of Kuwait is at hand and that fighting will continue until the last Iraqi unit is forcibly ejected from that captured nation.
• Teams of Special Forces fan out in the Euphrates River valley, Iraq, seeking intelligence as to Iraqi troop movements. The three-man team headed by Master Sergeant Jeffrey Sims is discovered and battles superior enemy forces for several hours until MH-60 Black Hawks of the 160th Special Operations Aviation Regiment (SOAR) swoop in to rescue them.
• In Kuwait, General H. Norman Schwarzkopf decides that Iraqi positions have been sufficiently "softened up" and the moment of decision to launch an all-out ground offensive is at hand.

MARINES: In Norway, reservists of the 2nd Marine Expeditionary Brigade conducts Exercise Battle Griffin 91 as part of a test of the Norway Airlanded MEB (NALMEB), as per the 1981 agreement to store prepositioned equipment and supplies.

February 24

AVIATION: Over the next three days, coalition aircraft are responsible for flying 3,000 combat sorties, including reconnaissance, close air support, and interdiction.

MILITARY: At 4:00 A.M., American and coalition ground forces under General H. Norman Schwarzkopf unleash their long-anticipated ground offensive against Iraqi forces holding Kuwait. The XVIII Airborne Corps under Lieutenant General Gary E. Luck, supported by the 82nd Airborne Division and the French 6th Light Armored Division, moves forward almost unopposed and easily takes its objectives. Simultaneously, the 101st Airborne Division employs 66 UH-60 Black Hawk and 39 CH-47 Chinook helicopters to air assault their way deep inside Iraqi territory and establish Forward Operating Base Cobra; 340 prisoners are seized in the process.

• As the flanking movement continues, General H. Norman Schwarzkopf orders his main strike force, VII Corps under Lieutenant General Tommy Franks, directly into the fray. Spearheaded by the 2nd Armored Cavalry Regiment, and preceded by a massive bombardment of 11,000 artillery rounds and 414 MLRS rockets, tanks and infantry of the 1st Infantry Regiment surge forward and breach Iraqi defenses. The only resistance comes from a handful of Iraqi T-55 tanks that are quickly dispatched by the 2nd Armored Cavalry. VII Corps seizes all its objectives in only two hours instead of the 18 hours anticipated.

MARINES: The I Marine Expeditionary Force, numbering 84,515 men, steps over the line during Operation Desert Storm. Here the 1st and 2nd Marine Divisions, assisted by armor of the Tiger Brigade, penetrate numerous belts of Iraqi defenses while advancing upon Kuwait City. Simultaneously, the 5th Marine Expeditionary Brigade disembarks to serve as the I Marine Expeditionary Force reserve. Other Marine units remain afloat in the Persian Gulf to act as a deception.

February 25

AVIATION: As Iraqi forces surround and prepare to attack an Army Special Forces team, they are struck by Air Force F-16Cs while a UH-60 Black Hawk helicopter swoops in to rescue the Americans.

• In Dhahran, Saudi Arabia, an Iraqi Scud missile slams into a warehouse occupied by the 14th Quartermaster Detachment, killing 28 soldiers (including the first enlisted female soldier to die in combat) and wounds 97. Nearby Patriot missile batteries were experiencing a software problem and proved unable to deal with incoming missiles.

MILITARY: As the VII Corps marches forward, General H. Norman Schwarzkopf grows concerned that the elite Iraqi Republican Guard is trying to escape. He orders Lieutenant General Franks to turn all units eastward and cut them off.

• Saddam Hussein takes to the air waves over Baghdad radio and orders his remaining forces out of Kuwait.

February 25–26
MILITARY: Colonel Robert Clark leads the 3rd Brigade, 101st Airborne Division, on a 150-mile penetration of Iraqi territory. This is not only the longest air assault in history, but it also severs Highway 8 and cuts off all enemy supplies and reinforcements below it.

February 26
AVIATION: The Iraqi Adnan Division is attacked by Lieutenant Colonel William Hatch and AH-64A Apaches of the 3rd Battalion, 1st Aviation Regiment. In a one-sided engagement, the Americans account for 38 T-72 tanks, 14 BMP fighting vehicles, and 70 trucks.
• As the bulk of surviving Iraqi forces abandons Kuwait, they are savaged by coalition force warplanes, killing thousands along what becomes known as the "Highway of Death." The four-lane passage is literally gutted by the wreckage of tanks, personnel carries, trucks, and looted civilian automobiles. The aerial attack stops on the orders of President George H. W. Bush.
MILITARY: At a region denoted as 73 Eastling, M1A1 Abrams tanks of the 2nd Armored Cavalry Regiment engage the Republican Guard Tawakalna Division in a stand-up fight; the Americans destroy 28 Russian-built T-72 tanks and 16 other armored vehicles at a cost of three dead. This encounter demonstrates in stark relief just how superior American armor is over its Soviet counterparts.
• At As Salman Airfield, Iraq, the 1st Platoon, Company A, 27th Engineering battalion suffers seven dead while clearing unexploded cluster bomb submunitions off a runway.

February 26–27
MILITARY: The Battle of Objective Norfolk unfolds as the 1st and 3rd Brigades, 1st Infantry Division, race through the 2nd Armored Cavalry Regiment and engage the Republican Guard Tawakalna Division and the 37th Brigade of the 12th Armored Division head on. The swirling engagement results in the destruction of both Iraqi brigades and scores of tanks, and hundreds are killed and injured. The Americans lose six dead along with a handful of Abrams and Bradleys, all through friendly fire.

February 27
AVIATION: The air force successfully delivers two 4,700-pound GPU-28 bombs that demolish the so-called impregnable Iraqi command bunker at Al Taji. Total air sorties mounted this day top 3,500–a new record.
• A UH-60 Black Hawk helicopter from the 2nd Battalion, 229th Aviation Regiment, en route to rescue a pilot downed behind enemy lines, is itself bagged by Iraqi forces. Five Americans die in the crash and three are captured; among the latter is Major Rhonda Cornum, flight surgeon, the second female prisoner of the war.
MILITARY: Along Medinah Ridge, the biggest tank fight of the war erupts as the 1st Armored Division rolls forward to engage the Republican Guard's Medinah Division and the remnants of the 12th Armored Division. Supported by artillery and helicopter fire, the Americans devastate their opponents, destroying more than 300 Iraqi vehicles; one American is killed and a handful of vehicles are damaged.

• Major General Barry R. McCaffrey leads the 24th Infantry Division (Mechanized) on a jaunt into Iraqi territory near Basrah, capturing Jalibah Air Base and destroying several MiG-29 fighters on the ground. They then dash down Highway 8, capturing several supply depots and sweeping aside resistance from remnants of the al-Faw, Nebuchadnezzar, and Hammurabi Divisions.

February 28

AVIATION: With the terminus of Operation Desert Storm at 8 A.M., the air force has flown 59 percent of all coalition force sorties, while its 2,000 aircraft represent 75 percent of all machines involved. For all their media celebrity, only 10 percent of ordnance dropped or fired were precision-guided "smart bombs." However, the elusive F-117s account for 40 percent of all Iraqi strategic targets knocked out by flying 1,270 combat sorties and dropping 2,041 tons of bombs. This is also the first "space war" judging from the extensive use of satellite technology involved.

• Jets, aircraft, and helicopters of the 3rd Marine Air Wing (3rd MAW) fly several hundred missions, mostly ground support. Their losses total four AV-8B Harriers and two OV10 Broncos shot down; five marine aviators are also captured and released within days.

• During the 100 hours of Desert Storm, the Air Force Space Command (AFSPACECOM) satellite systems were extremely active in relaying meteorological information to combat headquarters along with alerts of short-range ballistic missile launches.

MILITARY: With Kuwait completely free of Iraqi units, President George H. W. Bush declares a unilateral cease-fire after only 100 hours of fighting. Considering the devastation wrought on Iraqi forces since January 17, the toll is astonishingly light: 98 dead (21 through friendly fire) and 352 wounded. A further 126 died in noncombat-related accidents. In sum, the army deployed 227,800 men in theater, of which 35,158 were from the Army Reserve and 37,692 came from National Guard formations.

MARINES: Operation Desert Storm concludes just as the I Marine Expeditionary Force recaptures Kuwait City along with 22,000 prisoners. Marine losses in the 100-hour campaign are 24 dead and 92 wounded.

March 1

AVIATION: C-5 Galaxies from the Military Airlift Command (MAC) carry 150 tons of relief supplies to Bucharest, Romania, to help restore order at a time of violent street confrontations and shortages.

March 2

MILITARY: As elements of the Hammurabi Division flee inland, they fire upon the 24th Infantry Division, whose return fire through tanks, artillery, and helicopters bags an additional 185 Iraqi armored vehicles, 400 trucks, and 34 pieces of artillery.

March 3

MILITARY: At Safwan, Iraq, General H. Norman Schwarzkopf and coalition leaders under Lieutenant General Khalid ibn Sukltan meet with their Iraqi counterparts to hammer out cease-fire terms, including immediate repatriation of all captives. Once concluded, U.S. Army civil affairs units swing into action, providing food, medicine, and shelter to thousands of Iraqi and Kuwaiti refugees while Engineer and Explosive Ordnance Disposal units begin the arduous task of disarming thousands of mines and unexploded ordnance still littered about the desert.

• At this juncture, Central Command (CENTCOM) estimates that coalition forces have accounted for 3,300 tanks, 2,100 armored vehicles, and 2,200 artillery pieces. A total of 80,000 Iraqi prisoners have also been taken although the death toll is less precise and looms upward of 100,000.

March 4

MILITARY: The Iraqis release 10 coalition prisoners.

March 4–12

MILITARY: At Khamisiyah, Iraq, engineers from the 82nd Airborne Division discover and destroy a huge Iraqi bunker complex/weapon cache. They are unaware that chemical weapons and nerve agents are present, exposing many soldiers to low-level doses. This is the origin of what becomes known as Gulf War Syndrome, which ultimately affects 100,000 service personnel.

March 5

MILITARY: Iraqi authorities release 35 coalition prisoners, including two female captives.

March 8

AVIATION: At Vandenberg Air Force Base, California, the first Martin Marietta, two-stage Titan IV heavy-lift booster is successfully launched for the first time.

MILITARY: With Operation Desert Storm successfully concluded, the first wave of army units slated for a return to the United States departs.

March 8–December

AVIATION: The Military Airlift Command (MAC) again demonstrates its strategic flexibility by flying a host of supplies, personnel, and even environmental cleanup equipment into the Persian Gulf region. Accordingly, 42 C-5 Galaxies and three C-141 Starlifters of the 60th and 436th Military Airlift Wings fly in over 1,000 tons of firefighting equipment and crews necessary to extinguish 517 oil wells set alight by retreating Iraqi forces. They also deliver 7,000 tons of relief supplies to Kurdish refugees in southeastern Turkey.

March 9

MARINES: The first units of the I Marine Expeditionary Force begin withdrawing to the United States; all have departed by August 27.

March 10

AVIATION: The Iraqis release a further 21 prisoners, including eight air force members.

• At Andrews Air Force Base, Maryland, returning POWs are personally greeted by Defense Secretary Dick Cheney and several thousand well-wishers.

March 12

MILITARY: In Washington, D.C., President George H. W. Bush authorizes the Southwest Asia Service Medal for any military personnel participating in Operations Desert Shield or Desert Storm.

March 18
NAVAL: At Norfolk, Virginia, the combat stores ship *Sylvania* is the first vessel supporting Operation Desert Storm to return to port. During a seven-month tour, it delivered 20,500 tons of supplies 31,000 piles of mail, and its helicopters performed 10 medical evacuations.

March 20
AVIATION: Over Iraq, an Su-22 caught violating the cease-fire agreement is promptly shot down by an F-16C.

March 31
MILITARY: In accordance with the 1987 IMF Treaty between the United States and the Soviet Union, the last of the Pershing II missiles are removed from Europe and sent home for destruction.

April
AVIATION: Two C-5 Galaxies from the 436th Military Airlift Wing convey 200 tons of medical supplies to Lima, Peru, in order to stave off a cholera epidemic afflicting 150,000 people.

April 6–July 24
MILITARY: In northern Iraq, Operation Provide Comfort is executed to bring humanitarian assistance to thousands of Kurdish refugees. Joint Task Force Provide Comfort consequently is created at Incirlik Air Base, Turkey, where elements of the 3rd Infantry Division (Mechanized) distribute food, water, and shelter. By the time the operation concludes, over 17,000 tons of relief supplies have been distributed.

April 7
AVIATION: U.S. warplanes commence Operation Provide Comfort to assist the Kurds in northern Iraq; part of this effort entails enforcing a no-fly zone above the 36th parallel.

April 11
DIPLOMACY: In New York, the United Nations Security Council declares a cease-fire ending the Persian Gulf War.
NAVAL: U.S. Navy vessels have destroyed 533 mines, intercepted 8,770 merchant ships, and boarded 590 suspected vessels.

April 12
AVIATION: Off the Alaskan coast, forward-deployed F-15 Eagles stationed at Galena Airport intercept a Soviet AN-74 Coaler transport aircraft for the first time.

April 15–July 19
AVIATION: Helicopters of Marine HMM-264 fly in elements of the 24th Marine Expeditionary Unit (SOC) to northern Iraq to assist Kurdish refugees.

April 18
AVIATION: At Vandenberg Air Force Base, California, the air force test launches a Martin Marietta/Boeing MGM-134A intercontinental ballistic missile for the first time. The vehicle splashes down 4,000 miles away near the Kwajalein Missile Range.

April 23
MILITARY: In light of the decisive nature of Operation Desert Storm, which does much to revive America's military spirits since the Vietnam War, Congress votes to award Generals Colin Powell and H. Norman Schwarzkopf a special gold medal.

April 24
MILITARY: President George H. W. Bush posthumously awards a Medal of Honor to Corporal Freddie Stowers, 371st Infantry, who was killed while leading a squad on September 28, 1918. He is the first African American of either world war to be so recognized.

May 10–June 13
AVIATION: After a tropical cyclone batters the coast of Bangladesh with 150-mile per hour winds, transports of the Military Airlift Command (MAC) begin Operation Sea Angel in carrying 3,000 tons of relief supplies to the city of Dacca.

May 15–May 28
MARINES: With Bangladesh still reeling from a violent cyclone two weeks earlier, the 5th Marine Expeditionary Brigade is diverted to the Indian Ocean to provide emergency relief. Operation Sea Angel continues over the next two weeks as part of an international relief effort.

May 16
MILITARY: In Germany, the 11th Armored Cavalry Regiment received orders to ship out to Kuwait as part of Operation Positive Force, the high-profile continuing presence of U.S. forces there.

May 20
GENERAL: Queen Elizabeth II grants General H. Norman Schwarzkopf an honorary knighthood for his command of coalition forces in the Gulf War.

May 31
AVIATION: At RAF Greenham Common, England, the Air Force inactivates the 501st Tactical Missile Wing, the final unit entirely armed with cruise missiles. Ironically, this was also the first GLCM unit deployed and activated in Europe.

June–September
AVIATION: Throughout this period, Military Airlift Command (MAC) transports fly 19 humanitarian missions to Addis Ababa, Ethiopia, to help mitigate the effect of a severe drought.

June 8
MILITARY: In Washington, D.C., a victory parade of thousands of sailors, soldiers, airmen, and marines who fought in Desert Storm is led by their commander, General H. Norman Schwarzkopf. The scene is repeated again two days later in New York City.

June 8–July 2
AVIATION: Clark Air Base, Philippines, is nearly destroyed by the eruption of nearby Mount Pinatubo. Operation Fiery Vigil is drawn up to evacuate 15,000 people from the disaster zone and bring in 2,000 tons of humanitarian relief.

This becomes the largest emergency evacuation since the fall of South Vietnam in 1975.

June 12
MARINES: In the Philippines, Operation Fiery Vigil unfolds as elements of the III Marine Expeditionary Force arrive to assist survivors of a major volcanic eruption at Mount Pinatubo. The destruction to American naval facilities at Subic Bay results in the abandonment of that post, first used in 1898. Over 19,000 people are evacuated.

June 13
MILITARY: In Kuwait, the 11th Armored Cavalry Regiment relieves the 1st Brigade, 3rd Armored Division, and assumes responsibility for the defense of that nation.

June 15
NAVAL: At Annapolis, Maryland, Rear Admiral Thomas C. Lynch gains appointment as the 54th superintendent of the U.S. Naval Academy.

June 21
MILITARY: In Washington, D.C., General Gordon R. Sullivan gains appointment as the 32nd chief of staff, U.S. Army.

June 25
AVIATION: Ongoing drought conditions in Kenya results in 60 tons of food and other supplies being delivered to Nairobi by transports of the 60th Military Airlift Wing.

June 28
MARINES: Sergeant Major Harold G. Overstreet is appointed the 12th sergeant major of the Marine Corps.

June 30
MARINES: At this time, marine personnel levels stand at 19,753 officers and 174,287 enlisted men and women.

July 1
MARINES: In Washington, D.C., General Carl E. Mundy, Jr., gains appointment as the 30th commandant of the Marine Corps.

July 3
MILITARY: In Washington, D.C., President George H. W. Bush awards the Presidential Medal of Freedom to Generals Colin Powell and H. Norman Schwarzkopf for outstanding military leadership during recent events in Kuwait.

July 4
NAVAL: At Norfolk, Virginia, the navy commissions the *Arleigh Burke,* the first of a new class of Aegis guided-missile destroyers of the same name, in honor of an accomplished destroyer commander. In an unusual mark of respect, the honor is conferred while Admiral Burke is still living.

July 7
AVIATION: Drought conditions, exacerbated by civil war, result in a 70-ton food delivery to N'Djamena, Chad, by transports of the 436th Military Airlift Wing.

1991

July 10
AVIATION: At Plattsburgh Air Force Base, New York, the last remaining FB-111A nuclear strike aircraft are retired and flown to desert storage at Davis Monthan Air Force Base, Arizona.

July 22
AVIATION: In a first for the U.S. Air Force, transports of the 730th Military Airlift Squadron and 445th Military Airlift Wing carry 20 tons of medical supplies to Ulan Batar, Mongolia, to assist in a time of acute shortages.

July 30
DIPLOMACY: In a major development, UN arms inspector Rolf Ekeus reports uncovering four times as many chemical and biological weapons than Iraq had previously declared owning.
MILITARY: Congress approves a bill to close 44 military bases in a cost-cutting measure that eliminates 80,000 military and 37,000 civilian positions.

July 31
AVIATION: In Washington, D.C., Congress amends the 1992 defense appropriations bill to allow women to fly combat missions in air force, navy, and marine warplanes.
DIPLOMACY: In Moscow, Soviet Union, President George H. W. Bush and President Mikhail Gorbachev sign the Strategic Arms Reduction Treaty (START I), which mandates a 25 to 30 percent reduction in their respective nuclear arsenals. Hereafter, both countries are entitled to 1,600 strategic nuclear delivery systems and 6,000 warheads. Provisions are also made for vigorous, on-site inspections.

August
MARINES: The cold war having ended, the Marine Corps begins a troop drawdown by eliminating the fourth rifle company of each battalion.

August 6–9
AVIATION: Transports of the Military Airlift Command carry 75 tons of blankets and medical supplies to Shanghai, China, in the wake of severe flooding throughout the interior regions.

August 22
AVIATION: The Gulf War Air Power Survey (GWAPS) is commenced by the air force to correctly evaluate its overall impact during recent hostilities.

September 6
MARINES: A formalized screening process is adopted by the Marine Corps to choose lieutenant colonels and colonels selected for command positions.

September 8
NAVAL: In Las Vegas, Nevada, the 35th annual Tailhook Convention of naval aviators goes amok when several women, including some active duty officers, are sexually harassed or groped. An investigation results in 69 officers being reprimanded. Moreover, the incident highlights the need for increased sexual sensitivity training in the armed forces.

September 11
NAVAL: At Yokosuka, Japan, the carrier *Midway* is replaced by the *Independence*; this becomes the navy's only forward-deployed carrier.

September 15
AVIATION: At Long Beach, California, the new Boeing C-17A Globemaster III performs its maiden flight by flying to Edwards Air Force Base. This aircraft is designed to replace the C-141s and C-5s, and can transport oversized cargo loads of the C-5 Galaxy to remote and primitive landing zones like the C-130 Hercules.
• At Edwards Air Force Base, California, the prototype Beech T-1A Jayhawk makes its maiden flight; in 1993 it becomes a standardized trainer for prospective tanker and transport pilots.

September 16
DIPLOMACY: In Manila, the Philippine senate declines to renew the U.S. lease of the Subic Bay Naval Facility despite the entreaties of President Corazon Aquino. The Americans have maintained a presence there since 1898.
MARINES: All charges are dropped against Lieutenant Colonel Oliver L. North for his role in the Iran-contra scandal.

September 27
AVIATION: In a symbolic move to suggest that the cold war is winding down, President George H. W. Bush orders the long-standing Strategic Air Command (SAC) alert discontinued. This has been a standard American military fixture since October 1957.
NAVAL: In Washington, D.C., President George H. W. Bush declares that the United States will unilaterally reduce its stock of nuclear weapons at sea, including air-launched munitions on aircraft carriers.

October–November
AVIATION: Once the former Soviet Union begins unraveling, air force transports begin delivering food and medical supplies to the needy in Russia, Armenia, and Byelorussia.
• The formerly Communist government of Angola, having concluded a bloody, 16-year civil war, accepts aid from the United States for the first time. Transports from the 436th Military Airlift Wing carry in 275 ton of relief supplies to the capital of Luanda.

October 2
AVIATION: Transports of the 834th Airlift Division fly an additional 15 pallets of medical supplies and eight ambulances into Ulan Bator, Mongolia, to thwart ongoing shortages caused by the collapse of the Soviet Union.

October 17
NAVAL: The navy, having conducted further investigations, exonerates sailor Clayton Hartwigg for the accidental explosion onboard the battleship *Iowa* and apologizes to his family for an earlier accusation.

October 23
AVIATION: Air force transports deliver 146 tons of medical supplies and relief cargo to Kiev, Ukraine, after its economy collapses with the fall of the Soviet Union.

1991

November

AVIATION: The Military Airlift Command (MAC) performs its 100th humanitarian flight by assisting Afghan refugees fleeing to camps in Pakistan. Since March 1986, air force transports have delivered over 1,000 tons of aid to the region.

November 1

AVIATION: A C-5 Galaxy from the Twenty Second Air Force flies to Thule, Greenland, with a 36-member search-and-rescue team and two MH-60G Pave Hawks. Once landed, the helicopters rescue the 13-man crew of a Canadian C-130 Hercules that crashed 300 miles from the North Pole.

November 14

AVIATION: The 436th Military Airlift Wing dispatches a C-5 Galaxy with 50 tons of medical and relief supplies to mitigate ongoing food shortages in Freetown, Sierra Leone.

November 15

NAVAL: All charges against Rear Admiral John M. Poindexter for his role in the Iran-contra scandal are ordered dropped by a U.S. federal appeals court.

November 22

MARINES: At Guantánamo Bay, Cuba, units from the II Marine Expeditionary Force prepare to assist displaced refugees on the island of Haiti, then in the throes of its latest political coup.

November 24

NAVAL: After the Philippine government refuses to renew its lease, the navy relinquishes Subic Bay and all its naval facilities. This ends an American naval presence in the islands going back to 1898.

November 26

AVIATION: The air force closes Clark Air Base, Philippines, ending a 90-year American military presence there. This was the largest overseas air force base while it operated.

December 6

AVIATION: Six C-130s of the 834th Airlift Division arrive at Kwajalein Atoll with humanitarian relief supplies, after Typhoon Zelda thoroughly battered its facilities.

December 8

NAVAL: At the Naval Air Station, Pensacola, Florida, the venerable training carrier *Lexington*, the last of the World War II *Essex*-class carriers, is decommissioned. It ends up as a floating museum in Corpus Christi, Texas.

December 8–21

DIPLOMACY: The Soviet Union, one of the world's most oppressive governments, collapses under the weight of its own tyranny and incompetence. A new entity, the Commonwealth of Independent States (CIS), takes the place of the Soviet Union.

December 17–22

AVIATION: In another sign that the cold war has ended, transports of the 436th, 438th, and 439th Airlift Wings deliver 238 tons of food and relief supplies to

Moscow and Saint Petersburg, Russia, Minsk in Byelorussia, and Yerevan in Armenia. Severe economic hardships are an indelible aftereffect of the Soviet Union's collapse.

December 21
Aviation: The prototype Rockwell AC-130U gunship performs its maiden flight. This new aircraft possesses updated sensors, increased firepower, and enhanced ability to locate ground targets.

December 25
Diplomacy: After the Soviet Union votes itself out of existence, President Mikhail S. Gorbachev resigns from office and declares the cold war over. Hopes are high for a "new world order."

1992

January
Military: With the cold war over, army personnel drops to 610,450 in 18 active service divisions.

January 17
Aviation: The air force, desiring to upgrade its fleet of training aircraft, accepts delivery of the first production model T-1A Jayhawk.

January 20–25
Aviation: Continuing medical shortages in Mongolia result in another C-5 Galaxy from the 60th Airlift Wing delivering 56 tons of supplies to Mongolia. They do so at the behest of the U.S. State Department to curry good relations with this former Soviet state.

January 30
Aviation: In the latest consolidation move, control of all Department of Defense satellites and management of the Air Force Satellite Control Network are handed to the Air Force Space Command (AFSPACECOM).

February
Marines: As a cost-cutting measure, the Marine Corps begins disbanding six permanent Marine Expeditionary Brigade headquarters.

February 1
Diplomacy: In Washington, D.C., President George H. W. Bush and Russian president Boris Yeltsin declare the cold war over, which ended in a decisive victory for the United States.

February 6
Aviation: The 435th Tactical Airlift Wing provides four C-130 Hercules transports, which carry food and medical supplies to the former Soviet state of Lithuania.

February 10–29
Aviation: The air force embarks upon Provide Hope I, a mass humanitarian mission delivering thousands of tons of food and medical supplies to the new Commonwealth of Independent States, which replaced the now defunct Soviet Union. C-5 Galaxies and C-141 Starlifters fly 65 missions to that end.

February 12

NAVAL: Off Wake Atoll in the mid-Pacific, the salvage vessel *Salvor* makes the deepest-known recovery by recovering parts of a helicopter from 17,250 feet.

February 29

AVIATION: Operation Provide Hope II commences as air force transports continue flying food and medicine into struggling former states of the defunct Soviet Union. Both the army and the navy also deliver cargo by sea and over land.

March 4

AVIATION: For the first time since World War II, American bombers are welcomed in Russia when two B-52s land on a friendship mission.

March 15

AVIATION: In the wake of a severe earthquake that rattles eastern Turkey, C-5 Galaxy and C-130 Hercules aircraft transport over 165 tons of medicine, blankets, clothing, and other relief supplies to the victims.

March 19

AVIATION: Alaska-based F-15s intercept two Russian Tu-95 Bears aircraft for the first time since the demise of the Soviet Union.

March 24

AVIATION: The Open Skies Treaty is signed by 24 nations to allow unarmed reconnaissance flights over their territory.
• In Spain, the final air force fighter units depart for home, ending a 26-year tenure there.

March 31

AVIATION: Lieutenant Commander Wendy B. Lawrence, a navy helicopter pilot, is the first female line officer selected to receive astronaut training.

April

AVIATION: After severe oil rig fires break out in Uzbekistan, five C-141 Starlifters are assigned to deliver several tons of fire-fighting equipment.

April 1

AVIATION: A C-141 Starlifter from the 437th Airlift Wing delivers 155 barrels of aviation fuel by parachute to a joint U.S.-Russian ice station in Antarctica for use by their helicopters.

April 7

DIPLOMACY: After the United States recognizes the former Yugoslavian states of Croatia and Slovenia, resident Serb populations rebel and internecine civil strife ensues.

April 17

AVIATION: After the United States recognized the former Yugoslavian states of Croatia and Slovenia as independent countries, C-141 Starlifters begin flying in humanitarian aid as regional centralized economies constrict.

1992

April 24
AVIATION: Peruvian Su-22 jet fighters attack an air force C-130H Hercules of the 310th Airlift Squadron in international air space, injuring six crewmen and killing one, who was sucked out of the cabin at 14,500 feet. The surviving crew manage to make an emergency landing in the damaged plane, winning a Mackay Trophy.

May 1–10
AVIATION: Transports of the Military Airlift Command (MAC) fly in troops and police to help quell an outbreak of racial violence in Los Angeles, California.
MILITARY: Severe rioting breaks out in Los Angeles due to the acquittal of police charged with the beating of Rodney King; consequently, the 7th Infantry Division (Light) and the National Guard 40th Infantry (Mechanized) are sent in to restore order. The toll is staggering: 54 dead, 2,383 injured, and damages estimated at $700 million.
MARINES: In the wake of riots occasioned by the acquittal of four police officers charged with beating a motorist, 1,500 marines are rushed to Los Angeles, California, from Camp Pendleton.

May 3–4
AVIATION: A coup in Sierra Leone prompts the deployment of C-141 Starlifters and C-130 aircraft to evacuate 350 citizens and foreign nationals from that West African nation.

May 7–8
AVIATION: In another sign of growing détente, the Air Force Reserve Command Band marches in a Moscow military parade.

May 12
AVIATION: Lockheed delivers its 2,000th C-130 Hercules, making it one of the most widely produced and successful air transports in history.

June 1
AVIATION: In a major organizational overhaul, the Strategic Air Command (SAC), the Tactical Air Command (TAC), and the Military Airlift Command (MAC) are discontinued and replaced by the new Air Combat Command (ACC), which operates SAC's bombers and missiles and TAC's fighters, and Air Mobility Command (AMC), which inherits MAC's transports and SAC's tanker aircraft.
• The Department of Defense creates the United States Strategic Command (USSTRATCOM) as the nation's newest unified command, to oversee U.S. nuclear forces and their long-range delivery systems. General George L. Butler, the final SAC commander, is appointed to take charge.

June 22
NAVAL: In Washington, D.C., Secretary of the Navy H. Lawrence Garrett III resigns due to vocal criticism of his handling of the so-called Tailhook scandal.

June 30
AVIATION: In accordance with President George H. W. Bush's Nuclear Forces Initiative, transports of the Air Mobility Command (AMC) withdraw all remaining stocks of nuclear artillery shells, Lance missile warheads, and nuclear depth charges from Europe.

July 1
AVIATION: The new Air Force Materiel Command (AFMC) is created from a consolidation of the former Air Force Logistics Command (AFLC) and Air Force Systems Command (AFSC).

July 1–March 15, 1996
AVIATION: In Sarajevo, Bosnia-Herzegovina, Operation Provide Promise unfolds as Air Mobility Command (AMC) transports continue delivering tens of thousands of tons of medicine and food to that impoverished region.

July 10
POLITICS: In Miami, Florida, a U.S. federal court sentences former Panamanian dictator Manuel Noriega, whose provocations precipitated Operation Just Cause in January 1990, to 40 years in jail for drug smuggling, money laundering, and racketeering.

July 20
AVIATION: Near Quantico, Virginia, a Bell/Textron V-22 Osprey crashes, killing three marines and four civilians. Flight testing of this revolutionary hybrid aircraft is suspended until an accident investigation concludes.

July 22
NAVAL: In Washington, D.C., a major reorganization scheme is announced when the office of the Assistant Chiefs of Naval Operations for Surface, Submarine, Air, and Naval Warfare are consolidated under the office of the Deputy Chief of Naval Operations for Resources, Warfare, Requirements, and Assessment.

July 24
NAVAL: In light of ethnic unrest in the former Yugoslavian state of Bosnia-Herzegovina, the carrier *Saratoga* becomes the first such vessel to conduct operations in the Adriatic Sea.

August–October
MILITARY: In the wake of Hurricane Andrew, troops from the 82nd Airborne and 10th Mountain Divisions are sent in to assist National Guard troops in disaster relief operations.

August 2–20
AVIATION: In Kuwait, Operation Intrinsic Action unfolds as transports of the Air Mobility Command (AMC) arrive with army reinforcements. The move is made in response to recent threats made to Kuwait by Iraq.

August 12
AVIATION: In Angola, the end of civil war prompts Air Mobility Command (AMC) transports to conduct Operation Provide Transition. These aircraft begin flying thousands of demobilized soldiers home to participate in that nation's first democratic elections.

August 21–December 9
AVIATION: Following the overthrow of General Mohamed Siad Barre, Operation Provide Relief commences as transports of the Air Mobility Command (AMC) begin flying food, medicine, and other relief supplies to Somalia, wracked by civil

wars, drought, and famine. By February 28, 1993, over 3,000 missions have been flown, which deliver over 23,000 tons of cargo. The overall effort is commanded by Marine Brigadier General Frank Libutti.

August 25–October 28
AVIATION: After Hurricane Andrew ravages southern Florida, Homestead Air Force Base is so severely damaged that it is abandoned. Damage in the Miami area is so severe that the Air Mobility Command (AMC) dispatches 13,500 relief workers and 21,000 tons of equipment and supplies in 724 transport missions.

August 26
AVIATION: Over Iraq, coalition aircraft commence Operation Southern Watch to enforce a no-fly zone to keep the Iraqi air force from flying below the 32nd parallel. Naval aircraft involved are also operating from the carrier *Independence*. This is undertaken to prevent Saddam Hussein from attacking the large Shiite community residing in the southern marshes of Iraq.

August 28
AVIATION: Air force RF-4C Phantom II operations conclude when the 67th Reconnaissance Squadron is deactivated at Bergstrom Air Force Base, Texas.
MILITARY: Typhoon Omar hits the U.S. territory of Guam in the Pacific, heavily damaging military installations there; damages are estimated at $250 million.

August 31
AVIATION: An Air Mobility Command (AMC) C-141 Starlifter transports 70 children stricken by cancer from the Chernobyl nuclear accident from Minsk, Byelorussia, to Brussels, Belgium, for treatment.

September 1–25
AVIATION: Transports of the Air Mobility Command (AMC) convey 750 relief workers and 2,000 tons of supplies to the island of Guam, still reeling from the effects of Typhoon Omar.

September 12–October 18
AVIATION: After Typhoon Iniki ravages Kauai, Hawaii, Air Mobility Command (AMC) and Air National Guard transports perform 600 missions to fly in 9,200 tons of relief supplies and 8,600 passengers.

September 13–29
AVIATION: Operation Impressive Lift unfolds as transports of the Air Mobility Command (AMC) convey UN peacekeeping forces from Pakistan to Somalia, delivering 974 soldiers and 1,168 tons of equipment.

September 23–25
AVIATION: Two C-130 Hercules aircraft evacuate 96 Americans from Liberia in the face of civil strife.

September 24
NAVAL: An official inquiry into the so-called Tailhook scandal reveals that several high-ranking officers tried to cover up the affair to avoid adverse publicity about the U.S. Navy. Consequently, two admirals are forced into retirement and one is reassigned.

September 28
Naval: In Washington, D.C., a policy statement entitled ". . . From the Sea" is drawn up to address pressing post–cold war requirements for the navy and marine corps. It is signed by the secretary of the navy and the commandant of the Marine Corps.

October 1
Naval: In the Mediterranean, a Sea Sparrow missile accidentally launched from the aircraft carrier *Saratoga* strikes the bridge of the Turkish destroyer *Muavenet,* killing five sailors, including the ship's captain.

October 2
Naval: In Washington, D.C., Sean O'Keefe gains appointment as the 69th secretary of the navy.

October 25
Aviation: A spate of civil unrest in the former Soviet Republic of Tajikistan prompts the arrival of an Air Mobility Command (AMC) C-141 Starlifter to evacuate U.S. citizens and foreign nationals.

November 4–11
Aviation: The Air Mobility Command (AMC) dispatches five C-5 Galaxies and one C-141 Starlifter to Armenia with 236 tons of flour to help relieve food shortages there.

November 10
Marines: On Guam, the Marine Barracks, which has seen continuous occupation since 1899, is disestablished.

November 24
Marines: Following the transfer of Subic Bay to the control of the Philippines, the few remaining marine units depart.

November 30
Aviation: Disaster strikes when two C-141 Starlifters of the 62nd Airlift Wing collide during a nighttime air refueling mission over Montana.

December 3
Military: The 10th Mountain Division (Light) under Major General Steven L. Arnold is ordered to Somalia to participate in Operation Restore Hope to assist that war-ravaged, famine-stricken nation.

December 4
Aviation: Air Mobility Command (AMC) transports commence Operation Restore Hope by performing the first of 1,000 airlift missions to Somalia while Air Force Reserve crews perform an additional 190 sorties. Over all, a total of 50,000 passengers and 40,000 short tons of cargo are conveyed to the region.

December 6–20
Aviation: The Air Mobility Command (AMC) dispatches six C-5 Galaxies to Islamabad, Pakistan, with 415 tons of engineering vehicles and supplies to combat recent floods.

December 9–10

AVIATION: Operation Restore Hope necessitates Air Mobility Command (AMC) transports to conduct over 1,000 sorties while carrying 50,000 passengers and 40,000 tons of cargo. Air Force Reserve crews also contribute to the relief effort by flying 190 sorties, carrying 1,076 passengers and 1,500 tons of cargo.

NAVAL: In Mogadishu, Somalia, land phases of Operation Restore Hope commences as SEAL and marine reconnaissance teams go ashore to facilitate the transfer of humanitarian aid to a starving, war-ravaged population. The efforts are guided offshore by the carrier *Ranger* and the supply vessel *Tripoli*, which also guide and monitor all air traffic in and out of the capital. These forces maintain a visible presence until the operation concludes in March 1994.

MARINES: The 24th Marine Expeditionary Unit (SOC) goes ashore at Mogadishu, Somalia, to secure ports and landing facilities for relief operations. Lieutenant General Robert B. Johnson of the I Marine Expeditionary Force takes command of all operations on land, which ultimately number 30,000 marines.

December 15

AVIATION: As a cost-cutting measure, England Air Force Base, Eaker Air Force Base, and George Air Force Base are ordered closed.

December 16

AVIATION: The new McDonnell-Douglas C-17 Globemaster III jet transport sets several altitude records with payload.

• A B-52 flown by Captain Jeffrey R. Swegel, 668th Bomb Squadron experiences a severe inflight emergency that knocks out all four engines of its left wing. By means of adroit flying and repairs, two engines are restarted and the bomber makes a safe emergency landing. Swegel and his crew win the Mackay Trophy for their efforts.

December 27

AVIATION: Over Iraq, an F-16C shoots down an Iraqi MiG-25 Foxbat that had violated the United Nations no-fly zone. This is also the first aircraft destroyed by the new AIM-120 AMRAAM air-to-air missile, or "Slammer," a weapon greatly extending the reach of F-16s and enhancing their lethality.

1993

January

MILITARY: Army personnel declines sharply to 572,423 officers and men while force structure dwindles from 18 to 16 divisions.

January 1

AVIATION: At Falcon Air Force Base, Colorado, the 7th Space Operations Squadron becomes the first Reserve space unit to be activated.

January 3

AVIATION: The second Strategic Arms Reduction Treaty (START II) is signed by President George H. W. Bush and President Boris Yeltsin of Russia. This new agreement eliminates all multiple, independently targeted reentry vehicles (MIRV) and also reduces the number of nuclear weapons bombers can carry.

January 12
MARINES: Near Mogadishu International Airport, Somalia, a local gang ambushes a marine patrol, killing Private First Class Domingo Arroya. He is the first American serviceman killed there.

January 13
AVIATION: Air Mobility Command (AMC) transports fly in forces to support Southern Watch II, the no-fly zone in southern Iraq near the border with Kuwait and Saudi Arabia.
• A force of 100 American, British, and French warplanes attack 32 Iraqi antiaircraft missile sites discovered south of the 32-degree north latitude line. Thirty-five of these are launched from the carrier *Kitty Hawk*.
• Another gender barrier falls when U.S. Air Force major Susan J. Helms becomes the first U.S. military female in space when she blasts aloft in the space shuttle *Endeavor*.

January 15
MILITARY: In Baledogle, Somalia, heavily armed militiamen engage in a firefight with Company E, 2nd Battalion, 87th Infantry (10th Mountain Division), losing six members; the Americans incur no losses.

January 15–November 26, 1994
NAVAL: Operation Able Manner unfolds as U.S. Coast Guard vessels intercept 40,000 Haitian economic migrants attempting to flee to the United States, most of whom are returned to Haiti.

January 17
AVIATION: Over Iraq, an F-16 tasked with covering a F-4G Wild Weasel mission against Iraqi antiaircraft sites, detects a MiG-23 and destroys it with an AIM-210 "Slammer" missile.
NAVAL: In the Persian Gulf, the destroyers *Caron, Hewitt,* and *Stump* launch 45 Tomahawk cruise missiles against the Iraqi Zaafaraniyah nuclear fabrication plant in Baghdad.

January 18
AVIATION: In separate actions, F-4G Wild Weasels return fire on an Iraqi missile site that fired upon them while F-16s bomb an airfield whose antiaircraft had fired upon them. They are joined by British and French aircraft.
• In Zagreb, Croatia, a joint air operations cell is established for coordinating the airlift of supplies by aircraft of the United States, the United Kingdom, Germany, France, and Canada.

January 20
MILITARY: In Washington, D.C., William J. Clinton is sworn in as the 42nd president of the United States and commander in chief.

January 21
MILITARY: In Washington, D.C., Les Aspin gains appointment as the 18th secretary of defense.

January 25
AVIATION: In Kismaayo, Somalia, AH-1 Cobra attack helicopters belonging to the 3rd Squadron, 17th Cavalry, attack six armed pickup trucks that belong to the local militia, or "Technicals," killing eight.

February 2
AVIATION: As ethnic fighting in the former states of Yugoslavia intensifies, air force transports deliver medical and humanitarian aid to Zagreb, Croatia. Within a few weeks, Operation Provide Promise expands this effort by providing direct air drops to Muslims fleeing a Serbian advance.

February 13–March 9
AVIATION: Air Mobility Command (AMC) transports commence Operation Provide Refuge by flying supplies from Hawaii to Kwajalein Atoll to support 535 Chinese sailors who sought political asylum after their vessel broke down.

February 19
AVIATION: The new T-1A Jayhawk trainer is introduced to student pilots by the 64th Flying Training Wing.

February 24–26
MILITARY: In Kismaayo, Somalia, a firefight erupts between local militia and the 2nd Battalion, 87th Infantry (10th Mountain Division), and 23 Somalis are slain. No American casualties result.

February 28
AVIATION: Over eastern Bosnia, Operation Provide Promise unfolds as transports from the 435th Airlift Wing begin airdrop missions for refugees fleeing Serb forces.

March 12
NAVAL: In Norfolk, Virginia, the Naval Doctrine Command is founded.

March 13–14
AVIATION: In Florida, helicopters of the 301st Rescue Squadron save 93 victims of heavy flooding brought on by a recent blizzard that blanketed the Gulf Coast region.

March 26
DIPLOMACY: In New York, the UN Security Council passes Resolution 814, which transforms the role of peacekeepers in Somalia by instructing them to begin disarming the numerous warlords and private armies in the region.

March 31
AVIATION: Operation Deny Flight, a no-fly zone over Bosnia, is established by the United Nations. It becomes effective on April 5 and is aimed at limiting Serbian use of airplanes in the Bosnian civil war.

April 12–December 1995
AVIATION: Over Bosnia-Herzegovina, the NATO-sponsored Operation Deny Flight commences to enforce a no-fly zone against Serbian aircraft. The carrier *Theodore Roosevelt* transfers 12 F/A-18 Hornets to NATO command as part of the operation.

April 19–24
AVIATION: In Siberia, elements of the Russian and U.S. Air Forces conduct joint rescue operations for the first time.

April 24
MARINES: The last remaining Marine Corps elements still at Mogadishu, Somalia, are withdrawn.

April 28
MILITARY: In Washington, D.C., Secretary of Defense Les Aspin announces a new policy allowing servicewomen more latitude in choosing occupational specialties, including the opportunity to serve as combat pilots and as crews of combat aircraft and warships.

May 4
MILITARY: In Somalia, army forces under Major General Thomas M. Montgomery carry out Operation Continue Hope, which assists local authorities in taking control of international relief and humanitarian missions. The Americans also enforce their peacekeeping mission with a Quick Reaction Force, 60 aircraft/helicopters, and 1,000 aviation personnel.
MARINES: In Somalia, the American role in Operation Restore Hope declines after Lieutenant General Robert B. Johnson turns over control to Turkish general Cevik Bir. The I Marine Expeditionary Force also departs the region.

May 17–29
AVIATION: The Air Mobility Command (AMC) C-5s and C-151 fly 24 missions while conveying UN troops to Cambodia to help supervise the first free elections since 1970.

May 20
AVIATION: At Camp Pendleton, California, the marines begin phasing out the Vietnam-era OV-10 Bronco light attack aircraft by deactivating VMO-2.

June 5
DIPLOMACY: After followers of General Mohamed Farrah Aidid ambush and kill 24 members of the Pakistani peacekeeping force, the UN Security Council passes Resolution 837, which calls on UN forces to apprehend those responsible for their deaths. The ensuing hunt for Aidid falls upon elite army troops requested by U.S. special envoy Jonathan Howe.

June 11
AVIATION: Over Somalia, AC-130 Spectre gunships participate in Operation Continue Hope by raiding outposts of Somali warlords who had attacked UN ground forces on June 5.

June 14
AVIATION: At Charleston Air Force Base, South Carolina, the 437th Airlift Wing accepts delivery of its first C-17A Globemaster III. This is the first air force transport capable of hauling oversized cargo loads to relatively short, unprepared runways.

June 15
NAVAL: In the Adriatic Sea, navy vessels embark on NATO's Operation Sharp Guard to enforce economic sanctions against Croatia, Serbia, and the Republic

of Yugoslavia. They are occupied with maritime intercept and airborne warning and control activities until the operation concludes on June 19, 1996, at which time 73,000 vessels have been challenged and 7,200 searched.

June 17
AVIATION: At Minot Air Force Base, North Dakota, Lieutenant Colonel Patricia Fornes is the first woman to command a combat missile unit when she assumes control of the 740th Missile Squadron.

June 21
AVIATION: At Cape Canaveral, Florida, Major Nancy Currie becomes the first female army astronaut in space when she lifts off onboard the space shuttle *Endeavor.*

June 24
MARINES: In light of increasing tension and hostility from local Somali warlords, the 24th Marine Expeditionary Unit arrives at Mogadishu to back up UN peace-keeping forces.

June 26
AVIATION: Navy vessels unleash 23 Tomahawk cruise missiles at the headquarters building of Iraqi intelligence in Baghdad, Iraq, killing eight persons and wounding a dozen. The strike comes in retaliation for an Iraqi plot to kill President George H.W. Bush while he visited Kuwait the previous April.

June 29
AVIATION: At Wright-Patterson Air Force Base, Ohio, the prototype OC-135B aircraft flies its maiden flight. This vehicle is designed to serve in nations that have signed the Open Skies Treaty.

July 1
AVIATION: The Air Training Command (ATC) and the Air University (AU) are incorporated into the new Air Education and Training Command (AETC).

A 53rd Fighter Squadron F-15C Eagle aircraft takes off on a mission during Operation Deny Flight over Boznia and Herzegovina. *(Department of Defense)*

• The Air Force Space Command (AFSPACECOM) accepts responsibility for the Twentieth Air Force, which controls and monitors daily operations of the intercontinental ballistic missile force.
• At Vandenberg Air Force Base, California, the Fourteenth Air Force assumes missile warning and space surveillance missions under the aegis of the Air Force Space Command (AFSPACECOM).

July 5–12
AVIATION: Transports of the Air Mobility Command (AMC) begin transporting Army troops and their equipment from Germany to Macedonia to bolster UN peacekeeping forces there.

July 11–August 1
AVIATION: A flood in the American Midwest inundates eight states along the Mississippi and Missouri Rivers. Air Force C-5 and C-141 transports respond by delivering 800 tons of relief equipment, including 1 million empty sandbags.

July 19
AVIATION: Marine aircraft of VMFA(AW)-533 begin patrolling the no-fly zone established in Bosnia as part of Operation Deny Flight. This operation aims to curb Serbian aggression against ethnic and religious minorities.
MILITARY: In a controversial move, President Bill Clinton removes a 50-year ban on homosexuals in the military and substitutes a "don't ask, don't tell" policy. This politically inspired move strains his relations with the military establishment.

July 22
NAVAL: In Washington, D.C., John H. Dalton gains appointment as the 70th secretary of the navy.

July 29
AVIATION: Over southern Iraq, Navy EA-6B Prowlers unleash HARM missiles at Iraqi antiaircraft sites after their radar locked onto them.

August 6
AVIATION: In Washington, D.C., another gender barrier falls when Dr. Sheila E. Widnall gains appointment as the secretary of the air force.

August 8
MILITARY: In Medina, Somalia, an army humvee strikes a mine, killing four soldiers.

August 11–15
AVIATION: The 436th Airlift Wing dispatches three C-5 Galaxies to Nepal after floodwaters wash out several bridges. They are carrying 190 tons of bridge components made in England.

August 18
AVIATION: At White Sands Missile Range, New Mexico, Air Force Space and Missile Center (SMC) personnel are present during the first launch of the Delta Clipper Experimental (DC-X) vertical takeoff and landing rocket.

August 28

MILITARY: In a major escalation, President William J. Clinton changes the mission of army troops in Somalia from peacekeeping to capturing senior Somali militia leader Mohamed Farrah Aidid. To this end, Task Force Ranger, consisting of Company B, 3rd Battalion, 75th Ranger Regiment, Delta Force members, the 160th SOAR, Navy SEALS, and Air Force Special Operations personnel are deployed there. However, Clinton refuses all requests to supply army units with tanks and other heavy equipment for fear of alienating the local population.

September 1

NAVAL: The navy releases its "Bottom Up Review," which stipulates that, to wage two major regional conflicts and one low-intensity conflict at the same time, the fleet should consist of 346 ships, including 11 carrier battle groups, and one training/reserve carrier battle group.

MARINES: In Washington, D.C., the Department of Defense releases its "Bottom Up Review," which calls for a standing establishment of 175,000 marines during the post–cold war drawdown. This is larger than the 159,000 originally projected.

September 11

NAVAL: At the Philadelphia Naval Yard, Pennsylvania, the first supercarrier *Forrestal*, which entered the service on October 1, 1955, is decommissioned.

September 20

MILITARY: In a cost-cutting measure, the Congressional Base Closure and Realignment Commission promulgates its plan to shut 130 bases and reduce 45 more nationwide.

September 26

AVIATION: In Mogadishu, Somalia, militants shoot down a UH-60 Blackhawk helicopter with an RPG-7 rocket-propelled grenade launcher. Three crewmen die in the crash and another three soldiers are wounded trying to rescue the survivors.

October 1

AVIATION: The new Joint Primary Aircraft Training Program begins with air force pilots going to Naval Air Station Whiting Field, Florida, and navy and marine pilots attending classes at Randolph Air Force Base, Texas.

•   At Barksdale, Louisiana, the Air Force Reserve operates its first-ever B-52 bomber unit when the 93rd Bomber Squadron is activated.

October 2–4

AVIATION: The Air Mobility Command dispatches two C-5 Galaxies to Bombay, India, which carry 1,000 rolls of plastic sheeting, 950 tents, and nearly 19,000 five-gallon water containers for survivors of recent earthquakes.

October 3–4

AVIATION: Air force pararescueman Technical Sergeant Tim Wilkerson helps rescue and treat five wounded Rangers in Mogadishu, Somalia, winning an Air Force Cross.

MILITARY: In Mogadishu, Somalia, Task Force Ranger is launched after receiving a tip that one of Mohamed Farrah Aidid's lieutenants is at the Olympic Hotel downtown. A mixed group of Delta Force soldiers and rangers flown in by MH-6 Little Bird and MH-60 Black Hawk helicopters apprehends their targets, who are placed in a humvee convoy and taken back to UN lines. However, they are fired upon by thousands of angry militiamen, who also down two Black Hawks with rocket-propelled grenades. Delta Force snipers Master Sergeant Gary Gordon and Sergeant First Class Randall Shugart arrive at the second crash site and fight off Somali militia until they are overwhelmed and killed, winning posthumous Medals of Honor. Chief Warrant officer Michael Durant is taken prisoner. Worse, although the convoy fights its way out, troops must be sent in to rescue the 100 rangers and Delta soldiers now trapped in the city. A rescue force made up of the 2nd Battalion, 14th Infantry, backed by Pakistani and Malaysian tanks, fights its way in and rescues them. American loses are 19 dead and 100 wounded; Somali casualties are estimated in the range of 1,000. Losses of such extent turn public opinion against further operations in Somalia, and, by the following March, all American forces have been withdrawn.

October 5–13
AVIATION: In Mogadishu, Somalia, Operation Restore Hope II unfolds as Air Mobility Command (AMC) C-5s and C-141 deliver 18 Abrams tanks, 44 Bradley fighting vehicles, and 1,300 troops to bolster the American presence there.

October 6
MILITARY: A mortar attack at Mogadishu Airport, Somalia, kills Special Forces Sergeant Matt Rierson; he is the last American soldier lost in Somalia.

October 7
DIPLOMACY: In the wake of heavy fighting and loss of life with Somali warlords, President Bill Clinton announces the withdrawal of all U.S. forces from Somalia by March 31, 1994.

MARINES: In light of recent American military deaths in Somalia, the government decides to deploy the 13th and 22nd Marine Expeditionary Units (SOC) to back up existing forces there.

October 8
AVIATION: Over Bosnia, Operation Provide Hope becomes the air force's longest, continuous airlift operation; only the Berlin airlift surpasses it in tonnage and sorties.

October 15
AVIATION: At the Naval Air Base Pensacola, Florida, the Officer Candidate School and the Aviation Officer Candidate School are consolidated. This results in the closure of the Officer Candidate School at Newport, Rhode Island.

NAVAL: Pentagon officials censor three admirals and 30 senior naval officers for failing to properly supervise the annual Tailhook Convention in Las Vegas, Nevada, during which a score of women officers were sexually groped and abused by naval aviators.

October 18
NAVAL: Navy and Coast Guard vessels of Task Force 120 begin enforcing United Nations sanctions against the military regime in Haiti by enacting Operation

Support Democracy and imposing an economic quarantine on the island nation. These sanctions will remain in place until the Haitian military accepts the return of President Aristide.

October 25
MILITARY: In Washington, D.C., General John M. Shalikashvili gains appointment as the 13th chairman, Joint Chiefs of Staff.

November
AVIATION: Lieutenant Colonel Betty Mullis becomes the first woman to command an Air Force Reserve unit when she takes control of the 336th Air Refueling Squadron.

November 22
MILITARY: In Washington, D.C., Togo West, Jr., is appointed the 16th secretary of the army.

November 30
NAVAL: In Washington, D.C., President William J. Clinton signs legislation allowing women to serve on navy combat vessels.

December 2–13
AVIATION: The space shuttle *Endeavor* blasts off from Cape Kennedy, Florida, under the command of U.S. Air Force colonel Richard O. Covey. Its mission is to repair the $2 billion Hubble space telescope, which is in need of a "contact lens" to correct its malformed main lens. Another repair mission is necessary before the Hubble can provide spectacular images of the universe.

December 3
RELIGION: At the Pentagon, Imam Abdul Rasheed Muhammad becomes the first Muslim chaplain sworn into duty with the U.S. military.

December 7
AVIATION: At Barksdale Air Force Base, Louisiana, the 917th Bombardment Wing becomes the first Air Force Reserve unit to receive B-52 Stratofortresses.

December 8
AVIATION: The air force begins destroying the first of 450 Minuteman II missile silos in accordance with the 1991 Strategic Arms Reduction Treaty.

December 12
MILITARY: Secretary of Defense Les Aspin, angered by criticism over his handling of military affairs in Mogadishu, Somalia, tenders his resignation.

December 17
AVIATION: At Whiteman Air Force Base, Missouri, the first B-2 Spirit bomber, titled *The Spirit of Missouri*, is delivered to the 393rd Bomb Squadron.

1994

January
AVIATION: The former Communist nations of Romania, Hungary, and Bulgaria grant air force F-16 overfly rights as they deploy from Germany to Turkey, reducing their flight time by two hours.

MILITARY: Army personnel has stabilized at 541,343 officers and men although the number of active divisions declines from 18 to 16.

January 1
MILITARY: In Arlington, Virginia, the Army Historical Foundation is activated under retired colonel Raymond K. Bluhm, Jr., to preserve both the history and the heritage of the American soldier.

January 4
AVIATION: The 435th Airlift Wing at Rhein-Main Air Base, Germany, dispatches a C-130 Hercules with relief supplies to Bosnia. This particular unit is comprised of both Reserve and Air National Guard members.

January 10
AVIATION: Off the coast of Iceland, a pair of HH-60G Pave Hawk helicopters from the 56th Rescue Squadron save six sailors from a stranded tugboat amidst heavy seas and strong winds. The crews of Air Rescue 206 and 208 subsequently receive a Mackay Trophy for their efforts.

January 13
AVIATION: The last remaining F-15s of the 32nd Fighter Group depart Soesterberg Air Base, the Netherlands, ending a 40-year American presence there.

January 17–25
AVIATION: After parts of Southern California are struck by a powerful earthquake, C-5s and C-141s deliver 150 tons of relief supplies and 270 medical personnel to the afflicted regions.

January 25
AVIATION: An air force Titan II rocket launcher hurls the lunar probe *Clementine I* toward the moon; this is the first lunar mission since 1972.

February
AVIATION: For the first time, five KC-135 tanker aircraft working to support Operation Deny Flight in Bosnia receive permission to overfly French airspace for the first time in 20 years.

February 3
MILITARY: In Washington, D.C., William Perry is appointed the 19th secretary of defense.

February 5
AVIATION: A crew from the 317th Airlift Squadron, an Air Force Reserve unit, checks out in a new C-17 Globemaster III for the first time.
• After a Serbian mortar attack in Sarajevo kills 68 and injures 200, four C-130s are dispatched to fly the wounded to medical facilities in Germany.

February 7
AVIATION: An air force Titan IV/Centaur rocket hoists the first Military Strategic and Tactical Relay Satellite into Earth orbit. This is part of a new system designed to enhance ready, secure communications around the world in any conflict.

February 10
AVIATION: Lieutenant Jeannie Flynn becomes the air force's first F-15E-qualified fighter pilot.

February 18
AVIATION: The last remaining F-4G Wild Weasels depart Spangdahlem Air Base, Germany, for Nellis Air Force Base, Nevada.

February 25
AVIATION: As the air force begins closing Bitburg Air Base, Germany, it begins transferring F-15s of the 53rd Fighter Squadron over to Spangdahlem Air Base.

February 27
AVIATION: On the carrier *Dwight D. Eisenhower*, Lieutenant Shannon Workman becomes the first female pilot to carrier qualify by landing her EA-6B Prowler in the traps.

February 28
AVIATION: Over Bosnia-Herzegovina, U.S. warplanes conduct NATO's first-ever military action during Operation Deny Flight when an F-16 flown by Lieutenant Robert Wright, 526th Fighter Squadron, spots four Serbian J-1 Galeb attack aircraft violating the no-fly zone. In quick succession, he brings down all three with Sidewinder and AIM-120 Slammer missiles. Another pilot downs a final Jastreb, bringing the F-16s aerial record to 69 kills and no losses.

March
AVIATION: The T-41 Mescalero trainer, which has been in service with the air force since 1964, is ordered replaced by the newer T-3A flight screening aircraft.
• At Edwards Air Force Base, California, an F-16 fighter fires an AGM-84 Harpoon antiship missile for the first time.

March 7
NAVAL: The carrier *Dwight D. Eisenhower* becomes the first navy warship to receive a permanent female complement after 67 women are ordered to report for duty there.

March 8
MILITARY: The army announces Force XXI, an ambitious project intending to incorporate the latest digital technology into current weapons systems, and in every respect to modernize the army for the challenges of the 21st century.

March 12
MILITARY: The last army unit, 2nd Battalion, 22nd Infantry (10th Mountain Division), is withdrawn from Somalia following a failed two-year mission to attempt to restore stability to the wartorn nation. The cost was 27 American soldiers killed in action, four dead in accidents, and over 100 wounded.

March 13
AVIATION: At Vandenberg Air Force Base, a Taurus booster rocket places two military satellites into orbit for the first time.

March 18
AVIATION: Norton Air Force Base, California, which has served as an important aircraft repair depot for 52 years, is closed down.

March 24
MARINES: As U.S. peacekeeping forces are withdrawn from Somalia, they are covered offshore by the *Inchon* and *Peleliu* amphibious ready groups. A further 55 marines remain behind at the U.S. embassy until its closure the following September.

March 25
AVIATION: An air force C-5 Galaxy departs Somalian airspace, ending Operation Restore Hope and removing the last American military personnel still there.
MARINES: In Mogadishu, Somalia, the last U.S. forces are withdrawn from that embattled country, guarded by the 24th Marine Expeditionary Unit (SOC). The Marine security guards at the embassy alone remain.

March 31
AVIATION: In view of ongoing aerial operations over Bosnia, two F-16s fighters arrive at Aviano Air Base, Italy, which is upgraded to become a NATO main operating base.

April
AVIATION: At Ellsworth Air Force Base, the final 150 Minuteman II missiles are removed in compliance with the 1992 Strategic Arms Reduction treaty.

April 6–12
AVIATION: In light of ethnic unrest in Rwanda, Operation Distant Runner commences as air force transports evacuate citizens and foreign nationals from Bujumbura, Burundi, to Nairobi, Kenya, and safety.

April 7–8
AVIATION: Operation Distant Runner unfolds as the amphibious assault craft *Peleliu*'s helicopters begin evacuating American and United Nations personnel from wartorn Rwanda, then in the throes of a genocidal civil war.
MARINES: A force of 330 marines from the 11th Marine Expeditionary Unit (SOC) flies 650 miles inland from the helicopter assault vessel *Peleliu* to Bujumbura, Burundi, to safeguard the evacuation of U.S. citizens and foreign nationals there. Some 230 people are assembled by the Marines for transportation by air force transports.

April 10
AVIATION: In retaliation for a Bosnian Serb attack on UN personnel, air force F-16s bomb a Serbian command post near Gorazde in NATO's first air-to-ground attack, and the first close support mission of Operation Deny Flight.

April 11
AVIATION: A pair of Marine Corps F/A-18 Hornets bomb Serbian targets in the Gorazde safe area in retaliation for continuing attacks on UN peacekeepers.

April 12
MARINES: In Rwanda, the 11th Marine Expeditionary Unit (SOC) is flown in to help evacuate 230 U.S. citizens and foreign nationals trapped by genocidal fighting between Hutu and Tutsi tribesmen.

April 14
AVIATION: In a major mishap over northern Iraq, air force F-15C fighters of the 53rd Fighter Squadron accidentally down two army UH-60 Black Hawk

helicopters in Iraq's northern no-fly zone, killing 15 Americans and 11 international observers. They were apparently misidentified as Russian-built Mi-24 Hind gunships of the Iraqi air force.

April 23
NAVAL: In Washington, D.C., Admiral Jeremy M. Boorda gains appointment as the 25th chief of naval operations. He is the first man to do so after rising from the enlisted ranks.

April 26
AVIATION: The marines phase out the last of their venerable OV-10D Broncos with the disbanding of VMO-4.

May 3
AVIATION: At Davis Monthan Air Force Base, Arizona, the last operational B-52G is retired. However, fan-jet powered B-52Hs continue to serve well into the 21st century.

May 6
AVIATION: At Tucson, Arizona, Lieutenant Leslie DeAnn Crosby becomes the first female Air Force Reserve fighter pilot after passing through the F–16 RTU.

May 7–9
AVIATION: The onset of civil war in Yemen prompts six Air Mobility Command (AMC) transports to evacuate 623 U.S. citizens and foreign nationals to safety.

May 8
AVIATION: The Air Mobility Command (MAC) dispatches five C-141 Starlifters from Germany to support Operation Provide Promise in Bosnia. By the time their participation ends on July 26, they will have delivered 7,000 tons of supplies.

May 11–17
AVIATION: In Turkey, Air Mobility Command (AMC) C-141 Starlifters convey 329 tons of relief supplies to the hundreds of thousands of refugees in Rwanda. Operation Provide Assistance ultimately delivers 10,000 rolls of plastic sheeting and 100,000 blankets.

May 20–February 8
MARINES: At Guantánamo Bay, Cuba, Operation Sea Signal unfolds as marines prepare a detention center for a mass Haitian exodus toward the United States. More than 40,000 people are processed and sent back to Haiti.

June–September
AVIATION: After raging forest fires consume 2 million acres in six western states, eight Air Force Reserve and Air National Guard C-130 aircraft begin dousing afflicted regions with 5 million gallons of fire retardant.

June 1
MARINES: In Washington, D.C., Brigadier General Carol A. Mutter becomes the first female marine promoted to major general.

June 15–23
MARINES: At Vladivostok, Russian Republic, Marine forces conduct landing exercises with their Russian counterparts for the first time.

June 22–30
AVIATION: In Germany, Air Mobility Command (AMC) dispatches C-5 Galaxies and C-141 Starlifters to Uganda to convey armored vehicles intended for UN peacekeeping forces in Rwanda.

June 24
AVIATION: The stealthy F-117 officially receives the designation "Nighthawk." Previously, air crews had referred to it as the "Wobblin' Goblin" and "Black Jet."

June 26
AVIATION: A C-5 Galaxy of the 60th Military Airlift Wing carries a 34-ton magnetic resonance imaging system to the Ukraine to assist victims of the 1986 nuclear accident at Chernobyl.

June 30
AVIATION: In Berlin, Germany, the air force deactivates Detachment I, 435th Airlift Wing, 46 years after the famous Berlin airlift.

July
AVIATION: The air force accepts delivery of the last production F-15 Eagle.
• After the Georgia coastline is inundated by Tropical Storm Alberto, the 507th Air Refueling Group flies in 1,000 pounds of supplies to assist flood victims.

July 1
AVIATION: The 184th Bomb Group becomes the first Air National Guard (Kansas ANG) unit equipped with B-1B Lancers.
• The Air Force Space Command (AFSPACECOM) accepts responsibility for the nation's nuclear ballistic missiles from the Air Combat Command (ACC), and now controls all missile warning, space surveillance, space launch, and satellite control functions.

July 21
AVIATION: Over Bosnia, a C-141 Starlifter is damaged by small arms fire from the ground and humanitarian operations are temporarily suspended. The aircraft returns to Rhein-Main Air Base, Germany, with 25 holes in its fuselage and wings.
• The Air Force concludes all fighter operations at Ramstein Air Base, Germany, in transferring F-16s of the 86th Fighter Wing to Aviano Air Base, Italy.
MARINES: On Okinawa, the 9th Marines are deactivated as part of the post–cold war drawdown.

July 24–October 6
AVIATION: Over Zaire, Air Mobility Command (AMC) transports commence Operation Support Hope to bring in humanitarian relief to thousands of Rwandan refugees. Aircraft from 22 airlift wings deliver a total of 3,660 tons of supplies.
MARINES: Elements of the 15th Marines Expeditionary Unit (SOC) are sent along with 2,000 other U.S. service personnel to assist a major refuge crisis in Rwanda.

July 31
AVIATION: Off the coast of California, Lieutenants Kara Hultgreen and Carey Dunai become the first women to qualify in the Grumman F-14 Tomcat by landing on the carrier *Constellation*.

August 1
NAVAL: In Annapolis, Maryland, Admiral Charles R. Larson gains appointment as the 55th superintendent of the U.S. Naval Academy, a post he also held between 1983 and 1986. Larson is the first individual to hold the position twice.

August 2
AVIATION: Two B-52s from the 2nd Bomb Wing fly a record world circumnavigation mission in 47 continuous hours and five aerial refuelings. They land in Kuwait on the fourth anniversary of the Iraqi invasion.

August 3
AVIATION: A Pegasus rocket launched by a B-52 at high altitude successfully places a satellite in Earth orbit.

August 4
AVIATION: Brigadier General Susan L. Pamerleau is the first female commander of the Air Force Reserve Officer Training Corps.

August 5
AVIATION: In Bosnia, two A-10 Thunderbolt IIs destroy a Serbian armored vehicle near Sarajevo after heavy weapons had been stolen from a UN compound.

August 19–24
NAVAL: Operation Able Vigil unfolds as Coast Guard vessels intercept 30,224 Cuban refugees attempting to escape Communist Cuba. The operation requires the active involvement of 38 cutters and nine naval vessels, making it the biggest Coast Guard operation since the Vietnam War.

August 24–25
AVIATION: Air force transports evacuate over 1,000 people from Johnston Island in the Pacific as a huge typhoon approaches.

August 25–31
AVIATION: The United States and Ukraine sponsor a joint Open Skies trial flight consistent with the Open Skies Agreement allowing unarmed reconnaissance flights.

August 31–September 6
MILITARY: In Berlin, Germany, American, British, French, and Russian forces are withdrawn from the city for the first time since the end of World War II.

August 31–September 10
AVIATION: Operation Safe Haven takes place as air force transports convey Cuban and Haitian refugees from crowded facilities at Guantánamo Bay to Panama.

September 8
MILITARY: In Berlin, Germany, the army's Berlin Brigade is disbanded; it had been on active service since 1945.

September 9
AVIATION: The space shuttle *Discovery* lifts off from Cape Kennedy, Florida, with a crew of six: four air force officers and two civilian technicians.

September 19
AVIATION: Air force transports supply logistical support throughout the life of Operation Uphold Democracy in Haiti.

1994

DIPLOMACY: To avoid the onset of violence with the Haitian military, a deputation consisting of former president Jimmy Carter, retired general Colin Powell, and Senator Sam Nunn of Georgia convince Haitian strongman General Manuel Cedras to accept political exile in Panama.

MILITARY: Lieutenant General Henry H. Shelton leads a multinational force into Haiti during Operation Uphold Democracy, to restore a constitutionally elected government under President Jean-Bertrand Aristide. Units involved include the XVIII Airborne Corps, 10th Mountain Division (Light), 3rd Special Force Group, and the 25th Infantry Division, among others.

NAVAL: A total of 24 navy vessels are taped to participate in Operation Support Democracy, including the carriers *Dwight D. Eisenhower* and *America,* which have removed their usual air groups for several army helicopters.

September 20
MARINES: At Cap Haitien, Haiti, the Special Purpose Marine Amphibious Group Task Force Carib (2nd Battalion, 2nd Marines and helicopters of HMM-264) is landed to provide humanitarian relief during Operation Uphold Democracy and maintain order ashore.

September 24
MARINES: In Haiti, a marine rifle squad engages Haitian military personnel at a police station, killing 10 and wounding one. A sailor is wounded in the exchange.

September 26
AVIATION: At Poltava Air Base, Ukraine, a B-52 Stratofortress, a B-1B Lancer, and a KC-10 Extender pay a goodwill visit. This is the first appearance by American warplanes since the shuttle bombing missions of World War II.

October 4
AVIATION: The air force replaces its last F-4G Wild Weasel air defense suppression aircraft with F-16 Falcons.

October 8–December 22
NAVAL: In light of recent Iraqi maneuvers near the Kuwaiti border, the guided-missile cruiser *Leyte Gulf,* the *George Washington* carrier battle group, and the *Tripoli* amphibious ready group begin deploying in the Red Sea region.

MARINES: The 15th Marine Expeditionary Unit (SOC) positions itself off Kuwait City in the Persian Gulf in the event of hostilities with Iraq.

October 10
AVIATION: Air force warplanes begin arriving in Kuwait during Operation Vigilant Warrior to deter possible Iraqi aggression in the Persian Gulf region. Within days, the number of aircraft in the theater has increased from 77 to 270, including F-15s, F-16s, and A-10s.

MILITARY: In response to recent Iraqi movements toward the Kuwaiti border, President Bill Clinton orders the deployment of 36,000 American troops to the Persian Gulf, backed by warships and hundreds of aircraft. Meanwhile, elements of the 24th Infantry Division (Mechanized) deploy with Kuwaiti units as a precaution.

October 14–16
AVIATION: At Langley Air Force Base, Virginia, a pair of C-17 Globemaster IIIs fly their first logistical mission by conveying military supplies to Saudi Arabia.

1994

October 25
AVIATION: Lieutenant Kara S. Hultgreen, the first woman to carrier qualify in an F-14 Tomcat, dies in a landing accident onboard the *Abraham Lincoln.*

October 26
AVIATION: In Washington, D.C., General Ronald R. Fogleman is appointed air force chief of staff; he is also the first Air Force Academy graduate to take charge of the force.

October 30
AVIATION: At Kadena Air Base, Japan, a C-141 Starlifter loaded with 20 tons of medical supplies, blankets, and tarpaulins lifts off for Vladivostok, Russia, to assist flood victims there.

October 31–November 1
AVIATION: At Ellsworth Air Force Base, North Dakota, a pair of B-1B Lancers fly nonstop for 25 hours to reach a bombing range in Kuwait. This mission also marks their operational debut in the Persian Gulf region.

November 6–8
AVIATION: Flash flooding in Egypt results in a pair of C-141 Starlifters being loaded with 37 tons of relief goods and dispatched to assist the victims.

November 15
AVIATION: Commander Donnie L. Cochran becomes the first African American to lead the navy's Blue Angels Flight Demonstration Squadron.

November 21–23
AVIATION: A Serb attack on Bihac, Bosnia, results in NATO and U.S. Air Force strikes against Serbian airfields and missile sites at Ubdina in occupied Croatia.
• Two C-5 Galaxies participate in Project Sapphire, which entails removing 1,300 pounds of enriched uranium from the Republic of Kazakhstan to the United States for safekeeping.

December 17–21
AVIATION: The 94th Air Lift Wing dispatches a C-130 Hercules loaded with five pallets of clothing, furniture, and beds to assist orphan shelters in Albania.

December 22
AVIATION: At Edwards Air Force Base, the first of three Lockheed SR-71 Blackbirds reactivated for research purposes with NASA arrives.

December 29
AVIATION: Off the coast of Ireland, helicopters from the 56th Rescue Squadron save eight Dutch sailors from a sinking vessel.

1995

January
MILITARY: Army personnel continues contracting to 508,559 officers and men while the number of active divisions drops by one for a total of 13.

January 12
NAVAL: The four mothballed *Iowa*-class battleships are stricken from the Naval Vessel Register, but these vessels will display a longevity that surprises many.

January 17
AVIATION: The 17th Airlift Squadron is the first Air Mobility Command (AMC) unit equipped with the C-17 Globemaster III for military service.

January 19
AVIATION: The 374th Airlift Wing at Yokota Air Base, Japan, begins humanitarian missions to assist earthquake victims in southwestern Japan.

February 1–20
AVIATION: Rioting at Cuban refugee camps in Panama leads to Operation Safe Passage, whereby C-5 Galaxy, C-141 Starlifter, and C-130 Hercules missions to transport 7,300 passengers back to Guantánamo Bay.

February 3
AVIATION: U.S. Air force colonel/astronaut Eileen M. Collins becomes the first female shuttle commander during her mission onboard the *Discovery*.

February 3–10
AVIATION: In Kathmandu, Nepal, eight C-141 Starlifters begin transporting 300 Nepalese troops to Haiti as part of UN peacekeeping efforts there.

February 27–March 3
NAVAL: Off Somalia, Operation United Shield unfolds as Marines from the *Essex* amphibious ready group and the Italian helicopter carrier *Garibaldi* cover UN forces as they withdraw. The overall commander is Lieutenant General Anthony C. Zinni and the evacuation goes off without major problems.
MARINES: In Somalia, Operation United Shield commences as the 13th Marine Amphibious Unit (SOC), assisted by Italian marines, participates withdrawing the last UN peacekeepers from that embattled nation.

March 2
AVIATION: At Cape Canaveral, Florida, Lieutenant Commander Wendy Lawrence becomes the first female naval aviator in space when she blasts off as part of the space shuttle *Endeavor* crew.

March 3
NAVAL: Off Mogadishu, Somalia, a multinational force, including the amphibious assault ship *Essex,* removes the last United Nations troops from that war-ravaged land.
MARINES: The final contingent of Marines is withdrawn from Mogadishu, Somalia, after failing in a two-year quest to restore order and stability to that fractious nation.

March 5
AVIATION: At Malmstrom Air Force Base, Montana, the first Russian arms inspectors arrive to monitor the disposal of Minuteman II intercontinental ballistic missiles (ICBMs). The visit is in accordance with the recent Strategic Arms Reduction Treaty (START II).

March 10
AVIATION: The 11th Space Warning Squadron becomes the first unit able to detect the launch of theater ballistic missiles and warn battlefield commanders of their approach.

1995

March 16
AVIATION: At Keflavík, Iceland, an HH-60 Pave Hawk helicopter of the 56th Rescue Squadron saves three skiers caught in a sudden blizzard.

March 24
AVIATION: At Vandenberg Air Force Base, California, the last remaining Atlas E booster rocket hoists a satellite into polar orbit.

March 31
AVIATION: At Barksdale Air Force Base, Louisiana, Lieutenant Kelly Flinn commences training to be the first female bomber pilot in the U.S. Air Force.

April 8
AVIATION: Over Sarajevo, Bosnia, a C-130 transport flying for Operation Provide Promise is hit 12 times by small arms fire from the ground.

April 19
TERRORISM: In Oklahoma City, Oklahoma, a bomb explodes outside the Alfred P. Murrah Federal Building, killing and injuring hundreds; two marine recruiters are killed and four wounded by the blast. Air force search-and-rescue teams and medical personnel are flown in from across the country to assist survivors.

April 27
AVIATION: The Global Positioning System (GPS) is declared operational by the Air Force Space Command (AFSPACECOM). This device provides accurate geographical coordinates for both navigation and guided-bomb delivery.

May 8–11
AVIATION: A deluge of rain in Louisiana results in Air National Guard units rescuing thousands of flood victims over a two-day period.

May 10–17
AVIATION: In the wake of an outbreak of the deadly Ebola virus in Central Africa, transports of the 60th and 349th Airlift Wings deliver several tons of medical supplies to Kinshasa, Zaire, for distribution.

May 25–26
AVIATION: The NATO high command commits itself to aircraft strikes against Serbian artillery emplacements presently shelling Sarajevo, Bosnia, and F-16s drop precision-guided munitions on gun emplacements. Marine aircraft also participate in air strikes against Serbian ammunition dumps near the town of Pale.

June 1
DIPLOMACY: The United States and Portugal conclude a treaty that allows American military aircraft to use Lajes Field in the Azores, for the next five years. This serves as a major staging areas for forces deploying in the Middle East.

June 2–3
AVIATION: A pair of B-1B Lancers flown by Lieutenant Colonel Doug Raaberg and Captain Gerald Goodfellow fly around the world in 36 hours, 13 minutes, and 36 seconds. En route, the bombers refuel six times, and they drop bombs on three ranges on three continents in two hemispheres. This display of global air power wins both air crews the Mackay Trophy.

Captain Scott F. O'Grady speaks at a press conference. (*U.S. Air Force*)

June 2–7
AVIATION: An F-16C flown by Captain Scott O'Grady is shot down by Serbian anti-aircraft fire over Banja Luka, Bosnia. He spends the next six days evading capture.

June 8
MARINES: Two marine CH-53E Super Stallions launched from the amphibious assault ship *Kearsarge* fly into Bosnian airspace and rescue Captain Scott O'Grady, U.S. Air Force. The helicopters are carrying teams from the 24th Marine Expeditionary Unit (SOC).

June 20
MILITARY: In Washington, D.C., General Dennis J. Reimer gains appointment as the 33rd army chief of staff.

June 27–July 7
AVIATION: In Earth orbit, Captain Robert Gibson directs the space shuttle *Atlantis* as it docks with the Russian *Mir* space station for the first time.
•   The first prototype of the Lockheed Martin F-22 Raptor, an advanced tactical fighter, is under construction.

June 30
MILITARY: Gene C. McKinney becomes the 10th sergeant major of the army; he is also the first African American so appointed.
MARINES: Sergeant Major Lewis G. Lee becomes the 13th sergeant major of the Marine Corps.

June 30–August 10
AVIATION: Operation Quick Lift unfolds as Air Mobility Command (AMC) C-5 Galaxies and C-141 Starlifters transport British and Dutch peacekeepers to Croatia.

July 1
NAVAL: The Fifth Fleet is established under the U.S. Central Command (CENT-COM) to exercise operational control of U.S. naval forces in the Persian Gulf and Indian Ocean region.

July 23
AVIATION: A C-5 Galaxy from the 433rd Airlift Wing conveys 20 tons of medical equipment, blankets, clothes, and other supplies to assist victims of economic deprivation in Belarus (Byelorussia).

July 27
MILITARY: In Washington, D.C., President William J. Clinton and Kim Young Sam attend ceremonies dedicating the new Korean War Memorial at the National Mall.

July 30
MARINES: In Washington, D.C., General Charles C. Krulak becomes the 31st commandant of the Marine Corps.

July 31
AVIATION: At Whiteman Air Force Base, Missouri, the final Minuteman II missile belonging to the 351st Missile Wing is deactivated.

August 4
AVIATION: A pair of EA-6B Prowlers from the carrier *Theodore Roosevelt* and two Marine Corps F/A-18 Hornets from Aviano, Italy, fire HARM missiles at Serbian mobile missile sites operating near Knin and Udbina, Croatia.

August 13
AVIATION: A C-5 Galaxy of the 60th Air Mobility Wing delivers 75 tons of food from Germany to Croatia to feed victims of the recent civil disturbances there.

August 16
MARINES: In a nod toward greater physical fitness, female marines are now required to run the same three-mile distance as males during testing.

August 17
AVIATION: The E-8C joint surveillance target attack radar system (JSTARS) begins final flight testing to replace pre-production models that saw service during the 1991 Gulf War.
NAVAL: Threatening Iraqi troops movements along the Kuwaiti border result in deployment of the *Abraham Lincoln* and *Independence* carrier battle groups, assisted by the *New Orleans* amphibious ready group. The carrier *Theodore Roosevelt* is also put on alert in the eastern Mediterranean.

August 20–21
AVIATION: A C-5 Galaxy flies from Ramstein Air Base, Germany, to Zagreb, Croatia, to assist refugees of the civil disturbances there.

August 25–29
AVIATION: In their first major exercise as an operational unit, 11 new C-17 Globemaster IIIs of the 315th and 437th Airlift Wings haul 300 tons of troops and equipment to Kuwait.

1995

August 30–September 21
AVIATION: In the Adriatic, Operation Deliberate Force commences as the carrier *Theodore Roosevelt* launches warplanes to bomb Serbian air defense missile sites, radar sites, and communication facilities. Air force fighter bombers begin hitting Serbian targets with precision-guided munitions at 2 A.M. The carrier *America* also contributes aircraft to the fracas, while on September 10 the guided-missile cruiser *Normandy* fires 13 Tomahawk cruise missiles. A total of 3,518 sorties are flown before the Serbs are cajoled into attending peace talks at Dayton, Ohio.
MARINES: VMFA(AW)-533 at Aviano, Italy, and VMFA-312 on the carrier *Theodore Roosevelt* attack Serbian formations in Bosnia as part of Operation Deliberate Force.

August 31
AVIATION: NATO warplanes continue hitting Serbian targets in and around Sarajevo, Bosnia, including air defense systems, ammunition dumps, and equipment storage facilities. However, a 24-hour suspension of aerial activities is imposed to support NATO peace negotiations with Serbian leaders.

September 1
AVIATION: The air force reactivates its remaining SR-71 Blackbird to resume strategic reconnaissance missions previously handled by satellites.

September 5
AVIATION: As peace negotiations between NATO and Serbian leaders break down, Operation Deliberate Force resumes in full fury against existing targets.

September 6
AVIATION: NATO warplanes, including Italian Tornadoes, strike at key bridges and chokepoints at the behest of theater commanders. At one point an air force F-16C from the 23rd Fighter Squadron detects a Serbian SA-6 radar site and destroys it with a combination HARM (High-Speed Anti-Radiation) Targeting Pod System and an AGM-88 missile.

September 7
AVIATION: NATO warplanes fly six strike packages against integrated targets, including six bridges and one chokepoint.

September 8
AVIATION: Operation Deliberate Force begins planning strike packages with stands of missiles against integrated air defense systems (IADS) in northwest Bosnia-Herzegovina.

September 9
AVIATION: Three strike packages are flown against Serb targets in Bosnia using HARM missiles and 2,000-pound GBU-15 precision-guided glide bombs.

September 10
AVIATION: American and NATO forces use Tomahawk Land Attack Missiles (TLAM), HARM, and related stand-off weapons to strike down Serbian antiaircraft defenses in northwestern Bosnia. Other sorties are flown in support of UN positions near the Tuzla airport, which are being shelled.

September 11
AVIATION: Operation Deliberate Force continues as four strike packages are planned and delivered under favorable weather conditions. Reconnaissance efforts are also stepped up to provide accurate bomb damage assessments.

September 12
AVIATION: NATO warplanes strike ammunition dumps and other facilities in the Doboj region northwest of Tuzla, Bosnia, to good effect.

September 14
AVIATION: Once Serbian factions come to terms with UN negotiators, NATO commanders order a halt to all aerial offensive operations.

September 14–30
AVIATION: The Air Mobility Command (MAC) orders transports at Charleston Air Force Base, South Carolina, to deliver 30 tons of medical supplies to Hanoi, Vietnam. This is the first American visit to Vietnam since the war ended in 1975.

September 15–21
AVIATION: Air Force, Reserve, and National Guard transports are mobilized in the wake of Hurricane Marilyn to bring humanitarian aid throughout the eastern Caribbean. The C-17 Globemaster IIIs flies for the first time in a disaster relief effort.

September 20
AVIATION: Operation Deliberate Force formally concludes, having forced tough and professional Serb forces out of Bosnia by air power alone.

September 22
AVIATION: An E-3B AWACS jet crashes on takeoff at Anchorage, Alaska, killing its crew of 22 Americans and two Canadians.

September 26
AVIATION: Lieutenant Sarah Deal qualifies to fly the CH-53E and joins HMH-466 as the Marine Corps's first female helicopter pilot.

September 30
AVIATION: Former Strategic Air Command (SAC) bases at Castle Air Force Base, California, and Plattsburgh Air Force Base, New York, are closed down. The 93rd Bombardment Group, the first air force unit to operate B-52 Stratofortresses, is also deactivated after 47 years of service.

October
AVIATION: At Marietta, Georgia, the first C-130J Hercules, an advanced technology version of the noted transport, rolls off the assembly line. It is recognizable by its six-bladed propellers.

October 1
AVIATION: Chief Master Sergeant Carol Smits becomes the first woman to serve as senior enlisted advisor in the Air Force Reserve.
MARINES: At Quantico, Virginia, the Marine Corps Warfighting Laboratory is created to develop and assess new tactics, concepts, and doctrines for possible adoption by the fleet Marine Force (FMF).

October 16–17
AVIATION: In the Gulf of Mexico, aircraft of the 53rd Weather Reconnaissance Squadron search for survivors of a Mexican pipe-laying barge that sank during Hurricane Roxanne. A single survivor floating on a raft is spotted and his location is relayed to the Coast Guard, who ultimately rescue 23 survivors.

October 28–December 18
AVIATION: In Bahrain, F-16Cs of the 20th and 357th Fighter Wings arrive as part of Operation Vigilant Sentinel. This is the first test of the air expeditionary force concept.

November 1
DIPLOMACY: At Wright-Patterson Air Force Base, Dayton, Ohio, representatives from Croatia, Bosnia, and Serbia, meet to hammer out a formal peace agreement between the former states of Yugoslavia.

November 13
TERRORISM: In Riyadh, Saudi Arabia, a bomb explodes outside a Saudi National Guard facility, killing a soldier and four civilians attached to the U.S. Army Materiel Command.

November 29
AVIATION: The navy's super-capable McDonnell-Douglas F/A-18E Super Hornet flies for the first time in St. Louis, Missouri.

December
AVIATION: In Washington, D.C., Dr. Gene McCall, Air Force Scientific Advisory Board (SAB), unveils the New World Vista, a forecast of air and space technology. Such a study was ordered by Secretary of the Air Force Dr. Sheila Widnall and U.S. Air Force chief of staff Ronald R. Fogleman.

December 6
AVIATION: In Bosnia, Air Mobility Command (AMC) transports commence Operation Joint Endeavor by delivering American peacekeeping troops and equipment in anticipation of a comprehensive peace treaty reached at Wright-Patterson Air Force Base.

December 14
MILITARY: In accordance with the Dayton Peace Accords, the 1st Armored Division deploys in Bosnia-Herzegovina as part of an international peacekeeping force under the aegis of Task Force Eagle. A total of 60,000 NATO troops, of which 20,000 are American, replace UN peacekeepers.

December 21
MILITARY: At Fort Bliss, Texas, the 2nd Battalion, 7th Air Defense Artillery receives the new patriot PAC-3 missiles, with enhanced capabilities against ballistic missiles such as the Soviet-built Scud.

December 29
MILITARY: The Defense Base Realignment and Closure Commission is terminated, having shut down 243 installations in a major belt-tightening measure.

December 31
MILITARY: In Bosnia-Herzegovina, engineers from the 1st Armored Division complete the world's longest pontoon bridge–620 meters–across the rain-swollen Sava River, prior to occupying its assigned peacekeeping region during Operation Joint Endeavor.

1996

January
MILITARY: Army personnel declines to 491,103 officers and men while the number of active divisions dwindles to only 12.

January 9
AVIATION: Over Bosnia-Herzegovina, Operation Provide Promise, the longest sustain humanitarian airlift in history, begins coming to an end. Air force transports have flown 4,597 sorties and delivered 62,000 metric tons of cargo to numerous refugees throughout the region.

January 17
MARINES: In Washington, D.C., the Commandant and Headquarters Marine Corps leave the navy's Pentagon Annex, where they have been stationed for five decades, and take up office space in the Pentagon itself.

January 22
NAVAL: A conundrum develops over the Department of Defense appropriations act signed on December 1, 1995, which expressly prohibits funds to restore any of the four *Iowa*-class battleships to the Naval Vessel Register as they are prohibitively expensive to maintain in mothballs. However, a defense appropriations act signed this day allows the navy to put the two best-preserved battleships back on the list. Naval authorities request clarification of the issue before proceeding further.

February 3
MILITARY: Near Gradacac, Bosnia-Herzegovina, a mine takes the life of Sergeant First Class Donald A. Dugan, Troop A, 1st Squadron, 1st Cavalry (1st Armored Division).

February 14
AVIATION: The E-8S JSTARS aircraft flies its 50th mission in support of Operation Joint Endeavor over former Yugoslavia. This is a highly advanced, joint surveillance and target attack radar aircraft.

February 24
AVIATION: Cuban MiG fighters shoot down two unharmed Cessna aircraft belonging to Miami-based Cuban exiles; President Bill Clinton subsequently suspends all air charter travel to that island.
NAVAL: Off the Cuban coast, the guided-missile cruiser *Mississippi* and the amphibious assault ship *Nassau* assist Coast Guard vessels in searching for survivors of two Cessna aircraft shot down by the Cuban air force.

March 5–24
NAVAL: Once the People's Republic of China closes part of the Taiwan Strait to conduct live-fire naval exercises on the eve of the Taiwan national election, the

Navy rushes the *Nimitz* and *Independence* carrier battle groups into the area as a sign of solidarity with the Nationalist regime.

March 19–20

AVIATION: The space shuttle *Endeavor*, commanded by U.S. Air Force colonel John R. Casper, complete a 10-day mission in orbit that includes several satellite rendezvouses. It returns after 240 hours and 39 minutes in space and 160 Earth orbits.

March 23

NAVAL: In the China Sea, the *Nimitz* and *Independence* carrier battle groups hasten to the vicinity of Taiwan after the People's Republic of China conducts live-fire exercises nearby.

March 29

AVIATION: In Washington, D.C., Vice President Albert Gore declares that the United States will open up its GPS satellite navigation system to commercial interests.

• At Edwards Air Force Base, California, the *Tier II Minus Dark Star* unmanned aerial vehicle (UAV) performs its maiden flight. This is intended as a stealthy, jet-propelled reconnaissance system but only five are built before the program is cancelled.

April

MARINES: The Marine Corps creates its Chemical Biological Incident Response Force to deal with terrorists who may be handling biological or chemical weapons.

April 3

AVIATION: An air force CT-43 transport jet from the 76th Airlift Squadron crashes into a mountain outside Dubrovnik, Croatia, killing Secretary of Commerce Ron Brown and 34 other passengers.

April 9–25

AVIATION: In Monrovia, Liberia, Operation Assured Response commences as air force AC-130s, MC-130s, C-130s, and MH-53J Pave Low helicopters fly 94 missions while evacuating 2,000 U.S. citizens and foreign nationals.

NAVAL: SEALS and other Special Forces are flown into Monrovia, Liberia, to facilitate implementation of Operation Assured Response, a major evacuation effort.

April 15

AVIATION: For the first time, navy and air force navigator trainees will study in a single class at Randolph Air Force Base, Texas.

April 17

DIPLOMACY: On Haiti, Operation Uphold Democracy concludes after an 18-month duration; only one soldier has died as a result of hostile fire.

April 18

AVIATION: A pair of C-17 Globemaster IIIs convey a pair of MH-53J Pave Low helicopters from Sierra Leone, Africa, to England and at a considerable savings in time and expense had they flown there under their own power.

April 20
NAVAL: Off Monrovia, Liberia, Operation Assured Response continues as the amphibious assault ship *Guam*, the amphibious transport dock *Trenton*, the dock landing ship *Portland*, and the guided-missile destroyer *Conolly* begin evacuating 1,250 Americans and foreign nationals from that war-ravaged nation.
MARINES: Units of the 22nd Marine Expeditionary Unit (SOC) are helicoptered into Monrovia, Liberia, for the purpose of evacuating Americans and foreign nationals during a period of civil strife.

April 30
AVIATION: The top secret Tacit Blue aircraft, from which the B-2 Spirit was developed, is publicly revealed for the first time.

May 1
AVIATION: At Holloman Air Force Base, New Mexico, a German officer takes charge of the German tactical training center for the first time. This is the first time that a foreign officer commands a unit on a base within the United States.

May 9
POLITICS: Several geography experts, examining Admiral Richard E. Byrd's diary for the first time, determine that he falsified his claim to be the first person to fly over the North Pole on May 9, 1926.

May 10
AVIATION: Over Camp Lejeune, California, a CH-46E helicopter collides with an AH-1W gunship, resulting in the deaths of 12 marines, one sailor, and a soldier.

May 13
NAVAL: In Washington, D.C., President William J. Clinton nominates Vice Admiral Paul Reason as the navy's first four-star admiral of African-American descent.

May 15
MILITARY: President Bill Clinton declares that U.S. troops will remain on peacekeeping duties in Bosnia for an additional 18 months.

May 16
NAVAL: In Washington, D.C., Chief of Naval Operations admiral Jeremy M. Boorda commits suicide after being accused of wearing Vietnam War combat decorations for which he was not entitled.

May 21–June 22
AVIATION: Marine Aerial Refueler Transport Squadron 252 evacuates 208 American citizens and 240 foreign nationals from Bangui, Central African Republic, during a period of political upheaval.
MARINES: In Bangui, Central African Republic, Operation Quick Response unfolds as marine helicopters from the amphibious assault ship *Guam* fly in the 22nd Marine Expeditionary Unit (SOC) to evacuate personnel from the U.S. embassy there. By the time the maneuver concludes, 208 Americans and 240 foreign nationals have been removed to safety.

May 31
AVIATION: The air force signs a $16.2 billion contract to secure an additional 80 C-17 Globemaster III transport jets to gradually phase out its aging C-141 Star-

lifters. This is also the most costly military order ever placed, bringing the total number of C-17s acquired to 120.

June 3
LAW: The U.S. Supreme Court rule 9–0 to uphold military death sentences.

June 4
AVIATION: In the Pacific, an A-6 Intruder from the carrier *Independence,* engaged in target towing activities, is accidentally shot down by the Japanese destroyer *Yuugiri*; both crewmen eject and are rescued.

June 6
AVIATION: Lieutenant Colonel Kai Lee Norwood becomes the first woman commander of a unit that maintains air force missiles when she assumes control of the 91st Logistic Group.

June 11
AVIATION: The first production Boeing E-8 JSTARS aircraft is delivered to the air force. Several pre-production models were active in Operations Desert Storm and Joint Endeavor.

June 13
MARINES: The Marine Corps contracts with the General Dynamics Corporation to develop a new Advanced Amphibious Assault Vehicle (AAAV) capable of 25 knots at sea or 50 miles per hour on hard road surfaces while carrying 18 marines. A total of 1,022 such vehicles will be procured through 2012.

June 21
AVIATION: Navy commander David J. Cheslak becomes the first naval officer to head up an air force squadron when he assumes control of the 562nd Flying Training Squadron at Randolph Air Force Base, Texas. This particular unit is responsible for training navigators for both services.

NAVAL: Congress, aghast that the highly capable *Seawolf* submarines cost $2.1 billion apiece, scales back procurement plans from 28 to only three. Its designated adversary, the Soviet navy, no longer exists.

June 25
TERRORISM: The Khobar Towers, an American apartment complex in Dhahran, Saudi Arabia, is struck by a terrorist truck bomb that kills 19 air force personnel and wounds 300. Most of casualties were present in support of Operation Southern Watch.

July 1
AVIATION: On the carrier *Constellation,* an air force crew flies an EA-6B Prowler off a deck for the first time. This aircraft is intended to replace the EF-111 as that service's radar jamming aircraft.

July 10
NAVAL: Rear Admiral Patricia Tracey gains promotion to vice admiral, becoming the first three-star female officer of any military service.

July 11
NAVAL: At Naval Air Station Fallon, Nevada, the Naval Strike Warfare Center, Navy Fighter Weapons School, and Carrier Airborne Early Warning Weapons School are all consolidated into the new Naval Strike and Air Warfare Center.

1996

July 17
NAVAL: Off the coast of New York, the Navy salvage ships *Grasp* and *Grapple,* assisted by the landing dock ship *Oak Hill,* comb the waters for wreckage from TWA Flight 800, which crashed shortly after takeoff.

July 23
MARINES: Major General Carol A. Mutter is the first female marine to gain promotion to lieutenant general, or three-star rank.

July 25
MARINES: Congress votes to increase flag officers in the armed services, so the Marine Corps acquires another 12 generals for a total of 80. This is one more than it possessed during World War II.

July 27
AVIATION: At Fort Worth, Texas, the air force retires the last of its General Dynamics F-111s from active duty at the same plant where the first model was accepted 30 years earlier. The last unit operating F-111s, the 524th Fighter Squadron at Cannon Air Force Base, New Mexico, drops them in favor of new F-16 Falcons. However, it remains a mainstay of the Royal Australian Air Force (RAAF) for several more years.

July 29
AVIATION: The 11th Reconnaissance Squadron is activated by the Air Combat Command (ACC), becoming the first unit to operate unmanned aerial vehicles (UAVs), in this instance, RQ-1B Predators.

July 30
MARINES: In an attempt to weed out weak recruits, Commandant Krulak increases Marine Corps basic training by introducing the Crucible. This is a 54-hour event near the end of boot camp that severely tests the mental and physical endurance of future marines.

August 5
NAVAL: In Washington, D.C., Admiral Jay L. Johnson, a former fighter pilot, gains appointment as the 26th chief of naval operations.

August 8
NAVAL: Lieutenant Manje Malak Abd Al Mut'a Ali Noe is commissioned as the first Muslim chaplain in the U.S. Navy.

August 22
MILITARY: The army begins destroying its stockpile of chemical weapons at a depot in Utah and the process is slated to take seven years.

September 3–4
AVIATION: Following the Iraqi seizure of the city of Ibril, two B-52Hs depart Guam on Operation Desert Strike, fly to the Middle East, and launch 13 cruise missiles against antiaircraft and command-and-control centers in Iraq. This action requires the assistance of 29 tanker aircraft and wins the crew of Duke 01 the Mackay Trophy. This is also the first combat mission of the B-52H.
• Reacting to an Iraqi occupation of Kurdish territory in northern Iraq, Operation Desert Storm commences as the guided-missile cruiser *Shiloh,* the guided-missile

destroyers *Laboon* and *Russell,* the destroyer *Hewitt,* and the nuclear-powered submarine *Jefferson City* fire 31 Tomahawk missiles against air defense targets.

September 3
AVIATION: In Bosnia-Herzegovina, the 11th Reconnaissance Squadron is the first air force unit to operate the new RQ-1 Predator unmanned aerial vehicle (UAV). It is there to enforce peace treaty arrangements.

September 4
AVIATION: In Washington, D.C., President William J. Clinton expands the northern no-fly zone in Iraq from the 32nd to the 33rd parallel. Great Britain agrees to the change but France protests and its aircraft will not patrol the new region.
• The 305th Air Mobility Wing dispatches a C-141 Starlifter from McGuire Air Force base to Bujumbura, Burundi, to assist in the evacuation of 30 foreign nationals during a period of civil strife.

September 14
AVIATION: During free elections in Bosnia-Herzegovina, air force security personnel are on hand to help provide security.

September 15–19
AVIATION: In northern Iraq, air force transports begin Operation Pacific Haven by conveying 2,000 Kurdish refugees for processing at Anderson Air Force Base, Guam, prior to settlement in the United States.

September 30
AVIATION: An important benchmark is reached when the Seventeenth Air Force is inactivated after four decades of service in Europe.
MARINES: The combined officer and enlisted personnel levels are 174,049.

November 13
MILITARY: At Fort Stewart, Georgia, the army loses another active combat unit when the 24th Infantry Division (Mechanized) is inactivated. The army now stands at its lowest point in terms of active divisions (10) since before the Korean War.

November 21
AVIATION: The policy projection paper "Global Reach, Global Power" is released to the public by Secretary of the Air Force Dr. Sheila Widnall. This work conceptualizes air force power over the next century.

December 17
MILITARY: In Europe, NATO ministers approve an American plan for troops of 24 nations to continue peacekeeping forces in wartorn Bosnia.

December 23
MEDICAL: The army agrees to investigate the precise nature of sickness among Gulf War veterans, especially if there are bacteriological causes. It is determined that thousands of service men have been exposed to low levels of Iraqi nerve agent as stockpiles were being destroyed.

December 30
MARINES: Female marines are now allowed to attend Marine Combat Training, a post–boot camp program intending to extend infantry training to those recruits slated for noninfantry specialties.

1997

January
MILITARY: Army strength remains steady at 491,707 officers and men but the number of active divisions has declined to 10.

January 1
AVIATION: In northern Iraq, Operation Provide Comfort is superseded by Operation Northern Watch to enforce no-fly zone conditions north of the 36th north latitude line.

January 6
AVIATION: Abdullah Hamza Al-Mubarek is commissioned as the first U.S. Air Force Muslim chaplain.

January 18
AVIATION: The Northrop A/F-18F Super Hornet performs its carrier sea trials onboard the *John C. Stennis.* This new model is available in both one- and two-seat versions, is 25 percent larger that earlier Hornets, and enjoys greater range, payload, and combat survivability. Roughly 800–1,000 will be purchased over the next decade.

January 24
MILITARY: In Washington, D.C., William S. Cohen is appointed the 20th secretary of defense.

January 31
AVIATION: The 31st Air Expeditionary Wing is instituted as the first air force AEW unit and can be deployed or rotated worldwide with little delay.

February 17
AVIATION: Due to the increasing importance of the Air Force Reserve to American national security, it receives the status of a major command.

February 18–March 3
AVIATION: In Liberia, Operation Assured Lift commences as five C-130s of the 37th Airlift Squadron transport 1,160 peacekeepers and 450 tons of cargo from several neighboring African nations.

March 1–14
MARINES: At Twenty-Nine Palms, California, exercise Hunter Warrior unfolds at the newly opened Warfighting Lab, which is dedicated to testing futuristic tactics and weapons.

March 13–18
NAVAL: In the Adriatic Sea, Operation Silver Wake commences as the *Nassau* amphibious ready group begins evacuating American citizens and foreign nationals from the capital of Tirana, Albania. Ultimately, 877 people are moved to the amphibious transport dock *Nashville.*
MARINES: In Albania, the 26th Marine Expeditionary Unit is on hand to evacuate U.S. citizens and foreign nationals after the Communist regime there collapses.

March 14
AVIATION: In Tirana, Albania, a Marine Corps AH-1 Sea Cobra eliminates an Albanian who had been shooting at American helicopters with shoulder-fired surface-to-air missiles.

March 17
AVIATION: In Zaire, units of the Special Operations Command (SOC) and Air Mobility Command (MAC) commence Operation Guardian Retrieval to evacuate 532 individuals threatened by political infighting. The mission required 57 sorties and employed a wide variety of aircraft and helicopters.

March 18
AVIATION: In California, an F/A-18 Hornet fires the Standoff Land Attack Missile-Expanded Response for the first time.

March 21
AVIATION: At the Boeing facility in Mesa, Arizona, the army receives its first prototype of the new AH-64D Apache Longbow attack helicopter with enhances senors, bigger engines, and better avionics.
• At Naval Air Station Pensacola, Florida, Lieutenant Colonel Marcelyn A. Atwood becomes the first air force officer to command a navy squadron.

April 1
AVIATION: At Whiteman Air Force Base, Missouri, the 509th Bomb Wing becomes the first operational B-2 Spirit unit with six bombers.
• All C-130 transports deployed in the continental United States with the Air Combat Command (ACC) are hereafter assigned to the Air Mobility Command (AMC).

April 2
MILITARY: In Washington, D.C., Major General Claudia J. Kennedy advances to lieutenant general; she is the first female three-star general in army history and she serves as deputy chief of staff for intelligence.

April 9
AVIATION: At Marietta, Georgia, the first production Lockheed-Martin-Boeing F-22 Raptor is rolled out of the factory in front of an audience of 3,000 attendees. This aircraft reflects the change in air force thinking from air superiority to air dominance.

May 19
NAVAL: In Washington, D.C., Secretary of Defense William S. Cohen unveils the Quadrennial Defense Review. This program allows the navy to retain 12 carrier battle groups and 12 amphibious ready groups, but it reduces the surface fleet from 128 to 116 vessels and also cuts back the number of attack submarines from 73 to 50. While acquisition of the navy's planned Joint Strike Fighter (JCF) is kept alive, the number of F/A-18E/F purchases is cut back by a third to between 548 to 785 aircraft. Finally, active duty naval personnel will be reduced by 18,000 while the Naval Reserve will decline by 4,100.

May 29
MARINES: As fighting in Zaire verges on the brink of civil war, the 22nd Marine Expeditionary Unit is flown in to help evacuate American citizens and foreign nationals.

May 30–June 4
NAVAL: Off the coast of Sierra Leone, Operation Noble Obelisk unfolds as the *Kearsarge* amphibious ready group, 22nd Marine Amphibious Unit (SOC) begins evacuating 2,500 American citizens and foreign nationals from that war-torn nation.

June 10
AVIATION: The Air Force Special Operations Command directs that an MC-130H Combat Talon II from the 352nd Special Operations Squadron fly a European political survey crew into Brazzaville, Republic of Congo, then experiencing a period of political instability. They depart from RAF Mildenhall, Great Britain, and the flight lasts 13 hours, including three aerial refuelings, and covers 3,179 nautical miles. Braving ground fire from rebels, the aircraft lands, drops off the survey team, and takes 56 people to safety. For their efforts, the crew of Lieutenant Colonel Frank J. Kisner receives a Mackay Trophy.

June 28
AVIATION: At Fort Hood, Texas, the 1st Battalion, 227th Aviation Regiment is the first unit to deploy the new AH-64 D Apache Longbow attack helicopters.

July 21
NAVAL: In Boston Harbor, Massachusetts, the venerable frigate *Constitution,* still the world's oldest warship in commission, sets out on a one-hour voyage following a three-year, $12 million restoration. This is the first time the vessel has put to sea in 116 years.

August 1
AVIATION: A significant aerospace merger occurs when McDonnell Douglas and Boeing become a single corporation employing over 220,000 people.

August 6
AVIATION: No sooner does Korean Air Lines Flight 802 crash after taking off from Guam than CH-53 helicopters fly to the jungle crash spot to rescue 30 remaining survivors.

September 1
AVIATION: In Washington, D.C., General Ralph Eberhart becomes temporary U.S. Air Force chief of staff to replace retiring general Ronald R. Fogleman.
• On the carrier *Nimitz,* the new Joint Stand Off Weapon (JSOW) deploys at sea for the first time.

September 7
AVIATION: At Dobbins Air Reserve Base, Georgia, the F-22 prototype makes its maiden flight with test pilot Paul Metz at the controls.

October 1
MILITARY: In Washington, D.C., General Hugh Shelton gains appointment as the 14th chairman, Joint Chiefs of Staff. He is also the third consecutive soldier to occupy that post.
• At Fort Hood, Texas, the 4th Infantry Division (Mechanized) becomes the first unit selected for conversion of all electronic equipment to a new, digital format.

1997

MARINES: The Naval Air Station at Miramar, California, is acquired by the Marine Corps.

October 6
AVIATION: In Washington, D.C., General Michael E. Ryan gains appointment as chief of staff, U.S. Air Force.

October 12
AVIATION: Three C-130s of the 153rd Airlift Wing, Wyoming Air National Guard, are dispatched to Indonesia to help fight fires. They are equipped with the Modular Airborne Fire Fighting System, capable of dropping 3,000 gallons of water or flame retardant per sortie.

October 21
MILITARY: Robert E. Hall becomes the 11th sergeant major of the army.

December 27–January 4, 1998
AVIATION: In the wake of Typhoon Paka, Air Mobility Command (AMC) C-5s, C-141s, C-130s, and KC-135s transport 2.5 million pounds of relief supplies to Andersen Air Force Base, Guam.

1998

January 12
MILITARY: In response to Saddam Hussein's refusal to admit a UN weapons inspection team, over 27,000 American and British troops are rushed to the Persian Gulf for possible action against Iraq.
NAVAL: The Guam amphibious ready group, 24th Marines Expeditionary Unit (SOC), deploys in the Persian Gulf in response to Iraqi opposition to weapons inspections.

January 31
MARINES: In a major development, the Marine Corps starts deactivating the last of its traditional shipboard detachments.

February 3
AVIATION: In Cavalese, Italy, a Marine Corps EA-6B jet accidentally severs a ski lift cable in the Dolomite Mountains, killing all 20 passengers when it drops 370 feet. The pilot and navigator are subsequently charged with manslaughter.

February 11
AVIATION: At China Lake, California, A B-1B Lancer drops a Joint Direct Attack Munition (JDAM) for the first time. This is a conventional bomb fitted with a satellite guidance system.

February 12
NAVAL: The Department of Defense Authorization Bill of January 22, 1996, mandates that the battleships *Wisconsin* and *New Jersey* be restored to the Naval Vessel Register.

February 23
AVIATION: At Whiteman, Missouri, B-2 Spirit bombers are dispatched to Andersen Air Force Base, Guam, on their first overseas deployment.

February 26–April 3
MILITARY: All four armed services participate in Joint Task Force Kenya, Operation Noble Response, which delivers 800 tons of food and supplies to that flood-ravaged nation.

February 28
AVIATION: At Edwards Air Force Base, the Teledyne Ryan Aeronautical Company RQ-4 Global Hawk unmanned aerial vehicle (UAV) performs its maiden flight. This jet-propelled device is designed as a reconnaissance platform capable of performing from altitudes as high as 65,000 feet and photographing an area as large as Kentucky in under 24 hours.

April 3
NAVAL: The carrier *George Washington* comes to port and then discharges its 26-man marine complement; hereafter marines will no longer serve on aircraft carriers.

May 4
NAVAL: At Pearl Harbor, Hawaii, the battleship *Missouri* is transferred to the USS *Missouri* Memorial Association as part of battleship row.

May 27
AVIATION: Over Mount Torbert, Alaska, an Air National Guard HH-60 Pave Hawk helicopter from the 210th Rescue Squadron assists six surveyors trapped inside an airplane that has crashed on the glacier. Braving high winds and extreme temperatures, the helicopter safely picks up the passengers, winning a Mackay Trophy.

June
NAVAL: This month an important threshold is passed when the landing dock ships *Mount Vernon, Carter Hall,* and *Gunston Hall,* the tank landing ship *La Moure County,* and the guided-missile frigate *Jarrett* have female commanding officers.

June 6
MARINES: In Eritrea, Tarawa amphibious ready group, the 11th Marine Expeditionary Unit (SOC) dispatches KC-130 Hercules transports to evacuate civilians in the wake of border clashes with Ethiopia. These units remove 105 Americans and 67 foreign nationals from Asmara to safety.

June 12
AVIATION: At Cape Canaveral, Florida, the space shuttle *Discovery* makes the ninth and final rendezvous with the Russian space station *Mir.*
NAVAL: The navy contracts with the Bath Iron Works and Ingalls Shipbuilding to construct the futuristic DD 21 *Zumwalt*-class destroyer capable of fighting at sea or assisting landing forces from the littoral. These 32 vessels are intended to replace the existing *Perry-* and *Spruance-* class destroyers by 2010 and feature a 155mm Advanced Gun System that can hit targets 100 miles distant.

July 2
MILITARY: In Washington, D.C., Louis Caldera gains appointment as the 17th secretary of the army. He is an attorney and a 1978 graduate of the U.S. Military Academy.

1998

July 18
NAVAL: In Yokosuka, Japan, the *Kitty Hawk* replaces the *Independence* as the nation's forward-deployed aircraft carrier.

August 7
TERRORISM: U.S. embassies in Nairobi, Kenya, and Dar es Salaam, Tanzania, are struck by truck bombs; 250 people are killed, including 11 Americans and one marine security guard. A further 1,100 are injured.

August 20
TERRORISM: The navy, reacting to a spate of terrorist bombings of American embassies in Kenya and Tanzania, launches 75 cruise missiles at suspected chemical weapons facilities at Khartoum, Sudan, and terrorist training camps in Afghanistan. Saudi terror leader Osama bin Laden is believed to be behind the actions.

September 4
NAVAL: The *South Carolina*, the navy's last operable nuclear-powered surface ship, is deactivated.

September 9
NAVAL: Off Nova Scotia, Canada, the salvage ship *Grapple* is called upon to help recover wreckage from crashed Swissair Flight 111.

September 22
AVIATION: In the wake of destructive Hurricane George, air force transports deliver food and medical supplies to victims on Puerto Rico and in the Dominican Republic and coastal Mississippi.

October 29
AVIATION: At Cape Kennedy, Florida, the space shuttle *Discovery* blasts off with former astronaut and now Ohio senator John H. Glenn. Glenn, at 76, is the oldest human to be placed in orbit, and he participates in experiments concerning the effects of zero gravity on the elderly.

November 6
AVIATION: Powerful Hurricane Mitch cuts a swath of destruction through Central America, leaving 10,000 dead. Air force transports begin a major airlift of 3,500 tons of relief supplies in 200 missions lasting until March 1999.

November 11
MILITARY: In Kuwait, Operation Desert Thunder unfolds as the 1st Brigade, 3rd Infantry Division deploys along the Iraq border to counter any threatening moves by Saddam Hussein.

November 14
AVIATION: In response to Iraqi refusal to allow further UN arms inspection teams into his country, the United States and Great Britain prepare to launch a wave of air strikes in retaliation. Only 20 minutes before the attacks begin, Saddam Hussein changes his mind and allows the teams in.

November 16
NAVAL: In Washington, D.C., Richard Danzig gains appointment as the 71st secretary of the navy.

December 4–15

AVIATION: At Cape Canaveral, Florida, the space shuttle *Endeavor* lifts several components for the future International Space Station into orbit. Over the next 11 days, the crew work to join the *Unity* module with its Russian counterpart, *Zarya.*

December 9

AVIATION: In Washington, D.C., Benjamin O. Davis attends ceremonies during which he receives his honorary fourth star while on the retired list.

December 16–20

AVIATION: Over Iraq, Operation Desert Fox commences in retaliation for Iraqi obstruction and deceit in connection with the UN arms inspection mission. Aircraft from the carrier *Enterprise,* assisted by 325 Tomahawk cruise missiles, strike at Iraqi nuclear, biological, and chemical weapons facilities. This is also the first time that female aviators fly combat missions. The Air Combat Command (ACC) contributes several B-1B Lancers to the operation, this being their combat debut in the Persian Gulf.

MARINES: The 31st Marine Expeditionary Force (SOC) and jets of VMFA-312 participate in Operation Desert Fox to coax Iraqi cooperation with UN nuclear inspectors. Considerable damage is inflicted, but Saddam Hussein still refuses to allow UN inspectors back into the country.

December 19

MARINES: In Damascus, Syria, marine guards use tear gas to disperse crowds protesting Operation Desert Fox against Iraq.

1999

January 4

NAVAL: The battleship *Iowa* replaces the *New Jersey* on the Naval Vessel Register as the latter vessel's guns were damaged by its demilitarization in 1995.

January 22

MILITARY: The Defense Department announces that it has discharged twice as many homosexuals from the military in 1998 than in 1993, before "don't ask, don't tell" was adopted.

January 24

AVIATION: Over Iraq, a navy EA-6B Prowler fires an AGM-154A standoff weapon (JSOW) at a hostile radar site near Mosul for the first time. After eight years of compliance, the regime of Saddam Hussein is beginning to challenge United Nations enforcement of Operation Northern Watch, a no-fly zone.

January 25

AVIATION: Operation Southern Watch commences over Iraq as U.S. and British warplanes continue pounding Iraqi antiaircraft missile sites near Basra. Navy F/A-18 Hornets of VFA-22 and VFA-94 launches the first AGM-154A Joint Standoff Weapons used in combat.

February 4

NAVAL: Off the Virginia coast, the destroyer *Arthur W. Radford* collides with a Saudi Arabian cargo vessel at night, suffering $24 million in damage. Ten months elapse before it is back in commission.

February 7
AVIATION: At Cape Canaveral, Florida, the space probe *Stardust*, intended to rendez-vous with a comet and return samples to Earth, is launched by a Delta II rocket.

February 17
AVIATION: At Keesler Air Force Base, Mississippi, the 403rd Wing accepts delivery of its first Lockheed C-130J, a high-tech version sporting six-bladed propellers.
NAVAL: The navy ends its presence in Antarctica with the departure of the Antarctic Development Squadron 6 (VXE-6), which had logged more than 200,000 hours since 1955.

February 24
AVIATION: At Naval Air Station Point Mugu, California, three navy LC-130R Hercules transports of Antarctic Development Squadron 6 (VXE-6) return to base after assisting the National Science Foundation's Operation Deep Freeze in Antarctica.

February 25
MILITARY: In Austria, the victims of a recent avalanche are attended to by army helicopters and personnel.

March 24–June 10
AVIATION: United States and NATO warplanes begin Operation Allied Force, a concerted air offensive against Serbian forces committing "ethnic cleansing" in Kosovo, formerly a part of Yugoslavia. The aviation segment, Operation Noble Anvil, is the largest aerial offensive in Europe since World War II and aims to stop the Serbs under President Slobodan Milošević from committing further atrocities. U.S. aircraft constitute 69 percent of aerial forces involved, or 723 out of 1,023 aircraft. This attack sees the combat debut of the B-2 Spirit bomber.
• Flying from Aviano, Istrana, and Gioia del Colle, Italy, marine F/A-18 Hornets and navy EA-6B Intruders attack radar sites, communication centers, and army installations throughout Yugoslavia.
• The cruiser *Philippine Sea*, destroyers *Gonzalez, Nicholson,* and *Thorn,* and submarines *Miami* and *Norfolk,* launch Tomahawk cruise missiles at various targets throughout Yugoslavia during Operation Allied Force.
• On the first day, an F-16C flown by Captain Jeffrey G. J. Hwang shoots down a pair of Serbian MiG-29s with AIM-120 AMRAAM missiles in a quick action, winning the Mackay Trophy.
MILITARY: The overall commander of Operation Allied Force is General Wesley K. Clark. This is also the first wartime action in NATO history.
MARINES: Harrier jump jets attached to the 24th Marine Expeditionary Unit participate in Operation Allied Force against Serbian forces in Kosovo.

March 26
AVIATION: A roving air force F-16C shoots down two Serbian MiG-29s over Bosnia-Herzegovina.

March 27
AVIATION: Serbian antiaircraft missiles shoot down a Lockheed F-117 stealth fighter, but the pilot is rescued after being spotted by A-10 pilot Captain John A. Cherrey; Cherrey receives a Silver Star for his assistance.

Operation Sustain Hope in Tirana, Albania *(Department of Defense)*

March 31
Military: Three American soldiers are taken prisoner by Serbian forces along the Macedonian-Serbian frontier; they are beaten and held in custody until May 2.

April 3
Aviation: The carrier *Theodore Roosevelt* arrives in the Adriatic and its air wings go on to fly 4,270 sorties as part of Operation Allied Force against Serbia.

April 4
Aviation: In Tirana, Albania, Operation Sustain Hope commences as Air Mobility Command (AMC) C-17 Globemaster III transports begin lifting the first of 3,000 tons of relief supplies from Dover Air Force Base, Delaware, to refugees in Kosovo.

April 11
Aviation: Off Kukes, Albania, Operation Shining Hope unfolds as MH-53 Sea Dragon and H-46 Seaknight helicopters from the amphibious assault ship *Inchon* deliver food, medicine, and other humanitarian aide to the swelling ranks of refugees there.

April 17
Aviation: Over Serbia, the unmanned RQ-1 Predator drone performs its first combat operation.

April 19
Naval: On Vieques Island, Puerto Rico, a bomb released by an F/A-18 Hornet during a live-fire exercise goes astray and kills a civilian security guard. Ensuing protests from the local population lead to a temporary halt in training there.

1999

April 21
AVIATION: The Socialist Party headquarters building in Yugoslavia is struck by two NATO missiles and destroyed.
MILITARY: Task Force Hawk, consisting of 5,100 heavily armed soldiers using Special Forces equipment, deploys to Tirana, Albania, as part of Operation Allied Force. Despite an exceedingly dangerous military environment, they never fire a shot in anger.

April 23
AVIATION: The headquarters of Serbian state television is struck by NATO bombs.
DIPLOMACY: An offer by Slobodan Milošević to create an "international presence" in Kosovo is rejected by NATO leaders.

April 30
MARINES: In Albania, elements of the 26th Marine Expeditionary Unit (SOC) go ashore to provide security and assistance to refugees fleeing from the fighting in nearby Kosovo.

May 1
AVIATION: The Air Force Reserve Command mobilizes its first tanker wing for active duty; this is the first of five such wings to face activation over the next five months.
• In Kosovo, a Serbian bus carrying 47 passengers plunges off a bridge recently bombed by NATO aircraft; there are no survivors.

May 2
AVIATION: An air force F-16 is shot down by Serbian ground forces, although the pilot is rescued by an MH-60 helicopter. This is the second and final aircraft lost during Operational Allied Force.

May 3
NAVAL: At the North Pole, the nuclear-powered submarine *Hawkbill* surfaces through the ice in this, the final joint Navy–National Science Foundation Science Ice Expedition.

May 4
AVIATION: A F-16C pilot shoots down a MiG-29 over Kosovo; this is the final air force victory of Operation Allied Force.

May 5
MILITARY: In Albania, an AH-64 Apache helicopter attached to Task Force Hawk crashes on a training flight; the crew of two is killed.

May 6
DIPLOMACY: Ministers from the Group of Eight (G8) agree to a peace plan that calls for the return of all refugees to Kosovo plus the deployment of an international peacekeeping force.

May 8
AVIATION: In Belgrade, Serbia, NATO missiles accidentally strike the Chinese embassy, killing three. Massive demonstrations break out in China as a result.

May 14
AVIATION: The first operational Bell/Textron V-22 Osprey is delivered to Marine Corps units. It is intended to serve as a combat troop carrier to replace the aging CH-46 Skyknight and CH-53 Sea Stallion helicopters. A total of 360 Ospreys will be purchased by the Marine Corps to that end.

May 17–November 17
AVIATION: Continuous Iraqi violations result in no less than four air strikes against antiaircraft positions and radar sites in the no-fly zone. The aircraft involved are navy F/A-18 Hornets and air force A-10 Thunderbolt IIs.

May 20
AVIATION: In Hungary, VMFA(AW)-332 and 533 commence flying operations in support of Operation Allied Force in Kosovo.

May 23
AVIATION: In Washington, D.C., President Bill Clinton cannot rule out a larger military intervention once Serb forces and Albanian police begin skirmishing along the borders.

May 26
MILITARY: NATO leaders agree that a future peacekeeping force in Kosovo must be no less than 45,000 troops in size.

May 30
DIPLOMACY: NATO leadership demands a clear and irrevocable statement from Slobodan Milošević that he accepts NATO peace terms before the air campaign is halted.

June 4–5
MILITARY: At Fort Carson, Colorado, the 7th Infantry Division becomes the first of two "integrated" divisions when several National Guard units are formally attached to it. It is followed by the 24th Infantry Division at Fort Riley, Kansas.

June 9
DIPLOMACY: NATO leaders and Serb military authorities conclude an agreement for the withdrawal of all Serb forces from Kosovo.

June 10–July 6
AVIATION: All NATO air raids are suspended in the wake of Serbian withdrawals from Kosovo. This is also the first war won by air power alone.
MARINES: Serbian forces begin withdrawing from Kosovo, bringing Operation Allied Force to a close. The 26th Marine Expeditionary Brigade is then sent ashore to enforce provisions of the peace agreement and assist refugees.

June 11
MILITARY: In Kosovo, Operation Joint Guardian unfolds as units of Task Force Falcon, comprising the 2nd Battalion, 505th Expeditionary Unit, and the 82nd Airborne Division occupy select positions in that wartorn region. They are joined shortly after by elements of the 1st Infantry Division (Mechanized).

June 16
AVIATION: In the southern no-fly zone of Iraq, Iraqi antiaircraft fire prompts a sharp riposte by navy F/A-18 Hornets and British GR-1 Tornadoes against two radar sites and a missile battery.

June 21
MILITARY: In Washington, D.C., General Eric K. Shinseki gains appointment as the army's 34th chief of staff; he is also the first Japanese-American to hold that position.

June 28
MARINES: Sergeant Major Alfred L. McMichael becomes the 14th sergeant major of the Marine Corps.

July 1
MARINES: In Washington, D.C., General James Jones gains appointment as the 32nd commandant of the Marine Corps.

July 2
MARINES: Pursuant to post–cold war reductions, Marine Corps bases at El Toro and Tustin, California, are deactivated.

July 23
AVIATION: In Putumayo Province, Colombia, an RC-7 reconnaissance aircraft crashes into a mountainside, killing five soldiers of the 204th Military Intelligence Battalion.

July 23–27
WOMEN: U.S. Air Force colonel Eileen M. Collins becomes the first woman to command a space shuttle flight when she lifts off with the *Columbia* to orbit the Chandra X-Ray Observatory.

August 10
AVIATION: In Iraq, antiaircraft fire directed at coalition aircraft enforcing the southern no-fly zone provokes a retaliatory counterattack as F-14D Tomcats, F/A-18 Hornets, and F-16C Falcons knock out offending missile and radar sites.

August 13
MILITARY: As Panama prepares to assume control of the Panama Canal Zone at the end of 1999, the headquarters of U.S. army South transfers to Fort Buchanan, Puerto Rico. This concludes nearly a century of army occupation duties in this strategic region.

August 23–September 12
NAVAL: In response to a recent 7.4-magnitude earthquake in Turkey, which killed an estimated 24,000 people, the *Kearsarge* amphibious ready group begins ferrying the necessary aid to the stricken area by helicopter.

September 2
NAVAL: The keel of the *Virginia*, the navy's newest class of nuclear attack submarines, is laid. This vessel is nuclear-powered, capable of launching Tomahawk cruise missiles, and is the first of 30 such vessels comprising the class. They will gradually replace older *Los Angeles*–class attack submarines over the next 18 years.

September 20
AVIATION: Transports of the Air Mobility Command (AMC) begin transporting Australian peacekeeping forces to Dili, East Timor.

MARINES: Off East Timor, helicopters of the 31st Marine Expeditionary Unit convey Australian peacekeeping forces ashore in the wake of post-election violence.

October 1

AVIATION: Aerospace Expeditionary Force 1 is sent to Southwest Asia for the first time. This new system is designed to permit more effective deployments around the world while also rendering them more predictable to increase unit morale.

October 6

AVIATION: In eastern North Dakota, the destruction of 150 Minuteman III silos commences in accordance with the Strategic Arms Reduction Treaty (START II) with Russia.

October 7–26

NAVAL: Off East Timor, the *Belleau Wood* amphibious ready group, 31st Marine Expeditionary Unit (SOC), stations itself in support of Australian peacekeepers during a period of civil unrest.

October 10

AVIATION: The U.S. Central Command (USCENTCOM) initiates Exercise Bright Star 99/100, a large coalition military exercise held in Southwest Asia.

October 12

MILITARY: In Washington, D.C., General Eric K. Shinseki unveils a major reorganization scheme intended to transform the army from a heavy force to a lighter, faster, and more flexible strategic ground force. This change will require a new class of wheeled vehicles presently under development. Brigades within the 3rd and 25th Infantry Divisions are slated to undergo this conversion first.

October 26–November 26

NAVAL: Off East Timor, the *Peleliu* amphibious ready group relieves the *Belleau Wood* as peacekeeping efforts continue on that island.

MARINES: The 11th Marine Expeditionary Unit (SOC) goes ashore on East Timor to relieve Australian peacekeeping forces.

October 28

NAVAL: Cryptologic Technician First Class Daniel King is arrested and charged with espionage for passing classified materials to the Russian embassy in Washington, D.C.

October 31

NAVAL: Off Nantucket, Massachusetts, the amphibious transport dock *Austin* and the salvage ship *Grapple* comb the waters for wreckage and survivors from the crashed Egyptian Air Flight 900.

November 2

AVIATION: In the Panama Canal Zone, the United States formally turns over Howard Air Base to Panamanian authorities. It has been an active American base for the past 82 years.

November 17

AVIATION: An F/A-18 Hornet patrolling the southern no-fly zone is locked on by an Iraqi missile radar, and retaliates by firing HARM missiles at it.

1999

December 3

NAVAL: On Puerto Rico, the government asks the navy to suspend live-fire exercises on the island of Vieques. It rejects the navy's suggestion to end such maneuvers five years hence.

December 20–28

AVIATION: In Venezuela, Air Mobility Command (AMC) C-5, C-141, and C-130 transports convey humanitarian aid supplies to 200,000 victims of severe flooding.

December 31

DIPLOMACY: The last remaining U.S. forces pull out of the Panama Canal Zone, as per the September 1977 treaty with that nation.

2000

January

MILITARY: A present, army troop strength stands at 480,000, backed by 208,000 reservists and 232,000 army civilians.

January 21

MILITARY: In Washington, D.C., President William J. Clinton bestows the Medal of Honor on 21 Asian-American soldiers, mostly from the 442nd Regimental Combat Team. Daniel K. Inouye, presently a U.S. senator from Hawaii, is among those honored.

January 31

NAVAL: In Puerto Rico, civilian authorities agree to a compromise allowing the navy to continue exercises on Vieques Island for the next three years, although nonexplosive ammunition must be used.

• Off Point Mugu, California, the destroyer *Fife*, the guided-missile frigate *Jarrett*, and the amphibious transport dock *Cleveland* sortie to comb the waters following the crash of Alaska Airlines Flight 261.

February

MILITARY: In Bosnia, the 49th Armored Division (Texas) becomes the first National Guard unit deployed with Task Force Eagle.

March 2

AVIATION: In consequence of severe flooding in Mozambique, Operation Atlas Response unfolds as Air Mobility Command (AMC) transports deliver humanitarian relief and supplies from bases in Europe to southern Africa.

April

MILITARY: Exercise New Horizons unfolds in Nicaragua as National Guard troops from Mississippi, Ohio, California, and Alabama deploy to assist the victims of recent hurricanes.

April 8

AVIATION: A Bell/Textron MV-22 Osprey transport plane crashes at Marana, Arizona, killing all 19 marines onboard. All Ospreys currently in service are grounded pending a thorough investigation.

May 3
AVIATION: General Joseph W. Ralston becomes the first air force officer in 37 years to serve as supreme allied commander of the North Atlantic Treaty Organization (NATO).

May 6
NAVAL: At Vieques, Puerto Rico, the destroyer *Stump* is the first vessel to conduct live-fire exercises there since April 1999.

May 8
AVIATION: At Cape Canaveral, Florida, a Titan IVB launcher places a Defense Support Program (DSP) satellite in orbit. These are designed as an early warning missile launching detection system with global coverage.

May 23
AVIATION: At Randolph Air Force Base, Texas, the first production T-6A Texan II turboprop trainer arrives. This new machine is intended to replace the Cessna T-37 and Beech T-34 as a primary pilot training aircraft.

May 25
AVIATION: The Marine Corps authorizes the MV-22 Osprey to resume flight testing, although only with aircrews on board.

June 23
MILITARY: Jack L. Tilley is promoted the 12th sergeant major of the army.

July 2
MILITARY: The U.S. Central Command (CENTCOM) at MacDill Air Force Base receives a new commander in the person of General Tommy Franks.

July 5
NAVAL: In Washington, D.C., the post of assistant chief of naval operations for missile defense is created; it is responsible for defenses against both ballistic and cruise-type missiles.

July 13
NAVAL: West of Oahu, Hawaii, the amphibious transport dock *Denver* collides with the Military Sealift Command oiler *Yukon,* resulting in $7 million in damages to both vessels.

July 15
AVIATION: At Whiteman Air Force Base, Missouri, the final production B-2 Spirit bomber deploys. The air force has no plans to add new heavy bombers to its inventory for the next 35 years (2035).

July 21
NAVAL: In Washington, D.C., Admiral Vern E. Clark gains appointment as the 27th chief of naval operations.

August 8
NAVAL: At Charleston Harbor, South Carolina, the Confederate submarine *H. L Hunley* is raised from the bottom for the first time since 1864 and taken ashore to be restored as a historic exhibit.

2000

August 27
NAVAL: Off the Virginia coast, the destroyer *Nicholson* and the combat support ship *Detroit* collide at night during a replenishment exercise. This being the sixth such mishap over the past 12 months, the chief of naval operations institutes a safety stand-down of all vessels.

September 18
AVIATION: At Edwards Air Force Base, California, the first air force CV-22 Osprey arrives for testing. This hybrid design rakes off and lands like a helicopter, but it flies like a regular airplane.

October 12
AVIATION: At Cape Canaveral, Florida, the space shuttle *Discovery* goes aloft carrying parts and supplies for the international space station. The crew also completes four space walks to get everything assembled.
NAVAL: At Aden, Yemen, a terrorist attack on the guided-missile destroyer *Cole* kills 17 sailors and wounds 39. The ship itself is also seriously damaged by an inflatable speedboat laden with a half-ton of high explosives, which rips out a 40-foot hole in its port side. The *Cole* returns to the United States atop of the Norwegian commercial heavy-lift ship *Blue Marlin,* and it is repaired at Pascagoula, Mississippi. The vessel resumes active duty with the fleet on April 19, 2002. Surprisingly, no terrorist network claims responsibility for the attack, but American intelligence points to fugitive Saudi Osama bin Laden.

October 15
AVIATION: Aircraft from the 75th Airlift Squadron and the 86th Aeromedical Evacuation Squadron fly 28 victims of the *Cole* bombing from Yemen to medical facilities at Norfolk, Virginia, on a 6,000-mile trip. Their efforts result in a Mackay Trophy.

October 16
MILITARY: In Washington, D.C., U.S. Army chief of staff general Eric R. Shinseki announces that all ranks will be permitted to wear black berets as an esprit de corps–raising measure. Army Rangers, who already wear black berets, switch to tan to preserve their unique identity. Meanwhile, Green Berets will go on wearing green and Airborne forces will continue with maroon.

October 24
AVIATION: At Palmdale, California, the new Lockheed XF-35A Joint Strike Fighter, ostensibly the world's most sophisticated warplane, makes its initial flight to Edwards Air Force Base.

October 27
MILITARY: To correct a historic wrong, Lieutenant William Clark of the Lewis and Clark Expedition is posthumously promoted to captain almost two centuries after he quit the military.

October 30
POLITICS: A "Sense of Congress" resolution signed by President William J. Clinton rehabilitates the military reputations of Admiral Husband E. Kimmel and Lieutenant Walter C. Short, scapegoats for the Japanese attack on Pearl Harbor.

The resolution maintains that neither commander received adequate information about the impending attack to act properly. Consequently, the personnel files of Kimmel and Short are amended and they are allowed to retire posthumously at their highest rank.

October 31
AVIATION: At the Balkonur Cosmodrome, Kazakhstan, an American astronaut accompanies two Russian cosmonauts into space as first residents of the International Space Station.

November 22
AVIATION: At Edwards Air Force Base, California, Lieutenant Colonel Paul Smith flies the XF-35A Joint Strike Fighter (JSF) at supersonic speeds to 34,000 feet. Once back at Palmdale, the craft begins its conversion into the XF-35B short takeoff and landing (STOL) version.

November 29
MILITARY: On Johnston Atoll, Pacific, the army declares that it has destroyed the last of its chemical weapons stocks, including 400,000 mines, rockets, artillery rounds, bombs, and several tons of nerve and blister agents.

December 11
AVIATION: A Bell/Textron MV-22 Osprey, a hybrid design that is half airplane and half helicopter, crashes during a test flight near Jacksonville, North Carolina; the four marines onboard are killed. This is the second crash in one year and leads to a suspension of MV-22 flights until problems can be rectified.

December 16
AVIATION: The prototype of the Lockheed Martin X-35C Joint Strike Fighter (JCF) performs its maiden flight. This is the navy version.

2001

January
MILITARY: Army recruiting efforts, buoyed by reenlistment bonuses and education programs, manages to keep current personnel levels at 487,780. At this juncture, 114,000 troops, nearly a fourth of the army, are deployed overseas.

January 11
MILITARY: The Army Recruiting Command unveils a new campaign theme entitled "An Army of One."

January 13
AVIATION: In Puerto Rico, newly elected governor Sila Maria Calderón of the Popular Democratic Party reneges on a pledge to allow bombing practice at the Vieques firing range. President Bill Clinton is unable to resolve the issue.

January 16
MILITARY: In Washington, D.C., former president Theodore Roosevelt is awarded a Medal of Honor for his role in the Battle of San Juan Heights in 1898. His great-grandson accepts the medal on his behalf.

January 20
MILITARY: In Washington, D.C., President George W. Bush is inaugurated as the 43rd president of the United States and commander in chief.
• Colin Powell, former general and chairman, Joint Chiefs of Staff, is appointed secretary of state by President George W. Bush.

January 23
AVIATION: At Palmdale, California, Lieutenant Colonel Paul Smith flies the XF-35C naval version of the Joint Strike Fighter (JCF) on an aerial refueling qualification mission.

January 26
MILITARY: In Washington, D.C., Donald W. Rumsfeld is again to serve as the 21st secretary of defense. He had previously occupied the office from 1975 to 1977.

February 3
AVIATION: On Guam, Air Mobility Command (AMC) C-17 Globemaster IIIs transport relief supplies and food to victims of a recent earthquake in India. They are refueled en route by KC-135s while traversing the Pacific and Indian Oceans.

February 9
NAVAL: The nuclear submarine *Greeneville* surfaces rapidly nine miles from Pearl Harbor, Hawaii, inadvertently striking the Japanese 190-foot fishing trawler *Ehime Maru,* killing nine passengers. The navy issues a formal apology, agrees to recover the bodies of the deceased, and pays out $11 million in restitution. A major investigation ensues.

February 16
AVIATION: Over Iraq, 24 aircraft from the carrier *Harry S. Truman* strike at radar sites and air-defense command centers in retaliation for a series of violations in the northern and southern no-fly zones. These improved sites were judged a potential menace to enforcing the no-fly zones; hence, they were neutralized.

February 21
AVIATION: At Nellis Air Force Base, Nevada, an RQ-1 Predator pilotless drone has been modified to carry a Hellfire missile, which it fires and destroys a target tank. This is the first unmanned aerial vehicle (UAV) to do so.

February 24
AVIATION: At March Air Force Base, California, Lieutenant Colonel Stayce D. Harris becomes the first African-American woman to command an air force squadron when she takes control of the 729th Airlift Squadron.

March 4
NAVAL: The new aircraft carrier *Ronald Reagan,* the first such vessel named after a living ex-president, is commissioned by former first lady Nancy Reagan.

March 12
AVIATION: In Kuwait, during Operation Desert Spring, a live-fire exercise at night, an F/A-18 Hornet from the carrier *Harry S. Truman* accidentally drops a

2001

500-pound bomb on allied personnel, killing five Americans and a New Zealand army officer; an additional five Americans and two Kuwaitis are injured.

March 16

Aviation: At Edwards Air Force Base, the prototype XF-35B STOVL begins testing over a specially designed hover pit to gauge lift forces at various power settings. This is the Marine Corps version.

April 1

Aviation: Off Hainan Island, China, an EP-3E *Aries II* reconnaissance craft collides with a J-8 Chinese jet fighter that had been recklessly buzzing it over the South China Sea. The fighter pilot dies in the ensuing crash but Lieutenant Shane Osborne manages to safely land his bucking aircraft at Lingshui military airfield on Hainan Island, where the crew is detained for 11 days. Their aircraft is also boarded and ransacked by the Chinese, then dismantled and returned on a Russian transport on July 5. For the Communists, this proves a military intelligence windfall for many automated systems are recovered intact and closely analyzed.

April 4

Naval: The navy announces that it has destroyed its last remaining stocks of napalm bombs in the United States.

April 12

Naval: Ignoring protests, the navy declares its intention to resume live-fire training exercises on Vieques, Puerto Rico, for the first time since December 2000.

April 23

Aviation: At Edwards Air Force Base, California, the RQ-4 Global Hawk flies to Edinburgh, Scotland, on the first transoceanic flight by an unmanned aerial vehicle (UAV). The RQ-4 covers the 7,500 miles journey in 23 hours, a new world's record.

Naval: An admiral's mast held by Admiral Thomas Fargo, commander in chief of the Pacific Fleet, finds Commander Scott Waddle of the submarine *Greeneville* guilty of neglect for his vessel's collision with a Japanese fishing trawler. Waddle receives a reprimand, a 50 percent reduction in pay, and is ordered to retire as of October 1.

April 24

Diplomacy: In a slap at Red China, most likely over its detention of an EP-3E reconnaissance aircraft, President George W. Bush announces his intention to sell the Nationalist regime on Taiwan conventional submarines and P-3 Orion maritime patrol aircraft for defensive purposes.

• In Puerto Rico, Governor Sila Maria Calderón files a lawsuit to stop the navy from conducting live-fire exercises on Vieques Island on grounds that it violates decibel level restrictions passed by the legislature. Again, the governor asks the navy and Department of Defense to postpone the exercises.

April 25

Naval: In Washington, D.C., Judge Gladys Kessler of the U.S. district court denies a request for a temporary restraining order by the governor of Puerto Rico to halt navy live-fire exercises at Vieques.

April 27–May 1
NAVAL: In Puerto Rico, anti-U.S. Navy demonstrators protest at Vieques to prevent a scheduled live-fire exercise held by the carrier *Enterprise* and the *Kearsarge* amphibious ready group. Security forces arrest 183 people and the demonstration ends.

May 1
AVIATION: At the National Defense University, Washington, D.C., President George W. Bush declares that the United States should build a viable antimissile defense system to protect itself from attack by rogue states (North Korea, Iran, Iraq). To that end, he is prepared to back out of the Anti-Ballistic Missile Treaty signed with the Soviet Union in 1972.

May 7
AVIATION: An RC-135 aircraft from Kadena Air Base, Okinawa, resumes intelligence flights in international air space off the Chinese coast.

May 8
AVIATION: In Washington, D.C., the secretary of defense declares that the air force is the sole executive agent for the Pentagon's activities in space.

May 24
NAVAL: In Washington, D.C., Gordon R. England gains appointment as the 72nd secretary of the navy.

May 31
MILITARY: In Washington, D.C., Thomas E. White gains appointment as the 18th secretary of the navy.

June 5
AVIATION: Major General James E. Sherrard, III, commander of the Air Force Reserve, gains his third star to lieutenant general. He espouses a "total force" concept, which closely integrates the Reserves into the regular U.S. Air Force.

June 12
NAVAL: In Washington, D.C., a panel on military effectiveness reports that the proposed *Zumwalt*-class DD 21 land-attack destroyer does not represent a substantial improvement of existing systems. The panel was appointed by Secretary of Defense Donald Rumsfeld and casts the future of the DD 21 in jeopardy.

June 15
NAVAL: In light of ongoing protests, Secretary of the Navy Gordon R. England announces that the navy will cease all training exercises on Vieques Island, Puerto Rico, as of May 1, 2003. This effectively negates a lawsuit filed by the island government against the navy and the Department of Defense.

June 24
AVIATION: At Edwards Air Force Base, California, test pilot Simon Hargreaves takes off vertically in the XF-35B to an altitude of 20 feet and hovers for 30 seconds for the first time.
MILITARY: This being the 226th birthday of the American army, all soldiers are authorized to wear the new black beret, unless their unit is authorized to wear other colors.

July 5

AVIATION: The navy EP-3 that was forced to land at Hainan Island, China, on April 1, is disassembled and loaded onboard a Russian AN-124 transport for a flight to Dobbins Air Reserve Base, Marietta, Georgia. The aircraft has since been reassembled and returned to active service.

July 12

NAVAL: The navy, acting in concert with a congressional resolution in the 2001 defense authorization act, places a document in the personnel record of Captain Charles B. McVay III, clearing him for the loss of the heavy cruiser *Indianapolis* in 1945.

July 13

AVIATION: Historic Kelly Air Force Base, Texas, one of the cradles of American military aviation, is closed due to budget cuts. McClellan Air Force Base, California, also shutters its doors.

July 16

NAVAL: Off Hatteras Island, North Carolina, the Navy–National Oceanic and Atmospheric Administration Team recovers the 30-ton steam engine from the Union ironclad *Monitor,* which sank there in a storm on December 31, 1862. The engine will be displayed at the Mariners' Museum in Newport News, Virginia.

August 6

AVIATION: Test pilot Tom Morgenfield flies the XF-35B from Edwards Air Force Base to Palmdale, California, signaling the end of another successful round of flight testing. En route, he reached an altitude of 34,000 feet at Mach 1.2 and sustained it for 3.7 hours, the longest flight of the test program so far.

August 10

AVIATION: Over Iraq, 50 F-14 and FA-18 aircraft launched from the carrier *Enterprise* join British jets in the latest round of punitive strikes against Iraqi antiaircraft emplacements southeast of Baghdad. This is the 25th strike in retaliation for Iraqi violations of Operations Northern Watch and Southern Watch.

August 13

AVIATION: The National Aeronautics and Space Administration (NASA) flies Helios, a solar-powered remotely control experimental aircraft to an altitude of 96,000 feet over a 17-hour maiden flight.

August 24

AVIATION: A cold war milestone passes when the final Minuteman III missile silo, which formed the backbone of American nuclear deterrence for three decades, is destroyed at Minot Air Force Base, North Dakota.

September 6

AVIATION: In Washington, D.C., General John P. Jumper gains appointment as chief of staff, U.S. Air Force.

September 11

MILITARY: In Washington, D.C., a hijacked airliner flown by terrorists slams into the Pentagon, killing 125 military and civilian personnel. Among them is Lieuten-

Two days after the 9/11 terrorist attacks, fires still burn amidst the rubble and debris of the World Trade Center in New York City in the area known as Ground Zero. *(Department of Defense)*

ant General Timothy J. Maude, deputy chief of staff for personnel and the highest-ranking fatality since World War II.

NAVAL: In the wake of devastating terrorist attacks in New York City and Washington, D.C., several navy vessels sortie to patrol coastal waters. The attack on the Pentagon took the lives of 33 sailors and six civilians, while wounding four sailors and two navy civilians.

TERRORISM: A defining tragedy in American history unfolds as two hijacked airliners, commanded by Muslim fanatics, crash into New York's World Trade Center, collapsing both towers and killing 3,000 people. Another airliner crashes into the Pentagon Building in Washington, D.C., while a fourth crashes into a field in rural Pennsylvania as the passengers attempt to wrest control from their abductors. President George W. Bush immediately declares this terrorist act, the largest in human history, to be the work of Saudi fugitive Osama bin Laden and his al-Qaeda ("The Base") terrorist network.

September 12
DIPLOMACY: In New York, a United Nations resolution calls for all nations to collaborate in punishing those parties responsible for the 9/11 terrorist attack.

2001

Aerial view of the Pentagon Building located in Washington, D.C., showing emergency crews responding to the destruction caused when a high-jacked commercial jetliner crashed into the southwest corner of the building, during the 9/11 terrorists attacks. *(Department of Defense)*

- In Washington, D.C., President George W. Bush addresses the nation on television to declare war on terrorism and all parties responsible for it.

September 14
MILITARY: In light of the recent terrorist attack, President George W. Bush calls up 50,000 reservists for active duty in the war on terror. Most of these are deployed in domestic security settings.
NAVAL: The hospital ship *Comfort* docks in New York City to lend medical assistance to survivors of the World Trade Center terrorist attacks.

September 15
MILITARY: In Washington, D.C., President George W. Bush authorizes Operation Noble Eagle, a partial mobilization of the National Guard. By December, roughly 17,000 men and women have been called to the colors to serve in various homeland security positions.

September 16
DIPLOMACY: In Washington, D.C., President George W. Bush addresses a joint session of Congress and issues an ultimatum to the Taliban in Afghanistan: either surrender fugitive terrorist Osama bin Laden or face war with the United States.

2001

September 19

AVIATION: The air force contracts with Lockheed Martin to obtain an initial production batch of 10 ultramodern F-22 Raptors.

September 20–21

DIPLOMACY: In his address to a special session of Congress, President George W. Bush demands that the Taliban regime of Afghanistan surrender Osama bin Laden or face immediate military action. The Taliban refuse to comply, setting the stage for a major military response.

September 27

AVIATION: In Washington, D.C., Secretary of War Donald Rumsfeld declares that President George W. Bush has authorized military aircraft to shoot down commercial airliners hijacked in American air space.

September 28

MILITARY: In Tampa, Florida, U.S. Army Reserve colonel George Trofimoff is sentenced to life imprisonment following his conviction on charges that he spied for the Soviet Union over the past 25 years. He remains the highest-ranking soldier to face charges of espionage.

September 29

AVIATION: At the Kodiak Launch Complex, Alaska, the air force launches a space satellite for the first time. Previously, all space launches were either in Florida or in California.

September 30

NAVAL: In Washington, D.C., the 2001 Quadrennial Defense Review (QDR) stipulates that the navy should increase carrier battle groups in the Pacific and also home port surface vessels and submarines in that region. It also suggests developing new concepts of amphibious warfare and shifting more marines and their equipment to the Indian Ocean to deal with any crisis in the strategic Middle East. At this time, the navy can field 12 carrier battle groups, 12 amphibious ready groups, 108 surface combatants, 55 attack submarines, three marine divisions, and three marine air wings.

MARINES: Manpower levels at the onset of the war on terrorism are 18,057 officers and 154,878 enlisted men and women.

October

AVIATION: The air force and the CIA jointly begin operations against the Taliban with unmanned, remotely guided RQ-1 Predator aircraft, each armed with deadly and accurate Hellfire missiles.

October 1

AVIATION: In Washington, D.C., General Richard B. Meyers becomes the first air force officer to head up the Joint Chiefs of Staff (JCS) in almost 20 years.
• The Air Materiel Space and Missile System Center becomes subordinated to the Air Force Space Command (AFSPACECOM), which now monopolizes all air force space concerns.

October 2

DIPLOMACY: Lord Robertson, secretary-general of NATO, finds evidence, submitted by the United States, proving that al-Qaeda is responsible for the 9/11 terrorist attack that is "clear and compelling." As a member nation that has been attacked, the United States requests military assistance against terrorist cells in Afghanistan and receives it.

October 7
AVIATION: U.S. and British warplanes begin Operation Enduring Freedom, a concerted aerial campaign to drive the Taliban and al-Qaeda from power in Afghanistan. The attacks are run in concert with the Northern Alliance, an anti-Taliban group, and they include aircraft from the carriers *Enterprise* and *Carl Vinson*; 50 Tomahawk cruise missiles are also launched from a variety of vessels. Lieutenant General Charles W. Wald serves as the Joint Force Air Component commander throughout this operation.
• B-2 Spirit bombers of the 509th Bomb Wing at Whiteman Air Force Base, Missouri, fly to Afghanistan and back on the longest bombing mission in aviation history.
• Marine squadrons VMFA-251 and 314, launching from the carriers *Theodore Roosevelt* and *John C. Stennis,* are joined by Harrier jump jets of the 15th Marine Expeditionary Unit (SOC) as part of Operation Enduring Freedom.
MILITARY: Special Forces teams arrive in northern Afghanistan to coordinate anti-Taliban efforts with the Tajiki-based Northern Alliance while also directing close support bombing missions.
• Elements of the 10th Mountain Division (Light) arrive in Uzbekistan to guard an airfield utilized by U.S. Special forces for search-and-rescue operations; this is the first American military unit deployed on territory of the former Soviet Union.

October 8
AVIATION: Over Afghanistan, C-17 Globemaster IIIs perform their first combat mission by air dropping pallets of humanitarian daily rations to territory controls by the Northern Alliance.
• Coalition aircraft begin around-the-clock air strikes against Taliban positions throughout Afghanistan. This enables the Northern Alliance to counterattack

October 9–May 16, 2002
AVIATION: Over the United States, NATO deploys seven AWACS aircraft to assist in security measures during Operation Eagle Assist. This is also NATO's first deployment in the United States since 1949.

October 10
MARINES: The 4th Marine Expedition Brigade (Antiterrorism) is organized from the Marine Security Force Battalion, the Marine Security Guard Battalion, and a special antiterrorism battalion.
TERRORISM: Three journalists in Boca Raton, Florida, test positive for anthrax exposure, which leads to a government investigation. Results are judged inconclusive.

October 12
NAVAL: In the Arabian Sea, the carrier *Kitty Hawk* deploys to serve as a floating base for forthcoming Special Forces operations in Afghanistan. To accomplish this, most of its air assets have been transferred ashore.

October 20
MILITARY: Southwest of Kandahar, Afghanistan, 100 men of the 75th Ranger Regiment deploy onto a Taliban-held airfield, find it deserted, then search all adjoining buildings for possible military intelligence. Once reinforced by a Delta Force unit, the Rangers subsequently capture a house used by a noted Taliban leader.

October 26
AVIATION: The Department of Defense awards the Lockheed Martin Corporation with a contract to develop the new and highly advanced F-35 Joint Strike Fighter (JSF) while Pratt and Whitney will develop the engine. This new aircraft will be deployed by air force, navy, and marine units. However, the navy version is to be strengthened for carrier operations while the marine variant will be equipped for short takeoff/vertical landing operations. The Royal Air Force will also acquire a version of its own.

October 28–November 4
AVIATION: Beginning this week Coalition Aircraft switch from bombing fixed assets of the Taliban and al-Qaeda to striking front-line units opposing the Northern Alliance.

November 1
NAVAL: In Washington, D.C., the Navy Department announces that it is scrapping plans to build the new DD 21 *Zumwalt*-class destroyer to replace its *Arleigh Burke*–class vessels in the 21st century. Instead, it opts to acquire the very advanced and highly capable DDX, featuring a gun system that can strike targets over 100 miles away and will present a radar cross-section that is a fraction of most vessels. Moreover, the technology developed also forms the basis for the new CGX missile cruiser and LCS Littoral Combat Vessel.
MARINES: In Tampa, Florida, Task Force 58 is activated by the Central Command to take charge of the 15th and 26th Marine Expeditionary Brigades (SOC). They are destined to play a role in Operation Enduring Freedom in Afghanistan.

November 2
AVIATION: In Afghanistan, the crew of an MH-53J Pave Low helicopter of the 20th Special Operations Squadron braves hazardous weather flying behind enemy lines to rescue the crew of another MH-53 that crashed. They are awarded a Mackay Trophy.

November 5–18
MILITARY: In Afghanistan, the Northern Alliance, buttressed by coalition air power, begins an offensive that quickly overruns half the country. This represents problems of its own as the alliance, based mostly on Tajik, Uzbek, and Hazara tribesmen, have great antipathy for the Pashtun people who occupy the eastern third of Afghanistan. Fortunately, alliance leaders agree to form an inclusive government once the fighting stops.

November 13
MILITARY: Backed by coalition air power, troops and tanks of the Northern Alliance roll into the Afghanistan capital of Kabul, while Saudi fugitive Osama bin Laden disappears from view. Taliban forces are also in full retreat.

November 13–27
DIPLOMACY: Presidents George W. Bush and Vladimir Putin agree to reduce their nuclear arsenals by two-thirds, leaving the United States with 1,700 warheads and the Russian Republic with 2,200.
MILITARY: The last stand by Taliban, al-Qaeda, and 3,000 foreign zealot fighters (Arabs, Pakistanis, Chechens) at Konduz withers under a steady hail of coalition aircraft bombs. By the time the city falls, the Northern Alliance seizes 6,000 Taliban.

November 14–December 2
MILITARY: In southern Afghanistan, Pashtun tribes under Gul Agra Shirzai and Hamid Karzai drive the Taliban from their spiritual capital at Kandahar. Both columns receive coalition air support.

November 18
NAVAL: Petty Officer Vincent Parker and Petty Officer Third Class Benjamin Johnson die onboard an Iraqi tanker when the dangerously overloaded vessel suddenly sinks in heavy seas. Previously, it had been halted by the destroyer *Peterson* on the suspicion that it had been smuggling oil out of Iraq.

November 25
MARINES: In Afghanistan, the 15th Marine Expeditionary Unit (SOC) from the *Peleliu* amphibious ready group helicopters 400 miles inland and deploys at an abandoned airstrip christened Forward Operating Base Rhino. From there the Marines begin patrolling the region for Taliban and al-Qaeda fighters as reinforcements are airlifted in from the 26th Marine Expeditionary Unit (SOC) from the Bataan amphibious ready group.

November 25–28
MILITARY: During a prison uprising in Mazar-e-Sharif, Afghanistan, air force jets drop bombs that accidentally wound five Special Forces soldiers; they are immediately evacuated to medical facilities at Landstuhl, Germany. CIA operative Johnny "Mike" Spann also becomes the first American to die in combat during the uprising. Nearly all 600 Taliban captives involved die in the fighting.

November 26
AVIATION: F-14Ds from the carrier *Carl Vinson* wipe out a 15-vehicle Taliban convoy after being directed to it by Marine AH-1W Super Cobra helicopters operating from Camp Rhino.

November 28
AVIATION: Operation Swift Freedom unfolds as Air Mobility Command (AMC) C-17 Globemaster III transports carry army and Special Forces troops to an airstrip near Kandahar, Afghanistan.
MILITARY: At Mazar-e-Sharif, Afghanistan, the first elements of the 10th Mountain Division become the first regular army units to deploy in theater.

November 30
TERRORISM: Special Forces fighting in Mazare-e-Sharif Province, Afghanistan, capture 84 Taliban fighters, among them 20-year-old John Walker Lindh, an American citizen apparently fighting alongside them. Once returned to the United States, he faces possible treason charges.

2001

These Afghan al-Qaeda members were captured from a battle in the Tora Bora mountains, 2001. *(Corbis)*

December 4

AVIATION: Coalition aircraft begin pounding the mountain refuge of Tora Bora, a heavily fortified cave complex 55 miles south of Jalalabad, which holds an estimated 2,000 al-Qaeda Arab fighters. Fugitive terrorist Osama bin Laden is thought to be among them.

December 5

AVIATION: In Afghanistan, a 2,000-pound bomb dropped by a B-52 accidentally strikes an American command post, killing three Special Forces soldiers and five Afghan allies. They are the first soldiers killed during Operation Enduring Freedom.

DIPLOMACY: The United States and Russia announce that they have reduced their respective nuclear arsenals to levels established by the START I Treaty.

MARINES: From Camp Rhino, Afghanistan, the 15th Marine Expeditionary Unit (SOC) conducts a motorized convoy of light armored vehicles below Kandahar to interdict any Taliban reinforcements entering the area.

December 6

POLITICS: At Königswinter, Germany, representatives from the four Afghan factions agree to an interim government headed by Pashtun leader Hamid Karzai for the next six months. After that, a grand council (loya jirga) will convene to form a new administration to sponsor free elections within two years.

December 7
MILITARY: Taliban forces, mercilessly harassed by coalition air power and Northern Alliance ground forces, abandon their traditional stronghold of Kandahar and melt into the mountains along the Pakistan border. Their regime fell after only 62 days of fighting, mostly aerial bombardment.

MARINES: In Afghanistan, marine forces ambush a Taliban convoy, killing seven fighters and destroying three trucks. Marine aircraft also account for several more vehicles.

December 11
MARINES: In Kabul, Afghanistan, the long-abandoned U.S. embassy is reclaimed by the 26th Marine Expeditionary Unit (SOC). Shortly after, they are relieved by the 4th Marine Expeditionary Brigade (AT).

December 12
AVIATION: Off Diego Garcia in the Indian Ocean, the guided-missile destroyer *Russell* rescues the crew of an air force B-1B bomber, which ditched en route to targets in Afghanistan. This is also the first B-1B lost in combat and the first lost during Operation Enduring Freedom.

NAVAL: In Washington, D.C., the Navy Department postpones any action on Vieques, Puerto Rico, after the House and Senate Armed Service Committees pass a resolution forbidding the navy from abandoning the test range until a suitable replacement can be found.

December 13
DIPLOMACY: President George W. Bush informs the Russian Republic that the United States is withdrawing from the 1972 Anti-Ballistic Missile (ABM) Treaty in order to develop an antimissile defense system against terrorist attacks.

December 14
MARINES: In Afghanistan, troops from the 26th Marine Expeditionary Unit (SOC) travel overland from Camp Rhino to seize Kandahar airfield. Soon after, this location becomes an important detention facility for Taliban captives of interest to U.S. military intelligence.

December 15
AVIATION: The carrier *Enterprise* is relieved by the *John C. Stennis* after its air groups have flown 4,200 sorties and dropped 2 million pounds of bombs on Taliban targets in Afghanistan.

December 16
MILITARY: Men of the Pashtun-based Eastern Alliance clear out remaining al-Qaeda pockets at Tora Bora after killing 200 and capturing 11. American and British Special Forces begin combing through the caves over intervening weeks, but no trace of Osama bin Laden is found.

December 17
AVIATION: At Istres Air Base, France, Air Mobility Command (MAC) C-17 Globemaster IIIs begin airlifting French military forces to Afghanistan as part of Operation Enduring Freedom.

DIPLOMACY: In Kabul, Afghanistan, the U.S. embassy, which had been closed since the Soviet withdrawal from Afghanistan on January 31, 1989, is reopened for business.

December 22
MILITARY: In Kabul, Afghanistan, General Tommy Franks arrives to attend ceremonies marking the inauguration of a new, interim government under Hamid Karzai, the acting prime minister. He is installed only 78 days following the commencement of Operation Enduring Freedom.

December 26
AVIATION: In Washington, D.C., Undersecretary of War Pete Aldrich announces that the Pentagon has approved acquisition of the one-ton Joint Air-to-Surface Standoff Missile, a precision-guided weapon that can destroy targets at distances of 200 miles.

December 27
NAVAL: In Washington, D.C., the Department of Defense announces that Taliban and al-Qaeda captives seized in Afghanistan will be interred in special facilities at Guantánamo Bay, Cuba.

December 28
CRIME: The United States begins drawing up rules for military tribunals to try terrorist suspects, although they can face the firing squad only through a unanimous tribunal vote.

December 31
AVIATION: By this date, navy aircraft have accounted for 72 percent of all tactical air strikes and over half of all precision-guided weapon, launched against Taliban and al-Qaeda forces in Afghanistan.

2002

January
MILITARY: The army's personnel strength rises to 479,026 following a spate of enlistments, while active division strength remains at 10. This year another 17,000 soldiers will be drawn from the Reserves and activated.

January 3
MARINES: In Afghanistan, Forward Operating Base (FOB) Rhino closes once the 15th Marine Expeditionary Unit ships back to its vessels.

January 9
AVIATION: In Pakistan, a KC-130R from VMGR-352 crashes near Shamsi military airfield in Pakistan, killing seven marines.

January 10
MILITARY: In the Philippines, the army dispatches an advanced team of soldiers to assist the Philippine military in their struggle with the violent Abu Sayyaf, a Muslim group with ties to al-Qaeda. Over the ensuing months a total of 600 Americans arrive.

January 11
AVIATION: At Guantánamo Bay, Cuba, a C-17 Globemaster III arrives with the first 20 of 371 Taliban and al-Qaeda detainees.

MARINES: In Guantánamo Bay, Cuba, terrorist detainees begin arriving for interrogation. The facilities are guarded by the II Marine Expeditionary Force.

January 12
AVIATION: When the Marine Corps commandant is alerted by a letter that the investigation of the April 2000 crash of an MV-22 Osprey had been mishandled, he orders a completely new investigation of the Osprey program.

January 19–February 8
MARINES: At Kandahar airfield, Afghanistan, the 26th Marine Expeditionary Unit is replaced by the 101st Airborne Division and begins shipping back to the *Bataan*. During these proceedings, a CH-53E Super Stallion crashes on January 20, killing two marines and injuring five.

January 21
AVIATION: After Iraqi antiaircraft weapons fire at coalition aircraft enforcing Operation Southern Watch, American and British jets retaliate by striking weapons emplacements at Tallil, 170 miles southeast of Baghdad.

January 29
DIPLOMACY: In Washington, D.C., President George W. Bush declares in his State of the Union address that rogue nations such as Iran, Iraq, and North Korea constitute an "axis of evil" in the world. Moreover, he pledges that none of them will be allowed to develop or possess nuclear weapons or other devices of mass destruction.

MILITARY: At Kandahar airfield, Afghanistan, the 3rd Brigade, 101st Airborne Division, deploys and replaces marines forces. Under the code name Task Force Rakkaan, it consists of three battalions of the 187th Infantry Regiment.

January 31
TERRORISM: In the southern Philippines, U.S. forces assist local troops in hunting down and fighting Abu Sayyaf, a Muslim terrorist group with links to al-Qaeda, which seeks to found an Islamic state of its own.

February 4
AVIATION: Over Afghanistan, an MQ-1B Predator unmanned aerial vehicle (UAV) fires a Hellfire missile at a group of senior al-Qaeda figures on the ground, killing them. This is the first combat missile launch by an UAV.

• Over Mosul, Iraq, Iraqi antiaircraft weapons fire at coalition aircraft enforcing Operation Northern Watch and are, in turn, attacked by American and British jets.

POLITICS: In Washington, D.C., President George W. Bush submits a budget calling for $379 billion to be spent of defense. This request, 14 percent higher that the 2001 budget request, is the largest hike in real defense spending since the Reagan administration.

February 21
MILITARY: At Basilan Island, Philippines, an MH-47E Chinook transport helicopter belonging to the 160th Special Operations Aviation regiment crashes, killing eight soldiers and two air force personnel. They had been assisting in joint U.S.-Philippine training exercises.

February 26
MARINES: In Tampa, Florida, Task Force 58, tasked with supervising the 15th and 26th Marine Expeditionary Groups, is deactivated.

February 27
MILITARY: At Fort Lauderdale, Florida, the army's new, wheeled, assault vehicle, the Stryker, is unveiled. Fast, heavily armed, and armored, they form the core of new Stryker Brigade Combat Teams (SBCT) and serve as the primary weapons platform. A total of five SBCTs are planned.

February 28
AVIATION: For the second time this year, Iraqi antiaircraft weapons at Mosul fire upon coalition aircraft enforcing Operation Northern Watch. U.S. and British jets counter by attacking air defense installations in the region.

March 1
AVIATION: At McGuire Air Force Base, New Jersey, Brigadier General Teresa M. Peterson becomes the first active female duty officer to command an operational flying wing when she assumes control of the 305th Air Mobility Wing.
• In Eastern Afghanistan, the aerial element of Operation Anaconda commences as air force B-52s, B-1Bs, AC-130s, A-10s, and F-15s support ground units attacking Muslim extremists near Gardez. Precision-guided weapons help keep civilian casualties to a minimum while thermobaric bombs are dropped in caves; these kill terrorists by depriving them of oxygen.

March 2–10
AVIATION: An air force AC-130 Spectre gunship is on hand to relieve a detachment of the 10th Mountain Division that was surrounded by enemy fighters. Afterward, two HH-60 Black Hawk helicopters rescue them from rough terrain. The AC-130 crew wins a Mackay Trophy for their timely support.
MILITARY: Approximately 1,200 army troops and Special Forces soldiers engage Taliban remnants in the Shah-i-Kot Valley, Afghanistan, and Operation Anaconda forces them from their strongpoint at Tora Bora. Present are the 1st Battalion, 87th Infantry (10th Mountain Division), the 3rd Brigade, 101st Airborne Division, and the 1st Battalion, 75th Ranger Regiment. The ensuing operation accounts for over 500 enemy dead at a cost of eight Americans killed and 40 wounded.

March 4
AVIATION: Near Gardenz, eastern Afghanistan, a helicopter assault on enemy troops results in the deaths of two airmen. They are the first air force combat losses during Operation Enduring Freedom.
NAVAL: During Operation Anaconda in eastern Afghanistan, Aviation Boatswain's Mate First Class Neil C. Roberts, a navy SEAL, is killed in action.

March 27
NAVAL: Near Kandahar, Afghanistan, Chief Hospital Corpsman Matthew J. Bourgeois, a Navy SEAL, is killed during a small unit training exercise.

April 1
NAVAL: Protests erupt in Puerto Rico once the *George Washington* carrier battle group resumes live-fire training exercises on Vieques Island offshore.

April 15
Military: In Kandahar, Afghanistan, four Explosive Ordnance Disposal soldiers die when a cache of 107mm rockets, apparently booby-trapped, explodes.

April 18
Aviation: At Hanscom Air Force Base, Massachusetts, the experimental MC2A-X performs its maiden flight. This vehicle is designed to provide electronic command and control over combat areas.
• In Afghanistan, an American warplane accidentally kills four Canadian soldiers and wounds eight others in an errant bomb drop south of Kandahar.

April 22
Aviation: The air force resorts to a new organizational scheme for wings and bases it on four groups: operations, maintenance, mission support, and medical.

May 8
Military: In Washington, D.C., Secretary of Defense Donald H. Rumsfeld cancels the army's new Crusader artillery system; it was an armored, self-propelled 155mm gun with its own resupply vehicle.

May 13
Diplomacy: The United States and Russia agree to a further two-thirds reduction in their nuclear arsenals.

May 21
Naval: Off San Diego, California, the research submarine *Dolphin* is engulfed by a fire and flooding. The guided-missile frigate *Thatch* arrives to assist the crew.

May 22
Aviation: At Edwards Air Force Base, California, the X-45A unmanned combat aerial vehicle (UCAV) performs its maiden flight. While stealthy and capable, the program is terminated in 2006.

May 31
Military: In Bagram, Afghanistan, Lieutenant General Dan K. McNeill assumes command of newly created Combine Joint Task Force 180; he is tasked with coordinating military moves by coalition forces in the country.

June 6
Naval: Off the North Carolina coast, the dock landing ship *Tortuga* runs aground at night but is refloated the following day.
Terrorism: Secretary of Defense Donald Rumsfeld asks NATO members to change their prevailing defensive strategy to reflect present-day realities. He calls for a new, more aggressive approach involving preemptive war against terrorists and rogue nations possessing weapons of mass destruction.

June 12
Naval: At the Naval War College in Newport, Rhode Island, U.S. Chief of Naval Operations admiral Vern Clark announces "Sea Power 21," which articulates his vision for the U.S. Navy during the new century. He posits three central concepts: Sea Strike, the ability to project power anywhere in the world; Sea Shield, projecting defense of the nation and its assets; and Sea Basing, to project and maintain sovereignty abroad.

2002

June 17
NAVAL: Off Oman, the guided-missile cruiser *Vicksburg* rescues 16 merchant sailors who had been adrift for 11 days.

July 22
AVIATION: At McConnell Air Force Base, Kansas, the prototype YAL-1A, or "Airborne Laser," performs its maiden flight. This weapons system employs a concentrated light beam to destroy enemy ICBMs while they are still being launched into the atmosphere (boost phase).

July 24
AVIATION: The new and highly capable F/A-18E Super Hornet begins its operational deployment with Attack Squadron VFA-115 on the carrier *Abraham Lincoln*.

July 26
NAVAL: Following the collapse of a mineshaft in Somerset, Pennsylvania, lying 240 feet below the surface, eight medical and diving experts from various navy commands are dispatched to operate a portable recompression chamber.

July 30
AVIATION: A Scramjet engine (air-breathing supersonic combustion engine) is successfully ignited at high altitude for the first time. This futuristic technology has the potential for revolutionizing air transportation.

August 18–26
MILITARY: Southeastern Afghanistan is the scene of Operation Mountain Sweep, conducted by men of the 82nd Airborne Division, the 75th Rangers, and accompanying aviation units. Several Taliban weapons caches are captured, but the fighters evade contact.

August 21
AVIATION: At Cape Canaveral, Florida, the Lockheed Martin Atlas V undergoes its first launch. This is part of the air forces's Evolved Expendable Launch Vehicle, which consists of a main rocket with strap-on boosters added as necessary for heavy payloads.

September 3
NAVAL: At Yokosuka, Japan, the captain of the forward-based carrier *Kitty Hawk* is relieved by the commander, Seventh Fleet.

September 4
NAVAL: During a live-fire training exercise on Vieques Island, Puerto Rico, by the *Harry S. Truman* carrier battle group, protestors pelt naval security personnel with rocks.

September 7–11
MILITARY: In the Bermel Valley, Afghanistan, 175 miles south of Kabul, the 1st Battalion, 504th Parachute Infantry (82nd Airborne Division) makes several ground sweeps, seizing suspected Taliban agents, weapons, and many documents.

September 8
NAVAL: In Washington, D.C., the secretary of the navy declares that the navy's newest *San Antonio*–class amphibious transport dock will be christened the *New York* in honor of the victims of 9/11.

September 10–11

TERRORISM: Al-Qaeda agent Ramzi bin al-Shibh, the suspected coordinator of the 9/11 terrorist attacks, is arrested in Karachi, Pakistan, and secretly transported to an American military base for questioning.

September 11

NAVAL: In honor of the first anniversary of the 9/11 terrorist attack, the secretary of the navy instructs all vessels to fly the first navy jack of 1775, consisting of 13 red and white stripes with the motto "Don't Tread on Me," until the war against terrorism has concluded.

September 13

DIPLOMACY: In New York, President George W. Bush addresses the United Nations General Assembly in calling Iraqi dictator Saddam Hussein a "grave and gathering danger" to world peace. He insists that the body pass a resolution requiring Iraq to readmit weapons inspectors and mandating that Iraq continue disarming. Failing that, Bush warns that the United States will intervene unilaterally, if necessary, to secure Iraqi compliance.

September 29

MILITARY: In southeastern Afghanistan, Operation Alamo Sweep begins as part of the 82nd Airborne Division, the Rangers, and other units, are airlifted to the Afghan-Pakistan border to root out any Taliban or al-Qaeda fighters lurking there.

October 1

AVIATION: The U.S. Northern Command is activated under General Ralph Eberhart and is responsible for the military security of North America. It consists of elements from all four U.S. armed services.
• A historical benchmark is reached when General John P. Jumper orders the Peacekeeper ICBM system deactivated. This was the largest and most capable intercontinental ballistic missile deployed by the United States during the cold war years.

October 2

MILITARY: In central Afghanistan, Special Forces, acting on a tip, uncover a hidden Taliban cache of nearly 500,000 rounds of ammunition.

October 4

TERRORISM: John Lindh Walker, who apparently fought alongside Taliban forces in Afghanistan, is sentenced to 20 years' imprisonment.

November 10

AVIATION: American warplanes begin a concerted series of attacks against Iraqi antiaircraft sites for violating UN-ordered no-fly zones.

November 13

NAVAL: In the mid-Atlantic, the nuclear attack submarine *Oklahoma City* collides with a Norwegian commercial vessel, suffering damage to its periscope and sail. The captain is subsequently relieved of command and reassigned.

November 17–18

AVIATION: Iraqi antiaircraft batteries fire on coalition aircraft patrolling the northern no-fly zone, which prompts a sharp response. Aircraft drop precision-guided munitions on all the offending positions. This comes in the wake of a UN resolution authorizing strong action against Iraqi transgressions.

November 18
TERRORISM: A videotape of Saudi fugitive Osama bin Laden surfaces on the Arabic language Al-Jazeera Network in Qatar, affording the first proof that the wanted terrorist is still alive.

December 6
NAVAL: In the North Arabian Gulf, the guided-missile destroyer *Paul Hamilton* accidentally collides with a merchant vessel and receives some damage.

December 8
AVIATION: The Air Mobility Command (AMC) commences a bevy of C-5 Galaxys into Andersen Air Force Base, Guam, bringing 1,200 tons of relief supplies to survivors of Typhoon Pongsona.

NAVAL: After Guam is ravaged by Typhoon Pongsona, with winds of over 180 miles per hour, Naval Mobile Construction Battalion 74 spends the next several days restoring water supplies to the inhabitants. A total of $4 million in relief supplies is also flown in.

December 9
NAVAL: In Washington, D.C., the secretary of the navy declares that the 10th *Nimitz*-class carrier will be named in honor of former president George H. W. Bush, a distinguished naval aviator of World War II.

December 12
AVIATION: By this time in their service life, F/A-18 Hornets have logged 5 million hours of flight time in navy and Marine Corps squadrons.

December 18
MILITARY: The United States begins deploying 50,000 additional troops in the Persian Gulf region in anticipation of a possible attack upon Iraq.

December 31
MILITARY: In an attempt to shore up Afghan civilian support for the war against terror, the army implements its first Provincial Reconstruction Team (PRT) as part of an ongoing civil-military effort to repair the nation's infrastructure. By broadening the reach of the central Afghan government, the PRTs also play a major role in enhancing national security.

2003

January
MILITARY: Army personnel hovers at 484,628 officers and men with 12 regular divisions activated, although two of these consist of National Guard brigades. The United States has also deployed 10,000 soldiers in the Persian Gulf in anticipation of renewed hostilities with Saddam Hussein in Iraq.

January 3
MILITARY: At Fort Stewart, Georgia, the remainder of 3rd Infantry Division is ordered to deploy to Kuwait and join the headquarters unit and 2nd Brigade already there. Live-fire exercises have already been completed there.

January 14
MILITARY: A detachment from the 5th Battalion, 7th Air Defense Artillery departs Hanau, Germany, for Israel for joint exercises testing air defense capacities.

January 16
MILITARY: In Colombia, South America, 60 members of the 7th Special Forces Group deploy to help train Colombian troops in antiterrorist tactics. They reinforce 10 Green Berets who are already instructing there.

January 20
MILITARY: At Fort Hood, Texas, the 4th infantry Division (Mechanized) is ordered to deploy to Turkey in anticipation of hostilities with Iraq. The division currently has three brigades at Fort Hood and another at Fort Carson, Colorado.

January 23
NAVAL: In Fremantle, Australia, the navy's Sea Swap Initiative begins, which allows three ship crews to rotate through a vessel to give it more time on station. The first participant is the destroyer *Fletcher,* which is re-crewed by personnel of the recently decommissioned *Kinkaid.*

January 24
NAVAL: In Washington, D.C., Gordon England relinquishes the post of secretary of the navy to serve as deputy secretary of the Department of Homeland Security. He is temporarily replaced by acting secretary of the navy Susan M. Livingston.

January 28
MILITARY: In Spin Boldak, Afghanistan, Special Forces and 82nd Airborne Division soldiers, backed by Afghan militia, begin clearing out caves in the Adi Gahr Mountains; 18 Al-Qaeda terrorists are slain without loss.
POLITICS: In his State of the Union address, President George W. Bush accuses Iraqi dictator Saddam Hussein of hiding biological and chemical weapons of mass destruction from United Nations inspectors. He also advises the United States to prepare for a possible conflict there to evict him, but gives no indication of the timetable.

February 1
AVIATION: The space shuttle *Columbia* breaks up in the atmosphere and disintegrates only 15 minutes from touchdown. All seven astronauts die, including Captain David M. Brown, Captain Laurel Clark, and Commander William C. McCool of the Navy and Lieutenant Colonel Michael Anderson and Colonel Rick Husband of the Air Force.

February 2
MILITARY: National Guard troops from Texas, Oklahoma, Arkansas, and Louisiana are mobilized in the search for fragments of the ill-fated *Columbia* space shuttle, which broke up during its descent from space a day earlier.

February 6
MILITARY: At Fort Campbell, Kentucky, the 101st Airborne Division is ordered to prepare to deploy abroad in the war against terrorism.

February 8
AVIATION: In anticipation of another war with Iraq, the Department of Defense begins contracting with commercial airlines to deliver troops and supplies to the Persian Gulf region. This also involves activation of the Civil Reserve Air Fleet (CRAF).

February 13
NAVAL: At Naval Station Mayport, Florida, President George W. Bush visits naval families and has lunch onboard the guided-missile cruiser *Philippine Sea.*

February 14
MILITARY: At Fort Carson, Colorado, the 3rd Armored Division is ordered to deploy to Kuwait.

February 16
MILITARY: At Daytona Beach, Florida, army recruiters enter the NASCAR business by sponsoring a racer sporting the motto "Army of One." This vehicle, driven by Jerry Nadeau, finishes 28th at the Daytona 500.

February 19–March 3
MILITARY: In the Baghran Valley, Afghanistan, soldiers from the 2nd Battalion, 504th Parachute Infantry, 82nd Airborne Division, air assault positions in the search for Taliban and al-Qaeda weapons caches. No resistance is encountered.

March 1
MILITARY: After the Turkish parliament denies the 4th Infantry Division access to Turkish territory for the purpose of invading Iraq, the unit is rerouted to Kuwait by 30 ships.

March 7
DIPLOMACY: After UN weapons inspector Hans Blix informs the Security Council that Iraqi disarmament will take several months, the U.S. and Great Britain present a draft resolution requiring Saddam Hussein to disarm by March 17 or face war.

March 10
NAVAL: In the Mediterranean, Operation Active Endeavor commences as the guided-missile cruiser *Halyburton* begins escorting civilian shipping through the Strait of Gibraltar. This activity is sponsored by NATO and includes maritime patrol aircraft from several member nations.

March 14
NAVAL: At Amphibious Naval Base Little Creek, Virginia, the Center for Naval Leadership is founded.

March 15
MILITARY: On the cusp of war with Iraq, the army deploys 57,500 men from the 3rd Infantry and 101st Airborne Divisions, while the 4th Infantry Division (Mechanized) is currently en route by water. The entire 3rd U.S. Army present in theater is commanded overall by Lieutenant General David D. McKiernan.

March 17
AVIATION: In Washington, D.C., President George W. Bush delivers an ultimatum requiring Saddam Hussein and his sons to depart from Iraq within 48 hours.

March 18–19

AVIATION: During the buildup to war, air force planes begin dropping informational leaflets on 20 civilian locations. An EC-130 Commando Solo aircraft also broadcasts messages to alert Iraqi citizens to take cover. Other aircraft begin bombing antiaircraft emplacements placed in violation of the southern no-fly zone.

March 19

AVIATION: In this first day of Operation Iraqi Freedom, naval vessels fire a total of 42 Tomahawk cruise missiles at various targets in Iraq. Several buildings thought to house Saddam Hussein, his two sons, and several ranking government officials are deliberately targeted. Air force F-117 Nighthawks also drop precision-guided munitions at communication and command centers. All told, coalition forces aircraft hit artillery, air defenses, and missile sites throughout the country.

MILITARY: Operation Iraqi Freedom begins as coalition forces, spearheaded by the United States, invade Iraq and topple the regime of dictator Saddam Hussein. Special Forces are already in theater to gather information and President George W. Bush declares that the goal of the war is the removal of Hussein from power, the destruction of all Iraqi weapons of mass destruction (WMDs), and the elimination of all terrorist elements within that country.

NAVAL: In the Persian Gulf, the guided-missile destroyers *Donald Cook* and *Milius,* the guided-missile cruisers *Cowpens* and *Bunker Hill,* and the attack submarines *Cheyenne* and *Montpelier* launch cruise missiles against Iraqi targets.

March 20

AVIATION: Approximately 500 coalition aircraft, mostly from Great Britain and the United States, begin swarming over Iraqi antiaircraft and missile radar defenses, along with command and control centers. All told, coalition air and sea forces unleash 1,000 Tomahawks and over 3,000 precision-guided munitions against Iraqi forces.

• In Kuwait, Patriot PAC-3 missiles fired by Battery D, 5th Battalion, 52nd Air Defense Artillery, shoots down two Iraqi Scud missiles headed toward 101st Airborne Division headquarters at Camp Thunder.

MILITARY: In Iraq, the 3rd Infantry Division under Major General Buford C. Blount III initiates the ground offensive by crossing into Iraq from Kuwait. Resistance is light and easily dispatched by AH-62 Apache gunships. That afternoon, the first enemy units are engaged by the 3rd Squadron, 7th Cavalry while the 3rd Battalion, 15th Infantry (3rd Division) neutralizes some enemy armored vehicles.

NAVAL: In the Persian Gulf, the guided-missile destroyer *John S. McCain* and the attack submarines *Columbia* and *Providence,* assisted by two British submarines, unleash an additional 50 Tomahawk missiles at select targets in Baghdad, Iraq. Teams of SEALS and Royal Marines are also helicoptered in for raids against the Kaabot and Mabot oil terminals.

March 20–March 27

MILITARY: In southern Afghanistan, men from the 2nd Battalion, 504th Parachute Infantry (82nd Airborne Division) under Lieutenant Colonel Charles A.

Flynn, conduct Operation Valiant Strike in the Sami Ghar Mountains. Resistance is slight and several weapons caches are seized.

March 21

AVIATION: Launching at night, aircraft from the carriers *Abraham Lincoln, Constellation, Harry S. Truman, Kitty Hawk,* and *Theodore Roosevelt* participate in the "shock and awe" campaign against the Iraqi capital of Baghdad. A further 320 Tomahawk cruise missiles are fired against various military targets.

• In the Arabian Gulf, an Iraqi fast attack patrol boat is detected and tracked by a Navy P-3 Orion of VP-46, then destroyed by an air force AC-130 Spectre gunship.

MILITARY: In southern Iraq, the 101st Airborne Division under Major General David H. Petraeus crosses the border in a mass of helicopters and ground vehicles.

• The 3rd Brigade, 3rd Infantry Division, having dashed over 100 miles into enemy territory, comes under attack at Nasiriya, Iraq. Their counterfire destroys the Iraqi 11th Infantry Division in short order and, once the 1st Brigade seizes Jalibah Airfield, it is handed over to the marines.

March 22

AVIATION: Coalition force aircraft launch over 1,000 sorties and a like number of cruise missiles at Iraqi military targets.

• Over the Arabian Gulf, two Royal Navy Sea King helicopters collide and crash; an exchange officer U.S. Navy lieutenant Thomas M. Adams, is among those killed.

MILITARY: In a news briefing, General Tommy R. Franks, commander, Central Command (CENTCOM), declares that Operation Iraqi Freedom will be waged as a campaign of "overwhelming force."

March 23

AVIATION: In the eastern Mediterranean, the long reach of the Tomahawk cruise missile is amply displayed when the guided-missile cruisers *Cape. St. George* and *Anzio,* and the guided-missile destroyer *Winston S. Churchill* begin launching missiles against targets in Iraq.

• Over Karbala, Iraq, an AH-64 Apache Longbow from the 1st Battalion, 227th Aviation regiment, is badly damaged by heavy fire from Republican Guard units and crash lands; the crew of two is captured. Chief Warrant Officer David S. Williams and Chief Warrant Officer Ronald Young are subsequently paraded in front of television.

• Over Kuwait, a Patriot antimissile battery fires and accidentally downs a Royal Air Force GR4 Tornado jet bomber. An American F-16 also knocks out a Patriot battery after its radar locks on to it; no casualties occur.

MILITARY: At Camp Pennsylvania, Kuwait, a disgruntled soldier lobs a grenade into tents, killing an Air National Guard officer and an intelligence officer. The attack wounds 14 others; the soldier is charged with two counts of premeditated murder and faces the death penalty.

• Near Nasiriya, Iraq, an 18-vehicle convoy from the 507th Maintenance Battalion goes down the wrong road and is ambushed. Of 33 soldiers present, 11 are killed and six are captured.

March 24

AVIATION: Coalition force aircraft bombard Iraqi military targets near the oil-producing center of Kirkuk for a 24-hour period.

MILITARY: Near Najaf, Iraq, the 1st Brigade, 3rd Infantry Division severs Highway 9 as Iraqi irregulars launch waves of suicide attacks against them. These are repelled with heavy losses, although the soldiers expend so much ammunition that they have to employ captured enemy weapons.

NAVAL: In the Khor Abd Allah waterway, Iraq, coalition naval forces board four Iraqi vessels carrying nearly 100 mines. The units involved come from the U.S. Navy and Army, and Coast Guard unit from Australia and Kuwait.

March 25

AVIATION: Over Iraq, a Lockheed S-3 Viking from Sea Control Squadron 38 (VS-38) directs a raid by F/A-18 Hornets from VFA-151. This is the first time the 30-year-old Viking design has seen combat and also the first time it released

Franks, Tommy   (1945–)
Army general

Tommy Ray Franks was born in Wynneville, Oklahoma, and raised in Midland, Texas. He attended the University of Texas, Austin, for two years, then dropped out to join the U.S. Army in 1965 as a private. After passing through the Artillery and Missile Officer Candidate School at Fort Sill, Oklahoma, Franks was commissioned a second lieutenant and assigned to the 9th Infantry Division in South Vietnam. He performed well under fire, winning three purple hearts, and, in 1968, he returned to Fort Sill to command an artillery battery. Franks subsequently acquired a degree in business administration from the University of Texas in 1971 and, following a three-year tour in West Germany with the 2nd Armored Cavalry Regiment, he attended the Armed Forces Staff College. In 1976 Franks served at the Pentagon as army inspector General, deployed again in Germany in 1981, and passed through the Army War College while receiving a master's degree in public administration from Shippensburg University, Pennsylvania. In 1987 he was posted as chief of staff with the 1st Cavalry Division and subsequently accompanied his unit to Saudi Arabia in 1990, seeing active duty during Operations Desert Shield/Storm. In 1995 Franks received command of the 2nd Infantry Division in South Korea, and subsequently he became commander of the Third Army Forces Central Command in Atlanta, Georgia.

In June 2000 Franks's career took a dramatic turn when he was assigned as commander, U.S. Central Command, in Tampa Florida. Since the terrorist attack upon the World Trade Center on September 11, 2001, he has played central and successful roles in the war on terrorism. Commencing in October 2001, he orchestrated Operation Enduring Freedom, which drove the

a laser-guided missile. Carrier aircraft also attack and sink the Iraqi presidential yacht *Al Mansur,* sinking it.

MILITARY: As elements begin crossing the Euphrates River at Samawah, Iraq, they are beset by intense sandstorms that makes rapid movement impossible. The advance on Baghdad slowly necessarily, and intelligence is received that Iraqi forces might employ chemical weapons against coalition forces as they approach the city.

March 26

AVIATION: In northern Iraq, Operation Northern Delay commences as 15 C-17 Globemaster IIIs insert 990 paratroopers and 20 heavy platforms onto Bashur Airfield. This act effectively opens up a second front and is also the first time that parachutists have dropped from C-17s. The crew of the lead aircraft also wins a Mackay Trophy for orchestrating such an intricate maneuver.

MILITARY: The city of Najaf, Iraq, is surrounded by two brigades of the 3rd Infantry Division; American losses are two M1A1 Abrams tanks and one M2 Bradley

Taliban regime from Afghanistan in less than 90 days with very few losses. In the spring of 2003 he was also called upon to direct Operation Iraqi Freedom to dispose of the dangerous dictator Saddam Hussein. Franks, who had been limited to only 140,000 men, conducted a lightning-quick campaign that crushed Iraqi defenses and occupied a country the size of California in less than a month. A major challenge occurred when the government of Turkey would not allow the crack 4th Division to operate from its territory. It was forced to be transported to Kuwait by boat only after the fighting subsided. At that juncture Franks sought to resign his command but he was persuaded by Secretary of Defense Donald Rumsfeld to stay on. At this time, Iraq was convulsed by several sectarian-based insurgencies and al-Qaeda terrorists, which the coalition occupation troops had difficulty suppressing. The problem was still ongoing when Franks was replaced by Lieutenant General Ricardo Sanchez in June

General Tommy Franks speaks with the media during the invasion of Iraq. (*Department of Defense*)

2003. Reputedly, he had been offered to serve as chief of staff, U.S. Army, but Franks declined. He currently resides in Roosevelt, Oklahoma, and serves on the Board of Directors of Bank of America and several other institutions. In 2004 he also published a best-selling memoir, *American Soldier.*

disabled, with one crewman killed. In time, the advances are joined by truckloads of men from the 101st Airborne Division, although the still intense sandstorms have grounded all that unit's helicopters.

• The 173rd Airborne Brigade drops nearly 1,000 parachute infantry over Bashur Airfield, Iraq, in that units first combat jump since Vietnam. They are assisted by roughly 150 men of the 10th Special Force Group (Airborne) who are helping direct air strikes against nearby targets.

March 27

AVIATION: Over Kuwait, a Patriot missile successfully intercepts and destroys an Iraqi Scud missile.

MILITARY: Once the sandstorms subside, the 3rd Infantry Division resumes its advance on Karbala, Iraq, while Iraqi irregulars tie down other units in severe fighting near Najaf.

• The 2nd Battalion, 505th Parachute Infantry (82nd Airborne Division) commences Operation Desert Lion by sweeping through the Kohe Safi Mountains near Bagram Air Base. Resistance is minimal and the soldiers uncover a large cache of 107mm rockets and machine gun munitions.

March 28

AVIATION: In the Persian Gulf, minesweeping operations are maintained by helicopters of Mine Countermeasures Squadron 14 (HN-14) and the Commander Task Unit (CMU). Consequently, the Royal Navy landing ship *Sir Galahad* is able to dock at Umm Qasr with tons of humanitarian aid for the locals.

MILITARY: Around Karbala, Iraq, AH-64 Apache Longbow helicopters from the 101st Airborne Division attack tanks belonging to the Republican Guard Medina Division.

March 29

MILITARY: At Najaf, Iraq, five soldiers from the 1st Brigade, 3rd Division, die at the hands of a suicide bomber.

• As units of the 3rd Infantry Division give battle to the Republican Guard Medina Division outside Najaf, they are increasingly harassed by irregular fedayeen fighters, who fire at them from schools, hospitals, and mosques. The irregulars are also quick to employ women and children as human shields.

NAVAL: In the Persian Gulf, the *Nassau* amphibious ready group unloads the 24th Marine Expeditionary Unit. This is the first sizable troop reinforcement to land in theater.

March 30–31

MILITARY: The American advance on Baghdad, Iraq, continues as the 2nd Brigade, 3rd Infantry Division, seizes a bridge over the Euphrates at Al Handiyah, only 50 miles from the capital. Meanwhile, the 101st Airborne Division captures the airfield at Najaf, along with several tanks and prisoners. To the rear, the 82nd Airborne Division, which is tasked with keeping American lines of supply and communication open, destroys several Iraqi artillery batteries with effective counterfire.

March 31

AVIATION: At Webster Field, St. Inigoes, Maryland, an NP-3C Orion electronically controls an Aerolight unmanned aerial vehicle (UAV). This is the first time that a fixed wing aircraft has utilized an auxiliary device for gathering military data during flight.

• Over northern Iraq, aircraft from the carrier *Theodore Roosevelt* bombard artillery emplacements, barracks, and surface-to-air missile installations.

MILITARY: In Washington, D.C., U.S. Army Chief of Staff general Eric K. Shinseki rejects proposed changes to the prevailing U.S. Army class A uniform, which has been in vogue since the late 1950s.

April

MILITARY: Throughout the United States, Operation Noble Eagle commences as National Guard and Army Reserve forces are mobilized and deployed at various sensitive areas and border regions to thwart possible terrorist attacks. This month 1.4 million soldiers have been called to the colors to keep the nation safe.

April 1

AVIATION: Over Iraq, a Patriot missile successfully shoots down an Iraqi Scud missile fired at American forces. This is also the first Patriot success outside of Kuwait.

MILITARY: A quick raid on the hospital at Nasiriya, Iraq, by Special Forces frees Private First Class Jessica Lynch, who had been wounded and captured when the 507th Maintenance Company was ambushed. A sweep of the hospital ground also uncovers the bodies of seven soldiers killed earlier.

NAVAL: The raid on the hospital at Nasiriya, Iraq, is assisted by Navy SEALS and Marine reconnaissance units.

April 2

AVIATION: Over Kuwait, a Patriot missile battery inadvertently locks onto a Navy F/A-18 Hornet jet fighter of VFA-195 (*Kitty Hawk*), killing the pilot. Apparently, a software error caused the radar to misidentify the aircraft as an incoming missile. Lieutenant Nathan White dies in consequence.

• Over Iraq, B-52s drop CBU-105 cluster bombs on Iraqi tank units. These are armor-piercing, sensor-fused weapons and deadly to massed tank formations.

MILITARY: In the latest friendly fire incident, three soldiers of the 1st Battalion, 39th Field Artillery are killed when an F-15C fighter bomber mistakes their MLRS missile launcher for a Soviet-designed Iraqi vehicle and directs a laser-guided GBU-12 to bomb to it.

April 3

MILITARY: The 1st Brigade, 3rd Infantry Division, rumbles through the Karaba Gap, seizes the Yasin al Khudayr bridge over the Euphrates River, and captures Saddam International Airport. Simultaneously, the 101st Airborne Division and the 2nd Brigade, 82nd Airborne Division, engage Iraqi irregular forces that have emerged in the 3rd Infantry Division's wake.

April 4

MILITARY: Men from the 1st Brigade, 3rd Infantry Division, attack and destroy members of the Special Republican Guards occupying Saddam International Airport. A 12-hour battle ensues during which the Americans lose one dead and eight wounded while enemy losses are estimated at 250.

- In the course of heavy fighting around Saddam International Airport, Sergeant First Class Paul R. Smith, Company B, 11th Engineer Battalion, is killed while manning a .50-caliber machine gun. However, he stopped several Republican Guard attacks while American wounded were being evacuated, and he is the only soldier from Operation Iraqi Freedom to be recommended for the Medal of Honor.

April 5

AVIATION: Off the California coast, the guided-missile destroyer *Stethem* launches the first Tactical Tomahawk, the navy's newest version of this potent weapon system.

MILITARY: The 3rd Infantry Division dispatches two battalions on a quick raid into downtown Baghdad, before withdrawing them to the west to join the 1st Brigade. Meanwhile, Central Command (CENTCOM) announces that 6,500 Iraqi prisoners are currently in their hands.

April 6

MILITARY: Near Ibril, northern Iraq, artillery attached to the 173rd Airborne Brigade silences Iraqi artillery positions in a short but deadly duel.

- On a plateau between Ibril and Makhmur, northern Iraq, a force of 31 Special Forces, reinforced by Kurdish guerrillas, repel attacks by Iraqi infantry and armor with Javelin missiles. Unfortunately, an errant bomb dropped by naval aircraft kills 19 Kurdish fighters and wounds 40.

April 7

AVIATION: Acting on a tip that Iraqi dictator Saddam Hussein and his two sons are lodged in a building in the Mansur district of Baghdad, Iraq, a B-1B Lancer from the 34th Bomb Squadron drops four GBU-31 satellite-guided joint direct attack munitions (JDAM) on the premises, destroying it. Hussein is not there but the attack kills several senior Iraqi leaders.

- A C-130 Hercules brings the first army troops into Baghdad International Airport under the over of darkness.

MILITARY: In a ferocious fight, the 2nd Brigade, 3rd Infantry Division advances into the heart of central Baghdad and crushes all resistance from the Republican Guards along Highway 8. Four Americans die and 30 are wounded in exchange for an estimated 600 Iraqis killed. The Republican Palace, the actual seat of Saddam Hussein's regime, is also captured and occupied.

April 8

AVIATION: Iraqi ground fire brings down an A-10 Thunderbolt II over Baghdad, although the pilot escapes capture and is secured by coalition forces near the airport. However, a surface-to-air missile destroys an F-15E Strike Eagle, killing both crewmen.

MILITARY: The balance of the 3rd Division consolidates its grip on Baghdad, Iraq, by occupying the west bank of the Tigris River. The Iraqis subsequently attack these positions in a variety of trucks, tanks, and buses, but they are repelled by the Americans, backed by U.S. Air Force close air support, losing several hundred men. Two journalists also die when an M1A1 Abrams tank alerted that there are Iraqis firing from the Palestine Hotel, opens fire.

April 9

MILITARY: As marines advance into Baghdad, Iraq, and link up with elements of the 3rd Division, the city is considered fully occupied. Jubilant Iraqis also tear down a massive statue of Saddam Hussein. The image is broadcast around the world.

April 10

MILITARY: As organized Iraqi resistance collapses, American Special Forces and Kurdish fighters occupy the northern city of Kirkuk. They are soon joined by the 173rd Airborne Brigade, which secures several gas-oil separation plants and oil wells. The 82nd and 101st Airborne Division continue with mop-up operations around Samawah and Karbala, respectively.

April 11

AVIATION: At Peterson Air Force Base, Colorado, the army activates the 1st Space Brigade, the army's first-ever space unit.
• Over Iraq, a B-52 resorts to a Litening II advanced airborne targeting and navigation pod to strike Iraqi facilities at an airfield.
MILITARY: Army and marine forces begin active patrols to discourage widespread looting in Baghdad and Kirkuk, Iraq. Meanwhile, Special Forces teams arrange a truce between themselves and the Iraqi V Corps near Mosul, while an Iraqi colonel surrenders the border crossing at Highways 10 and 11 near Syria. An active hunt for weapons caches in the area ensues, which turns up several tons of ballistic missiles and heavy weapons.
NAVAL: At Naval Amphibious Base Little Creek, Virginia, the amphibious dock landing ship *Portland* is the first vessel to return from active duty during Operation Iraqi Freedom.

April 12

MILITARY: American efforts to restore law and order are thwarted by an epidemic of looting in Baghdad, Kirkuk, and Mosul, Iraq. General Amir Saadi is also captured, becoming the highest-ranking Iraqi captured, while the 3rd Infantry Division skirmishes with various militia groups.

April 13

MILITARY: Near Samarra, Iraq, several American captives have been released by the Iraqis and are found walking along a road until discovered by marines combing the area. They include the two Apache crewmen shot down on March 23.

April 14

MILITARY: CENTCOM leader General Tommy Franks declares that all organized resistance has ended in Iraq and that all major towns and cities are under coalition control. Army troops are occupied with searching for weapons of mass destruction while engineers begin the task of rebuilding the country's shattered infrastructure. As a bonus, Special Forces and 3rd Infantry Division soldiers capture Mohammed Abas (Abu Abbas) who had masterminded the highjacking of the Italian liner *Achille Lauro* and murdered American citizen Leon Klinghofer.
• A rather tardy 4th Infantry Division under Major General Raymond T. Odierno crosses into Iraq from assembly areas in Kuwait. It subsequently forms the core of Task Force Iron Horse in concert with other armored units.

April 16
Aviation: At Baghdad International Airport, Iraq, a P-3 Orion patrol plane of VP-46 is the first navy aircraft to land there. It is carrying the commander, U.S. Naval Forces Central Command, Vice Admiral Timothy Keating.
Diplomacy: In Washington, D.C., President George W. Bush calls upon the UN Security Council to end all sanctions imposed against Iraq.
Military: General Tommy Franks, the senior American ground commander, enters Baghdad for the first time.

April 19
Military: The 4th Division, advancing northward, encounters pockets of resistance from Iraqi paramilitaries between Taji and Samara; they destroy eight armed trucks and seize 30 prisoners. An unmanned surveillance drone also captures television images of fedayeen guerrillas loading ammunition stores onto trucks.
•   In Baghdad, Iraq, soldiers from the 3rd Infantry Division uncover a stash of $656 million in U.S. $100 bills. The neighborhood in question is home to many high-ranking Iraqi officials.

April 20
Military: With the Iraqi missile threat to Israel over, troops of the 5th battalion, 7th Air Defense Artillery begin rotating back to bases in Hanau, Germany.

April 22
Naval: In Hawaii, the guided-missile frigate *Crommelin* reports to home base after a six-month cruise during which it seized six tons of narcotics worth $183 million, and also rescued 157 Ecuadorians from their sinking vessel and transported them home.

April 25
Military: In Washington, D.C., Leslie Brownlee becomes acting secretary of the army to replace outgoing Thomas White, who has enjoyed stormy relations with Secretary of Defense Donald Rumsfeld.

April 30
Naval: On Puerto Rico, the navy transfers all its property on the eastern end of Vieques Island to the Department of the Interior, which intends to develop it into a wildlife refuge.

May
Aviation: The air force declares its intention to lease 100 Boeing KC-767 tankers to replace its aging fleet of KC-135s.

May 1
Aviation: Operation Northern Watch, begun as a no-fly zone over northern Iraq on January 1, 1997, ends.
Naval: President George W. Bush lands onboard the deck of the carrier *Abraham Lincoln* off the California coast and announces an end to all offensive military operations in Iraq. "Mission accomplished!" he declares to loud applause.

May 4
Military: In the wake of tornadoes and flooding in Missouri, Kansas, Tennessee, and Alabama, National Guard troops are called into action to assist in disaster relief efforts.

May 6
Naval: At Bremerton, Washington, the carrier *Abraham Lincoln* returns to port after 10 months at sea, a record deployment for a nuclear-powered carrier. During this period the vessel and its aircrews participated in Operation Southern Watch, Enduring Freedom, and Iraqi Freedom—then capped efforts off by briefly hosting the commander in chief.

May 7
Military: In Washington, D.C., Air Force Secretary James G. Roche is nominated to serve as the new secretary of the army.

May 13
Military: The army makes public an incident along the Demilitarized Zone (DMS), South Korea, when a laser was flashed at pilots of a pair of AH-64 Apache helicopters on patrol. Military intelligence suggests that the device was Chinese in origin and specifically designed to injure human eyesight.

May 14
Military: Redeployment of the 3rd Infantry Division is halted in the face of continuing unrest and violence throughout Baghdad, Iraq. Security of the city is the responsibility of the 1st Armored Division under Major General Ricardo S. Sanchez, but the 3rd Infantry will now assist with that task.

May 15
Military: In northern Iraq, Operation Planet X in executed by the 1st Brigade, 4th Infantry Division, against a village 11 miles south of Tikrit. They seize 260 suspected Baath Party members along with General Mahdi Adil Abdallah, one of the coalition's most wanted.

June 1
Military: Iranians seize four soldiers of the 1092nd Engineer Battalion as they cruised along the Shatt al Arab waterway separating Iran from Iraq. The men were blindfolded and interrogated, then released the following day.

June 3
Military: In Baghdad, Iraq, army engineers begin searching a large bomb crater for any trace of Saddam Hussein's remains.

June 9–13
Military: In Balad, Iraq, Operation Peninsula Strike unfolds as Task Force Iron Horse, including the 3rd Brigade, 4th Infantry Division, the 173rd Airborne Brigade, and the 3rd Squadron, 7th Cavalry (3rd Infantry Division), execute raids to seize any remaining Baath Party members. On the final day of operations, the 3rd Squadron engages a force of armed Iraqis, killing 20 in a one-sided firefight.

June 14
Military: In Baghdad, Iraq, Major General Ricardo S. Sanchez, commanding the 1st Armored Division, gains promotion to lieutenant general in charge of V Corps. He also succeeds General Tommy Franks as head of the Multi-National Force–Iraq.

June 16
Military: In Baghdad, Iraq, Brigadier General Martin E. Dempsey is appointed the new commander of the 1st Armored Division.

Thirty-foot tall bronze sculptures of former Iraqi dictator Saddam Hussein rest on the grounds of the Republican Palace, in the International Zone located in Central Baghdad, Iraq. The sculptures once capped the towers of the palace but have since been removed, following the overthrow of the Saddam Hussein regime. *(Department of Defense)*

June 18
MILITARY: North of Baghdad, Iraq, soldiers of the 4th Infantry Division raid two farmhouses and uncover $8.5 million in U.S. dollars and $400 million in Iraqi dinars. They also take into custody 20 men, including several of Saddam's personal body guard, and seize weapons and another $1 million in jewelry.

June 29–July 7
MILITARY: In light of continuing insurgent attacks against American convoys on Highways 1 and 2 north of Baghdad, Operation Sidewinder is undertaken by the 4th Division to apprehend the transgressors. When the operation concludes, a total of 282 prisoners have been secured along with many weapons and tons of ammunition.

July 7
MILITARY: In Baghdad, Iraq, General Tommy Franks is replaced as CENTCOM commander by General John P. Abizaid, former deputy head of Combined Forces Command.

July 9
TERRORISM: The U.S. Court of Appeals upholds the president's right to designate American citizens captured in combat as "enemy combatants," and subject them to indefinite confinement without legal representation.

Sanchez, Ricardo   (1951–)
Army general

Ricardo Sanchez was born at Fort Myer, Florida, in 1951 and raised in Rio Grande City, Texas, a son of Hispanic parents. He enrolled in the Reserve Officer Training Corps (ROTC) while attending the University of Texas–Kingsville, and he was commissioned a second lieutenant in 1973. While in school Sanchez was named a Distinguished Military Graduate, an honor reserved for the top 10 percent of all ROTC graduates. He initially served as a platoon leader in the elite 82nd Airborne Division although in 1977 he transferred to the armor branch. When Operation Desert Storm commenced in January 1991, Sanchez commanded the 197th Infantry Brigade (Mechanized), which assisted in the capture of the Iraqi port of Basra. Soon afterward he advanced to colonel in charge of the 2nd Brigade, 1st Infantry Division. Sanchez left field operations to accept a position within the U.S. Southern Command as deputy chief of staff and director of operations. He then rose to major general and accepted command of the elite 1st Armored Division as part of the V Corps in Germany. He served there for two years before assuming command of the entire V Corps. It was while acting at this post that he received the most daunting challenge of his career in June 2003: commander of the Multi-National Force–Iraq.

Iraq had been ruled by dictator Saddam Hussein, who quickly eliminated political or religious dissenters, whether they were Arab or Kurd, Shia or Sunni. After he was deposed following Operation Iraqi Freedom, these simmering resentments surfaced

General Ricardo Sanchez (*U.S. Army*)

in an intractable insurgency aimed at occupying forces and each other. The Americans, previously greeted as liberators, now found themselves under increasing attack. As commander, it was Sanchez's responsibility to maintain order and orchestrate reconstruction efforts, a task made doubly difficult by his strained relations with L. Paul Bremer, head of the Coalition Provisional Authority. Worse, news of American misconduct toward Iraqi prisoners held at the Abu Ghraib prison came to light and Sanchez, though he denied any culpability, was nonetheless in charge and held respon-

(continues)

(continued)

sible for it. The Americans scored some notable success against al-Qaeda operatives in Iraq, as well as capturing Saddam and killing his two sons, but Sanchez could not shake the stigma of Abu Ghraib. After relinquishing control to General George Casey in June 2004, he resumed commanding the V Corps in Germany, longer than any other incumbent, but he was denied his fourth star to full general. On September 6, 2006, he turned over the V Corps to a superior officer, rather than to a successor, and he ended a distinguished 33 years of military service by resigning. Sanchez presently resides in Texas. Sanchez afterward launched a personal campaign in which he lambasted the media for its "sensationalist tendencies." In 2008 he also published his memoir, *Wiser In Battle: A Soldier's Story,* which excoriates President George W. Bush's policies and handling of affairs in Iraq.

July 12–17

MILITARY: In northern Iraq, Operation Soda Mountain is launched by the 4th Division, the 101st Infantry Division, and the 3rd Armored Cavalry to capture insurgents and their cadres. In 141 raids throughout the region, 600 prisoners are seized, including 62 former regime leaders, along with weapons and ammunition.

July 16

MILITARY: In Baghdad, Iraq, General John P. Abizaid declares that the Americans are now engaged in a guerrilla war with supporters of the previous regime, whose tactics and attacks are increasingly sophisticated. Fanatical Muslims fighting under the banner of al-Qaeda are also entering Iraq from abroad to commit acts of terrorism. In light of declining morale in the 3rd Infantry Division, the general also states that it will be rotating back to the United States by September.

July 22

MILITARY: Detachments from the 101st Airborne Division track down and kill Saddam Hussein's two brutal sons, Uday and Qusay, in Mosul, northern Iraq. They received an anonymous tip as to their whereabouts from the local populace.

August 3

MILITARY: In Washington, D.C., General Peter J. Schoomaker, previously commander of the U.S. Special Operations School, is appointed the new army chief of staff.

August 6

MILITARY: In Baghdad, Iraq, men of the 4th Infantry Division discover a large cache of rockets, mortar rounds, small arms, and ammunition.

August 18

MILITARY: At Fort Benning, Georgia, Specialist Liana Bombardier is the first woman to win the National Long-Range Rifle Championship in the century-old history of the competition. She walks off with the prestigious Billy C. Atkins Trophy.

• In Baghdad, Iraq, men of the 2nd Brigade, 1st Armored Division, uncover a large weapons cache, including 20 pounds of C-4 plastic explosives, outside their lines.

August 22

MILITARY: The last elements of the 3rd Infantry Division return to Fort Stewart, Georgia, following a two-year deployment in the Middle East in the war against terrorism.

August 24

MILITARY: Near Missoula, Montana, men of the 82nd Field Artillery, 1st Cavalry Division, assist in the containment of a large wildfire.

August 26

MILITARY: In Khalis, Iraq, the 2nd Brigade, 4th Infantry Division under Colonel David Hogg commences Operation Ivy Needle to corral a gang of criminals who have been attacking coalition forces and Iraqi police; 24 members are rounded up.

August 29

AVIATION: The last of 14 Defense Satellite Communications System (DSCS III) satellites is placed in orbit, finishing a project that was begun in 1981.

August 31

MILITARY: At the Anniston Army Depot, Alabama, workers begin burning stocks of chemical weapons, especially the nerve agent Sarin, from 600 M55 rockets. This also marks the first time that the army has deactivated chemical weapons in a populated area.

September 10

MILITARY: At Guantánamo, Cuba, James Yee, a Muslim chaplin, is arrested and charged with espionage in connection with aiding Islamic terrorists in captivity and carrying classified information. Yee is a former West Point graduate. All charges against him are eventually dropped.

September 12

MILITARY: At Fort Stewart, Georgia, President George W. Bush awards a Presidential Unit Citation to the 3rd Infantry Division for its lengthy service in Iraq.

September 30

MILITARY: The headquarters of U.S. Army South transfers from Puerto Rico to Fort Sam Houston, Texas, where it also changes from a Major Army Command to a Major Subordinate Army Command within the U.S. Forces Command.

• In Bosnia-Herzegovina, a unit of 1,100 soldiers from the 34th Infantry Division, Minnesota National Guard, are deployed for service as part of NATO's Stabilization Force (SFOR). For the 34th Division, this is the largest single overseas deployment since World War II.

October 1

MILITARY: The army, responding to the new National Call to Service Act passed by Congress in 2002, initiates a pilot program allowing new recruits to sign on for only 15 months of active duty. They remain at liberty to enlist for the usual two, three, four, five, or six years.

Abizaid, John P.   (1951–)
Army general

John Philip Abizaid was born in Coleville, California, on April 1, 1951, and he graduated from the U.S. Military Academy in 1973. He served as a second lieutenant in the 504th Parachute Infantry Regiment, rose to command a company, and distinguished himself during the U.S.-led invasion of Grenada in 1983. During the first Gulf War of 1991, Abizaid commanded a battalion in the 325th Airborne Regimental Combat Team stationed at Vicenza, Italy, and he subsequently served in northern Iraq while assisting the Kurds. Abizaid handled his affairs adroitly and commanded a brigade in the elite 82nd Airborne Division and also served as assistant commander of the 1st Armored Division in Bosnia-Herzegovina. In 1997 Abizaid returned to West Point as its 66th commandant, where he updated the curricula and clamped down on hazing abuses. He subsequently returned to Bosnia commanding the famous 1st Infantry Division,

parts of which deployed there as part of a UN-sponsored peacekeeping mission. At various times in his career, Abizaid studied at the Armed Forces Staff College, the U.S. Army War College, and he also received a master's degree in Middle Eastern studies from Harvard University. Abizaid is one of a handful of senior army officers to attain fluency in Arabic, having studied at the University of Jordan in Amman.

During the initial phases of Operation Iraqi Freedom in the spring of 2003, Abizaid served with the Deputy Command (Forward), Combined Forces Command, U.S. Central Command. On July 7, 2003, he gained promotion to full general and succeeded outgoing General Tommy Franks as commander of the Central Command. This command organization oversees the activities of 250,000 U.S. troops across a 27-nation arc stretching from the Horn of Africa, through the Arabian Peninsula, to South and Central Asia. It figures promi-

October 2
TERRORISM: David Kay, the chief U.S. weapons inspector, informs Congress that the Iraq Survey Group has yet to uncover demonstrable proof of weapons of mass destruction (WMD), be they biological, chemical, or nuclear.

October 2–5
MILITARY: The army's Total Personnel Command and the Reserve Personnel Command are joined as the new U.S. Army Human Resources Command; shortly afterward, the U.S. Army Civilian Human Resources Agency also is created.

October 31
MILITARY: A protracted insurgency rages in occupied Iraq, resulting in the deaths of 120 American personnel and 1,100 wounded by this date. The most insidious weapon used is the improvised explosive device (IED) placed alongside roadways and detonated when military columns pass by.

2003

nently in military matters pertaining to the war on terror. No armchair general, Abizaid was a frequent visitor to Iraq and Afghanistan to help direct operations against Muslim extremists and terrorists operating in that region. For four years he helped to craft the strategy necessary to fight al-Qaeda in Iraq and the Taliban, based in Pakistan, with varying degrees of success. Like most senior American leaders, Abizaid was taken aback by the tenacity of the insurgents, who suffered heavy losses at the hands of coalition troops but were never quite eradicated. He expressed his unhappiness with the current affairs before the Senate Armed Services Committee in August 2006, and he admitted that civil war in Iraq seemed very likely. Concurrently, Abizaid also contended with a rising tide of Muslim piracy in the Persian Gulf and Red Sea regions, which further threatened to undermine regional security and stability. On December 20, 2006, Abizaid announced his retirement from Central Command. He was replaced by

General John Abizaid (U.S. Army)

Admiral William J. Fallon. He serves as a Fellow at the Hoover Institute at Stanford University, California.

November 2
AVIATION: Over Fallujah, Iraq, a shoulder-fired surface-to-air missile brings down an army CH-47 Chinook helicopter, killing 16 soldiers and injuring 26.

November 5
MILITARY: The army releases a new rotation plan to move troops stationed stateside and in Germany to Iraq and Afghanistan. These plans entail the services of 37,000 National Guard forces.

November 12
MILITARY: In Kuwait, the 3rd Brigade, 2nd Infantry Division arrives under the aegis of Colonel Michael E. Rounds. This is also the first organized Stryker brigade deployed abroad; in light of the Iraqi insurgency, many of the wheeled Strykers are equipped with slatted armor to protect them against rocket-propelled grenades.

November 15
AVIATION: Over Mosul, Iraq, a pair of UH-60 Black Hawk helicopters crash, killing 17 soldiers and injuring five. The reasons behind the accident are unexplained.

November 27
MILITARY: In Baghdad, Iraq, President George W. Bush makes a surprise Thanksgiving appearance at Baghdad International Airport, and he enjoys dinner with members of the 101st Airborne Division.

December 4
MILITARY: At Abu Gjurayb, Iraq, Operation Bulldog Mammoth unfolds as the 2nd Battalion, 70th Armor (4th Division), 1st Battalion, 325th Airborne Infantry (82nd Airborne Division) and the 70th Military Police Battalion raid apartment complexes northwest of Baghdad looking for terror suspects; 40 individuals are taken into custody along with numerous weapons.

December 6
MILITARY: In Philadelphia, Pennsylvania, the U.S. Military Academy football team completes its worst-ever season by losing to U.S. Navy 34-6, and ending the year 0-13.

December 8
MILITARY: In Ad Duluyiyah, Iraq, two soldiers from the 3rd Brigade, 2nd Infantry Division are killed when their Stryker vehicle accidentally rolls down an embankment and into a canal. While not combat-related, these are the 2nd Infantry Division's first fatalities.

December 13
MILITARY: Soldiers belonging to the 1st Brigade, 4th Division (Mechanized), commence Operation Red dawn by searching the village of Ad Dawr, southeast of Tikrit. They capture fugitive Iraqi president Saddam Hussein as he hides in his "spider hole."

December 15
AVIATION: In Washington, D.C., the Stephen F. Udar-Hazt Center is opened to the public by the National Air and Space Museum, Smithsonian Institution. Located near Dulles International Airport, it is destined to house 80 percent of the Smithsonian's aircraft collection.

December 17
MILITARY: At Camp Lemonier, Djibouti, Company B, 3rd Infantry, deploys as part of Combined Joint Task Force–Horn of Africa. This is the unit's first overseas hitch since the Vietnam War, and they are there to perform humanitarian aid work as well as to help defeat terrorist activities.

December 29
MILITARY: *Time* magazine votes "The American Soldier" as "Person of the Year." So far this year 450 Americans have been killed in combat operations in Iraq while 8,000 have been wounded in fighting a protracted Sunni-based insurgency.

2003

2004

January

MILITARY: Army personnel rates are steady at 494,000 officers and men, although over 100,000 of these are deployed overseas. Iraq and Afghanistan remain the military's largest source of operations.

January 2

AVIATION: Near Fallujah, Iraq, ground fire downs an OH-58D Kiowa Warrior helicopter belonging to the 1st Battalion, 82nd Aviation Regiment. Captain and pilot Kimberly N. Hampton is the first female helicopter pilot to die in Operation Iraqi Freedom.

January 8

AVIATION: Over Fallujah, a medivac UH-60 Black Hawk helicopter of C Troop, 1st Squadron, 17th Cavalry goes down, apparently after being hit by a ground-launched missile; all nine occupants are killed.

January 12

MILITARY: The government announces a plan to provide Mauritania and Mali with $100 million in military assistance. Within a month members of the 1st Battalion, 10th Special Forces, will deploy there as advisers.

January 15

MILITARY: Kenneth O. Preston becomes the army's 13th sergeant major of the army.

January 16

MILITARY: Negotiations between the United States and South Korea result in an agreement allowing the Americans to redeploy south of the Demilitarized Zone (DMZ) for the first time since 1953. Most army units will be concentrated outside of Seoul at Camp Humphreys.

January 19

MILITARY: At Fort Bragg, North Carolina, the 2nd Brigade, 82nd Airborne Division arrives home after a long tour of duty in Iraq.

January 28

MILITARY: In Washington, D.C. General Peter J. Shoolmaker explains the army's new organization plan to the House Armed Services Committee. Under this scheme, each of the 10 divisional headquarters will be retained but each division will now consist of four brigades, each with permanently assigned field artillery, signal, and engineering components.

January 29

MILITARY: In Gahzni, Afghanistan, seven soldiers die when a weapons cache accidentally explodes.

February

AVIATION: Over Edwards Air Force Base, California, an F/A-22 aircraft undergoes an icing test at altitude by being sprayed with water from a modified KC-135 tanker. This is the first aircraft employed for such testing.

February 1

MILITARY: In Würzburg, Germany, the first elements of the 1st Infantry Division begin departing for a tour in Iraq under Major General John R. S. Batiste. Most of the division's heavy equipment will remain behind as it will be utilizing armored humvees and small arms to combat the insurgency. These troops, in concert with the 2nd Brigade, 25th Infantry Division and the 30th Separate Heavy Brigade, will also form the core element of Task Force Iron Danger to replace Task Force Iron Horse.

February 6

MILITARY: In Washington, D.C., the Department of Defense creates a Korean Service Medal for all military personnel who served in Korea after the Korean conflict (1950–53).

February 12

MILITARY: At Fort Lewis, Washington, National Guard Specialist Ryan G. Anderson, Company A, 1st Battalion, 303rd Armor Regiment, is arrested for attempting to pass classified information to al-Qaeda.

• At Fallujah, Iraq, General John P. Abizaid comes under hostile rocket and small arms fire while visiting a civil defense post. Soldiers of the 82nd Airborne Division fire back, but no casualties are incurred.

February 14

AVIATION: At Elmendorf Air Force Base, Alaska, F-15 fighters and 150 ground support crews begin deploying to Gwalior Air Force Station, India, for training exercises with the Indian air force. This constitutes the first such joint venture between the two services in 40 years.

MILITARY: At Fort Campbell, Kentucky, the 101st Airborne Division under Major General David Petraeus rotates home after a lengthy tour of duty in Iraq; the division suffered 58 fatalities during Operation Iraqi Freedom.

February 16

MILITARY: At Fort Benning, Georgia, the prototype XM-8 rifle undergoes vigorous testing at the Infantry Center. The army is seeking a replacement for its M-16 rifle, which has seen steady service since the Vietnam War.

February 23

MILITARY: After 20 years in development and $20 billion spent, General Peter J. Shoolmaker cancels the army's RAH-66 Comanche helicopter program, leaving the service to contend with existing AH-64 Apaches and OH-58D Kiowa Warriors.

February 26

MILITARY: In Washington, D.C., the War Department approves the Global War on Terrorism Expeditionary Medal for personnel deployed to Afghanistan or Iraq, and the Global War on Terrorism Service Medal for those who participated in any homeland security activities.

March 4

MILITARY: At Fort Stewart, Georgia, the 3rd Infantry Division returns after a lengthy tour of duty in Iraq. However, personnel are notified that they will be redeployed there commencing November 2004.

March 6
MILITARY: Near the Afghan-Pakistani border, nine Taliban fighters are killed after a group of 40 tries to overrun a Special Forces sniper outpost.

March 10
MILITARY: In Washington, D.C., James Roche, smarting over the fact that he has been kept waiting for Senate confirmation of his appointment as secretary of the army, withdraws his name from consideration.

March 10–23
MILITARY: In Athens, Greece, 400 Special Forces personnel participate in Operation Shield of Hercules to provide security during the 2004 Olympics there.

March 14
MILITARY: In northeastern Iraq, a patrol from the 4th Infantry Division exchanges fire with Iranian border guards; no casualties result.

March 26–April 10
MILITARY: At the National Training Center, Fort Urwin, California, the 2nd Brigade, 3rd Infantry Division becomes the first unit selected to be reorganized and tested under the new tactical structure. It is also slated for deployment in Iraq in the fall.

March 28
MILITARY: In Ghanzi, Afghanistan, men of the 10th Mountain Division uncover a cache of Taliban grenades, mines, and mortar rounds. Simultaneously, a detachment from the 3rd Battalion, 6th Field Artillery discovers 2,000 rifles and stores of ammunition while searching a house in Kandahar.

March 31
MILITARY: In Baghdad, Iraq, the advanced elements of the 1st Cavalry Division under Major General Peter W. Chiarelli arrive in Iraq to replace the 1st Armored Division. Meanwhile, the 1st Brigade, 1st Infantry Division, and the National Guard 81st Armored Brigade join the 1st Marine Expeditionary Force in a sweep against militant strongholds in Fallujah and Ramadi.

April 2
MILITARY: The army announces that its recruitment goals have been met for the previous year, despite the ongoing conflicts in Iraq and Afghanistan. Moreover, it is well on its way to meet the current year's goals as well.

April 4
MILITARY: In Baghdad, Iraq, men of the 1st Brigade, 1st Cavalry Division shoot it out with a large insurgent force in the downtown area; seven Americans die and 51 are injured. Enemy losses are unknown.

April 9
MILITARY: Two soldiers from the 724th Transportation Company are captured by Iraqi insurgents after an ambush; both are subsequently murdered in captivity.
• In Baghdad, Iraq, Specialist Michelle Witmer, 32nd Military Police Company (Wisconsin) is killed by an improvised explosive device; she is the first female National Guard soldier killed in army history and the first Wisconsin National Guard member to die since World War II.

April 15

MILITARY: An upsurge in violence throughout Iraq results in extended tours for 20,000 soldiers previously scheduled to be rotated home. All have their tours of duty extended by 90 days.

April 16

AVIATION: Near Kharbut, Iraq, two CH-47 Chinook helicopters crash in a sandstorm but the crew are rescued by MH-53Js. During the operation, the helicopters had to dodge surface-to-air missiles fired from below, along with blinding sand that reduced visibility to zero. The rescue crews win the Mackay Trophy.

April 22

MILITARY: At Fort Hood, Texas, the 4th Infantry Division (Mechanized) comes home after a tour of duty in Iraq; it lost 79 soldiers in combat operations.

Casey, George W.   (1948–   )
Army general

George William Casey, Jr., was born in Sendai, Japan, on July 22, 1948, during the U.S. occupation of that country. His father, George W. Casey, Sr., was a West Point graduate who rose to major general and died in Vietnam when his helicopter crashed in July 1970. Casey grew up in south Boston, Massachusetts, and enrolled in Reserve Officer Training Course (ROTC) while acquiring his bachelor's degree from Georgetown University. As a second lieutenant, he served the initial part of his career with the Mechanized Infantry, rising to brigadier general commanding the 3rd brigade of the 1st Cavalry Division. Casey subsequently served as the assistant division commander of the 1st Armored Division in Germany, and he deployed with his men in Bosnia-Herzegovina between July 1996 and August 1997 for peacekeeping duties. He rose to major general and assumed control of the 1st Armored Division in July 1999, performing

competently for the next two years. In July 2001 Casey transferred to the Pentagon to serve as director of strategic plans and policy with the Joint Chiefs of Staff. In January 2003 he joined the Joint Staff as its director, and he became the 30th vice chief of staff of the army in October 2003. He held that post until June 2004 when he received the challenging appointment to command the Multinational Force Iraq.

Casey replaced outgoing Lieutenant General Ricardo Sanchez in Baghdad and was compelled to grapple with the same problems as his predecessor. Warring ethnic and religious factions within Iraqi society were attacking each other while Sunni-based al-Qaeda terrorists attacked occupation troops and Shia-based terrorists, armed and agitated by Iran, were also active. Casey's sought to encourage Iraqis to shoulder increasing responsibility for their own security. To that end he focused on train-

April 29
MILITARY: In Washington, D.C., the National World War II Memorial opens at the National Mall. It was constructed at a cost of $172 million and will be officially commemorated on May 29, during Memorial Day weekend.

June 7–16
AVIATION: In Alaska, over 9,000 airmen, sailors, marines, soldiers, and men of the coast Guard are mustered in to participate in Operation Northern Edge, that state's largest annual exercise.

June 23
AVIATION: At Cape Canaveral, a Delta II, three-stage launch vehicle places a replacement satellite for the Air Force Global Positioning System (GPS).

July 23
AVIATION: In the Caribbean, an HC-130 from the 38th Rescue Squadron airdrops two pararescue men who deploy a rubber boat and paddle to a Chinese fishing vessel to treat a crewman who had sustained a life-threatening chest injury.

ing the demoralized Iraqi military, and he kept U.S. forces in the background. He also publicly stated that the national elections of December 2005 held the potential to unify that nation and allow for an expedited withdrawal of American forces, but his expectations were dashed by increased sectarian violence. When President George W. Bush announced his plans for a troop "surge" to reinforce occupying forces in January 2007, Casey went on record opposing it, feeling that a heightened American visibility might actually fuel the insurgency. He was replaced as coalition commander on February 10, 2007, by General David H. Petraeus. Two days earlier, however, the Senate approved his appointment as the new chief of staff of the army in Washington, D.C., replacing General Peter Schoomaker. In September 2007, Casey raised political eyebrows again by stating that the concurrent deployments in Iraq and Afghanistan were wearing the army thin and taking a toll on military families, who were enduring 15-month tours of duty. As

General George Casey, Jr. *(U.S. Army)*

the army's top officer, he remains a blunt and outspoken advocate for that service and its members.

August 7–17

MARINES: Marines surround and attack supporters of Shiite leader Moktada al-Sadr in the holy city of Najaf, Iraq, killing nearly 600 fighters.

September 4–8

AVIATION: After a hurricane strikes Patrick Air Force Base, members of the 45th Space Wing response team begin surveying the damage.

September 14

AVIATION: During a Thunderbird exhibition at Mountain Home Air Force Base, Idaho, an F-16 suddenly bursts into flames and the pilot is forced to eject. None of the 60,000 spectators below are hurt.

September 15

AVIATION: In Washington, D.C., ground-breaking ceremonies are held for the site of the Air Force Memorial. It is located near the Potomac River, directly across from the Pentagon.

November 7–18

MILITARY: Army troops numbering upward of 15,000 surround the Sunni stronghold of Fallujah, Iraq, and attack, systematically killing 1,600 Muslim terrorists at a cost of 38 dead and 275 wounded. This action breaks the back of the armed insurgency in this region.

December 3

AVIATION: Over Edwards Air Force Base, California, the Airborne Laser (ABL) aircraft flies for the first time with an integrated battle management and Beam Control/Fire Control (BC/FC) systems in place. This aircraft is designed to shoot down missiles while they are still in the launch phase.

December 12

AVIATION: At Edwards Air Force Base, California, the Airborne Laser (ABL) team announces a successful series of tests with its high-energy beam weapon.

2005

January 1

NAVAL: The carrier *Abraham Lincoln* and its escort vessel arrive off Aceh Province, Indonesia, devastated by a tidal wave, to support humanitarian efforts. Onboard helicopters begin rushing medicine and supplies ashore.

January 3–8

AVIATION: In Sri Lanka, A C-17 Globemaster III aircraft delivers a pair of HH-60G Pave Hawk helicopters to facilitate rescue efforts following a destructive tsunami there. Concurrently, C-130s fly in from Japan to bring 145 tons of relief supplies.

January 12

MILITARY: The United States formally concludes its search for weapons of mass destruction (WMD) in Iraq, one of the main reasons for the American invasion there; none are ever found.

January 14

MILITARY: A court-martial at Fort Hood finds U.S. Army Reserve Specialist Charles Graner guilty of abusing Iraqi captives at Abu Ghraib prison and he draws a 10-years sentence of imprisonment along with a dishonorable discharge.

January 20
MILITARY: In Washington, D.C., George W. Bush is sworn in to serve a second term as president of the United States and commander in chief.

January 26
MARINES: A helicopter crashes near the border of Jordan in a sandstorm, killing 30 marines.

February 3–7
DIPLOMACY: Secretary of State Condoleezza Rice arrives in Europe to mend relations damaged by the recent war in Iraq, with additional stops in Turkey and Israel.

February 14
MILITARY: A test of the National Missile Defense (NMD) is unsuccessful when an intercepting rocket fails to hit its target due to software deficiencies.

March 25
DIPLOMACY: President George W. Bush announces that his administration will sell highly advanced General Dynamics F-16 fighters to Pakistan, a valuable ally in the war against terror.

April 28
MILITARY: In Fort Bragg, North Carolina, a military jury sentences U.S. Army sergeant Hasan Akbar, a Muslim American, to death for the murder of two fellow soldiers at Camp Pennsylvania, Kuwait, in March 2003.

May 12
AVIATION: At Langley Air Force Base, Virginia, the first operational F-22A Raptor is delivered to the 27th Fighter Squadron, 1st Fighter Wing. This aircraft remains the most advanced fighter plane in the world, incorporating such novel technologies as stealth and "super cruise."

May 13
AVIATION: Over Charleston Air Force Base, South Carolina, a massed formation of C-17 Globemaster IIIs flies to Biggs Army Air Field, Texas. This is also the largest C-17 formation to ever fly cross-country.
MILITARY: The Pentagon releases a list of 33 bases it sought to close as a cost-cutting measure, although members of Congress resist any base closings in their peculiar state or district.

June 16
AVIATION: The Thunderbirds aerobatic team announces that Captain Nicole Malachowski is joining as the first female demonstration pilot of any U.S. military high-performance jet team.

June 22
AVIATION: Over Southwest Asia a U-2 aircraft from the 9th Reconnaissance Squadron experiences a catastrophic failure and crashes, killing the pilot.

June 28
MILITARY: An army helicopter attempting to rescue a stranded party of Navy SEALS in Afghanistan is shot down and crashes, killing all 19 service members onboard.

2005

Murphy, Michael P. (1976–2005)
Naval officer

Michael Patrick Murphy was born in Smithtown, New York, on May 7, 1976, the son of a district attorney. He graduated from Pennsylvania State University in 1988 with degrees in political science and psychology and was considering law school, but he opted to attend SEAL (Sea/Air/Land) monitoring classes at the United States Merchant Marine Academy. SEALs are a small and highly elite force of combat specialists capable of deploying behind enemy lines by submarine, small boat, or parachute. Murphy proved himself adept in military matters so, in September 2000, he accepted a slot with the U.S. Navy Officer Candidate School at Pensacola, Florida. That December he received his ensign's commission and transferred to the Basic Underwater Demolition/SEAL school at Coronado, California, from which he graduated in January 2001. Murphy continued his quest to become an elite soldier by attending the Army Jump School, the SEAL Qualification Training and SEAL Delivery Vehicle (SDV) school. Murphy survived this rigorous routine and earned his Trident as a Navy SEAL in July 2002. That fall he reported for duty at Pearl Harbor, Hawaii, and he saw routine tours of duty in Jordan, Qatar, and Djibouti as part of forces assigned to wage the war against terrorism.

In spring 2005 Murphy arrived in Afghanistan as assistant officer in charge of ALFA Platoon. He was here to support Operation Enduring Freedom, the ongoing campaign to rid that country of al-Qaeda and Taliban terrorists. The effort had been ongoing since the fall of the Taliban regime in the fall of 2001, and it proved frustratingly difficult because of the rough terrain of Afghanistan and relative porous borders of Pakistan, both of which afforded the terrorists ample cover. In June 2005 Murphy participated in Operation Red Wing, which

July 13
TERRORISM: U.S. Air Force general Randall Schmidt appears before the Senate Armed Services Committee and testifies that terrorist suspects ("detainees") at Guantánamo, Cuba, are being held under safe and humane conditions.

July 29
AVIATION: In Rwanda, U.S. Air Force transports convey 1,200 soldiers to Sudan on a UN peacekeeping mission.

August 23–29
AVIATION: Hurricane Katrina causes massive damage along the Gulf of Mexico, and many air force bases in the region are evacuated in advance.

September 2
AVIATION: In Washington, D.C., General T. Michael Moseley gains appointment as chief of staff, U.S. Air Force.

★ ★ ★ ★ ★ ★ ★ ★ ★ ★ ★ ★ ★

was intended to locate and eliminate a noted Taliban leader called Ahmad Shah. His four-man reconnaissance team was helicoptered into the rugged mountains of Kunar Province, near Asadabad, along the Pakistani border to find their quarry. However, while performing their mission, they were discovered by hostile local tribesmen, who alerted nearby Taliban units of their presence. Murphy and his three men deployed in a rough section of terrain and engaged a force estimated at between 100 and 200 men for several hours, while calling for reinforcements. When it was discovered that their cell phone would not operate properly from behind cover, Murphy assumed a more exposed position and eventually contacted the relief team. However, he and three SEALs were mortally wounded in the firefight and several days passed before the lone survivor, Leading Petty Officer Marcus Lutrell, could be rescued. For heroically sacrificing himself to save his team, Murphy became the first

Navy SEALs in Afghanistan while participating in Operation Red Wing, June 28, 2005. Murphy is to the far right. *(U.S. Navy)*

American soldier to receive a Medal of Honor in Afghanistan. On May 7, 2008, Secretary of the Navy Donald C. Winter announced that an *Arleigh Burke*–class destroyer, DDG-112, would also be christened the USS *Michael Murphy* in his memory.

September 10
AVIATION: An all-female crew flies the first C-130 combat mission over Southwest Asia.

September 24
AVIATION: In the wake of Hurricane Rita, the Civil Air Patrol begins assessing damage in the Houston, Texas, area while flying new GA-8 Airvan aircraft.

October 1–7
MILITARY: A force of 1,000 U.S. Army troops commences Operation "Iron Fist" to attack and root out Iraqi terrorists in the town of Sadah, near the Syrian border, killing 50.

October 15–18
AVIATION: At Langley Air Force Base, Virginia, the 27th Fighter Squadron flies its F-22A Raptors to Hill Air Force Base, Utah, as part of Operation Combat Hammer. There they drop their first JDAMs on a target range.

October 16
MILITARY: An attack by U.S. forces on Iraqi insurgents handling artillery shells kills 20 guerrillas.

November 5
AVIATION: At Randolph Air Force Base, Texas, the first operational TH-1H Huey training helicopters are delivered.

November–January 2006
AVIATION: Air force C-130s support military exercises at Camp Lemonier, Africa, as part of the Combined Joint Task Force–Horn of Africa.

2006

January 8
MARINES: The *New York Times* reports that 80 percent of marines killed by torso wounds in Iraq might have been saved had they been equipped with proper body armor.

January 14
AVIATION: At the San Antonio Monster Jam, Texas, the air force enters a monster truck called *Afterburner* in a car-smashing contest; it loses to an equally huge competitor named *Grave Digger*.

January 15
AVIATION: A U.S. air strike in the Bajaur tribal region of northwest Pakistan, targeted at Ayman al-Zawahiri, the al-Qaeda second in command, kills several terrorists along with 18 civilians.

January 19
TERRORISM: Terrorist Osama bin Laden releases a video tape declaring his intention to attack the United States soon, but he also makes the offer of a truce.

January 29
AVIATION: An all-Iraqi air force crew flies a C-130E while carrying Minister of the Interior Bayan Jabr to a summit in Tunisia. This is one of three C-130s operated by the 23rd Transport Squadron, based at Tallil Air Base, which is jointly staffed by American personnel.
MILITARY: ABC reporter Bob Woodruff and cameraman Dick Vogel are injured when their vehicle is struck by a roadside bomb in northwest Baghdad.

February 3
AVIATION: At Al Kasik Training Station, Iraq, Captain LeeAnn Roberts becomes the first female instructor performing firearms instruction for Iraqi trainees.

February 8
AVIATION: At Hickham Air Force Base, Hawaii, the first C-17 Globemaster III deploys as part of the first operational C-17 unit based in that state.

February 22–25
AVIATION: Off Okinawa, Japan, four F-15s from the 18th Fighter Wing simultaneously target and fire at aerial decoys during a three-day aerial exercise there.

March 16
MILITARY: U.S. forces attack Iraqi insurgents near Samarra, utilizing the largest air strike employed since the beginning of the war.

March 22
AVIATION: At Davis Monthan Force Base, Arizona, A-10 Thunderbolt IIs arrive for their annual ground support exercise, "Hawgsmoke 2006."

May 29
JOURNALISM: CBS reporters Paul Douglas and James Brotan are killed by a roadside bomb in Baghdad while reporter Kimberly Dozier is badly injured.

June
AVIATION: Former astronaut Susan J. Helms gains promotion to brigadier general and takes command of the 45th Space Wing.

June 7
AVIATION: U.S. Special Forces direct an air strike by two air force F-16s that kills terrorist ring leader Abu Musab al-Zarqawi at his hiding place near Baqubah, Iraq. This removes a senior al-Qaeda figure from the fighting. He had earned the ire of senior leaders by his willingness to kill civilians, and they may have betrayed his location to the Americans.

June 16
POLITICS: By wide margins, the Senate and House reject calls for an Iraq timetable for withdrawing American forces.

June 19
MILITARY: Three soldiers are accused of murdering three Iraqi detainees and also of threatening a fourth soldier if he confessed to investigators.

July 3
MILITARY: The U.S. Army accuses former soldier Steven D. Green, previously dismissed for a "personality disorder," with the rape and murder of an Iraqi girl and her family in March 2006.

July 31
MILITARY: The United States formally transfers military control of Afghanistan to NATO, which is now responsible for fighting off Taliban extremists and local drug lords.

September 1
MILITARY: The Pentagon announces the successful test of the Missile Defense System; in this instance, an interceptor rocket shot from California destroys a target missile heading in from Alaska.

September 3
MILITARY: U.S. forces capture Hamid Juma Faris, a senior al-Qaeda operative, in Iraq. He is best known for orchestrating the deadly attack against the Shiite Askariya Shrine last February.

September 6
TERRORISM: President George W. Bush announces that 14 high-level terrorists have been transferred from abroad to detention pens at Guantánamo Bay, Cuba. He awaits congressional authorization to conduct military tribunals.

September 8
TERRORISM: A car bomb explodes outside the U.S. embassy in Kabul, Afghanistan, killing 16 people, including five Americans.

2006

October 3
MILITARY: Eight American soldiers die in Iraq today, victims of roadside bombs.

October 17
TERRORISM: In Washington, D.C., President George W. Bush signs legislation under which rules for interrogating and prosecuting terrorists are differentiated from those that apply to criminals.

November 8
POLITICS: In Washington, D.C., Secretary of Defense Donald Rumsfeld resigns from office in the wake of unfavorable midterm elections for the Republicans. He is succeeded by former CIA director Robert Gates.

November 17
MILITARY: In Washington, D.C., General John Abizaid of the U.S. Central Command (CENTCOM) testifies before the Senate Armed Services Committee. He argues for an increase in American troop strength in Iraq and against a timetable for an American withdrawal.

November 25
MILITARY: North of Baghdad, Iraq, American troops, backed by Iraqi security forces, kill 22 insurgents.

December 6
MILITARY: In Washington, D.C., Robert M. Gates is confirmed by the U.S. Senate on a 95–2 vote to serve as the new Secretary of Defense. He had previously testified that, while the United States is not winning the struggle in Iraq, neither is it losing and he urges patience.

December 21
MARINES: The government accuses four marines of committing atrocities against civilians at Haditha, Iraq; they are to face court-martials for murder.

December 31
MILITARY: The government announces that the death toll for U.S. forces in Iraq has reached 3,000; the number of dead Iraqi civilians killed at the hands of numerous insurgent groups ranges from 30,000 to a high of 650,000.

2007

January 7
AVIATION: An air force AC-130H Spectre gunship attacks a suspected al-Qaeda training camp in Somalia.

January 10
MILITARY: In Washington, D.C., President George W. Bush announces the impending dispatch of 20,000 additional troops to Iraq in the hopes that this "surge" will lead to lessened outbreaks of violence there. Democrats who control Congress cannot muster sufficient votes to oppose him.

January 12
POLITICS: In Washington, D.C. Secretary of State Condoleezza Rice announces that President George W. Bush has authorized attacks on known Iranian agents operating in Iraq and training terrorists teams there.

January 18
AVIATION: The U.S. government announces that the Chinese have recently destroyed an old weather satellite with a new antisatellite weapon.

January 20
AVIATION: Over northern Baghdad, Iraq, a UH-60 Black Hawk helicopter crashes, possibly from insurgent fire; all 13 passengers are killed.

January 23
POLITICS: During his annual State of the Union address, President George W. Bush reiterates his plan to dispatch 20,000 additional troops to Iraq, confident that this "surge" will bring ongoing violence there to a halt.

January 24
AVIATION: Air force gunships conduct a second round of strikes against suspected al-Qaeda terrorist training camps in Somalia.

January 27
MILITARY: In Washington, D.C., the U.S. Senate unanimously approves Lieutenant General David H. Petraeus to serve as the new top commander of occupation forces in Iraq. He replaces General George W. Casey, Jr.

January 28
TERRORISM: Near Najaf, Iraq, U.S. troops and Iraqi ground forces battle a group of Sunni insurgents who are bent on attacking and killing Shiite religious pilgrims celebrating the festival of Ashura; an estimated 250 terrorists are slain.

February 6
MILITARY: In Washington, D.C., Secretary of Defense Robert M. Gates declares that the United States is establishing a new Africa Command by 2008. Presently, responsibility for that continent is shared by three other commands.

February 7
AVIATION: Near Baghdad, Iraq, a Marine Corps helicopter crashes, apparently after taking ground fire.

February 10
MILITARY: In Iraq, Lieutenant General David H. Petraeus replaces Lieutenant General George W. Casey, Jr., as head of coalition occupation forces.

February 11
MILITARY: In Baghdad, military authorities display evidence of Iranian involvement in terrorist activities throughout Iraq. They also state that recent raids by American forces in Baghdad have netted six members of the elite Iranian Revolutionary Guards. These have long been suspected of aiding and abetting unrest among the sizable Shiite population.

March 2
MILITARY: In Washington, D.C., Secretary of Defense Robert M. Gates relieves U.S. Army secretary Francis J. Harvey over allegations of poor conditions at Walter Reed Army Medical Center. General Kevin Kiley also loses his job as Army Surgeon General.

March 16
MILITARY: General John P. Abizaid is replaced by Admiral William J. Fallon as head of the U.S. Central Command (CENTCOM).

March 26
MILITARY: Four generals are rebuked by Pentagon officials for their role in covering up the friendly fire death of former football hero Pat Tillman in Afghanistan.

April 10
MILITARY: In Washington, D.C., General George W. Casey, Jr., is sworn in as the new chief of staff of the army.

April 11
MILITARY: In Washington, D.C., Secretary of Defense Robert M. Gates announces that military tours in Iraq and Afghanistan will be extended three months to a total of 15 months.

May 13
MILITARY: In Helmand Province, Afghanistan, U.S., NATO, and Afghan security forces kill Mullah Dadullah. He is one of the highest-ranking Taliban leaders to die in combat.

May 15
MILITARY: In Washington, D.C., President George W. Bush nominates Lieutenant General Douglas Lute to serve as "war czar" for coordinating military matters in Iraq and Afghanistan.

May 23
MARINES: The Japanese government agrees to pay the United States $6 billion to relocate 6,000 marines from Okinawa to the island of Guam; the Americans will also contribute $4 billion to the project.

May 24
MILITARY: In Washington, D.C., the Democratic-controlled Congress yields to the Republican administration of President George W. Bush by approving billions of dollars for the war there without attaching a timetable for withdrawal. Antiwar groups responsible for the Democratic victory cry foul and bemoan the decision.

June 15
MILITARY: In Washington, D.C., the Department of Defense announces that the 28,500-man "surge" in Iraq is now complete, boosting American strength in that country to 160,000 men and women.

September 3
DIPLOMACY: In Baghdad, Iraq, President George W. Bush makes a surprise visit to confer with Prime Minister Nouri al-Maliki and Sunni tribal leaders who wish to join coalition forces in the fight against insurgents.

September 11
MILITARY: In Washington, D.C., Lieutenant General David H. Petraeus testifies before a joint committee in Congress that the military "surge" of late has greatly reduced violence levels in Iraq.

2007

Petraeus, David H.   (1952–   )
Army general

David Howell Petraeus was born in Corn-wall-on-Hudson, New York, and he gradu-ated from the U.S. Military Academy in 1974 with the top 5 percent of his class. His first assignment was with the 509th Air-borne Battalion Combat Team in Vicenza, Italy, and he became closely identified with light infantry. Petraeus proved himself an adept officer, and, in 1981, he became aide-de-camp to the commanding general of the 24th Infantry Division (Mechanized). He also continued his education by attending the Command and General Staff College in 1983, graduating top in his class, and also received a doctorate in International Rela-tions from Princeton University in 1987. In 1993 he served as the assistant chief of staff with the elite 101st Airborne Division, and he participated in several peacekeeping and nation-building ventures in Haiti and Bosnia during that decade. Petraeus com-manded the 101st Airborne Division during Operation Iraqi Freedom, which overcame stiff enemy resistance and occupied the city of Mosul. He was successful at both coun-terinsurgency warfare and civic relations to isolate the insurgents from the greater population. In February 2004, Petraeus accompanied his men back to the United States and, the following June, he was promoted to lieutenant general command-ing the Multi-National Security Transition Command Iraq.

Back in Iraq, Petraeus was tasked with rebuilding that nation's shattered military and security apparatus. His methodical methods made considerable progress, but at too slow a rate for many in Congress,

General David Petraeus *(Department of Defense)*

who wanted to withdraw from Iraq. To this end he testified before Congress several times and urged patience with the delicate task he was orchestrating. On January 27, 2007, Petraeus became a full general and replaced General George C. Casey as head of the Multi-National Force-Iraq. He employed an additional 20,000 soldiers sent to Iraq by President George W. Bush as a military "surge." Petraeus also placed greater responsibilities on the Iraqis for their own security while also securing tribal alliances against the al-Qaeda ter-ror network. The results were spectacular

(continues)

(continued)

and terrorist violence declined nearly 80 percent from the previous year. However, Petraeus was under no illusions. He insisted that more work needed to be done before the Americans could withdraw. On September 16, 2008, he handed his responsibilities over to General Raymond T. Odierno and returned home. The following month, he accepted command of the U.S. Central Command, headquartered in Tampa, Florida, where he is tasked with directing military operations in 20 nations stretching from Egypt to Pakistan, as well as the ongoing Operations Enduring Free in Afghanistan and Iraqi Freedom in Iraq. In the words of Secretary of Defense Robert Gates, "He is the preeminent soldier-scholar-statesman of our generation and precisely the man we need in this command at this time."

November
MILITARY: By mid-month, American combat fatalities in Afghanistan exceed 100, the highest annual total since the conflict began in October 2001.

November 6
MILITARY: The recent loss of six Americans makes 2007 the deadliest year for fighting in Iraq, bringing the total number of dead to 852.

November 18
TERRORISM: In Iraq, the monthly U.S. combat fatalities drop to 37, down from a high of 126 in May 2007. Thanks to the recent troop surge, the level of terrorist attacks against American troops has declined to its lowest level since January 2006.

November 24
MILITARY: In Diyala Province, Iraq, a brigade of 5,000 American soldiers is withdrawn and sent home, leaving overall troop strength at 157,000.

December 10
MILITARY: U.S., NATO, and Afghan forces recapture the Taliban stronghold of Musa Qala in Helmand Province. This town in one of the main poppy-growing regions in southern Afghanistan, and a major source of income from the drug trade.

December 29
MILITARY: In Iraq, Lieutenant General David H. Petraeus reports that car bombings and other terrorist attacks have fallen by 60 percent since the start of the military "surge" in June 2007. This translates into 899 killed, which, ironically, also makes this the deadliest year for American forces. Petraeus nonetheless considers al-Qaeda the greatest menace facing Iraqi stability and reconciliation.

December 31
MILITARY: The Associated Press reports that 100 American soldiers have died in Afghanistan this year, the highest number since Operation Enduring Freedom

began in October 2001. The war has also claimed an estimated 4,500 militants and 925 Afghan police.

2008

January 8
MILITARY: In Diyala Province, Iraq, U.S. and Iraqi forces conduct Operation Iron Harvest, which is aimed at eliminating final pockets of guerrillas from the region.

January 15
MARINES: In Washington, D.C., the Defense Department announces a one-time deployment of 3,200 marines to Afghanistan to help thwart any possibility of a spring offensive by the Taliban. This temporarily raises the total number of American troops there to 30,000; they are assisted by an additional 28,000 NATO troops.

January 29
AVIATION: A missile strike launched by an unmanned Predator drone kills wanted terrorist leader Abu Laith al-Libi in northwestern Pakistan.

February 20
AVIATION: It is announced that a U.S. missile successfully destroys a falling spy satellite in order to destroy its fuel tank before it might contaminate parts of the Earth.

March 19
POLITICS: In Washington, D.C., President George W. Bush marks the fifth anniversary of Operation Iraqi Freedom by reiterating that the war was correct and that it will continue until absolute victory is attained. To date American losses are over 4,000 dead and 29,600 wounded.

March 23
MILITARY: In Baghdad, Iraq, an improvised explosive device (IED) kills four U.S. soldiers, raising the total number of war-related fatalities to 4,000.

April 6
MILITARY: In Afghanistan, a team under Captain Kyle Walton from the 3rd Battalion, 3rd Special Forces Group engages 200 dug-in Taliban militants in the Shok Valley, a violent encounter that results in 10 Silver Stars being awarded.

April 8–9
POLITICS: In Washington, D.C., General David H. Petraeus testifies before Congress that significant progress continues to be made at reducing violence levels in Iraq but that success remains fragile. He therefore recommends that after the troop presence drops to its pre-surge level of 140,000 men, all future withdrawals be suspended for an additional 45 days.

May
MILITARY: In Iraq, American troop deaths are reported at 19, the lowest level since the war commenced in March 2003.

June
MILITARY: The Associated Press reports that 45 coalition troops, including 27 Americans, were killed in Afghanistan; this is the highest one month total since

Operation Enduring Freedom began in October 2001. This number also outstrips the number of troops killed in Iraq, which totals 31, including 29 Americans.

June 5
AVIATION: In a major shake-up, Secretary of Defense Robert Gates dismisses Secretary of the Air Force Michael W. Wynne and Air Force Chief of Staff T. Michael Moseley. They are relieved due to an August 2007 incident during which a B-52 bomber had accidentally flown with six nuclear-tipped cruise missiles from Minot Air Force Base, North Dakota, to Barksdale Air Force Base, Louisiana.

June 10
MILITARY: In Afghanistan, U.S. forces engage in a fight with Taliban militants just astride the Pakistani border. This is followed by an airstike in that border region, which the Pakistani government claims killed 11 paramilitary soldiers.

Odierno, Raymond T.   (1954–   )
Army general

Raymond T. Odierno was raised in Rockaway, New Jersey, and he graduated from the U.S. Military Academy in June 1976. His first assignment was with the 41st Field Artillery and he became closely associated with that arm. In 1986 Odierno received a master's degree in nuclear effects engineering and, in 1990, he also successfully completed the staff course at the Naval War College. For many years thereafter Odierno held various ranks with the Seventh Army in Germany, and, between 1997 and 1998, he served as chief of staff to the V Corps. The following year he accompanied the 1st Armored Division to Albania as part of Operation Allied Force, and, in 1999, he relocated to the Pentagon for work in the Office of the Deputy Chief of Staff for Operations and Plans. In October 1991 he was made commanding officer of the 4th Infantry Division, (Mechanized) and, in this post, he was assigned to fight in Operation Iraqi Freedom. His division was supposed to operate from Turkey and invade northern Iraq, but when the Turkish government refused, the force was shipped through the Suez Canal and entered Iraq from Kuwait. Consequently, Odierno saw no combat in the conquest of Iraq, but he received one of the toughest postwar occupations by being assigned to the so-called Sunni Triangle around Tikrit and Mosul.

The 4th Division dealt with its share of attacks while stationed in the north, but Odierno's tough and methodical approach to suppressing insurgents paid dividends when his men captured fugitive dictator Saddam Hussein in his hometown of Tikrit in December 2003. He was next reassigned to serve as special assistant to the vice chief of staff, U.S. Army, in Washington, D.C., in August 2004, and he also acted as military adviser to Secretary of State Condoleezza Rice until May 2006. In December of

June 12
POLITICS: In Washington, D.C., a ruling by the U.S. Supreme Court invalidates the Military Commissions Act of 2006, thereby allowing detainees kept at Guantánamo Bay, Cuba, to challenge their detention in federal court.

July
MILITARY: In Iraq, the monthly death toll of American troops falls to 13, the lowest since Operation Iraqi Freedom commenced in March 2003.

July 6
AVIATION: In Nangahar Province, Afghanistan, an American air strike kills several Taliban militants. However, Afghan government officials complain that 47 civilians at a nearby wedding party also died.

that year he returned to Iraq commanding the III Corps and, the following spring, he joined his superior, General David H. Petraeus, in cultivating the "Sunni awakening," which turned many tribes and former insurgents against the fanatical al-Qaeda terrorists. This effort, in concert with the military "surge" of five additional combat brigades, greatly reduced levels of violence in heretofore unstable Anwar Province, and the trend continued throughout the countryside. Odierno left Iraq a second time in February 2008 to command the III Corps at Fort Hood Texas, but he returned that September and replaced Petraeus as commander, Multi-National Force–Iraq. He remains tasked with sustaining recent gains in security while preparing to reduce and ultimately end the coalition presence in that nation. To this end, he is continuing his predecessor's policy of not only aggressively acting against insurgents, but also training and encouraging Iraqi military and police to look after their own matters. Odierno also works to protect the local population

General Raymond Odierno *(U.S. Army)*

from harm, and he encourages self-rule. Despite his success, Odierno cautions that Iran remains a destabilizing factor, a nation requiring constant monitoring.

July 13

MILITARY: A remote American outpost in southeast Afghanistan, along Pakistan's lawless border, is attacked by an estimated 200 Taliban fighters. The attack is repulsed but nine Americans are killed in the fighting.

August 22

AVIATION: In northern Iraq, an army UH-60 Black Hawk helicopter crashes, killing all 14 soldiers onboard; the accident is ascribed to mechanical failure.

• In western Herat Province, Afghanistan, an American air strike on the village of Azizabad kills several Taliban militants. However, Afghan government officials claim that 90 civilians also died in the attack.

August 25

DIPLOMACY: In Baghdad, Iraq, Prime Minister Nouri al-Maliki calls for the complete withdrawal of all occupation forces by 2011. Apparently, this deadline was reached in advance with American authorities.

September 1

MILITARY: In Anbar Province, Iraq, U.S. military authorities turn over control to the Iraqi military. This area was formerly a center of the Sunni insurgency, but the so-called Sunni awakening induced many tribes and former insurgents to take up arms against al-Qaeda terrorists.

September 16

MILITARY: In Iraq, Lieutenant General David H. Petraeus turns command of the Multi-National Force–Iraq over General Raymond T. Odierno.

October 5

MILITARY: In Mosul, Iraq, a raid by American troops acting on a tip from the locals leads to the death of Abu Qaswarah, a Moroccan who was also the second most important al-Qaeda leader; four other militants are also killed.

October 31

MILITARY: Lieutenant General David H. Petraeus is promoted to full general and placed in charge of the U.S. Central Command, Tampa, Florida. From here he will direct all military actions relative to Iraq, Afghanistan, and the Middle East.

November 14

MILITARY: In Washington, D.C., Major General Ann E. Dunwoody receives her fourth star to become the first American woman promoted to full general. She will command the U.S. Army Materiel Command.

December 20

MILITARY: The Associated Press reports that, since Operation Iraqi Freedom began in March 2003, 4,209 members of the U.S. military had been killed in combat. Of coalition forces, Britain has lost, 176; Italy, 33; Ukraine, 18; Poland, 21; Bulgaria, 13; Spain, 11, Denmark, seven; El Salvador, five; Latvia and Georgia, three apiece; Estonia, Netherlands, Thailand and Romania, two each; and Austria, Hungary, Kazakhstan and South Korea, one each.

December 29

AVIATION: A Marine Corps AV-8B Harrier jump jet crashes near Havelock, North Carolina, killing the pilot.

Dunwoody, Ann E.   (1953–   )
Army General

Ann E. Dunwoody was born at Fort Belvoir, Virginia, in 1953, the daughter of a career army officer. She comes from a family long active in the military, commencing with her great-grandfather, Brigadier General Henry C. Dunwoody, who graduated from West Point in 1862 and served in the Civil War and Spanish-American conflict. Her father and brother are also West Point graduates with distinguished combat records from World War II and Vietnam. Dunwoody attended the State University of New York College at Cortland, and, after graduating in 1975 with a degree in physical education, she commissioned into the Women's Army Corps as a second lieutenant. She subsequently held leadership positions in various maintenance companies and service battalions, at Fort Sill, Oklahoma, Fort Drum, New York, and Fort Bragg, North Carolina. Dunwoody proved herself to be a conscientious officer and she received staff assignments with the 82nd Airborne Division, which she accompanied to Saudi Arabia during Operations Desert Shield/Storm in 1990–91. During Operation Enduring Freedom in the fall of 2001, Dunwoody commanded the 1st Corps Support Command that was responsible for deploying logistics in Uzbekistan to support operations in neighboring Afghanistan. In the course of her career she has received numerous decorations, including the Distinguished Service Medal and the Defense Superior Service Medal.

Dunwoody's litany of firsts include the first female officer to command a battalion in the 82nd Airborne Division, Fort

Ann Dunwoody during the ceremony promoting her to a general, the first four-star female officer in the U.S. military. *(Department of Defense)*

Bragg's first female general officer in 2000, and the first female to command the Combined Arms Support Command at Fort Lee, Virginia, in 2004. In 2005 Dunwoody became the first woman general to achieve three-star rank since Lieutenant General Claudia Kennedy in 2000. At the time she served as the army's top-ranking woman leader and deputy chief of staff for logistics. On June 23, 2008, Dunwoody made American military history by becoming the first female officer nominated for four-star, full general rank. The Senate confirmed her promotion on November 13, 2008, and she received her fourth star at Fort Belvoir on November 14, 2008. The ceremony was

(continues)

(continued)

widely attended by ranking military figures, including Army Chief of Staff George W. Casey and Secretary of Defense Robert Gates. In an emotional speech to those gathered, Dunwoody modestly attributed her success to her father, an army brigadier general, who always taught her to set personal objectives, then never quit and never accept defeat. About her husband of 19 years, retired U.S. Air Force colonel Craig Brotchie, she noted, "There is no one more surprised than I—except of course, my husband. You know what they say, 'Behind every successful woman there is an astonished man.'" As a full general, Dunwoody now leads the Army Materiel Command, numbering 130,000 service members at 150 locations around the world, which is tasked with equipping and arming American soldiers for battle.

2009

January 1
AVIATION: A missile launched from a U.S. Predator drone kills two senior al-Qaeda leaders, Usama al-Kini and Sheikh Salim Swedan at an undisclosed location.
MILITARY: The U.S. Army formally turns over the Green Zone in Baghdad, Iraq, to the Iraqi military as the United States makes another incremental step to restore that nation's sovereignty.

January 9
MILITARY: The U.S. Army Experience Center at Franklin Mills, Philadelphia, Pennsylvania, has so far recruited 33 full-time soldiers and five reservists. This is a $12 million high-tech, arcade game-style recruiting center that uses state-of-the-art video games to lure in prospective recruits and, to date, its performance approximates those of traditional recruiting centers.

January 13
MILITARY: A military court charges Sergeant Joseph P. Mayo, 18th Infantry Regiment, with killing four Iraqi prisoners in the spring of 2007, then dumping their bodies in a canal. He is one of seven soldiers implicated in their deaths.

January 20
MILITARY: In Washington, D.C., Barack Obama is sworn in as the nation's 44th president and commander in chief. He previously pledged to change the focus of the war on terrorism by shifting thousands of troops from Iraq to Afghanistan.

January 23
AVIATION: At least five missiles fired in two U.S. Predator drone attacks kill 14 Taliban militants in North and South Waziristan, Pakistan. These are the first such attacks since President Barack Obama took office and he signaled that they will continue.

January 26
Aviation: Two U.S. Army OH-58D Kiowa helicopters belonging to the 10th Mountain Division collide near Kirkuk, Iraq, killing all four crewmen. An investigation is launched to determine the cause.

January 29
Military: The Pentagon recalls 16,000 sets of U.S. Army body armor out of concerns for wearers under combat conditions. Apparently the equipment was not properly tested for stopping bullets and other projectiles.

February 11
Military: The U.S. Army Corps of Engineers has been put to work scouring Long Beach Island, New Jersey, for live munitions discarded there during World War I. It is feared that the ordnance, previously dumped overboard by naval vessels, then pumped ashore as part of a beach replenishment program, might pose a hazard to vacationers.

Naval: The guided missile cruiser *Vella Gulf* apprehends seven suspected pirates in the Gulf of Aden after a passing merchant ship sends out a distress signal that they were attempting to board it.

February 14
Aviation: Two missiles by a U.S. Predator drone near the town of Makeen, South Waziristan, Pakistan, kills an estimated 30 Taliban militants.

February 16
Aviation: Missiles fired by U.S. Predator drones kill an estimated 30 Taliban militants in the Kurram Valley, Pakistan.

February 27
Aviation: The Army determines that hostile gunfire near Kirkuk, Iraq, caused the crash to two Army OH-58D Kiowa helicopters, which apparently collided while dodging the attack.

March 1
Aviation: Missiles fired from U.S. Predator drones kill seven Taliban militants in Saraogha village, South Waziristan, Pakistan.

March 3
Marines: Lance Corporal Patrick Malone is accidentally shot and killed by Corporal Mathew Nelson during a "confidence game" in Anbar Province, Afghanistan. The latter is arrested and charged with involuntary manslaughter.

March 8
Naval: The Naval survey ship *Impeccable,* dangling a sono buoy as part of a routine intelligence gathering mission, is harassed by several small Chinese vessels 75 miles off the South China coast. At one point, crew members of the *Impeccable* turned a water hose on a Chinese vessel passing with 25 feet of it.

March 12
Aviation: Missiles fired from a U.S. Predator drone kill an estimated 24 Taliban militants in Berju, Kurram Agency, Pakistan.

March 15
Aviation: Missiles fired from U.S. Predator drones kill four Taliban operatives at Jani Khel, North-West Frontier Province, Pakistan.

March 20

NAVAL: In the Persian Gulf, the 24,000-ton amphibious ship *New Orleans* collides with the nuclear submarine *Hartford* near the Straits of Hormuz, sustaining a ruptured fuel and ballast tank.

March 25

AVIATION: Over Edwards Air Force Base, California, an ultra-modern F-22A Raptor jet fighter crashes, killing the pilot.
• Missiles fired from a U.S. Predator drone kill seven Taliban militants riding in two vehicles near Makin, South Waziristan, Pakistan.

March 26

AVIATION: A missile fired from a U.S. Predator drone kills four Taliban militants in Essokhel, North Waziristan, Pakistan.

March 31

NAVAL: The privately-owned U.S. Naval Institute announces the existence of a Chinese "kill weapon" specifically designed to sink U.S. Navy carriers at a range of 1,240 miles. A Navy spokesman, while acknowledging the Chinese device, states that it can be defeated in flight by existing Aegis missile defense systems.

April 1

AVIATION: A missile strike by a U.S. Predator drone kills 14 Taliban militants in the Orakzai tribal area, Pakistan.

April 4

AVIATION: A missile launched from a U.S. Predator drone kills 13 suspected Taliban in North Waziristan, Pakistan.

April 8

AVIATION: A missile launched from a U.S. Predator drone kills four Taliban militants in a vehicle in Gangi Khel, South Waziristan, Pakistan.

April 9

NAVAL: Off Somalia, the destroyer *Bainbridge* responds to the hijacking of the freighter *Masersk Alabama* by positioning itself nearby. The latter's captain, Richard Phillips, is being held hostage in a lifeboat by four Somali pirates.

April 12

NAVAL: On the destroyer *Bainbridge,* Snipers from SEAL Team Six shoot and kill three of four Somali pirates holding Captain Richard Phillips in a lifeboat, freeing him. A fourth pirate is taken into custody.

April 16

MILITARY: An Army court in Vilseck, Germany, sentences Sergeant John Haley to life imprisonment for the murder of four Iraqi civilians in 2007.

April 19

AVIATION: A missile launched from a U.S. Predator drone kills three suspected Taliban militants in South Waziristan, Pakistan.

April 20

MILITARY: In Iraq, 500 men of the 4th Engineer Battalion, who specialize in clearing roads of explosives, begin packing their equipment for a tour of duty in

Afghanistan. They are part of the 17,000 additional combat troops ordered there by President Barack Obama.

April 23
AVIATION: The U.S. Army begins testing its Autonomous Rotocraft Sniper System (ARSS), which is a remote-controlled Vigilante robot armed with a self-stabilizing turret and a 338-caliber high velocity gun.

April 25
NAVAL: In North Charleston, South Carolina, the new guided-missile destroyer *Truxtun* is commissioned at the Charleston Naval Weapons Station.

April 27
MILITARY: Word surfaces that the U.S. Army is researching a unique "Double Laser" system, literally a beam within a beam, that can destroy roadside bombs and explosive-laden vehicles at a distance.

April 29
AVIATION: A missile launched from a U.S. Predator drone kills six Taliban militants in Kanni Garam village, South Waziristan, Pakistan.

May 2
AVIATION: In Canberra, Australia, Prime Minister Kevin Rudd announces that his government will purchase 100 Lockheed F-35 Lighting II Joint Strike Fighters as part of an overall military buildup.

May 4–5
MILITARY: A fire fight between U.S., Afghan security forces, and Taliban insurgents in Farah Province, Afghanistan, results in the death of 26 civilians. President Hamid Karzai begin pressuring the United States to modify its rules of engagement to cut down on civilian losses.

May 5
NAVAL: The new high-tech warship *Freedom* is revealed to the public by the U.S. Navy for the first time. This sophisticated vessel is manned by only 40 sailors, yet can engage larger enemy fleets at speeds of up to 45 miles per hour. This is the first of a new generation of warships and is expected to perform effectively in the fight against international piracy.

May 9
AVIATION: A missile launched by a U.S. Predator drone kills six Taliban militants in Saraogha, South Waziristan, Pakistan.

May 11
AVIATION: The Marine Corps announces that it is deploying at least one of its new MV-22 tilt rotor transport squadrons to combat operations in Afghanistan. This hybrid helicopter/aircraft transport lifts off vertically and flies horizontally while carrying 24 fully equipped combat troops.

May 12
AVIATION: A missile launched from a U.S. Predator drone kills eight Taliban militants in Sra Khawra village, South Waziristan, Pakistan.

May 16
AVIATION: Missiles fired from a U.S. Predator drone kills 25 Taliban militants in the village of Sarkai Naki, North Waziristan, Pakistan.

May 17
MILITARY: Defense Secretary Robert Gates, upon being interviewed on CBS News, declares that it will require U.S. forces another two to four years to make Afghan security forces capable of defending their own country.

May 20
AVIATION: A Navy HH-60 Seahawk helicopter crashes 13 miles off San Diego; all five passengers are missing and presumed dead.

May 21
MILITARY: A bomb explosion in the Dora district of Baghdad, Iraq, takes the lives of three U.S. Army soldiers.
• U.S. and Afghan security forces storm into the village of Marjah, Helmand Province, Afghanistan, killing 34 Taliban insurgents and seizing 16.5 tons of illegal drugs.

May 22
AVIATION: An Air Force T-38 Talon jet trainer crashes at Edwards Air Force Base, California, killing the pilot.

May 25
MILITARY: In Mosul, Iraq, a suicide bomber attacks an American military convoy, killing one U.S. Army soldier. However, military spokesman Major General David Perkins declares to journalists that terrorist attacks against military and civilian targets are down 60 percent from a year ago.

May 26
MILITARY: In Washington, D.C., Army chief of staff General George Casey declares that the United States has to be ready to remain in Iraq for at least 10 years for the situation to fully stabilize itself. This is despite a recent agreement with that government to withdraw all military forces no later than 2012.

May 27
NAVAL: The former transport *General Hoyt S. Vandenberg*, which was employed by the U.S. Air Force for many years to track missile and spacecraft, is sunk off Key West, Florida, to serve as an artificial reef. It settles into 140 feet of water minutes after scuttling charges were detonated.

May 28
MILITARY: Fighting in Paktia Province, Afghanistan, between U.S. troops and Taliban guerrillas results in the death of at least 34 insurgents.

May 29
MILITARY: U.S. forces combing through Zabul Province, Afghanistan, manage to engage and kill 35 Taliban operatives after an Afghan security patrol was ambushed.

June 1
MILITARY: The government reports that four U.S. Army troops have been killed in Wardak Province, Afghanistan, by two Taliban roadside bombs that struck separate vehicles a mile apart.

June 4

AVIATION: The Air Force announces that its new Counter-Electronics High-Powered Microwave Advanced Missile Project could revolutionize electronic warfare. This new weapon is a cruise missile that emits focused bursts of high power microwaves (HMP) capable of frying enemy electronic without harming their operators. A working prototype, costing $40 million, is expected to be operational within five years or less.

June 6

AVIATION: The Air Force reveals that its top secret X-37B unmanned space plane is being stored in a housing facility at Cape Canaveral, Florida, in anticipation of a January 2010 launch. The five-ton craft is only 27 feet long and 15 feet across, yet capable of performing a variety of classified missions and experiments.

NAVAL: The U.S. Navy is dispatching Towed Pinger Locators to help recover the black box flight recorders of an Air France jetliner that crashed in the North Atlantic after taking off from Brazil. If salvaged, it is hoped the black boxes will reveal the cause of Airbus 330-200's crash.

June 7

MILITARY: U.S., coalition, and Afghan security forces operating in Zabul Province, Afghanistan, engage and kill 30 Taliban insurgents.

June 8

MARINES: A Force of 7,000 newly deployed Marines begins sweeping through Helmand Province, Afghanistan. The troops are from the 2nd Marine Expeditionary Brigade and are the first of 21,000 troops to be added by President Barack Obama.

June 11

NAVAL: In the South China Sea, a Chinese submarine collides with a towed sonar array attached to the destroyer *John S. McCain.* This is part of a pattern of increasing incidents between U.S. and Chinese naval forces in the region.

June 12

MILITARY: In Washington, D.C., General David Petraeus admits that Taliban-style attacks are at an all-time high in Afghanistan, which attributes to the new strategy of rooting out enemy sanctuaries and safe havens.

June 14

AVIATION: Missiles fired from a U.S. Predator drone kill five Taliban militants in a vehicle in South Waziristan, Pakistan.

June 15

MILITARY: Newly appointed General Stanley McChrystal assumes command of all anti-insurgent operations in Afghanistan. Given his background in special warfare, he is expected to take an unconventional but effective approach at suppressing Taliban operatives.

June 17

MILITARY: At the U.S. Central Command in Tampa, Florida, General David Petraeus informs French journalists that "tough fighting" can be expected in Afghanistan over the next months.

June 18

AVIATION: A suspected U.S. missile strike in northwest Pakistan kills eight people at the villages of Gharlamal and Nandaran; most were apparently Taliban guerrillas but at least two dozen villagers may have been injured.

MILITARY: Throughout Iraq, U.S. Army troops are being withdrawn from cities and urban areas in order for their replacement by Iraqi security forces. Presently, 90 of 138 military sites have been turned over to the Iraqis.

June 21

MILITARY: A Taliban missile attack upon Bagram air base, 25 miles northeast of Kabul, Afghanistan, results in the deaths of two U.S. Army troops from the 82nd Airborne Division.

June 22

AVIATION: The Air Force announces that it has developed a new bomb rack for the B-2 stealth bomber which enables it to carry advanced MOP (Massive Ordnance Penetrator) weighing 30,000 pounds.

• A train crash near Washington, D.C., takes the life of General David F. Wherley, Jr., who commanded the district National Guard from 2003 to 2008. During the terrorist attack of September 11, 2001, he headed the 113th Fighter Wing at Andrews Air Force base and sent jets aloft to protect the capital after the attack.

MILITARY: In Afghanistan, commander General Stanley McChrystal announces new restriction on U.S. and NATO forces in an attempt to cut down on civilian casualties. Henceforth, fighting and aerial attacks will not be allowed near Afghan homes and villages, regardless if Taliban troops are active there.

June 23

AVIATION: In Makeen, South Waziristan, Pakistan, a U.S. Predator drone launches several missiles at a Taliban funeral for fallen leader Niaz Wali, killing 45 guerrillas in attendance. Another missile strike in Neej Narai also kills eight suspected Taliban militants.

June 24

MILITARY: In southern Afghanistan, U.S., coalition, and Afghan security force report killing 23 Taliban militants, including Mullah Ismail.

June 25

MILITARY: Throughout Iraq, a new wave of terrorist bombings takes the lives of nine U.S. Army troops; they died in two roadside attacks in eastern Baghdad.

June 28

MILITARY: In Baghdad, Iraq, General Ray Odierno accuses Iran of interfering with events in Iraq by training Shiite insurgents and paying surrogates to advance their interests. Despite the provocation, he insisted "I am not authorized to do anything outside the borders of Iraq."

June 29

AVIATION: The Air Force test launches a Minuteman 3 ICBM from Vandenberg Air Force Base, California, to collect data and check the weapon system's reliability and accuracy. The dummy warhead fell on the test range near Kwajalein Atoll in the Marshall Islands.

June 30
AVIATION: It is reported at U.S. airstrikes in Khost province, along the Afghan-Pakistani border, have killed 12 Taliban militants hiding in a bunker complex.
MILITARY: A roadside bomb in Baghdad, Iraq, takes the lives of four U.S. Army troops just as coalition forces are preparing to evacuate Iraqi cities to their own security forces.

July 1
MARINES: A force of 4,000 Marines commence an offensive along the Lower Helmand River Valley, Afghanistan, in an attempt to root out Taliban forces lurking there. The assault is code named Operation Khanjar (Strike of the Sword) and is conducted in concert with 650 Afghan security personnel and police.

July 2
MILITARY: The U.S. Army begins testing tethered blimps as a means of detecting incoming enemy cruise missiles, which travel low under the control of terrain-guiding radars. This is part of the $1.4 billion Joint Land Attack Cruise Missile Defense Elevated Netted Sensor System (JLENS) being developed by Raytheon.
MARINES: In southern Afghanistan, gunfire erupts as 4,000 Marines continue with Operation Khanjar in Helmand Province, Afghanistan. This is a major Taliban stronghold and the world's largest opium poppy-producing region. One Marine is reported killed in action.

July 3
AVIATION: A U.S. Predator drone launches missiles at Taliban training facilities in Pakistan, killing 17 people and wounding 27 others. The facility was operated by Baitullah Mehsud, who is wanted by the Pakistani government for the assassination of former prime minister Benazir Bhutto.

July 4
AVIATION: The Air Force announces that it is upgrading all F-22 Raptor jet fighters for ground attack missions. This comes as a result of modifying the onboard AN/APG-77 radar to allow it to see realistic photo images on the ground.
MILITARY: Taliban forces bombard a U.S. Army base in Paktia Province, Afghanistan, killing two soldiers.

July 6
MILITARY: Two roadside bombs detonated in Kunduz Province, Afghanistan, kill 6 U.S. Army troops in their vehicles.

July 7
AVIATION: A U.S. Predator drone strike against Taliban targets in the Makeen area of South Waziristan, Pakistan, killing 12 militants associated with the band of Baitullah Mehsud.

July 8
AVIATION: A U.S. Predator drone launches missiles at a Taliban target in South Waziristan, Pakistan, critically wounding noted leader Maulana Fazullah and killing 45 of his associates.

MARINES: In southern Afghanistan, Brigadier General Larry Nicholson declares that more Afghan police and security forces are needed in order to completely contain the Taliban insurgency.

MILITARY: In Nuristan, Farah Province, Afghanistan, a U.S. soldier is killed in a clash with Taliban militants.

July 9

MILITARY: Lieutenant General James Dubik, who spent several months training and equipping Iraqi security forces since June, 2007, states that their progress is mixed and so they may require additional help throughout the near-distant future. The Iraqi army has expanded from 444,000 to 566,000 but still lacks qualified, experienced officers at every level.

July 10

AVIATION: A U.S. airstrike in Ghazni Province, Afghanistan, results in the deaths of 22 Taliban insurgents.

July 12

MILITARY: Coalition forces attack a Taliban compound in Uruzgan Province, Afghanistan, killing 12 militants.

MARINES: Roadside bombs take the lives of four Marines in Helmand Province, Afghanistan, as a major offensive continues through the southern part of that nation.

July 13

MILITARY: In Baghdad, Iraq, a roadside bomb wounds seven U.S. Army troops and their Iraqi translator. This is the first major attack since American forces turned over urban centers to Iraqi security forces.

July 14

MARINES: As U.S., coalition, and Afghan security forces push through Helmand Province, Afghanistan, two Marines are killed by sporadic gunfire.

NAVAL: In the Black Sea region, the guided-missile destroyer *Stout* drops anchor off Batumi, Georgia, ahead of joint military exercises. These are the first held since the Russian invasion in Ossetia in 2008.

July 16

MILITARY: Defense Secretary Robert Gates visits Fort Drum, New York, for a question-and-answer session from personnel of the 10th Mountain Division stationed there. At the time he notes there is a good chance additional troops would be deployed in Afghanistan, and he might also call for an increase in the U.S. Army's manpower ceilings.

July 17

AVIATION: A missile launched by a U.S. Predator drone strikes the home of militant Abdul Majid and kills five Taliban militants in Garhiwam Bahadur Khel, North Waziristan, Pakistan.

• In Washington, D.C., Senators Carl Levin and John McCain argue for striking additional funding for the F-22 jet fighter; President Barack Obama has threatened to veto any defense appropriation bill containing more money than for the 187 aircraft requested.

MILITARY: Iraqi insurgents shell the Contingency Operating Base in Basra, Iraq, killing three U.S. Army soldiers.

2009

July 18
AVIATION: An Air Force F-15E Strike Eagle inexplicably crashes in eastern Afghanistan, killing its two crew members. The case of the crash remains speculative but enemy action is ruled out.

NAVAL: At Pascagoula, Mississippi, the Northrop Grumman company lays the keel of the first LHA-6 amphibious assault vessel, which is intended to replace vessels of the older *Tarawa* class.

MILITARY: In Afghanistan, the Taliban release a video of Private Bowe R. Bergdahl, 501st Parachute Infantry Regiment, whom they claim to have captured after he strayed from his base.

July 20
MILITARY: A roadside bomb explodes in eastern Afghanistan, killing four U.S. Army troops. This brings the total number of coalition deaths to 55, making July the deadliest month of the Afghan war thus far. At least 30 of these deaths have been American.

July 23
AVIATION: A missile launched from a U.S. Predator drone reputedly kills the son of Saudi terrorist Osama bin Laden at an undisclosed location in Pakistan.

July 24
MILITARY: In Washington, D.C., President Barack Obama awards Staff Sergeant Jared Monti, 10th Mountain Division a posthumous Medal of Honor. He was killed on June 21, 2008 near Gowardesh, Afghanistan, while attempting to rescue a fellow soldier.
• Two U.S. Army troops are killed by a roadside bomb in southern Afghanistan.

July 30
AVIATION: In a major policy shift, U.S. Predator drone attacks will be refocused from neutralizing Al-Qaeda targets in Pakistan to local Taliban efforts. The change is undertaken to help shore up the Pakistani regime in the face of a protracted radical insurgency.

July 31
MILITARY: A U.S. Army soldier is killed in fighting in southern Afghanistan during a firefight with Taliban insurgents. This brings the total number of American slain in July to 40, making it the deadliest month of the Afghan conflict.

August 1
MILITARY: In southern Kandahar Province, Afghanistan, roadside bombings take the lives of three U.S. Army troops.

August 2
NAVAL: In southern Iraq, the remains of Lieutenant Commander Michael "Scott" Speicher are found and identified. His F/A-18 Hornet jet was shot down on January 17, 1991, on the first night of the Persian Gulf War.

August 4
AVIATION: The Quinnipac poll organization releases a national survey that found 61 percent of the American public support the dropping of atomic bombs on Hiroshima and Nagasaki in August 1945. Twenty-two percent said it was wrong and 16 percent were undecided.

August 5
AVIATION: A missile launched by a U.S. Predator drone strikes the home of wanted Taliban leader Baitullah Mehsud in South Waziristan, Pakistan, killing one of his two wives.

August 6
MARINES: A roadside bomb strikes a vehicle and kills four Marines in western Afghanistan. Casualties continue to rise as U.S. and coalition forces push deeper into Taliban territory.

August 7
AVIATION: A missile launched from a U.S. Predator drone kills Taliban leader Baitullah Mehsud as he laid on a rooftop in South Waziristan. Mehsud, who suffered from diabetes, was observed having his legs massaged—a clear indication of who it was—when the missile struck his father-in-law's house.

August 8
AVIATION: The Canadian government announces that it has possibly found the wreckage of a U.S. Army OA-10A Catalina amphibian aircraft that crashed in the St. Lawrence River on November 2, 1942. The United States and Canada will work together to recover the wreckage and any human remains still extant.
MILITARY: President Barack Obama asks Congress to shift at least $1 billion from next year's defense budget to recruiting an additional 15,000 troops for the U.S. Army. This addition will raise the number of active duty personnel from 547,000 to 562,400.

August 10
AVIATION: The U.S. Air Force revives the concept of the Strategic Air Command (SAC), which was disbanded in 1992 following the collapse of the Soviet Union. The new organization is called the Global Strike Command.
• In Afghanistan, U.S. and coalition officials point to declining numbers of Afghan civilian casualties due to new restrictions and rules of engagement for dropping bombs on Taliban targets. Taliban militants routinely use civilians as "human shields" to evade bombing attacks, but the trade off in terms of better public relations is viewed as worth the sacrifice.

August 11
AVIATION: A missile launched from a U.S. Predator drone strikes a house used by Taliban militants in Kani Guram, South Waziristan, Pakistan, killing 14 people.

August 12
MARINES: The town of Dahaneh, Helmand Province, Afghanistan, is assaulted by 500 helicopter-borne of the 2nd Battalion, 3rd Marines backed by AV-8B Harrier jump jets. The Taliban in town resist fiercely, losing eight fighters in a stand-up firefight, then withdraw into the countryside.

August 13
MARINES: In southern Afghanistan, Marines continue assaulting Dahaneh, Afghanistan, securing it from resident Taliban units that refuse to abandon their strong point.

August 14
NAVAL: The remains of Lieutenant Commander Scott Speicher are laid to rest in Jacksonville, Florida, following his death 18 years earlier in the 1991 Gulf War.

August 17
MILITARY: General Ray Odierno expressed his desire to keep U.S. forces in contested areas of the country separating the Arabs and Kurds to the north. This represents a departure from an earlier security arrangement requiring American forces to leave all urban areas by June 30, but the general maintains this is a temporary "confidence-building" measure intending to enhance local security there.
MARINES: A roadside bomb kills a Marine in southern Afghanistan, bringing to 22 the number of Americans killed this month.

August 19
AVIATION: A U.S. Army UH-60 Black Hawk helicopter crashes on the slopes of 14,421-foot tall Mount Massive, Colorado, killing all four soldiers onboard.
MILITARY: The U.S. government reveals that the American death toll in Iraq stands at 4,332 since Operation Iraqi Freedom commenced in March 2003. Of this total, 3,465 were killed in hostile actions.
• A roadside bomb in Kabul, Afghanistan, takes the life of 59-year old First Sergeant Jose San Nicolas Crisostomo of Spanaway, Washington State. He is the oldest soldier to die in action there.

August 21
AVIATION: A missile launched from a U.S. Predator drone strikes a suspected Taliban hideout in Dande Darpa Khel, North Waziristan, Pakistan, killing 11 insurgents. This town is the stronghold of militant leader Sirajuddin Haqqani, who reputedly has close connections to the terrorist group Al-Qaeda.
MILITARY: In Iraq, four U.S. Army sergeants are charged with cruelty and maltreatment of their troops. They are identified as Enoch Chatman, Bob Clements, Jarett Taylor, and Daniel Weber of B Troop, 2nd Squadron, 13th Cavalry Regiment from Fort Bliss, Texas.
MARINES: Adrien E. Augustin, a 20-year old recruit from Kenton, Kentucky, collapses and dies during a fitness test at the Marine Corps Recruit Depot at Parris Island, South Carolina.

August 23
AVIATION: The Air Force test launches another Minuteman 3 ICBM from Vandenberg Air Force Base, California, which splashes down at a target range in the Kwajalein Atoll, 4,200 miles distant.

August 25
MILITARY: A bomb blast at Kandahar, southern Afghanistan, takes the lives of four U.S. Army soldiers.

August 27
AVIATION: A helicopter from the guided-missile cruiser *Chancellorsville* is fired on by Somali pirates in the Gulf of Aden.
• A missile launched by a U.S. Predator drone strikes a Taliban hideout operated by Waliur Rehman in Tapar Ghar, South Waziristan, Pakistan, killing six militants.

August 28
MILITARY: A roadside bomb kills a U.S. Army soldier in eastern Afghanistan, bringing the total number of Americans killed this month to 45. August is now the deadliest month of Operation Enduring Freedom, with a total of 732 dead American since the war began in October 2001.

August 31
MILITARY: Two separate bombing incidents in southern Afghanistan take the lives of two U.S. servicemen, bringing the monthly total to 47 dead Americans.
• In Kabul, General Stanley McChrystal, commanding all U.S. and coalition forces in Afghanistan, calls for a new strategy to defeat the Taliban, one which will include an increase in the number of U.S. forces there.

September 3
MILITARY: An improvised explosive device (IED) takes the life of two American servicemen in southern Afghanistan as they were on patrol.

September 4
MILITARY: The Pentagon announces that tours of the 82nd Airborne Division in Afghanistan will be extended from 12 to 14 months. This is being done to allow newly returning members of the 101st Airborne Division a full 12 months at home.

September 6
MILITARY: A bomb blast in southern Afghanistan takes the life of a U.S. serviceman.

September 7
AVIATION: A missile launched from a U.S. Predator drone strikes a Taliban compound in the village of Machi Khel, North Waziristan, Pakistan, killing five militants. It is suspected that al-Qaeda leaders Ilyas Kashmiri and Mustafa al Jaziri also died.
MILITARY: Soldiers from the 10th Mountain Division break into a hospital in Wardak Province, Afghanistan, searching for fleeing Taliban operatives. Afterwards, members of a Swedish charity who operated the facility accuse the Americans of violating Muslim customs by entering female wards.

September 8
MILITARY: A roadside bomb detonated in southern Baghdad, Iraq, strikes a U.S. Army patrol, killing one soldier. Three more subsequently die in a similar attack in northern Iraq. This brings the total number of American dead since March 2003 to 4,343.
• Defense officials declare that a U.S. Army patrol caught up in a "complex attack" in Afghanistan loses four soldiers dead.

September 9
MARINES: Defense Secretary Gates condemns as "appalling" a decision by the Associated Press (AP) to release photographs of a mortally wounded Marine lane corporal Joshua M. Bernard, who died of his wounds following an April 14 ambush in Helmand Province, Afghanistan.

September 11
MILITARY: Senate Armed Services Chairman Senator Carl Levin advised President Barack Obama to refrain from sending additional U.S. troops to Afghanistan

until more Afghan security forces have been trained and deployed. He also added that additional equipment can be shifted there from Iraq as the military commitment winds down.

MARINES: A court-martial sentences Corporal Mathew Nelson to eight years in prison, demotion to private, and a bad-conduct discharge for the death of Lane Corporal Patrick Malone during a hazing incident in Anbar Province, Iraq, on March 3, 2009.

September 12

MILITARY: Two roadside bombings in Afghanistan take the lives of five U.S. Army troops.

September 13

AVIATION: Airstrikes by U.S. and coalition warplanes kill several dozen Taliban militants in the Bala Baluk district of Farah Province, Afghanistan.

MILITARY: Taliban forces ambush a U.S. Army patrol in Farah Province, Afghanistan, killing three Americans and seven Afghan troops. Air power is called in with deadly results to the attackers.

September 14

AVIATION: A missile launched from a U.S. Predator drone strikes a car in the town of Mir Ali, North Waziristan, Pakistan, killing four Taliban militants.

• A Muslim terrorist opens fire at an American military helicopter near Tal Abta, Iraq, and is killed after the helicopter fired back.

September 15

MILITARY: Admiral Mike Mullen, chairman of the Joint Chiefs of Staff (JCS), goes on record today as favoring the immediate deployment of additional combat forces to Afghanistan.

September 16

MILITARY: President Barack Obama, feeling pressure from Democrat Party liberals not to send additional forces into Afghanistan, declares that there is "no immediate decision pending."

• The U.S. military closes its largest detention camp at Bucca in Iraq, having released or transferred several thousand detainees to Iraqi control. The camp was christened after Ronald Bucca, a former Green Beret and New York City fire marshal who died in the September 11, 2001 attack on the World Trade Center.

September 17

AVIATION: A missile fired by a U.S. Predator drone kills two dangerous al-Qaeda leaders in Pakistan. One, Najmiddin Kamolitdinovich Jalolov, was from Uzbekistan and apparent head of the ultra violent Islamic Jihad Union.

September 20

AVIATION: An Army UH-60 Black Hawk helicopter crashes near Balad Air Base, Iraq, killing a U.S. service member and injuring 12 others.

MILITARY: Fighting and a roadside bombing in southern Afghanistan takes the lives of the three American servicemen.

September 21

MILITARY: General Stanley McChrystal, commander of all U.S. forces in Afghanistan, submits a 66-page report to President Barack Obama, outlining the case for sending additional troops there. He warns the commander in chief that underresourcing the war effort could lose that country to an ongoing Taliban insurgency.

Marines: Sergeant David Budwah is charged by Marine Corps officials with faking war injuries for personal gain. The 34-year old native of Springhill, Louisiana, is to face a court-martial for claiming to have served in Afghanistan, when he actually spent all his time on Okinawa.

September 24
Aviation: A missile launched from a U.S. Predator drone kills 12 Taliban militants in the village of Dande Darpa Khel, North Waziristan, Pakistan.

September 25
Military: A combination of firefights and roadside bombings throughout southern Afghanistan takes the lives of five more U.S. service personnel.

September 28
Aviation: An amateur historian conducting a sonar search off the Southern California coast discovered the wreckage of a Lockheed T-33 jet trainer that had been missing since October 15, 1955.

Military: A large raid in Farah Province, Afghanistan, by U.S. Army troops and Afghan security forces results in the deaths of at least 30 Taliban fighters.

• General Stanley McChrystal, during an interview on CBS television, admits that he has conferred only once with President Barack Obama over the past 70 days. This revelation fuels ongoing political speculation that the president is waiting too long to deal with the general's request for additional troops in Afghanistan.

September 29
Aviation: Missiles launched from a U.S. Predator drone strike two buildings operated by Taliban militants in North and South Waziristan, Pakistan, killing 13 people including commander Irfan Mehsud.

Military: General Ray Odierno announces that he is prepared to send 4,000 U.S. troops home from Iraq by the end of October. He cites the dramatic reduction in terrorist activity, dropping from 4,000 attacks per month in August 2007 to 600 in August 2009.

• A line mine detonated by the al-Qaeda linked Abu Sayyaf group kills two U.S. Army soldiers in the Muslim-dominated southern Philippines.

Marines: A Marine judge has dismissed murder charges against Sergeant Jermaine Nelson after he agreed to a plea bargain that included no jail time and an honorable discharge. Previously, he and three other Marines had been accused of killing an unarmed Iraqi detainee in heavy fighting at Fallujah in 2004.

September 30
Aviation: In Washington, D.C., the U.S. Senate brushes aside criticism by Defense Secretary Robert M. Gates and votes $2.5 billion to continue production of the Boeing C-17 transport jet; another 10 aircraft will be procured to keep the assembly lines open.

Military: General Ray Odierno, top U.S. commander in Iraq, addresses a Congressional committee and warns them not to lose sight of the ongoing problems in that region. He also declares that the controversial troop surge in 2007 has greatly enhanced Iraqi security against terrorism.

• The Ibn Sina hospital in Baghdad, Iraq, which had been administered by the U.S. Army as an emergency medical facility for wounded soldiers, is turned over to Iraqi authorities.

• A U.S. Army soldier is killed by a suicide bomber in Khost Province, Afghanistan, raising the total number of fatalities for that month to 43.

October 1

MILITARY: General Ray Odierno, addressing reporters at a Pentagon news briefing, said he doubts that the United States can declare victory by the time all U.S. forces are withdrawn from that country in 2011. He feels that five or even ten years will pass before the true extent of Iraqi national security can be determined.

October 2

MILITARY: In Copenhagen, Denmark, President Barack Obama schedules an impromptu conference with General Stanley McChrystal on Air Force One to discuss the recent turn of events in Afghanistan. The general had previously delivered a speech in London, England, whereby he rejected a call to scale back the war against the Taliban in favor of concentrating upon al-Qaeda.

• A suicide bomber in eastern Afghanistan strikes a U.S. Army convoy, killing two U.S. Army soldiers.

October 3

TERRORISM: In Wardak Province, Afghanistan, an Afghan policeman, possibly a Taliban infiltrator, kills two U.S. servicemen then flees.

October 4–6

MILITARY: In Nuristan Province, Afghanistan, U.S. forces engage in a protracted engagement with Taliban operatives, killing more than 100 foreign fighters; eight Americans are killed in a major attack on their remote outpost near the Pakistani border.

October 5

MILITARY: In Washington, D.C., President Barack Obama concurs that withdrawal from Afghanistan is not an option.

October 6

MILITARY: In Nuristan Province, Afghanistan, U.S. and Afghan security forces engage Taliban militants in mountainous terrain, killing at least 40.

October 14

DIPLOMACY: In Baghdad, Iraq, the government all but accuses Syria of having aided and abetted the series of large truck bombings the previous August and asks that the United Nations step in and help investigate. Former Baathist extremists are suspected of being responsible for the blasts.

MILITARY: In London, England, Prime Minister Gordon Brown declares his willingness to dispatch additional 500 British troops to Afghanistan, but only on condition that NATO and the Afghan government also commit more resources to fighting the Taliban insurgency. At the time, Britain is deploying 9,000 troops in Afghanistan.

• In Washington, D.C., excerpts of General Stanley McChrystal's assessment of Afghanistan are released, wherein he states that even the addition of as many as 80,000 additional troops many not win the war unless there is a major crackdown

on Afghan government corruption. He feels that the Afghan government's indifference to it own populace is forcing many desperate citizens to assist the Taliban.
TERRORISM: In Baghdad, Iraq, the government human rights agency releases a report that declares 85,694 Iraqi citizens have been killed in acts of terrorism between 2004 and 2008. The toll includes 263 college professors, 21 judges, 95 lawyers, and 269 journalists, all of whom appear to have been targeted.

October 16
MILITARY: In Washington, D.C., the Department of the Army cancels plans to deploy a brigade of 3,500 troops from the 10th Mountain Division to Iraq, citing the improved security situation there. This renders them available for deployment in Afghanistan, however.

October 20
MILITARY: In Baghdad, Iraq, top U.S. commander General Raymond T. Odierno predicts a very rapid drawdown of U.S. forces from the country following the January 2010 elections. He intends to withdraw all combat forces by August of that year, with a complete withdrawal no later than 2011.

October 26
AVIATION: In Badghis Province, Afghanistan, a U.S. Army UH-60 Black Hawk helicopter crashes, killing 14 Americans on board. To the south, two other helicopters collide in midair, killing four troops and injuring two others. The cause of the accident is not known.

October 27
AVIATION: In Nuristan Province, Afghanistan, NATO forces uncover the wreckage of a U.S. Army C-12 Huron transport aircraft that crashed two weeks earlier. Enemy action is ruled out, so the accident is attributed to the violent downdrafts common in the region's mountain ranges.
TERRORISM: In Iraq, the militant Sunni group al-Qaeda in Iraq claims responsibility for the bombing in Baghdad two days earlier.
• In Afghanistan, a rash of roadside bombing takes the lives of eight American servicemen.

November 4
TERRORISM: In Helmand Province, Afghanistan, an Afghan policeman, most likely a Taliban infiltrator, kills five British soldiers. Six other soldiers are wounded, in addition to two Afghan policemen.

November 6
MILITARY: In Ottawa, Canada, Chief of the Defence Staff General Walter Natynczyk announces that Canada will commence pulling its 2,800 troops out of Afghanistan beginning in the summer of 2011.

November 8
MILITARY: In Washington, D.C., army chief of staff General George Casey endorses President Barack Obama's plan to deploy additional forces to Afghanistan to combat the Taliban insurgency.

December 1
MILITARY: In Washington, D.C., Pentagon officials declare that marines will constitute the majority of 35,000 reinforcements to be sent to Afghanistan by the

spring. This is part of President Barack Obama's "surge" for the region once American forces in Iraq begin to withdraw.

December 4

AVIATION: In Helmand Province, Afghanistan, MV-22 transports drop the 3rd Battalion, 4th Marines behind Taliban lines at Now Zad. A second column of marines simultaneously pushes northward from their Forward Operating Base (FOB) at Now Zad, penetrating Taliban minefields with armored steamrollers. This is also the first major Afghan operation undertaken since the surge was announced the previous spring.

December 9

MILITARY: In Washington, D.C., General David H. Petraeus informs a congressional committee that progress against the Taliban in Afghanistan is likely to be slower than the military surge in Iraq was two years previous. He anticipates that at least 18 months will lapse before real progress can be measured in terms of reducing terror attacks against civilians and Coalition personnel.

December 18

TERRORISM: In Baghdad, Iraq, a series of coordinated car bombings kills 118 people and wounds 261 more. Officials begin to question if the Sunni-based al-Qaeda insurgency, largely dormant, is making a comeback.

December 21

AVIATION: In Afghanistan, it is reported that the first MC-12W spyplanes, which are highly advanced and classified, are due to be deployed under the aegis of the U.S. Air Force. This four-crew, twin-engined aircraft is equipped with video cameras and other senors and is capable of beaming real-time intelligence to troops on the ground.

December 25

TERRORISM: In Afghanistan, the Taliban release a videotape of captured Idaho National Guard private Bowe Bergdahl, who made anti-American statements, presumably under duress.

December 30

TERRORISM: In Kandahar Province, Afghanistan, an improvised explosive device strikes a Canadian armored vehicle, killing four soldiers and a female journalist.
• In Khost Province, Afghanistan, an apparent Taliban double agent recruited by the Central Intelligence Agency (CIA) strolls into CIA headquarters at Forward Operating Base Chapman and detonates himself, killing seven agents and injuring six more.
• In Anbar Province, Iraq, a bomb explodes in Ramadi, killing 23 people, 13 of them policemen.

December 31

MILITARY: For the first time since 2003, the month of December sees no recorded American combat-related fatalities in Iraq. "That is a very significant milestone for us as we continue to move forward," General Raymond T. Odierno declares, "And I think it also speaks to the level of violence and how it has decreased over time." Since the beginning of Operation Iraqi Freedom, 4,373 U.S. service personnel have been killed, including 898 from noncombat incidents. The Iraqi Interior

Ministry also notes that 2,773 civilians were killed and 8,900 wounded—the lowest toll since 2003. The story is reversed in Afghanistan, where 304 U.S. service members were killed in the previous year, 151 more fatalities sustained than in 2008. This brings the death toll of Operation Enduring Freedom, launched in October 2001, to 933 service members. Among coalition partners, Canada is second in fatalities, with 32 deaths, while 2,021 Afghan civilians are also reported killed—465 of these by U.S. and Coalition forces.

MAPS

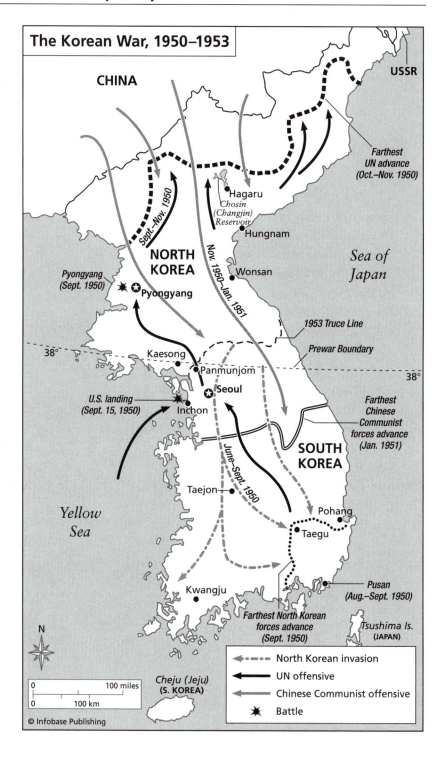

The Korean War, 1950–1953

CHINA

USSR

Farthest
UN advance
(Oct.–Nov. 1950)

Sept.–Nov. 1950

Hagaru
Chosin
(Changjin)
Reservoir
Hungnam

NORTH
KOREA

Sea of
Japan

Nov. 1950–Jan. 1951

Wonsan

Pyongyang
(Sept. 1950)

Pyongyang

1953 Truce Line

Prewar Boundary

38°

Kaesong

Panmunjom

38°

Seoul

Farthest
Chinese
Communist
forces advance
(Jan. 1951)

U.S. landing
(Sept. 15, 1950)

Inchon

June–Sept. 1950

SOUTH
KOREA

Yellow
Sea

Taejon

Pohang

Taegu

Kwangju

Pusan
(Aug.–Sept. 1950)

Farthest North Korean
forces advance
(Sept. 1950)

Tsushima Is.
(JAPAN)

N

North Korean invasion

UN offensive

Chinese Communist offensive

Battle

0   100 miles
0   100 km

Cheju (Jeju)
(S. KOREA)

© Infobase Publishing

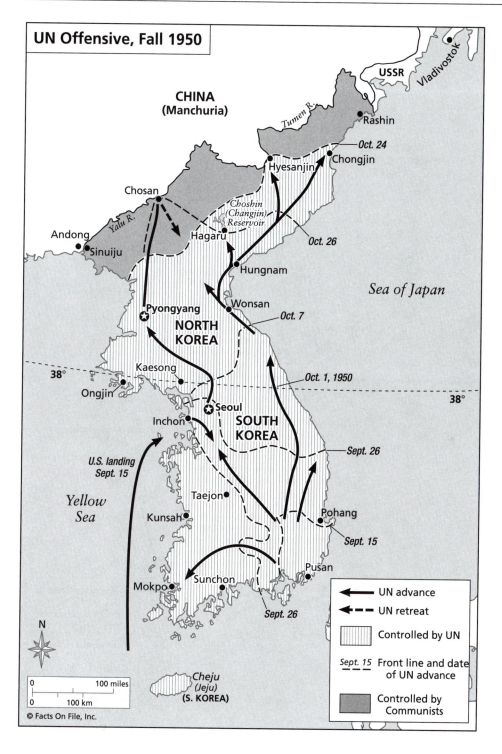

UN Offensive, Fall 1950

CHINA
(Manchuria)

USSR

Vladivostok

Tumen R.

Rashin

Oct. 24

Chongjin

Hyesanjin

Chosan

*Choshin
(Changjin)
Reservoir*

Yalu R.

Hagaru

Oct. 26

Andong

Sinuiju

Hungnam

Sea of Japan

Wonsan

Pyongyang

Oct. 7

**NORTH
KOREA**

Kaesong

Oct. 1, 1950

38°   38°

Ongjin

Inchon

Seoul

**SOUTH
KOREA**

Sept. 26

*U.S. landing
Sept. 15*

*Yellow
Sea*

Taejon

Pohang

Kunsah

Sept. 15

Mokpo   Sunchon

Pusan

Sept. 26

N

Legend:

← UN advance

◀--- UN retreat

▓ Controlled by UN

Sept. 15 Front line and date
of UN advance

▒ Controlled by
Communists

0   100 miles
0   100 km

© Facts On File, Inc.

*Cheju
(Jeju)*
(S. KOREA)

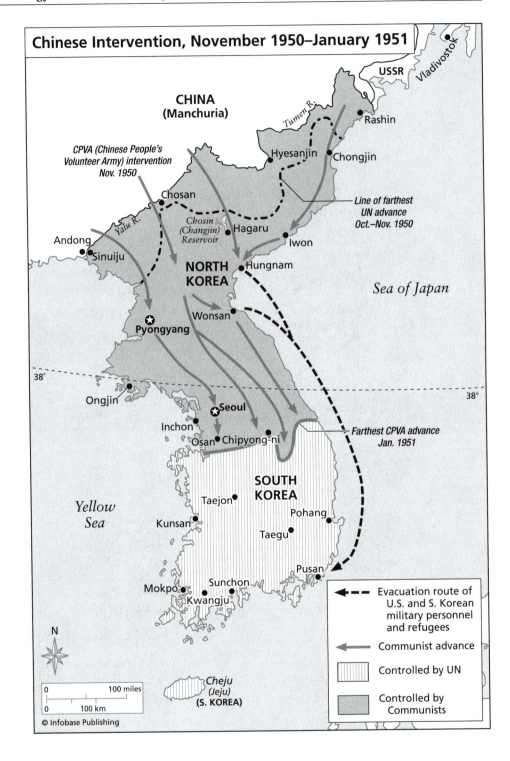

Chinese Intervention, November 1950–January 1951

CHINA (Manchuria)

USSR

Vladivostok

Tumen R.

Rashin

CPVA (Chinese People's Volunteer Army) intervention Nov. 1950

Hyesanjin

Chongjin

Chosan

Line of farthest UN advance Oct.–Nov. 1950

Yalu R.

Chosin (Changjin) Reservoir

Hagaru

Andong

Sinuiju

Iwon

NORTH KOREA

Hungnam

Sea of Japan

Wonsan

Pyongyang

38°

38°

Ongjin

Seoul

Inchon

Chipyong-ni

Farthest CPVA advance Jan. 1951

Osan

SOUTH KOREA

Yellow Sea

Taejon

Pohang

Kunsan

Taegu

Pusan

Mokpo

Sunchon

Kwangju

N

Cheju (Jeju) (S. KOREA)

0   100 miles
0   100 km

© Infobase Publishing

- ◀ - - Evacuation route of U.S. and S. Korean military personnel and refugees
- ◀─── Communist advance
- Controlled by UN
- Controlled by Communists

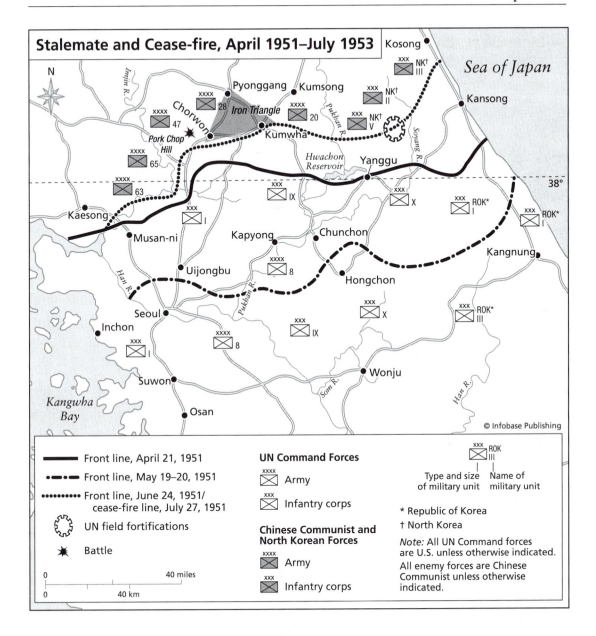

Stalemate and Cease-fire, April 1951–July 1953

N

Sea of Japan

Kosong

Pyonggang • Kumsong

Chorwon

Iron Triangle

Kumwha

Kansong

Pork Chop Hill

Hwachon Reservoir

Yanggu

38°

Kaesong

Musan-ni

Kapyong

Chunchon

Kangnung

Uijongbu

Hongchon

Seoul

Inchon

Wonju

Suwon

Kangwha Bay

Osan

Imjin R.
Pukhan R.
Soyang R.
Han R.
Pukhan R.
Som R.
Han R.

© Infobase Publishing

Legend:

— Front line, April 21, 1951

-•-•- Front line, May 19–20, 1951

••••••••• Front line, June 24, 1951/
cease-fire line, July 27, 1951

UN field fortifications

✳ Battle

0 — 40 miles
0 — 40 km

UN Command Forces

Army

Infantry corps

Chinese Communist and North Korean Forces

Army

Infantry corps

Type and size of military unit | Name of military unit

* Republic of Korea
† North Korea

Note: All UN Command forces are U.S. unless otherwise indicated.

All enemy forces are Chinese Communist unless otherwise indicated.

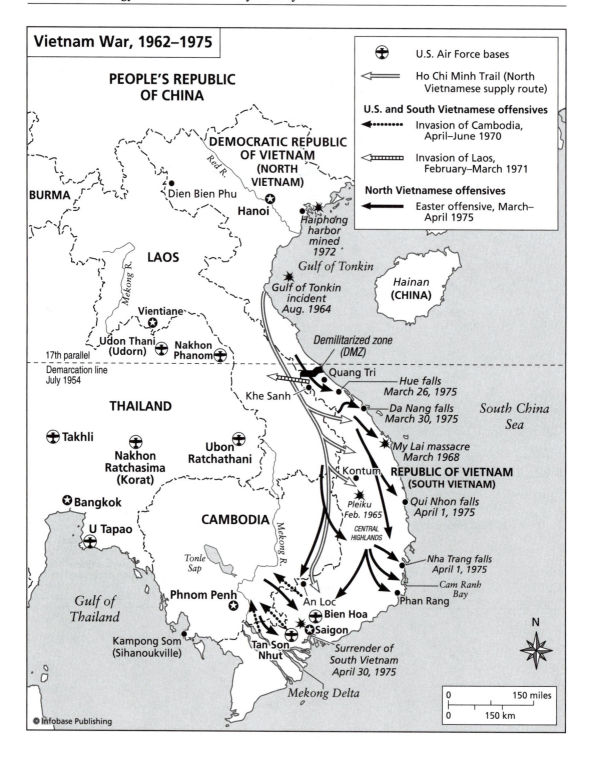

Vietnam War, 1962–1975

Legend:
- ⊕ U.S. Air Force bases
- ⇐ Ho Chi Minh Trail (North Vietnamese supply route)

U.S. and South Vietnamese offensives
- ◄······· Invasion of Cambodia, April–June 1970
- ⇐▭▭▭ Invasion of Laos, February–March 1971

North Vietnamese offensives
- ◄━━━ Easter offensive, March–April 1975

PEOPLE'S REPUBLIC OF CHINA

DEMOCRATIC REPUBLIC OF VIETNAM (NORTH VIETNAM)

Red R.

BURMA

Dien Bien Phu

Hanoi

Haiphong harbor mined 1972

Gulf of Tonkin

LAOS

Mekong R.

Gulf of Tonkin incident Aug. 1964

Hainan (CHINA)

Vientiane

Udon Thani (Udorn)   Nakhon Phanom

17th parallel
Demarcation line
July 1954

Demilitarized zone (DMZ)

Quang Tri

Hue falls March 26, 1975

Khe Sanh

Da Nang falls March 30, 1975

THAILAND

South China Sea

⊕ Takhli

Ubon Ratchathani

Nakhon Ratchasima (Korat)

My Lai massacre March 1968

Kontum

REPUBLIC OF VIETNAM (SOUTH VIETNAM)

⊕ Bangkok

CAMBODIA

Mekong R.

Pleiku Feb. 1965

Qui Nhon falls April 1, 1975

⊕ U Tapao

CENTRAL HIGHLANDS

Tonle Sap

Nha Trang falls April 1, 1975

Cam Ranh Bay

Phnom Penh

An Loc

Phan Rang

Gulf of Thailand

Bien Hoa

Saigon

N

Kampong Som (Sihanoukville)

Tan Son Nhut

Surrender of South Vietnam April 30, 1975

Mekong Delta

© Infobase Publishing

| 0 | 150 miles |
| 0 | 150 km |

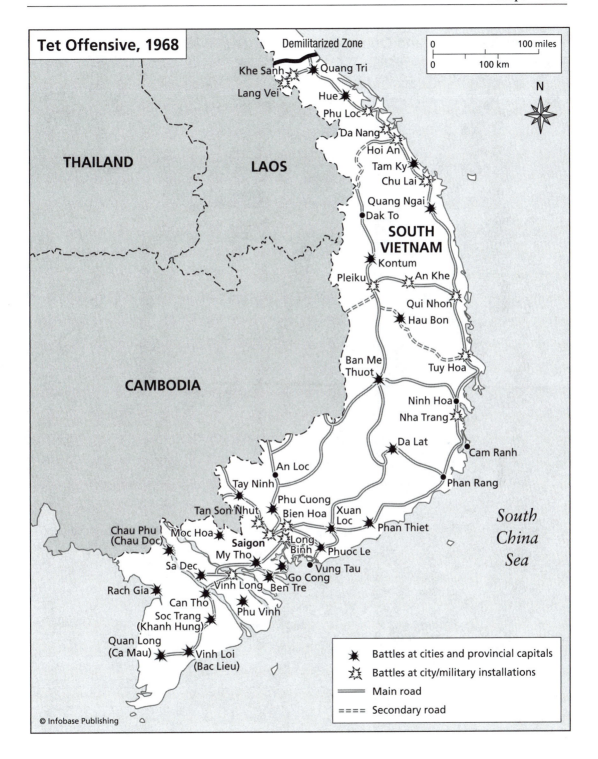

Tet Offensive, 1968

Demilitarized Zone

0 _____ 100 miles
0 _____ 100 km

N

Khe Sanh
Quang Tri
Lang Vei
Hue
Phu Loc
Da Nang
Hoi An
Tam Ky
Chu Lai
Quang Ngai
Dak To

THAILAND

LAOS

SOUTH VIETNAM

Kontum
Pleiku
An Khe
Qui Nhon
Hau Bon

Ban Me Thuot
Tuy Hoa

CAMBODIA

Ninh Hoa
Nha Trang

Da Lat
Cam Ranh

An Loc
Tay Ninh
Phan Rang

Phu Cuong
Tan Son Nhut
Bien Hoa
Xuan Loc
Phan Thiet

South China Sea

Chau Phu (Chau Doc)
Moc Hoa
Saigon
Long Binh
Phuoc Le
My Tho
Vung Tau
Sa Dec
Go Cong
Rach Gia
Vinh Long
Ben Tre
Can Tho
Phu Vinh
Soc Trang (Khanh Hung)
Quan Long (Ca Mau)
Vinh Loi (Bac Lieu)

✳ Battles at cities and provincial capitals
✳ Battles at city/military installations
——— Main road
==== Secondary road

© Infobase Publishing

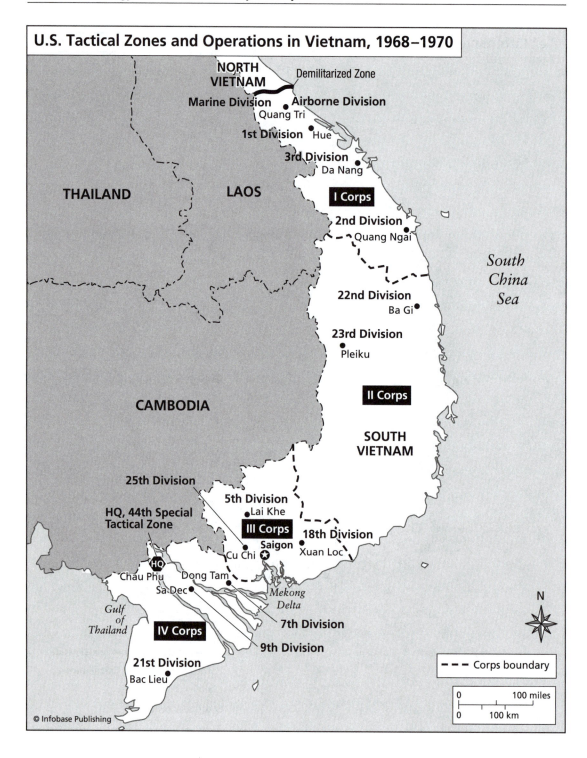

U.S. Tactical Zones and Operations in Vietnam, 1968–1970

NORTH VIETNAM

Demilitarized Zone

Marine Division   Airborne Division
Quang Tri

1st Division   Hue

3rd Division
Da Nang

I Corps

THAILAND   LAOS

2nd Division
Quang Ngai

South China Sea

22nd Division
Ba Gi

23rd Division
Pleiku

CAMBODIA

II Corps

SOUTH VIETNAM

25th Division

HQ, 44th Special Tactical Zone

5th Division
Lai Khe

III Corps   18th Division
Saigon   Xuan Loc
Cu Chi

HQ
Chau Phu   Dong Tam
Sa Dec   Mekong Delta

Gulf of Thailand   7th Division

IV Corps   9th Division

21st Division
Bac Lieu

N

– – – Corps boundary

0   100 miles
0   100 km

© Infobase Publishing

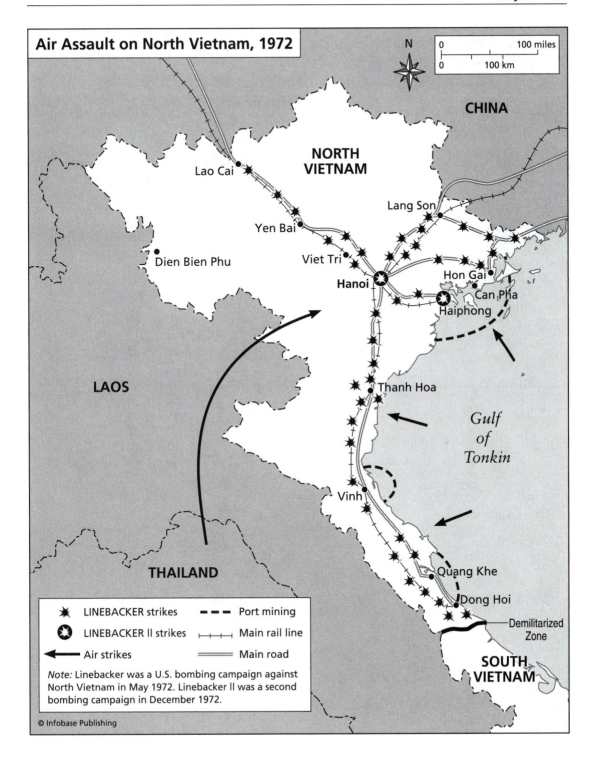

Air Assault on North Vietnam, 1972

N

| 0 | | 100 miles |
| 0 | | 100 km |

CHINA

NORTH VIETNAM

Lao Cai

Lang Son

Yen Bai

Viet Tri

Dien Bien Phu

Hanoi

Hon Gai

Can Pha

Haiphong

LAOS

Thanh Hoa

Gulf
of
Tonkin

Vinh

THAILAND

Quang Khe

Dong Hoi

Demilitarized Zone

SOUTH VIETNAM

✸ LINEBACKER strikes

✪ LINEBACKER II strikes

➙ Air strikes

– – – Port mining

+++++ Main rail line

═══ Main road

Note: Linebacker was a U.S. bombing campaign against North Vietnam in May 1972. Linebacker II was a second bombing campaign in December 1972.

© Infobase Publishing

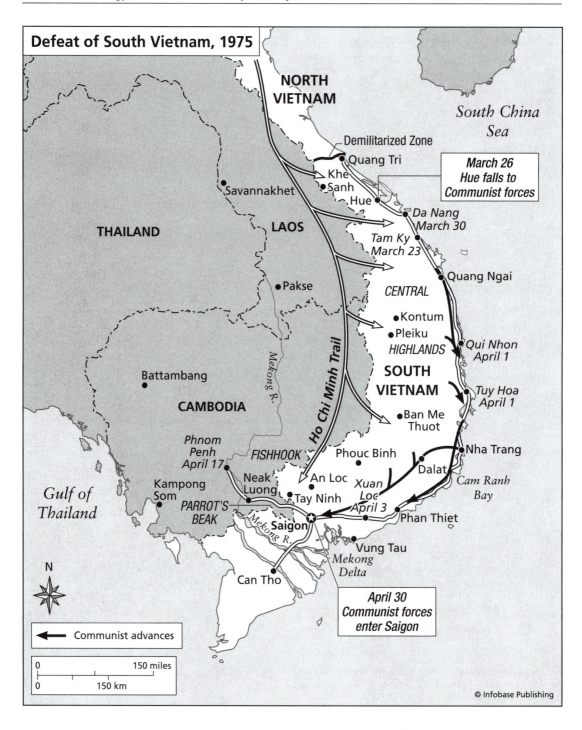

Defeat of South Vietnam, 1975

NORTH VIETNAM

South China Sea

Demilitarized Zone

Quang Tri

Khe Sanh

March 26 Hue falls to Communist forces

Savannakhet

Hue

Da Nang *March 30*

THAILAND

LAOS

Tam Ky *March 23*

Quang Ngai

CENTRAL

Pakse

Kontum

Pleiku

HIGHLANDS

Qui Nhon *April 1*

Mekong R.

SOUTH VIETNAM

Battambang

Ho Chi Minh Trail

Tuy Hoa *April 1*

CAMBODIA

Ban Me Thuot

Nha Trang

Phnom Penh *April 17*

FISHHOOK

Phouc Binh

Dalat

Cam Ranh Bay

Kampong Som

Neak Luong

An Loc

Xuan Loc April 3

Gulf of Thailand

PARROT'S BEAK

Tay Ninh

Mekong R.

Saigon

Phan Thiet

N

Vung Tau

Mekong Delta

Can Tho

April 30 Communist forces enter Saigon

← Communist advances

| 0 | 150 miles |
| 0 | 150 km |

© Infobase Publishing

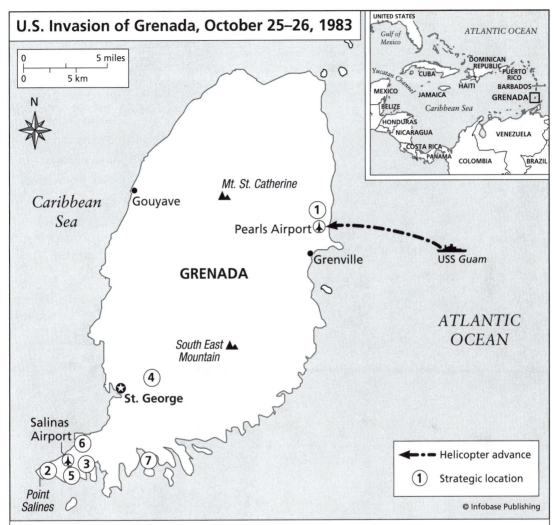

U.S. Invasion of Grenada, October 25–26, 1983

1. **October 25, 5:00 A.M.:** Helicopters with 400 U.S. Marines leave the USS *Guam* and commence an assault on Pearls Airport. They secure the airport within two hours, and the Guam then moves to the west coast.

2. **October 25, 5:36 A.M.:** Flying from a staging area in Barbados, hundreds of U.S. Army Rangers parachute into the Point Salines area. They meet heavy resistance, but by 7:15 A.M. the airport is secured.

3. **October 25, 8:50 A.M.:** Rangers secure the True Blue campus of the St. George's University School of Medicine.

4. **October 25, 7:30 P.M.:** In the St. George's area, the Governor's House is secured after 250 U.S. Marines land with five tanks and 13 amphibious vehicles; later Richmond

Hill Prison and Fort Frederick nearby are captured. By this time, the island is overrun by a combined force of 2,200 U.S. and Organization of Eastern Caribbean States troops. Pockets of resistance from some Cuban troops continue.

5. **October 26, 9:00 A.M.:** The evacuation of medical students begins from Salinas Airport. Meanwhile, additional troops arrive from Barbados; the invading force will eventually exceed 5,000.

6. **October 26, 4:00 P.M.:** Following a helicopter assault on the Grand Anse medical campus, students are evacuated.

7. **October 26, late afternoon:** U.S. planes strafe positions still occupied by Cuban soldiers. However, the fighting is effectively over, and the entire island is soon secured.

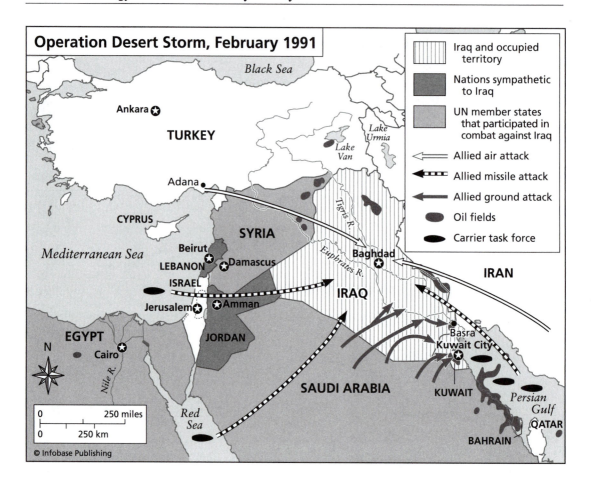

Operation Desert Storm, February 1991

Legend:
- Iraq and occupied territory
- Nations sympathetic to Iraq
- UN member states that participated in combat against Iraq
- Allied air attack
- Allied missile attack
- Allied ground attack
- Oil fields
- Carrier task force

Black Sea

Ankara

TURKEY

Lake Urmia

Lake Van

Adana

CYPRUS

SYRIA

Tigris R.

Beirut

Euphrates R.

Baghdad

IRAN

LEBANON   Damascus

Mediterranean Sea

ISRAEL

IRAQ

Jerusalem   Amman

EGYPT

N

Cairo

JORDAN

Basra

Kuwait City

SAUDI ARABIA

KUWAIT

Persian Gulf

QATAR

Nile R.

0   250 miles

0   250 km

Red Sea

BAHRAIN

© Infobase Publishing

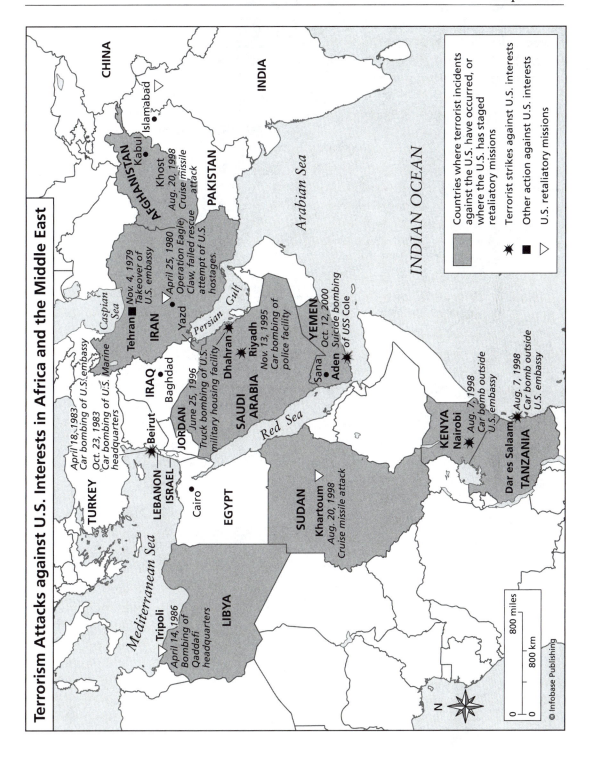

Terrorism Attacks against U.S. Interests in Africa and the Middle East

Legend:
- Countries where terrorist incidents against the U.S. have occurred, or where the U.S. has staged retaliatory missions
- ✴ Terrorist strikes against U.S. interests
- ■ Other action against U.S. interests
- ▷ U.S. retaliatory missions

CHINA

INDIA

Arabian Sea

INDIAN OCEAN

PAKISTAN

AFGHANISTAN

Kabul

Islamabad

Khost
Aug. 20, 1998
Cruise missile attack

Nov. 4, 1979
Takeover of U.S. embassy

April 25, 1980
Operation Eagle Claw, failed rescue attempt of U.S. hostages.

Tehran ■ IRAN

Yazd ▷

Caspian Sea

Persian Gulf

Dhahran
June 25, 1996
Truck bombing of U.S. military housing facility

Riyadh
Nov. 13, 1995
Car bombing of police facility

SAUDI ARABIA

YEMEN

Sana
Aden
Oct. 12, 2000
Suicide bombing of USS Cole

IRAQ

Baghdad

JORDAN

ISRAEL

LEBANON

Beirut ✴

April 18, 1983
Car bombing of U.S. embassy

Oct. 23, 1983
Car bombing of U.S. Marine headquarters

TURKEY

Mediterranean Sea

Cairo

EGYPT

Red Sea

SUDAN

Khartoum ▷
Aug. 20, 1998
Cruise missile attack

LIBYA

Tripoli ▷
April 14, 1986
Bombing of Qaddafi headquarters

KENYA

Nairobi ✴
Aug. 7, 1998
Car bomb outside U.S. embassy

TANZANIA

Dar es Salaam ✴
Aug. 7, 1998
Car bomb outside U.S. embassy

N

0   800 miles
0   800 km

© Infobase Publishing

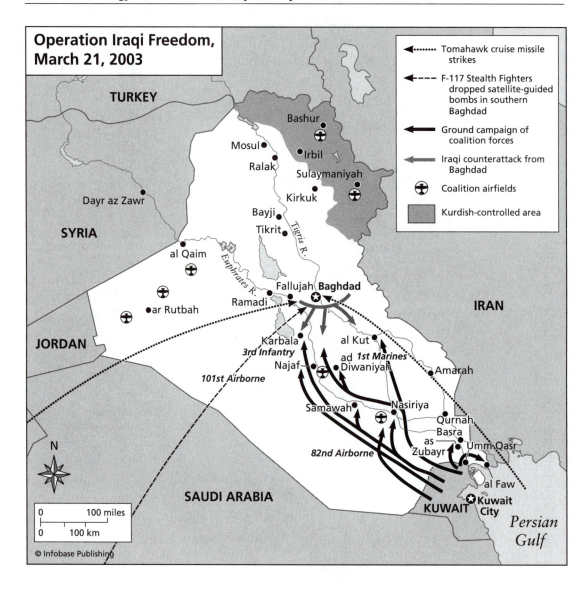

Operation Iraqi Freedom, March 21, 2003

Legend:
- ◄┄┄┄ Tomahawk cruise missile strikes
- ◄----- F-117 Stealth Fighters dropped satellite-guided bombs in southern Baghdad
- ◄━━━ Ground campaign of coalition forces
- ◄━━━ Iraqi counterattack from Baghdad
- ✛ Coalition airfields
- ▓ Kurdish-controlled area

TURKEY

SYRIA

JORDAN

SAUDI ARABIA

IRAN

KUWAIT

Persian Gulf

Bashur
Mosul
Irbil
Ralak
Sulaymaniyah
Dayr az Zawr
Kirkuk
Bayji
Tikrit
al Qaim
Fallujah
Baghdad
Ramadi
ar Rutbah
Karbala
al Kut
3rd Infantry
Najaf
ad
1st Marines
Diwaniyah
Amarah
101st Airborne
Samawah
Nasiriya
Qurnah
Basra
as Zubayr
Umm Qasr
82nd Airborne
al Faw
Kuwait City

Euphrates R.
Tigris R.

N

0   100 miles
0   100 km

© Infobase Publishing

Operation Iraqi Freedom, March 26, 2003

◀┅┅┅ UK ground forces

◀━━━ U.S. ground forces

◀•••• Kurdish U.S.-backed forces

⛛ Special operations forces

▨ Kurdish-controlled areas

⛏ Oil refineries

🏛 Presidential palaces

0 ——— 100 miles
0 ——— 100 km

TURKEY

Bashur

Mosul   •Irbil

Ralak

Euphrates R.

Quayyarah

Sulaymaniyah

Kirkuk

Dayr az Zawr•

SYRIA

Bayji

•al Qaim

Tikrit

Jabal Makhul

•Hadithah

US Marines

Ramadi   Fallujah

Baghdad

⛛ ar Rutbah

Daura

al Kut

JORDAN

Karbala

Najaf

US Marines

IRAN

N

•ad Diwaniyah

Amarah

Samawah

US 3rd Infantry

Qurnah

Nasiriya

Tigris R.

Basra

UK forces:
3rd Commando Brigade
7th Armored Brigade

Umm Qasr

al Faw

KUWAIT   ✪ Kuwait City

Persian Gulf

SAUDI ARABIA

© Infobase Publishing

Baghdad

N

🏛 Al-Azimiyah

🏛 Abbasid

Republican 🏛

Radwaniyah
Presidential
Palace

🏛 Sijood

Tigris

🏛 Abu Ghurayb

0 ——— 5 miles
0 ——— 5 km

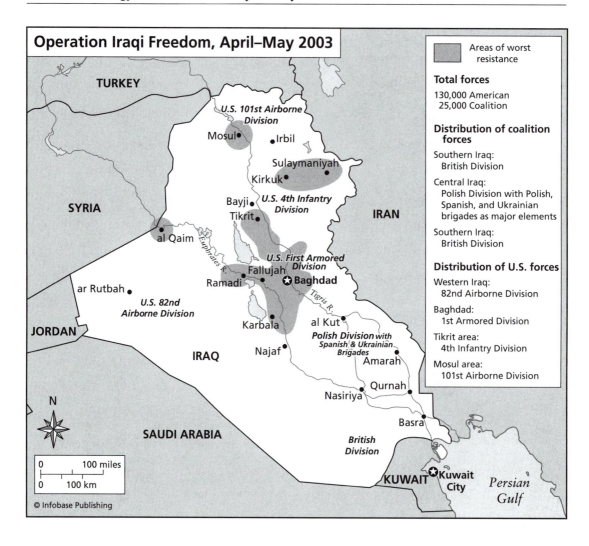

Operation Iraqi Freedom, April–May 2003

Areas of worst resistance

Total forces
130,000 American
25,000 Coalition

Distribution of coalition forces

Southern Iraq:
British Division

Central Iraq:
Polish Division with Polish, Spanish, and Ukrainian brigades as major elements

Southern Iraq:
British Division

Distribution of U.S. forces

Western Iraq:
82nd Airborne Division

Baghdad:
1st Armored Division

Tikrit area:
4th Infantry Division

Mosul area:
101st Airborne Division

TURKEY

Mosul
Irbil
U.S. 101st Airborne Division
Sulaymaniyah
Kirkuk
Bayji
Tikrit
U.S. 4th Infantry Division

SYRIA

al Qaim
Euphrates R.

IRAN

ar Rutbah
U.S. 82nd Airborne Division
Ramadi
Fallujah
U.S. First Armored Division
Baghdad
Tigris R.

JORDAN

IRAQ
Karbala
al Kut
Najaf
Polish Division with Spanish & Ukrainian Brigades
Amarah
Qurnah
Nasiriya

Basra

N

SAUDI ARABIA

British Division

0   100 miles
0   100 km

© Infobase Publishing

KUWAIT
Kuwait City
Persian Gulf

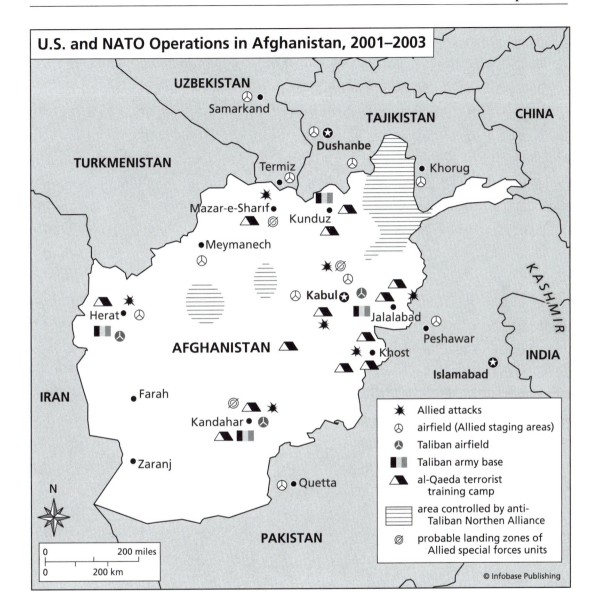

U.S. and NATO Operations in Afghanistan, 2001–2003

UZBEKISTAN

Samarkand

TAJIKISTAN

CHINA

TURKMENISTAN

Dushanbe

Termiz

Khorug

Mazar-e-Sharif

Kunduz

Meymanech

KASHMIR

Herat

Kabul

Jalalabad

Peshawar

AFGHANISTAN

Khost

Islamabad

INDIA

IRAN

Farah

Kandahar

Zaranj

Quetta

N

PAKISTAN

Legend:
- ✳ Allied attacks
- ⊕ airfield (Allied staging areas)
- ◉ Taliban airfield
- ▮▮ Taliban army base
- ◣◤ al-Qaeda terrorist training camp
- ▤ area controlled by anti-Taliban Northen Alliance
- ⊘ probable landing zones of Allied special forces units

0   200 miles
0   200 km

© Infobase Publishing

BIBLIOGRAPHY

General

Allison, William T., Jeffrey Grey, and Janet G. Valentine. *American Military History: A Survey from Colonial Times to the Present.* Upper Saddle River, N. J.: Pearson Prentice Hall, 2007.

Alvah, Donna. *Unofficial Ambassadors: American Military Families Overseas and the Cold War, 1946–1965.* New York: New York University Press, 2007.

Arnold, James R. *Jungle of Snakes: A Century of Counterinsurgency Warfare from the Philippines to Iraq.* New York: Bloomsbury Press, 2009.

Bacevich, Andrew J., ed. *The Long War: A History of U.S. National Security Policy since World War II.* New York: Columbia University Press, 2007.

Biank, Tanya. *Under the Sabers: The Unwritten Code of Army Wives.* New York: St. Martin's Press, 2006.

Binnendijk, Hans. *Seeing the Elephant: The U.S. Role in Global Security.* Washington, D.C.: Potomac Books, 2006.

Buckley, Mary, and Robert Singh, eds. *The Bush Doctrine and the War on Terrorism: Global Responses, Global Consequences.* New York: Routledge, 2006.

Carroll, John M., and Colin F. Baxter. *The American Military Tradition: From Colonial Times to the Present.* Lanham, Md.: Rowman & Littlefield, 2007.

Eberwein, Robert T. *Armed Forces: Masculinity and Sexuality in the American War Film.* New Brunswick, N.J.: Rutgers University Press, 2007.

Fagan, George V. *Air Force Academy Heritage: The Early Years.* Golden, Colo.: Fulcrum Publishing, 2006.

Greene, Benjamin P. *Eisenhower, Science Advice, and the Nuclear Test-Ban Debate, 1945–1963.* Stanford, Calif.: Stanford University Press, 2007.

Hacker, Barton C. *American Military Technology: The Life Story of a Technology.* Westport, Conn.: Greenwood Press, 2006.

Hawkins, Walter L. *Black Military Leaders: A Biographical Dictionary.* Jefferson, N.C.: McFarland, 2007.

Heng, Yee-Kuang. *War as Risk Management: Strategy and Conflict in an Age of Globalized Risks.* New York: Routledge, 2006.

Kagan, Frederick W. *Finding the Target: The Transformation of American Military Policy.* New York: Encounter Books, 2006.

Kaplan, Robert D. *Hog Pilots, Blue Water Grunts: The American Military in the Air, at Sea, and on the Ground.* New York: Random House, 2007.

Laver, Harry S., and Jeffrey J. Matthews. *The Art of Command: Military Leadership from George Washington to Colin Powell.* Lexington: University Press of Kentucky, 2008.

Lewis, Adrian R. *The American Culture of War: The History of U.S. Military Force from World War II to Operation Iraqi Freedom.* New York: Routledge, 2006.

Lind, Michael. *The American Way of Strategy.* New York: Oxford University Press, 2006.

Lock-Pullan, Richard. *U.S. Intervention Policy and Army Innovation: From Vietnam to Iraq.* New York: Routledge, 2006.

Mahnken, Thomas G. *Technology and the American Way of War since 1945.* New York: Columbia University Press, 2008.

Martel, William C. *Victory in War: Foundations of Modern Military Policy.* New York: Cambridge University Press, 2006.

Miller, Mark J., and Boyka Stefanova, eds. *The War on Terror in Comparative Perspective: U.S. Security and Foreign Policy after 9/11.* New York: Palgrave Macmillan, 2007.

Miscamble, Wilson D. *From Roosevelt to Truman: Potsdam, Hiroshima, and the Cold War.* New York: Cambridge University Press, 2006.

Perry, Mark. *Partners in Command: George Marshall and Dwight Eisenhower in War and Peace.* New York: Penguin Press, 2007.

Polar, Norman. *The U.S. Nuclear Arsenal: A History of Weapons and Delivery Systems.* Annapolis, Md.: Naval Institute Press, 2009.

Sapolsky, Harvey M. *U.S. Military Innovation since the Cold War: Creation with Destruction.* New York: Routledge, 2009.

Sarkesian, Sam C. *The U.S. Military Profession in the Twenty-first Century: War, Peace, and Politics.* New York: Routledge, 2006.

Schwab, Orrin. *A Clash of Cultures: Civil-Military Relations during the Vietnam War.* Westport, Conn.: Praeger, 2006.

Schweikart, Larry. *America's Victories: Why the U.S. Wins Wars and Will Win the War on Terror.* New York: Sentinel, 2006.

Shapiro, Ian. *Containment: Rebuilding a Strategy against Global Terror.* Princeton, N.J.: Princeton University Press, 2007.

Soundhaus, Lawrence, and A. James Fuller, eds. *America, War, and Power: Defining the State, 1775–2005.* New York: Routledge, 2007.

Stevenson, Charles A. *Warriors and Politicians: U.S. Civil-Military Relations under Stress.* New York: Routledge, 2006.

Stone, David J. *Wars of the Cold War: Campaigns and Conflicts, 1945–1990.* Havertown, Pa.: Casemate, 2004.

Tomes, U.S. *Defense Strategy from Vietnam to Operation Iraqi Freedom: Military Innovation and the New American Way of War, 1973–2003.* New York: Routledge, 2006.

Worley, D. Robert. *Shaping U.S. Military Forces: Revolution or Relevance in a Post–Cold War World.* Westport, Conn.: Praeger Security International, 2006.

Air Force

Anderegg, C. R. *Sierra Hotel: Flying Air Force Fighters in the Decade after Vietnam.* Washington, D.C.: Air Force History and Museum Program, United States Air Force, 2001.

Boyne, Walter J. *Beyond the Wild Blue: A History of the United States Air Force, 1947–2007.* New York: Thomas Dunne Books/St. Martin's Press, 2007.

Casey, Aloysius G., and Patrick Casey. *Velocity: Speed with Direction: The Professional Career of General Jerome F. O'Malley.* Maxwell Air Force Base, Ala.: Air University Press, 2007.

Collins, Martin W. *Cold War Laboratory: RAND, the Air Force, and the American State, 1945–1950.* Washington, D.C.: Smithsonian Institution Press, 2002.

Davies, Steve. *Red Eagles: The Top Secret Acquisition and Testing of Soviet Combat Aircraft in the Cold War by the USAF.* Stroud, U.K.: Sutton, 2006.

——. *America's Secret Migs.* Oxford: Osprey, 2008.

Engel, Jeffrey A. *Cold War at 30,000 Feet: The Anglo-American Fight for Aviation Supremacy.* Cambridge, Mass.: Harvard University Press, 2007.

Gordon, Doug. *Tactical Reconnaissance in the Cold War: 1945 to Korea, Cuba, Vietnam, and the Iron Curtain.* Barnsley, U.K.: Pen & Sword Aviation, 2006.

Hagedorn, Dan. *North American AT-6: A Definitive History of the World's Most Famous Trainer.* North Branch, Minn.: Specialty Press, 2009.

Hall, R. Cargill, and Clayton R. Laurie, eds. *Early Cold War Overflights, 1950–1956: Symposium Proceedings.* Washington, D.C.: Office of the Historian, National Reconnaissance Office, 2003.

Hirsch, Michael. *None Braver: U.S. Air Force Pararescuemen in the War on Terrorism.* New York: New American Library, 2003.

Houchin, Roy F. *U.S. Hypersonic Research and Development: The Rise and Fall of Dyna-Soar, 1944–1963.* New York: Routledge, 2006.

Jenkins, Dennis R., and Tony Landis. *Experimental and Prototype U.S. Air Force Jet Fighters.* North Branch, Minn.: Specialty Press, 2008.

Kennedy, Gregory P. *Touching Space: The Story of Project Manhigh.* Atglen, Pa.: Schiffer Military History, 2007.

Lenderman, Laura L. *The Rise of Air Mobility and Its Generals.* Maxwell Air Force Base, Ala.: Air University Press, 2008.

Marrett, George. *Testing Death: Hughes Aircraft Test Pilots and Cold War Weaponry.* Annapolis, Md.: Naval Institute Press, 2006.

——. *Contrails over the Mojave: The Golden Age of Jet Fighter Flight Testing at Edwards Air Force Base.* Annapolis, Md.: Naval Institute Press, 2008.

Meilinger, Philip K. *Hubert R. Harmon: Airman, Officer, Father of the Air Force Academy.* Golden, Colo.: Fulcrum Group, 2009.

Natola, Mark, ed. *Boeing B-47 Stratojet: True Stories of the Cold War in the Air.* Atglen, Pa.: Schiffer Publishing, 2002.

Rodriques, Rick. *Aircraft Markings of the Strategic Air Command, 1946–1953.* Jefferson, N.C.: McFarland, 2006.

Samuel, Wolfgang W. E. *I Always Wanted to Fly: America's Cold War Airmen.* Jackson: University of Mississippi Press, 2001.

Tillman, Barrett. *LeMay.* New York: Palgrave Macmillan, 2007.

Wallwork, Ellery D., and Kathyrn A. Wilcoxson. *Operation Deep Freeze: 50 Years of U.S. Air Force Airlift in Antarctica.* Scott Air Force Base, Ill.: Office of History, Military Airlift Command, 2007.

Withington, Thomas. *Wild Weasel Fighter Attack: The Story of Suppression of Enemy Air Defenses.* Barnsley, U.K.: Pen & Sword Aviation, 2008.

Army

Adams, Thomas K. *The Army after Next: The First Postindustrial Army.* Stanford, Calif.: Stanford Security Studies, 2008.

Bahmanyar, Mir. *Shadow Warriors: A History of the U.S. Army Rangers.* Westminster, Md.: Osprey Direct, 2006.

Bluhm, Raymond K., ed. *The U.S. Army: A Complete History.* Westport, Conn.: Hugh Lauter Levin Associates, 2004.

Buhite, Russell D. *Douglas MacArthur: Statecraft and Stagecraft in America's East Asian Policy.* Lanham, Md.: Rowman & Littlefield, 2008.

Clark, Wesley K. *A Time to Lead: For Duty Honor and Country.* New York: Palgrave Macmillan, 2007.

Davis, Robert T. *The Change of Adaptation: The U.S. Army in the Aftermath of Conflict, 1953–2000.* Fort Leavenworth, Kan.: Combat Studies Institute Press, 2008.

Harper, John P. *Army of Hope, Army of Alienation: Culture and Contradiction in the American Army Communities of Cold War Germany.* Tuscaloosa: University of Alabama Press, 2005.

Hogan, David W. *The Story of the Noncommissioned Officer Corps: The Backbone of the Army.* Washington, D.C.: Center of Military History, United States Army, 2007.

Kaplan, Robert D. *Imperial Grunts: The American Military on the Ground.* New York: Random House, 2005.

Linn, Brian M. *Echo of Battle: The Army's Way of War.* Cambridge, Mass.: Harvard University Press, 2007.

Pegler, Martin. *Sniper: A History of the U.S. Marksmen.* Oxford: Osprey, 2009.

O'Sullivan, Christopher D. *Colin Powell, American Power, and Intervention from Vietnam to Iraq.* Lanham, Md.: Rowman & Littlefield, 2009.

Pushies, Fred J. *82nd Airborne.* Minneapolis, Minn.: MBI Publishing, 2008.

Rearman, Mark J., and Jeffrey Charlton. *From Transformation to Combat: The First Stryker Brigade at War.* Washington, D.C.: Center of Military History, United States Army, 2007.

Sanchez, Ricardo S. *Wiser in Battle: A Soldier's Story.* New York: HarperCollins, 2009.

Ucko, David H. *The New Counterinsurgency Era: Transforming the U.S. Military for Modern Wars.* Washington, D.C.: Georgetown University Press, 2009.

Wheeler, James S. *The Big Red One: America's Legendary 1st Infantry Division from World War I to Desert Storm.* Lawrence: University Press of Kansas, 2007.

Wright, Donald P. *The United States Army in Operation Iraqi Freedom, May 2003–January 2005.* Fort Leavenworth, Kan.: Combat Studies Institute, 2008.

Coast Guard

Helvarg, Davis. *Rescue Warriors: The U.S. Coast Guard, America's Forgotten Heroes.* New York: Thomas Dunne Books, 2009.

Marines

Brady, James. *Why Marines Fight.* New York: Thomas Dunne/St. Martin's Press, 2007.

Daugherty, Leo J. *The Marine Corps and the State Department: Enduring Partners in U.S. Foreign Policy, 1790–2007.* Jefferson, N.C.: McFarland, 2009.

Gilbert, Oscar E. *The U.S. Marine Corps in the Vietnam War: III Marine Amphibious Force, 1965–1975.* Oxford: Osprey, 2006.

——. *Marine Corps Tank Battles in Vietnam.* Havertown, Pa.: Casemate, 2007.

Jones, Charles V. *Boys of 67: From Vietnam to Iraq, the Extraordinary Story of a Few Good Men.* Mechanicsburg, Pa.: Stackpole Books, 2007.

Lowry, Richard S., and Howard Gerrard. *U.S. Marines in Iraq: Operation Iraqi Freedom, 2003.* New York: Osprey Publishing, 2006.

Michael, G. J. *Tip of the Spear: U.S. Marine Light Armor in the Gulf War.* Annapolis, Md.: Naval Institute Press, 2008.

O'Hara, Thomas Q. *The Marines at Twentynine Palms.* Charleston, S.C.: Arcadia Publishing, 2007.

Simonsen, Robert A. *Marines Dodging Death: Sixty-Two Accounts of Close Calls in World War II, Korea, Vietnam, Lebanon, Iraq, and Afghanistan.* Jefferson, N.C.: McFarland, 2009.

Venzon, Anne C., and Gordon K. Martin. *Leaders of Men: Ten Marines Who Changed the Corps.* Lanham, Md.: Scarecrow Press, 2008.

Warren, James A. *American Spartans: A Combat History from Iwo Jima to Iraq.* New York: Pocket Books/Simon & Schuster, 2007.

Wise, James E. *The Navy Cross: Extraordinary Heroism in Iraq, Afghanistan, and Other Conflicts.* Annapolis, Md.: Naval Institute Press, 2007.

Zinni, Anthony C. *The Battle for Peace: A Frontline Vision of America's Power and Purpose.* New York: Palgrave Macmillan, 2006.

National Guard

Donnelly, William M. *Under Army Orders: The Army National Guard during the Korean War.* College Station: Texas A&M University Press, 2001.

Navy

Barlow, Jeffrey G. *From Hot War to Cold War: The U.S. Navy and National Security Affairs, 1945–1955.* Stanford, Calif.: Stanford University Press, 2009.

Holloway, James L. *Aircraft Carriers at War: A Personal Retrospective of Korea, Vietnam, and the Soviet Confrontation.* Annapolis, Md.: Naval Institute Press, 2007.

Knoblock, Glenn A. *Black Submariners in the United States Navy, 1940–1975.* Jefferson, N.C.: McFarland, 2005.

Lambeth, Benjamin S. *American Carrier Air Power at the Dawn of a New Century.* Santa Monica, Calif.: RAND, National Defense Research Institute, 2005.

Nalty, Bernard C. *Long Passage to Korea: Black Sailors and the Integration of the U.S. Navy.* Washington, D.C.: Naval Historical Center, 2003.

O'Rourke, Ronald. *The Impact of Chinese Naval Modernization on the Future of the United States Navy.* New York: Nova Science Publishers, 2006.

Puryear, Edgar F. *American Admiralship: The Moral Imperatives of Naval Command.* Annapolis, Md.: Naval Institute Press, 2006.

Reardon, Carol. *Launch the Intruders: A Naval Attack Squadron in the Vietnam War, 1972.* Lawrence: University Press of Kansas, 2005.

Riker, H. Jay. *The Silent Service. Seawolf Class.* New York: Avon Books, 2002.

Schneller, Robert S. *Blue & Gold and Black: Racial Integration of the U.S. Naval Academy.* College Station: Texas A&M University Press, 2008.

Sherwood, John D. *Black Sailor, White Navy: Racial Unrest in the Fleet during the Vietnam War Era.* New York: New York University Press, 2007.

———. *Nixon's Trident: Naval Power in Southeast Asia, 1968–1972.* Washington, D.C.: Naval Historical Center, Department of the Navy, 2008.

Trimble, William F. *Attack from the Sea: A History of the U.S. Navy's Seaplane Striking Force.* Annapolis, Md.: Naval Institute Press, 2005.

Zichek, Hared A. *Secret Aerospace Projects of the U.S. Navy: The Incredible Attack Aircraft of the USS United States, 1948–1949.* Atglen, Pa.: Schiffer Publishing, 2009.

Special Forces

Blaber, Pete. *The Mission, the Men, and Me: Lessons from a Former Delta Force Commander.* New York: Berkley Caliber, 2008.

Carney, John T., and Benjamin F. Schemmer. *No Room for Error: The Covert Operations of America's Special Tactics Units from Iran to Afghanistan.* New York: Ballantine Books, 2002.

Couch, Dick. *Sheriff of Ramadi: Navy SEALS and the Winning of Al-Anbar.* Annapolis, Md.: Naval Institute Press, 2008.

Durant, Michael J. *The Night Stalkers: Top Secret Missions of the U.S. Army's Special Operations Aviation Regiment.* New York: G.P. Putnam's Sons, 2007.

Finlan, Alastair. *Special Forces, Strategy, and the War on Terror: Warfare by Other Means.* New York: Routledge, 2007.

Fury, Dalton. *Kill Bin Laden: A Delta Force Commander's Account of the Hunt for the World's Most Wanted Man.* New York: St. Martin's Press, 2008.

Griswold, Terry. *Delta: America's Elite Counterterrorist Force.* St. Paul, Minn.: Zenith Press, 2005.

Halberstadt, Hans. *Trigger Men: Shadow Team, Spider-Man, the Magnificent Bastards, and the American Combat Sniper.* New York: St. Martin's Press, 2008.

Haney, Eric L. *Inside Delta Force: The Story of America's Elite Counterterrorist Unit.* New York: Delta Trade Paperbacks, 2005.

LeBleu, Joe. *Long Rifle: A Sniper's Story in Iraq and Afghanistan.* Guilford, Conn.: Lyons Press, 2008.

McKinney, Mike. *Chariots of the Damned: Helicopter Special Operations from Vietnam to Kosovo.* New York: Thomas Dunne/St. Martin's Press, 2002.

Pushies, Fred J. *U.S. Air Force Special Ops.* St. Paul, Minn.: Zenith Press, 2007.

Rosenau, William. *Special Operation Forces and Elusive Enemy Ground Targets: Lessons from Vietnam and the Persian Gulf War.* Santa Monica, Calif.: RAND, 2001.

Schumacher, Gerald. *To Be a U.S. Army Green Beret.* St. Paul, Minn.: Zenith Press, 2005.

Smith, Michael. *Killer Elite: The Inside Story of America's Most Secret Special Operations Team.* New York: St. Martin's Press, 2008.

Zapata, Regulo. *Desperate Lands: The War on Terror through the Eyes of a Special Forces Soldier.* Gilroy, Calif.: Nadores & Research, 2007.

Zimmerman, Dwight J., and John D. Gresham. *Beyond Hell and Back: How America's Special Operations Forces Became the World's Greatest Fighting Unit.* New York: St. Martin's Press, 2007.

Korean War

Anderson, Christopher J. *The War in Korea: The U.S. Army in Korea, 1950–1953.* Mechanicsburg, Pa.: Stackpole Books, 2001.

Ballenger, Lee. *The Final Crucible: U.S. Marines in Korea.* Dulles, Va.: Potomac, 2001.

Blair, Clay. *The Forgotten Men: American in Korea, 1950–1953.* Annapolis, Md.: Naval Institute Press, 2003.

Boose, Donald W. *Over the Beach: U.S. Army Amphibious Operations in the Korean War.* Fort Leavenworth, Kan.: Combat Studies Institute Press, 2008.

Buell, Thomas B. *Naval Leadership in Korea: The First Six Months.* Washington, D.C.: Naval Historical Center, 2002.

Bussey, Charles M. *Firefight at Yechon: Courage and Racism in the Korean War.* Lincoln: University of Nebraska Press, 2002.

Drury, Bob. *The Last Stand of Fox Company: A True Story of U.S. Marines in Combat.* New York: Atlantic Monthly Press, 2005.

Edwards, Paul M. *The Korean War.* Westport, Conn.: Greenwood Press, 2006.

———. *The Hill Wars of the Korean Conflict: A Dictionary of Hills, Outposts, and Other Sites of Military Action.* Jefferson, N.C.: McFarland, 2006.

———. *Korean War Almanac.* New York: Facts On File, 2006.

Endicott, Judith G., ed. *The USAF in Korea: Campaigns, Units, and Stations, 1950–1953.* Washington, D.C.: Air Force History and Museums Program, 2001.

Greene, Robert E. *The Black Presence in the Korean War, 1950–1953.* Fort Washington, Md.: R.E. Greene, 2003.

Hallion, Richard P., ed. *Silver Wings, Golden Valor: The USAF Remembers Korea.* Washington, D.C.: Air Force History and Museums Program, 2006.

Hammel, Eric M. *Chosin: Heroic Ideal of the Korean War.* St. Paul, Minn.: Zenith Press, 2007.

Knott, Richard C. *Attack from the Sky: Naval Air Operations in the Korean War.* Washington, D.C.: Naval Historical Center, Department of the Navy, 2004.

Kolb, Richard K., ed. *Battle of the Korean War: Americans Engage in Deadly Combat, 1950–1953.* Kansas City, Mo.: Veterans of Foreign Wars of the United States, 2003.

Mesko, Jim. *Air War over Korea.* Carrollton, Tex.: Squadron/Signal Publications, 2000.

Muir, Malcolm. *Sea Power on Call: Fleet Operations, June 1951–July 1953.* Washington, D.C.: Naval Historical Center, Department of the Navy, 2005.

Thompson, Warren. *F-86 Sabre Aces of the 4th Fighter Wing.* Oxford: Osprey, 2006.

Y'Blood, William T. *MiG Alley: The Fight for Air Superiority.* Washington, D.C.: Air Force History and Museums Program, 2000.

———. *Down in the Weeds: Close Air Support in Korea.* Washington, D.C.: Air Force History and Museums Program, 2002.

Vietnam

Allison, William T. *Military Justice in Vietnam: The Rule of Law in an American War.* Lawrence: University Press of Kansas, 2006.

Anderson, Christopher J. *Marines in Vietnam.* Mechanicsburg, Pa.: Stackpole Books, 2002.

Arthurs, Ted. *Land with No Sun: A Year in Vietnam with the 173rd Airborne.* Mechanicsburg, Pa.: Stackpole Books, 2006.

Burgess, Richard R. *A-1 Skyraiders of the Vietnam War.* Oxford: Osprey, 2009.

Chambers, Larry. *Recondo: LRRPs in the 101st.* New York: Random House, 2004.

Clodfelter, Mark. *The Limits of Air Power: The American Bombing of North Vietnam.* Lincoln: University of Nebraska Press, 2006.

Cosmas, Graham A. *MACV: The Joint Command in the Years of Escalation, 1962–1967.* Washington, D.C.: Center of Military History, United States Army, 2006.

———. *MACV: The Joint Command in the Years of Withdrawal, 1968–1973.* Washington, D.C.: Center of Military History, United States Army, 2007.

Dumbrell, John, and David Ryan, eds. *Vietnam in Iraq: Tactics, Lessons, Legacies, and Ghosts.* New York: Routledge, 2007.

Dunstan, Simon. *1st Air Cavalry in Vietnam: the "First Team."* Haverton, Pa.: Casemate Publishing, 2004.

Elward, Brad A. *U.S. Navy F-4 Phantom II MiG Killers: 1965–1970.* New York: Osprey Aviation, 2001.

Frankum, Ronald B. *Like Rolling Thunder: The Air War in Vietnam, 1964–1975.* Lanham, Md.: Rowman & Littlefield, 2005.

Goodspeed, Michael. *When Reason Fails: Portraits of Armies at War: America, Britain, Israel, and the Future.* Westport, Conn.: Praeger, 2002.

Ha, Mai Viet. *Steel and Blood: South Vietnamese Armor and the War for Southeast Asia.* Annapolis, Md.: Naval Institute Press, 2008.

Hammel, Eric M. *Marines in Hue City: A Portrait of Urban Combat, Tet 1968.* St. Paul, Minn.: Zenith, 2007.

Henderson, Charles. *Jungle Rules: A True Story of Marine Justice in Vietnam.* New York: Berkley Caliber, 2006.

Hendon, Bill. *An Enormous Crime: The Definitive Account of American POWs Abandoned in Southeast Asia.* New York: Thomas Dunne Books, 2007.

Ives, Christopher K. *U.S. Special Forces and Counterinsurgency in Vietnam: Military Innovation and Institutional Failure, 1961–63.* New York: Routledge, 2007.

Keeter, Hunter. *American Air Forces in the Vietnam War.* Milwaukee, Wis.: World Almanac Library, 2005.

Lehrack, Otto J. *The First Battle: Operation Starlight and the Beginning of the Blood Debt in Vietnam.* Novato, Calif.: Presidio, 2006.

Mardola, Edward J. *The Approaching Storm: Conflict in Asia, 1945–1965.* Washington, D.C.: Naval Historical Center, Department of the Navy, 2008.

McCarthy, Donald J. *MiG Killers: A Chronology of U.S. Shoot Downs in Vietnam, 1965–1973.* North Branch, Minn.: Specialty Press, 2009.

Moyar, Mark. *Triumph Forsaken: The Vietnam War, 1954–1965.* New York: Cambridge University Press, 2006.

Murphy, Edward F. *Dak To: America's Sky Soldiers in South Vietnam's Central Highlands.* New York: Ballantine Books, 2007.

Nalty, Bernard C. *The War against Trucks: Aerial Interdiction in Southern Laos, 1968–1972.* Washington, D.C.: Air Force History and Museum Program, United States Air Force, 2005.

Nolan, Keith W. *House to House: Playing the Enemy's Game in Saigon, May 1968.* St. Paul, Minn.: Zenith Press, 2006.

Phillips, Rufus. *Why Vietnam Matters: An Eyewitness Account of Lessons Not Learned.* Annapolis, Md.: Naval Institute Press, 2008.

Prados, John. *Vietnam: The History of an Unwinnable War, 1945–1975.* Lawrence: University Press of Kansas, 2009.

Randolph, Stephen P. *Powerful and Brutal Weapons: Nixon, Kissinger, and the Eastern Offensive.* Cambridge, Mass.: Harvard University Press, 2007.

Rottman, Gordon L. *Vietnam Riverine Craft, 1958–75.* Oxford: Osprey, 2006.

——. *Mobile Strike Forces in Vietnam, 1966–70.* New York: Osprey, 2007.

——. *Vietnam Airmobile Warfare Tactics.* New York: Osprey, 2007.

———. *The U.S. Army in the Vietnam War, 1965–73*. New York: Osprey, 2008.

Sharpe, Mike. *101st Airborne Division in Vietnam: The Screaming Eagles*. Haverton, Pa.: Casemate Publishing, 2005.

Stanton, Shelby L. *Vietnam Order of Battle*. Mechanicsburg, Pa.: Stackpole Books, 2003.

Stoffey, Robert E. *Fighting to Leave: The Final Years of America's War in Vietnam, 1972–1973*. Minneapolis, Minn.: MBI Publishing, 2008.

Van Staaveren, Jacob. *Gradual Failure: The Air War over North Vietnam, 1965–1966*. Washington, D.C.: Air Force History and Museums Program, 2002.

Cold War

Bonner, Kit. *Cold War at Sea: An Illustrated History*. Osceola, Wis.: MBI Publishing, 2000.

Burrows, William E. *By Any Means Possible: America's Secret Air War in the Cold War*. New York: Farrar, Straus, & Giroux, 2001.

Craven, John P. *The Silent War: The Cold War Battle Beneath the Sea*. New York: Simon & Schuster, 2001.

Huchthausen, Peter A., and Alexandre Sheldon-Duplaix. *Hide and Seek: The Untold Story of Cold War Espionage at Sea*. Hoboken, N.J.: John Wiley & Sons, 2008.

Johnson, Stephen R. *Silent Steel: The Mysterious Death of the Nuclear Attack Submarine USS Scorpion*. Hoboken, N.J.: John Wiley & Sons, 2006.

Lindgren, David T. *Trust but Verify: Imagery Analysis in the Cold War*. Annapolis, Md.: Naval Institute Press, 2000.

McHale, Gannon. *Stealth Boat: Fighting the Cold War in a Fast Attack Submarine*. Annapolis, Md.: Naval Institute Press, 2008.

Offley, Edward. *Scorpion Down: Sunk by the Soviets, Buried by the Pentagon: The Untold Story of the USS Scorpion*. New York: Basic Books, 2007.

Peebles, Curtis. *Twilight Warriors: Covert Air Operations against the USSR*. Annapolis, Md.: Naval Institute Press, 2005.

Sasgen, Peter T. *Stalking the Red Bear: The True Story of a U.S. Cold War Submarine's Covert Operations against the Soviet Union*. New York: St. Martin's Press, 2008.

Sewell, Kenneth R. *All Hands Down: The True Story of the Soviet Attack on the USS Scorpion*. New York: Simon & Schuster, 2008.

Stanton, Shelby L. *U.S. Army Uniforms of the Cold War. 1948–1973*. Mechanicsburg, Pa.: Stackpole Books, 1994.

Tart, Larry. *The Price of Vigilance: Attacks on American Surveillance Flights*. New York: Ballantine Books, 2001.

Taubman, Philip. *Secret Empire: Eisenhower, the CIA, and the Hidden Story of America's Space Espionage*. New York: Simon & Schuster, 2003.

Trauschweitzer, Ingo. *The Cold War U.S. Army: Building Deterrence for Limited War*. Lawrence: University Press of Kansas, 2008.

Winkler, David F. *Cold War at Sea: High-Seas Confrontation between the United States and the Soviet Union*. Annapolis, Md.: Naval Institute Press, 2000.

Grenada

William, Gary. *U.S.-Grenada Relations: Revolution and Intervention in the Backyard.* New York: Palgrave Macmillan, 2007.

Panama

Yates, Lawrence A. *The U.S. Military Intervention in Panama: Origins, Planning, and Crisis Management, June 1987–December 1989.* Washington, D.C.: Center of Military History, United States Army, 2008.

Gulf War

Bacevich, Andrew J., and Efraim Inbar, eds. *The Gulf War of 1991 Reconsidered.* Portland, Ore.: Frank Cass, 2003.

Bourque, Stephen A. *Jayhawk! The VII Corps in the Persian Gulf War.* Washington, D.C.: Department of the Army, 2002.

Carlisle, Rodney P. *Persian Gulf War.* New York: Facts On File, 2003.

Crawford, Steve. *The First Gulf War.* Redding, Conn.: Brown Bear Books, 2009.

Davis, Richard G. *On Target: Organizing and Executing the Strategic Air Campaign against Iraq.* Washington, D.C.: Air Force History and Museums Program, United States Air Force, 2002.

Evans, Anthony A. *Gulf War: Desert Shield and Desert Storm, 1990–1991.* London: Greenhill Books, 2003.

Finlan, Alastair. *The Gulf War 1991.* Oxford: Osprey, 2003.

Kagan, Frederick W., and Christian Kubik, eds. *Leaders in War: West Point Remembers the 1991 Gulf War.* New York: Frank Cass, 2005.

Lehrack, Otto J. *America's Battalion: Marines in the First Gulf War.* Tuscaloosa: University of Alabama Press, 2005.

Mardola, Edward J., and Robert J. Schneller, eds. *Shield and Sword: The United States Navy in the Persian Gulf War.* Annapolis, Md.: Naval Historical Center, 2001.

Olsen, John A. *Strategic Air Power in Desert Storm.* Portland, Ore.: Frank Cass, 2003.

Putney, Diane T. *Airpower Advantage: Planning the Gulf War Air Campaign, 1998–1991.* Washington, D.C.: Air Force History and Museums Program, United States Air Force, 2004.

Rice, Earle. *Overview of the Persian Gulf War, 1990.* Hockessin, Del.: Mitchell Lane Publishers, 2008.

Schwab, Orrin. *The Gulf Wars and the United States: Shaping the Twenty-first Century.* Westport, Conn.: Praeger Security International, 2008.

Toomey, Charles L. *XVIII Airborne Corps in Desert Storm: From Planning to Victory.* Central Point, Ore.: Hellgate Press, 2004.

Whitcomb, Darrell D. *Combat Search and Rescue in Desert Storm.* Maxwell Air Force Base, Ala.: Air University Press, 2006.

Woods, Kevin M. *The Mother of All Battles: Saddam Hussein's Strategic Plan for the Gulf War.* Annapolis, Md.: Naval Institute Press, 2008.

Yetiv, Steven A. *The Absence of Grand Strategy: The United States in the Persian Gulf, 1972–2005.* Baltimore, Md.: Johns Hopkins University Press, 2008.

Kosovo

Haave, Christopher E., and Phil M. Haun, eds. *A-10s over Kosovo: The Victory of Airpower over a Fielded Force as Told by the Airmen Who Fought in Operation Allied Force.* Maxwell Air Force Base, Ala.: Air University Press, 2003.

Hendriksen, Dag. *NATO's Gamble: Combining Diplomacy and Airpower in the Kosovo Crisis, 1988–1999.* Annapolis, Md.: Naval Institute Press, 2007.

Lambeth, Benjamin S. *NATO's Air War Kosovo: A Strategic and Operational Assessment.* Santa Monica, Calif.: RAND, 2001.

Latawski, Paul C. *The Kosovo Crisis and the Evolution of Post–Cold War European Security.* New York: Manchester University Press, 2003.

Phillips, R. Cody. *Operation Joint Guardian: The U.S. Army in Kosovo.* Washington, D.C.: Center of Military History, United States Army, 2007.

Siani-Davies, Peter. *International Intervention in the Balkans since 1995.* New York: Routledge, 2003.

Afghanistan

Carroll, Andrew. *Operation Homecoming: Iraq, Afghanistan, and the Home Front, in the Words of U.S. Troops and Their Families.* Chicago: University of Chicago Press, 2008.

Grant, Rebecca. *The First 600 Days of Combat.* Washington, D.C.: IRIS Press, 2004.

Holmes, Tony. *F-14 Tomcat Units of Operation Enduring Freedom.* New York: Osprey Publishing, 2008.

Jacobson, Sidney. *After 9/11: America's War of Terror (2001–).* New York: Hill & Wang, 2008.

Jones, Seth G. *Counterinsurgency in Afghanistan.* Santa Monica, Calif.: RAND National Defense Research Institute, 2008.

Koontz, Christopher N., ed. *Enduring Voices: Oral Histories of the U.S. Army Experience in Afghanistan, 2003–2005.* Washington, D.C.: Center of Military History, United States Army, 2008.

Lambeth, Benjamin S. *Air Power against Terror: America's Conduct of Operation Enduring Freedom.* Santa Monica, Calif.: RAND, 2005.

Loyn, David. *In Afghanistan: 200 Years of British, Russian, and American Occupation.* New York: Palgrave Macmillan, 2009.

Luttrell, Marcus. *Lone Survivor: The Eyewitness Account of Operation Redwing and the Lost Heroes of SEAL Team 10.* New York: Little, Brown, 2007.

Moorcraft, Paul, ed. *The New Wars of the West: Anglo-American Voices on the War on Terror.* Havertown, Pa.: Casemate, 2005.

Morgan, Matthew J. *A Democracy Is Born: An Insider's Account of the Battle against Terrorism in Afghanistan.* Westport, Conn.: Praeger Security International, 2007.

Iraq

Borden, Arthur M. *A Better Country: Why America Was Right to Confront Iraq.* Lanham, Md.: Hamilton Books, 2008.

Burden, Matthew C. *The Blog of War: Front-Line Dispatches from Soldiers in Iraq and Afghanistan.* New York: Simon & Schuster Paperbacks, 2006.

Cerf, Christopher. *Mission Accomplished! Or How We Won the War in Iraq: the Experts Speak.* New York: Simon & Schuster Paperbacks, 2008.

Collins, Joseph J. *Choosing War: The Decision to Invade Iraq and Its Aftermath.* Washington, D.C.: National Defense University Press, 2008.

Cordesman, Anthony H. *Iraq's Insurgency and the Road to Civil Conflict.* Westport, Conn.: Praeger Security International, 2008.

DeLong, Michael. *A General Speaks Out: The Truth about the Wars in Afghanistan and Iraq.* St. Paul, Minn.: Zenith Press, 2007.

Earle, Robert. *Nights in the Pink Motel: A Strategist's Pursuits of Peace in Iraq.* Annapolis, Md.: Naval Institute Press, 2008.

Gray, Wesley R. *Embedded: A Marine Corps Advisor Inside the Iraqi Army.* Annapolis, Md.: Naval Institute Press, 2009.

Groen, Michael S. *With the 1st Marine Division in Iraq, 2003: No Greater Friend, No Worse Enemy.* Quantico, Va.: History Division, Marine Corps University, 2006.

Knights, Michael. *Cradle of Conflict: Iraq and the Birth of Modern U.S. Military Power.* Annapolis, Md.: Naval Institute Press, 2005.

——, ed. *Operation Iraqi Freedom and the New Iraq: Insights and Forecasts.* Washington, D.C.: Washington Institute for Near East Policy, 2004.

Mansoor, Peter R. *Baghdad at Sunrise: A Brigade Commander's War in Iraq.* New Haven, Conn.: Yale University Press, 2008.

Mills, Dan. *Sniper One: On Scope and Under Siege with a Sniper Team in Iraq.* New York: St. Martin's Press, 2008.

Mockaitis, Thomas R. *Iraq and the Challenge of Counterinsurgency.* Westport, Conn.: Praeger Security International, 2008.

Moore, Robin. *Hunting Down Saddam: The Inside Story of the Search and Capture.* New York: St. Martin's Press, 2004.

Munson, Peter J. *Iraq in Transition: The Legacy of Dictatorship and the Prospects of Democracy.* Washington, D.C.: Potomac Books, 2009.

O'Donnell, Patrick K. *We Were One: Shoulder to Shoulder with the Marines Who Took Fallujah.* Cambridge, Mass.: DaCapo, 2006.

Ricks, Thomas E. *The Gamble: General David Petraeus and the American Military Adventure in Iraq, 2006–2008.* New York: Penguin Press, 2009.

Scheuer, Michael. *Marching towards Hell: America and Islam after Iraq.* New York: Free Press, 2008.

Schwab, Orrin. *The Gulf Wars and the United States: Shaping the Twenty-first Century.* Westport, Conn.: Praeger Security International, 2008.

Swansborough, Robert H. *Test by Fire: The War Presidency of George W. Bush.* New York: Palgrave Macmillan, 2008.

Tucker, Mike. *Ronin: A Marine Scout/Sniper Platoon in Iraq.* Mechanicsburg, Pa.: Stackpole Books, 2008.

Weinberger, Caspar W. *Home of the Brave: Honoring the Unsung Heroes in the War on Terror.* New York: Forge, 2006.

INDEX

Note: *Italic* page numbers indicate illustrations; **boldface** page numbers indicate boxed biographical features; page numbers followed by *m* indicate maps.

A

ABC-1 Plan 1042–1043, 1055, 1070
Abercrombie, Robert 83, 141, 156
Abizaid, John P. 1972, 1974, **1976–1977**, *1977*, 1980, 1990, 1992
Abrams, Creighton W. 1242, 1665–1667, **1666**, 1672, 1682, 1722, 1730, 1733, 1749
Abu Ghraib prison 1973–1974, 1984
Abu Sayyaf 1953–1954, 2014
Achille Lauro 1824, 1969
Adams, Buck 1748–1749
Adams, John 8–9, 21, 24, 79, 170, 189–191, 201
Adams, John Quincy 79, 305
Adams, Samuel 2–3
Adjutant General's Department 803, 810
Admiralty Islands 1182, 1185, 1235–1236
advance base operations 788, 952
Advance Base School 828
Advanced Amphibious Assault Vehicles (AAAVs) 1921
advanced medium-range air-to-air missiles (AMRAAM) 1852, 1894
Advanced Research Projects Agency (ARPA) 1522, 1540
Advanced Tactical Fighter (ATF) 1864
Aeronautical Engine Laboratory 962
Aerospace Corporation 1545

Afghanistan 1781, 1784, 1839, 1929, 1994
Afghanistan war (2001–) 1946–2018, 2035*m*
 Afghan security forces in 2004, 2008
 Canada in 2016–2018
 casualties in (*See* casualties)
 deployment duration in 1992, 2012
 detainees from 1950, 1952–1954
 friendly fire in 1956, 1992, 2001
 IEDs in 2012, 2017
 Kandahar in 1950–1952
 Mazar-e-sharif in 1950
 NATO in 1989, 2015
 Northern Alliance in 1948–1950, 1952
 Pakistan in 1995–1996, 2001–2014
 precision-guided weapons in 1955
 reconstruction in 1959
 roadside bombs in 2004, 2007–2016
 start of 1946–1948
 Taliban's fall in 1946–1952
 Taliban's resurgence in 1996–2017
 Tora Bora in 1951–1952
 UAVs in 1947, 1954, 1995, 2000–2014
 U.S. troop increases in 1995, 2003, 2005, 2012–2017

Africa. *See also* North Africa; *specific countries*
 terrorist attacks in 1929, 2031*m*
 in World War II 1086, 1185
African Americans. *See also* Civil War
 in Air Force 1372, 1494, 1535, 1861, 1941
 in American revolution 14, 19–20, 22, 26, 28, 42, 78, 89, 95
 in Bicycle Corps 718, 752
 in Blue Angels 1910
 at Brownsville 808–809, 815
 discrimination against 1346, 1390, 1718
 drafting of 1037
 in draft riots 534
 flight training for 1024
 on frontlines 1242, 1247
 Gillem Report on 1346
 integration of 1258, 1377, 1453, 1515, 1566, 1570, 1731
 in Korean War *1467*
 in marines 1090, 1300, 1378, 1388, 1390, 1650, 1731
 medals to 536, 581, 685, 1883
 in National Guard 899
 at Naval Academy 691, 1386
 in navy 193, 1358, 1716, 1920
 as officers 577, 793, 1300, 1650
 as pilots 1024, 1037, 1043, 1050